2/2

LIBERTY U
LY

POLITICAL AND
LEGAL STUDIES

JOSEPH F. COSTANZO, S.J.

POLITICAL AND LEGAL STUDIES

Volume

Two

STUDIES IN AMERICAN
CONSTITUTIONAL LAW

By

JOSEPH F. COSTANZO, S.J.

THE CHRISTOPHER PUBLISHING HOUSE
WEST HANOVER, MASSACHUSETTS
02339

COPYRIGHT © 1982
BY JOSEPH F. COSTANZO, S.J.
Library of Congress Catalog Card Number 81-69217
ISBN: 0–8158–0407–5

*Tibi se cor meum totum subjicit
quia, te contemplans, totum deficit*

To commemorate his fiftieth anniversary in the Society of Jesus (September 16, 1931-1981), relatives, friends and former graduate students of Father Joseph F. Costanzo, S.J. have collated together into two volumes a selection of his scholarly publications in European and American Journals and Quarterlies. Many of us recall the wealth of erudition, and disciplined pedagogy of his learned lectures, and above all the inspiration that he gave us for the high vocation of teaching. On occasion he would remind us that the usual form in which Our Lord was addressed by the disciples during His earthly life was *didaskalos* — "teacher," (eight times in Mark, twelve times in Matthew, fifteen times in Luke). Most of Father Costanzo's publications were related to his graduate courses in the History of Political Philosophy, American Constitutional Law, Historical Jurisprudence, Church and State.

We are grateful to Sister Mary Ruth Murphy, CCVI, Mary and Caesar Costanzo who served as principals and by whose persevering efforts these two volumes were published.

CONTENTS

(Volume Two — American Constitutional Law)

PART B

Religious Heritage of American Democracy	1
Civil Liberties	23
Public Protest and Civil Disobedience, Moral and Legal Considerations	47
Loyalty Oaths Affidavit	85
Jefferson, Religious Education and Public Law	99
Federal Aid to Education and Religious Liberty	133
Religious Schools and Secular Subjects	187
Prayer in Public Schools	259
Wholesome Neutrality: Law and Education	275

PART C — Conscience, the Academy and the City

Academic Freedom and the Intellectual	337
The Academy and the City	353
The Divided Allegiance of the Catholic	369
Public Law and the University Campus	383

PART D — Of War and Peace

Pacificism Is Not Peace	389
Conscription and the Conscientious Objector	399
Vita	467

CONTENTS

(Volume One – Politeia)

PART A

The Graeco-Roman Politeia 1
Christian Politeia I 41
Christian Politeia II 111
Juridic Origins of Representation I 163
Juridic Origins of Representation II 191
Plato: Republic, Books VI and VII 221
Il Principio Agostiniano di Egualita 231
La Dottrina Agostiniana Sull'Integrita della Natura Umana .. 243
Justice in St. Augustine's Definition of the State 255
Lo Studioso Cattolico e la Liberta Scientifica 271
Liberta Scientifica e Liberta Sociale 285
The "De Monarchia" of Dante Alighieri 297
A Critique of Immanuel Kant's Principles of Politics 337

RELIGIOUS HERITAGE OF AMERICAN DEMOCRACY*

I

American political democracy was conceived and established within the terms of the theology of politics. Throughout our national history this relevance has been consistently and authoritatively affirmed in numerous corporate and individual official acts of the three branches of our government. Further, this nexus has been predicated not only about the origins of our Republic but also for its survival and prosperity. Now, to ignore or to deny this relation is to separate in effect the superstructure from the foundation which sustains it and confers upon it its unique spiritual meaning.

Some prefatory remarks on the manner of conceiving the relationship of religion and polity in pagan and Christian societies will draw our perspective into focus. In antiquity such a relevance meant to the Greek philosophers that the ideals and values of the City derived their validity from Platonic vision of the Exemplary Good, the heavenly paradeigma of the due order of being and truth; or, with Aristotle, the City is the embodiment of ethical purposes. The *politeia* is a way of life, *ti biou*. For want of an adequate metaphysics (with the embarrassing disability of a confounding array of mythological gods) pagan theology was at best the philosophers' order of suprasensibles, of first principles and of ultimate origins of all that is as they are meant to be. The Graeco-Roman statecraft was the constant endeavor to reconstruct in human affairs an abiding order of peace and justice in obedience to eternal laws.

With the advent of Christianity, man was supernaturally revealed as an image of divine personality endowed with authentic and tran-

---

*THOUGHT, Vol. xxx, n. 119. Winter 1955-1956, pp. 485-507. Paper read at the American Political Science Convention at the University of Colorado, Denver, 1955.

scendent purposes and accordingly invested with original responsibilities and connatural rights. As a consequence the prerogatives of the pagan state as the supreme moralizing force were radically undermined and the identity of the Ultimate Good with the common good of the City was cancelled. The acknowledgement of a higher law, of which the State is no longer the oracle, and the revelation of the divine guarantee of eternal beatitude, liberated man from the self-enclosed system of nature of which man was wholly a part and the City his fulfillment. Man was freed from the Promethean struggle between the spiritual aspiration for liberty and the pagan cosmological necessitarianism.[1] The Christian martyrs, the Fathers of the Church, and the Church apologetes brought the divine inheritance of men to bear upon the absolute Roman *imperium* so as to render it ministerial of justice in obedience to the fiduciary function of authority. It was to the credit of St. Augustine, Bishop of Hippo, to have expressed in theological terms the metaphysical necessity for the consent of the governed and to have brought out its new significance as a delimiting principle upon law and authority.[2] As a ferment Christian doctrine operated to the transformation of political ideas and practices to the gradual evolution of a constitutionalism of medieval provenance. As the eminent Carlyle brothers have abundantly shown in their monumental work, *History of Political Theory in the West,* this Christian tradition of law and government maintained that the immediate source of political authority is in the community; law and authority are both purposively ordained to the advantage of the governed conceived as justice and commonweal; that the contractual relation between ruler and ruled is reciprocally binding and its conditions mutually inviolable; that the supremacy of law rests juridically, as Hincmar of Rheims pointed out, upon the consent of the governed.

The central truths which energized this historic process were the inviolability of human personality and its indestructible rights,[3] the equality of men in the divine adoption and the correlative doctrine of consent for governance, and the transtemporal value of human affairs. Now, it is within the context of this Christian tradition of the influence of religious truths upon law and government that the history of the birth of the American Republic took place.

By religion, I understand man's total dependency, ontological and moral, upon God, His Creator. These divine-creature relations I take to be the proper objects of intellection and assent given either by motivation of Divine Revelation or under the compelling persuasion of reason. To the Hebrew of the Old Testament, religion is God, the Decalogue, and the Messianic Promise; to the Christian, the fulfillment of the divinely inspired scriptural prophecies in the Incarnation, and generally speaking, institutionalized Christianity. There is, too, a natural theology constructed by a rational analysis of the universe. Within a wide comprehension, these "believers" are called theists to distinguish them from deists. For the theists hold to the immortality of the soul and eternal reward by divine judgment, to God's special providence for man and the efficacy of intercessory prayer.

Our national history is abundantly rich with evidence that our American political democracy was conceived in theological terms, and through the years to this day the relevance has been asserted and reaffirmed authoritatively and officially as the genuine foundation for the prosperity and endurance of our Republic. Far am I from suggesting that every American has held to religious beliefs as the spiritual wellspring of our democracy. From the days of Washington, there is clear evidence of a secularist concept of our national experiment.[4] But I do maintain that the secular tradition is not the only American tradition; on the contrary, the religious tradition is the *original* and *prevailing* one; it is *authentic* in the very fiber of our body politic and as such constitutes the *genuine* American consensus. Such an admission must be made with as much compelling force as that with which a sojourner in the Soviet State, wholly unsympathetic to it, must allow that the Red State was conceived and founded upon the dialectical materialism of Karl Marx. Nonbelievers were not the controlling promoters of American Independence nor were they the leading and responsible architects of the New Republic.

The historical record of our Colonial and Revolutionary period, the Acts of the Continental Congress, the Declaration of Independence, the Northwest Ordinance, the Constitution, the *Federalist* papers, the Bill of Rights, the long course of Presidential utterances, Congressional acts, and determinations of our Supreme Judicature, are constant reiterating affirmations that our American political democracy was conceived and must rest for its survival on moral and religious foundations.

II

If we inquire what was the original American consensus, we shall find in what has been so aptly called the *Seedtime of the Republic*

(1765-1776) the prevailing practice of the colonists to resort to a "higher law" in justification of their campaign of protest, resistance, and revolt.

Clinton Rossiter writes[5] of the "habit, in which most colonists indulged to excess, of recurring to first principles." Scarcely any specific issue was argued.

> without first calling upon rules of justice that were considered to apply to all men everywhere. These rules, of course, were the ancient body of political assumptions known as natural law and natural rights. The great political philosophy of the Western world enjoyed one of its proudest seasons in this time of resistance and revolution... few people have made such effective use of the recourse to first principles.
>
> The Declaration of Independence was written, the Constitution adopted, and the Republic launched in an age when most men, whether subtle or simple, believed unequivocally in higher law, generally called "the law of nature."

Exemplary illustrations of the polemic use of the natural law doctrine are James Otis' *Rights of the Colonists Asserted* (1764), John Dickinson's fourth *Letter to the Inhabitants of the British Colonies in America* (1774), and James Wilson's *Considerations on the Nature and Extent of the Legislative Authority of the British Parliament* (1774). Whatever may be the variant versions as to the ultimate source of natural law then extant, be it the divine natural law, or the secularized natural law of an indifferent and unconcerned deism, or the nonmetaphysical, utilitarian, historically inductive law said to be "higher" because of a value proved constant by experience, it was the language of the theist which prevailed authentically in the Declaration of Independence.

The more frequently we study the Declaration of Independence, the more deeply we appreciate its profound theological and philosophical presuppositions. The Preamble is a public official confession of the all-inclusive comprehension of the divine moral order over the consciences and affairs of men and nations. Such a profession rests on truths which are declared to be self-evident, not indeed because they are immediately or intuitively known, but because of the clarity of their evidential intelligibility. Realism engenders the certitude for the cause of freedom. Since realism was for our

Founding Fathers the source of personal liberty, it was for the same reasons the only guaranty of social and political liberty. Political freedom does not ensue from doubts, conjectures, empirical hypothesis, but from philosophical certitude. *We hold these truths to be self-evident* will equate by the conclusion of the argument "the truth has made us free."

The Declaration then pronounces the theological major in justification of the revolutionary cause. It does not vaguely assert "all men are equal" nor affirm the equality of men by the mere fact of birth. But with precision it specifies the equality of the natures of men which is ensured unfailingly and immutably by divine creative action. Men are equal by reason of their relationship to God. Human nature is divinely endowed with rights which because of their connatural inherence foreclose all alienability whatsoever to any superior temporal force or power. To those who would read any utilitarian ideas into "life, liberty, and the pursuit of happiness," let them carefully regard James Madison's reflections on this very point. Writing to James Monroe, he observed:

> There is no maxim, in my opinion, which is more liable to be misapplied, and which, therefore, more needs elucidation, than the current one, that the interest of the majority is the political standard of right and wrong. Taking the word "interest" as synonymous with "ultimate happiness," in which sense it is qualified with every necessary moral ingredient, the proposition is no doubt true. But taking it in the popular sense as referring to immediate augmentation of property and wealth nothing could be more false. In the latter, it would be the interest of the majority in every community to despoil and enslave the minority of individuals.[6]

It was precisely on this basis of interest as qualified by every moral ingredient that John Dickinson and James Wilson had understood "ultimate happiness" two years before the Declaration as the principle of reconciliation between English rule and colonial claims. Because of his inherent obligation in natural law to pursue his ultimate happiness, man has an inalienable right to all the necessary means to the attainment of that end. Hence, the profound significance of the illation "that to secure these rights, Governments are instituted among men." The origin of politics is situated four-square in the theology of man. Governments are established primarily to *secure, not grant* such divinely endowed rights which are protective of the inviolability of the human personality and accordingly define the purposive direction of public authority.

The all-comprehensive divine moral order completes its arch in the Declaration when it asserts that the powers that derive from the consent of the governed must be "just." Consent as a practical source of power was recognized as far back as Solon. But the subjection of popular consent to a higher law dates with the Christian revelation that "all power is from God." Unjust laws are not properly laws; arbitrary government is simply tyrany; unconstitutional exercise of power is usurpation; and the unrestricted sovereignty which the Colonials rejected in the British rule they would also deny for themselves in the guise of popular sovereignty *Vox populi vox Dei*—the absolutizing of popular sovereignty is not part of our early American consensus. The people are collectively as well as individually dependent upon God and therefore they can exist and act only as second cause, never as ultimate original source of all power. Even in the limited sphere of their sovereignty they may be sovereign only in a derivative, secondary sense; never absolute sovereign in their own independent right.

As a minor to the theological-moral premise, the Declaration catalogues a listing of repeated abuses and usurpations by reason of which both the natural law and the law of Englishmen justify in conscience not only the right but also the compelling duty—such as obtains whenever any Form of Government becomes destructive of its proper ends—to institute a new government.

Implicitly, the revolutionary argument is that from the rights of God over men shall we better know the rights among men. We have Jefferson's own testimony that the Declaration is the embodiment of the original American consensus. Fifty years after the event, in a letter to Henry Lee he wrote:

> With respect to our rights, and the acts of the British government contravening those rights, there was but one opinion on this side of the water. All American whigs thought alike on these subjects. When forced, therefore, to resort to arms for redress, an appeal to the tribunal of the world was deemed proper for our justification. This was the object of the Declaration of Independence. Not to find out new principles, or new

arguments, never before thought of, not merely to say things which had never been said before; but to place before mankind the common sense of the subject, in terms so plain and firm as to commend their assent, and to justify ourselves in the independent stand we are compelled to take. Neither aiming at originality of principle or sentiment, nor yet copied from any particular or previous writing, it was intended to be the expression of the American mind, and to give to that expression the proper tone and spirit called for it by the occasion. All its authority rests then on the harmonizing sentiments of the day, whether expressed in conversation, in letters, printed essays, or in the elementary books of public right, as Aristotle, Cicero, Locke, Sidney, etc.

There is a story which portrays Jefferson in the throes of authorship, and discloses a critical Congress wholly bent on their dictation:

During the debate, Jefferson was sitting by Benjamin Franklin, who consoled him by telling the story of John Thompson, the hatter. That tradesman, having composed an inscription for the signboard of his shop, submitted it to his friends for criticism; after their amendments nothing remained but his name and the picture of a hat.[7]

The historical explanation for the American concordance (on the theological-moral presuppositions of the birth of a nation) lies in the fact that the American experiment took place wholly within the broad Christian tradition of the divine natural law doctrine which had coursed its way from medieval Christendom through English Common Law and Whiggism to the new land.

Unlike the artificial theories of the eighteenth century and the French Enlightenment, which deformed rather than illustrated the natural law, the natural law of the Declaration is wholly operative upon the practicalities of human affairs because it ensues from the Divine Author whose sovereignty is complete over nations as well as over individuals. There is no secularized substitute for the God-centered authority for law and government. Hence the correct distinction and necessary relation in the Declaration between the law of nature and human positive law. Both in the events leading up to the Revolution and in the theological preamble of the Declaration, the claim is first made to the rights of Englishmen and, this failing, the reference is then made to God's law because in the natural law the colonists had a right to their positive legal claims. This polarity of natural and human law was the very point made by Edmund Burke as he espoused the American cause, much to the dismay of the New Whigs who a decade and a half later accused him of inconsistency. They failed to appreciate the radical difference between the American and French Revolutions, as one between real and abstract rights. In his speech on *Conciliation* Burke summed up the Colonists' rightful claim to separation when he said that the Colonists were "not only devoted to liberty, but to liberty according to English ideas, and English principles. Abstract liberty like other mere abstractions is not to be found. Liberty inheres in some sensible object."[8]

III

The Declaration is hardly the instant creation of idealistic revolutionary leaders. It is the most remarkable epitome of the theology of politics proclaimed within the concrete context of American history, and the most fruitful application of the theological convictions of the prevailing colonial mind to their cause. A year before, the Continental Congress, fully aware of the choice they must soon make between peace and war, made a public confession of total dependence upon divine providence, of the necessity of adoration, of intercessory prayer, of the confession and forgiveness of sins, and appointed July 20 as a

> day of public humiliation, fasting, and prayer for preserving the union and securing just rights and privileges of the Colonies, that virtue and true religion may revive and flourish throughout our land; and that America may soon behold the gracious interposition of heaven for the redress of her many grievances, for the restoration of her invaded rights, for a reconciliation with the Parent State on terms constitutional and honorable to both; and that her civil and religious privileges may be secured to the latest posterity.[9]

The Proclamation of June 12, 1775, one of the four fast-day proclamations of the Continental Congress prior to its first thanksgiving, had for its object the strengthening of the religious foundations of colonial union as it was being molded into a nation. It coupled with marked significance civil and religious privileges. The Northwest Ordinance of 1787 enacted by the last Congress of the Confederation, reaffirms this nexus: "Religion, morality, and knowledge, being necessary to good government and the happiness of mankind, schools and the means of education shall forever be encouraged."

The language of the official corporate proclamations of our Founding Fathers is unmistakably that of traditional Christianity. Of the Thanksgiving Proclamations, the 1777 enactment of the Continental Congress is strikingly noticeable for its Trinitarian confession. In later Federal and State Proclamations, it is generally omitted with the obvious intent to apply equally to all believers. Such a deliberate change is in line with the consensus to band together all theists in spiritual support of American polity.

Wholly in accord with this original corporate and official profession of the religious foundations of our Democracy are the individual official pronouncements of our highest government officers from the very beginnings of the American Republic. To those cynics and political scientists of a wholly empirical bent who discount the long tradition of Presidential utterances and especially the Presidential Proclamations of Thanksgiving Days as expedient pious exhortations divested of personal conviction or as official actions made perhaps in rare instances under duress, we would reply that they unwittingly give testimony to the strength of the American consensus that it *must* be officially acknowledged and promoted.

The Inaugural Addresses, Messages to Congress, the Proclamations of Thanksgiving Days of our Chief Executives, from our first President to our own day have set an incontrovertible historical record of the religious presuppositions of our national existence and endurance. In his memorable Farewell Address, Washington pointedly warned against the deceptive insufficiency of a laic morality: "Of all the dispositions and habits which lead to political prosperity, religion and morality are indispensable supports.... And let us with caution indulge the supposition that morality can be maintained without religion."[10]

In his First Inaugural Address of March 4, 1797, John Adams gave similar vigorous expression when he listed the qualifications for the executive office.

... a love of science and letters and a wish to patronize every rational effort to encourage schools, colleges, universities, academies, and every institution for propagating knowledge, virtue, and religion among all classes of people, not only for their benign influence on the happiness of life in all its stages and classes, and society in all its forms, *but as the only means of preserving our Constitution from its natural enemies.* ...[11]

Perhaps the most characteristically Christian and strikingly supernatural Presidential utterance is John Adams' first Proclamation of Thanksgiving of March 23, 1798:

As the safety and prosperity of nations ultimately and essentially depend on the protection and the blessing of Almighty God, and the national acknowledgment of this truth is not only an indispensable duty which the people owe to Him, but a duty whose natural influence is favorable to the promotion of that morality and piety without which social happiness cannot exist nor the blessings of a free government be enjoyed; and as this duty, at all times incumbent, is so especially in seasons of difficulty or of danger... I do hereby recommend that ... 9 day of May ... be observed throughout the United States as a day of solemn humiliation, fasting, and prayer; ... to the Father of Mercies ... that all religious congregations do ... acknowledge before God the manifold sins and transgressions with which we are justly chargeable as individuals and as a nation, beseeching Him ... through the Redeemer of the World, freely to remit all our offenses, and to incline us by His Holy Spirit so that sincere repentance and reformation ... that our *civil and religious* privileges may be preserved inviolate and perpetuated to the latest generations ... that the principles of genuine piety and sound morality may influence the minds and govern the lives of every description of our citizens, and that the blessings of peace, freedom, and pure religion may be speedily extended to all nations of the earth.[12]

This Presidential expression of the dependence of social happiness of free government, of civil and religious liberties, as a national acknowledgment of an indispensable truth incumbent upon nations as well as upon individuals clearly establishes the original American religious consensus as authentic. Both Washington and Adams significantly spoke in sharp rejection of the alien importation of Jacobin atheism both in the guise of French revolutionary totalitarian democracy and of Napoleonic supreme sovereignty. On March 6, 1799, President Adams warned of the subversive dangers of religious neutrality when, repeating his former insistence on the nation's acknowledgment as a society of its dependence upon God, he added:

> ... the most precious interests of the people of the United States are still held in jeopardy by the hostile designs and insidious acts of a foreign nation, as well as by the dissemination among them of those principles, subversive of the foundations of all religious, moral, and social obligations, that have produced incalculable mischief and misery in other countries.[13]

Clearly in our earliest history as a New Republic secularism is officially declared alien to the American religious affirmation and inimical to it. There is no need to collect here all these Presidential testimonials to the American consensus. Lincoln's "this nation under God" gives focal point to the prevailing American tradition. In our freshest recollections, Presidents Roosevelt, Truman and Eisenhower have voiced this tradition as the authentic American affirmation. We choose one last illustration of Presidential witness. On January 4, 1939, President Roosevelt gave his Annual Message to Congress in person. He identified the "ancient" American faith with the one prevailing "now as always." In his words:

> Storms from abroad directly challenge three institutions indispensable to Americans, now as always. The first is religion. It is the source of the other two—democracy and international good faith.
> Religion, by teaching man his relationship to God, gives the individual a sense of his own dignity and teaches him to respect himself by respecting his neighbors....
> In a modern civilization, all three—religion, democracy, and international good faith—complement and support each other. Where freedom of religion has been attacked, the attack has come from sources opposed to democracy. Where democracy has been overthrown, the spirit of free worship has disappeared. And where religion and democracy have vanished, good faith

and reason in international affairs have given way to strident ambition and brute force.

An ordering of society which relegates religion, democracy and good faith among nations to the background can find no place within it for the ideals of the Prince of Peace. The United States rejects such an ordering, and retains its ancient faith.[14]

Far are we from denying the protestations of the secularist or "neutralist" (as he would fain be known) through the course of our national history; but his is not the voice of the American religious and political heritage; he is not giving witness to the original, authentic, and still prevailing American affirmation. In a distinctly nonprophetic sense, his is the voice crying in the wilderness. It is the voice of dissent; it is a protest against our "ancient faith"—prevailing "now as always."

IV

That our nation was conceived under God, with a religious view of human rights and the purpose of government, is abundantly evident in our early national history and in the vigorous tradition carried on by every incumbent of the President's office. Now we inquire if and in what way the religious conception of government entered into the very fabric of our federal government, that is to say, in the Federal Constitution. Presupposing the sound doctrine of the distinction and necessary relation of human positive law to the divine natural law as expressed in the declaration, the Constitution as a juridical document is a superstructure built upon that foundation and, as such, does not need to affirm explicitly this referral.

We should bear in mind that the very men who guided the Colonists within the Christian tradition of natural law doctrine to Independence were generally those same men who either participated in the momentous discussions of the Federal Convention or helped advance the ratification of the Constitution in their several states.

In the first place, the procedure adopted for the ratification of the Constitution conformed to every ethical requirement of the natural law. Chief Justice Marshall in *McCulloch v. Maryland* took juridical notice of the due regard had for the "consent of the governed," in the construction of a new federal government directly binding upon individuals as well as states when he recounted the mode of proceeding followed by the convention which framed the Constitution and by the Congress which submitted it upon recommendation of the Federal Convention to the States for acceptance by conventions chosen in each State by the people thereof, and the juridical binding effect of popular determination upon the State sovereignties as well as upon the people of the new United States. The Federal Government in very truth proceeds directly from the people, deriving its powers from them. Hardly ever in history was the principle of the "consent of the governed" observed with such scrupulous care as in the ratification of the Constitution.

Secondly, American sovereignty is not that of totalitarian democracy, not indeed the unrestricted sovereign of Rousseau's *Contrat Social;* for this instead of presupposing natural law is held itself to be the original source of morality; whereas the right of the people to choose their own form of government necessarily presupposes the major premise in natural law, that civil government is necessary to "life, liberty and the pursuit of happiness." A government of limited powers fixed in a written constitution is wholly in accord with the sovereignty of God over states as well as over individual persons. Plenary but not absolute, derivative and not original, American popular sovereignty is under God from whom whom all power descends, nor again, as with Rousseau, is sovereignty assumed to reside ultimately and inalienably in the people.

Thirdly, in the institutional structure of our Constitution, e.g., the distribution and balance of empowerments, in the delegation of limited and enumerated powers, with a supreme judicature to arrest ventures beyond the prescribed limits, the Constitution provides the institutional securities and restraints for the supremacy of the rule of law over the rule by men. The area of human presumption for tyrannical exercise of power or the usurpation of power itself is doubly restricted both by supremacy of law and the adequate institutional safeguards.

Fourthly, American supremacy of law is neither legal autocracy nor mere legal process; it is medial for the prosecution of substantive civil goods. American political democracy has a substantive content as well as a procedural course. The Preamble proclaims the purpose of the establishment of the federal government to be the "establishment of justice, the promotion of the General Welfare, and the blessings of Liberty." Substantive ethical goods are those rights and purposes of the law of human nature which have been historically and juridically secured even beyond human disowning. For the medievalist Bracton's dictum *sub Deo et lege* operated to the gradual realization of *homo liber et legalis*. Herein lies the radical significance of the American Bill of Rights. They juridically secure by the best tried precedents of history those freedoms which the divinely endowed spiritual nature of man demands. The moral order enters concretely into human law and asserts that by no majoritarian or authoritarian determination will we deprive a man of the free exercise of religious conscience and of worship; that before the bar of justice, laws will be fairly and equally applied; that free speech and free press, the right to assemble peaceably and to petition the government are rational exigencies not only of the spiritual nature of man but of the moral imperatives of society itself. What else are preferred rights, due process, equal protection touching upon life, liberty, and property but the acknowledgment by law and the will of the people of that immunity from the arbitrary to which the spiritual nature of man is entitled.

American political democracy is more than a form of government, a species of governance; it is a content as well as a process. But in the American context it is doubly so, by reason of its unique historical genesis and actualities as we have summarily seen as well as by reason of the purposive prerogative claims of the democratic *politeia*. The higher advantages of the democratic form of government rest on the political maturity of its citizens, who are called upon to participate responsibly in the direction and ultimate control of governmental policies; its broad purpose is the larger diffusion of opportunities for moral and material benefits. Both these ethical objectives and rational procedures are consequent to a philosophy of man or as Aristotle said, "a way of life." Democratic collaboration is self-defeating without commonly accepted principles, a fundamental creed, without a common denominator of beliefs, without certain imperishable values which are beyond question. Surely there is sound democracy and unsound democracy, and its soundness depends on its accordance with the ultimates of man's nature. There can be a totalitarian democracy, just as brutal and arbitrary, as there have been totalitarian dictatorships. "Nothing above the State, nothing outside the State, nothing against the State" applies equally to both. But American political democracy says there is something outside the State—God and His laws; there are many realities beyond the competence and the dominance of the State — the Church, the family, and the countless number of free associations of human endeavor in arts and science and of all sorts of cultural and recreational pursuits; there are many realities delimiting upon the State, such as the prior rights and prerogatives of individuals and of associations which arise from the law of man's nature and of societies. To the preservation and prospering growth of these substantial moral values, to the guarantee of the immunity of these human properties, American democracy as a process is wholly medial. In the American historical context, a substantive deposit, known as the American heritage, has been continuously asserted and reaffirmed in diverse ways, politically, juridically, and socially.

V

Without a philosophy of freedom and of order we shall have neither a free order nor an ordered freedom. To maintain that the core of American democracy is procedural, to say that there are no human values beyond change by majoritarian vote save the supreme value of fair and peaceable competition in the open market of ideas and wholly free election is to affirm that there are no political truths or wrongs to which men and societies are committed or if they exist they are not humanly cognizable. But Americans have with unquestionable certitude held truths as self-evident and in this faith and conviction a new nation has been conceived and has endured under God.

When the Federal Constitution affirms the equality of all men before the law, it recognizes that there are equal rights not held from the law, but from the Divine Author of men and societies, and therefore rights which governments must secure with the full efficacy of human law, and of civil power. Legal expedients which have historically been tried and proven efficacious for the security of fundamental rights were retained from our English heritage. The substantive and procedural rights of the American Bill of Rights and of the Fourteenth Amendment are historical reassertions and juridical securities of man's personal dignity and for the fuller expression of his capacity for freedom. Anglo-American Constitutional history is the continuous record of the development of the secondary nature of man (to borrow from Burke) in accordance with his first nature. The writ of habeas corpus, for example, has a theological presupposition. The writ asserts the right of an individual; but a right presupposes a value outside the reach of any power to cancel. True, the theology of man does not say there must be a writ of habeas corpus; it does say that law must provide proper and adequate means for securing that immunity from the arbitrary which accords with the personal dignity of man. Due process means that persons, rights, and possessions must be treated with reverence even when they are chargeable with crime. The Constitution does not explicitly say man is a child of God. But in those lands and governments which explicitly or in effect deny man is a child of God we shall look in vain for adequate securities for man's immunity from governmental arbitrary action. In such countries there is no writ of habeas corpus. We need only compare the trial of Cardinal Mindszenty and the trial of Communist leaders under Judge Medina to appreciate the vast difference which derives from ultimate theological roots. Negativewise, due process is a legal restraint upon that presumption of pride born of Original Sin that the alleged criminal can be mobbed and lynched at popular demand. In theological terms, what is arbitrary discrimination but the vicious doctrine of election? The use in Supreme Court decisions of the words "unreasonable," reasonable," "arbitrary," "capricious," "justice," "equity" transcends the bifocal thinking of positive jurists and empirical political scientists.

There is throughout our whole American Constitutional history the underlying affirmation of a "higher law" of which the State is not the oracle. The First Amendment declares the inherent disability of legislative power in matters of mind and soul and in so doing confesses to the independence and supremacy of the spiritual nature of man. The American State neither originates nor concedes the right of freedom of religion; it recognizes that this right descends from a source superior to itself and is thereby inviolable, and consequently, it is obligated to protect it. The freedoms of speech and press, of peaceable assembly and petition are not indeed the Voltairean absolutes but rights fully in accord with man's participation in society and to provide the means for a larger scope of democratic responsibilities contributory to the national welfare. There is no more striking feature of the American system than its expressed recognition that the government is one of limited powers, not indeed because power is said to corrupt but because power by reason of its divine descent is limited to the very purposes of the divine grant. Lastly, our Constitution is remarkably viable in accord with the dictates of sound reason. It provides the method of peaceable change, of identity through growth, analogously to the natural law which is immutable in its fundamental principles and progressive in its effects. To amend is to preserve the substance for posterity not to annul it, not to subvert it least of all by the very provision inherent in the Constitution that makes possible the adaptations to the growth of our nation. "To form a more perfect union" is ever toward a more indissoluble survival.

A word about the *Federalist* papers is relevant to our discussion. Besides being a profound compendium of political wisdom on the basic problems of government it enjoys the unique distinction of being frequently cited by our Supreme Court as to the genuine meaning of disputed provisions in the Constitution. The argument of the eighty-five papers is to show that the Constitution is apt and necessary for the proper coherence of liberties and authority, of stability and energy in government (No. 1 and No. 37). But what is directly relevant to our purpose is the admission that the superstructure of government must rest on ultimates which precede and should determine human choice and contrivance. Wrote Hamilton (No. 31):

> In disquisitions of every kind, there are certain primary truths, or first principles, upon which all subsequent reasonings must depend. These contain an internal evidence which, antecedent to all reflections or combination, commands the assent of the mind.

The American judiciary has repeatedly recognized the religious character of our nation as bearing upon American law and government. State and Federal Courts have declared that "Christianity is part of the law of the land," "We are a Christian people,"[15] "This is a Christian nation."[16] These judicial notices obviously do not mean to contradict the First Amendment (as Justice Storey observed[17]) much less to intrude upon and embarrass non-Christians. They simply acknowledge the Christian genesis and quality of American law. There is scarcely anything in our legal system offensive to Christianity and there is much in accordance with its moral standards. Our law incorporates the sociological exigencies of the religious life of our nation. When the eminent scholar, Dr. Corwin, sharply criticized the McCollum decision on historical and constitutional grounds, he asked in conclusion a question to which in response he pointed to the testimonial evidence of American history:

> Is the decision favorable to democracy? Primarily democracy is a system of ethical values, and that this system of values so far as the American people are concerned is grounded in religion will not be denied by anyone who knows the historical record.[18]

To which almost in response are the concurring voices of the New York State Court of Appeals[19] and the Federal Supreme Court[20] in the *Zorach v. Clauson* Case.

> We are a religious people whose institutions presuppose a Supreme Being. We guarantee the freedom of worship as one chooses. . . . When the state encourages religious instruction or cooperates with religious authorities by adjusting the schedule of public events to sectarian needs, it follows the best of our tradition. For then it respects the religious nature of our people and accommodates the public service to their spiritual needs. . . . We cannot read into the Bill of Rights (such) a philosophy of hostility to religion.

We draw to a conclusion the broad lines of our argument and affirm that the American consensus as to the religious foundations of our American political democracy is substantially and abundantly evidenced by the testimony of our Founding Fathers in the Continental Congress, in the drafting of the Declaration of Independence, in the construction of the Federal Constitution, in the long tradition of Presidential utterances which helped perpetrate the spiritual wellsprings of our Republic, and in the judicial recognition of the religious experience of our nation. The long history of legislative acts in favor of cooperation with religious life is a vast and consoling study in itself and presupposes the theological convictions underlying our democracy. Far are we from denying the secularistic stream in American history; but we do deny their claim that it is the only American tradition; what is more we deny it is the original American tradition; much less is it the prevailing one and certainly not the genuine and authentic one. In the light of the historical record, the secularist claim is wholly alien to the American mind and as such continues a dissent and a protestation.

VI

There are certain practical considerations which follow upon this study. Since the days of the Northwest Ordinance the moral, educational, and political have been conceived as necessarily intertwined. Can American democracy survive without its original theological and moral foundations? Will it endure on secularistic substitutes for God-centered values? Educators and political scientists who follow their own intellectual prepossessions and rewrite American history falsify the record. What shall we say of those who teach that American political democracy is essentially a process, wholly a method whereby any change may be effected provided it be done peaceably (without violence) and according to the rules in the contest of ideas and by the majoritarian determination of the suffrage?[21] Or shall we insist that the democratic process is medial for the conservation and enjoyment of substantive ethical ends which are beyond debate and capricious change?[22] In the light of the answer to be given this question the problems of national security and the many issues concerning loyalty and subversion must be faced.[23]

About a year ago Congress reaffirmed that patriotic duty and national allegiance are not religiously neutral, and accordingly inserted (what had always been taken for granted) "under God" into the official formula of salute to our national flag. On March 28 of this year,[24] the New York State Board of Regents spoke out in unequivocal terms against the secularism which has crept into the public schools under guise of religious neutrality. In the statement titled, "Fundamental Beliefs, Liberty Under God, Respect of Dignity and Rights of Each Individual, Devotion to Freedom, the Brotherhood of Man under the Fatherhood of God," the Board urged that schools devote frequent periods to the teaching of the country's moral and spiritual heritage and to this purpose recommended intensive study of American documents and pronouncements by Presidents and other national leaders which provide:

> ...an understanding and appreciation of his role as an individual endowed by his Creator with inalienable rights and as a member of a group similarly endowed, of respect for others, particularly parents and teachers, of devotion to freedom and reverence for Almighty God.

Of the Declaration of Independence the Regents had this to say:

> "All men are created equal" is the basic principle of the brotherhood of man and "endowment by their Creator with

life, liberty, and the pursuit of happiness" is recognition of the fatherhood of God and that these most precious rights come from the Creator and not from kings, princes, or other men.

And so as not to leave any doubt as to the relevance of religious beliefs to American political democracy the Regents cited as the traditional Presidential affirmation of the original and authentic and still prevailing consensus the words of President Eisenhower:

> Without God there could be no American form of government, nor an American way of life. . . . Thus the Founding Fathers saw it; and thus, with God's help, it will continue to be. . . . Each day we must ask that Almighty God will set and keep His protecting hand over us so that we may pass on to those who come after us the heritage of a free people, secure in their God-given rights and in full control of a government dedicated to the preservation of those rights.

The freedom of man has come with divine revelation; it was not conceived in philosophical agnosticism, nor in religious indifference, nor in rational skepticism, least of all in scientific empiricism. Doubts, uncertainties, and ignorance have never offered effective barriers in the minds of men nor provided the inspiration to fight usurpations of power. The threat to liberties comes from those who deny the sovereignty of God over nations as well as over persons. This is the meaning of "the Truth shall make you free," for God is truth.

The survival of American political democracy will not rest solely on a prosperous economy and military preparedness; it requires the religious perception that the insidious crime against the spiritual content of political liberty is indifference. There is no religious neutral ground between God and man for society.

EDITOR'S NOTE: In its original form this paper was read at the Fifty-first Annual Meeting of the American Political Science Association which convened at the University of Colorado, Boulder, September 7-9.

FOOTNOTES AND REFERENCES

1. *Cambridge Medieval History,* XX, 592-3: "The effects of the Church upon the Empire may be summed up in one word, 'freedom'. In a word, authority was seen to be a form of service according to God's will and such service was freedom. It was, however, not from Seneca but from Christ and St. Paul that the Fathers took their constant theme of the essential equality of men before which slavery could not stand.... Not only did the Fathers establish the primitive unity and dignity of man, but seeing slavery as the result of the Fall, they found in the sacrifice of Christ a road to freedom that was closed to Stoicism."

2. Consent as the *practical* source of power was recognized since the days of Solon. But the idea of the proper and due relationship between Government and governed necessarily presupposes the prior consideration of the specific equality of men understood not only in terms of the constitution and exigencies of man's nature but also in the light of man's transcendental destiny. This more enlarged and definite view of man's essential nature is the metaphysical basis of the doctrine of inherent and inalienable rights which, because they are a divine investiture, render man inviolable (the connatural right of immunity from the arbitrary) and condition the use of consent. Not consent alone but consent involving reservations of the law of human nature provides the basis of government. By conjoining the doctrine of the divine origin and descent of authority to the doctrine of the equality of men, St. Augustine provided the initial premise for the development of constitutional limitation in medieval history, not merely as a limitation upon wrongdoing but also as a limitation inherent in the power itself.

3. Otto von Gierke, *Political Theories of the Middle Ages,* (Maitland's trans., 1927), pp. 81-2: "In this Medieval Doctrine was already filled with the thought of the inborn and indestructible rights of the individual. The formulation and classification of such rights belonged to a later stage in the growth of the theory of the Natural Law. Still, as a matter of principle, a recognition of their existence may be found already in the medieval Philosophy of Right when it attributes an absolute and objective validity to the highest maxims of Natural and Divine Law. Moreover, a fugitive glance at Medieval Doctrine suffices to perceive how throughout it all, in sharp contrast to the theories of Antiquity, runs the thought of the absolute and imperishable value of the Individual; a thought revealed by Christianity. ... That every individual by virtue of his eternal destiny is at the core somewhat holy and indestructible even in relation to the Highest Power; that the smallest part had a value of its own, and not merely because it is a part of a whole; that every man is to be regarded by the Community, never as a mere instrument, but also as an end; all this is not merely suggested, but is more or less clearly expressed.

4. The earliest expressions of secularism in America are to be found in the writings of Tom Paine, John Taylor, and Benjamin Rush. The current widened with the victory of Jeffersonian Democracy in 1800. All sort of philosophical isms have dominated most of our high institutions of learnings and have seriously threatened to secularize our nation culture.

5. Clinton Rossiter, *Seedtime of the Republic* (New York: Harcourt Brace, 1953), p. 352.

6. Works, Congress ed., I, 250, 251.

7. Edward Dumbauld, *The Declaration of Independence and What It Means Today.* (University of Oklahoma Press, 1950), p. 19.

8. *The Works of Burke* (Oxford University Press), II, 185.

9. Anson Phelps Stokes, *Church and State in the United States* (Harper, 1950, 3 vols.), I, 451.

10. *Messages and Papers of the Presidents,* compiled and edited by James D. Richardson (1897), I, 212.

11. *Ibid.,* p. 221.

12. *Ibid.,* p. 258.

13. *Ibid.,* p. 275.

14. *The Public Papers and Addresses of Franklin Delano Roosevelt,* compiled and collected by Samuel Rosenman, 1939 volume (1941), pp. 1-2.

15. Chief Justice Kent in *People v. Ruggles* 1811 8 Johns. 290. Also p. 296 that the Constitution "never meant to withdraw religion in general, and with it the best sanctions of moral and social obligation, from all consideration and notice of the law."

16. Justice Brewer in *Church of the Holy Trinity v. United States* 143 U.S. 457.

17. Joseph Storey, *Commentaries on the Constitution, ##1874 (1833): "Probably at the adoption of the Constitution, and of the amendment to it, now under consideration, the general, if not the universal sentiment in America was, that Christianity ought to receive encouragement from the state, so far as was not incompatible with the private rights of conscience, and the freedom of religious worship. An attempt to level all religions, and to make it a matter of state policy to hold all in utter indifference, would have created universal disapprobation if not universal indignation."

18. "The Supreme Court as National School Board" in 14 *Law and Contemporary Problems* 21 (1949).

19. *Zorach et al v. Clauson et al.,* Court of Appeals of New York, 1951, 100 N.E. 2d 463. Cf. Judge Desmond's concurring opinion.

20. U.S. 306 1952.

21. See, for example, J. Roland Pennock, "Reason, Value, and the Theory of Democracy," *American Political Science Review,* October, 1944, pp. 855-875; Willmore Kendall, "Prolegomena to Any Future Work on Majority Rule," *Journal of Politics,* XII, 694-713 (Nov., 1950); J. Austin Ranney, "Toward a More Responsible Two-Party System: a Commentary," *American Political Science Review,* XLV, 488-99 (June, 1951); J. Austin Ranney and Willmore Kendall, "Democracy: Confusion and Agreement," *Western Political Quarterly,* IV, 430-39 (Sept., 1951); Sidney Hook, *Heresy, Yes – Conspiracy, No* (New York: John Day Co., 1953).

22. For example, Justice Cardozo in *Palko v. Connecticut* spoke of "immunities implied in the concept of ordered liberty" and lists the four freedoms. 302 U.S. 319, 324-5.

23. There are other grave and complex questions of the greatest significance to our nation which will be seriously affected by the admission or denial of a political substance of American democracy which is resonant with religious and spiritual verities and values: Should public education be religiously neutral? What should be the nature and extent of cooperation in Church and State relations in America? Is not the religious neutrality of public education contrary to the official and authoritative professions of the religious foundations of American democracy? Can patriotic loyalty survive without adherence to the religious orientation of American democracy?; etc.

24. *New York Times,* March 29, 1955.

CIVIL LIBERTIES*

In the most comprehensive sense, civil liberties constitute that broad and changing body of substantive liberties and procedural safeguards that Justice Benjamin Cardozo once referred to as "of the essence of a scheme of ordered liberty" [*Palko v. Connecticut,* 302 U. S. 319 (1937)]. This vast complexus is customarily differentiated according to the nature of the freedoms guaranteed or the obstructions to their free enjoyment. Constitutional liberties are protected against government in the interest of individual freedom. *Civil rights give rise to reciprocal obligations enforceable against private persons. These in turn admit of two categories. The first category comprises all those private rights recognized in the law of torts, contract, and property and protected also by criminal law, as well as the further specification and extension of these rights by legislation, e.g., in rights to be secure against bodily assault, to be free to enter into contracts and to have them enforced, and to deny trespass on private property. Such rights generally have their origin in common law or statute; and any individual, without regard to group identity, may assert them against infringement by government or by private action. In the second category are political liberties and rights ensuing freedom to participate in the political processes of government and in the privileges of citizenship, e.g., the franchise, eligibility for public office, the freedom of speech and press to criticize governmental activities and the conduct of public officials, the right of the people peaceably to assemble, and the right to petition government for the redress of grievances. Human rights are such as are guaranteed to all without regard to citizenship, e.g., the requirements of

---

*NEW CATHOLIC ENCYCLOPEDIA, vol. iii, pp. 897-906.

due process of law in the administration of justice in court proceedings, the right to be unmolested in person and property. Depending on the context of reference, constitutional, political, and human rights and liberties may also be denoted as civil liberties or civil rights.

MORAL AND LEGAL FOUNDATIONS

The basic documents of the American Union, the Declaration of Independence and the Constitution of the U.S., are explicit with reference to the moral and legal bases of civil liberties.

Moral Basis. The ultimate moral foundations on which the inviolability of the human personality is predicated in American constitutional law are the Hebraic-Christian beliefs and natural-law doctrines that hold, in the words of the Declaration,

> that all men are created equal, that they are endowed by their Creator with certain unalienable Rights, that among these are Life, Liberty, and the pursuit of Happiness. —That to secure these rights, Governments are instituted among Men, deriving their just powers from the consent of the governed. —That whenever any Form of Government becomes destructive of these ends, it is the Right of the People to alter or to abolish it, and to institute new Government, laying its foundations on such principles and organizing its powers in such form, as to them shall seem most likely to effect their Safety and Happiness.

So prevalent among the colonists were the philosophical convictions thus expressed that Thomas Jefferson could write to Henry Lee 50 years after the event that the Declaration was "intended to be an expression of the American mind" and that "All its authority rests then on the harmonizing sentiments of the day" [*Writings* (Washington, D.C. 1903) 118]. *See POLITICAL THOUGHT,* AMERICAN.

Legal Sources. The dominant theme of the Constitutional Convention was that a national government limited by a written constitution to specific enumerated powers delegated by the people, and structured by the division of functions, separation of powers, and checks and balances, would be legally incompetent and practically unable to make encroachments on basic human rights and liberties that were beyond the reach of governmental authority. Nonetheless, the framers of the Constitution set down in the original organic act certain guarantees of civil liberties, namely, protection against suspension of the writ of habeas corpus (Art. 1, sec. 9), prohibition of bills of attainder or ex post facto laws by Congress (Art. 1, sec. 9) or by the states (Art. 1, sec. 10), the ban on religious tests as a qualification for public office (Art. 6), the requirement of trial by jury (Art. 3, sec. 2), restrictions on convictions for treason (Art. 3, sec. 3), and the guarantee to the citizens of each state of all privileges and immunities of citizens in the several states (Art. 4, sec. 2).

During the public debates in the state ratifying conventions, it became evident that adoption of the Constitution by some states would be on the condition that specific guarantees of liberties against Federal encroachment would be added. At the insistence of Roger Sherman of Connecticut the celebrated Bill of Rights was appended to the Constitution in the form of amendments, so as to emphasize the insertion of these guarantees as express and deliberate limitations on Federal power, something that might not have been accomplished by incorporating them in the body of the document, as James Madison had proposed. More than 20 specific provisions may be singled out in the first eight amendments. The First Amendment guarantees freedom of speech, press, assembly, and religion. The Second and Third Amendments on the right of the peoples to keep and bear arms and on the quartering of soldiers in private homes are significant mainly for disclosing certain deeply felt necessities and grievances of the new nation. The Fourth to Eighth Amendments have to do in great part with procedural protections in criminal trials, with other provisions on the right to privacy, and with government compensation for the taking of private property for public use. The 10th Amendment is simply declaratory of an existing constitutional arrangement on the division and delegation of powers to the Federal and state governments by the people. The Ninth Amendment, which provides that the enumeration of rights in the Constitution shall not be construed to deny or disparage others retained by the people suggests that basic human rights are broader than those specifically guaranteed and, by implication, these rights are no less inviolable against government encroachment.

Despite the reliance of Alexander Hamilton on the restriction of governmental powers in a written constitution, and the contention of the constitutional historian William W. Crosskey that the addition of the Bill of Rights was unnecessary and was actually intended to allay the fears aroused by the opponents of centralized national sovereignty *(Politics and the Constitution in the History of the United*

States, Chicago 1953), the significance of these amendments for the constitutional development of civil rights and liberties is beyond doubt, especially since the U.S. Supreme Court has made them applicable to the states through the 14th Amendment.

CLASSIFICATION

The whole aggregate of substantive and procedural civil rights and liberties can be divided into two categories on the basis of their origin. The basic distinction is between those rights and liberties that are protected by the language of the 14th Amendment against infringement or denial by the states and those Federally created rights and liberties that owe their origin to explicit or inferred provisions of the Constitution or to congressional enactment. This basic distinction between "protected" and "Federally created constitutional liberties" has great bearing in determining the proper agency, state or Federal, for the effective guarantee of their free exercise. The role of Congress in the area of "protected" rights and liberties is limited to authorizing corrective devices whereby the judicial and executive branches of government can ensure the unhampered enjoyment of civil liberties. Congress has a broader function in regard to Federally created rights and liberties by reason of its constitutionally endowed powers to originate these rights and to prescribe means of enforcement (see 14th Amendment, sec. 5). In this creative legislative role the actions of Congress are further strengthened by the interpretative and enforcement functions of the courts. To the Department of Justice of the executive branch falls the responsibility of the general enforcement of the laws of the U.S. as well as such specific functions committed to it by congressional authorization.

Protected Rights and Liberties. The 14th Amendment enjoins, "nor shall any State deprive any person of life, liberty, or property without due process of law, nor deny to any person within its jurisdiction the equal protection of the laws" (sec. 1). The Supreme Court in the *Civil Rights Cases,* 109 U.S. 3 (1883), found unconstitutional the Civil Rights Act of 1875 prohibiting racial discrimination in inns, public conveyances, and places of amusement; the Congress, it ruled, was not empowered under the 14th Amendment to enact positive legislation with respect to civil rights and to secure equality in the enjoyment of rights as against interference by private persons, but only to enforce these provisions against state action (sec. 5). Thus, since the enforcement power conferred is only corrective, Congress is not authorized to enact positive legislation governing private action in public facilities not owned or operated by a state government. Because of the precision of this ruling the constitutionality of Federal civil rights legislation may have to rest on both the 14th Amendment and the interstate commerce clause, on the supposition that discriminatory practices in privately owned public accommodations entail in some responsible way state complicity, or that the denial of these services affects substantially interstate commerce, which Congress has the constitutional power to regulate. The Federal government may also discourage discriminatory racial practices indirectly by withholding funds from local community projects.

Because the Court construed narrowly the 14th Amendment's grant of power to Congress to embrace no more than remedial and corrective legislation, the task of giving positive content and meaning to the "due process" and "equal protection" clauses of this amendment has devolved on the judiciary. It is what the Supreme Court says is required by due process and equal protection that constitutes these protected rights against state impairment. In addition to what the Court declares these protected rights to be as restraints on state action, the Court has also read into the meaning of "liberty" in the 14th Amendment elements of the Bill of Rights so that the incorporated liberty has become an identical limitation on state and Federal power.

Application to States. Although the history of the drafting and adoption of the Bill of Rights gives strong evidence that it was intended to restrict only the Federal government, in only two amendments is a limitation specifically directed against the national government, namely, in the First Amendment, which by its wording is made applicable only to Congress, and in one clause of the Seventh Amendment that stipulates that "no fact tried by a jury, shall be otherwise reexamined in any Court of the United States, than according to the rules of the common law." The limitation was settled beyond doubt in a unanimous opinion written by Chief Justice John Marshall in *Barron v. Baltimore,* 7 Pet. 243 (1833), in which the Court ruled that general provisions of the Constitution, including guarantees of the Bill of Rights, apply only to the Federal government. Arguing from history and textual interpretation, Marshall pointed out that whenever the organic act intended to reach state action it did so by explicit reference; e.g., sec. 9 and 10 of art. 1 both contain series of prohibitions on legislative action, but in section 9 these are expressed in general language, whereas in section 10 all the prohibitions imposed on the states are mentioned specifically. "Whenever the Constitutional provision was meant to affect the states," Marshall concluded, "words are employed which directly express that intent. . . . These amendments contain no expression indicating an intention to apply them to the state governments."

Although the adoption of the 14th Amendment did not affect the *Barron* ruling, it provided the legal instrumentality by which the Court could incorporate certain specifics of the first eight amendments into the meaning of "liberty" under the 14th Amendment and, accordingly, guarantee the identical rights protected against Federal encroachment equally against state interference. This judicial process of incorporation began in *Gitlow v. New York,* 268 U.S. 652 (1925), when the Court said that for "present purposes we may and do assume that freedom of speech and of the press—which are protected by the First Amendment from abridgment by Congress—are among the fundamental personal rights and 'liberties' protected by the due process clause of the Fourteenth Amendment from impairment by the states." Later decisions added religion [*Hamilton v. Regents of the University of California,* 293 U.S. 245 (1934), and *Cantwell v. Connecticut,* 310 U.S. 296 (1940)] and assembly and petition [*De Jonge v. Oregon,* 229 U.S. 353 (1937)]. The right of a criminally accused person to the benefit of counsel in capital cases was upheld in *Powell v. Alabama,* 287 U.S. 45 (1932). In *Gideon v. Wainwright,* 372 U.S. 335 (1963), this assurance was extended to all types of criminal cases. In *Mapp v. Ohio,* 367 U.S. 643 (1961), the Court added to the "included" rights the freedom from unreasonable search and seizure of the Fourth Amendment; in *Robinson v. California,* 370 U.S. 660 (1962), it added the prohibition against cruel and unusual punishments of the Eighth Amendment. On June 15, 1964 the Court overruled the precedent established in *Twining v. New Jersey,* 211 U.S. 78 (1908), when it held that the privilege of the Fifth Amendment applied in state as well as in Federal proceedings. The Federal standard of mere claim of liability to self-incrimination thus supercedes the general standard of state laws, according to which a mere claim of self-incrimination without explanation was regarded as insufficient and trial judges could determine whether there was reasonable ground to apprehend danger of criminal liability from compelled testimony. Another precedent was overruled on the same day when the Court held that a grant of immunity by either state or Federal government in order to compel testimony would preclude prosecutional action by the other as well (on the basis of the testimony given).

Fundamental Liberties. A distinction may be drawn between two sorts of rights and liberties that the Court has incorporated into the clauses of the 14th Amendment. Certain liberties are said to be "fundamental" and "basic" [cf. *Near v. Minnesota*, 283 U.S. 697 (1931)], so that they inhere in the concept of ordered liberty enunciated in *Palko v. Connecticut* and are equally restrictive of Federal and state action. These "fundamental" rights and liberties may coincide with their equivalent legal formulation in the Bill of Rights, as in the case of the First Amendment liberties, but as fundamental liberties they do not owe their origin to the Federal Constitution; among these are trial by jury in controversies in which $21 is at stake (Seventh Amendment) and criminal accusation on a presentment or indictment of a grand jury (Fifth Amendment). There is a substantial difference between the First Amendment freedoms that are incorporated in the 14th Amendment against state action by judicial construction and those liberties that are incorporated in the 14th Amendment because they are fundamental freedoms, basic and implicit in the concept of ordered liberty, although they may also coincide with First Amendment liberties. Although both sorts are operative upon the states, the manner of judicial determination differs in each case. The First Amendment freedoms enjoy a preferred status or, according to a minority of justices, an absolute status. Any law infringing upon these liberties is initially viewed by the Court with presumptive invalidity that only grave reasons of national security and public order may overcome under the "clear and present danger" norm. Fundamental freedoms rest solely on the due process clause of the 14th Amendment and, conceived as related to ordered liberty, are subject to the reasonable exercise of police power in the legitimate requirements of public order. In litigation on fundamental liberties the Court will either defer to legislative determination or weigh in a balance of interests the private claim of constitutional liberty against the gravity of national security under the "reasonable man" theory of judicial review.

Usually, however, the incorporation theory has reference to the absorption of specifics of the Bill of Rights into the clauses of the 14th Amendment. Within the Court, justices have divided by the narrowest of margins on the question whether the inclusion of Bill of Rights liberties and guarantees is only partial or total. In *Adamson v. California*, 332 U.S. 46 (1947), the Court, relying on the Twining and Palko decisions, held through Justice Stanley Reed that "the due process clause of the Fourteenth Amendment does not draw all the rights of the federal Bill of Rights under its protection." Justice Felix Frankfurter, in a concurring opinion, maintained that the 14th Amendment does not apply to the states "a shorthand summary of the first eight amendments, but rather protects from invasion by the States through the due process clause only those basic freedoms which are implicit in the concept of ordered liberty" and such as are in accordance with "those canons of decency and fairness which express the notions of justice of English-speaking peoples." At times the Court, independently of the incorporation process by which a universal application is affirmed, will rule in an *ad hoc* instance with sole reliance on due process that in a particular set of circumstances the requirements of essential justice or fairness have not been met. Thus, long before the Gideon case (1963), the Court held in *Powell v. Alabama* (1932) that "in a capital case, where the defendant is unable to employ counsel, and is incapable adequately of making his own defense because of ignorance, feeblemindedness, illiteracy or the like it is the duty of the court, whether requested or not, to assign counsel for him as a necessary requisite of due process of law." The actual holding was limited to the specific facts of the case without relating the due process clause of the 14th Amendment to the 6th Amendment. The continuing expansion of "fundamental" rights that correspond with those enumerated in the Bill of Rights, together with the gradual absorption of the formally defined liberties and guarantees of the Bill of Rights into the clauses of the 14th Amendment, may bring about an almost total parallelism just short of those specifics of the Bill of Rights for which state laws may have alternate or even superior provisions as in requirements for a jury trial in civil suits or in the manner of criminal indictment.

Judicial Standards for Civil Liberties Litigation. Certain rights, such as the franchise and trial by jury, are specific in kind and in the manner of their enjoyment cannot conceivably pose any threat to the rights of others and to the legitimate and reasonable exercise of police power. But First Amendment freedoms of religion, press, speech, and assembly admit a variety of expression that under certain circumstances and conditions may pose a grave challenge to the just requirements of national security and public order. The Constitution does not forbid Congress to abridge speech, press, etc.; rather, it denies to Congress the power to abridge the freedom of speech, etc. The Court has at different times formulated diverse canons of construction with which to mark off the area of inviolable freedom and the legitimate and reasonable functioning of police power.

The theory that prevailed in the trials brought under the Alien and Sedition Acts (1798) was taken from the English common law carried over into American law by way of Blackstone's *Commentaries*. It defined freedom of expression as freedom from previous restraint from a licensing power but with liability to punishment for the very fact of adverse criticism of the government and of its officers. Although the expiration of these two repressive statutes by their own terms kept them from an adjudication by the Supreme Court, the common-law freedom from previous restraint subject to the punitive consequences of the law received occasional affirmation well into the 1930s. In *Patterson v. Colorado*, 205 U.S. 454 (1907), Justice Oliver Wendell Holmes, better known for the "clear and present danger" test he developed years later, held that "the main purpose of such constitutional provisions (the First Amendment) is to 'prevent all such *previous restraints* upon publications as had been practiced by other governments,' and they do not prevent the subsequent punishment of such as may be deemed contrary to the public welfare." Not until *Grosjean v. American Press Co.*, 297 U.S. 233 (1936), did the Court abandon the narrow construction that the freedom consisted only in immunity from previous censorship.

In the meantime the Court forged another test with which to distinguish legitimate freedoms of speech and press from license. It had applied the "reasonable tendency" rule in World War I espionage cases that involved either pamphlets or foreign-language newspapers critical of the war effort and in the State Criminal Syndicalism Act cases of the 1920s. In these instances the Court looked to the reasonable tendency of the acts done to influence or bring about the effects and consequences forbidden by law. While this test held sway a new norm, the "clear and present danger" test, was formulated by Holmes in *Schenck v. United States*, 249 U.S. 47 (1919):

The question in every case is whether the words used are used in such circumstances and are of such a nature as to create a clear and present danger that will bring about the substantive evils that Congress has a right to prevent. It is a question of proximity and degree. When a nation is at war many things that might be said in time of peace are such a hindrance to its effort that their utterance will not be endured so long as men fight and that no court could regard them as protected by any constitutional right.

When Chief Justice Charles Evans Hughes, in *Near v. Minnesota* (1931), revitalized the "no previous restraint" theory in its broader meaning, disengaged from summary consequences of law for adverse criticism, it prevailed during the decade of the 1930s in place of the "bad tendency" theory of the 1920s and of the "clear and present danger" theory. The Holmesian norm finally achieved majority status in the 1940s. It was extended beyond cases involving national security to uphold picketing; to strike down statutes and municipal ordinances that interfered with the activities of the Jehovah's Witnesses; to contempt of court cases, state and Federal, that arose from public criticism about the conduct of pending trials; and even to defend the right to make provocative public utterances, critical and contemptuous of the creed of casual auditors.

The alarming successes of the Communist worldwide conspiracy brought about a substantial modification of the "clear and present danger" test in *Dennis v. United States*, 341 U.S. 494 (1951), when the Court adopted the formula that Justice Learned Hand had used in the Court of Appeals: "Whether the gravity of the evil, discounted by its improbability, justifies such invasion of free speech as is necessary to avoid the danger." The substitution of "probability" for "remoteness" seemed to require something more than "reasonable tendency" but something less than a "clear and present danger." This rephrasing of the concept of danger to be weighed was not used subsequently as a rule of decision by a plurality or majority of the Court. In the early 1960s, when an apparent conflict arose between the First Amendment freedoms of belief, expression, and association and congressional investigatory powers and legislation on subversive activities and membership, a narrowly divided Court resorted to the norm of "balancing of interest." The restrictions that governmental regulations imposed on the entire freedom of individual action were weighed against the value to the public of the ends that the regulations were intended to achieve.

Each of these judicial canons of construction presupposes a concept of the status of the freedoms in question and an attitude toward legislative findings. Absolutists such as Justice Hugo Black insist on a strict literal acceptance of the First Amendment prohibition so that Congress may not under any circumstances impinge upon the unrestricted or absolute enjoyment of these liberties. A modified version of the absolutist position is to exclude from the definition of a protected freedom certain types of self-expression. In the Roth and Albert cases (1957) the Court ruled that obscene publications are not the type of self-expression protected by the free press guarantees of the First Amendment. At times the Court has given a preferred status to these liberties so that any law restricting them is viewed with presumptive invalidity and government has had the burden of justifying before the Court the restrictive regulation on grounds of "clear and present danger" or by a show of substantive and grave danger. The "reasonable man" theory that is employed usually in a balancing of private versus public interest generally defers to legislative determinations. By the early 1960s the Court was inclined to approach First Amendment issues by considering them as questions of evidence rather than as requiring decision on constitutional grounds. In *Garner v. Louisiana,* 368 U.S. 157 (1961), a "sit-in" case, the Court chose to rest its decision on whether the petitioners' convictions were justified by evidence "which would support a finding that the petitioners' acts caused a disturbance of the peace." All these diverse canons of construction on First Amendment freedoms seem ultimately to involve some sort of balancing of interests, the difference in approach being prompted by an appraisal of contemporary social conditions.

Federal Rights and Liberties. In addition to the "protected" rights guaranteed against state impairment by the 14th Amerndment, there is the category of Federally established constitutional rights and liberties. These originate either in the Constitution or in Federal legislation and treaties. They are protected by the Federal government not only against encroachment by Federal and state governments but also against interference by private persons. These Federally created rights and liberties may be said to be incident to national citizenship. As guarantees against private obstruction, they are considered as civil rights; as against governmental infringement they are called civil liberties. Since they originate formally in the Constitution or owe their existence to the constitutional powers of the Federal government, its laws and treaties, they are generally called constitutional liberties. Although there has been no complete official enumeration of them, a listing of many may be found in a Federal court of appeals case, *Brewer v. Hoxie,* 238 F. 2d 91 (1956).

Originating in the Constitution. Specifically designated in the Constitution are the right to vote for congressmen (Art. 1, sec. 2) and senators (17th Amendment). Qualified Federal electors are those who become eligible electors under state law subject, however, to constitutional prohibitions against exclusion based on race (15th Amendment) or sex (19th Amendment) and to the requirements of the equal protection clause of the 14th Amendment. Because of their distinctly Federal character, Congress may take appropriate measures to protect these rights against state and private hindrance [*United States v. Classic,* 313 U.S. 299 (1941)]. Congress also has the power expressly granted to it by the Constitution to "make or alter" regulations on the "Times, Places and Manner of holding Elections" for Federal officers (Art. 1, sec. 4).

Federal rights that constitute the privileges and immunities of national citizenship are the right to interstate travel; the right of access to the Federal government and its officers against violence in the enjoyment of the decrees of a Federal court, in testifying before a Federal tribunal, and in fulfilling the duties of a Federal office to which one has been lawfully elected; and the right of the people peaceably to assemble to petition Congress for a redress of grievances. It is a matter of judicial determination to affirm what rights and liberties are among the privileges and immunities of Federal citizenship.

Originating in Federal Legislation and Treaties. Federal rights that are a product of congressional legislation embrace three categories.

First, by virtue of its sumptuary legislative power over Federal territories Congress may legislate against discriminatory practices in employment, public facilities, and privately owned public accommodations and impose criminal and civil sanctions for noncompliance [*District of Columbia v. John R. Thompson Co.,* 346 U.S. 100 (1953)].

Second, by its power to regulate interstate commerce Congress has enacted the National Labor Relations Act, establishing the statutory right of collective bargaining, and rights to strike and picket within limits set by Congress (29 U.S.C.A., sec. 610), and the Federal Communications Act (47 U.S.C.A., sec. 605), defining the rights to secrecy and privacy of the mails and electronic communications and immunity against the use of unlawfully intercepted communications in Federal court proceedings. Congressional statutes forbid interstate carriers to discriminate in their services for reasons of race or color or to enforce regulations of these statutes that prescribe racial segregation [49 U.S.C.A., secs. 216 (d) and 316 (d)]. On the basis of these statutes the Supreme Court in *Boynton v. Virginia,* 364 U.S. 454 (1960), forbade restauranteurs who service interstate passengers from discriminating against Negroes. On a broad interpretation of interstate commerce in conjunction with the 14th Amendment, Congress enacted the Civil Rights Act of 1964 to bar racial discrimination in employment and in use of public facilities and of privately owned accommodations on the ground that certain discriminatory practices bear a substantive impact on interstate commerce that Congress has the power to regulate.

Third, there is the spending power of Congress exercised for the promotion of civil rights by withdrawing or denying Federal funds for the construction of both public and private housing, schools, or hospitals where business enterprises or communities persist in racially discriminatory practices. Similar provisions may be stipulated in government contracts with private industries. The Federal denial of these fiscal benefits is to be distinguished from the corrective power that the 14th Amendment confers on the Congress for the enforcement of the due process and equal protection clauses. Civil liberties and rights that originate in congressional legislation have their own statutory remedies and sanctions. A manufacturer, for example, whose products are engaged in interstate commerce and who practices racial discrimination in employment contrary to congressional legislation may be subject to criminal sanctions for violating the act, may be liable to civil damages, may be restrained by an injunctive remedy, or may be held to an administrative hearing for determination of the unfair labor practices.

The difference between the "protected" rights and the Federally created rights differentiates the role of Congress in relation to these liberties. In regard to the "protected" rights Congress is limited by the narrow interpretation of the 14th Amendment in the *Civil Rights Cases.* Its function is broader, however, when it exercises one of its several constitutionally granted substantive powers to legislate positively in the creation of rights and liberties and thereby establish a Federal cause of action in favor of persons injured by private individuals as well as by state action through the abridgment of Federally created constitutional rights.

ENFORCEMENT

All three branches of government necessarily participate in the enforcement of civil liberties. Also, some private organizations, such as the American Civil Liberties Union, are devoted specifically to the cause of civil liberties.

Judicial. The principal instrumentality by which the judiciary ensures the independence of its own judicial process and the carrying out of its decisions is the exercise of the Federal equity power to issue restraining orders or injunctions and court decrees commanding that an action be done. It is a very effective remedial device, since it can be issued without delay and it subjects persons guilty of violating court decrees to summary contempt procedure and to fines and imprisonment or both without a jury trial. Progress against the obstructive tactics of state officials in defiance of the school desegregation ruling was made principally through the employment of the injunctive power. It also has the advantage of reaching private individuals, whose obstructive tactics are not subject as are state actions to the equal protection clause of the 14th Amendment, on the grounds that they are thereby interfering with Federal court orders or with the enjoyment of Federally created rights based on Federal court decrees [*Kasper v. Brittain,* 245 F. 2d (6th Cir.1957)]. Consequently, intimidations, threats, and physical and economic reprisals by private individuals to keep citizens from the free exercise of their civil liberties – e.g., by registering and voting in Federal elections or attending a public school integrated by a local school board with the sanction of a Federal court decree – may be enjoined to desist and so be brought within range of the contempt power of the Federal courts. Where massive resistance to court decrees renders the regular officers of the court, the marshals, incapable of enforcing the court orders, statutory law empowers the President to use Federal troops in order to remove obstructions to the carrying out of the decree of the Federal court (Sec. 333, 10 U.S.C.A.).

The most creative action of the judiciary in the cause of civil liberties has been the practical consequence of its narrow construction of the 14th Amendment in the *Civil Rights Cases.* The judiciary thereby assumed the principal role of determining the essential content of due process and equal protection of the 14th Amendment and of the rights they embrace. In this creative function, the Court has defined the rights of the accused in state criminal proceedings, the guarantee of counsel in capital cases, the selection of impartial juries, admissible evidence, and, above all, the momentous ruling on equal protection in the school desegregation cases. To these must be added the element of the Bill of Rights incorporated into the "liberty" of the 14th Amendment as well as the designation of fundamental human rights operative with equal and identical restriction on state as well as on Federal governmental power.

Legislative. Congress possesses vast reservoirs of substantive powers for the protection and creation of civil liberties and rights. The 14th Amendment confers on Congress the power to enact corrective legislation against state denial of civil liberties and, in addition, the Constitution delegates to Congress several independent legislative powers that may be directly or indirectly employed for the promotion of civil liberties and rights — power over interstate commerce, the spending power — and sumptuary legislative powers over Federal territories.

Until 1957 the constitutional history of congressional legislation on civil rights and liberties had been almost wholly a record of frustration and ineffectiveness. The Civil Rights Act of 1866 that became law over the veto of Pres. Andrew Johnson provided in part:

> That all persons born in the United States and not subject to any foreign power, excluding Indians not taxed, are hereby declared to be citizens of the United States, and such citizens, of every race and color, without regard to any previous condition of slavery or involuntary servitude except as a punishment for crime whereof the party shall have been duly convicted, shall have the same right, in every State and Territory in the United States, to make and enforce contracts, to sue, be parties, and give evidence, to inherit, purchase, lease, sell, hold, and convey real and personal property, and to full and equal benefit of all laws and proceedings for the security of person and property, as is enjoyed by white citizens, and shall be subject to like punishment, pains and penalties, and to none other, any law, statute, ordinance, regulation, or custom to the contrary notwithstanding. [Act of April 9, 1866, 14 Stat. 27.]

Serious doubts raised about the constitutionality of this act led to the adoption of the 14th Amendment in 1868. It defined citizenship and enjoined the states from abridging the privileges or immunities of citizens of the U.S.; depriving any persons of life, liberty, or property without due process of the law; or denying any person equal protection of the laws. The 15th Amendment of 1870 declared that the right of citizens of the U.S. to vote shall not be denied or abridged by the U.S. or by any state on account of race, color, or previous condition of servitude.

Enforcement Acts. In 1870 Congress passed the First Enforcement Act (Act of may 31, 1870, 16 Stat. 140) in order to implement the 14th and 15th Amendments. It declared that all citizens of the U.S. who are otherwise entitled to vote in any state election, municipality, or other subdivision shall be entitled to vote without distinction of race, color, or previous condition of servitude. State prerequisites for voting were to apply to all citizens with equal opportunity. Persons hindering, obstructing, or exercising control over qualified electors in the exercise of their franchise were made subject to fine, imprisonment, or both. Violators were to be prosecuted in the courts of the U.S. and all Federal officials were to cooperate in the enforcement of the law. On Feb. 28, 1871, Congress passed the Second Enforcement Act. It provided that supervisors of elections were to be appointed by Federal courts so that any interference with the discharge of their duties constituted a Federal offense. Elections and supervisors and their work were placed under the jurisdiction of the Federal courts (16 Stat. 433). On April 20, 1871, Congress passed the Third Enforcement Act (17 Stat. 13) generally known as the "Ku Klux Act" because sections of it were directed against the clandestine activities of secret societies such as the Klan.

When the disputed presidential election of 1876 was resolved in favor of Republican Rutherford B. Hayes by the close vote of eight to seven on strict party lines in a special electoral commission, the acceptance of this decision by Southern Democrats was made contingent on the promise that Federal troops would be withdrawn from the South and that a Southerner would be appointed to the cabinet. The withdrawal of the last Federal troops from the South in 1877 was the start of a succession of reversals that rendered the newly adopted constitutional amendments and congressional statutes wholly incapable of any effective implementation and enforcement. In 1880 Congress enacted legislation that forbade the employment of military forces in elections (Act of May 4, 1880, 21 Stat. 113), and in 1894 it repealed those portions of the First Enforcement Act that required qualifications to be equal for all persons, obliged election officials to receive the vote of all qualified electors, and provided punishment for any person found guilty of obstructing the exercise of the franchise. Congress also repealed the provisions of the Second Enforcement Act that stipulated the conditions and manner under which Federal elections were to be supervised.

Of the remaining legislation, two important sections of the Third Enforcement Act that have since been incorporated under title 18 of the U. S. Criminal Code have been sustained by the Supreme Court. Section 241 provides a fine of up to $5,000 and imprisonment of up to 10 years or both for a conspiracy by two or more persons to "injure, oppress, threaten or intimidate any citizen in the free exercise or enjoyment of any right or privilege secured to him by the Constitution or laws of the United States, or because of his having so exercised the same." Under this section, private persons who are guilty of infraction of Federally created rights, including the rights of citizenship, can be punished. On June 26, 1964, agents of the Federal Bureau of Investigation arrested three men in Mississippi for violating this section by interfering with the right to engage in voter-registration activities. The other criminal statute, sect. 242, provides a $1,000 fine or 1 year in prison, or both, for any person who acting "under color of any law, statute, ordinance, regulation, or custom, willfully subjects any inhabitant of any State, Territory or District to the deprivation of any rights, privileges, or immunities secured or protected by the Constitution or laws of the United States." "Under color of law" means not only action exercised by virtue of the authority of public office [*Ex parte Virginia*, 100 U.S. 339 (1880)] but also "misuse of power, possessed by virtue of state law and made possible only because the wrongdoer is clothed with the authority of state law" (*United States v. Classic*). A state police officer could be indicted under sec. 242 for causing the death of a prisoner in his custody even if his action was totally lawless in violation of state law [*Screws v. United States*, 325 U. S. 91 (1945)].

Parallel to these two criminal action statutes are two civil suit statutes. Section 1985 of title 42 allows a damage suit against two or more persons who deprive or conspire to deprive "any person or class of persons of the equal protection of the laws, or of equal privileges and immunities under the laws." This statute incongruously sets remedial damage action against private persons for obstructing the equal protection of laws, which according to the Court's interpretation of the 14th Amendment are restraints only on state activities. Section 1983 of title 42 provides for civil suits against state officers by making them liable to monetary damages for "unlawful law enforcement," such as officially enforcing segregation ordinances and practices in public schools, buses, and parks. These criminal and civil liability statutes have not proved very effective in the guarantee of either "protected" or Federally created "secured rights." The prospects of an adverse verdict from a local jury in some communities have not been such as to discourage seriously further violations of civil liberties. Monetary compensation does not correct the actual denial of a liberty and ordinarily the financial assets of a state officer scarcely allow more than a nominal award.

Civil Rights Act of 1875. The Civil Rights Act of 1875 declared that all persons within the jurisdiction of the U. S. "shall be entitled to the full and equal enjoyment of the accommodations, advantages, facilities and privileges of inns, public conveyances on land and water, theatres, and other places of public amusement; subject only to the conditions and limitations established by law and applicable alike to citizens of every race and color, regardless of any previous condition of servitude" (Act of March 1, 1875, 18 Stat. 335). In its historic decision declaring this act unconstitutional, the Court, as already noted, restricted Congress to appropriate legislation to enforce the prohibitions that sec. 1 placed on the states, thus limiting the enforcement power to a corrective, remedial function and denying to Congress the role of defining in positive terms the content of individual rights that the states were prohibited to deny.

Civil Rights Act of 1957. Impetus for the Civil Rights Act of 1957 (71 Stat. 634) gathered momentum as a consequence of the *Segregation Cases* of 1954. The act authorized the Federal government to bring civil suits in its own name to obtain injunctive relief in order to protect the right to vote from hindrance. While this relieved the offended person from the expense of litigation, it also effectively brought within the reach of Federal contempt proceedings registration officals who persisted in discriminatory practices. The use of the criminal contempt power as an instrument for enforcing an equitable decree is intended to eliminate frustrating delays by avoiding a jury trial with the exception, however, that in the event of a conviction exceeding a fine of $300 or a jail sentence of

40 days, the defendant is entitled to a trial *de novo* before a jury (42 U.S.C.A. sec. 1995). The Federal district courts were given jurisdiction over these civil proceedings without first requiring recourse to state remedies. The civil rights section of the Department of Justice was granted the statutory status of a new division with the appointment of an assistant attorney general. The act established a civil rights section of the Department of Justice was granted the statutory status of a new division with the appointment of an assistant attorney general. The act established a civil rights commission, the first of its kind in American history (42 U.S.C.A. sec 1975) with powers of subpoena to investigate allegations of denials of civil rights, to gather information, and to make reports and recommendations on needed legislation. In *Hannah v. Larche*, 363 U.S. 420 (1960), the Supreme Court upheld the commission's power to conduct hearings on the basis of information given by secret informers without disclosing their names. However, the effectiveness of the 1957 act was seriously impaired by the new evasive tactics of resigning state registrars and the unavailability of registration and voting records to Federal inspectors.

Civil Rights Acts of 1960. By the Civil Rights Act of 1960 (74 Stat. 86) Congress provided that discriminatory practices of registrars would be deemed also acts of the state, which might therefore be enjoined as a party defendant. In the event of the resignation of a registrar, the proceeding may still be instituted against the state. Voting records are required to be preserved for 22 months following an election, and the attorney general has the right of inspection and copying in order to determine whether a suit should be instituted. Federal district courts are authorized to appoint Federal voting referees to weigh the complaints of qualified electors alleging that they were prevented from registration and voting. If the referee reports to the court the existence of obstructive tactics, the court may then issue a decree ordering that the qualified elector be permitted to vote. Defiance of the decree is punishable as contempt of court (74 Stat. 86). By this new device of court-appointed voting referees, the Federal government entered into a process normally under state control. In a number of litigations, the constitutionality of "interpretation tests" of state constitutions that some prospective voters had to pass to the satisfaction of registrars were successfully challenged in Federal district courts.

Civil Rights Act of 1964. In 1964 Congress enacted another Civil

Rights Act (78 Stat. 241), wherein it extended the reach of Federal power by granting to the attorney general authority to initiate suits in areas other than voting, to request trials before a statutory three-judge Federal court in order to avoid the prejudiced rulings of sectionally minded judges, and to approve of summary criminal contempt proceedings without trial by jury under certain prescribed limits.

Title 1, on voting, was intended to remove the arbitrary obstacles placed in the way of Negro voting applicants and to hasten the process of judicial remedies. It prohibits registrars from applying different standards to white and Negro citizens. It strikes at the arbitrary literacy and law interpretation tests Negroes were required to pass to the discretionary satisfaction of the registrars by making a sixth-grade education a rebuttable presumption of literacy. No one is to suffer disqualification because of inconsequential errors on the forms. By provision of the Third Enforcement Act of 1871 (42 U. S. A. sec. 1983), aggrieved individuals could institute civil damage suits against state officers for depriving them of their constitutional rights of sec. 131. The Civil Rights Act of 1957 authorized the Federal government to bring civil suits in its own name to obtain injunctive relief when any person is denied or threatened in his right to vote, since many were unable to support the financial cost of protracted litigation. Section 601 of the Civil Rights Act of 1960 authorized Federal district courts to ascertain on request of the attorney general whether deprivation of voting is pursuant to a pattern or practice, and also the use of Federal court-appointed voting referees to receive applications from prospective voters who claim to have been denied free and equal opportunity to register and vote. If the referee reports to the court that the complaint of the prospective elector is proved, then the court will issue a decree ordering that the qualified voter be permitted to vote, thus relieving him of the personal responsibility of initiating civil suit himself. Refusal to honor the decree is punishable as contempt of court. Reflecting the endeavor of Congress to further expedite the judicial remedies, title 1 of the Civil Rights Act of 1964 permits the attorney general to apply to the courts for relief wherever a pattern of discrimination exists, and allows him or the defendant state officials to request trial by a three-judge court—of whom one must be a circuit judge—with precedence for voting cases on the calendar. In the absence of an established pattern of discrimination, the aggrieved person must sue for his rights.

Title 2 of the act of 1964 bans discrimination and refusal of service on ground of race, color, religion, or national origin in privately owned public accommodations, such as, hotels, motels, restaurants, gasoline stations, and places of amusement if their operation affects interstate commerce or if their discriminatory practices are supported by state action. Excluded are beauty parlors and owner-occupied rooming houses with no more than five rooms. When there has been an attempted or actual deprivation of these rights, civil action for preventive relief may be instituted by the aggrieved person and the court may in its discretion permit the attorney general to intervene if the case is of general public importance. Waiting periods are required before instituting a private suit in a Federal court to permit states with antidiscrimination laws to settle the issue or to allow the Federal community relations service to bring about voluntary compliance in states without such laws. Further, the attorney general is empowered to initiate suits promptly without a waiting period (as in private suits) only when he finds patterns or practices of resistance without first receiving complaints as is required under the titles for public facilities and public schools. This title does not permit the attorney general to file suits on behalf of individuals as he is permitted to do for citizens who are unable to sue effectively under titles for public facilities and public schools. The attorney general may also request trial by a three-judge court.

Title 3 requires that no one may be denied, on the ground of race, color, religion, or national origin, equal utilization of any publicly owned or operated facilities other than public schools, such as parks, swimming pools, and libraries. Whereas formerly the aggrieved person had to sue for his own rights, the attorney general is permitted to initiate suits on behalf of the aggrieved but only after receiving a written complaint from one whom he judges unable to sue effectively.

Under title 4 the attorney general is empowered to institute suits to compel desegregation in public schools under the same conditions as in title 3. Furthermore, the Federal government is authorized to provide limited financial and technical aid to school districts to assist in the process of desegregation. This title specifically excludes correction of racial imbalance in public schools by compulsory busing of pupils.

Title 5 extended the life of the civil rights commission to Jan. 1, 1968.

Title 6 declares that no person shall be subjected to racial discrimination "under any program or activity receiving federal financial assistance." It directs Federal agencies in charge of certain programs, not including Federal insurance activities, to take definite steps to eliminate existing discriminatory practices and if necessary, as a last resort, to terminate aid to the culpable local institution or community. Any final decision to stop Federal funds is made subject to judicial review.

Title 7 established an equal employment opportunity commission with authority to investigate complaints of discrimination by employers or unions with 100 or more employees or members in the first year the act was effective, this number to be reduced over a 4-year transitional period to 25 or more. The attorney general is authorized to sue in the Federal courts if he believes any person or group is engaged in a pattern or practice of resistance to the title and the offending employer or union cannot be persuaded to end discrimination voluntarily. He is also empowered to ask for trial by a three-judge court.

Title 8 directs the census bureau to ascertain the number of persons eligible to vote in areas designated by the civil rights commission. Such information might be used to enforce the provision of the 14th Amendment that states that discriminate in voting shall lose seats in the House of Representatives.

Title 9 was intended to cope with the frustration felt by defendants in state criminal trials who have, on a show of jeopardy to their civil rights in state tribunals, been allowed to remove their cases to the Federal courts, with the result, more often than not, that lower Federal judges have remanded these cases back to the state courts and the decisions to remand have been held unappealable. Title 9 also allows appellate review of such orders.

Title 10 established in the U.S. Department of Commerce a community relations service to mediate racial disputes.

Title 11 guarantees jury trials for criminal contempt under any part of the act except Title 1 and provides that the statute shall not invalidate state laws with consistent purposes and that it shall not impair any existing power of Federal officials.

The Civil Rights Acts of 1957, 1960, and 1964, and other measures such as the Voting Rights Act of 1965, disclose amply what a large reservoir of diverse substantive powers Congress possesses not only for legislating remedial and corrective measures for the guarantee of the unhampered exercise of "protected" rights and liberties, but also for the exercise of a positive function of creating Federal rights and liberties with adequate and effective enforcement procedures against both private and public impairment. The Voting Rights Act of 1965 condemns poll taxes in state and local elections, instructs the attorney general to move in the courts to invalidate discriminatory poll taxes, provides Federal machinery for registration of Negroes in Southern states, and extends the presumption of literacy to persons whose native tongue is not English but who have had at least six grades in an "American flag school" (e.g., Puerto Ricans).

Executive. The role of the executive in relation to civil rights and liberties is, apart from moral leadership and in the recommendation and promotion of congressional legislation for their advancement, to ensure the independence of court proceedings and the carrying out of their decrees, even to the extent, as a last resort, of summoning armed forces to ensure freedom of judicial action and compliance (Sec. 333, 10 U.S.C.A.). The Department of Justice is invested with the power to initiate criminal actions under sections 241 and 242 of the criminal code, title 18; and under the terms of the Civil Rights Acts of 1957, 1960, and 1964 it is also authorized to institute civil suits in its own name to obtain injunctive relief to enforce the provisions of these laws and to intervene in certain specified instances.

American Civil Liberties Union. A number of private organizations have dedicated themselves to the cause of civil rights and liberties. Some, such as the National Association for the Advancement of Colored People, have labored for the protection of individual rights against denials based on race, color, religion, or national origin. The American Civil Liberties Union (ACLU) has had from its establishment a broader range of rights and activities to defend. Since its foundation in 1917 by Roger Baldwin, it has come to the support of the rights of conscience and self-expression of others against antievolution laws and Federal antisedition statutes, and it has supported the right of labor to organize, to bargain collectively, and to strike. On First Amendment liberties, it tends to favor unrestricted freedom of expression, opposing the Smith Act of 1940, the Federal loyalty programs, and laws against obscene literature as threats to civil liberties. It has upheld conscientious objectors to military service and to flag saluting and has fought against zoning laws excluding religious institutions from residential areas. On the relations of Church and State it has committed itself unequivocally to total neutrality, toward the elimination of any religious exercise or manifestation in public schools – prayer, Bible reading, crèches, religious festivities — and to the denial of any aid in any form to church-related schools. It disagrees with and hopes for the reversal of the decision in *Everson v. Board of Education,* 330 U.S. 1 (1947), which upheld free bus transportation to pupils of parochial schools, and the ruling in *Zorach v. Clauson,* U.S. 306 (1952), allowing released time off school premises for religious instructions. The ACLU has an admirable record in fighting for the elimination of segregation in travel, housing, employment, and schooling. Some of its more significant achievements have been in the enlargement of the rights of the accused in court proceedings and of witnesses before congressional investigatory committees, and of the protection that should be accorded aliens. The ACLU has fought for civil rights and civil liberties without reference to group identity.

Bibliography: W. M. Beaney, *The Right to Counsel in American Courts* (Ann Arbor 1955). *The Constitution of the United States of America,* ed. E. S. Corwin (Washington 1953). D. Fellman, *The Constitutional Right of Association* (Chicago 1963); *The Defendant's Rights* (New York 1958). E. G. Hudson, *Freedom of Speech and Press in America* (Washington 1963). P. G. Kauper, *Civil Liberties and the Constitution* (Ann Arbor 1962). C. B. Swisher, *American Constitutional Development* (2d ed. Boston 1954). U.S. Commission on Civil Rights, *Freedom to the Free, Century of Emancipation 1863-1963: A Report to the President* (Washington 1963).

PUBLIC PROTEST AND CIVIL DISOBEDIENCE MORAL AND LEGAL CONSIDERATIONS*

It is surely not inappropriate to discourse on public protest and civil disobedience in the state of Louisiana. In the last six years some of the more memorable court tests relevant to these twin questions originated in this state: *Garner v. Louisiana*,[1] (1961), *Taylor v. Louisiana*[2] (1962); *Cox v. Louisiana*[3] (1965), and *Brown v. Louisiana*[4] (1966). And if we recall reaching into the past, we shall find historically cognate, the *Slaughter House*[5] cases (1873), *Hall v. De Cuir*[6] (1878), *United States v. Classic*[7] (1941).

We have now in recent years witnessed a mass phenomenon of public protests and civil disobedience in almost every geographic sector of the country. The public fact of protest and dissent is not novel in American history. One need only recall the anti-war protests during the first World war, the labor picketing cases, and the large cluster of Jehovah's Witnesses. What distinguishes the mass demonstrations of today from these earlier experiences,—apart from the present-day arguable opposition to American combat participation in Vietnam and the more questionable activities on university campuses—is that they are an anguished cry for social and racial justice to which generally speaking the consciences of the vast majority of the American community and of state and federal governments have responded albeit in an uneven manner. It is not the interest of a particular category of labor, of the intelligentsia, or of the pacifist—that cries out for recognition and remedy, but the soul stirring demand that we accord to our fellowmen, whatever their ethnic or racial identity, that equality which we so devoutly confess to in our Christian faith.

---

*LOYOLA LAW REVIEW (New Orleans). Vol. xiii, nos. 1 and 2, 1966-1967, pp. 21-56. Lecture given at the Loyola University Law School (New Orleans).

My discourse this evening turns upon the moral and legal presuppositions by which we may distinguish permissible from impermissible forms of public protest and civil disobedience whether in support of the civil rights movement or in opposition to it in the name of conscience and one's own convictions of what constitutional law ought to be. Nothing could be more misleading than to suppose that my tentative reflections are directed solely to the advocates of the civil rights cause. They should apply with equal force—if valid—to opposing dissidents and protestants.

THE APPEAL TO CONSCIENCE

The ultimate moral justification for acts of public protest and civil disobedience to existent law is the appeal to conscience. The real and full meaning, however, of the uncontroverted axiom, conscience is always binding,—is not altogether self-evident. It may have, as it generally does, a religious referral,—"we ought to obey God rather than men"—or the appeal may be to an objective standard of moral justice in the light of which certain dispositions of man-made law are judged to be a legal imposition of injustice,—prescinding or disavowing the divine origination of the universal moral law. The subject may then claim not to be bound to compliance with the human law and for such as these, the Anglo-American and generally most western legal systems provide exemptions for conscientious objectors whose religious creed or its equivalent is contrary to combative military service.

Our problem is a much larger one. The political, social, economic, and legal circumstances of a people may be so intolerable that they may have recourse to such acts of public agitation as to induce a change by law, if necessary, to correct the inequities and injustices visited upon them by the general public in a pattern of discriminatory activities.

"Conscience is always binding" means at least this, that a person who is about to act of his own accord, that is, he is not coerced by others to do what he would not otherwise do. Such a person does not choose a course of action unless impelled to it by a practical judgment that motivates him to choose to do so in obedience to a moral imperative as he personally understands it. There are several limitations attendant upon this ethical axiom. To admit as much as we have stated is not to say that a man's judgment and choice of action

are invested with moral rectitude. The subjective conscience however firm in its personal sense of moral correctness may be objectively in error. Obedience to such a conscience may excuse from sin, from moral culpability, but not from punitive consequences if its outward expression injures another. In a word, because conscience is fallible, its personal dictates are not as absolutely controlling in the presence of others as it may be in solitary existence. While the generality of mankind admits to primary principles of morality, the hazard of disagreement enlarges as we proceed to the secondary and tertiary principles wherein the immediacy of self-evident truths diminish as a matter of human experience. The problem is further compounded when a particular moral precept is made to bear on specific instances within the order of public law, and doubly compounded when opposing claims of conscience are made on the proper role and reach of public law on the regulation of human relations. Of course, the appeal to conscience must, to win acceptance, also be coupled with the appeal to reason. And while human intelligences are open to persuasion and enlightenment, they can be impervious to conversion. The duty to obey the dictates of conscience within a public order may be ultimate but never absolute.

CONSCIENCE AND THE ORDER OF RIGHTS

As we have noted, the dictates of conscience are absolutely controlling in a solitary existence such as that of the fabled Robinson Crusoe. However, once he noticed the footprints of man Friday on the sands of the seashore, a human relationship emerged and with it an order of rights and duties. Human rights and duties, moral and legal, presuppose the presence of other men. For an authentic right is a claim to an action or to a possession as against a contrary claim and against arbitrary interference from another. We must therefore distinguish between claims of conscience in themselves and claim of conscience which engender subject rights only in the midst of others. The whole complexus of human rights and immunities which originate ultimately in men's social and political capacities which we call the "unalienable rights" of man constitute the objective moral order, and the human safeguards and guarantees that are correspondent and commensurate with social and political co-existence constitute the juridical order.

A POSTULATE OF REASON

We do not speak of *abstract* rights, immunities, and liberties. We speak of *real* rights and duties. Rights, duties, and liberties inhere in a concrete object, – in human persons as they are existentially related to one another.

Since we are historically and legally situated in the Republic of America, we must either accept the postulate that we *can* remedy, however sluggishly, injustices and inequities by the processes of law as embodied in our political and legal institutions or we shall have to speak within the context of a revolution wherein a people opposes with armed forces a government and its supporters or within the context of a civil war wherein a nation is divided in half and each strives to prevail by force of arms. In America we have known both experiences. I cling hopefully to that postulate not only for myself but also for all Americans, however diverse and contrary their views of moral and legal justice. I am not unmindful that for the greater time of our national history our governments – including the judiciary – held to and enforced a contrary proposition on racial relations, on moral and constitutional grounds which in the last three decades they have just as earnestly endeavored to reverse. Either on all sides we shall abide by that postulate of hope and adjust our differences in the manner that comports with civilized living or we shall take to the violence and destruction of warriors, who have abandoned all hope in the efficacy of political and legal processes.

Granted this postulate of reasonable hopefulness in the orderly processes of law, our government under law requires obedience to its laws as long as they are not repealed or judicially repudiated. Of course, a law which is not supported by general acceptance and is in practice rejected, even by habitually law-abiding citizens, cannot be effectively enforced and results in disastrous consequences, such as for example, the Eighteenth Amendment and the Volstead Act. But laws are ordinarily promulgated with the expectation that they will be obeyed by the generality of the citizenry and not broken. Even so, the requirement of compliance to existent laws admits of two differing degrees of obedience. A statutory law which has not yet been submitted to judicial review may or may not be constitutional, whereas, a law that has been judicially upheld as constitutional can only be superseded by repeal through the process of amendment or by a reversal by the United States Supreme Court. A judicially untried law is not entitled to the same degree of compliance as a judicially reviewed law and the minimal act of civil disobedience is reasonably allowable in order to test its presumptive constitutionality, with the expectation and willingness to submit to the penalty consequent to its violation. There are, besides legally permissible forms of public protest whose intent is to advertise the alleged inequity and injustice and stir the conscience of the community out of its complacence with the existent pattern of social conduct.

The advocacy and the actual practice of violence must be eschewed in a civilized rule of law in a government where change and remedy are available through legally prescribed methods. When such methods are not adequate or are too costly or too prolonged and conclude too late, then the recourse may be had to legally permissible and protected forms of public demonstration within the constitutional guarantees of the right to peaceable assembly and the right to petition government for the redress of grievances or for the correction of the inadequacies of law. Even in the context of a revolutionary or civil war, acts of violence may be justifiably directed only upon the armed opposition and upon such civilians who are immediately and actively collaborators of the militant forces. That is why the moral obligation to a claim of conscience within a public order may be ultimate but never absolute, — save for the singular exception of the freedom of religious belief and worship.[8]

THE CONSTITUTIONAL QUESTION

Legally, the basis for dissent and protest are the First Amendment freedoms. What the Constitution forbids is not the abridgment of speech and press, etc., for in fact and in virtue of law the government does abridge a diverse variety of certain expressions of speech and press in times of peace as well as in times of war. The First Amendment rather denies to the government the constitutional power to abridge the *freedom* of these expressions. It is the judicial definition of constitutional freedom that is controlling. The Court, for example, has denied that obscenity is within the constitutional guaranteed freedom of speech and press.

There are three categories of self-expression relevant to our discussion: (a) the pure speech and press freedoms which some members of the high tribunal distinguish from speech — mixed — with conduct. The Court is divided on whether the identical constitutional protective guarantees extend to both kinds; (b) a variety of forms of peaceable public protest and demonstrations, — parades, marches, large rallies, sit-ins, — in a word, direct actions,[9] non-violent in conduct, initiated outside the remedial provisions of law, and customarily designated as "self-helps." Such activities must cope with statutes on breach of peace, criminal trespass, obstructing public passageways, and picketing near a courthouse. These controlling statutes are subject to review under the due process and equal protection requirements of the Fourteenth Amendment. These forms of "self-helps" however well intentioned and peaceable must be considerate of time, place, and manner of action in order to warrant legal permissiveness; (c) acts of civil disobedience, unlike the two preceding categories, deliberately intend the violation of a law with expectation and acceptance of punishment for the avowed purpose of inducing the legislature to enact new laws or to force a court test of constitutionality or to advertise a pattern of grievances that enjoys the protection of law one way or another. While every act of civil disobedience is a form of direct action, not every direct action is civil disobedience. All forms of direct action are predicated on the appeal of conscience to a higher moral law or to a higher human law, against "legal" injustices or against alleged moral injustices not yet corrected by man-made law.

DECISIONAL LAW

An analytic survey of United States Supreme Court decisions will disclose a gradually emerging doctrine of constitutional law that is correspondent to the natural law presuppositions we have sketched above.

In 1897, the Court unanimously upheld an ordinance of the city of Boston which provided that "no person shall, in or upon any of the public grounds, make any public address," etc., "except in accordance with a permit of the Mayor,"[10] quoting with approval Justice Holmes, still on the Massachusetts Supreme Judicial Court:

> For the Legislature absolutely or conditionally to forbid public speaking in a highway or public park is no more an infringement of the rights of a member of the public than for the owner of a private house to forbid it in the house. When no proprietary rights interferes the legislature may end the right of the public to enter upon the public place by putting an end to the dedica-

tion to public uses. So it may take the less step of limiting the public use to certain purposes.[11]

To which Chief Justice White added:

The right to absolutely exclude all right to use, necessarily includes the authority to determine under what circumstances such use may be availed of, as the greater power contains the lesser.[12]

The plenary power rationale of the *Davis* case survived until 1939. In *Hague v. C.I.O.*,[13] the question at issue was the validity of a Jersey City ordinance requiring a permit for a public assembly in or upon the public streets, highways, public parks, or public buildings of the city and authorizing the director of public safety to refuse to grant a permit if, in his appraisal of all the facts and circumstances, the purpose was to prevent rioting, disturbances, or disorderly assemblage. Justice Roberts speaking for the Court rejected the city's claim that its ordinance was justified by the plenary power argument of *Davis:*

Whenever the title of street and parks may rest, they have immemorially been held in trust for the use of the public and time out of mind, have been used for purposes of assembly, communicating thoughts between citizens, and discussing public questions. Such use of the streets and public places has from ancient times, been a part of the privileges, immunities, rights, and liberties of citizens.[14]

This broad generous affirmation of immemorial rights is more suggestive of a legislative and judicial deference that should obtain when such rights are at issue than a precise guideline of the extent of their exercise. Besides, Justice Roberts was quick to add that these immemorial rights must be related to other uses of public places and to the legitimate requirements of public order.[15] Nonetheless, the rejection of the *Davis* plenary power rationale has shifted the problem of First Amendment freedoms in public places to a balancing of reasonable regulation for other uses of public places and the requirements of public order as against the weightier necessities of free speech on the public properties.

In *Schneider v. State*,[16] that same year, Justice Roberts applied his dictum in *Hague* for the first time. The defendants, Jehovah's Witnesses, had been convicted of violating municipal ordinances which flatly prohibited the distribution of handbills, circulars, etc., in public places for the avowed purpose of preventing the littering of the streets. Again, Justice Roberts balanced the historic significance of the public distribution of pamphlets for the cause of liberty and how fundamental freedom of speech and press are to personal rights and liberties as against the circumstantial consequences of these rights to public order.[17] Public inconvenience is not so substantial a reason for restraints upon the exercise of these rights:

> In every case, therefore, where legislative abridgement of the rights is asserted, the courts should be astute to examine the effect of the challenged legislation. Mere legislative preference or beliefs respecting matters of public convenience may well support regulation directed at other personal activities but be insufficient to justify such as diminishes the exercise of rights so vital to the maintenance of democratic institutions. And so, as the cases arise, the delicate and difficult task falls upon the courts to weigh the circumstances and to appraise the substantiality of the reasons advanced in support of the regulation of the free enjoyment of the rights.
> We are of the opinion that the purpose to keep the streets clean and of good appearance is insufficient to justify an ordinance which prohibits a person rightfully on a public street from handing literature to one willing to receive it. Any burden imposed upon the city authorities in cleaning and caring for the streets as an indirect consequence of such distribution results from the constitutional protection of the freedom of speech and press.[18]

This balancing of interests in terms of what is gained and what is lost need not turn upon the "preferred position" and its controversial challenges even within the Court.

Two years later, the same Court that had ruled on *Hague* and *Schneider* with but one substitution, — Justice Murphy succeeded Justice Butler, — unanimously upheld the conviction of Jehovah's Witnesses who had violated the ordinance of the city of Manchester, New Hampshire, which required a permit for any "theatrical or dramatic representation... parade or procession upon any public street or way." The Court adopted the construction placed upon the ordinance by the New Hampshire Supreme Court that the discretion in granting permits was restricted to considerations of time, place, and manner, — in a word, the discretion was to be exercised solely for the purposes of proper policing and not as a ban upon activities.[19] Besides, the case for the defendants labored embarrassingly from the fact that two parades were overlapping one another on the same place and at the same time. Chief Justice Hughes brought *Hague* and *Schneider* rulings to bear upon the instant issue:

> As regulation of the use of the streets for parades and processions is a traditional exercise of control by local government, the question in the particular case is whether that control is exerted so as not to deny or unwarrantedly abridge the right of assembly and the opportunities for the communication of thought and the discussion of public questions immemorially associated with resort to public places.
> The defendants had a right under the Act to a license to march, when, where, and as they did, if after a required investigation it was found that the convenience of the public in the use of streets would not thereby be unduly disturbed, upon such changes in conditions or changes in time, place, and manner as would avoid disturbance.[20]

It is obvious that not every exercise of free speech is identical in kind. While speech is a form of action, not every activity subsumed under freedom of speech is purely speech but speech-mixed-with action. The consequences attendant upon these diverse forms of free speech may be substantially different and therefore may call into play other factors and considerations of law and of police power. *Cox v. New Hampshire* is not so much a balancing of conflicting interests ruling as an issue of reasonable accommodation of speech-mixed-with action with the basic requirements of public order.

Two years later, Justice Roberts speaking for an unanimous Court gave added strength to his reasonings in *Hague* and *Schneider*.

> This court has unequivocally held that the streets are proper places for the exercise of the freedom of communicating information and disseminating opinion and that through the states

and municipalities may appropriately regulate the privilege in the public interest, they may not unduly burden or proscribe its employment in these public thoroughfares.[21]

But in the instant case the ordinance prohibiting the distribution of handbills and circulars was limited to commercial and advertising matter and in such a matter the Court deferred to the legislative judgment on the appropriate accommodation of public use of streets to the claims of business advertising.[22] Business advertising while a form of free speech does not enjoy the same latitude of constitutional coverage as free speech on public issues, the sole exception of a private interest being a species of religious liberty advertisement that proselytizes, as the numerous Jehovah's Witness cases attest. This religious advertising even when coupled with the solicitation cannot be equated with commercial speech.[23]

In *Niemotko v. Maryland*, Justice Frankfurter after an elaborate study of all the public-place cases to that time concluded that the issue was

> how to reconcile the interest in allowing free expression in public places with the protection of ... the primary uses of streets and parks.[24]

Members of the Jehovah's Witnesses had been found guilty of disorderly conduct because of an attempt to hold a meeting in a municipal park without a permit. The Court noted that there was no evidence of disorder. Officials had refused the appellant's request for a permit acting in accord with a local custom of nonstatutory character under which permits had been granted to other religious and fraternal organizations. The Court observed that the Witnesses had been interrogated as to their religious beliefs and concluded that the officials had denied them use of the park because of their dislike for the religious views of the appellants. Such a discriminatory refusal of a permit was denial of equal protection of the laws, in the exercise of those freedoms of speech and religion protected by the First and Fourteenth Amendments.

The immunity that constitutionally surrounds the freedom of speech in the form of leaflet distribution[25] was forcibly accented in *Talley v. California*,[26] where the Court struck down an ordinance which prohibited distribution of handbills which did not identify the name and address of the author, printer, and sponsor. The Court lauded the virtues of anonymity in the cause of freedom against the merits of the contention of the state that its requirement of disclosure of sponsorship was for the purpose of protecting the public from fraud.

RACIAL PROTESTS AND DEMONSTRATIONS

In the 1960's all the pent up frustrations which the Negro community had endured with long suffering patience and humiliation broke out in widespread protests and demonstrations across the country. Their most frequent expression took the form of peaceable sit-ins at lunch counters. Those cases which ultimately reached the United States Supreme Court for final ruling may be broadly classified in two groups: those whose convictions were reviewed in the light of the local ordinances and statutes on breach of peace, criminal trespass, obstructing public passageways, and picketing near a courthouse or by referral to a higher overriding federal law, such as the provisions of the Interstate Commerce Act; the second group comprised those convictions which were obtained prior to the passage of the Civil Rights Act of 1964 but were reviewed by the Court after its enactment and by referral to the public accommodations provisions of Title II of the Act. These were disposed of by a construction that upheld the legal permissiveness of such peaceable direct actions as not precluded by the "exclusive" remedies stipulated in the Act and by a doctrine of abatement that reached such cases as were still in the appellate process by the time of the enactment of the new Civil Rights Act.

In *Boynton v. Virginia*,[27] an interstate bus passenger was denied service at a bus terminal lunch counter on the basis of race, and because he refused to leave he was convicted of criminal trespass. The Court ruled that the restaurant management had violated its statutory obligation in denying the defendant lunch service on a nonsegregated basis. Accordingly the conviction under the criminal trespass statute was void simply because the passenger was asserting by his conduct a protected right secured to him by the federal statute.

The *Boynton* case is distinguishable from other sit-ins which protested against racial discriminatory practices which were not yet specifically proscribed by state or federal statute. In a number of these cases[28] convictions were reversed because the Court found state complicity in one form or another inconsistent with the guarantees of the Fourteenth Amendment. In others, the Court found fault with statutes under which convictions were obtained, for failing to comply with the requirements of the due process clause of the Fourteenth Amendment. General criminal statutes which proscribe breach of the peace without specifically defining the illegal acts involved deny protestants advance notice that their contemplated conduct is criminal. Besides, the latitude of discretionary power that local officials may exercise under these generalized statutes may invite discriminatory application contrary to the imperative of the Equal Protection clause of the Fourteenth Amendment. And, finally, such incertitude may inhibit personal initiative in the exercise of the freedom of speech, assembly and petition, which is so basic for the protection of other rights and for the betterment of government. Because of the hazards and inequities potentially inherent under general statutes or common law rules, the legislature should all the more exert itself to a more precise determination of illegal conduct out of that customary deference for the First Amendment freedoms.[29]

PUBLIC DEMONSTRATIONS

The constitutional problematics of peaceable sit-ins at privately owned lunch counters has, as we shall shortly observe, been settled for the future under the protective coverage of the Civil Rights Act of 1964 and the *Hamm* and *Lupper* rulings of 1965. In *Edwards v. South Carolina*,[30] the Court addressed itself with the constitutional questions raised by Negro demonstrations in public places. As a subject of study, *Edwards* discloses the underlining and, as yet, unresolved contending considerations, to which different Justices of the Court attach diverse emphasis.

On March 2, 1961, 179 high school and college students of the Negro race gathered at the Zion Baptist Church in Columbia. About noon they proceeded to walk in groups of fifteen to the South Carolina State House grounds which are open to the general public. Their avowed purpose was

> to submit a protest to the citizens of South Carolina, along with the Legislative Bodies of South Carolina, our feelings and our dissatisfaction with present conditions of discriminatory

actions against Negroes, in general, and to let them know we were dissatisfied and that we would like for the laws which prohibited Negro privileges in this State to be removed.[31]

When the demonstrators arrived at the State House grounds there were already present there some thirty law enforcement officers who had been apprised of their coming. Law enforcement officials informed the demonstrators that they had a right as citizens to go through the State House grounds as long as they were peaceful. A large crowd of white onlookers gathered and after about forty-five minutes, the demonstrators were ordered to disperse within fifteen minutes. They were arrested when they refused to do so. The charge on which they were convicted was for breach of peace. Justice Stewart, speaking for the Court, in an 8 to 1 reversal of the convictions, pointed to the absence of a narrowly drawn statutory offense. He observed that there had been no violence by the demonstators or by the onlookers and there was no recorded evidence of provocative and antagonizing words spoken that might augur the outbreak of disorder.

What is notable in *Edwards* are the different attitudes of the Justices to a situation as it is appraised in its actuality or as a potential crisis. Justice Clark, in his lone dissent, wrote that the situation

> "was by no means the passive demonstration which this Court relates.... The question... seems to me whether a State is constitutionally prohibited from enforcing laws to prevent breach of the peace in a situation where city officials in good faith believe, and the record shows, that disorder and violence are imminent merely because the activities constituting that breach contain claimed elements of constitutionally protected speech and assembly. To me the answer under our cases is clearly in the negative.... It is my belief that anyone conversant with the almost spontaneous combustion in some Southern communities in such a situation will agree that the City Manager's action may well have averted a major catastrophe.[32]

Justice Clark's focus on tensions between races in a community as providing justifiable grounds for preventive action on the part of law enforcement officers for the sake of public order was to be re-echoed in two subsequent South Carolina cases[33] which the United

States Supreme Court would remand to the State Supreme Court for consideration in the light of *Edwards.* In *Henry v. City of Rock Hill,* the State Justices reaffirmed the convictions expressing their astonishment that the high tribunal could have meant "to hold that one has an absolute right to commit a breach of peace, provided one is engaged at the time in the exercise of a right protected by the First Amendment to the United States Constitution."[34]

The counterpoint to the inherent potentials of a situation is to be found in the strong affirmation of the Court, speaking through Justice Stewart, on the high prerogatives of the First Amendment freedoms that peals with the resonances of Justice Robert's dictum in *Hague.*

> South Carolina infringed the petitioners' constitutionally protected rights of free speech, free assembly, and freedom to petition for redress of grievances.
>
> The circumstances of this case reflect an exercise of these basic constitutional rights in their most pristine and classic form.[35]

It may be that Justice Stewart was moved to this conjunction of First Amendment freedoms and a broad breach of peace statute by Justice Harlan's concurring opinion in the *Garner* sit-ins case where he held the sit-in as a type of First Amendment freedom that could not be constitutionally penalized under a general breach of peace statute. But there are significant differences. In the sit-in *Garner* case, the speech action is a non-verbal protest in a privately owned lunch counter, and thus suggesting the First Amendment protection of free speech, can find expression in conduct. On the other hand, Justice Harlan would subordinate such an actionable expression to the requirements of a properly and narrowly drawn breach of peace statute[36] that established a clear and present danger norm.[37] In *Edwards,* the protest is vocal and on state property that was open to the public. The availability of public property for the expression of First Amendment freedoms, however, has posed distinct questions which the Court has since evaluated in *ad hoc* decisions, that is, without any broad proposition as to the extent and coverage of public facilities that may be used for such purposes of protest. Justice Black, who concurred in *Edwards,* in his concurring opinion in the later *Cox* case, was to refer to the earlier case and state his position that there is no public law requirement that the government provide such facilities any more than a private property owner is so obliged.

> *Edwards,* however, as I understand it, did not hold that either private property owners or the States are constitutionally required to supply a place for people to exercise freedom of speech or assembly.[38]

The proper correlation of First Amendment freedoms, of the potential dangers inherent in community racial tensions, of the permissible use of public facilities other than their primary purposes of public convenience, and the requirements of public order will prove to be more cautiously resolved in specific determinations than in any doctrinaire generalization under which every ostensibly peaceable activity of protest can be automatically subsumed.

NARROW AND BROAD GROUNDS OF JUDICIAL DETERMINATION

In the first sit-in case to be reviewed by the Supreme Court, *Garner v. Louisiana,* 1961, the convictions were reversed without reaching the problem of state action under the Equal Protection Clause. Rather, the Court relied on *Thompson v. Louisville,*[39] and ruled that convictions were "so totally devoid of evidentiary support as to render them unconstitutional under the Due Process Clause of the Fourteenth Amendment."[40] Its rationale is somewhat similar to the faulting of generalized statutes. In 1963, the Court ruled on five sit-in cases again without reaching broad constitutional issues.[41] In *Peterson, Gober* and *Avent,* petitioners were convicted under criminal trespass laws and not under the city ordinance requiring segregation in restaurants, against which they were protesting. Chief Justice Warren, nonetheless, held for the Court that the State's criminal processes were being employed in a way which enforced the discrimination mandated by its ordinances in palpable violation of the Fourteenth Amendment, "even assuming that the management would have acted as he did independently of the existence of the ordinance."[42] In the fourth case, *Lombard v. Louisiana*[43] there was no law requiring restaurant segregation and the sit-ins were convicted under a criminal mischief statute. Because the police chief and the Mayor denounced the demonstrators the Court ruled that "the City must be treated exactly as if it had an ordinance prohibiting such conduct."[44] In the fifth case, *Shuttlesworth v. City of Birmingham*,[45] Reverend Shuttlesworth and the Reverend Charles Billups, were convicted of "aiding and abetting" a violation of the city trespass laws by encouraging students to conduct sit-ins. The Chief Justice said it could not be a crime to aid or abet something that was not a crime. The constitutional ban on racial discrimination had always been held to cover only official public activity. Private persons and businesses had been free to discriminate as they chose. But in a long series of cases the Court had also made it clear that Government may be so involved with a private business-financially, for example,—that private discriminatory practices by these enterprises would make it, legally, public discrimination. The 1963 sit-ins rulings enlarged the doctrine further. Even if municipalities repeal their local ordinances on segregated services at lunch counters, a proprietor who chose to discriminate racially could not call upon the local law enforcement officers to dislodge sit-in demonstrators under a criminal trespass statute.

In 1964, in another group of five companion cases the Court reviewed the convictions of sit-in demonstrators and again as in the decisions of 1961 and 1963 the convictions were reversed on a "narrow" ground.[46] In one, *Bell v. Maryland*,[47] six Justices reached the "broad" constitutional issues but only to divide evenly, and thereby left the determination of the instant case to rely upon a narrow basis. The broad issue that was in effect avoided was whether prosecution of persons excluded on racial grounds by private businesses, in the absence of other state participation in the discrimination, violated the requirement of the Fourteenth Amendment that "No State shall . . . deny to any person the equal protection of the laws." Justice Brennan, in the opinion of the Court, stated:

> We do not reach the questions that have been argued under the Equal Protection and Due Process Clauses of the Fourteenth Amendment. It appears that a significant change has taken place in the applicable law of Maryland since these convictions were affirmed by the Court of Appeals . . . Petitioners' convictions were affirmed by the Maryland Court of Appeals on January 9, 1962. Since that date, Maryland has enacted laws that abolish the crime of which petitioners were convicted. . . .

It is not for us ... to ignore the supervening change in state law.... We have long followed a uniform practice where a supervening event raises a question of state law pertaining to a case pending on review here. That practice is to vacate and reverse the judgment and remand the case to the state court, so that it may reconsider it in the light of the supervening change in state law....[48]

Justice Douglas in a twenty-two page opinion in which Justice Goldberg concurred, objected to this remand, and protested that the Court was "avoiding decision of the basic issue by an obvious pretense."[49] He argued that the convictions should be reversed for violation of the Equal Protection Clause. He contended that racial discrimination by any privately owned commercial establishment anywhere is unconstitutional, regardless of state or local law or "custom," because these operate under some form of government license. "The right to be served in places of public accommodations is an incident of national citizenship and of the right to travel."[50] In a less vibrant but no less compelling argument, Justice Goldberg, besides concurring with Justice Douglas' opinion, wrote his own seventeen-page opinion in which he was joined by Chief Justice Warren and Justice Douglas, in which he gave further reasons for the identical position. For the opposing side, Justice Black, joined by Justice Harlan and White, submitted a sixteen page opinion that held that the Equal Protection Clause by itself did not forbid convictions for trespass in such sit-in demonstrations.

At this point of time, then, the Court has confined its ban on customer exclusion to privately owned, public marketing facilities in two areas; one, where any state or local ordinance stipulates them; two, where, even in the absence of such ordinances, the Court concluded by a process of deduction that the actual sources of these discriminatory practices was a policy of "coercion" by state or local authorities under the pretext of breach of peace or criminal trespass.

Ten days after the Court handed down its rulings in the 1964 sit-in cases, President Johnson on July 2, signed the Civil Rights Act of 1964. On December 14, that same year, the Court upheld the constitutionality of the Public Accommodations provisions of Title II in the *Atlanta Motel* and *Mc Clung* cases. That same day, the Court also handed down its rulings in the *Hamm* and *Lupper* cases that turned on the impact of the 1964 Act on sit-in arrests and convictions before the passage of the congressional law. Again the Court found it unnecessary to settle the broad constitutional problem. Justice Clark, in his opinion for the Court, concluded that the 1964 Civil Rights Act, though passed subsequent to convictions for trespass and their affirmances in the state courts abated these actions.

SELF-HELP AND STATUTORY REMEDIES

In the *Hamm* and *Lupper* cases[51] the Court reversed the convictions of Negro demonstrators who had insisted to be served at luncheon counters in southern retail stores. It practically, by its rationale, removed from judicial review all peaceable sit-ins at establishments covered by the Civil Rights Act of 1964. These convictions had been obtained under state trespass laws prior to the enactment of the Act and were reversed by the Court subsequent to its passage by Congress. Speaking for a five to four majority, Justice Clark argued that trespass prosecutions for peaceable sit-ins at lunch counters conducted in an identical way as had the defendants that occurred after the enactment of the law would be impermissible because of the federal statutory rights created by section 201 (a) and 203;[52] secondly, that these convictions would be abated had they occurred under a federal statute; thirdly, such convictions obtained under a state law but which were still in the appellate process would also be abated under the Supremacy Clause of the Constitution. But before the doctrine of abatement could be applicable in the instant companion cases, Justice Clark had to contend with the literally explicit provision of section 207 (b): "The remedies provided in this title shall be exclusive means of enforcing the rights based on this title. . . ." By an analysis and conjunction of the substantive requirements of sections 201, 202, 203,[53] he concluded that the literal provision of "exclusive remedies" of section 207 (b) did not preclude direct, self-help action. In effect, then, the Civil Rights Act of 1964 created federal statutory immunity from state prosecution under criminal trespass laws of persons who refused to leave the premises of an establishment covered by the Act when the proprietor refuses to serve customers solely because of their "race, color, religion, or national origin."

The dissenting reactions of Justices Black, Harlan, White and Stewart varied in the intensity of opinions. All of them disagreed with the majority in reading any such intention of abatement in the congressional history of the Act. All, excepting Justice Stewart, seriously doubted that Congress was constitutionally empowered to do just that even if it had such an intention. Justice Stewart did not call into question the power of Congress under the Supremacy Clause, but he reasoned, the silence of Congress warranted remanding the judgments to the state courts for application of state abatement.

Justice Black who had previously rejected[54] the contention argued at great length by Justice Goldberg in the *Bell* case, that the Fourteenth Amendment precludes criminal trespass convictions relating to public accommodations, vigorously opposed the reasoning of the Court:

> I do not understand from what the Court says that it interprets these provisions of the Civil Rights Act which give a right to be served without discrimination in an establishment which the Act covers as also authorizing persons who are unlawfully refused service a 'right' to take the law into their own hands by sitting down and occupying the premises for as long as they choose to stay. I think one of the chief purposes of the 1964 Civil Rights Act was to take such disputes out of the streets and restaurants and into the courts, which Congress had granted power to provide an adequate and orderly judicial remedy.

The Court's narrow approach in the *Hamm* and *Lupper* cases kept it from facing squarely the broad Fourteenth Ameendment issue. Justice Stewart's recommendation that the judgments be remanded to the state courts for application of state abatement principles would only have delayed this confrontation if the state courts, in such a hypothesis, had denied abatement under state rules. Justice Goldberg's generous proposition[56] in *Bell* that the Fourteenth Amendment established a positive obligation on the states to assure nondiscriminatory treatment in public accommodations, however arguable, in the light of the Black-Harlan-White opposing contentions is now invested by the Civil Rights Act of 1964 with those substantive rights that he had found therein prior to the Act. Whether the coverage of establishments should be as comprehensive as Justice Douglas maintained in *Bell* — presumably beyond those covered by the Act — as incidents of national citizenship and of the right to travel — is a constitutional thesis that is not yet widely shared by members of the Court nor of Congress.

That same day on which the *Hamm* and *Lupper* cases were decided, the Court in *Heart of Atlanta Motel v. United States*[57] affirmed a three-judge district court decision sustaining the validity of the public accommodations section of the Civil Rights Act of 1964. In the companion case of *Katzenbach v. McClung*[58] the Court reversed a lower federal court determination of unconstitutionality. The *Atlanta Motel* serviced a substantial number of inter-state truck drivers. *Mc Clung's* restaurant neither solicited nor catered to interstate travellers; rather it came within the Act only because an appreciable amount of the food served had moved in interstate commerce. The *Atlanta Motel* case was litigated in order to remove a pattern of discriminatory practices wherein Negroes were denied accommodations solely because of their race. The substantive impact on interstate commerce within the coverage of the Civil Rights Act however must be calculated in terms of a collective computation of similar motels and hotels. Surely, no single restaurant or motel by itself could depress interstate business by its policy of racial exclusion. Justice Clark, speaking for an unanimous Court, sustained the constitutionality of the Act by relying solely upon the Commerce Clause. The motel proprietor's appeal to the Civil Rights Cases which declared provisions of the Civil Rights Act of 1875 unconstitutional was declared to be without any precedential value because that earlier Act had broadly proscribed discrimination without limiting the categories of affected business to those impinging upon interstate commerce. The Commerce Clause justification on *Mc Clung* is much broader than in *Atlanta Motel*. It was subsumed under the Act of 1964 not because it served or was likely to serve interstate customers, — but only because a substantial portion of the food served had moved in interstate commerce.

Both Justices Douglas and Goldberg each wrote separate concurring opinions. Justice Douglas, reiterating his position in the *Bell* and *Lombard* cases, would prefer to rest on the assertion of legislative power contained in Section 5 of the Fourteenth Amendment to proscribe "state action" which results when a state's machinery is employed to enforce private discrimination that is under color of any law or local custom. Justice Goldberg would stress the primary purpose of the Act, which in its legal form is the underlying one, namely, "the vindication of human dignities and not mere economics." And to this end, the reliance upon the Fourteenth Amendment is more in accord, while the Commerce Clause provides Congress with the comprehensive means to constrain conduct that offends the human person.

The disparity between the Douglas-Goldberg and the Black-Harlan-White rationale on the efficacy and reach of the Fourteenth Amendment with or without congressional specificatory statute becomes by the ruling in *Atlanta Motel* and *Mc Clung* quite academic as far as public accommodations are concerned. However, this basic cleavage will persist in regard to other as yet unresolved situations on public protest. *Cox v. Louisiana*[59] the following year will again bring to the surface the deep divergent constitutional points of reference as to the adequacy of legal recourse that still divides the Court.

On December 14, 1961, twenty-three students from Southern University, a Negro College, were arrested in downtown Baton Rouge, Louisiana, for picketing stores that maintained segregated lunch counters. The next day the students left the campus in mass and marched five miles to Baton Rouge to demonstrate in front of the courthouse in protest of segregation and the arrest and imprisonment of the picketers who were being held in the parish jail located on the upper floor of the courthouse building. When the student leader was arrested for violation of an anti-noise statute while using a sound truck, the defendant Cox, took up the leadership. The students, about 1,500 of them, who were assembed at the site of the old State Capitol Building two and a half blocks from the courthouse, were counselled by Cox to keep to one side of the sidewalk as they proceeded to the courthouse. At the block opposite the courthouse, Cox was allegedly told by the chief of police that it was permissible for the demonstrators to remain on the side of the street opposite the courthouse. Justice Goldberg, in the majority opinion, noted that the group did not obstruct the street, sang patriotic songs and religious hymns and displayed picket signs. The students who were jailed responded to the singing of the demonstrators. Several hundred onlookers gathered about and some eighty police and firemen were in attendance. When Cox eventually urged the demonstrators to stage sit-ins at segregated lunch counters without any show of violence, the police dispersed the protest group and arrested Cox[60] the following day.

Cox had been indicted and convicted on three charges. The first, for breach of the peace, was reversed unanimously by the Court. The Louisiana Supreme Court had evaluated the situation differently. It held that the collection of over 1,500 Negroes in a predominantly white business district was potentially so explosive as to constitute "an inherent breach of the peace." The United States Supreme Court simply noted that the police were fully in control of the situation. While the Court also reversed the convictions on the second and third charges, the diversity of numerical concurrence and more so, the divergent rationales given by the Justices, highlight the deep radical cleavages among the members of the Court as to the ultimate controlling constitutional premise. To this must be added, the tempered language of Justice Goldberg and admonitory statements of Justice Black that sit apparently incongruously with the pacific detailing of the demonstration. In retrospect, the constraint the Court set upon civil rights demonstrators in the *Adderley v. Florida* case of November 1966 now appears to be less surprising.

The second charge was based on a statutory violation for obstructing a public passageway.[61] Justices White and Harlan upheld the conviction. Of the remaining seven, Justices Black and Clark ruled against the statute because in exempting labor picketing from its prohibition, it contravened the requirements of the Equal Protection Clause. But more significantly, both justices insisted on the constitutionality of a statute that would proscribe all such activity. The five remaining Justices took no cogniziance of the Black-Clark equal protection and total prohibition stances. They based their reversal of the conviction on the alleged admission of the chief of police that parades and demonstrations are allowable after arrangements are made with officials. The majority opinion ruled that the statute did not specifically delineate the exercise of this licensing permission and accordingly found the statute faulty.

The third charge was for statutory violation for picketing near a courthouse.[62] Justice Goldberg, speaking for a five to four split decision, found the colloquy between the police official and Cox to be the decisive factor. Justice Goldberg construed the official's instruction to Cox that it was permissible for the protestants to remain on the street "opposite" the courthouse into an equivalent of the word "near" of the statute. This, he argued, stopped the state from prosecuting. The four dissenters, holding with the majority that the statute was constitutional, would confirm the conviction and denied that the instruction of the police official added up to entrapment.

Despite Justice Goldberg's pacific appraisal of the protestants activity, he does omniously speak of the "influence or domination by either a hostile or friendly mob"[63] and "mob law is the very antithesis of due process."[64] Is he mindful of riotous and violent outbursts in the name of civil rights that were occurring in various parts of the country but were hardly the issue in the instant case or was he fearful that in reversing the conviction of Cox, protest groups may take heart and feel that the rightness of their cause practically, in effect, immunized them against public order statutes?

> From these decisions certain clear principles emerge. The rights of free speech and assembly, while fundamental in our democratic society, still do not mean that everyone with opinions or beliefs to express may address a group at any public place and at any time. The constitutional guarantee of liberty implies the existence of an organized society maintaining public order, without which liberty itself would be lost in the excesses of anarchy. The control of travel on the streets is a clear example of governmental responsibility to insure this necessary order. A restriction in that relation, designed to promote the public convenience in the interest of all, and not susceptible to abuses of discriminatory application, cannot be disregarded by the attempted exercise of some civil right which, in other circumstances, would be entitled to protection. One would not be justified in ignoring the familiar red light because this was thought to be a means of social protest. Nor would one, contrary to traffic regulations, insist upon a street meeting in the middle of Times Square at the rush hour as a form of freedom of speech or assembly. Government authorities have the duty and responsibility to keep their streets open and available for movement. A group of demonstrators could not insist upon the right to cordon off a street, or entrance to a public or private building, and allow no one to pass who did not agree to listen to their exhortations.
> We emphatically reject the notion urged by appellant that the First and Fourteenth Amendments afford the same kind of freedom to those who would communicate ideas by conduct such as patrolling, marching, and picketing on streets and highways, as these amendments afford to those who communicate ideas by pure speech. . . . We affirm the statement of the Court in Giboney v. Empire Storage & Ice Co. (336 U.S. 490), that "it has never been deemed an abridgement of freedom of speech or press to make a course of conduct illegal merely because the

conduct was in part initiated, evidenced, or carried out by means of language, either spoken, written or printed.[65]

In a case, where the Court, through Justice Goldberg, had discounted community tension as constituting "an inherent breach of peace" as the Louisiana State Supreme Court had held, and whose detailing of the record is devoid of any real danger to public order, and whose appraisal of the orderly and pacific conduct of the protestants seems unquestioned, save in the mind of Justice Clark, the above admonitory qualifications upon speech-protest may signal a balancing of the generous protestations of the prerogatives of free speech in public places earlier pronounced by Justice Roberts in *Hague* and Justice Stewart in *Edwards* by "other" rights, — the requirements of public order and of the "primary uses" of public passageways. The cursory reference to reasonable regulation that Justice Roberts admitted to in *Hague* and reaffirmed by Justice Frankfurter in *Niemotko* become more clearly etched by the Court majority prodded by the insistent reiteration by Justice Black.

Justice Black, while concurring in the Court's opinion in reversing the conviction for violation of the Louisiana statutes prohibiting breach of peace and obstructing public passages, does so, however, for reasons which differ somewhat from those stated in the Court's opinion. He finds fault with the breach of peace statute because it is not narrowly drawn against the hazards of arbitrary discretion and with the obstruction of passageways statute because in exempting similar activity by labor groups it contravened the impartiality of the Equal Protection Clause. But he would sustain the conviction for picketing near a courthouse. But his underlying rationale is broader in its reach. He distinguishes between pure speech and speech mixed with conduct, as he had done in earlier cases, and holds that government can constitutionally proscribe all such public demonstrations, granted recourse to and redress by the courts. What he had maintained in *Bell v. Maryland,* the denial of First Amendment protective coverage for sit-in protests on private property, he now unequivocally and broadly translates as applicable to public property, narrowing thereby the import of *Edwards* to a constitutional permissiveness.

> *Edwards,* however, as I understand it, did not hold that either private property owners or the States are constitutionally required to supply a place for people to exercise freedom of speech or assembly.

The First and Fourteenth Amendments, I think, take away from government, state and federal, all power to restrict freedom of speech, press, and assembly *where people have a right to be for such purposes.* This does not mean, however, that these amendments also grant a constitutional right to engage in the conduct of picketing or patrolling, whether on publicly owned streets or on privately owned property.... Picketing, though it may be utilized to communicate ideas, is not speech and therefore is not of itself protected by the First Amendment....

Those who encourage minority groups to believe that the United States Constitution and federal laws give them a right to patrol and picket in the streets whenever they choose, in order to advance what they think to be a just and noble end, do no service to those minority groups, their cause, or their country.[66] (Italics original)

Standing, patrolling, or marching back and forth on streets is conduct not speech, and as conduct can be regulated and prohibited.[67]

It is apparent that in *Cox v. Louisiana* the Court has veered from a concentration on the prerogatives of First Amendment freedoms to the faulting of statutes either directly or indirectly in their application, which, if otherwise properly drawn for a reasonable regulation in the interest of public order would be constitutionally upheld as valid and, if impartially administered, would sustain convictions for violations. Rights are related to "other" rights and to public responsibilities. Justice Goldberg concluded:

Nothing we have said here or in No. 24, ante, is to be interpreted as sanctioning riotous conduct in any form or demonstrations, however peaceful their conduct or commendable their motives, which conflict with properly drawn statutes and ordinances designed to promote law and order, protect the community against disorder, regulate traffic, safeguard legitimate interests in private and public property, or protect the administration of justice and other essential governmental functions.[68]

On July 5, 1966, the District of Columbia Court of Appeals affirmed the conviction of seven persons who had entered the White House as tourists and after they got to the hallway in front of the library they sat down blocking the flow of tourists and causing the building to be closed.[69] They were convicted in the District of Columbia's trial court for a violation of a statute making it a misdemeanor for any person who "without lawful authority to remain (in a public building) shall refuse to quit the same on the demand of the lawful occupant, or of the person lawfully in charge thereof."[70] Calling the comment relevant to its case, the Court of Appeals quoted from Justice Fortas's concurring opinion in *Shuttlesworth v. City of Birmingham,* 382 U.S. 87 (1965).

> Civil Rights leaders, like all other persons, are subject to the law and must comply with it. Their calling carries no immunity. Their cause confers no privilege to break or disregard the law.[71]

On November 14, 1966, the United States Supreme Court upheld for the first time the trespass convictions of thirty-two civil rights demonstrators in Florida after a five year record of consistently reversing sit-ins and trespass convictions in privately owned lunch counters and on public property. Justice Black, who wrote the opinion for the five to four majority and who is known to be one of the stalwart advocates of free speech, had, in his concurring support in preceding cases, nonetheless warned that the reversals were not to be related to a broad constitutional premise which entitled anyone to give public expression to his grievances anywhere anytime without regard to the rights and immunities of private and public proprietors. In fact, he maintained that a flat prohibition of all such public demonstrations that is impartially applied would be constituional within the terms of the Fourteenth Amendment. The five man majority was made possible when Justice Byron White who had been the swingman in preceding five to four decisions sided with Justices Black, Tom Clark, John Harlan, and Potter Stewart.

The court ruled that the county sheriff, the legal custodian of the jail and jail grounds in Tallahassee, Florida, acted legally when he arrested thirty-two demonstrators for trespassing, after the Negro demonstrators had refused the sheriff's order to leave the jail house grounds.[72] Because the petitioners relied upon *Edwards v. South Carolina* and *Cox v. Louisiana* for reversal of their convictions, Justice Black set down the disparities between the preceding and the instant case. In *Edwards,* the demonstrators collected together on the state capitol grounds which were open to the public. Jails, which are built for security purposes, are not. In *Edwards,* the demonstrators had gone through a public driveway and were informed by state officials they had a right to go through the State House grounds as long as they were peaceful. In *Adderley,* the protestants had entered the jail grounds through a driveway used only for jail purposes and without warning to or permission from the sheriff. In *Edwards,* South Carolina had prosecuted the demonstrators by charging them with the common-law crime of breach of peace which the Court found to be indefinite, loose, and so broad and all-embracing as to jeopardize the exercise of First Amendment freedoms. And it was on this same ground of vagueness that, in *Cox v. Louisiana,* the state breach of the peace law used to prosecute Cox was invalidated. The Florida trespass statute is aimed at conduct of one limited kind, for one person or persons to trespass upon the property of another with a malicious or mischievous intent.[73] The doctrine of abatement employed by the Court in *Hamm v. City of Rock Hill* is hardly applicable in *Adderley* because jails and jail house grounds are not the establishments comprehended by the Civil Rights Act of 1964, Title II, on Public Accommodations.

Summarizing the propositions which he had expounded repeatedly in previous cases, Justice Black concluded:

> Nothing in the Constitution of the United States prevents Florida from even-handed enforcement of its general trespass statute against those refusing to obey the sheriff's order to remove themselves from what amounted to the curtilage of the jailhouse. The State, no less than a private owner of property, has power to preserve the property under its control for the use to which it is lawfully dedicated. For this reason there is no merit to the petitioners' argument that they had a constitutional right to stay on the property, over the jail custodian's objections, because the "area chosen for the peaceful civil rights demonstration was not only reasonable but also particularly appropriate. . . ." Such an argument has as its major unarticulated premise the assumption that people who want to propagandize protests or views have a constitutional right to do so whenever and however and wherever they please. That concept of constitutional law was vigorously and forthrightly rejected in two of the cases petitioners rely on *Cox v. Louisiana, supra,* at 554-555 and 563-564. We reject it again. The United States Constitution does not forbid a State to control the use of its own property for its own lawful non-discriminatory purpose.[74]

DECISIONAL LAW-INFERENCES AND CONCLUSIONS

When the states incorporated the Bill of Rights into the Constitution, the First Amendment guarantee of "the right of the people peaceably to assemble, and to petition the Government for a redress of grievances" left undefined the place where such activities could legally be conducted. This question became a highly controversial issue during the 1930's and 1940's when the Jehovah's Witnesses insisted upon exercising the freedom of speech and religion in public places. A large collection of Supreme Court decisions established the broad principle that public property, – parks, sidewalks, streets, – could not be denied to people who wished to express their convictions peaceably in the public area, subject, of course to reasonable restrictions, such as, notifying the authorities in advance and obtaining a permit for a parade provided that these local ordinance requirements were narrowly drawn to obviate wide discretionary exercise and were impartially applied without discrimination. The intent was to allow the widest latitude of public expression compatible with the minimum requirements of public order and convenience.

The mass civil rights demonstrations of the 1960's posed problems which in terms of numbers and collective conduct could scarcely be comparable to the activities of the Jehovah's Witnesses. The degree of inconveneince to the public, the dangers to private and public property, and to the security of persons was of a magnitude and complexity that the precedents of the few harmless religious pamphleteers could offer no assurance of an equally facile solution. When the champions of Negro rights developed the technique of peaceable sit-ins and collective mass demonstrations to bring about desegregation of public facilities, effective legal provisions for the exercise of voting rights, and nondiscriminatory opportunities for employment, their successes with the national and state legislatures encouraged them to widen their protest movement. Convictions under breach of peace and criminal trespass ordinances were overruled by the Court by finding fault either with the statute or its application. Besides, so long-sufferingly had a large part of the American community endured the indignities and humiliations of racial prejudice that the generality of the American people were awakened to an acute sense of conscience to redress the wrongs so callously inflicted upon their brethren.

Two facts set in to contain their almost unrestrained exuberance for justice for all men. First, the goodwill which the nonviolent technique of demonstration had engendered was being undone in great part by riotous and bloody racial outbreaks in cities throughout the country and no explanation about the frustrations of people crowded in ghettos could convince other people whose safety, property, and lives were endangered that the cause of racial justice was still right in itself and should not suffer from these acts of senseless destruction. The other fact was a contest of constitutional construction going on among the members of the Court even in the very act of upending convictions. In particular, Justice Black insisted on the necessity of national legislation supplementary to the Fourteenth Amendment in order to provide the justifiable legal basis for certain activities. And he also insisted on the right of the state to regulate with properly drawn statutes such activities on public properties as within the general empowerment of the state to prohibit them altogether as being no less than the rights of a private proprietor to govern the use of his property.

> The state no less than a private owner of property has power to preserve the property under its control for the use to which it is lawfully dedicated.[75]

The ruling in *Adderley* applies only to publicly owned property. In the *Edwards* case, demonstrators may conduct their peaceful protests on state grounds which are open to the public. The reversal of convictions for picketing near a courthouse in *Cox* did not settle that issue since the reversal was based on a doctrine of "entrapment" and presumably without that implied official collusion the statute prohibiting such picketing near a courthouse would be constitutionally upheld concerning an unambiguous act of violation. There may be no trespassing on jailhouse yards. But the extent of public places that may be subsumed under the guarantee of freedom of assembly is still largely an unanswered question. It would seem that the Court would not uphold the legal permissiveness of sit-ins in the White House and in other public offices designated for public services, the Governor's office, the Board of Education, the Mayor's office, the Post Office, etc., Justice Douglas to the contrary.

As for privately owned property that is open for business to the public in general but closed to Negroes, which come within the coverage of the Civil Rights Act of 1964, the ruling in *Hamm, Lupper,*

Atlanta Motel, and *Mc Clung* have settled that question. The Court has not yet ruled whether Negroes can be constitutionally arrested for trespass for entering privately owned property that serves the public on a segregated basis but are not within the classification of establishment defined in Title II of the Act.

What then may we speculate with reasonable expectation about the future?

Convictions under generalized statutes proscribing breach of the peace will be reversed because their broad and vague criteria are susceptible to discriminatory application. Protestants are not forewarned what specific behavior is prohibited. Such an uncertainty may inhibit a right of public protest that is constitutionally guaranteed and protected in the First Amendment and so deprive a democratic community of those necessary means for the betterment of the administration of justice. A properly drawn breach of peace statute would be upheld.

In regard to criminal trespass statutes, we must note that prior to the enactment of the Civil Rights Act of 1964 with its coverage of establishments of public accommodations the Court avoided definitive resolution of the broad constitutional question whether the Fourteenth Amendment and Section 6 thereof did, as Justices Douglas and Goldberg maintained, or did not by itself, as Justice Black, Harlan, and White held, warrant peaceful trespassing on privately owned public facilities and on government owned property. Predictably this constitutional question was met within a wide range by the Federal legislature in 1964 by the statutory provisions of Title II. Because the broad equal protection problems will persist, the Court resolution of cases will most likely continue to be settled on narrow grounds. Nonetheless the Equal Protection Clause bore significantly in the *Hamm* and *Lupper* cases. Though section 207 of Title II designated the stipulated civil remedies as "exclusive," Justice Clark, in the opinion of the Court, conjoined the "full and equal enjoyment" provision of section 201 (a), the state complicity provision of section 202, and the non-interference interdictions of section 203 to uphold direct, self-help actions apart from the "exclusive" civil remedies of section 207. But even here the legality of a self-help action may turn on the appropriateness of the conduct to the purpose. For example, peaceable sit-ins at lunch counters are permissible whereas lying down on the floor of the restaurant would be considered impermissible. Peaceable and orderly demonstrations outside the Board of Education building to protest de facto segregation in public schools are permissible but chaining oneself to stairways inside the building would not be allowable. On the other hand, while a sit-in at a lunch counter covered by a state or federal statute is legal, a sit-in at a private club open only to restricted membership would not be.

In regard to statutes prohibiting the obstruction of public passageways, the most relevant rationale is that of *Cox v. New Hampshire* in which the Court upheld a properly drawn statute that is limited to a reasonable consideration of time, place, and manner for the purpose of adjusting public order and convenience in the primary uses of public streets with the opportunity of expressing dissent. Obstruction of traffic to the entrance of a bridge would not be tolerated nor would an otherwise orderly street demonstration permit the dumping of garbage on a public thoroughfare. An orderly march to protest the war in Vietnam with reasonable advance notice and arrangement with the local officials is legally protected but obstructing the movement of trains with supplies or troops is not. New York police, citing traffic problems, banned meetings in mid-town Manhatten. Opponents of the Vietnam war, contending that a rally in suburbia would be pointless, staged a protest speech near Times Square. The police arrested its leaders and the case will be reviewed by the Court. Notwithstanding Justice Douglas' reasoning in his dissent in *Adderley*,[76] it is our conjecture that the convictions will not be reversed. The undoubted advantage of protesting in a manner as to make a dramatic impact on a community and draw the widest possible advertisement of a cause through the communication media must be weighed against grave and minimal necessities of public order. One cannot generalize easily *a priori*. The Supreme Court rulings are based on specific sets of facts of an instant case. Still there is discernible a trend in Court decisions which seem to turn away from the broad right of protest upheld in recent years. It may be that at first the stability of public order warranted this broader exercise of protest against inequities and injustices that humiliated the Negro community. But the passage of Civil Rights Acts of 1964 and 1965 on the one hand and, on the other, the rash outburst of violent and destructive conduct in many of our major cities may have led the courts to draw all contending rights, personal and public, more nearly within the concept of ordered liberties.

The fourth observation concerns the statutes on court picketing.

Though Justice Goldberg in *Cox v. Louisiana* ingeniously construed entrapment to reverse the conviction, he and all the other members of the Court would without doubt uphold properly drawn statutes that protect the administration of justice by the courts from outside influence. To conclude on the above four categories of legal restriction of public self-expression, the Court emphasized in *Cox v. Louisiana:*

> It is, of course, undisputed that appropriate, limited discretion, under properly drawn statutes or ordinances, concerning the time, place, duration, or manner of use of the streets for public assemblies may be vested in administrative officials, provided that such limited discretion is exercised with "uniformity of method of treatment upon the facts of each application, free from improper or inappropriate considerations and from unfair discrimination"... (and with) a systematic, consistent and just order of treatment, with reference to the convenience of public use of the highways...."[77]

The distinction between pure speech and speech mixed with conduct is controlling. The First Amendment coverage for the first does not apply identically to the second.

> The rights of free speech and assembly, while fundamental in our democratic society, still do not mean that anyone with opinions or beliefs to express may address a group at any public place and at any time. The constitutional guarantee of liberty implies the existence of an organized society maintaining public order, without which liberty itself would be lost in the excesses of anarchy.... A group of demonstrators could not insist upon the right to cordon off a street, or entrance to a public or private building, and allow no one to pass who did not agree to listen to their exhortations.[78]
>
> The conduct which is the subject of this statute — picketing and parading — is subject to regulation even though interveined with expression and association. The examples are many of the application by this Court of the principle that certain forms of conduct mixed with speech may be regulated or prohibited.[79]

The regulation of speech mixed with conduct is for the sake of liberty itself.

THE MORAL - LEGAL CONTINUUM

It is our thesis that the development of the Court's doctrine of public protest within the necessities of public order ever since in *Hague,* it disengaged itself from the plenary power rationale of *Davis* corresponds with the natural law premises as we have outlined them in the earlier part of this article. Liberties are to be exercised without gravely endangering the public order wherein liberties themselves find their own protection. And at the same time the requirements of public order must allow the widest possible lattitude of freedom of expression compatible with civilized society. This supposition of civilized conduct is to be measured against the hope of legal redress as embodied in political and juridical institutions of a community. We hold that in the matter of civil rights this supposition is more surely embodied in the Civil Rights Acts of 1964 and 1965 than ever before. Legal rights and duties are neither relative nor absolute. They are correlative. They sustain one another. Within such a context, other Civil Rights Acts for the correction of still enduring inequities and racial discriminatory practices will be forthcoming despite the resistance of many in the American community. What we must frankly acknowledge is that there is a type of resistance that requires more than a legal prescription to the contrary; it requires a moral conversion that makes possible that social acceptance of our fellowmen without which the efficacy of law will meet with endless obstruction and a spiritual antagonism.

Violence must be denounced as immoral as well as criminal by all responsible leaders of the civil rights movement. It will not do to explain away acts of racial violence in terms of social, economic, and political frustration of a people. Leaders must realize that their exhortations to judge what laws are unjust and to disobey them may be based on false assumptions. A claim of conscience does not give one the right to be a law unto himself, not to take the law into one's hands save for the minimal requirements of civil disobedience in order to test the law by the processes of the court. The moral claims of subjective conscience to a higher moral law as against an existent human law is ultimate but not absolute save the one unique exception of religious beliefs and worship. Claims of conscience within a social order may have to contend with contrary claims of conscience. Either these conflicts are resolved peaceably through the processes of law or recourse will be had to circumstances of revolutionary war or civil war. But even in these circumstances of armed conflict, violence is not to be directed to the unarmed civilians of the opposing camp. To equate the riots of Watts to the dumping of tea in a Boston Harbor is to exercise in a facile rhetoric of the flimsiest sort of analogy. This is not to deny that in a civilized society the use of violence may bring about material advantages that had been denied. After Watts, the inhabitants of the area did receive aid from government agencies and private industry but that did not bring back to life the fireman who was shot in the back nor the Mexican-American who was yanked forcibly out of his vehicle and mauled to death. No doubt the savage murder of over one hundred Negroes in the South will intimidate many not to exercise their legally guaranteed rights and frighten others who may be willing to cooperate in bettering racial relations. But the laws are not changed thereby. Morally and legally murder has been committed. The dead do not come back to life again. The dependents are left disconsolate. No conscientious claim to states' rights can possibly justify these acts of brutal violence in the name of sanity.

The way a cause is advocated may be self-defeating. The dogs at Selma aroused the nation to a sense of outrage and the murder of Mrs. Liuzzi and other civil rights advocates has done more than anything else to discredit a concept of state-federal constitutional structure that some southerners may have held in great earnestness of learning and conviction. The mob riots across the land with destruction of property and senseless killing has brought undoubted consequences in the national elections.

A word about gradualism. There is a gradualism which is a deliberate strategm of obstructionism and with it the agencies of law must contend. But such a gradualism is to be distinguished from the gradualism that is inherent in the inheritance of prejudices that must be dissipated, of unequal aptitudes and skills that must be corrected, of disparities and disabilities that separate communities and must be remedied. Not to acknowledge this inevitable gradualism of improvement, of correction, of adjustment is to be blind to hard core problems and to be blinding in the abstract answers that are so facilely proffered. To admit to this social, economic, and moral disordination and to cope with it as humans must is not to disown the original responsibility of the pattern of injustices imposed but rather to exercise that responsibility now in redress of that original culpability.

We humans are a sluggish species. We may be wise, not so wise. We may be foolish, sinful, malicious, perverse. For those of us who confess to the Fatherhood of God, to the redemption of mankind by Christ Jesus, we shall have to exert ourselves fully as the First Commandment exhorts us with our whole heart, with all our strength, and with all our souls to sanctify ourselves by our love for our fellowmen. God will judge the earnestness in our hearts whatever the outward result. Men will judge us as Christians by the substantive effort to achieve in public fact what we have in mind and the good will to do.

FOOTNOTES AND REFERENCES

1. 368 U.S. 157 (1961).
2. 370 U.S. 154 (1962).
3. 379 U.S. 536 (1965).
4. 383 U.S. 131 (1966).
5. 83 U.S. 36 (1873).
6. 95 U.S. 485 (1877).
7. 313 U.S. 299 (1941).
8. Reference by Civil Rights leaders to a religious right to violate the law by appealing to St. Paul (Romans, XIII), to St. Peter (Acts V, 29), to the early christian martyrs and to St. Augustine are strictly speaking misapropos. Early christians were generally exhorted to obey the laws even of a pagan ruler of state with the sole exception of the supreme fidelity to God in matters of worship and belief. Whatever they may have felt about particular laws, there is no evidence of any exhortation to engage in acts of civil disobedience or the equivalent of modern sit-ins and mass demonstrations. The *lex iniusta non lex* of St. Augustine and St. Thomas was more an affirmation of what constituted the objective order of justice than a claim of subjective conscience to decide tor itself what laws are just and what are unjust. The stress and emphasis from the Advent of Christianity through medieval christendom was on the prerogatives of authority and on the moral influence of christian virtue to improve civil law. Undoubtedly, from these propositions of Scripture, of the Fathers, and of the Schoolmen, very distinct premises at that, by a process of historical and legal development one can arrive at the formulation of a theory of civil disobedience. St. Thomas' stress on the obligation to comply with one's own conscience must be understood within a historical situation wherein the faithful admitted to the magisterium of the Church to help form their consciences and to defer to Her authoritative directives. In modern times increased studies on the psychology of conscience and motivation has contributed in no small part to personal freedom of expression in the civil and religious areas of human conduct.
9. Public protest demonstrations did not originate with the civil rights movement. Much of labor's gains through national and state legislations were brought about by such activities in order to advertise their grievances and to influence the governments by appealing directly to the electorate for support. Labor sit-ins at industrial plants were a familiar experience.
10. Davis v. Massachusetts, 167 U.S. 43 (1897).
11. *Id.* at 47.
12. *Id.* at 48.
13. 307 U.S. 496 (1939).
14. *Id.* at 515.
15. "The privilege of a citizen of the United States to use the streets and parks for communication of views on national questions may be regulated in the interest of all; it is not absolute, but relative, and must be exercised in subordination to the general comfort and convenience, and in consonance with peace and good order; but it must not, in the guise of regulation, be abridged or denied. We think the court below was right in holding the ordinance quoted in Note 1 void upon its face. It does not make comfort or convenience in the

use of streets or parks the standard of official action. It enables the Director of Safety to refuse a permit on his mere opinion that such refusal will prevent 'riots, disturbances or disorderly assemblages.' It can thus, as the record discloses, be made the instrument of arbitrary suppression of free expression of views on national affairs for the prohibition of all speaking will undoubtedly 'prevent' such eventualities. But uncontrolled official suppression of the privilege cannot be made a substitute for the duty to maintain order in connection with the exercise of the right." 307 U.S. 496. 515-516 (1939). Two other Justices also invoked the Due Process Clause of the Fourteenth Amendment, and thereby made applicable to aliens as well as citizens the claim of right of assembly, 307 U.S. at 525.

16. 308 U.S. 147 (1939).
17. *Id.* at 160, 161.
18. *Id.* at 162.
19. New Hampshire v. Cox, 91 N.H. 137, 148, 16 A.2d 508, 516 (1940): "A license to permit its enjoyment may not be required as a form of censorship, but a license to permit its enjoyment in fair adjustment with the enjoyment of other relations and conditions is not understood to be under the ban of the federal constitution."
20. Cox v. New Hampshire, 312 U.S. 569, 576 (1941).
21. Valentine v. Chrestenson, 316 U.S. 52, 54 (1942).
22. *Id.* at 54-55: "The question is not whether the legislative body may interfere with the harmless pursuit of a lawful business, but whether it must permit such pursuit by what it deems an undesirable invasion of, or interference with the full and free use of the highways by the people in fulfillment of the public use to which the streets are dedicated.
23. Jamison v. Texas, 318 U.S. 413 (1943). But Justice Black, speaking for the Court, upheld this right in a context of orderly conduct. "But one who is rightfully on a street . . . carries with him there as elsewhere the constitutional right to express his views in an orderly fashion. This right extends to the communication of ideas by handbills and literature as well as by spoken word." 318 U.S. at 416.
24. 340 U.S. 268, 276 (1951).
25. Our sampling of leaflet distribution cases seems a more appropriate introduction to peaceable and orderly civil rights protests than the sound truck cases of Saia v. New York, 334 U.S. 558 (1948) and Kovacs v. Cooper, 336 U.S. 77 (1949).
26. 362 U.S. 60 (1960).
27. 364 U.S. 454 (1960).
28. Robinson v. Florida, 378 U.S. 153 (1964); Griffin v. Maryland, 378 U.S. 130 (1964), amusement park case; Peterson v. City of Greenville, 373 U.S. 244 (1963); Lombard v. Louisiana, 373 U.S. 267 (1963); Gober v. Birmingham, 373 U.S. 374 (1963); Avent v. North Carolina, 373 U.S. 375 (1963).
29. Bouie v. City of Columbia, 378 U.S. 347 (1964); Barr v. City of Columbia, 378 U.S. 146 (1964); Garner v. Louisiana, 368 157 (1961).

Justice Harlan, in his concurring opinion in Garner voted to reverse the conviction by subsuming within the free speech guarantee of the First Amendment a nonverbal form of protest, a sit-in, and that on private property.

Justice Stewart's court opinion in Edwards is strikingly similar to that of Justice Harlan in Garner with, of course, the noted difference that Edwards involved public property. Justice Black, to the contrary in his dissenting opinion in Bell v. Maryland, 378 U.S. at 325, 344 46 (1964), would not allow that the free speech guarantee extends to the place as well. "Unquestionably petitioners have a constitutional right to express these views wherever they had an unquestioned legal right to be." And in Cox v. Louisiana, 379 U.S. 536, 559 (1965) both Justices Black and Clark would uphold as constitutional a total ban on public picketing provided it accorded with the impartiality requirement of the Equal Protection clause of the Fourteenth Amendment.

30. 372 U.S. 229 (1963).
31. *Id.* at 230-31.
32. *Id.* at 238-39.
33. Cases revolving on community tension as constituting inherent breach of peace were Fields v. South Carolina, 375 U.S. 44 (1963) and Henry v. City of Rock Hill, 376 U.S. 776 (1964). Both were remanded by the Court for reconsiderations by the state supreme courts in the light of Edwards.

34. 244 S.C. 74, 78 135 S.E. 2d 718, 720 (1963). The Supreme Court reversed in a per curiam opinion. 376 U.S. 776 (1964).
35. 372 U.S. at 235.
36. Justice Harlan's contrived construction of an implied consent because the proprietors did not request the sit-ins to depart within the context of a general breach of peace statute is arguable. However, even with consent present, he would uphold the convictions under a narrowly drawn statute, if, as in the instant case, the initiative for the arrests was taken by the police officers.
37. Garner v. Louisiana, 368 U.S. at 202 (1961).
38. Cox v. Louisiana, 379 U.S. 536, 578-79 (1965).
39. 362 U.S. 199 (1960).
40. 368 U.S. 157, 163 (1961).
41. See Note 21 *supra.* See also, Shurrlesworth v. City of Birmingham, 373 U.S. 262 (1963).
42. 373 U.S. 244, 248 (1963).
43. 373 U.S. 267 (1963).
44. *Id.* at 273.
45. 376 U.S. 339 (1963).
46. See Note 30 *supra.*
47. 378 U.S. 226 (1964).
48. 378 U.S. 226, 228 (1964).
49. *Id.* at 243 (1964).
50. *Id.* at 250 (1964).
51. 379 U.S. 306 (1964).
52. Public Law 88-352, 78 Stat. 243, July 2, 1964. Title II — Injunctive Relief Against Discrimination in Places of Public Accommodation. Sec. 201. (a) All persons shall be entitled to the full and equal enjoyment of the goods, services, facilities, privileges, advantages, and accommodations of any place of public accommodation, as defined in this section, without discrimination or segregation on the ground of race, color, religion, or national origin.
Sec. 203. No person shall (a) withhold, deny, or attempt to withhold or deny or deprive or attempt to deprive, any person of any right of privilege secured by section 201 or 202, or (b) intimidate, threaten, or coerce, or attempt to intimidate, threaten or coerce any person with the purpose of interfering with any right or privilege secured by section 201 or 202, or (c) punish or attempt to punish any person for exercising or attempting to exercise any right or privilege secured by Section 201 or 202.
53. Sec. 202. All persons shall be entitled to be free, at any establishment or place, from discrimination or segregation of any kind on the ground of race, color, religion, or natural origin. If such discrimination or segregation is or purports to be required by any law, statute, ordinance, regulation, rule, or order of a State or agency or political subdivision thereof.
54. Justices Harlan and White had concurred with Justice Black's dissenting opinion in Bell v. Maryland, 378 U.S. 226 (1964) in denying that the Fourteenth Amendment, interdicted criminal trespass convictions relating to public accommodations. In *Hamm* and *Lupper* they objected strenuously to Justice Clark's employment of the abatement doctrine.
55. 379 U.S. at 318-19. Justice White would have looked to an undoubted congressional intent embodied in "unmistakable language" for the ratification of "massive disobedience to the law, so often attended by violence." And he would distinguish the problems of conscientious motivations of civil disobedients from the duties of the court. "Whether persons or groups should engage in nonviolent disobedience to laws with which they disagree perhaps defies any categorical answer for the guidance of every individual in every circumstance. But whether a court should give it wholesale sanction is a wholly different question which calls for only one answer." *Id.* at 328.
56. "In spite of this, the dissent intimates that its view best comports with the needs of law and order. Thus it is said: "It would betray our whole plan for a tranquil and orderly society to say that a citizen, because of his personal prejudices, habits, attitudes, or beliefs, is cast outside the law's protections and cannot call for the aid of officers sworn to uphold the law and preserve the peace." . . . This statement, to which all will readily agree, slides

over the critical question. Whose conduct is entitled to the "law's protection?" Of course every member of this Court agrees that law and order must prevail; the question is whether the weight and protective strength of law and order will be cast in favor of the claims of the proprietors or in favor of the claims of petitioners. In my view the Fourteenth Amendment resolved this question in favor of the right of the petitioners to public accommodations and it follows that in the exercise of that constitutionally granted right they are entitled to the "law's protection." Bell v. Atlanta Motel and Mc Clung that the Civil Rights Acts of 1875 on public accommodations was invalidated in the Civil Rights Cases of 1883 for resting broadly on the Fourteenth Amendment without the narrowing stipulations of the 1964 Act and the accompanying empowerment of the Commerce Clause.

57. 379 U.S. 241 (1964).
58. 379 U.S. 294 (1964).
59. 379 U.S. 436 (1965).
60. *Id.* at 538-43. Justice Clark, to the contrary, described the event as the "staging of a modern Donnybrook Fair across from the courthouse. . . ." 379 U.S. at 585.
61. La. R.S. 14:100.1 (Cum. Supp. 1962).
62. La. R.S. 14:101 (Cum. Supp. 1962).
63. 379 U.S. at 562.
64. *Ibid.*
65. *Id.* at 554-55.
66. *Id.* at 578-79.
67. *Id.* at 581.
68. *Id.* at 574.
69. Jalbert v. Dist. of Columbia, 221 A. 2d 94 (1966).
70. D.C. Code, Sec. 22-1121 (1961).
71. Whittlesey v. United States, 221 A. 2d 86 (D.C. 1966), District of Columbia Court of Appeals, July 5, 1966, *rehearing denied* August 9, 1966, Hood, C.J.
72. Adderley v. Florida, 385 U.S. 39, 87 Sup. Ct. 242, 17 L. ed. 2d 149 (1966).
73. "Every trespass upon the property of another, committed with a malicious and mischievous intent, the punishment of which is not especially provided for, shall be punished by imprisonment not exceeding three months, or by fine not exceeding one hundred dollars." Fla. Stat. ## 821.18 (1965). Justice Black explains in note 2 that by "malicious" is meant "the act was done knowingly and willfully and without any legal justification" and by "mischievous" is meant "that the alleged trespass shall be inclined to cause petty and trivial trouble, annoyance and vexation to others. . . ." 385 U.S. 39, 87 S. Ct. 242, 245, 177 L. ed. 149, 153 (1966).
74. 385 U.S. 39,...., 875 S. Ct. 242, 247, 17 L. ed. 2d 149, 156 (1966). The latter part of this quotation is directed against the sharp dissent of Justice Douglas. The quotations from Cox v. Louisiana are appended by Justice Black in Notes 6 and 7. Justice Black's court opinion in Adderley was predictable in the light of his dissent in Cox to uphold the conviction for picketing near the courthouse as against the ingenious device of "entrapment" contrived by Justice Goldberg.
75. 385 U.S. 39, 87 S. Ct. 242, 247, 17 L. ed. 2d 149, 156 (1966).
76. Justice Douglas in dissent: "Those who do not control television and radio, those who cannot afford to advertise in newspapers or circulate elaborate pamphlets may have only a more limited type of access to public officials. Their methods should not be condemned as tactics of obstruction and harassment so long as the assembly and petition are peaceable, as these were." 385 U.S. 39, 87 Sup. Ct. 242, 249, 17 L. ed. 149, 158 (1966).
77. Cox v. Louisiana, 379 U.S. 536, 558 (1965).
78. *Id.* at 554-55.
79. *Id.* at 563.

LOYALTY OATH AFFIDAVIT*

Scarcely two years ago Congress passed the National Defense Education Act of 1958.[1] Hailed from the start as a magnanimous and imaginative government program of financial assistance for the cause of education, it also engendered from the very beginning a controversy over section 1001 (f). It reads:

> No part of any funds appropriated or otherwise made available for expenditure under authority of this Act shall be used to make payments or loans to any individual unless such individual (1) *has executed and filed with the Commissioner an affidavit that he does not believe in, and is not a member of and does not support any organization that believes in or teaches, the overthrow of the United States Government by force or violence or by any illegal or unconstitutional methods, and* (2) *has taken and subscribed to an oath or affirmation in the following form:* "*I do solemnly swear (or affirm) that I will bear true faith and allegiance to the United States of America and will support and defend the Constitution and laws of the United States against all its enemies, foreign and domestic.*" The provisions of section 1001 of title 18, United States Code, shall be applicable with respect to such affidavits.[2]

The target of criticism is the requirement of a loyalty oath affidavit disclaiming subversive affiliation and activity in addition to the oath of allegiance, an affirmative protestation of patriotic fealty and support of the United States of America, its Constitution and its

---

*UNIVERSITY OF DETROIT LAW JOURNAL. Vol. 37, n. 5, June 1960, pp. 718-728.

laws. A few of the institutions of higher learning refused from the outset to participate in the program,[3] several have withdrawn in the intervening time since the passage of the Act,[4] some have voiced their objections but continue to administer the government student loan plan,[5] and the overwhelming majority have accepted the program without criticism and in a number of instances their spokesmen have declared their agreement with the requirement of the two oaths and expressed bewilderment with the critics.[6]

Since there is every likelihood that Congress will reconsider[7] the requirement of the loyalty oath affidavit (there is also a movement on foot urging repeal of both oaths of allegiance and loyalty)[8] and what is of more immediate consequence, deserving and needy students are being denied the benefits of government loans at universities which have withdrawn from the program without consulting their wishes,[9] it may be well to weigh the criticisms levelled at the loyalty affidavit.

THE ARGUMENT OF HISTORICAL CONTEXT

An argument takes on deeper significance when posited in an historical context. It becomes less doctrinaire and escapes the hidden pitfalls of purely conceptual theorizing. One need only recall the heavenly premises from which by purely deductive reasoning Plato drew some very unearthly (and inhuman) conclusions. Situated in time and place a problematic takes on human dimensions invested with all the rational and nonrational factors within which it originally arose. It is in the midst of these human forces that a principle of justice and righteousness must vindicate its claims on human conduct, neither compromising itself thereby nor by its transcendence be wholly indifferent to the potentials of human nature. Frequently in posing a modern problem we have recourse to the lessons of the past. This judicious practice rests on the reasonable assumption that human experiences reviewed at some distance may be studied less passionately and more wisely. But at times the historical reference to the past does less than justice to the understanding of the present problematic and bears within itself still less light for the future. Many past experiences however similar on the surface to a modern problem have a coloring of sympathies, antagonisms, and of generally accepted practices wholly alien to our modern way of thinking and are not as likely to be approved or even tolerated by us. They bear a symbolism which rather obfuscates than enlightens our own problematic however similar they may seem at first sight. Thus, for example, in Elizabethan England (for that matter, in other parts of the civilized west of the time) the range of criminal penalties was far greater than would be imaginable today and they frequently took the form of mutilation of the body, whose parts might be stuck on pikes for public view in the town square or at its gates. Is it really helpful in the present controversy about the disclaimer affidavit to conjure up the lurid memories of the English Court of High Commission or of the Spanish Inquisition, or of any of the oppressive religious and political oath tests of the past?[10] We have grown out of the generally accepted practices of those days with a deep sigh of relief. The historical advance of civil liberties, religious and political, in the Anglo-American tradition has been steadfastly, however slowly, forward and continues to progress perseveringly and grudgingly ahead. Political and religious oath tests were in the past usually intertwined so that political allegiance was generally inconceivable without religious uniformity. These oaths posed a problematic which in its complexities and contemporary significances is a far cry from our present discussion. A study of the the loyalty oath affidavit should proceed within the framework of its own distinctive historical context within which it bears its own unique meaning.

Title I—sec. 191 of the National Defense Education Act of 1958 reads:

> The Congress hereby finds and declares that the *security* of the Nation *requires* the fullest development of the mental resources and technical skills of its young men and women. *The present emergency demands* that additional and more adequate educational opportunities be made available. *The defense of this Nation depends* upon the mastery of modern techniques developed from complex scientific principles. It depends as well upon the discovery and development of new principles, new techniques, and new knowledge.
>
> We must increase our efforts to identify and educate more of the talent of our Nation. This requires programs that will give assurance that no student of ability will be denied an opportunity for higher education because of financial need; will correct as rapidly as possible the existing imbalances in our educational programs which have led to an insufficient proportion of our

88 *Political and Legal Studies*

population educated in science, mathematics, and modern foreign languages and trained in technology.

The Congress reaffirms the principle and declares that the States and local communities have and must retain control over and primary responsibility for public education. *The national interest requires, however, that the Federal Government give assistance to education for programs which are important to our defense.*

To meet the present educational *emergency* requires additional effort at all levels of government. *It is therefore the purpose of this Act* to provide substantial assistance in various forms to individuals, and to States and their subdivisions, in order to ensure trained manpower of sufficient quality and quantity *to meet the national defense needs of the United States.* (Italics supplied.)[11]

It is obvious from the plain reading of the *Findings and Declaration Policy* of section 101 that this government education program is distinguishable from past government programs and from those presently contemplated. The declaration of national emergency is related to the needs for increased knowledge of the technical sciences which are calculated to relieve the relative deficiencies of our national defense and security. Therefore Congress set up a $900,000,000 Federal-aid program including loans for undergraduates and grants for graduate study in order to spur science education primarily though not exclusively. It is in the light of such a specifically defined purpose and within the context of a national emergency engendered by a grave world-wide struggle for the survival of free society versus a dominated society that the intention and significance of the loyalty oath affidavit ought to be considered. Reference to the odious and oppressive religious and political oath tests, we respectfully submit, is not only irrelevant but far from enlightening as they evoke frightening memories and antagonisms wholly alien to the modern American scene. The danger of similar developments today or the risk of tending in that direction by retaining the loyalty oath affidavit is more gratuitously assumed than probable.

THE QUESTION OF DISCRIMINATION

It has been charged that the requirement of the disclaimer affadavit in addition to the oath of allegiance from the recipients of federal loans is "discriminatory since it singles out students alone in our population—and, among students, the neediest—as subjects of special distrust."[12]

A question of fact is here involved. What Americans are required to subscribe to a similar loyalty affidavit separate and distinct from the oath of allegiance?

a) An identical loyalty affidavit and oath of allegiance have been required for nearly ten years by Section 15(d) of the National Science Foundation Act of 1950.[13] That Act likewise makes the penal provisions of Title 18 U.S.C. Section 1001 applicable with respect to false statements in such affidavits.

b) Until quite recently, the eligibility of labor unions to avail themselves of the facilities of the National Labor Relations Board has been conditioned upon their compliance with Section 9 (h) of the Labor Management Relations Act of 1947.[14] Before a union could be certified by the Board as being in compliance, it was necessary for each of its officers to file an affidavit of Noncommunist Union Officer (NLRB Form 1081). The affidavit included a denial of present membership in and affiliation with the Communist Party. Section 9(h) was repealed by the Labor Management Reporting and Disclosure Act of 1959.[15]

c) While we do not claim to have a comprehensive list of all the groups from whom some form of loyalty affadavit or certificate is required the following come to mind immediately:

1. All applicants for Federal civilian employment;

2. All personnel of the armed forces, including the Reserve components;

3. All employees of defense contractors for whom it is necessary to obtain access to classified information;

4. All persons accepted for Federal employment at the time of their entry into such employment.

Although the forms of affidavit or certificate may vary among individual agencies, as a minimum they require the denial, or disclosure as the case may be, of present and past membership in the Communist Party. In addition, many also require similar representations with respect to present or past membership in, affiliation with or attendance at meetings of Communist organizations, subversive organizations, or organizations designated by the Attorney General.

More specifically under the above categories, all ambassadors, ministers, diplomatic secretaries, consular officers, and foreign service officers are required, at the time of acceptance of their appointments, to execute under oath an affidavit of this type. This requirement applies generally to all officers and employees of the Federal Government and is imposed pursuant to the provisions of Section 2 of the Act of August 9, 1955.[16]

Standard forms of appointment affidavits are employed by federal agencies including the Department of State. While there are some minor variations in the forms, those executed by ambassadors and other diplomatic officers are identical in essential respects with those required of other Government employees. In either case, the standard forms include the oath of office (of which the oath of allegiance is a component part) and the affidavits as to subversive activity and affiliation and striking against the Federal Government which are required under the above statute.

These are some of the facts and precedents for the controversial affidavit and considering its extension to hundreds of thousands and even millions (counting the armed services) one may well hesitate to accept the charge that the loyalty oath affidavit of the N.D.E.A. of September 2, 1958 is discriminatory in "singling out students alone in our population—and, among students, the neediest—as subjects of special distrust." Students are singled out because the Congressional Act singles them out as its beneficiaries in an education program geared to national defense and security. Why should anyone consider the requirement of the nonsubversive affidavit from the recipients of federal loans as a mark of special distrust for them more than or differently from the hundreds of thousands who subscribe to it for salaried employment in federal service? Those in federal service are called upon to confirm their oath of allegiance with an explicit disavowal of disloyal conspiratorial intent. The prospective recipients of government loans are being considered as engaged in the same work of trust and greater reliance. They are being grouped symbolically with those who are in federal service as contrasted with other government beneficiaries such as farmers *et alii* whose relevance to national security and defense is not defined by Congress with the same degree of immediacy as education in the technical sciences. Deserving and needy students are offered loans on most reasonable terms. Their repayment to the government is so generously conditioned that they can scarcely impose any financial distress or burden to the borrower. Should the recipient subsequently serve as a full time teacher in a public elementary or secondary school in any State, up to fifty percent of such loan (plus interest) is "forgiven."[17] The *A fortiori* argument is in place here. If the salaried personnel in federal employment are required to subscribe to a non-subversive disclaimer, should not those who receive financial assistance in a program of national defense be equally privileged?

At times semantics can work prejudice on reason. The word "discriminatory" has hardened into a pejorative connotation even when discrimination is favorable. If an argument of any sort is to be drawn from practice why should anyone choose to refer to farmers who are beneficiaries of the government as the term of comparison with students any more than those federal employees, civilian and military, who by far outnumber the farmers? I am of the opinion that discrimination is objectionable when a good is directed to one group arbitrarily to the exclusion of others who are equally apt as candidates for the same benefit, or for imposing a burden upon one group and exempting others of the same condition and to whom identical reasons would apply. (Our income taxes are graduated to a wage scale as an instance of reasonable discrimination dictated by equity.)

The comparatively few university officials who object to the disclaimer affidavit distinguish the National Science Foundation Act with which they have concurred for nearly a decade from the National Defense Education Act. In the student loan program of 1958, they point out, the educational institution is required to invest 10 percent of its own funds in each loan,[18] and to administer the disclaimer affidavit and oath of allegiance to each borrower. The National Science Foundation Act did not require any financial complement from the educational institution. While some weight may be allowed to this argument of financial involvement as a starting point for distinguishing compliance with the one Act from noncooperation with the other, the argument thins out too soon. It cannot wholly explain away nearly ten years' cooperation whereby under the terms of the National Science Foundation Act the colleges and universities made available their research facilities in return for a financial recompense. Such concurrence seems to go beyond reluctant acquiescence.

The Taft-Hartley Act required all union officers to file noncommunist affidavits with the National Labor Relations Board.[19]

The penalty for non-compliance fell, not on the officers, but on their unions, which were denied the services of the Board. There was no similar provision for the employers. Notice is taken that Section 9 (h) of the Act of 1947 prescribing the disclaimer affidavit was repealed by Section 201 (d) of the Labor Management Reporting and Disclosure Act of 1959.[20] No inference may be drawn as to the congressional intent in repealing the requirement of a disclaimer affidavit from union officials that would give consolation to those who now urge its repeal for students under the federal loan program of the National Defense Education Act. On the contrary, the provisions of Section 9 (h) of the Act of 1947 which were repealed by Section 201 (d) of the Act of 1959 were superseded by those contained in Section 504. What the affidavit proviso stipulated as a condition for the eligibility of labor unions to avail themselves of the facilities of the National Labor Relations Board, Section 504 proscribes categorically with a much wider applicability. The new law substitutes a complete ban on Communist office-holding in unions. No member of the Communist Party, the law reads, may serve

> as an officer, director, trustee, member of any executive board or similar governing body, business agent, manager, organizer or other employee (other than as an employee performing exclusively clerical or custodial duties) of any labor organization.[21]

The same ban applies to ex-Communists for a period of five years following the termination of their party membership. Nor are only trade unions covered. The prohibition also affects labor-relations consultants hired by employers and employer associations. Section 504 (a) 2. For wilful violation of this section of the law, which applies to those who knowingly permit employment of the Communists as well as to the Communists themselves, the penalty is a fine of not more than $10,000 or imprisonment for not more than one year, or both. Section 504 (a) 2 (b). If the present critics who urge the repeal of the nonsubversive affidavit for students applying for government loans should point to its cancellation for labor union officials, would they as readily argue to a parallel substitution in law?

FACTS AND SYMBOLISM

Seventeen institutions are known to have withdrawn or to have refused to join the loan program. About a dozen colleges and universities have publicly registered their protest and urge the repeal of the disclaimer affidavit but continue to participate in the federal loan program. The overwhelming majority about 1,370 educational institutions with a total student body of more than 85 percent are cooperating in the administration of the National Defense Education Act and several of their spokesmen have publicly defended the loyalty affidavit and at times expressed their misgivings and bewilderment about the contrary criticisms. Should not their wishes and choice in the matter bear favorable comparison with the dissenting few? Nor will it do to say simply, let each institution decide for itself. What of the wishes and choice of the deserving and needy students who are not only willing but might also be proud to subscribe to the loyalty affidavit? The students' freedom of choice should not be entirely foreclosed by the dissenting university authorities because of their ten percent financial investment. The students' investment is far greater. In such a conflict of interest and rights to freedom of choice there should be an equitable weighing of claims and benefits and an observation as to whose greater benefit is being denied and who will suffer the greater deprivation. By its very profession, the Academy symbolizes freedom of expression. A wholly one-sided determination by the Academy may operate to a discrimination against the willing student and deny him his freedom of choice and expression in the very circumstances where sensitive regard for it may be expected.

One might moralize *onerosa sunt restringenda*. Oath taking is always a serious matter but it does not always incur a *grave incommodum*. In time of war a patriot who is apprehended by the enemy in the process of gathering information about their military installations for transmission to his own country will suffer a *grave incommodum* if he admits to his true allegiance. Such a confession will most certainly mean torture and death. A sincere oath of allegiance alone bears out this consequence in such circumstances. But it is difficult to see where the *grave incommodum* is for the student who is required to subscribe to an affidavit which disavows disloyalty against the very government from whom he asks a loan. Spontaneity is a quality of devotion, both patriotic and familial. To press the argument and say that a subversive would not hesitate to lie about his real allegiance and subversive intentions only brings out in sharp focus its real need and utility. It provides a legal catch for the perjurer. Every card-carrying American Communist will in his caution reasonably allow that there is an excellent chance that he is known to undercover agents of the FBI. And even if he is confident that he has escaped their detection, nothing can insure him against the risk of exposure by some present fellow-Communist who turns against the Party before the statute of limitations has run on any perjury that may have been committed. More than likely that may be the reason why so few Communists are convicted for perjury. They sedulously avoid this legal trap. It is therefore far from convincing to contend that the loyalty oath affidavit is "inherently futile." To refer with disdain to the disclaimer as a "negative affidavit" is really to do it simple justice. It is a legal instrument complementary to the oath of allegiance to increase the chances of apprehending and convicting the perjurer. As such it makes no pretense to instil, coerce, or compel patriotism. The blunt significance of the disclaimer proviso is the refusal of our federal government to educate against its own undoing.

Finally, the critics argue that the affidavit proviso constitutes a threat to academic freedom. Historically, the freedom of the Academy has meant the corporate right to regulate its faculties and disciplines independently of political dictation and control. This obtains even in educational institutions which are established by public law and supported by public funds. This is no less true of private colleges and universities, church-affiliated or not, even when they are the recipients of government financial assistance of various sorts. It is not easy to appreciate the doctrinaire position—and one must earnestly strive to do so—that it is congruous with the free pursuit of truth to insist that those who would destroy our free society by deceit and force for the sake of a politically dominated society should under no condition be excluded from a national defense educational program which is intentionally directed against such a subversive world force. On the contrary, one might expect a free Academy to cooperate with the federal loan program in a symbolic affirmation that its own survival and prosperity depend on the survival of a free society. We do not pretend to say that the repeal of the proviso would bring about in time the destruction of our American liberties by breeding a festering nest of subversives on our campuses. This would be as pretentious a logism as to contend that the retention of the proviso smacks of the odious religious and political oaths of the absolute state which would throttle the freedom of learning. Such reasoning leads only to confusion of historical realities by intellectual association. The loyalty oath affidavit is surely not a religious test although, unfortunately, the word "believes" appears twice in Section 1001(f) and its critics add to the misunderstanding by speaking of the oath of "disbelief." The religious connotation of the word stirs extremely sensitive resonances. Nor is the oath in the tradition of the old political tests. The student is not being asked to support any regime or political party or an administration. Nor is he being asked to forego or disown completely any intention of changing the Constitution and our form of government. He is simply being told that unless he disavows deceitful and conspiratorial intentions and activities to "overthrow our government and its laws by force or violence or by any illegal or unconstitutional methods," he may not be a beneficiary of the federal loan plan.

The controversy really centers on two considerations: may the United States Government choose to exclude from its beneficiaries of a national defense education program those students who are unwilling to disavow disloyalty? Secondly, should the university authorities who object to the nonsubversive disclaimer do so to the extent of depriving deserving and needy students of the right to make their own choice at their institutions unimpeded?

Nor should we see in the affidavit proviso a potential tendency to presumptive statism which gradually assumes to itself the control of education. The Act of 1958 makes its own disclaimer on this precise point in Title I, Section 102:

> Nothing contained in this Act shall be construed to authorize any department, agency, officer, or employee of the United States to exercise any direction, supervision, or control over the curriculum, program of instruction, administration, or personnel of any educational institution or school system.[22]

Besides, it is rather late in the history of American governmental aid to education to raise that ghostly spectre, what with greater demands presently being made on government subvention. Congressmen as well as educators have contributed to the deepening of the tradition of independence of our colleges and universities.

Fortunately no one is obfuscating the atmosphere of discussion by imputing or insinuating less patriotism to any of the critics—a charge which we think would be undeserved as well as irrelevant to the rational merits of their position. My own considered opinion is that it is not even a question of right or wrong. I personally find the reasons justifying the retention of the loyalty oath affidavit more convincing than the reasons urging its repeal, and in several instances I find their criticisms misleading. It is heartening to observe that no fast and clear line divides the supporters of the proviso from its critics, public from private institutions of higher learning, religious or church-affiliated schools from those which are neither officially. Dissenters are found within the same religious profession and even amongst educational institutions of the same religious order. Statistically the overwhelming number of schools cooperating with the federal loan plan as it is, is sharply in contrast with the relatively few who oppose it.

One last reflection. The argument that the loyalty oath affidavit "represents an affront to freedom of belief and conscience" bears within itself a premise of assault upon the oath of allegiance—a dialectical nexus that has not been lost altogether on at least one Senator and a university group which is urging the repeal of both in the National Defense Education Act. We are of the opinion that the validity of the manner of reasoning and logic rooted in a doctrinaire conception of freedom will not stand the test of reflection. Academics are not exempt citizens.

FOOTNOTES AND REFERENCES

1. 72 Stat. 1581-1605, 5 U.S.C. 401-589 (1958).
2. *Id.* at 1602, 20 U.S.C. at 581. Section 1001 of Title 18, United States Code reads:

> Whoever, in any matter within the jurisdiction of any department or agency of the United States knowingly and wilfully falsifies, conceals or covers up by any trick, scheme, or device a material fact, or makes any false, fictitious or fraudulent statements or representations, or makes or uses any false writing or document knowing the same to contain any false, fictitious or fraudulent statements or representations, or makes or uses any false writing or document knowing the same to contain any false, fictitious or fraudulent statement or entry, shall be fined not more than $10,000 or imprisoned not more than five years, or both.

3. Bryn Mawr, Haverford, Swarthmore.
4. Amherst, Antioch, Bennington, Goucher, Grinnell, Harvard, Oberlin, Princeton, Reed, Sarah Lawrence, St. John's of Maryland, Wilmington of Ohio, Yale.
5. Bates, Bowdoin, and Colby in Maine, Smith College, University of Chicago.
6. For example, Sister M. Madeleva, president of St. Mary's College at South Bend, Ind.: "The college has been proud to present the affirmative oath of allegiance to the United States and the accompanying affidavit to the students. The students consider it an honor to take the same oath that every service man takes." "Loyalty Oath Termed An Honor,"

New York Times, Dec. 15, 1959. Also, Dr. Robert L. Johnson, chancellor of Temple University, on November 24 said: "It is high time that someone in higher education pointed out that it is hard for many of us to comprehend the controversy . . . as to whether or not young people borrowing money from the Federal Government should be required to support the Constitution and to swear that they are not members of any organization striving to overthrow our country." See too, letter to the editor by Rev. Robert Grewen, S.J., president of Le Moyne College, in AMERICA, January 16, 1960. Also NATIONAL REVIEW, February 27, 1960 citing Professor Ernest van den Haag of New York University and Professor E. Merrill Root of Earlham. See Rabbi Aaron Sadowsky, letter to *New York Times*, "Student Loyalty Oath Upheld," November 27, 1959.

7. Dates of governmental action: Passage of the Act, September 2, 1958. Under Pressure from education officials, Arthur S. Fleming, Secretary of Health, Education, and Welfare, urged the repeal of the disclaimer affidavit in December, 1958. Hearings were heard by a Senate Education subcommittee on a proposal to amend the act and the Senate voted in July, 1959 against repeal. On January 28 of this year, 1960, Senator John Kennedy reintroduced in Congress his bill designed to remove the nonsubversive affadavit. Numbered S. 2929, it was reported favorably, February 2, by the Senate Labor and Welfare Committee, "Senate Unit Backs Red Oath's Repeal," *New York Times*, February 3, 1960. This year's bill is a modified version of the Kennedy-Clark bill of the last session of Congress which asked that both the affidavit and the oath of allegiance be removed from the N.D.E.A.

8. A Committee for the Repeal of 1001(f) has been organized by Harvard students under the chairmanship of Professor David Riesman and is currently lobbying for congressional action to eliminate the loyalty oath and disclaimer affidavit requirements from the N.D.E.A.

9. "Student Loan Aid Held Endangered," *New York Times*, November 29, 1959.

10. *Cf.* letters of protest referred to by the *New York Times*, "University Heads Hit Loyalty Oath," January 25, 1959; *cf.* letters of withdrawal from the educational program cited by *New York Times*, November 18, 1959, "Yale, Harvard Spurn U.S. Loans"; *cf. New York Times*, November 22, 1959, letters cited in "Loyalty Oath Stirs Objections"; see too, *New York Times* magazine section, December 20, 1959, "Loyalty: An Issue of Academic Freedom" by A. Whitney Griswold.

11. 72 Stat. 1581, 20 U.S.C. 401 (1958).

12. Letter of Dr. Pusey to Dr. Derthik, Commissioner of Education, cited in *New York Times*, November 22, 1959, "Loyalty Oath Stirs Objections."

13. 64 Stat 156 (1950), 42 U.S.C.   1874(d) (1958).

14. 29 U.S.C.   159(h) (1958).

15. Pub. L. No. 257, 86th Cong, 1st Sess.   201d (1959).

16. 69 Stat 624, 5, U.S.C.   118(q) (1958).

17. 72 Stat. 1581, 1856, 20 U.S.C.   401, 425(b) (3) (1958).

18. *Id.* at 1584, 20 U.S.C. at 424(2).

19. Section 9(h):

> No investigation shall be made by the Board of any question affecting commerce concerning the representation of employees, raised by a labor organization under subsection (c) of this section, no petition under section 9(e) (1) shall be entertained, and no complaint shall be issued pursuant to a charge made by a labor organization under subsection (b) of section 10, unless there is on file with the Board an affidavit executed contemporaneously or within the preceding twelve-month period by each officer of such labor organization and the officers of any national or international labor organization of which it is an affiliate or constituent unit that he is not a member of the Communist Party or affiliated with such party, and that he does not believe in, and is not a member of or supports any organization that believes in or teaches, the overthrow of the United States Government by force or by any illegal or unconstitutional methods. The provisions of section 35A of the Criminal Code shall be applicable in respect to such affidavits.

20. *Supra* note 15.

21. *Supra* note 15 at   504(a)1.

22. 72 Stat 1581, 1582, 20 U.S.C.   401, 402 (1958).

THOMAS JEFFERSON, RELIGIOUS EDUCATION AND PUBLIC LAW*

The majority opinion delivered by Justice Douglas in the *Zorach*[1] case of 1952 made no mention of the Jeffersonian metaphor, "wall of separation" which members of the Court in their several opinions cited in the earlier *Everson*[2] and *McCollum*[3] cases of 1947 and 1948 respectively. The Court, rather, strove sedulously to contrive a formula of separation of church and state without resorting to the metaphor of masonry. Perhaps the late Justice Jackson's caustic remarks about the "serpentine wall" and that "the wall which the Court was professing to erect between church and state has become even more warped and twisted than I had expected" — may have stung some members of the high tribunal to less confidence about the masonic symbolism.

The three Court rulings were the occasions of widespread national controversies[4] and so thoroughly were the complex issues debated that a contestant today could anticipate the opposing argument. There is, however, one aspect remaining which, I think, has not been adequately explored, namely, the bearing of Jefferson's personal religious convictions, which he freely expressed in his private correspondence, to his stand on public law provisions for religious liberty, especially in the area of religious education. The contrast is, paradoxical as it may seem, an illuminating revelation of Jefferson's conception of the scope and function of public law. With highminded restraint motivated by principles of great statesmanship, he did not allow his own prejudices and animosities as well as his own convictions on religious matters to color his actions either as statesman or educator.

---

*JOURNAL OF PUBLIC LAW. Emory University Law School. Vol. 8, n. 1, 1959, pp. 81-108.

I. INTRODUCTION

On August 6, 1816 the sage of Monticello wrote to Mrs. Samuel Harrison Smith[5] that he had been variously charged with being "atheist, deist, or devil" and he countered these accusations by declaring that it was nobody's business what he was, religion being "a concern purely between our God and our consciences, for which we are accountable to Him." Notwithstanding Jefferson's frequent insistence on the privacy of religious beliefs he did write freely about his own convictions to a number of correspondents. There is no evidence that he was being coaxed to do so; on the contrary, on occasion he would urge his own canons for the discernment of religious truths upon his confidants. What is more, Jefferson was far from inhibited in passing judgment upon the creeds of others. That Jefferson was taunted atheist, devil or infidel is to be attributed to the animosity which flamed with evident mutual relish between the federalist-clerical hierarchies of New England and himself.

The disclosures in his own letters about his personal religious convictions allow really only two questions: Was Jefferson a deist or a theist? Was Jefferson a Christian? The answers to these questions rest on certain presuppositions. By religion, I understand, man's acknowledgment of his total dependency upon God, his Creator. These divine-creature relations, ontological and moral, I take to be the proper objects of intellection and assent given either by motivation of divine revelation or under the compelling evidence of the universe. To the Hebrew of the Old Testament, religion is God, the Decalogue, and the Messianic Promise; to the Christian, the fulfillment of the divinely inspired scriptural prophecies in the Incarnation, and generally speaking, institutionalized Christianity. Deism I take to be a rationalistic naturalism which discounts the supernatural, whatever is not discernible by reason alone. It is characterized by a spirit of criticism directed against the nature and content of traditional religious dogmas, viz., Trinity, Incarnation, Original Sin, Redemption, against ecclesiastical, magisterial and disciplinary authority in matters of faith and morals, and against the ministry of the sacraments. Deism took its rise and flourished amongst the individualistic freethinkers of seventeenth- and eighteenth-century England. In France, under the impact of the Voltairean Age of Enlightenment, deism dispensed with the personal deity and survived only as a rationalist moralism of an enthroned all-self-sufficient "reason." Denunciations of the "superstitions" and "corruptions" of "priestcraft" abound in the writing of deists and they leave no doubt as to the alleged source of the various forms of Christianity and their practices. "God is in His heaven and all is well with the universe" epitomized the deist conception of the Architect who leaves his creatures to fend for themselves with what he has bountifully given to them. Theism comprehends broadly all those who by natural or positive theology or both admit to a special as well as general divine providence, the efficacy of intercessory prayer, immortality, and eternal life according to divine judgment. Ready thumb rules for distinguishing theists from deists are the doctrines of special providence and the efficacy of intercessory prayer. Obviously, the denial of the first renders the other useless. Theists who are not also supernaturalists are generally favorably disposed towards organized religion for its beneficent effects upon society. Theists may be adherents of a particular Christian church or they may simply profess latitudinarian Christianity.

In ascertaining whether Jefferson was a theist or a deist, it is necessary to acknowledge the difference between an individual's avowal of a religious tenet and his attempts to think as a theologian or philosopher about his religious professions. A believer's incompetence to think congruously and convincingly as a philosopher or theologian should not discredit the sincerity of his beliefs especially if his conduct conforms with the virtues of his faith. In this wise we shall spare not only Jefferson, who was never embarrassed or hesitant to expound on theological matters with an extraordinary sense of competence beyond his learning, but so many others, from the justifiable censures of reason and logic.

The central marks of theism are contained in Jefferson's second inaugural address of 1805:

> I shall need, too, the favor of that Being in whose hands we are, who led our forefathers, as Israel of old, from their native land, and planted them in a country flowing with all the necessaries and comforts of life; who has covered our infancy with his providence, and our riper years with his wisdom and power; and to whose goodness I ask you to join with me in supplications, that he will so enlighten the minds of your servants, guide their councils, and prosper their measures, that whatsoever they do, shall result in your good, and shall secure to you the peace, friendship, and approbation of all nations.[6]

In the report of the commissioners for the University of Virginia to the legislature of the state, which Jefferson wrote, we read of "God, the creator, preserver, and supreme ruler of the universe, the author of all the relations of morality, and of the laws and obligations these infer."[7] These moral precepts our Creator has indelibly impressed in our hearts.[8] From his earliest writings and continuing to his declining years, Jefferson repeatedly affirmed the self-sufficiency of reason alone to know truth, including the existence of God.[9] When Jefferson insisted on the independence of inquiry and freedom of thought, he meant freedom from external constraints in order that reason may have unimpeded access to evidence. His argument for the disestablishment in Virginia in 1779 is introduced with the statement:

> Well aware that the opinions and belief of men depend on their own will, *but follow involuntarily the evidence proposed to their minds*. . . .[10]

There is no doubt in his mind about the intelligibility and demonstrability of the existence of God[11] and though this would allow the possibilities for the science of natural theology, Jefferson himself never did elaborate nor for that matter examine and weigh the various arguments for the existence of God and His divine attributes. Perhaps he was conscious of his shortcomings as a philosopher. That God is a transcendent being appears from his frequent reference to God as Creator. However, he does not seem to allow the possibility that such a God may choose to make direct revelations of truths otherwise inaccessible to human intelligence. Reason and reason alone is the only avenue to truth. With this he forecloses all possibilities of divine revelation and the various expressions of supernaturalism therein contained. In 1820, he wrote to John Adams that God was "an ethereal gas"[12] and that same year to W. Short: "I am a Materialist."[13] Here we must recall the difference between Jefferson's religious professions and his inept and clumsy efforts at philosophizing. Metaphysics was decidedly not Jefferson's forte; on the contrary, he had a deep-grained aversion for speculative philosophy except in moral studies and even here to a very limited extent. His constant appeal to "simple" doctrines and fundamentalist residues of common agreement and aceptance reveals his impatience with complex and intricate thinking. The theological incongruity between

God, the Creator, the author of all morality, and a gaseous substance would escape him entirely. This unembarrassed statement of crude materialism may be traced to the stoic physics which Jefferson very likely imbibed without much reflection during his sojourn in France in the salons where Voltairean discourse dominated. Jefferson ought not to be taken with more seriousness than he did himself.[14] He believed in the immortality of the soul, accountability to God for our conduct on earth, and a future state of rewards and punishments. He conceived the work of salvation wholly as an individual and private endeavor: "If I could not go to heaven but with a party, I would not go there at all."[15] Despite his intense dislike for organized religion and his opposition to the support of the clergy with public funds he is known to have contributed liberally to the support of the clergy, and was a frequent attendant and participant at church services.[16]

For himself and others, Jefferson set the processes of reason alone as the exclusive and sufficient avenue to religious as well as other truths. Yet we find no elaborate argument, or a developed system of reasoning, establishing with demonstrative force any of his religious confessions — the existence of God and His attributes, as "creator, preserver, and supreme ruler of the universe, the author of all relations of morality, and of the laws and obligations these infer," the spirituality and immortality of the soul, etc. Thus he may oddly enough be termed a believer in what are objectively rational truths. Perhaps Jefferson sensed the inadequacy of his *fideism* and consequently made personal conduct the credentials of a faith; but this too involves certain rational discomforts. While, indeed, true belief should issue into good works, goodness itself is no surrogate for truth. For a believer of the true faith may fail to live according to his faith, and the believer of a false faith or a nonbeliever for that matter may live a good life out of generous impulses and unselfish qualities of character. Be that as it may, Jefferson does write of a moral law which is imprinted in our hearts by the Author of our being. But here too his repugnance for absolutes and dogmas carry over from his theological creed such as it was, and to hold to a morality whose highest commendation is its utility conditioned by geographic and environmental factors even to the point of contrariety.

> Some men are born without the organs of sight, or of hearing, or without hands. Yet it would be wrong to say that man is

born without these faculties, and sight, hearing and hands may with truth enter into the general definition of man. The want or imperfection of the moral sense in some men, like the want or imperfection of the sense of sight and hearing in others, is no proof that it is a general characteristic of the species. When it is wanting, we endeavor to supply the defect by education, by appeals to reason and calculation, by presenting to the being so unhappily conformed, other motives to do good and to eschew evil, such as the love, or the hatred, or rejection of those among whom he lives, and whose society is necessary to his happiness and even existence; demonstrations by sound calculation that *honesty promotes interest in the long run; the rewards and penalties* established by the laws; and ultimately the *prospects* of a future state *of retribution* for the evil as the good done while here. These are the *correctives* which are supplied by education, and which exercise the functions of the moralist, the preacher, and legislator. . . . Some have argued against the existence of a moral sense, by saying that if nature had given us such a sense . . . then nature would also have designated, by some particular ear-marks, the two sets of actions which are, in themselves, the one virtuous and the other vicious. Whereas, we find, in fact, that the same actions are deemed virtuous in one country and vicious in another. The answer is that *nature has constituted utility to man the standard and test of virtue. Men living in different countries, under different circumstances, different habits and regimens, may have different utilities; the same act, therefore, may be useful, and consequently virtuous in one country which is injurious and vicious in another differently circumstanced.* I sincerely, then, *believe* . . . in the general existence of a moral *instinct.* I think it the brightest gem with which the human character is studded, and the want of it as more degrading than the most hideous of the bodily deformities.[17]

Apart from the misleading parallel and inferences drawn by Jefferson between the physical complement of the human body and the totality of spiritual faculties in man, inclusive of a moral sense, the appeal to the efficacy of education and the weighing of practical motivations may serve in some instances as apt instruments for the awakening and development of a moral conscience in those in whom it is seriously deficient. But Jefferson capitulates completely to utilitarianism and moral relativism when he constitutes utility the norm of virtue and virtue itself and evil interchangeable according to geographic location. There is not even a suspicion of the malice of sin as an offense against God, and of virtue as a conformity of human will with the divine out of love of God to whom we creatures owe adoration and obedience. There is no higher motive put forth for useful moral conduct than consequents, advantages, correctives. He scarcely advocates a universal and uniform utility, a very discouraging premise for international relations! For all his vaunted rationalism, Jefferson turns out to be a moral sensist:

> He who made us would have been a pitiful bungler, if he had made the rules of our moral conduct a matter of science. For one man of science, there are thousands who are not. What would become of them? *Man was destined for society. His morality, therefore, was to be formed to this object.* He was endowed with *a sense* of right and wrong, *merely relative to this.* This *sense* is as much a part of his nature, *as the sense of hearing, seeing, feeling;* it is the true foundation of morality, and *not* the *tokalon, truth,* etc., as fanciful writers have imagined.... This *sense* is submitted, indeed, *in some degree*, to the guidance of reason; *but it is a small stock which is required for this: even a less one than what we call common sense.*"[18]

Far are we from denying that the Author of our being meant the moral law to be useful and enjoyable to man, otherwise human life would be extremely uncomfortable and well-nigh impossible. But we do deny that law or action is good only because it is useful, but rather that utility is merely one of the several positive social consequences of morality. Men may be called upon by the divine laws to sacrifice their properties and even their lives rather than violate them grievously, a sacrifice hardly useful in this life. Nor for that matter can it be said to be a utility ordained to eternal happiness since beatitude is a companionable enjoyment of God, not a use of God. This misconception has led utilitarians to include religious life within the narrow principle of self-interest.

Jefferson finds the answer to the hazards of moral relativism in a general and prevailing consensus amongst the dogmatically differing faiths. This effort is inexorably guaranteed by the divine action which has destined man to live in a well-ordered society and has impressed indelibly on human hearts those moral precepts whose observance are foreordained to this end. The inevitable emergence of this general consensus is categorically affirmed by Jefferson in the interests of society despite the fact that "[t]he varieties in structure and action of the human mind as in those of the body, are the work of our Creator, against which it cannot be a religious duty to erect the standard of uniformity."[19]

Jefferson should not be wholly to blame for elliptical and incoherent reasoning. He is exercising the independence of the freethinker whose mind has been not only emancipated by the Age of Enlightenment from the assumption of supernaturalism, the "personal inspiration" in the Reformers' "private judgment," but also cut from its ontological moorings by the discredit which eighteenth-century empiricism visited upon speculative philosophy. Such a mind was content to acknowledge perforce the inexorable laws of physics and mathematics because nature was thereby made to yield its secrets to human calculation and to the utility of mankind.[20] While then Jefferson would not allow that God created man capable of arriving at the same speculative truths — such an intellectual agreement might conduce to that dreadful spectre of uniformity — he would nonetheless hold fast that God imprinted indelibly in our hearts moral precepts which even the "varieties in structure and action of the human mind" could not keep us from sensing. The content of this sensist moralism coincides with the moral precepts of Jesus and the obligation for observance it derives from no higher motive than the interests of society. The reasonableness of the law is in its utility.

II. WAS JEFFERSON A CHRISTIAN?

In 1816 Jefferson wrote to Charles Thomson:

I am a *real Christian,* that is to say, a disciple of the doctrines of Jesus, very different from the Platonists, who call *me* infidel and *themselves* Christians and preachers of the gospel, while they draw all their characteristic dogmas from what its author never said nor saw. They have compounded from the heathen mysteries a system beyond the comprehension of man, of which the great reformer of the vicious ethics of deism of the Jews, were he to return on earth, would not recognize one feature.[21]

Since Jefferson distinguishes himself, a *real Christian* — the italics are in the original — from, presumably, the putative ones, in what sense was he a Christian, or, in other words what did he think of Christ? He always insists that he is a Christian in the only sense in which he (Christ) wished anyone to be. With this, he denies that Christ ever claimed divinity though "ascribing to himself every *human* excellence."[22] With the rejection of the dogma of the Incarnation, Jefferson discounts, too, the trinitarian dogma which he describes as the confection of platonizing priests.[23] Jefferson's enthusiasm and admiration for the man Jesus is unbounded[24] even with the admission of certain limitations, excusable, Jefferson thinks, in him. Christ, reared within the Jewish tradition of divine favors and gifted with an "eloquence which had not been taught him, he might readily mistake the coruscations of his own fine genius for inspirations of an higher order."[25] Jefferson further allows that Jesus, in order to escape the snares of the "priests of... superstition... was justifiable, therefore, in avoiding these by evasions, by sophisms, by misconstructions and misapplications of scraps of the prophets, and in defending himself with these their own weapons, as sufficient, *ad homines,* at least."[26] Of course, he has his differences with Christ:

> It is not to be understood that I am with him [Jesus] in all his doctrines. I am a Materialist; he takes the side of Spiritualism; he preaches the efficacy of repentance towards forgiveness of sin; I require a counterpoise of good works to redeem it, etc.[27]

Jefferson exults in the purity, sublimity, benevolence of Christ's moral teaching — "purest system of morals ever preached to man." All his references to it are in the superlative. Christ's moral teaching was a necessary corrective of the inferior ethics of the Jews,[28] superior to any taught by the pagan philosophers, and never excelled by anyone since. But his sublime and simple doctrines were "adulterated and sophisticated by artificial constructions" of the clergy "into a mere contrivance to filch wealth and power to themselves." Whereupon Jefferson urges several of his correspondents to join him in "extracting the pure principles" of Christ from the distortions and accretions that have been visited upon it since the days of Paul. It is a scissor and paste job, "cutting verse from verse out of the printed book, and arranging the matter which is evidently his [Christ's]."[29] Others take to his suggestion before he does and when he does complete his own compilation, news of it stirs speculation that there is a "change" in his religious life.

One may be amazed at the degree of self-assurance with which Jefferson pontificates as a textual critic of the New Testament. The original manuscripts had long since decayed and the fragments still extant were dispersed in distant European libraries. Countless translations of the original Aramaic and Hellenic Greek differed in the choice of idiom as to establish variant dogmatic interpretations. Yet Jefferson never doubts his own competence to penetrate to the original teachings of Christ. His canon for selectivity is remarkably uncomplicated: moral simplicity; everything else is disregarded. The most profound religious dogmas were registered in the words of Christ. Nonetheless Jefferson can, without any qualms, counsel John Adams "select, *even from them* [evangelists], the very words of Jesus" and arrange "the matter *which is evidently his* [Christ's]."[30] Really, Jefferson's purpose was to expurgate all record of the supernatural in the New Testament and abbreviate it to a summary compilation of the "morals of Jesus" as he called it, but what is now more properly known as the *Thomas Jefferson Bible*.[31] It is not unlikely that Jefferson saw his own role similar to that of Christ. Just as Jesus was the great reformer of the ethics of the Jews so too he would undertake the restoration of Christ's original teaching.

Despite his repeated protestation that religion is a private concern between man and his Maker and his occasional avowal that he does not scrutinize the beliefs of others, Jefferson's private correspondence discloses a facile inclination to do just that. He was far from reticent about his own religious convictions and not at all indifferent about the beliefs of others. On the contrary, he judged and at times even ridiculed the religious tenets of other creeds.

He was unrestrained in his contempt for the clergy. They were motivated by self-interest and power; worse, they had adulterated the simple teachings of Christ; worse still, they had judged him not to be a Christian, but infidel, and even atheist. In his denunciations his language is uninhibited and unsparing. He is unalterably opposed to all expressions of the supernatural. The trinitarian dogma he dismissed as the confection of platonizing clergy. Any dogma as such was divisive. He never seems to have entertained the thought that a truth may be divisive of those who accept it and those who reject it, such as, for example, on a lower plane, the justice of a revolutionary cause which he himself helped to embody in the Declaration of

Independence. Nor did he examine the possibility that God, the Creator, might favor mankind with truths which could not otherwise be known by reason alone.

In particular, he vented his spleen against St. Paul, no less, "the great Coryphaeus, and the first corruptor of the doctrine of Jesus,"[32] and Athanasius whom he brackets with Calvin as "impious dogmatists."[33] He was scornful of metaphysicians of the stature of Plato and Aristotle, but quite partial to Epicurus, a diminutive in comparison.[34]

Of his criticisms of particular creeds, we observe that his judgments are caustic rather than critical, temerarious rather than judicious.[35] His strongest strictures are directed against the Jews and the Calvinists. Jefferson's brusque evaluation of Judaic beliefs and moral code may have derived in no small measure from the Voltairean derision current in the France of his sojourn as well as from his aversion for the rigidity of the Old Testament Calvinist theocracy which took rootage early in the northern colonies. He misses completely the profound significance of the divine insertion into human history, the prophecies, the messianic promise, the decalogue, the beauty and sublimity of the psalms and the many divine revelations and commissions to the patriarchs and prophets of the Old Testament. One must carefully guard against any suspicion that Jefferson was anti-Semitic. On the contrary he had a genuine and sensitive concern for the extension of social and civil rights to the Jews,[36] and for the suffering they had everywhere endured from religious persecution and oppression.[37] By far his sharpest darts are directed against Calvinism.

> I can never join Calvin in addressing *his God.* He was indeed an atheist, which I can never be; or rather his religion was daemonism. If ever a man worshipped a false God, he did. The being described in his five points, is not the God whom you and I acknowledge and adore, the creator and benevolent governor of the world; but a daemon of malignant spirit. It would be more pardonable to believe in no God at all, than to blaspheme him by the atrocious attributes of Calvin.[38]

His sentiments toward the Presbyterians are in the same vein.[39]

It would seem that no purpose would be served in registering Jefferson's judgments upon the religious beliefs of others except to weigh how critical and judicious a theologian he was. Actually our intention points to a remarkable and, for all Americans, a highly profitable paradox. Jefferson rejects all forms and expressions of supernaturalism, either as dogmas or ministries. His language is sharp, caustic, and many times without the tempered restraint that accords with scientific and specialized learning and scholarly canons of criticism. Truly amazing is the confidence of his own competence to review before the bar of his personal judgment the Old and New Testament, the Greek philosophers, Plato and Aristotle, amongst the Fathers, Athanasius, no less, the faith of his contemporaries, and above all an infallible ability to pierce to the original teachings of Christ. Yet he could write as late at 1816, "I have never told my own religion nor scrutinized that of another." The remarkable paradox is this: Jefferson is dogmatically intolerant — he is very sure he is right and his critics wrong, just as wrong as they think he is and more so. He has no doubt that *he* is the *real* Christian and they the infidels and atheists. Jefferson's own religious dogmatism seemingly is in contrast with his equally uncompromising public political tolerance of all religious creeds and consciences. This apparent contrast is fundamentally sound and harmonious. Whoever holds to religious truths does so by an unshaken belief in their veracity. No one willingly would hold to error. Even scepticism is not a denial of truth but rather a doubt whether truth, if it exists, is available to human intelligence. Jefferson's aversion to dogma is not to dogma as such, but to dogma harnessed to the physical compulsions and coercions which interfere with free inquiry.

> That if there be but one [religion] right, and ours that one, we should wish to see the nine hundred and ninety-nine wandering sects gathered into the fold of truth. But against such a majority *we cannot effect this by force. Reason and persuasion are the only practical instruments. To make way for these, free inquiry must be indulged; and how can we wish others to indulge it while we refuse it ourselves.*[40]

Here we have the key to Jefferson's thought. He is not an agnostic and he does not subscribe to religious indifferentism. The *Notes on the State of Virginia* were written shortly after his bill for disestablishment to Virginia had been submitted. Jefferson felt no incongruity between personal religious dogmatism and the *corresponding need for public law tolerance* which for him serves a double purpose; to secure by law the rights of religious conscience, and to provide the suitable, free circumstances for making possible rational persuasion to the claimed true religion. This Jeffersonian conviction contrasts sharply with many who today deny the compatibility of religious dogmatism and public religious liberty for all. This is the underlying premise of his bill of 1779.

> [T]ruth is great and will prevail if left to herself; and that she is the proper and sufficient antagonist to error, and has nothing to fear from the conflict unless by human interposition disarmed of her natural weapons, free argument and debate; errors ceasing to be dangerous when it is permitted freely to contradict them.[41]

Throughout his whole life he never abandoned this fundamental position. Religious liberty meant for Jefferson, not only the guarantee of the rights of religious conscience but also the rationally suitable provision for the freedom to search for religious truths as well as the best circumstances to propagate them by persuasion. This is what he meant when he stated the necessity of *"fixing every essential right on a legal basis."* Therefore it should not be surprising that in his program for education in Virginia, he was meticulous to guard against any "surprise" encroachments upon religious conscience of students. At the same time he would provide by state financial support facilities for the teaching and worship in the various religious creeds by their own ministries and doctors of divinity on state university grounds and in state university rooms — creeds and ministries whose dogmas of supernaturalism and authoritative ministry he castigated and ridiculed in his private correspondence. These letters are *dated contemporarily* with his universal provisions for sectarian religious teaching and worship in the Virginia educational system. Yet some have seen as change of principle what was in fact a reasoned disposition to bring his provisions more in line with his unwavering conception of religious liberty.

III. RELIGION, EDUCATION AND PUBLIC LAW

The unalterable principle of religious liberty which underlies Jefferson's educational programs in Virginia was a conviction which he possessed from the earliest year of his public life. The clarity of the principle never dimmed in his mind. The application of it to the conditions of state education may stir unforeseen difficulties but this does not induce him either to compromise the principle or to shirk the responsibility of working out an equitable application wholly within the terms of that principle. The frequency with which he attends to the problem (which may be broadly described as public law and religious life) attests to his constant concern not to seek easy subterfuge or escape in a "neutral" position with all its concealed prejudices and discriminations.

A. Notes on Religion, October 1776 (Circa)

In a manuscript[42] which is a compound of "notes" to be used by Jefferson in speeches and petitions in the Virginia House of Delegates, particularly in connection with the disestablishment of the Episcopal Church, the young patriot of 1776 goes directly to the heart of the matter when he inquires what is a heretic. Since he does not allow the possibility of a divinely established church as guardian and teacher of the true faith, he is firmly convinced that the numerous Christian sects are all equally of human origin and invention. He finds the source of religious liberty in the "right of chusing and the necessity of deliberating to which we will conform" — but he continues, "if we chuse for ourselves, *we must allow others to chuse also, and to reciprocally* [sic]."[43] Jefferson's extreme religious individualism is as emphatically egalitarian. What we claim for ourselves we must vindicate for others too. Once within an ecclesiastical communion, how far does the duty of toleration extend? Jefferson answers, "No church is bound by duty of toleration to retain within her bosom obstinate offenders against her laws,"[44] and she has the right to exercise her proper power of expulsion or excommunication. However, "we have no right to prejudice another in his *civil* enjoyments because he is of another church."[45] Jefferson holds fast to the individual right of religious conscience to choose its religious communion and to the corporate right and freedom of action of the communion to the exercise of its proper jurisdiction over its adherents. Jefferson then guards the freedom of the churches from interference from one another, by denying to any church the coercive arm of the civil magistrate. This denial is based on the dictates of reason. Force is ineffective for the salvation of souls because "God himself will not save men against their wills."[46]

Compulsion in religion is distinguished peculiarly from compulsion in every other thing. I may grow rich by art I am compelled to follow, I may recover health by medicines I am compelled to take against my own judgment, but I cannot be saved by a worship I disbelieve or abhor.[47]

Further, the civil magistrate is incompetent in the ways of salvation and therefore cannot have jurisdiction therein. Nor can the people confer such jurisdiction upon the magistrate. The magistrate's jurisdictions extend only to civil rights. The compulsions of the secular arm are ineffective and incompetent in the ways of salvation. Besides such presumptions usually entail incidents of civil inequality, religious favoritism, civil incapacitations, exclusion from office, the denial of the franchise, the exaction of a tax contrary to religious conscience. Therefore "all partial distinctions, exclusions and incapacitations [are to be] removed."[48]

B. A Bill for Establishing Religious Freedom (1779)

On June 13, 1779, when Jefferson introduced into the Virginia Assembly his bill for the disestablishment of the Episcopal Church it aroused much opposition. Its passage was delayed until 1786 when Madison, encouraged with his own success against Patrick Henry's bill for the state support of the teachers of the Christian religion, reintroduced Jefferson's original bill. It was adopted with certain changes.

Summarily, Jefferson states: God has created the mind free, subject only to the compulsions of evidence. Its freedom consists in unimpeded access to evidence. Governmental coercions beget hypocrisy and presume to do what God himself will not do. It is the "impious presumption" of fallible men to set up as infallible their own opinions and impose them upon others. Such imposition has perpetuated false religions. Compulsions may take the form of a fiscal exaction for the support of a religious teacher of a faith other than the one of personal choice. "[O]ur civil rights have no dependence on our religious opinions. . . . [I]t is time enough for the rightful purposes of civil government for its officers to interfere when principles break out into overt acts against peace and good order."[49]

Jefferson safeguards liberty simply by denying that the civil power has any competence and jurisdiction to dictate in religious matters. He is equally insistent that the cause of religion is best served by religious liberty, and the most appropriate avenue to the true religion is free inquiry.[50]

C. Notes on Religion (1780-1785)

The following year Jefferson, as governor of his home state, repeats his arguments against governmental compulsion in religion in his answers to the questionnaire which Francois Marbois of the French legation in Philadelphia had addressed to the several American states. The limits and limitation of civil power: "The legitimate powers of government extend only to such acts only as are injurious to others." The harm that coercion works upon religion itself: "Constraint may make him worse by making him a hypocrite. . . . It may fix him obstinately in his errors." Besides, the use of force is by men who are themselves fallible and may thereby perpetuate falsehood rather than truth. Jefferson never tires of stressing both the theoretical fallacy and historical failure of governmental coercion to achieve religious uniformity. The appropriate avenues to truth are reason and free inquiry. And then the logical inference of egalitarian individualism (so characteristic of Jefferson's natural rights doctrine): "[*H*]*ow can we wish others to indulge it* [free inquiry] *while we refuse it ourselves."* Hence the necessity of *"fixing every essential right on a legal basis."*[51]

Underlying these repeated and ever enlarging affirmations of the proper objectives of civil power and of the appropriate conditions for religious life, there gradually emerges a concept of the scope and function of public law which will attain its maturity when Jefferson in later life copes with the problems of education in the state of Virginia. There is, however, discernible at this early stage Jefferson's profound insight that the social order and political allegiance is not contingent upon religious conformity. At the same time he affirms in explicit words the theological basis of human liberties.[52]

D, Jefferson's Metaphor and Historic Commentaries

On January 1, 1802, Jefferson wrote his celebrated letter with the most often quoted metaphor in American legal debate. A committee of the Danbury Baptist Association, in the state of Connecticut, had sent him a letter of high esteem and good wishes. If we bear in mind his fight for disestablishment in Virginia, his recurring arguments against all the discriminatory incidents of establishment in favor of one faith to the disadvantage of the nonconformists, that the Baptists to whom he addressed his answer were in such a disadvantageous status within the terms of the Congregationalist establishment in Connecticut—a situation that would endure until 1818, then his letter, while clearly obvious in its intention and explicit meaning, should not suffer the slightest misconstruction.[53] That same day Jefferson penned a note to Attorney General Levi Lincoln and referred to his letter. "The Baptist address, now enclosed, admits of a condemnation of the *alliance* between Church and State, under the authority of the constitution.... I know it will give great offense to the New England clergy; but the advocate of religious freedom is to expect neither peace nor forgiveness from them."[54]

The meaning of a figure of speech is not self-contained; it is derivative. It loses its meaning if it is excised from its historical context and from its literal composition. Much less ought we to ignore the author's consistent conduct and thinking. The meaning of a figure of speech is wholly in its referral to related thinking on the subject. Seven years later Jefferson had a similar occasion to respond to a letter of approbation and good wishes from the Society of the Methodist Episcopal Church at New London, Connecticut, in close vicinity to the Danbury Baptists.

> No provision in our constitution ought to be dearer to man than that which *protects the rights of conscience against the enterprises of the civil authority. It has not left the religion of its citizens under the power of its public functionaries*, were it possible that any of these should consider a conquest over the consciences of men either attainable or applicable to any desirable purpose. To me no information would be more welcome than that the minutes of the several religious societies should prove, of late, larger additions than have been usual, to their several associations, and I trust that the whole course of my life had proved me *a sincere friend to religious as well as civil liberty.*[55]

Years before all the states cancelled their church establishments and decades before the Supreme Court would make the First Amendment meaning of religious liberty operative upon the states through the Fourteenth Amendment, Jefferson is looking forward to the day when state governments would follow the example of the federal Constitution and guarantee by law equality of religious freedom.

But a more immediate commentary upon the Jefferson metaphor of the "wall of separation" is the treaty with the Kaskaskia Indians which he sent to the Senate on October 31, 1803, scarcely two years after his letter to the Danbury Baptists.

> *And whereas* the greater part of the said tribe have been baptised and received into the Catholic church, to which they are much attached, *the United States will give annually, for seven years one hundred dollars toward the support of a priest of that religion, who will engage to perform for said tribe the duties of his office*, and also to instruct as many of their children as possible, in the rudiments of literature. And the United States will further give the sum of *three hundred dollars*, to assist the said tribe *in the erection of a church.* [56]

This action of Jefferson during his presidency of the United States is remarkably significant and highlights with a precision that leaves no doubt as to his meaning of the First Amendment religious clauses. Before the federal union came into existence, Jefferson had fought for equality of religious freedom by removing church establishment in Virginia. In his correspondence with the Danbury Baptists and with the Methodist Episcopal Church of New London, he hoped for the same in Connecticut. As President of the United States he refrained from proclamations of national days of fasting and prayer because, as he saw it, he would be prescribing religious exercises and discipline beyond the constitutional empowerments of his office. Yet in his second year as chief executive of the national government, he signs a treaty which provides federal financial subvention of a Catholic priest for seven years for his own personal support and three hundred dollars for the construction of a church of worship in order that he may instruct his faithful in their religious life as well as in literature. A more intimate involvement of the federal government with a particular faith could scarcely be contrived without violation of the no-establishment clause of the First Amendment.

The primary and paramount purpose of Jefferson is obvious— the provision of conditions favorable to the free exercise of their

Thomas Jefferson, Religous Education and Public Life 117

faith by the Indians under federal jurisdiction. Washington, before Jefferson, had made similar provisions.[57] The striking significance of this presidential act cannot be minimized. It took place in the midst of a flurry of private correspondence wherein Jefferson never tried to inveigh against various expressions of supernaturalism. Here he pens his signature to the financial subvention of a cleric (whose faith claimed to be divinely revealed and divinely commissioned, no less). Nor is there any record of any doubts or pause in Jefferson's mind as to its constitutionality. The gradual emergence of Jefferson's conception of public law on equality of religious freedom has been marked with two characteristics, uniformity and universality secured by the proscription of establishment and the constitutional guarantee of free *exercise* of religious beliefs and worship. The essential ingredient of universality is impartiality and this is in no wise compromised when the federal government assists in certain circumstances a particular faith. Jefferson, on the contrary, saw this action as an application of governmental action to render actual the free exercise of religion. Nor did Jefferson construe his own action as an act of favoritism or discrimination since in fact there were no other missionaries in similar circumstances with identical needs—surely none to come to his consideration. Jefferson's sense of the universality of religious liberty and its impartiality even when governmental support is directed by reason of circumstances to a particular faith, is remarkably premature in American history and marks him as a farseeing statesman of great stature.

E. Public Law, Education and Religion

From the year that Jefferson left the presidential office in 1809 to his death in 1826, two preoccupations seem paramount amongst his many varied interests. First, to establish that he is the real Christian and his clerical critics the infidels. He has obviously been nettled by their charges that he is either devil, infidel, or atheist. Jefferson answers his religious opponents to the effect that their norm of judgment is wholly arbitrary and unwarranted since the gospels were the manufacture of platonizing clergy through the centuries succeeding upon the "primitive christians" and the "unlettered apostles." In order to vindicate himself as the *real* Christian and to establish *their* heresy, he urges in private correspondence several of his friends to join him in extracting the "simple" "unadulterated" "genuine" moral teachings of Jesus from the "travesties," "sophistications," "artificial constructions" which the clergy in their greed for power and wealth grafted on to the "pure" teachings of Jesus. Concurrent with this personal concernment, there is another interest which preoccupies Jefferson's major efforts— the planning of state educational systems in Virginia. Inevitably the two became intertwined. From his own deep conviction of the theological basis of society, he insists on religious instructions at least in higher education. His own conception of the "complete circle of the useful sciences" includes sectarian teaching (and worship). The necessary involvement of sectarian religious learning in state educational institutions raises a knotty problem to whose resolution he applies himself with great discretion and discernment. As we review Jefferson's educational proposals of 1814, 1817, 1818, 1822 and 1824, we will observe that despite his own dogmatic intolerance of creeds of supernaturalism which he repeatedly ridicules in his private correspondence, he preserves inviolate the equal and impartial protection and provision by public law of freedom for all faiths in institutions of learning. Just as he would not allow a man's faith to suffer "civil incapacitations" neither would he allow a man's faith to incur inequality of circumstances and benefits in state schools.

On September 7, 1814, Jefferson wrote to his nephew, Peter Carr, outlining a comprehensive plan of education for "our native state" to be supported by state funds.[58] He provides for three specified types of schools—the elementary, general, and professional. Amongst the provisions for the last, he stipulates a department for "Theology and Ecclesiastical History" to which the "ecclesiastic" will repair as the lawyer, physician, and militaryman, the agricultor, etc., to his own appropriate studies. In this plan there is no mention of religious instruction in the curriculum of the elementary school. Jefferson is here silent on the question perhaps because he felt that the provision for Theology and Ecclesiastical History was safer for the professional grades than a similar provision for youngsters who would be no match for any "surprise" indoctrination by a teacher of a faith other than theirs. This conjecture is confirmed by the terms of his draft of an "Act for Establishing Elementary Schools" which he submitted to the General Assembly of Virginia September 9, 1817.[59]

[N]o religious reading, instruction or exercise, shall be pre-

Thomas Jefferson, Religious Education and Public Law 119

scribed or practiced *inconsistent with the tenets of any religious sect or denomination.*[60]

Evidently Jefferson has thought of this particular problem during the intervening three years. He is careful to guard the religious conscience of all minors against the more learned persuasion of adult instructors. In the light of his insistence in private letters on the teaching of religious truths acceptable to all, it would seem that Jefferson proscribes only what is inconsistent with the tenets of any religious denomination and not all religious reference and inculcation.

The following year the commissioners for the University of Virginia convened in Rockfish Gap, on the Blue Ridge, to draw up a report which Jefferson wrote for submission to the legislature of the state.[61] In the tentative outline of 1814 Jefferson had provided for a department of Theology and Ecclesiastical History to which the ecclesiastic could repair as other professionals would to their studies. In 1818, in the formal planning of the curriculum for the University of Virginia he abandons this earlier provision and explains the change in terms of principles to which he has constantly referred for the rational justification of any concrete implementation. Now he argues against the provision of sectarian teaching by the state itself.

In conformity with the principles of our Constitution, which places all sects of religion on an equal footing, with the jealousies of the different sects in *guarding that equality from encroachment and surprise* and *with the sentiments of the Legislature in favor of freedom of religion*, manifested on former occasions, *we have proposed no professor of divinity* . . . rather as the proofs of . . . God, the creator, preserver, and supreme ruler of the universe, the author of all the relations of morality, and of the laws and obligations these infer, will be *within the province of the professor of ethics*; to which adding the developments of these moral obligations, of those *in which all sects agree*, with a knowledge of the languages, Hebrew, Greek, and Latin, a basis will be formed *common to all sects.* Proceeding thus far *without offense to the Constitution*, we have thought it proper at this point *to leave every sect to provide*, as they think fittest, the means of further *instruction in their own peculiar tenets.*[62]

This passage is undoubtedly the end result of much reasoned deliberation amongst the commissioners and Jefferson is anxious to make clear that the cause for the change of his own proposal of 1814 are reasons of principle. Referring first to the state constitution which abandoned church establishment by the Acts of 1786, he argues that a professor of divinity of *one* sect would be offensive to religious equality. The implied argument points to the immense practical financial difficulty of providing professors of divinity of *every* denomination that a concrete implementation in accord with religious equality would entail. This forbidding prospect leaves the alternative, let every sect provide the instruction in their own peculiar tenets. However, the teaching of the proofs of God and His moral law by the professor of ethics whose appeal is not to revealed theology but to the construction of natural theology and ethics on the unitive basis of reason wherein all sects can agree is presented as the proper and sufficient surrogate.

But the abandonment in 1818 of the provision for a professor of divinity in the tentative outline of 1814, however painstakingly explained and justified in the cause of equality of religious liberty in education, was misconstrued as a disparagement of the place of religion in a state education, much to the annoyance of Jefferson.

Four years later, Jefferson in his report to the legislature,[63] reexamines the position of 1818 to make clear that on the contrary, despite misrepresentation, a totally nonreligious education is a defective one, and he goes on to work out in greater detail than in 1818 the close cooperation that should obtain between the University of Virginia and the sectarian religions. In the 1818 report, the occasion for possible intrusion upon religious conscience and the danger of religious favoritism are eliminated. In the 1822 report a positive plan in favor of religious education is put forth in detail with sensitive concern for impartiality. In effect, what Jefferson establishes is that neutrality, total abstention, is not the only universal, impartial disposition by law to avoid inequities; rather, a positive construction impartially and universally applied may be the more desirable alternative. What should determine the choice is the value involved, the rights of religious conscience in all areas of human conduct regulated by law. It is obvious that Jefferson is annoyed with the misrepresentation of the 1818 report.

He quotes verbatim, with the necessary variation in tense and pronouns, from the Report of 1818, "in conformity with the principles of constitution" etc. to the conclusion of that passage "they had left, at this point, to every sect to take into their own hands the office of further instruction in the peculiar tenet of each."[64] Obviously, he has before him a copy of the earlier report and may well wonder how it could have been misunderstood. And then he adds immediately, as if to foreclose any further misconstruction:

It was not, however, to be understood that instruction in religious opinion and duties was meant to be precluded by the public authorities, as indifferent to the interests of society. On the contrary, the relations which exist between man and his Maker, and the duties resulting from those relations, are the most interesting and important to every human being, and the most incumbent on his study and investigation. *The want of instruction in the various creeds of religious faith existing among our citizens presents, therefore, a chasm in a general institution of the useful sciences.* But it was thought that this want, and the entrustment to each society of instruction in its own doctrine, were evils of less danger than a permission to the public authorities to dictate modes or principles of religious instruction, or than opportunities furnished them by giving countenance or ascendency to any one sect over another.[65]

The tentative proposal for a professor of divinity had been dropped only because such a provision would necessarily be sectarian, and unless all the denominations were equally to have faculties of their own within the university theology department, a partial provision would be offensive to the state constitutional guarantee of equality of religious freedom and exercise which, for Jefferson, extends into education itself. At that time ("at this point") the commissioners were satisfied that religious truths which are an essential ingredient of the Jeffersonian conception of education could be taught by the professor of ethics on the universal basis of rational persuasion as distinct from the dogmas peculiar to various creeds. In the earlier report of 1818, Jefferson saw the dangers of preferment in one or some sectarian teaching by state law. In 1822 Jefferson goes further: "The want of instruction in the various creeds of religious faith ... presents, therefore, a *chasm* in a general institution of the useful sciences."[66] The significance of this very serious judgment on instruction in the various creeds is sharpened by the sentiments which

Jefferson at that time was expressing in private correspondence. Scarcely four months earlier, he had written to Dr. Benjamin Waterhouse venting his spleen against "impious dogmatists" and "false shepherds" who had adulterated the genuine doctrine of Jesus with "the *deliria* of crazy imaginations," and he "trusts that there is not a *young man* now living in the United States who will not die an Unitarian."[67]

The dogmatically intolerant Jefferson could insist in the full stature of a great statesman on the equal right of all the faiths before the law and, as an educator, appreciate the beneficent effects of bringing the various faiths together on a university level. In 1818, his solution to the knotty problem was to be content with religious study and investigation by the ethics professor and leave it to each sect to provide further instruction in their own peculiar tenets. In 1822, Jefferson studiously formulates a remedy that is as positive in its provisions in favor of religious studies as it should be in guarding against favoritism that encroaches upon anyone's religious conscience. The detailed suggestions are: that the various denominations "establish their religious schools *on the confines of the University,*"[68] —in 1818 they were asked to attend to their own peculiar instructions without the present specific invitation that they do so on state university property; that their students have "ready and convenient access and attendance on the scientific lectures of the university; that students of the university may have reciprocally equal access to the "*religious exercises* with the professor of their particular sect, either in the building still to be erected ... or in the lecturing room of such professor." The visitors of the university "*would think it their duty to give every encouragement, by assuring to those who might choose such a location for their schools, that the regulations of the University should be so modified and accommodated as to give every facility of access and attendance to their students*, with such regulated use also as may be permitted to the other students, *of the library* which may hereafter be acquired, either by public or private munificence."[69] And then Jefferson concludes, with the inviolable principles and premises within which all such dispositions must take place:

> But always understanding *that these schools shall be independent of the University and of each other.*[70]

He is satisfied that "such an arrangement would complete the circle of the useful sciences embarked by this institution, and fill the chasm now existing, on principles which would leave inviolate the constitutional freedom of religion."[71] Let us bear in mind that Jefferson is writing not only for himself but also for the commissioners (of whom ex-President James Madison was one) and the visitors of the university. A more compact epitome of the intricate and necessarily involved relations between religious beliefs and state schools expressed with a more precise constitutional guarantee of the equality of religious freedom and its exercise in education can scarcely be imagined. The 1822 report is the most telling commentary by Jefferson on his metaphor of the "wall of separation of church and state." The problem of religious freedom and public education engaged Jefferson's mind tenaciously, and with the patience of a great statesman he resolved it without seeking refuge in educational neutralism, which, let it be noted, is far from neutral and decidedly offensive to the religious conscience.

Jefferson can hardly contain his resentment and anger at the misconstruction placed on his educational provisions despite the meticulous care with which he explains his reasons.[72] Three weeks later, on November 2, he wrote to Thomas Cooper:

> In our university you know, there is no Professorship of Divinity. *A handle has been made of this, to disseminate an idea that this is an institution, not merely of no religion, but against all religion.* [And then he lists the recommendations of October 7, perhaps asking his friend how could he possibly be misunderstood.] In our annual report to the legislature, ... we suggest the expediency of encouraging the different ... sects to establish, each for itself, a professorship of their own tenets, on the confines of the university, so near as that their students may attend the lectures there, and have the free use of our library, and every other accommodation we can give them; preserving, however, their independence of us and of each other. This fills the chasm objected to [in] ours, as a defect in an institution professing to give instruction in *all* useful sciences.[73]

And what is equally puzzling is that Jefferson's clear record should have been construed a century later contrary to his explicit meaning by members of the highest tribunal in the American judiciary. The wry irony is that Jefferson's appointment of Cooper, a scientist, to the university faculty was to be blocked by the hue and cry raised by the Virginia Presbyterians for *his* religious views.

In 1824 Jefferson, now rector of the State University of Virginia, draws up the regulations[74] for the university which is scheduled to open within a year. It had taken six years to build and it would not actually open its doors until March of 1825 after a postponement of its original date, February 1, because the faculty members from across the ocean had not yet arrived. One would think that he had amply disposed of the university cooperation with religious education in his 1822 report. But he recurs to it again with stronger stipulations. In the 1818 plan, the proper solution was "to leave every sect to provide ... further instruction in their own peculiar tenets."[75] In 1822, the "[v]isitors [of the University] ... think it their *duty to give every encouragement*, by assuring those who might choose such a location for their schools, that the regulations of the University should be so modified and accommodated as to give every facility, etc."[76]

In 1824, the opportunity offered to the religious sects to build on the university grounds is referred to as "according to the *invitation* held out to them."[77] In 1822, the arrangements and accommodations are to be such as to provide "greater advantage of *enabling* the students of the University to attend religious exercises."[78] In 1824, "the students of the University will be free, and *expected* to attend religious worship at the establishment of their respective sects, in the morning, and in time to meet their school in the University at its stated hour."[79] A very pointed commentary on those who today object to realeased-time programs on and off public school property and in the same breath quote Jefferson's "wall of separation"! In 1822, the religious schools may build "*on the confines of the University*."[80] In 1824, they are invited to build "*within or adjacent to* the precincts of the University, schools for instruction in the religion of their sect."[81] And as if to erase every doubt as to the status of the students of divinity who also attend any school of the University, they "shall be considered as students of the University, subject to the *same* regulations, and entitled to the *same* rights and privileges."[82] Conscientious reading of the various educational plans of Jefferson, 1814, 1817, 1818, 1822 and 1824 should leave no room for the misconstruction with which Jefferson has been visited in our times. And if the students of religion should be in want of a room for religious worship as well as for lectures and examinations, the 1824 regulations provide that "one of its [university's] larger elliptical rooms" may be used for such purposes.[83] A year after its opening, Jefferson was to breathe his last on the Fourth of July, 1826, fifty years after he had penned the theological premises justifying the American Declaration of Independence — forty years after discriminatory preferments of the Church establishment in Virginia were annulled. In 1822 and 1824 he had worked towards a positive construction of a formula and its special detailed concrete implementation for the free exercise of religion in education just as assiduously as he had labored for the removal of the impediments for the equality of religious freedom for all creeds.

IV. THE MODERN PROBLEM

Two considerations remain for our final reflections. Any reference to Jefferson's position on the relations of religious rights and state-supported education must be historically correct. It was a problem to which he gave repeated attention and he was not content to avoid the difficulties of formulating a solution by withdrawing into a specious neutrality. As an individual, he was as firmly convinced of his own religious correctness as he was certain that the "various creeds," "sects," and "denominations" were in their expressions of supernaturalism decidedly wrong and a falsification of the "genuine teachings of Jesus." He was, in a word, personally, dogmatically intolerant. He was opposed to error in any form. He was neither a sceptic nor indifferent in religious matters. On the contrary, he held firmly to the ability of reason to attain to religious truths. He saw, however, no contradiction in his mind that public law provisions should guarantee equality of religious freedom for all these creeds, however obnoxious they were to him. That Jefferson was misunderstood in his own time, as he complains in his letter to Cooper, may be explained — and at that, weakly — by the limitations of publication in his day. There is no such excuse for scholars today — nor for that matter, for jurists on and off the bench who engage in quoting Jefferson.

The second consideration is, what would Jefferson hold today: He would definitely not compromise the two principles he held inviolable — the equality of religious freedom for all believers and the rights of religious conscience and their free exercise, guaranteed by law, in education. Would he hold today for the same concrete implementations he specified in his own times for the public schools of Virginia? The answer may vary from an affirmative to that of a doubt — a doubt that would extend to most all of his thoughts — namely, would Jefferson be as "Jeffersonian" today, a century and a half after his own historic times? This is a question which we think no one can settle convincingly about any historical personage. But there are certain lessons which we can learn from the Jefferson of a century and a half ago which we think to be abiding and permanent characteristics of the American formula of church-state relations.

The "wall" that keeps governmental powers from preferential treatment of a religion must be impregnably high. The "wall" that protects the free exercise of religion must be uniformly nondiscriminatory, universally applicable, and impartially favorable. Neutrality is not impartiality[84] and that ghostly evasive reference should be confined to limbo once and for all. Nor should the baffling difficulties of implementing the two inviolable principles afford any rational excuse for retreating into that neutrality which is the benign disguise for wholly secular education. Such education besides being defective, as Jefferson held, cannot but be a contrary influence upon the necessary religious involvements of some disciplines, viz., literature, history, philosophy, value-judgments, political science and so on.

Legally the problem today is how to adjust legislative and judicial action to the resolution of the thorny problem of satisfying the legal requirements of the American type of separation of church and state in a manner to accord with the social and religious demands of American history. The problem is complicated not only by the difference in federal and states' history[85] on church-state relations but also by the operation of the religious clauses of the First Amendment through the Fourteenth upon states who disagree amongst themselves on the constructive interpretation of financial aids.[86]

We must be as confident as Jefferson was in working out an implementation that satisfies all requirements of principle and law. And above all the suspicion that the dogmatically intolerant, *the non-believer as well as the believer* cannot be politically tolerant, through the provision of public law, should be dispelled by the example of Jefferson who formulated detailed accommodations of state university facilities for the benefit of the various religious denominations whose supernaturalism he disparaged so relentlessly in private correspondence. Jefferson's stature as a statesman, as to the function and scope of public law touching on religious life, is more than matched by the grandeur and nobility of his character.

FOOTNOTES AND REFERENCES

1. Zorach v. Clauson 343 U.S. 306 (1952).
2. Everson v. Board of Education, 330 U.S. 1 (1947).
3. McCollum v. Board of Education, 333 U.S. 203 (1948).
4. Costanzo, Federal Aid to Education and Religious Liberty, 36 U. Det. L.J. 1 (1958).
5. Padover, The Complete Jefferson 955 (1943). She was the wife of the newspaper publisher whom Jefferson induced to transplant his printing establishment from Philadelphia to Washington. Rumor had divulged the contents of Jefferson's letter to Thomson earlier that same year that he had compiled a scrapbook of the teachings of Christ and speculations stirred that Jefferson had "changed" to Christianity.
6. Ibid., at 414. Consult too his letter to David Barrow on May 1, 1815: "We are not in a world ungoverned by the laws and the power of a superior agent. Our efforts are in his hand, and directed by it; and he will give them their effect in his own time." 9 The Writings of Thomas Jefferson 516 (Ford ed., 1892-1898).
7. Padover, The Complete Jefferson 1104 (1943).
8. Padover, Democracy by Thomas Jefferson 178 (1939), in a letter to J. Fishback written in 1809.
9. "Reason and free enquiry are the only effectual agents against error. Give a loose to them, they will support the true religion by bringing every false one to their tribunal, to the test of their investigation." Jefferson, Notes on the State of Virginia c. 17 (Stockdale ed., 1787). These notes had their origin in the fall of 1780 when Jefferson, as governor of Virginia, undertook to reply to a questionnaire addressed to the several American states by Francois Marbois of the French legation in Philadelphia. Jefferson's replies to Marbois' twenty-two inquiries are a valuable sourcebook on eighteenth-century Virginia. In three pages Jefferson states his argument for freedom of religion based upon natural rights, the fallibility of governments in religious matters, the futility of control and suppression, the inevitability of truth and the competence of reason if left free of hindrance, of compulsion and of coercion. These notes were first published privately in Paris in 1785 and later edited and published at Jefferson's request by John Stockdale on London in 1787. For a rather recent American edition based on Stockdale, see Jefferson, Notes on the State of Virginia (Peden ed., 1955).

"Your own reason is the only oracle given you by heaven, and you are answerable not [only] for the rightness but the uprightness of the decision." So Jefferson counselled his own nephew in searching for religious truths. 4 The Writings of Thomas Jefferson 432 (Ford ed., 1892-1899); consult too, Padover, The Complete Jefferson 1104 (1943), about the "proofs of the being of a God, creator, etc.," to be "within the province of the professor of ethics."

10. Padover, The Complete Jefferson 946 (1943) (italics added).
11. Padover, Democracy by Thomas Jefferson 184 (1939), in a letter to Adams written in 1823.
12. 15 The Writings of Thomas Jefferson 274-275 (Bergh and Lipscombe ed., 1904).
13. Padover, Democracy by Thomas Jefferson 184 (1939). A year earlier, he had written to Short that he was an epicurean in philosophy, adding that he meant "epicurean" in the genuine and original sense. 15 The Writings of Thomas Jefferson 219 (Bergh and Lipscombe ed., 1903-1905). The next month, he repeated the same to John Adams. Padover, The Complete Jefferson 1036 (1943), in a letter dated November 7, 1819.

14. For a contrary appraisal consult Koch, The Philosophy of Thomas Jefferson 34 (1943), where Jefferson is set down as a "conservative materialist" – an odd conjunction of political and philosophical terminology.

15. Padover, Democracy by Thomas Jefferson 187 (1939), in a letter to Hopkinson written in 1789. Also consult a letter to E. Styles written in 1819: "I am of a sect by myself as far as I know." Ibid., at 188.

16. Bowers, Jefferson and Hamilton 103 (1930): "He planned at least one church and contributed to the erection of others, gave freely to Bible Societies, and liberally to the support of the clergy. He attended church with normal regularity, taking his prayer book to the services and joining in the responses and prayers of the congregation." Consult also, Smith, The First Forty Years of Washington Society 13 (1906). During the winter of 1800, before the regular Sunday services were established in the capitol, Jefferson was a frequent attendant of the small Episcopal church in Washington.

17. Padover, The Complete Jefferson 1032-1034 (italics added), in a letter to Thomas Law dated June 13, 1814.

18. Padover, The Complete Jefferson 1057-1058 (1943) (italics added), in a letter to Peter Carr dated August 10, 1787. Scarcely adequate cognizance has been taken of the influence of the Scottish school upon Jefferson especially in his earlier years. In his memoirs, Jefferson speaks of his early education at William and Mary College under Dr. William Small of Scotland who gave him his "first views of the expansion of science, and of the system of things in which we are placed." 2 Memoir, Correspondence, & Miscellanies, from the Papers of Thomas Jefferson 2 (2d Randolph ed., 1830). The philosophy of common sense which was worked up in Scotland by Reid and Beattie in opposition to Hume and Berkeley held that there are certain first principles or dictates of common sense which are either simple perceptions or seen with intuitive evidence. This Scottish school had its stalwart advocate in colonial times in the person of John Witherspoon who had come over from Scotland and become president of Princeton. Jefferson's preference was obviously not for the Scottish thinkers of the antisceptical and nonsentimental type but for the moral *sense* of Shaftesbury, Hutcheson and Hume, which was but a modification of the same, minus all assumptions of the supernatural (the Reformer's "personal inspiration") and with the additional identification of moral sentiment with utility.

19. Padover, Democracy by Thomas Jefferson 177-178 (1939), in a letter to Fishback written in 1809: "Reading, reflection and time have convinced me that the interests of society require the observation of those moral precepts only in which all religions agree (for all forbid us to murder, steal, plunder, or bear false witness) and that we should not intermeddle with the particular dogmas in which all religions differ, and which are totally unconnected with morality. . . . The varieties in structure and action of the human mind as in those of the body, are the work of our Creator, against which it cannot be a religious duty to erect the standard of uniformity. The practice of morality being necessary for the well-being of society, he has taken care to impress its precepts so indelibly on our hearts that they shall not be effaced by the subtleties of our brain. We all agree in the obligation of the moral precepts of Jesus."

20. In his first inaugural, Jefferson in listing "the essential principles of our government," made vigorous affirmation of what he called the "vital principle of republics" – "absolute acquiescence in the decisions of the majority." But what are the other "essential principles" of his enumeration but a bill of exceptions to this "vital principle?" They were in fact, a catalogue of rights placed out of the reach of the majority, for fear that the majority might destroy them. In the same address, Jefferson even declared explicitly that though the will of the majority was "in all cases" to prevail, that will "to be rightful must be reasonable." "The minority possess their equal rights . . . and to violate [them] would be oppression." If the will of the majority was entitled to "absolute acquiescence," if it was "in all cases" to prevail, what safeguard was there for the rights of the minorities? Yet if minorities were indulged in their claims, how was the maintenance of their "equal rights" to be restrained from leading to minority rule? This basic ambiguity was to stir Jefferson from his earliest years in public service, and his inability to resolve it may be explained partly by the fact that he was the heir of a tradition from whose charm he could not escape. It was the problem of depositing in the right place the freedom of the mind and its perfection in "following" involuntarily the evidence proposed to it. And the eventuality of uniformity amongst

minds conforming to the same evidence – another word for absolutes, dogmas – ultimately arose from the congenital capacity in all men to attain alone or usually with the enlightening assistance of others to the necessary truths of life.

21. Padover, Democracy by Thomas Jefferson 187 (1939).
22. Padover, The Complete Jefferson 955 (1943), in a letter to Dr. Benjamin Rush dated April 21, 1803; also Padover, Democracy by Thomas Jefferson 186 (1939), in a letter to W. Short written in 1820.
23. Padover, Democracy by Thomas Jefferson 181 (1939).
24. Ibid., at 185: "It is the innocence of his character, the purity and sublimity of his moral precepts, the eloquences of his inculcations, the beauty of the apologues in which he conveys them, that I so much admire." Consult also Padover, The Complete Jefferson 949 (1943): "His parentage was obscure; his condition poor; his education null; his natural endowments great; his life correct and innocent; he was meek, benevolent, patient, firm, disinterested, and of the sublimest eloquence."
25. Padover, Democracy by Thomas Jefferson 186 (1939).
26. Ibid., at 185-186.
27. Ibid., at 184-185.
28. Padover, The Complete Jefferson 948 (1943): "Their ethics were not only imperfect, but often irreconciliable [sic] with the sound dictates of reason and morality, as they respect intercourse with those around us; and repulsive and anti-social, as respecting other nations. They needed reformation, therefore, in an eminent degree."
29. Padover, The Complete Jefferson 951 (1943), in a letter to John Adams dated October 13, 1813; 10 The Writings of Thomas Jefferson 294 (Ford ed., 1892-1899); 1816; as late as 1820, he is still calling for this work of restoration. Padover, Democracy by Thomas Jefferson 181 (1939), in a letter to Van der Kemp written in 1820.
30. Padover, The Complete Jefferson 951 (1943).
31. His final achievement is "an octavo of forty-six pages, of pure and unsophisticated doctrines" which are easily distinguished as "diamonds in a dunghill" from what he called "the *deliria* of crazy imaginations," referring to st. Athanasius, no less. Padover, The Complete Jefferson 951 (1943).
32. Padover, Democracy by Thomas Jefferson 185 (1939), in a letter to W. Short written in 1820.
33. Padover, The Complete Jefferson 956 (1943), in a letter to Dr. Benjamin Waterhouse written in 1822.
34. His untiring complaint was that the "simple religion of Jesus" was disfigured beyond recognition by Christ himself by the "jargon of Plato, of Aristotle, and other mystics." Padover, Democracy by Thomas Jefferson 180 (1939).
35. Consult Padover, The Complete Jefferson 948-950 (1943). (Syllabus of an Estimate of the merit of the Doctrines of Jesus Compared with those of others), written in April, 1803; Ibid., at 950-951, in a letter to John Adams dated October 13, 1813; Padover, Democracy by Thomas Jefferson 187 (1939), in a letter to C. Thomson written in 1816; Ibid., at 188, in a letter to E. Styles written in 1819; Ibid., at 185, in a letter to W. Short written in 1820.
36. Padover, Democracy by Thomas Jefferson 179 (1939), in a letter to De la Motte written in 1820: "[I am] happy, in the restoration, of the Jews particularly, to their social rights, and hope they will be seen taking their seats on the benches of science, as preparatory to their doing the same at the board of government."
37. Ibid., at 179, in a letter to Joseph Marx.
38. Ibid., at 184, in a letter to John Adams written in 1823.
39. Ibid., at 183, in a letter to Short written in 1820: "The Presbyterian clergy are the loudest; the most intolerant of all sects, the most tyrannical and ambitious; ready at the word of the lawgiver, if such a word could be now obtained, to put the torch to the pile, and to rekindle in this virgin hemisphere, the flames in which their oracle Calvin consumed the poor Servetus, because he could not find in his Euclid the proposition which has demonstrated that three are one and the one is three, nor subscribe to that of Calvin, that magistrates have a right to exterminate all heretics to Calvinistic Creed."
40. Jefferson, Notes on the State of Virginia c. 17 (Stockdale ed., 1787) (italics added).
41. Padover, The Complete Jefferson 947 (1943).

42. Ibid., at 397-946 (italics added). The date is not certain. Jefferson dated the manuscript "scraps" early in the revolution.
43. Ibid., at 942.
44. Ibid.
45. Ibid.
46. Ibid., at 943.
47. Ibid., at 944.
48. Ibid., at 946.
49. Ibid., at 946-947.
50. A telling commentary on Jefferson's bill of 1779 is Madison's Memorial and Remonstrance of 1785: "Who does not see that the same authority which can establish Christianity, in exclusion of all other religions, may establish with the same ease any particular sect of christians, in exclusion of all other sects? That the same authority which can force a citizen to contribute three pence only of his property for the support of any one establishment, may force him to conform to any other establishment in all other cases whatsoever?" Madison, like Jefferson fought against the *discriminatory,* exclusive support of one religion in preference to others. Madison, Religious Freedom (1819). Despite the clarity of Madison's text, Justice Rutledge in his dissenting opinion in the Everson case construed Madison's thought (apart from its irrelevance to the First Amendment of the federal Constitution ratified six years later) as forbidding financial support of religion as such. Everson v. Board of Education, 330 U.S. 1, 28 (1947).
51. Padover, Democracy by Thomas Jefferson 168-171 (1839); Jefferson, Notes on the State of Virginia c. 17 (Peden ed., 1955).
52. "Can the liberties of a nation be thought secure, when we have removed their only firm basis, a conviction in the minds of the people that these liberties are the gifts of God?" Morris, Christian Life and Character of the Civil Institutions of the United States Developed in the Official and Historical Annals of the United States 35 (1864).
53. Padover, The Complete Jefferson 518-519 (1913).
54. Padover, Democracy by Thomas Jefferson 177 (1939) (italics added); consult too his letter to Elbridge Gerry written 1799: "I am for freedom of religion, and against all maneuvers to bring about a legal ascendancy of one sect over another." 10 The Writings of Thomas Jefferson 78 (Lipscombe ed., 1904); and in the following year, 1800, he listed amongst his services to his country, "I proposed the demolition of the church establishment, and the freedom of religion." Padover, The Complete Jefferson 1288 (1943).

In the same letter to Levi Lincoln referred to above, Jefferson says that he had hoped to explain in the same letter to the Danbury Baptists why he had not continued the practice of his presidential predecessors of proclaiming days of fasting and thanksgiving. Padover, Democracy by Thomas Jefferson 177 (1939). (The occasion was not opportune.)

He repeats his stand again during his second inaugural address of March 4, 1805; but it is not until January 23, 1808 that he explains in a letter to Reverend Samuel Miller that he considers such an act on his part as "intermeddling with religious institutions, their doctrines, discipline [and] exercises," and let us note, while he allows such practice to be within the proper jurisdiction of state governments, he, as President of the United States, has "no authority to direct the religious exercises of his constituents." Ibid.

Whatever may be the merits of Jefferson's rationale on a practice which, with the added exception of Grant, has continued uninterrupted into the proclamations of days of prayer and thanksgiving by all subsequent presidents, we must not lose sight of Jefferson's sensitive concern against interference with anyone's religious conscience. We might reflect that Jefferson's eudaemonism hardly inclined him to penitential practices. Ibid., at 184-86, in a letter to W. Short dated 1820.

Jefferson's contemporaries did not share his construction of the powers of the presidential office. The day – September 24, 1789 – that both Houses adopted a resolution to recommend the new amendments to the states, a resolution was adopted that a joint committee of both houses request the President to proclaim a day of thanksgiving and prayer.
55. Padover, The Complete Jefferson 544 (1943) (italics added).
56. 1 Am. State Papers 687 (1803) (italics added).
57. 4 Am. State Papers 687 (1803). (In 1789 the first Congress appropriated funds for

the support of Christian missionaries amongst the Indians in implementation of a recommendation made by General Knox, the Secretary of War, and approved by President Washington): "The object of this establishment would be the happiness of Indians, *teaching them the great duties of religion and morality,* and to inculcate a friendship and an attachment to the United States" (italics added).

58. Padover, The Complete Jefferson 1064-1069 (1943).
59. Ibid., at 1072-1076.
60. Ibid., at 1076 (italics added).
61. Ibid., at 1097-1105 (italics added).
62. Ibid., at 1104.
63. Ibid., at 957.
64. Ibid.
65. Ibid. (italics added).
66. Ibid., at 957-958.
67. Ibid., at 956.
68. Ibid., at 958.
69. Ibid. (italics added).
70. Ibid. (italics added).
71. Ibid.
72. Ibid., at 956-957, in a letter to Dr. Benjamin Waterhouse dated June 26, 1822.
73. 10 The Writings of Thomas Jefferson 243 (Ford ed., 1892-1899), in a letter to Thomas Cooper dated November 2, 1822 (italics added).
74. Padover, The Complete Jefferson 1106-1112 (1943).
75. Ibid., at 1104.
76. Ibid., at 958.
77. Ibid., at 1110 (italics added).
78. Ibid., at 958.
79. Ibid., at 1110.
80. Ibid., at 958.
81. Ibid., at 1110.
82. Ibid.
83. Ibid., at 1111.
84. Costanzo, Religion in Public School Education, 31 Thought, No. 121, at 1 (1956).
85. The First Amendment couples an express declaration of no delegation whatsoever of power to the Congress to pass laws respecting religion with just as strong an affirmation of religious freedom – no preference and no interference. The amendment prohibits not only "establishment" but also any other encroachment upon religious liberties. It is the broad federal meaning of religious liberty which is transferable through the Fourteenth Amendment, not the meaning of any particular state law of any time in our national history. Historically part of the explanation of the bizarre pattern of discriminatory and nondiscriminatory practices in the states, and, comparatively, among the states, derives from the fact that the states, unlike the federal government, began with establishments and disestablishments and the transition has been from religious liberty, scarcely discernible from tolerance. Further, they have maintained through the decades, until recent times, religious tests and qualifications for state public office. The federal government, on the other hand, began with a clear and clean slate of no establishment, no restriction on religious freedom and no religious test for federal office. Consequently it was able to adopt more easily from the beginning, a policy of nondiscriminatory financial assistance to religion, religious activity, and religious institutions. The federal government was therefore able to escape the consequences of the tensions of a pluralist religious society which came to the fore whenever a church or a religion has enjoyed a preferred status in law and the other churches and religious societies strove to obtain (with an increase in numbers) an equality before the law. Federal incompetence and impotence to prefer a religion or church and to interfere with the free exercise of religious conscience has never meant, in law and in fact, federal neutrality toward religious life.
86. Costanzo, Federal Aid to Education and Religious Liberty, 36 U. Det. L. J. 1 (1958).

FEDERAL AID TO EDUCATION
AND RELIGIOUS LIBERTY*

The present day controversy on federal aid to education differs vastly from the sharper debates which raged in the 1940's. Then constitutional issues were involved; today, seemingly, only matters of policy and advisability. The restriction in 1957 by the Eisenhower Administration of federal aid to capital outlays for construction apparently evades the more sensitive constitutional issues of a decade ago and the open avowal of ecclesiastical authorities that they do not wish nor expect direct federal aid for church-affiliated schools reduces the area of contentious claims. In this comparatively more tranquil atmosphere, the present writer would survey the complex and intricate question of federal aid to education broadly considered — direct, indirect, auxiliary — and mark out with precision the distinctly different issues and the premises from which each issue legitimately depends and validly may derive its force of rational persuasion. From such an analytical-critical examination the conclusion will emerge that whatever may be the political determination of our national congress on federal aid to education in no wise should its legislative policy portend an interpretation of the religious clause of the First Amendment contrary to its authentic meaning. Part of the responsibility for conjoining these two questions rests with the Supreme Court which in the *Everson*[1] and *McCollum*[2] decisions stirred up blinding confusion about what kind of "aid to religion" the First Amendment allowed. The Court upheld in 1947 the constitutionality of a New Jersey statute which provided at public expense bus transportation to all school children whether they attended

---

*UNIVERSITY OF DETROIT LAW JOURNAL. Vol. 36, n. 1, October 1958. Paper read to the Catholic Lawyers Guild, New York City.

governmental or non-governmental schools, as a legitimate exercise of state police power. Benefits of public welfare legislation were extended "to all its citizens without regard to their religious belief." Not content with satisfying the requirements of law, the Court, in acknowledgment of the appellant's contention, also considered whether public aid to religion was constructively a violation of the First Amendment:

> The establishment of religion clause of the First Amendment means at least this: Neither a state nor the Federal Government can set up a church. Neither can pass laws which aid one religion, aid all religions, or prefer one religion over another. Neither can force nor influence a person to go or to remain away from church against his will or force him to profess a belief or disbelief in any religion. No person can be punished for entertaining or professing religious beliefs or disbeliefs, for church attendance or non-attendance. No tax in any amount, large or small, can be levied to support any religious activities or institutions, whatever they may be called, or whatever form they may adopt to teach or practice religion.[3]

Even at first reading a glaring incongruity affronts the reasonable mind. Government establishment of religion, which the Court correctly identifies with the legal preferential status of one state established church or religion and its concomitant incidents of coercion and civil incapacitations for nonconformists, is simultaneously equated in the same breath with impartial governmental aid of all religions! On the basis of such reasoning, the Court should have consistently voided the New Jersey statute. The following year in *McCollum v. Board of Education*[4] the high tribunal adopted Justice Rutledge's construction of absolute separation as enunciated in his dissent in the *Everson*[5] case with full logical consistency by declaring unconstitutional a released time religious program on public school property.

Notwithstanding the Court's improvised proscription of "any" aid "large or small" to "all religions" and "any religious activities" in "whatever form," our state and federal authorities are confronted with a vast panorama of governmental aid, "large and small," to "all religions" and "religious activities" – especially in our national history – in varied forms, financial and non-financial, direct and indirect. Nonetheless, the Court's doctrinaire pronouncement of no governmental aid at all to all religions has caused confusion in the minds of congressmen and state officials. Amongst the states, where all with but one exception, the state of Vermont,[6] rule out indirect as well as direct aid to sectarian schools and denominational institutions — some provide or allow auxiliary services and others do not, and even where permitted, a bizarre and inconsistent pattern prevails. Surely, auxiliary services may very properly be distinguished from indirect aids inasmuch as they are intended to relive the nonreligious needs of school children. But in the place of clearly established and reasonably well founded definitions of law, supreme, uniform, and universal, we find instead the exercise of discretionary judgments of state attorney generals or of local school boards.

In 1952, in *Zorach v. Clauson*[7] the Court retreated somewhat from Rutledge's revolutionary doctrine on church and state to explain the specific type of separation implied in the First Amendment:

The First Amendment within the scope of its coverage permits no exception; the prohibition is absolute. The First Amendment, however, does *not* say that *in every and all respects* there shall be a separation of Church and State. Rather, it studiously defines the manner, the specific ways, in which there shall be no concert or union or dependency one on the other. . . .

We are a religious people whose institutions presuppose a Supreme Being. We guarantee the freedom to worship as one chooses. We make room for as wide a variety of beliefs and creeds as the spiritual needs of man deem necessary. We sponsor an attitude on the part of government that shows *no partiality* to any one group and that lets each flourish according to the zeal of its adherents and the appeal of its dogma. When the state *encourages* religious instruction or cooperates with religious authorities by adjusting the schedule of public events to sectarian needs, it follows the *best of our traditions.* For it then respects the religious nature of our people and accommodates the public service to their spiritual needs. To hold that it may not would be to find in the Constitution a requirement that the government show a *callous indifference* to religious groups. *That would be preferring those who believe in no religion over those who do believe.* Government may not finance religious groups nor undertake religious instruction nor blend secular and sectarian education nor use secular institutions to force one or some religion on any person. But we find no constitutional requirement which makes it necessary for government to be *hostile to religion and throw its weight against efforts to widen the effective scope of religious influence.* The government must be neutral when it comes to competition between sects. It may not thrust any sect on any person. It may not make a religious observance compulsory. It may not coerce anyone to attend church. . . .[8]

The *Zorach* decision marks a retreat from the reasonings of the *Everson* and *McCollum* cases. The Court upheld governmental "encouragement" and "accommodation" with religious life because our "institutions presuppose a Supreme Being." While rejecting unequivocally "partiality", "compulsion", "coercion" or "force" in favor of one religion, it disowns governmental neutrality between believer and unbeliever as the equivalent of preferential treatment for nonbelievers. Further, the Court finds no constitutional requirement that conduces the government to throw "its weight against efforts to widen the effective scope of religious influence." Now, then, frankly admitting that religious education is an effort (perhaps one of its strongest) to widen the effective scope of religious influence, does governmental "encouragement" and "accommodation" allow the inclusion of federal financial aid to it? And if so, what sort? What would or would not be lawfully permissible? Surely, religious education is one of the "forms" of religious exercise and the First Amendment guarantees "the free exercise thereof" of which one vindication is the constitutionality of church-affiliated schools upheld in *Pierce v. Society of Sisters.*[9] Yet the Court said in *Everson:*

No tax in any amount . . . can be levied to support any religious activities, whatever they may be called, or whatever form they may adopt to teach or practice religion.[9a]

It seems to us that the question of religious education is involved in the "free exercise thereof" clause of the First Amendment. Whether or not the exclusion of religious education from a federal aid bill – and what separate answers may be given to the different sorts of aid – is a reduction of that freedom constitutionally guaranteed, and constitutes a preferential status for secularized educa-

Federal Aid to Education and Religious Liberty 137

tion, and discrimination against publicly accredited education precisely because it is religious as well as secular, or church-affiliated — cannot conclusively be resolved from the *Everson-McCollum-Zorach* reasonings. We must turn to American constitutional history to ascertain what have been the governmental relations to religious exercise and in this studious endeavor subject the rulings of the present Court to a critical appraisal. From the high tribunal have come words of encouragement. Justice Frankfurter in his dissent in *Bridges v. California* said:

> . . . (J)udges must be kept mindful of their limitations and of their ultimate public responsibility by a vigorous stream of criticism expressed with candor however blunt.[10]

CONSTITUTIONAL CONSENSUS

A. Legislative History — Textual Evidence and Intentions

A careful scrutiny of the various drafts of the religious Amendment submitted to either or both Houses of Congress discloses the meaning which the framers strove to fix into legal language. Such a responsible task against a vivid background of state establishments and disestablishments and the use of concepts and words clearly intelligible to their contemporaries, to the framers and to the adopters of the First Amendment, would reveal through the various successive versions proposed prima facie and inferentially the original and authentic meaning of the First Amendment.[11]

Since in our times an alleged principle of absolute "separation of church and state" is rhythmically chanted without surcease, it is remarkable that neither "separation" nor "church" nor "state" (in the generic meaning) occurred at all to the men who strove with great care to express their meaning with literal accuracy. A reflective rereading of the various versions discloses these constants: the Congress of the federal government is declared impotent to legislate into existence a "national religion", that is to say, "articles of faith or a mode of worship", "One Religious sect or Society in preference to others", "particular denomination in preference to another" — or simply, a preferential status by law to one religion or church to the disadvantage of all the others. The uniform intention underlying all the various versions of "no establishment" is to guarantee the equality of all religions and churches in two complementary ways, one, indirectly by rendering the national government impotent to bring about an inequality of religions before the law by political "establishment"; and secondly, the over-all preoccupation of the First Congress to guarantee inviolable the "free exercise thereof," under federal jurisdiction, that is to say, not only freedom of belief is secured against national conformism of religious profession, but also religious worship and activities, the outward exercise of religious belief, is guaranteed freedom of public expression. In view of the reference made today in discussions of federal aid to education, of religious education to the First Amendment, let us observe a matter of fact and a question of interpretation. The *fact* is there was absolutely no mention at all made in any way of education, religious or non-religious, nor aid for it, in the entire deliberations of the Congress on the First Amendment. Now the question of interpretation. Educational naturalists and secularists are wont to read, on their own, federal aid to religious education into the prohibition of the "no establishment" clause. An interpretative construction which would refer the question of federal aid to non-governmental schools of religious affiliation to the First Amendment can reasonably do so only by including it within the "free exercise thereof" clause. Religious education is in response to the dictates of religious conscience and it is undoubtedly an exercise of religious liberty which the law better preserves by removing the possibility of establishment and its inhibiting incidence. The paramount principle of the First Amendment was a federal guarantee of religious liberty and the "no establishment" clause was a political decision of a public policy instrumental for the insurance of this religious liberty on the federal level.

B. *Madisonian Federalism and Religious Liberty*

There is much ado in the federal aid controversy about James Madison's mind on church-state relations and much more ado about what is relevant and non-relevant from his lifetime testimony and actions. However, no one may reasonably question the telling evidence of the Annals of the First Congress which has preserved for us Madison's mind on the religious amendment. It is to his lasting credit that despite his personal doubts on the constitutional necessity for such an amendment, he championed its passage. Madison initiated the congressional proceedings of the subject with his own formula:

Federal Aid to Education and Religious Liberty

> The civil rights of none shall be abridged..., nor shall any national religion be established, nor shall the full and equal rights of conscience be in any manner, or on any pretext, infringed.[12]

When the House debated an altered version of Madison's which omitted his adjectival "national," questions arose which seem to have justified Madison's original inclusion of the term. Mr. Sylvester of New York feared the amendment "... might be thought to have a tendency to abolish religion altogether."[13]

> Mr. MADISON said, he apprehended the meaning of the words to be, that Congress should not establish a religion, and enforce the legal observation of it by law, nor compel men to worship God in any manner contrary to their conscience. Whether the words are necessary or not, he did not mean to say, but they had been required by some of the State Conventions, who seemed to entertain an opinion that... the clause of the Constitution, which gave power to Congress to make all laws necessary and proper to carry into execution the Constitution, and the laws made under it, enabled them to make laws of such a nature as might infringe the rights of conscience, and establish a national religion; to prevent these effects he presumed the amendment was intended, and he thought it as well expressed as the nature of the language would admit.[14]

In his response, Madison discloses what is paramount in his mind, namely, the constitutional guarantee of religious liberty affirming explicitly what the original organic act achieved by its omission, the legislative impotence of the federal government to confer a preferential status on the one religion together with the accompanying restraints of religious and civil liberties for nonconformers. He stresses the federalist character of the proposed amendment to assure those who feared it might operate to intrude into each state's own settlements on religion.[15]

That same day, August 15, 1789, Representative Huntington of Connecticut averred that he personally understood Madison's meaning clearly but he feared "... that the words might be taken in such latitude as to be extremely hurtful to the cause of religion..." by others who "... might find it convenient to put another construction upon it."[16] Mr. Huntington voiced the fear that a federal court might not uphold local by-laws which authorized the financial support of "ministers" and the "building of places of worship" by their congregation.

> He hoped, therefore, the amendment would be made in such a way as to secure the rights of conscience, and a free exercise of the rights of religion, but not to patronize those who preferred no religion at all.[17]

Madison's rejoinder reiterates the federalist character of the law, the technical meaning of establishment, and the over-all purpose of securing religious liberty against governmental religious dictation.

> Mr. MADISON thought, if the word "national" was inserted before religion, it would satisfy the minds of the honorable gentlemen. He believed that the people feared one sect might obtain a preeminence, or two combine together, and establish a religion to which they would compel others to conform. He thought if the word "national" was introduced, it would point the amendment directly to the object it was intended to prevent.[18]

Madison's insistence on the federalist character of the amendment and the inviolability of the sovereignty of the states should foreclose any endeavor to read the dispositions of one state on church-state relations (settled upon three years before the ratification of the Constitution) into the federal organic act. The blunt historical fact is that the Virginian legislature found the amendment "totally inadequate, and betrays an unreasonable, unjustifiable, but a studied departure from the amendment proposed by Virginia. . . ."[19] The supposition of continuity between Madison's conception of Church-state relations in his own state of Virginia brought about three years before the ratification of the Constitution, and Madison's meaning of the First Amendment is only possible by a process of thinking unrelated to reality.

In Colonial times, the Anglican Church was the established church in Virginia with the attendant incidents of the legal preferential status, civil privileges, tax support, and for the dissenters, compulsory religious attendance, occasional penalties, and civil disabilities.

Even, toleration, at first an unavoidable concession to a growing society of religious pluralism, and the beneficient consequence to the common cause against England, still retained many of the disabilities of the existing establishment. But, when the increasing number of dissenters reduced the Anglicans to a minority, Patrick Henry in 1784 proposed to the Virginia Assembly, a "Bill Establishing a Provision for Teachers of the Christian Religion" with the expectation that such a comprehensive tax support would find favor with all Christians whether of the establishment or not to take place of the abrogated provision for the support of the Anglican ministers alone. It was against this preference through tax support of *a* religion, the Christian one, under the benign mantle of the Anglican establishment that Madison directed his famed *Memorial and Remonstrance Against Religious Assessments* of 1785. The reading of the text[20] makes evident that Madison's primary concern is religious liberty for all through equality for all beliefs before the law and he considers tax support of *one* religion (latitudinarian) Christianity, in itself or (incongruously) as part of the Anglican establishment then still existing in Virginia, as a violation of that equality before the law which he considered a pre-condition of religious liberty. Madison's success in defeating the religious assessment bill encouraged him to reintroduce Jefferson's Bill for Religious Freedom of 1779, and its passage on January 16, 1786 brought to an end the establishment in Virginia.

Justice Rutledge's enterprising manipulation of Madison's *Memorial and Remonstrance* to mean no governmental aid at all to religion *as such* and to infuse this meaning into the federal First Amendment of four years later has drawn Edward Corwin to comment:

> All in all, it is fairly evident that Justice Rutledge sold his brethren a bill of goods when he persuaded them that the "establishment of religion" clause of the First Amendment was intended to rule out all governmental "aid to *all* religion."[21]

C. *The Jeffersonian "Handle"*

On June 13, 1779 Jefferson introduced a Bill for Establishing Religious Freedom into the Virginia Assembly[22] and because of the opposition it aroused, its passage was delayed until Madison reintroduced it successfully in 1786. Since in the previous year Madison's *Memorial and Remonstrance* had prevailed against state favoritism of one religion, latitudinarian Christianity, in his home state, the persuasion of logic, from the greater to the less, brought about the end of the establishment of the Anglican church in Virginia. For Jefferson as for Madison, church establishment epitomized the compulsions, coercions, and disabilities whereby religious liberty might be discouraged, diminished, or even destroyed. Disestablishment for both was instrumental and subservient to the paramount right of religious liberty.

Today we are confronted with an unusually remarkable fact. Educational neutralists and secularists, who, with rhythmic choral chant, quote Jefferson's "wall of separation" (a very admirable metaphor), ignore Jefferson's expressly defined mind on state relations with religious education, the very precise issue before us. Not once but several times and hammering upon the same issue, Jefferson has not only stated his position with argumentative reasoning but pointedly warned his contemporaries against the very misrepresentation that he is being subjected to by the educational neutralists and secularists of our times.

1. Plan for An Educational System, A Letter to Peter Carr, September 7, 1814[23]

In this letter, Jefferson fulfills a promise made to the "trustees" for a plan of education for "our native State" to be supported by state public funds for three specified types of schools, the elementary, general, and professional. Amongst the several provisions for the latter, he stipulates a department for "Theology and Ecclesiastical History" to which "the ecclesiastic" will repair as the "lawyer", "physician", the "military man", the "agricultor", etc., to his own appropriate studies.

2. An Act For Establishing Elementary Schools, September 9, 1817

Jefferson's draft for the establishment of state-supported elementary schools passed the Virginia Assembly three years later. The 11th provision of the Act registered a change in the original plan of 1814:

> The said teachers shall, in all things relating to education and government of their pupils, be under the direction and control

of the visitors; but no religious reading, instruction or exercise, shall be prescribed or practiced *inconsistent with the tenets of any religious sect or denomination.*[24]

Clearly Jefferson is careful to preserve inviolable the rights of religious conscience against *sectarian* teaching in a state-supported school that would be offensive to pupils of other faiths.

3. The University of Virginia, Aim and Curriculum, August 10, 1818

The following year, Jefferson drew up a plan for the University of Virginia in which he makes a notable change from the tentative proposals of 1814. Then he had provided for a Department of Theology and Ecclesiastical History to which the ecclesiastic could repair as the lawyer, physician, etc., would to his own studies. Now he argues against state provision of sectarian teaching:

In conformity with the principles of our *Constitution, which places all sects of religion on an equal footing,* with the jealousies of the different sects *in guarding that equality from encroachment and surprise* and with the sentiments of the *Legislature in favor of freedom of religion,* manifested on former occasions, *we have proposed no professor of divinity;* rather, as the proofs of the being of God, the creator, preserver, and supreme ruler of the universe, the author of all the relations of morality, and of the laws and obligations these infer, will be *within the province of the professor of ethics;* to which adding the developments of these moral obligations, of those *in which all sects agree,* with a knowledge of the languages, Hebrew, Greek, and Latin, *a basis will be formed common to all sects.* Proceeding thus far without offense to the Constitution, we have thought it proper at this point *to leave every sect to provide,* as they think fittest, the means of further *instruction in their own peculiar tenets.*[25]

The change from the 1814 plan is most reasonably explained with due regard for the equal rights of an inviolable religious conscience and for the laws that guard "that equality from encroachment." There is no change in principle but only in prudential choice to guard against the "surprise" that may compromise religious liberty.

Further, Jefferson makes it clear that the fundamental truths, theological and moral, philosophically knowable, will be taught by the professor of ethics, who, as a professor of a branch of philosophy is bound to follow the light of reason in his expositions as distinguished from the evidences of supernatural revelation, the proper province of a professor of divinity.

4. *The Freedom of Religion at the University of Virginia, October 7, 1822*[26]

In 1814 Jefferson included a Department of Theology and Ecclesiastical history within his state-supported educational system for the training of clergymen, In 1817 Jefferson advised against *such* religious instruction for elementary schools as would be violative of the rights of religious conscience of any sect or denomination. In 1818, moved above all by the supreme concern for religious liberty for every sect, Jefferson withdrew his original proposal for a school of divinity in the 1814 plan while he retained the study of the ontological and moral relations of man to God as within the proper domain of philosophy wherein human reason can ascertain those truths which are cognizable by the intelligence of any believer. Because his change of plan was being misunderstood despite his clear and painstaking explanation on the basis of principle, Jefferson four years later in his Report to the Legislature defined his position in words and content which no educational neutralist and secularist could receive with satisfaction. No one should infer from his change of plan that public authorities are unconcerned about the relevance to society of man's relations to God. A totally nonreligious education is a defective one. If the dangers imminent in the public provision of religious instructions ("ascendency of any sect over another") are to be removed on the one hand, on the other a remedy is proposed for this total abstention (which he describes as *"evils* of less danger") by a cooperative relationship between religious life and studies and the state, a type of cooperation that is equivalent to the "full benefit the public provisions made for the instruction in the other branches of science." This cooperation is filled out in detail within the two broad premises that public authority acknowledges the place of religious life in society, and that religious studies are necessary to an integral concept of education. The details suggested are: that believers "established" their religious schools *"on the con-*

fines of the university" so that students attending these religious schools may have "convenient access" to other University lectures; that other University students may "attend religious exercises with the professor of their particular sect, either in the rooms of the building still to be erected . . . or in the lecturing room of such professor"; those "who might choose such a location for their schools (sectarian schools of divinity on the confines of the University) are to be assured that the University regulations will be modified in order to accommodate those divinity students with the same facilities as the other University students," such as, access to and use of the University library. And then the telling line: *"But always understanding that these schools shall be independent of the University and of each other."* The facilities on state property which the State University offers the sectarian schools of divinity established on the confines of the University are to entail no compromise of their independence. As he began his explanation so he ends:

> Such an arrangement would complete the circle of the useful sciences embraced by this institution, and would fill the chasm now existing, on principles which would leave inviolate the constitutional freedom of religion, the most inalienable and sacred of all human rights, over which the people and authorities of this state, individually and publicly, have ever manifested the most watchful jealousy....[27]

5. *Letter to Thomas Cooper, November 2, 1822*[28]

That same year Jefferson felt compelled in private correspondence to express his resentment against the misconstruction which was being placed upon his change of plans for the University of Virginia. "In our university you know there is no Professorship of Divinity. *A handle has been made of this, to disseminate an idea that this is an institution, not merely of no religion, but against all religion."*[29]

Here Jefferson singles out his opponents, educational neutralists ("not merely of no religion") and secularists ("but against all religion") as the ones who are seizing upon a part of his proposal as a *handle* to misconstrue his purpose and to confound the people. In his letter to Thomas Cooper, Jefferson repeats almost verbatim the provisions of the new plan to remedy the "chasm" which the withdrawal of the professorship of divinity might bring about.[30]

6. Regulations for the University, October 4, 1824[31]

Two years later, Jefferson, as Rector of the State University of Virginia, again sets down the cordial and cooperative relations between the sectarian schools of divinity established "within, or adjacent to, the precincts of the University." He is not content to say only that the University students are "free to attend religious worship at the establishment of their respective sects" but they are "expected" to do so. Students of the religious schools are to be "considered as students of the University, subject to the same regulations, and *entitled to the same rights and privileges.*"[32] University classrooms are made available for theology lectures and religious worship when the facilities of the divinity schools do not suffice!

7. Letter to the Danbury Baptists, January 1, 1802[33]

In the second year of his presidential office, Jefferson received an address of congratulations and good wishes from a Committee of the Danbury Baptist Association of the State of Connecticut. If we bear in mind that Connecticut did not disestablish its Congregational church until 1818, sixteen years later, that Jefferson was the original author of the proposal for the disestablishment of the church in Virginia, that he was the constant foe of the privileged status of a religion or church in law, that he repeatedly championed equality of religion before the law (and especially so in education), the patent meaning of Jefferson's use of the metaphor of the "wall of separation between church and state" was to express his disapproval of the disadvantageous status of the Baptists within the terms of the Congregationalist establishment in Connecticut. He objected, in a word, to state support, not indeed of religion (for which his educational plans provided) but to a discriminatory favoritism of one religion with rights and privileges denied to non-conformists and dissenters. He therefore studies "with sincere satisfaction the progress of those sentiments which tend to restore to man all his natural rights (the rights of conscience) convinced that man has no natural right in opposition to his social duties." If the educational neutralists and secularists whom Jefferson resentfully marked as his interpolators could seize upon a "handle" in Jefferson's own lifetime, it is not surprising that their modern heirs do so with more boldness many decades after his demise with a metaphor taken out of context.

FEDERAL AID TO RELIGION

Across the panorama of American history hangs a brilliant rainbow of religious dedication spangled with multitudinous professions, lay and official, individual and corporate, of dependence upon and gratitude to divine providence. In response to the religious life of our nation, and in the continuous acknowledgment of individual, social, and political dependence upon the providence of God, federal and state governments in numerous and different ways have financially supported and encouraged religious activities.

The federal tradition has its authentic beginnings in the Continental Congress' Ordinance for the Government of the Northwest Territory. The statesmen of the time give expression to the prevailing religious convictions of their day in Article III of the Ordinance of 1787:

Religion, morality and knowledge, being necessary to good government and the happiness of mankind, schools and the means of education shall forever be encouraged....[34]

Lot Number 16 of every township, including 640 acres, was set aside for the support of the schools (at that time characteristically religious and for that reason supported), Lot Number 29 for the support of religion, and two townships for the benefit of a university. The provisions of the Northwest and the later Southwest Ordinances are highly meaningful because they were incorporated into the constitutions of the several states which arose from these territories. For example, the Ohio Constitution of 1802, twelve years after the adoption of the First Amendment, provided in Section 26:

The laws shall be passed by the legislature which shall secure *to each and every denomination* of religious societies in each surveyed township which now is or may hereafter be formed in the State, *an equal participation, according to their number of adherents, of the profits arising from the land granted by the Congress for the support of religion,* agreeably to the ordinance or act of Congress making the appropriation.[35]

It was not until 1860 that the land grants for higher education were restricted to the "State University" and the grant for schools only to "common schools" which though officially undenominational were under the direction, control, and publicly avowed influence of Protestant Christianity. In 1789 the First Congress appropriated funds for the support of Christian missionaries amongst the Indians in implementation of a recommendation made by General Knox, the Secretary of War, and approved by President Washington. "The object of this establishment would be the happiness of Indians, *teaching them the great duties of religion and morality,* and to inculcate a friendship and attachment to the United States."[36]

President Thomas Jefferson continued this government policy of supporting, with public funds, religious education, and religious worship when in 1803 he asked the Senate to ratify the treaty with the Kaskasia Indians which included the following passage:

> And whereas the greater part of said tribe have been baptized and received into the Catholic Church, to which they are much attached, the United States will give annually, for seven years, one hundred dollars toward the support of a priest of that religion, who will engage to perform for said tribe the duties of his office, and also to instruct as many of their children as possible, in the rudiments of literature, and the United States will further give the sum of three hundred dollars, to assist the said tribe in the erection of a church.[37]

In this historic instance the President and Congress supported the subvention of one religion and one church without any intent or effect of conferring upon it a preferential status in law or discriminating advantages by benefit of law. In 1897 Congress abandoned this century-old policy of subsidizing Christian Missions amongst the Indians and by the Act of June 7th[38] decided no longer to make appropriations for sectarian education with a proviso, however, that such financial assistance continue in diminishing sums until 1900. There was no question raised about the constitutionality of the century-old practice and the change was one of policy unless someone would rather infer that the National Congress legislated a three-year moratorium on constitutionality. It is easier to point to federal support of a congressional chaplain, of the support of chaplains in the armed services, on land and sea, in peace and in war, and the construction at federal cost of chapels on government property. Religious publications enjoy mailing privileges. Federal and state penitentiaries provide facilities for preserving uncompromised

Federal Aid to Education and Religious Liberty 149

the constitutional guarantee of religious liberty in circumstances where the exercise of other civil rights is gravely curtailed. A number of Congressional financing programs have been directed to remedying a need defined and acknowledged whatever its religious or proprietary affiliation. The National Youth Administration program of 1935,[39] the Reserve Officers Training Corps program,[40] the Federal school-lunch program,[41] the G.I. Bill of Rights[42] (which included education for the ministry and rabbinate), the Legislative Reorganization Act of 1946[43] — all provided out of federal funds financial assistance, military opportunities, food, and education with due respect for the personal choice made in accordance with individual conscience. Federal projects of research are assigned to institutions of higher learning with or without any avowed religious affiliation. The Hill-Burton Act[44] makes federal funds available to *any* hospital on the basis of predefined need and demonstrated fiscal ability. The seemingly endless enumeration of specific illustrations of programs of federal aid which consistently has maintained throughout our national history the traditional policy of absolute equity in sensitive deference to rights of conscience is an exceptionally agreeable instance of etceteration. This policy is not only authoritative (the effect of national legislation), it is also authentic, the representatives of the nation acting in response to the national religious mind. The strength and vigor of this federal policy prevailed in the 1870's over the challenges of President Grant and Congressman Blaine and again against the proposal of Congressman Bryson[45] in 1947. Amendments to the Constitution have been proposed to prohibit the extension of federal aid to religious institutions and in every instance the Congress refused. Opponents of federal aid to religious schools, having failed for almost a century to change the Constitution to achieve their objective, now pin their hopes on a realignment of nine justices of the Supreme Court to interpret the First Amendment contrary to its authentic meaning. Their hopes rested with the potentialities of the reasoning in the *Everson* case in 1947 and soared with the triumph of the Rutledge doctrine in the *McCollum* case the following year. But the American constitutional consensus reasserted itself when a year after the *McCollum* decision President Truman signed a Congressional bill which appropriated $500,000 for the construction of a chapel at the Merchant Marine Academy, Kings Point, New York.[46]

CATEGORIES OF AID

Government financial support of religion is ordained directly for religious life *as such*, that is to say, no one church or religion is singled out exclusively for preferential treatment to the disadvantage of the others. In acknowledgment of the religious foundations of our country and in recognition, public and official, of the need for divine guidance for the just government, prosperity, and preservation of our Republic, federal funds provide for chaplains and chapels for congress and the military, and make available facilities for religious exercise and worship in penal institutions. Public funds pay for the printing of the annual Presidential Thanksgiving Proclamations and, in recent years, for the Army Character Guidance Program and the United States Air Force training manual which state without hesitance the religious presuppositions of the American way of life.[47] Technically and in the strict meaning of words tax-exemption and tax-deductible benefits are not considered direct positive aids in law. Only the appropriation and subtraction from public revenue and its conveyance to an institution fulfills the meaning of financial support by law. These exceptional benefits befall churches and synagogues, schools of divinity, universities, hospitals, orphanages, etc., inasmuch as they are included within those benevolent nonprofit making institutions and associations, educational,[48] cultural, charitable, scientific, literary, which the law sets apart.

Government financial aid is said to be *indirect* when the disbursements of an authorized appropriation of public funds are directly ordained for the remedy, alleviation, amelioration, of a predefined good by whomsoever it is achieved, whether the agency and its affiliation be religious (of any denomination) or nonreligious.[49] Indirect aids are said to be *incidental* to express the indirection by which the institutional agency may benefit as a consequence of the aid directly given to a defined objective. The G.I. Bill of Rights, the N.Y.A., R.O.T.C., Hill-Burton Act, government research projects, etc., while ordained for the good of individuals regardless of their faith or lack of it, may result in some advantages to the institutional agency. Indirect aids at times are described as *accidental* aids to emphasize that it is by chance, it is not part of the legislative intention, that a particular denomination of the institutional agency is indirectly benefited. The indirect assistance chances to be the operation of an unavoidable double effect.

"*Auxiliary aids*" "help out" financially *all* needy schoolchildren with governmental provision of free bus transportation, lunches, health and welfare services, nonsectarian textbooks for the purpose of equalizing educational opportunities in a democratic society and with due reverence for the rights of conscience in education. The Supreme Court has refused to consider "auxiliary aids" with the category of "indirect aids" which almost all state constitutions proscribe and the States through their courts and attorney generals are fairly evenly divided on this point and not always consistently within each state. At present the federal government provides free lunches to needy schoolchildren either with state cooperation or through a federal administrator. State governments either provide some, or all, or none of the auxiliary aids. The Supreme Court has upheld the constitutionality of state supplied non-sectarian textbooks to *all* schoolchildren in *Cochran v Board of Education*[50] as a legitimate exercise of state police power for public welfare. In the *Cochran* case, the Court denied the contention of the appellants that inclusion of school children attending privately owned schools, constituted the taking of public property for a private purpose in violation of the due process of the Fourteenth Amendment. In the *Everson* case, the Court rejected the contention that provision at public cost of bus service to children attending religious schools was constructive of "establishment" within the meaning of the First Amendment. In this case, too, the Court for the first time in its entire history raised the non-relevant position (since it upheld the bus service as a legitimate exercise of police power for public welfare) in recognition of the appellant's contention, whether *any* tax support of all religion was constructive of "establishment" and in the face of past and present history, held that it did. On the identical ground of police power for public purpose, the health and welfare services provided by some states would, if ever contested before the court, be equally upheld. Opponents of federal provision of "auxiliary services" for children attending church-affiliated schools object to federal provision of other auxiliary services besides school lunches on the ground that it would be violative of the First Amendment when as a matter of fact the Supreme Court has already upheld their constitutionality.

SECULARIZATION OF STATE SCHOOLS

Today all states, with the possible exception of Vermont, prescribe, one way or another in constitutional or statutory law, that no direct or indirect state financial aid may go to a sectarian school or denominational institution. Despite this express prohibition, many states grant or permit one or more of the auxiliary aids and these practices have been upheld by state courts and attorneys general and further confirmed by the Supreme Court of the United States. These states do not agree with other states that "auxiliary aids" are to be counted amongst the proscribed indirect aids and rightly so since auxiliary aids provide nourishment, safety, medical care, and textbooks for the benefit of the child in alleviation of a predefined need wheresoever it is found without prejudice to creed.

What has been the story of public support of religious education in the states?

In the history of public support of education, federal and state policies have been neither identical nor consistently parallel to one another. The traditional federal policy has been uniformly and universally non-discriminatory. State policies, on the other hand, whether in law or practice, have been discriminatory. The earliest American schools were church schools. With disestablishment, the intermingling of religiously pluralist population, and the growing need for making education more available, the financial limitations of the church groups could no longer support the educational burdens adequately, nor could various religious groups agree on the religious influence that was to dominate. In 1818 Connecticut first introduced the public or common school which is not by proprietary title under church control. From 1820 to 1870 the states assumed more and more the responsibilities of education by supporting from public funds their own public schools and other non-church schools sponsored by school societies. All these schools were, in the original American tradition of education, religiously orientated and where one denomination predominated, its sectarian beliefs were taught. But where the frictions of religious pluralism would not countenance such a partisan dictation, a compromise amongst the Protestants settled upon the teaching of fundamentalist doctrines of Protestant Christianity. Horace Mann is looked upon as the champion of non-sectarian religious public schools and his plan for Massachusetts which precluded public funds from nonpublic schools was widely adopted by other states. But what of the Catholics? The teaching of nonsectarian Protestant Christianity in state-supported schools was a matter of public policy and approved in some instances expressly by law and at times upheld in some places by the local courts, even in the absence of positive law. With the influx of the Catholic immigrants, Catholics voiced publicly a rightful protest against the imposition of fundamentalist Protestantism upon their children attending state schools. Since they were being asked to support a public school system which Protestantism—if not officially prescribed at least authoritatively permitted or even approved[51]—controlled and influenced, it is not surprising that members of the Catholic hierarchy would request to participate equitably in the disbursement of state funds earmarked for compulsory education. While Protestants and Catholics agreed that education is religious, Protestants would not allow the application of state funds except for the support of public education that was under the influence of Protestant Christianity. The episcopal requests in the cities of New York and Philadelphia aroused the rage of nativists of the 1840's and again in the 1850's of the Know-Nothings, and in Philadelphia and Boston, Catholics were assaulted and killed and church properties destroyed.[52] The ugliness of the Know-Nothing's *animus* moved President Abraham Lincoln to write to Joshua Speed, under date of August 24, 1855:

> I am not a Know-Nothing, that is certain. How could I be? How can any man who abhors oppression of negroes be in favour of degrading classes of white people? Our progress in degeneracy appears to me pretty rapid. As a nation we began by declaring that "All men are created equal." We now practically read it "All men are created equal, except negroes." When the Know-Nothings get control, it will read "All men are created equal except negroes and foreigners and Catholics." When it comes to this, I shall prefer emigrating to some country where they make no pretence of loving liberty.[53]

In *A History of Freedom of Teaching in American Schools*, Howard K. Beale has given us a trenchant account of the religious educational tensions in the mid-nineteenth century:

> While sectarianism was increasingly discouraged, practically

all schools still included religion in their curricula. School opened with prayer. The Bible was read and portions of it memorized. Hymns were sung. The principles of Protestant Christianity, so far as they were accepted by all Trinitarian sects, were instilled into children....[54] These religious requirements of schools decidedly affected teachers. In religious schools where children were now allowed to attend the worship of their parents' choosing, teachers were still expected, on the contrary, to adhere to the denomination that controlled the school. In many communities local public opinion, even in the face of a state prohibition of sectarianism for the pupils, still required public school teachers to be orthodox according to the local conception of orthodoxy. In places where the sects were mixed, sectarian restrictions disappeared, but a teacher still had to be a fundamentalist Protestant Christian without Unitarian taint. Most states had constitutional provisions guaranteeing religious liberty. But this had not yet come to mean religious equality. If it had really been interpreted to mean what it said, most early state constitution makers would have opposed as destructive of the integrity of the state that provision of the Wisconsin Constitution of 1848 that declared that "no religious test shall be required as a qualification for any office of public trust under the State." But "religious tests" usually meant only sectarian tests among Protestant Christians. Most original constitutions included restrictions that violated this principle in regard to important state functionaries. It is doubtful whether local public opinion permitted its fulfillment in regard to teachers even in Wisconsin in 1848. In any case, the public school requirements concerning religious instruction, Bible reading, and prayers would have made it impossible for the teachers to accept, and unwise for the school to offer, a position to any but orthodox Protestant Christians....[55]

All would have been well, however, in the best of Protestant school worlds, had not this period brought a great influx of Roman Catholic immigrants who objected to Protestant schools and who had the power in some cases to make men heed their objections. There had always been a few Catholics, a few Jews, a few deists, and many who were indifferent to religion. But the indifferent had not objected to a system that excluded them from teaching and taught their children Protestant Christianity.

Federal Aid to Education and Religious Liberty 155

The indifferent had merely accepted the situation, because, after all, religion did no harm. The Jews, Catholics, and deists had accepted the situation because they did not have the power to alter it. The Protestant sects, therefore, had been able to meet the religious problem by agreeing to teach in the schools not the sectarian dogmas on which they disagreed but the Protestant Christian principles upon which they could unite. . . . The Catholics had always had a few schools of their own. As democratic influence increased their desire for education, they built more. When thousands of new Catholics arrived from Europe, they built still more. In days when all education was in private hands, this arrangement had been satisfactory. Their teachers and their children had been on equal terms with Protestants. Under a system of public education, however, they contributed in taxes to the support of schools in which their teachers were not allowed to teach and could not have taught the required subjects anyway without violating their own consciences. Furthermore, the Catholics were not satisfied to have religion excluded from the schools. Like the Protestants, they wanted to teach religion to children, but, again like the Protestants, they wanted to teach their own religion. Since in America Catholic control of the public schools seemed impossible, they preferred a parochial school system in which each denomination trained its own children and supplied its own teachers. If, however, they were to be taxed for the support of the public schools, then, since schools that taught Protestant religion could not satisfy them, they demanded a share of the school fund to pay their own teachers to teach their own children in schools that taught Catholic doctrine. There were American precedents for state aid to religious schools. But Protestants objected to having public tax money used to spread "dangerous" Papist power, and nationalist democracy objected to contributing to schools that were controlled neither by the local community nor by the nation but by a "foreign sovereign."[56]. . . The net result of all this agitation was that the status of the teacher remained about what it had been. A Catholic teacher was still barred from the public schools, as was a Jew, and in many places a deist or a Unitarian. Trinitarian Protestant Christians, however, retained the liberty to teach the Bible and the general principles of Protestant Christianity in the schools with no further restraint upon them than the prohibitions against sectarianism. Here was freedom for a particular group — freedom that in many places is denied today, but freedom exercised at the expense of other groups. In this controversy, the first blows were struck in a struggle that was to bring sufficient secularization of the school curriculum so that some day men could be qualified to teach in public schools whatever their religious views might be.[57]

Where the multiplicity of sects made the dominance of public schooling by one sect difficult to assert itself, the contrivance was attempted to funnel the disbursement of tax funds through a Public School Society. But since this organization was under Protestant domination and indeed chartered to forward fundamentalist Protestant tenets, not only were church-affiliated "religious" schools thereby excluded from participation in public funds allotted to education, but the public schools were avowedly stamped with the religious character of nonsectarian Protestant Christianity.

The abandonment of state support for religious education in public schools was historically not motivated by any "principle" of "separation of church and state" or the "wall of separation" nor the fear of the camel's nose, but the phantasmagoria of papist, popish plots that danced in revelry in the minds of nativists and Know-Nothings and their progeny in succeeding decades. Expediency dictated a forced compromise. True, prior to the adoption of the Fourteenth Amendment in 1868, there was no limitation in the Constitution upon the powers of the States on the subject of religion. After its adoption, even then, it was not until 1940 that the Suprme Court in *Cantwell v. Connecticut*[58] handed down the first decision categorically holding that the religious freedom embraced in the First Amendment was applicable to the States. It was in 1947 that the Supreme Court for the first time in its entire history considered *any* governmental aid to religion constructive of "establishment" within the prohibited meaning of the First Amendment.

FEDERAL AID TO EDUCATION

There is no mention of education in the Constitution and despite some earnest talk of a national university in the Convention of 1787 and for some years thereafter in and out of Congress, nothing came of it. The original governmental policy dating from the Northwest and Southwest Ordinances, and continuing to the middle of the nineteenth century, was financial support in the form of land grants and the income deriving therefrom for general education. In the earlier years the general education was neither general in curriculum nor generally available. Theological and moral studies predominated. In the 1860's, a new governmental policy was initiated which has continued to our times. The Morrill Act of 1862[59] set the first precedent of land-grant colleges and universities for the benefit of agricultural and mechanical arts. Since that time the federal government has established state agricultural and mechanical arts colleges, experiment stations, vocational promotions, extension services, and financed a variety of specialized training programs and numerous research projects both in private and government owned schools of higher learning. The aftermath of the Civil War and the two World Wars awakened the national conscience to the promotion of a federal program of aid for general education. American citizens who never had the equivalent of even an elementary education, the newly enfranchised Negro population, and the successive waves of immigration to our country posed a grave problem of educating citizens to their responsibilities of achieving a decent minimum of literacy, and of satisfying a legitimate demand for a process of Americanization amongst diverse ethnic groups of varied national origins.

In the 1880's Senator Blair successfully championed several federal aid programs for general education in the Senate but none of his bills ever reached the House. After the First World War, and more insistently since the Second World War, scores of bills were introduced in both Houses, which generally have expired from constant revisions in response to criticisms, or failed to win the vote in either or both Houses of Congress. Summarily and cumulatively the objections which have frustrated the passage of a federal aid bill for general education are as follows: the express or effective exclusion of religious schools from the benefits of federal general aid programs or the exclusion of even auxiliary aids for parochial schoolchildren; fear of federal control of education incident to or, if provided against by the terms of the legislation, inherently potential in the power of the purse which court interpretation might uphold as legitimate jurisdictional supervision and direction; opposition to "creeping socialism" in government; suspicion of federal encroachments in a domain traditionally entrusted to local communities and states; the dread of increased taxation; and, most recently, the stipulation that federal funds be available only to such states as manifest concrete evidence of a gradual and effective co-operation with the desegregation decision. Our study concentrates only on an examination of the constitutional question which turns upon the inclusion or exclusion of parochial schoolchildren as beneficiaries of "auxiliary services" provided by a federal grant aid bill and secondarily, the broader, all comprehensive, underlying fundamental question of constitutionality of governmental support for education whatever its proprietary or religious affiliation.

A. Divisions and Distinctions

Specific federal aid to education may be for a specialized type of education and since the 1860's the federal government has to this day established a large variety of such programs. Specific aid may also be earmarked for an auxiliary aid and as such it is not an aid to education but a general welfare benefit for the remedy of a need and also one type of equalization of educational opportunities.

General federal aid to education was the original tradition which gradually diminished toward the middle of the nineteenth century as local communities assumed the responsibility for providing public school education and after the 1870's institutions of higher learning were increasingly founded by individual philanthropists and by the states. *General aid* is a comprehensive term which may reach out to any expenditure-building construction, provision, extension, and improvement of facilities, scholastic and athletic, libraries, laboratories, and the supplementation of teachers' salaries. *General aid* may be restricted to "current expenditures" which may or may not include auxiliary aids and if provided, may or may not extend to children attending nongovernmental schools. Federal grants in aid to the states and government territories for educational purposes have been established in principle. The policy, however, of fixing upon the revenue resources, the methods of allocation, and the procedures and distribution formulae varied in the different legislations and proposals in response to a variety of circumstances. Suffice for our study to designate the general usages and preferred kinds. Prior to the middle of the nineteenth century federal support of education was in the form of land-grants and the revenue deriving therefrom allocated to the states on the basis of uniform amounts to defined geographical units. This was the original pattern of financing education which began with the Northwest and Southwest Ordinances and which continued in practice as the Western territories were incorporated as states in the Union. Approximately three-fourths of the states were beneficiaries under the federal land grant plans. In the 1880's the federal government followed a *new* policy of money grants which were distributed in proportion to population figures, and this type of grant and method of allocation had been the general practice for subsidization of the various specialized educational programs as well as for the School Lunch program. These money grants may be outright, flat grants or as in recent years, follow an equalization formula. In order to relieve the poorer states the grants are made on a per capita basis but inversely in proportion to financial ability. The Hill-Burton Act[60] by which the federal government aids *all* hospitals whatever their affiliation on the basis of defined and demonstrated needs and supplementary to local fiscal capacity is an exemplary illustration of this inverse relationship. Most of the federal aid to education bills which have been proposed unsuccessfully for the past twenty years have followed the equalization formula.

B. The Problems Presented

The fact is that the federal government in a long line of valid acts has supported directly and indirectly religion, religious activity, and church-affiliated institutions of a great variety. On the other hand, almost all the states have laws, constitutional or statutory, which expressly forbid in one way or another, direct and indirect aid from state revenue to sectarian schools and denominational institutions. Many of the states do not consider auxiliary aids (we concur in this interpretation), one or the other or all of them, within that prohibition. Other states do. *Since the contemplated bills for general aid to education require that federal funds be made available to the states provided that the states match such funds from their own fiscal resources, the problem arises how to resolve the conflict between the federal laws which constitutionally allow extension of these benefits to children attending church-affiliated schools and those state laws which expressly or interpretively forbid such an application.* In cooperatively financed programs the problem is real and inevitable and a just solution must respect the supremacy of laws and legitimate jurisdictions within the proper domain of federal and state governments. Neither one nor the other should be compromised.

The complexity of the problem and the facility with which different issues deriving their legitimacy from disparate sources are unwittingly confounded establishes the necessity for raising questions in order to ascertain the nature and significance of the many issues of the problem. *Is* there a grave need for financial assistance for education from sources beyond the local communities and state supplementary to their own provisions?[61] *Should* there be federal subsidization for education? That is a matter of political decision. No one questions that the legislation providing appropriation for education is one for the National Congress to decide upon by the political process of majority decision. *Must* these aids — and of what sort — extend to church-affiliated schools? *Should* auxiliary needs, which are not properly educational aids nor for that matter even indirect aids for sectarian schools but, as the Supreme Court has upheld, constitutionally valid child welfare programs — should these auxiliary aids be extended to children attending church-affiliated schools by the federal government in an interlocking federal-state educational program? In a conflict of laws which may arise in a federal-state cooperatively financed program, equity and distributive justice would so dictate. There is no legal compulsion to include nor legal requirement to exclude. Here again, it is one of political decision embodying a policy which binds in legal justice because of the general will of a democratic society to abide by majority decisions. An equitable solution should satisfy the jurisdictional rights and responsibilities of state and federal governments.

Many factors besides legality enter into the promotion of legislation. Is the contemplated measure desirable, expedient, wise, feasible? These are strongly felt considerations and any combination of them can effectively block the passage of the proposal. Should we allow the federal government to enter into a domain traditionally a concern of the local communities and states? Will not federal subventions entail supervision and direction that potentially and gradually may assume the proportions of control or dominance of education? Will not the American taxpayer be overburdened directly by an increase on income and realty taxes, or indirectly by taxes attached to commodities and luxuries? Should the disbursement of federal funds be contingent upon state cooperation with the desegregation decision? What of the animus surely of *some* secularists and educational neutralists toward any federal beneficence however related to church-affiliated schools? What of the fears of a "creeping socialism"? Whatever may be the degree of reasonableness of each of these considerations and the substance of reality behind them — they can block a measure because of the emotional climate they engender and the strength of will to choose as one pleases. However, we are concerned in this study solely with the question of constitutional law.

THE CONSTITUTIONAL QUESTION

A. The Basis of Opposition

The constitutional issues raised by the controversialists on federal aid to education touch upon several provisions and amendments to the United States Constitution. These are:

Article I. Section 8: The Congress shall have power to lay and collect taxes, duties, imposts, and excises, to pay the debts and provide for the common defense and general welfare of the United States;

Article VI. This Constitution, and the laws of the United States which shall be made in pursuance thereof . . . shall be the supreme law of the land;

Amendment I. Congress shall make no law respecting an establishment of religion, or prohibiting the free exercise thereof;

Amendment V. No person shall . . . be deprived of life, liberty, or property, without due process of law;

Amendment X. The powers not delegated to the United States by the Constitution, nor prohibited by it to the States are reserved to the States respectively, or to the people.

Amendment XIV. Section 1. All persons born or naturalized in the United States, and subject to the jurisdiction thereof, are citizens of the United States and of the State wherein they reside.

No State shall make or enforce any law which shall abridge the privileges or immunities of citizens of the United States; nor shall any State deprive any person of life, liberty, or property, without due process of law; nor deny to any person within its jurisdiction the equal protection of the laws.

B. The Key to the Solution

The key to the solution is to be found in the constitutional prescriptions of American federalist government and dual citizenship. A conflict, therefore, between what the federal laws and what state laws prohibit is not only legally possible, but also, strange as it may seem, legally compatible. Two sovereignties converge upon one and the same individual. Both invested with their own proper plenary powers – the federal government with its delegated and enumerated powers, expressed and implied, and the states retaining what was never delegated. The American citizen owes obedience to the laws of both governments which the general will of their respective constituents brought to pass through their duly elected representatives. Each individual citizen enjoys privileges and immunities corresponding to his dual citizenship and not infrequently there is also a concurrence.

Within these constitutional premises, federal aid to religious education – interlocked with state finance – is not only feasible but also legally possible. The National School Lunch Act aids *all* children who attend publicly accredited non-profit schools whatever their proprietary and religious affiliation. The federal government offers to the states funds in proportion to the population of all school children which the states must match dollar for dollar from its own resources for the provision of free lunches. In twenty-nine states where state laws prohibiting direct and indirect aid to sectarian education are interpreted by their own courts and attorneys general to preclude such a matching arrangement, the National School Lunch Act stipulates that a federal administrator withhold the amount proportional to the number of school children in church-affiliated and private schools and then dispurse the amount withheld directly to the parochial and private schools who then in turn supplement the federal contribution for the expenses incurred *in toto* in serving lunches to their school children. This withholding proviso preserves intact the traditional federal policy of non-discriminatory benefactions while at the same time it does not interfere with contrary state practices. Another model statute which embodies this same nondiscriminatory policy of the federal government is the Hill-Burton Survey and Construction Act of 1946. Congress provides an annual appropriation for the construction and expansion of facilities and equipment of nonprofit hospitals whatever their proprietary or religious affiliation on the basis of defined minimum standards and demonstrated needs relative to the community and in inverse proportion to the respondents' fiscal ability. Both these legislative enactments of 1946 have been highly successful in their objective, and are exemplary embodiments of the traditional federal policy of nondiscriminatory action, and on that basis, of the governmental acknowledgement of the right to participate equitably in the disbursement of federal funds, of the governmental definition of a good whatever the affiliation of the agency, and of the equality before the law of the institutions serving such a good.

C. States' Rights

Almost all of the numerous proposals concerning federal aid fall into one of three categories on the point here under study. The Taft-Thomas bills[62] provided a federal offer of funds to the states to be matched by them on an equalization basis so that the poorer states receive a greater proportion of funds per capita than the richer states. They embodied no withholding of funds but rather left it to the states to decide whether any part of the federal funds received by them should reach church-affiliated schools for the provision of auxiliary services. A second and meager class of proposals, the Aiken-Mead proposal of 1945,[63] the first of its kind, extended to all children attending state and private schools the auxiliary services which were specifically included in the appropriation for current expenditures. Where the interpretation of state laws would not allow this disbursement because of the federal-state cooperatively financed benefit, the federal government empowered a National Board of Apportionment to make the allotment of funds directly to the nongovernmental schools. This bill, too, followed the equalization formula. Foremost amongst the opponents of the Aiken-Mead bill was the National Education Association. In general, the third category includes the pre-Taft proposals and the Barden bill.[64] Whereas the Taft-Thomas type left it to the states to decide whether any share of the federal allotments should reach the children of nongovernmental schools, the pre-Taft proposals generally excluded the nongovernmental schools from any sort of benefit from the public funds, auxiliary or otherwise. The ignominious Barden bill has the singular and unenviable distinction of frank discriminatory definition. It was a general aid bill limited to "current expenditures" a term which as customarily used has included auxiliary services. The Barden bill explicitly incorporated a restriction of its own, with obvious intention, that "current expenditures" does not include in the definition given the auxiliary services. In two other ways the bill excluded children of nongovernmental schools from the federal benefits that would otherwise have accrued to them in the absence of the inserted restriction. In the apportionment of funds the total school children population from five to seventeen years of age, in each state, attending parochial schools as well as state schools are counted in, but in the disbursement of funds, the children of the church-affiliated schools are counted out. To make certain a third time the exclusion of children attending parochial schools, a judicial review section empowers a taxpayer to proceed to a federal court on one count: when in his judgment any of the money appropriated is being applied to nongovernmental school children. The Barden bill foreclosed entirely not only what the nondiscriminatory School Health-Services Bill[65] (introduced by Senator Thomas as subsidiary to the Thomas General Aid bill and approved by the Senate) provided universally to all school-children — it incorporated the "withholding proviso" of the School Lunch Act of 1946 — but it also would not allow what the Taft-Thomas proposals would leave to the states to decide for themselves. The Representative from North Carolina did not trust even the alleged states' rights argument! This proposal deservedly never left the full House Committee on Labor and Education. It was repeatedly affirmed that the underlying principles of the Taft-Thomas general aid bills were in accord with states' rights. Leaving it to the states to decide whether any of the federal funds should be allocated for the children attending nongovernmental schools was a respectful regard of the sovereign jurisdiction of each state and of its laws. To incorporate a withholding proviso such as the School Lunch Act of 1946 had embodied, and to disburse funds directly to the institutional agency on an equalization formula such as both the School Lunch Act and the Hill-Burton Acts of 1946 provided was denounced as "by-passing" the states, "side-stepping" the states, "diverting" public funds. Besides, such a pattern of federal allocation of its own funds was a violation of the "principle" of non-interference with the educational systems of the states! We must bear in mind that in the controversies of the 1940's the benefactions in question were auxiliary services such as bus transportation, nonreligious textbooks, medical services, and school lunches, which the

Supreme Court had repeatedly upheld as legitimate expressions of the police power of the state for the nondiscriminatory provision of public welfare benefits. All of these services, with the exception of the textbooks, are noneducational in purpose. They are welfare and safety measures. There is no whisper at all here of direct or indirect aids to religious institutions in a federal-state interlocking financing program, aids which the federal government by itself has and does provide in a variety and number of ways.

D. Federal Rights

The antinomy of federal vs. states' rights is unnecessary and artificial. We should all be advocates of states' rights but we should all be equally advocates of federal rights. Within the context of our American federalism there is no irreconcilable conflict between the two. National citizenship is primary and paramount over state citizenship, and the Constitution and the laws of the United States made in pursuance thereto are the supreme law of the land. Where an apparent conflict emerges it is for the courts to ascertain whether the federal government is usurping powers reserved to the states or whether the states are encroaching upon the powers delegated to the federal government. And where both sovereign powers legislate for the same individual in a field of action which the law has not pre-empted exclusively to one jurisdiction or the other, the concurrence of responsibilities and rights must be mutually preserved intact through the function of the judiciary. Both governments for obvious reasons have a serious interest in and corresponding grave duties for the education of an intelligent and responsible citizenry; and the federal government can help to equalize the educational opportunities amongst the poorer and wealthier states. Traditionally it is left to the states and their local communities to determine their own educational *systems*. There is no discernible conflict between state educational *systems* and federal nondiscriminatory legislative *policy* of financial aid for education *as such*. In an interlocking federal-state financial program for education, the federal government may not require that states match the federal offer of funds in disregard of state laws and policies. But neither should the laws and policies of any state interfere with the laws and policies of a higher sovereignty of the federal government. The "withholding proviso," far from "bypassing" and "side-stepping" the states, assiduously respects the laws and policies of each state while at the same time it preserves undamaged with equal reverence the laws and legislative policies of a higher jurisdiction and of a superior law operating for the benefit of a higher citizenship. "Leaving it to the states" is in fact a surrender of federal responsibilities and subordination by default to the unilateral dictation of state laws and policies. The real difference is between federal nondiscriminatory legislative policy in the disbursement of federal benefits for education — as witness the G.I. Bill of Rights, R.O.T.C., N.Y.A., National Reorganization Legislative Act, federal research programs, the School Lunch Act, etc. — and state policy which discriminates between state and nongovernmental schools as the beneficiaries of state direct and indirect aid in education. But this real difference is not a conflicting one since the federal government can pursue its own policy and at the same time leave untouched the state laws and policies by means of a "withholding proviso" in any federal-state fund matching subsidization of educational needs.

E. Rights of Citizens

As the middle term of all exercise of authority and operation of laws and policies, stands the American citizen endowed with federal and state rights. Invested with citizenship, he is entitled to the rights and the benefits of both governments as he is without arbitary exception to obey the laws, pay the taxes, be subject to military duty, and fulfill all the obligations which each government may rightly demand of him. The most prized of the constitutional rights is the "exercise of religious freedom."[66] In American law, religious liberty means the right to believe and the right not to believe. The wording of "exercise" of religious freedom was sedulously chosen by the drafters of the amendment to embrace not only artciles of faith which may be contained within one's conscience and mind, and modes of worship which as external manifestations are locally expressed in houses of prayer and worship, but also all such human conduct and activity which the religious conscience may dictate in conformity with the dogmas of its faith with due regard to the legitimate demands of social order and peace. The Supreme Court has upheld the constitutionality of religious schools which comply with state requirements to satisfy the state compulsory school attendance laws.[67] While it did not expressly rest its ruling on the free exercise clause (and it did not do so until 1940),[68] the Court declared inviolable "the liberty of parents and guardians to direct the upbringing and education of children under their control." No one can seriously contest that the motive of parents for sending their children to parochial school is religious, since in fact, the parents' compliance with state compulsory attendance laws by sending their charges to public schools would be at no financial burden to themselves. The significance of the Court's striking down state education compulsory laws seems to be completely lost on those who recognize only state education as *the* truly American type of education.[69] Equally lost on public school advocates is the implication which the Court drew from any pattern of state monopoly of education: "The child is not the mere creature of the State; those who nurture him and direct his destiny have the right, coupled with the high duty, to recognize and prepare him for additional obligations."[70] Since 1940, when *Cantwell v. Connecticut* categorically included for the first time the "free exercise" clause of the First Amendment, the Court has jealously guarded religious "exercise" even to uphold in *West Virginia Board of Education v. Barnette,* as an expression of that free exercise, an objectively wrong conscience on the significance of flag-saluting provided in the given instance there is no danger to public order. While scarcely anyone would openly contest the rights of parents to send their children to a parochial school in response to the dictates of religious conscience, in the matter of federal aid even when restricted to auxiliary aids, there are many who would place a disabling price upon such religious liberty. Attendance at church-affiliated schools becomes *eo ipso* for these opponents a liability before the law. Contrary to the intentions of the framers of the First Amendment and its subsequent history, they would insert an antinomy into the "preferred" right of religious liberty. What the "no establishment" clause intended to do — to remove any actual or potential impediments to religious liberty and to the equality before the law of all believers — these opponents would annul by converting the right of free exercise of religion in education into a religious test of exclusion from the disbursement of federal aids. National and state governments are enjoined by the Fifth and Fourteenth Amendments from depriving a person of life, liberty, or property without due process of law. Not only is religious liberty in education contracted by the proponenets of exclusion without any culpability before the law, but the right to property is conditioned in the disbursement of federal funds on a discriminatory basis of religious affiliation. In the words of Cardinal Spellman, this is equivalent to "taxation without participation." Let us bear clearly in mind we are still restricting our discussion to auxiliary aids which are vital services — health, welfare, and safety — for the child, not for the church-affiliated school, for the alleviation of needs, not for the support of a creed. To say that government responsibilities to children cease, when in compliance with their religious conscience, they attend parochial schools, is to pervert our national law and the underlying moral principles which have inspired the federal non-discriminatory policies traditional in our history. Furthermore, the "leave it to the states" argument seriously jeopardizes impartiality in federal government. Since there is no consistent and uniform pattern amongst the states, and even within each state, on auxiliary services, the federal government in a federal-state financing program would become accessory to their bizarre variations. If the federal government permitted its own share of funds to be disbursed in accordance with the contradictory policies that exist amongst the states, it would be partner to the unequal treatment of its own federal citizens.

F. American Constitutional Consensus

A general and summary review of the American constitutional consensus of the national government's relation to religion and religious institutions readily brings to mind the more obviously known facts:

1. Direct Financial Support

In the Ordinances for the Northwest and Southwest territories in the period immediately prior to and continuing after adoption of the Constitution, land grants were set aside for the support of religious education. From the presidency of Washington and Jefferson until 1900 Congress has supported with tax funds religious education by Christian missionaries amongst the Indians. Throughout our national history, chapels and chaplains for Congress (a system which Madison helped establish) and for the armed services on land and sea in war and peace have been traditional. One month after the *McCollum* decision, Congress passed and President Truman signed a bill which appropriated public funds for the construction of a chapel at the Merchant Marine Academy at King's Point. In circumstances where the exercise of civil rights are justly restrained by due process of law, provisions for religious exercise in penal institutions are conscientiously made for the privileged right of religious liberty.

2. Indirect Financial Support

The National Youth Administration Act of 1935 extended public fund benefits to all high school and college students whatever the school of their choice. The Reserve Officers Training Corps program conducted by the military may be incorporated into the curriculum of any college. The Legislative Reorganization Act of 1946 provided at federal cost for the choice of religious education of congressional pages in the District of Columbia.[71] War surplus at nominal prices was available to religious institutions as well as to other defined nonprofit organizations. And above all, the G.I. Bill of Rights provided at federal cost for the higher education of veterans at any educational institution of their choice not excluding preparation for the ministry and rabbinate. The federal government supports numerous research projects at institutions of higher learning whatever their proprietary and religious affiliation. The Hill-Burton Act extends federal funds to all nonprofit hospitals for the expansion and improvement of their facilities regardless of their proprietary and religious affiliation.

Not the least significant admission of the constitutionality of federal aid to religion and its free exercise is the unsuccessful and repeated action of those who would alter the Constitution by amendment in order to reverse the government's traditional policy of nondiscriminatory disbursements.

3. Auxiliary Services

The Supreme Court has upheld the constitutionality of auxiliary aids by the states as a legitimate exercise of police power for the nondiscriminatory provision of public welfare benefits. The Court upheld the state statutes as neither violative of state law, prohibiting direct and indirect aid to sectarian schools and denominational institutions, nor of the First and Fourteenth Amendments of the Constitution. At present non-religious textbooks are provided free by the states to *all* schoolchildren in Louisiana, Mississippi, New

Mexico, Oregon, and in Kansas and in West Virginia only to indigent parochial school children. Free transportation is provided by twenty states: California, Colorado, Connecticut, Illinois, Indiana, Kansas, Kentucky, Louisiana, Maryland, Massachusetts, Michigan, New Hampshire, New Jersey, New Mexico, New York, Ohio, Oregon, Rhode Island, West Virginia, and Wyoming. The exemplary Federal School Lunch Act provides free lunches to children whatever the school of their choice either directly through a Federal Administrator in twenty-eight states, or in cooperation with the other twenty states whose policy of disbursement concurs in this instance with the federal government's. The Supreme Court has upheld the free textbooks and bus transportation. The Federal School Lunch Act has so far not been contested and it is to date the only federal auxiliary provision. In the 1940's many insisted that health and welfare benefits, bus transportation, and free non-religious textbooks be included amongst the federal provision of auxiliary services and extended to all children without discrimination.

Such has been the magnificent panorama of the federal government's support of religion — not to mention the countless evidences of the authoritative and official professions of our country's dependence on divine providence for its foundation, survival, and prosperity. Scarcely the masonry of a wall of *absolute* separation (which Jefferson disowned as a misleading "handle" for the understanding of his thought on the subject), it is more like the corridor constituted by two walls, political government and religion, each a distinct jurisdiction and proper competency, mutually respectful and cooperative for the benefit of one and the same individual citizen and believer.

G. What Is Education?

One of the many slogans which are with accordian-like insistence repeated in the public debates on federal aid is the constant reference to the "American *type*" of education, as if parochial schools are not quite as much American as the state schools. As a matter of fact, the parochial schools are a more indigenous development in America than in any other part of the religious world, and a pro-religious oriented education was the original prevailing American conception of education which has suffered by default in the state schools because of unresolved religious tension. We may properly speak of the English school system, the German *gymnasium*, and the French *lyceum,* namely, a distinctive pattern of intellectual disciplines directed to an academic achievement. Broadly speaking, there is only one American system of education in the sense that all publicly accredited schools, state and privately owned, must comply with the required standards of teaching, of curriculum, and of school facilities, and generally, pass the final examinations provided by the State educational authorities. For this reason the student of any publicly accredited school is given recognition in a transfer to another school before or after graduation. The differences that exist between state schools and church-affiliated schools do not affect these common standards and requirements. Both schools are obviously under the greater supervision incident to proprietary and religious affiliation. The slogan of the "American type of education" is supposedly bolstered by invoking in the same voice the "American principle of separation of Church and State." There is an American type of separation which precludes presumptuous interference beyond the competence of one jurisdiction upon the other, which differentiates it from say, the French absolute separation of the laic state and, within the context, a subordinate church. But the conjunction of these two slogans makes a seriously misleading assumption that the relation of government to church is the same as the relation of the government to education.

In the American type of separation, two separate jurisdictions are recognized by law, each supreme in its own domain, and between the two a traditional policy of cooperation and mutual assistance, moral and fiscal, has been a standing testimonial that the two separate jurisdictions must operate in harmony for the integral good of citizen and believer. On the other hand, the government has real jurisdiction, although not an exclusive one, as well as an interest in education so much a constituent part of general welfare. The conjunction of these slogans has logically led to the insertion of a religious test in the definition of education, of educational needs, and of the common good to which education contributes. Does education become less educational and less American because it *also* provides religious instruction? Do educational needs cease to be needs and lose their significance because of the religious affiliation of the school? Do schools lose their efficacy to contribute to the common good because their students are taught the love and fear of God? And if an appeal be made to Americanism, well then, which of the schools, the secularized state schools or the religious schools are in accord with the religious heritage of America and with the religious nature of our people, whose institutions, as the Court said in the *Zorach* case, presuppose a Supreme Being? Which of the two educational arrangements, religious or secularized education, "complete the circle of the useful sciences... and fills the chasm" which Jefferson decried in a school which did not provide for religious instruction and facilities, let us note, for religious exercise and worship on state property? Jefferson held that the students of religious education on or near the confines of the State University should be *"entitled to the same rights and privileges."* Yet a new brand of Americanism ignores Jefferson on governmental aid to religious education, rejects the nondiscriminatory policy traditional in the federal government, and is remarkably divisive by inserting a religious test in a general federal aid bill!

H. Federal Aid to Education and Religious Liberty

One consideration emerges as paramount with increasing clarity from this study: one cannot totally separate the problem of federal aid to education from religious liberty. If the objective is to assist education, remedy educational needs, and equalize the educational opportunities amongst the poorer and richer states, for the good of the American nation, then it is extremely difficult and potentially dangerous to settle upon a norm of participation, of inclusion and exclusion, by reason of religious affiliation. The exercise of religious liberty must not become a liability before the law in the disbursement of the benefits of law.[72] To allow this is to incur through the exercise of religious liberties one of "civil incapacitations" of which Jefferson spoke as the incidents of a state established church. In a reverse spin, the First Amendment, originally intended to deny the national legislature any power to grant a preferential status in law for a church or a religion, comes now to mean that Congress shall have the power to pass laws that may operate to the disadvantage of the exercise of religious liberty. *The controlling provision of the constitutional organic act for federal aid to education is the general welfare clause of Article I, 8.* The First Amendment is a guarantee that the exercise of federal power for general welfare should not abridge the free exercise of religion. The Court in the highly controversial *Everson* reasoning felt the artificial tensions which it had created for itself when it incorporated in its reasoning the novel

Rutledge doctrine of absolute separation. It would not allow that a religious test be controlling in the exercise of a general welfare provision:

> New Jersey cannot consistently with the "establishment of religion" clause of the First Amendment contribute tax-raised funds to the support of an institution which teaches the tenets and faith of any church. On the other hand, other language of the amendment commands that New Jersey cannot hamper its citizens in the free exercise of their own religion. Consequently, it cannot exclude individual Catholics, Lutherans, Mohammedans, Baptists, Jews, Methodists, Non-believers, Presbyterians, or the members of any other faith, *because of their faith, or lack of it,* from receiving the benefits of public welfare legislation. *While we do not mean to intimate that a state could not provide transportation only to children attending public schools, we must be careful, in protecting the citizens of New Jersey against state-established churches, to be sure that we do not inadvertently prohibit New Jersey from extending its general state law benefits to all its clients without regard to their religious beliefs.*[73]

The Court therefore does not deny that a state may adopt a restricted policy in the disbursement of public welfare benefactions, but it refuses to allow that the motive for such a restriction be a religious test. In the *Zorach* case, the Court tries earnestly to extricate itself from the unreality of the Rutledge "absolute" doctrine and to reaffirm in broad sweep the American constitutional consensus on the relation of government to religion. It rejects the conception of absolute separation as one which would connote preference for those "who believe in no religion over those who do believe."

I. Law and Policy

Constitutionally there is no real problem at all for the federal provision of *auxiliary* services to all schoolchildren. Constitutionally, there has not been any real problem on federal *indirect* aid to religious educational institutions. In fact, the practices of the national government are lavishly uniform and universal. What of *direct* federal aid to religious educational institutions? One would think that no *legal* objection would be raised for doing the *less* when in fact the federal government has from the inception of the Republic done the *greater,* the provisions of chapels and chaplaincies which is a direct financial support of religion.

During the war, the federal government constructed "temporary" buildings on the campus of private educational institutions whatever their religious or proprietary affiliation. Yet there may be reasons of great weight why there should not be a policy of direct federal aid to religious schools; certainly not a policy of equal aid to all schools. Ecclesiastical authorities have made advance disclaimers of participation in any federal bill of direct support, such as capital outlays for construction, payment of teachers' salaries, etc. But such a disclaimer, we respectfully submit, may be for prudential reasons, for reasons other than constitutional. It is here precisely where the unsuccessful Kelley Bill[74] for "construction", and other similar ones about to be proposed fail to meet the constitutional issue. They think to evade the issue; actually they submerge it. May educational institutions of religious affiliations be included constitutionally? We submit that they may. Must they be so included? There is no legal compulsion to do so, but likewise there is no legal barrier against such an inclusion. *The reason and motive for noninclusion must never be the fact of religious affiliation.* Concretely, there might never be a bill proposed or promoted by anyone for direct financial aid to religious educational institutions. But the answer must be unequivocally given even if it never descends from the speculative to the order of actual events for the supreme purpose of keeping the authentic meaning of the First Amendment inviolate from misconstruction. The choice by the democratic political process of majority decision of one policy in preference to others must always be within the comprehension of the law. The choice of a specific policy or the change of a prevailing policy is usually motivated by a combination of conditioning factors, expediency, wisdom, desirability, feasibility, fiscal and social, etc. But if ever the choice of restricted policy of disbursement of general welfare benefactions to education, direct, indirect, or auxiliary should operate in the concrete to interfere with religious liberty, conduce to inequalities before the law, as to constitute a discriminatory preferential status against believers, then we hold it to be the solemn duty of the courts to affirm the *primacy* of religious liberty *before* the law. The courts have yet to decide whether restricted general welfare policies can in certain circumstances be constructive of the violation of the "free exercise thereof" clause.

J. An Argument of Law

One of the causes contributing to the confusion in many minds on the problems of federal aid to education is the unjustifiable reference to a so-called Catholic position. A careful survey of expressions by Catholics on the rights to participate in federal aid will disclose no unanimity on the extent of federal aid to parochial schools. There are Catholics who would rather rely completely on the resources and generosity of the parish for all the school needs, including the "auxiliary" services. In rejecting any sort of public aid they are not questioning its constitutionality. Many Catholics and non-Catholics insist upon the legality and provision of auxiliary aids for all school children but either will not allow or do not want any direct public support for the school itself which is church-affiliated. There are Catholics who share with many non-Catholics the conviction that government intrusion into the educational field should be restricted only to necessary aid for the needy areas in the economically poorer states. Here, there is a difference of opinion whether such necessary aid should be applicable to all publicly accredited schools or not. I have discovered so far only one instance of a Catholic claim for full public support of religious schools.[75] My own position is as follows: The controlling constitutional provision for federal aid to schools is the "general welfare clause" of the organic act. The determination of the provision and extent of federal aid to schools is a matter of *policy* which is fixed upon by the democratic process of majority decision. The Supreme Court has sustained the constitutionality of state provision of auxiliary services in the Louisiana textbook case and the *Everson* bus fare case. On the same grounds it would uphold, if challenged, the federal provision of free school lunches both directly to the children through a federal administrator and where, interpretation of state laws allows, through state cooperative finance and distribution. There is no question about the constitutional consensus of the federal direct support of religion in Congress and in the armed services. The problem centers on support of religious schools. There is no question on federal indirect aid to religious schools. The federal policy of nondiscriminatory indirect aid to religious institutions of learning is an established policy and thriving in our times. What of federal support of religious institutions? In the noneducational area, the Hill-Burton Act provides federal supplementary aid for the construction extension, and maintenance of hospital facilities on a nondiscriminatory basis. The pointed question: What of *direct* federal aid to religious *educational* institutions? My position unequivocally stated, is that the noninclusion of religious educational institutions may not be motivated by an objection to its religious profession and affiliation. This would be a violation of the religious liberty guarantee of the First Amendment, and if the appeal be to the First Amendment, it constitutes a misconstruction of the authentic meaning of the entire amendment. I personally prefer that religious educational institutions draw their vigor from the free financial support of the faithful. Where avoidable, I maintain it would be wiser not to have governmental support because of the governmental control it may entail and for other reasons mentioned elsewhere. But I do insist that this additional question be asked and duly considered: Whether, in any given concrete circumstance, the exclusion of a religious school from direct public support does or does not operate as a restriction of the exercise of religious liberty in education. The courts have not to date faced this issue. But it has not gone wholly without notice amongst jurists. Professor Wilber G. Katz has reflected:

> No case in the Supreme Court has directly involved the question of the validity, under the First Amendment, of tax support for parochial schools. In the New Jersey bus fare case, however, both the majority and the minority clearly assumed that such support is unconstitutional. Until recently, it seemed to me that this assumption was a sound application of the "no aid" rule. It seemed to me that direct payment for educational costs was something more than action to avoid discrimination against religion. Two years ago, I suggested that to protect the freedom of parents in their choice of schools, a tax deduction of some kind for tuition paid to such schools would be permissible. It seemed to me, however, that affirmative aid to religion would be avoided only if religious schools were limited to the support of individuals paying tuition and voluntary contributions.
>
> This position no longer appears to me to be tenable. The "no aid to religion" rule is a rule prescribing neutrality, forbid-

ding action which aids those who profess religion as compared with those who do not. If one assumes that the religious schools meet the state's standards for education in secular subjects, it is not aid to religion to apply tax funds toward the cost of such education in public and private schools without discrimination. Like the dissenters in the bus fare case, I am not now able to distinguish between the minor payments there involved and payments for educational costs. I believe, therefore, that none of such nondiscriminatory uses of tax funds are forbidden by the First Amendment.[76]

If the Supreme Court may consider, as it needlessly did in the *Everson* case, whether any public support of religion may be construed a violation of "no establishment" clause—and it did so in the face of American constitutional consensus to the contrary—then it may with greater relevance ask itself whether the exclusion of a religious school in a federal policy of aid to schools does or does not operate to a real government restriction and intervention of the "free exercise thereof" clause. It is my opinion that neither natural nor legal justice requires equal aid, uniform and in the same amount to all schools in a nondiscriminatory policy of aid to schools. But distributive justice does require that there be equal right to proportionate aid the computation of which rests on a number of confluent factors. The Hill-Burton Act is an exemplary illustration of one such sort of computation for all hospitals whatever its proprietary or religious affiliation.

Federal aid to education which excludes religious schools from its beneficiaries precisely because of their religious profession and affiliation may place Congress in the incongruous role of promulgating a law prejudicial to the "free exercise thereof" clause; of establishing a preferential status for a secularized education as more worthy of its benefits than religious education, and find itself in the unenviable position of constructively setting a religious test as a norm for inclusion amongst the beneficiaries in the exercise of its general welfare powers, and, lastly, allow, if not actually intend, that exercise of religious liberty in education become a liability before the law in the disbursement of the benefits of the law. This would convert the "no establishment" clause into an *affirmative* official action in favor of nonreligious education.[77]

K. The Residual and Delegated Rights to Educate

The rights of parents to educate their children is primary, personal and inalienable. The high tribunal has acknowledged this connatural investiture of parents, and in 1944 the court noted: "It is cardinal with us that the custody, care and nurture of the child reside first in the parents, whose primary function and freedom include preparation for obligations the state can neither supply nor hinder."[78] When therefore, parents cannot provide a private education, they delegate some of their responsibilities to the government whose right to exist derives in great measure from the purpose of civil society to implement the inadequacy of means and the incompetence of parents to fulfill their parental obligations. Besides, the state has its own stake in education. The common good is the realization of a good society and this moral excellence derives from the moral development of its citizens. When the government aids education which also provides religious instruction it is assisting itself. For the government would otherwise have to provide at public cost the classrooms which religious communities are providing at their own expense. If indeed, as all agree, it is an expression of social justice when the government provides the total cost of public school education, why should the lesser provision of partial support of nonprofit private schools be offensive to anyone? The Canadian, Dutch, and English educational systems make these provisions to the consternation of no one in countries predominantly Protestant. We maintain the controlling constitutional premise for federal aid to education is the "general welfare" clause of the organic act. The First Amendment is secondary and qualifying. The motive for the non-inclusion of church-affiliated schools in a governmental policy of aid to education may not be the religious profession and affiliation.

All must jealously guard the "wall of separation" for the sake of religious freedom. Civil and religious jurisdictions must be kept distinct and separate. Neither the political nor the ecclesiastical authorities should be allowed to encroach upon the legitimate and proper jurisdiction of the other. Neither one should hinder the operations of the other. This is a two-faced coin. All, too, should in their vigilance be just as jealously sensitive against any sort of educational establishment which would be prejudicial to and diminish the exercise of religious liberty that the "no establishment" clause was intended to secure. Even those who for many good reasons of policy — and these number amongst the different faiths — are opposed to federal direct aid to religious education should be just as responsive to the effects of such a policy. Any evidence — not abstract or hypothetical, but real and substantive — which shows that the exercise of religious liberty in education becomes a liability before the law and operates as a sort of religious test, results in an inequality before the law for the benefits of law should arouse the anxieties of all on both sides of the debate. The civil rights of believers should not be abridged because the first civil right is exercised. Federal educational favoritism of an educational policy cannot be justified in reason or law to the disadvantage of religious liberty in education. *To date, the courts have yet to weigh this consideration.*

The distinctive meaning of the First Amendment, which Madison helped define and explain, is that the Federal Congress is declared impotent to legislate on establishment which may be such as to infringe upon the religious liberty (as state constitutions allowed for many years) and to ensure against a restricted liberty, the free exercise thereof clause was inserted. When the First Amendment is taken, as it should be, together with the "no religious" test of the organic act, its meaning has a sharper precision than the religious liberty guaranteed by the state constitutions which in its earliest history was scarcely distinguishable from tolerance and which for decades prescribed in some form or another a religious profession for public office. The incorporation therefore of the freedom of religious exercises of the First Amendment into the liberty of the Fourteenth if it is to convey the original and authentic meaning of the First should be equally prohibitive of any state action in the field of education no less than in any other human activity that would constructively operate as a religious test as a liability before the law for the benefits of the law. In the absence of such a conformity will we find the radical reason for the disparity between the traditionally uniform federal policy of nondiscriminatory beneficence, and the bizarre patterns of partly discriminatory and partly nondiscriminatory policies and laws of the states. It is precisely at this juncture that the unsuccessful Kelley Bill and other like it to be proposed fail to conform with the authentic purpose of the First Amendment. A bill which for very good and valid reasons does not include religious schools within its capital outlays should make some acknowledgment of their contribution to American education and in this way or another officially disown that the reason for their non-inclusion is not their religious affiliation.

State and federal courts have at various times upheld in the interest of religious freedom governmental administration or provision of funds in such circumstances which favored religious education. In *Quick Bear v. Leupp*,[79] the Supreme Court sustained the authorization of the Commissioner of Indian Affairs to pay from "treaty funds" for the education provided by the Bureau of Catholic Indian Missions lest the free exercise of religion be otherwise constrained amongst the Indians. On this same constitutional principle courts have upheld state statutes which committed delinquent, neglected or dependant minors to institutions under the auspices of the same religious profession as the child and to which the state paid from public funds for their care. The courts have struck at the restriction of religious liberty even when freedom of movement is controlled by government authority; *it has not spelt out entirely how far government may favor religion positively*. The high tribunal has upheld auxiliary services; the federal government provides many indirect aids to religious education; the federal government gives direct financial support to religion in Congress and in the armed forces. How far may it go in direct subsidy of religious education, if at all? *No one really knows the answer.*

L. How Far?

The affirmation of a constitutional right is not disowned because of the advance disclaimers to benefit by that right. Nor does the validity of a constitutional right lose meaning because the question how far it extends, has not yet been answered. Within the broad comprehensive scope of the general welfare clause of the constitutional organic act, the federal government may choose for valid reasons of expediency, feasibility, wisdom, social considerations, economy, underlying religious tensions – not to extend direct aid to church-affiliated schools in a general federal aid program for education. But we emphasize that this restriction may not derive from the First Amendment. Such an appeal would be a serious distortion of the original and authentic meaning of the amendment. Secondly, since the *Cantwell v. Connecticut* ruling of 1940, the religious liberty guarantee of the First Amendment was categorically made operative through the Fourteenth Amendment upon the States. May not the broader meaning of the federal free exercise of religion at least suggest that it serve as a normative correction of the state laws and correspondingly, their policies, on governmental relations with religious activities not excepting religious education? May not the traditional federal policy of nondiscriminatory benefits through the efficacy of the operation of the First Amendment upon the states, achieve a corresponding nondiscriminatory state practice, at least as far as auxiliary services are concerned, services which the high tribunal has already upheld as in no way offensive to federal and state laws? Finally, the Supreme Court has yet to consider if a federal aid program limited exclusively to government schools (and let us grant, for valid reasons) may not operate in a particular concrete circumstance to an "unreasonable interference" with religious liberty exercised in education. This last consideration should engage the serious reflections of jurists and nonjurists for the preservation of the original and authentic meaning of the First Amendment and its relevance as a qualifier upon the exercise of the general welfare clause of the Federal Constitution for aid to education.

FOOTNOTES AND REFERENCES

1. Everson v. Board of Educ., 330 U.S. 1 (1947).
2. McCollum v. Board of Educ., 333 U.S. 203 (1948).
3. Everson v. Board of Educ., 330 U.S. 1, 15-16 (1947).
4. 333 U.S. 203 (1948).
5. 330 U.S. at 28-74.
6. The Vermont Constitution is silent on this point.
7. 343 U.S. 306 (1952). (Emphasis added.)
8. *Id.* at 312.
9. 268 U.S. 510 (1925).
9a. 330 U.S. 1, 16 (1947).
10. 314 U.S. 252, 289 (1941).
11. Six versions were proposed: (1) "The civil rights of none shall be abridged on account of religious belief, nor shall any national religion be established, nor shall the full and equal rights of conscience in any manner or on any pretext be infringed." 1 ANNALS OF CONG. 434 (1789). (2) ". . . No religion shall be established by law, nor shall the equal rights of conscience be infringed." *Id.* at 729. (3) ". . . Congress shall make no laws touching religion, or infringing the rights of conscience." *Id.* at 731. (4) ". . . Congress shall make no law establishing religion, or to prevent the free exercise thereof, or to infringe the rights of conscience." *Id.* at 766. (5) "Congress shall make no laws establishing articles of faith or a mode of worship, or prohibiting the free exercise of religion." JOURNAL OF THE FIRST SENATE 77 (Gates and Seaton ed. 1820). (6) "Congress shall make no laws respecting an establishment of religion, or prohibiting the free exercise thereof. . . ." 1 ANNALS OF CONG. 913 (1789). After the House approved of the sixth version on the 24th of September and the Senate the following day, it was sent to President Washington for submission to the states. See 1 ANNALS OF CONG. 913-14 (1789). The first four versions were either proposed, altered or adopted by the House alone, and rejected by the Senate. In response to the House's fourth version which was forwarded to the Senate for its concurrence, the Senate adopted its own formula, the fifth version, which the House in turn rejected. A committee of three from each House of Congress settled upon the final text, our present First Amendment.

12. 1 ANNALS OF CONG. 434 (1789).
13. *Id.* at 729.
14. *Id.* at 730.
15. To point out more sharply the unique Madisonian meaning for the federal religious guarantee, namely, the instrumental subordination of "no establishment" to the "free exercise thereof" we may recall that Madison's original fifth amendment guaranteed religious freedom against encroachment by the states without at the same time requiring state disestablishment. See 1 ANNALS OF CONG. 435 (1789).
16. 1 ANNALS OF CONG. 730 (1789).
17. *Id.* at 730-31.
18. *Id.* at 731. Despite Madison's repeated reassurances that the federal amendment left untouched state dispositions of religious life we find today the converse attributed to him, that his mind on the disposition of religious matters in his own state of Virginia, expressed in his *Memorial and Remonstrance* of 1785, six years before the final ratification of the ten amendments, as interpretative of the intent of the federal First Amendment!
19. JOURNAL OF THE VIRGINIA SENATE (1789) 63 (1828 ed.).
20. We remonstrate against the said Bill, because we hold for a fundamental and undeniable truth, "that Religion or the duty which we owe to our Creator and the Manner of discharging it can be directed only by reason and conviction, *not by force or violence"*. . . . We maintain therefore in matters of Religion, no man's right is abridged by the institution of Civil Society . . . that the majority may (not) trespass on the rights of the minority . . . if religion be exempt from the authority of the Society at large, still less can it be *subject to that of the Legislative Body.* . . . Who does not see that the same authority which can *establish Christianity, in exclusion of all other Religions, may establish* with the same ease *any particular sect of Christians, in exclusion of all other Sects?* That the same authority which can *force* a citizen *to contribute* three pence only of his property for the support of any one establishment, may force him to conform to any other establishment in all cases whatsoever? . . . the bill *violates* that equality which ought to be the basis of every law . . . all men are to be considered as entering into Society on *equal conditions;* as relinquishing no more, and therefore retaining no less, one than another, of their natural rights. Above all are they to be considered as retaining an *equal title to the free exercise of Religion* according to the dictates of conscience. . . . As the Bill *violates equality by subjecting* some to particular burdens; so it violates the same principle, by *granting to others pecuniary exemptions* . . . the bill implies either that the Civil Magistrate is a competent Judge of Religious truth; or that he may employ religion as an engine of Civil policy. . . . It (the Bill) *degrades from the equal rank* of Citizens all those whose opinions in Religion do not bend to those of the Legislative Authority. 2 THE WRITINGS OF JAMES MADISON 184-88 (Hunt ed. 1901). (Emphasis added.)
21. Corwin, *The Supreme Court as National School Board*, 14 LAW & CONTEMP. PROB. 3, 16 (1949).
22. After the Preamble of Section 1 which set forth in fourteen statements the incidents usual in an establishment, the inequities and injustices visited upon dissenters and nonconformists as well as the hypocrisy it may engender, Section II reads:

....We the General Assembly of Virginia do enact (1) that no man shall be compelled to frequent or support any religious worship, place, or ministry whatsoever, (2) nor shall be enforced, restrained, molested, or burthened in his body or goods, or shall otherwise suffer, on account of his religious opinions or belief; but (3) that all men shall be free to profess, and by argument to maintain, their opinions in matters of religion, and (4) that the same shall in no wise diminish, enlarge, or affect their civil capacities.

See Padover, THE COMPLETE JEFFERSON 947 (1943). Like Madison, Jefferson's opposition to "establishment" in Virginia was inspired by the dominating idea of religious freedom "I am for freedom of religion, and against all maneuvers to bring about the legal ascendency of one sect over another. . . ." Letter to Elbridge Gerry, 1700, 7 THE WRITINGS OF THOMAS JEFFERSON 328 (Ford ed. 1896).
23. Padover, THE COMPLETE JEFFERSON 1064-69 (1943).
24. *Id.* at 1076. (Emphasis added.)
25. *Id.* at 1104. (Emphasis added.)
26. *Id.* at 957-58.
27. *Id.* at 958.

28. 10 THE WRITINGS OF THOMAS JEFFERSON 242 (Ford ed. 1899).
29. *Id.* at 243. (Emphasis added.)
30. In our annual report to the legislature, . . . we suggest the expediency of encouraging the different sects to establish, each for itself, a professorship of their own tenets, on the confines of the university, so near as that their students may attend the lectures there, and have the free use of our library, and every other accommodation we can give them; preserving, however, their independence of us and of each other. This fills the chasm objected to in ours, as a defect in an institution professing to give instruction in *all* useful sciences. *Ibid.* (Emphasis added.)
31. Padover, *op. cit. supra* note 24, at 1106-11.
32. *Id.* at 1110. (Emphasis added.)
33. *Id.* at 518-19.
34. See 1 Stokes, CHURCH AND STATE IN THE UNITED STATES 480 (1950).
35. *Id.* at 481. (Emphasis added.)
36. 4 AM. STATE PAPERS, Class 2, Indian Affairs 54 (Cong. 1832). (Emphasis added.)
37. 1 AM. STATE PAPERS, Class 2, Indian Affairs 687 (Cong. 1803).
38. 25 U.S.C. 278 (1928).
39. Exec. Order 7086 (June 26, 1935).
40. 10 U.S.C. 381 (1927).
41. 42 U.S.C. 1751-60 (1952).
42. Servicemen's Readjustment Act, 58 Stat. 284, 290 (1944).
43. 60 Stat 812 (1946).
44. 42 U.S.C. 291 (1952).
45. 93 CONG. REC. 4459 (1947).
46. 62 Stat. 172 (1948).
47. Dept. of Army Pam. 16-8 (1950): ". . . the character development programs stress . . . the moral principles that sustain the philosophy of American freedom, particularly as it is set forth in the opening paragraph of the Declaration of Independence. That philosophy regards man as a creature of God."

Air Force 50-21, Living for Leadership (1955): "There is an objective truth which we can discover with our own intellects concerning the nature of man, and of society, and of the purpose of life. There is a natural law and order. . . . There is a God who has created man with rights and duties and a purpose in life."

48. The courts have on numerous occasions insisted that the determining factor whether the school was parochial or public was *who controlled it.* Control must be distinguished from supervision and inspection which ascertains the conformity to state prescribed standards in order to be a publicly accredited school, attendance at which satisfies the requirements of the state compulsory school attendance laws. Control is a concomitant right of a proprietary title. Though the courses of study are prescribed and supervised by the state, and their pupils' attendance at church-related schools is a compliance with state compulsory attendance laws, this does not constitute control. Cochran v. Louisiana State Board of Educ., 281 U.S. 370 (1930).

Viewing the statute as having the effect thus attributed to it, we cannot doubt that the taxing power of the state is exerted for a public purpose. The legislation does not segregate private schools, or their pupils, as its beneficiaries or attempt to interfere with any matters of exclusively private concern. Its interest is education, broadly; its method, comprehensive. Individual interests are aided only as the common interest is safeguarded. *Id.* at 375.

49. See National Citizens Committee for Public Schools, FINANCING PUBLIC EDUCATION IN THE DECADE AHEAD (1954); Freeman, FEDERAL AID TO EDUCATION – BOON OR BANE? (American Enterprise Ass'n Inc., Washington, D.C., 1955); National Citizens Comm'n for Public Schools, HOW DO WE PAY FOR OUR SCHOOLS? (1954); Comm'n of Intergovernmental Relations, FEDERAL RESPONSIBILITY IN THE FIELD OF EDUCATION (1955); A Report Prepared in the Legislative Reference Service of the Library of Congress for the Subcommittee on Education of the Senate Committee on Labor and Public Welfare, ACTION BY THE 83rd CONGRESS AFFECTING EDUCATION AND EDUCATORS (U.S. Gov't Printing Office, 1955); A Report Prepared in the Legislative Reference Service of the Library of Congress by Charles A. Quattlebaum, Specialist in Ed-

ucation, FEDERAL AID FOR SCHOOL CONSTRUCTION (U.S. Govt. Printing Office, 1955); A Report Prepared in the Legislative Reference Service of the Library of Congress by Charles A. Quattlebaum, EDUCATIONAL ISSUES OF CONCERN TO THE 84th CONGRESS (U.S. Govt. Printing Office); A Report Prepared in the Legislative Reference Service of the Library of Congress at the Request of Senator John Sherman Cooper, Chairman, Subcommittee on Education of the Committee on Labor and Public Welfare, FEDERAL AID TO STATES AND LOCAL SCHOOL DISTRICTS FOR ELEMENTARY AND SECONDARY EDUCATION (U.S. Govt. Printing Office, 1954).

50. 281 U.S. 370 (1930).

51. In 1854 the Maine Supreme Judicial Court upheld the expulsion of a Catholic child from school for refusing to read the Protestant Bible. Donahue v. Richards, 38 Me. 379 (1854).

52. See Billington, THE PROTESTANT CRUSADE 1800-1860 (1938); Myers, HISTORY OF BIGOTRY IN THE UNITED STATES (1943).

53. 2 COMPLETE WORKS OF ABRAHAM LINCOLN 287 (Nicolay and Hay ed. 1905). See also Bates, RELIGIOUS LIBERTY 363 (1945).

54. Beale, A HISTORY OF FREEDOM OF TEACHING IN AMERICAN SCHOOLS 95 (1941).

55. *Id.* at 97.

56. *Id.* at 98-99.

57. *Id.* at 104-05.

58. 310 U.S. 296 (1940).

59. 7 U.S.C. 301 (1946).

60. 42 U.S.C. 291 (1952). In Kentucky the Court of Appeals upheld the federal statute against the contention that the federal-state grant to church-affiliated hospitals violated both federal and state constitutions.

... (4) private agency may be utilized as the pipe-line through which a public expenditure is made, the test being not who receives the money but the character of the use for which it is expended. ... The fact that members of the governing board of these hospitals, which perform a recognized public service to all people regardless of faith or creed, are all of one religious faith does not signify that the money allotted the hospitals is to aid their particular denominations. ... Courts will look to the use to which these funds are put rather than the conduits through which they run. If that use is a public one... it will not be held in contravention of sec. 5 merely because the hospitals carry the name or are governed by the members of a particular faith.

Kentucky Bldg. Comm'n v. Effron, 310 Ky. 355, 358-59, 220 S.W. 2d 836, 837-38 (1949). In Mississippi, the State Supreme Court also upheld the federal-state interlocking subsidization of a church-affiliated hospital on the same constitutional grounds of public service. Craig v. Mercy Hospital, 209 Miss. 427, 45 So. 2d 427 (1950).

61. The education of its citizens is no less a concern and responsibility of the federal government as it is for the states. An illiterate and politically irresponsible citizen may be a liability to the federal as well as to the state governments.

62. *Cf.* Harrison-Thomas Bill, S. 1305, 76th Cong., 1st Sess. (1939); Harrison-Thomas Bill, S. 1313, 77th Cong., 1st Sess. (1941); Hill-Thomas Bill, S. 637, 78th Cong., 1st Sess. (1943); Thomas-Hill-Ramspeck Bill, S. 181, 79th Cong., 1st Sess. (1945); Taft-Hill-Thomas Bill, S. 472, 80th Cong., 1st Sess. (1947).

63. S. 717, 79th Cong., 1st Sess. (1945).

64. H.R. 7160, 81st Cong., 2d Sess. (1950).

Expenditures of Funds and Judicial Review Sec. 5. Amounts paid to any State under this Act shall be expended only for current expenditures for public elementary and secondary schools within such State....

(2) ... Whenever in the judgment of any member of the board, or commission of education or equivalent agency of such State, or of any member of any local school board or equivalent agency of such State, any person has engaged, or is about to engage, in any acts or practices which constitute or will constitute a violation of any provision of the first four sentences of this section, such member may make application to the appropriate United States district court... for an order enjoining such acts and practices, or for an order enjoining compliance with the provision of the first four sentences of this section. Upon a showing that such person has engaged, or is about to engage, in any such acts or practices,

a permanent or temporary injunction, restraining order, or other order may be granted.

Definitions. Sec. 7. For the Purpose of this Act —

(2) The term 'current expenditures' includes only expenditures for salaries of teachers and of school supervisory, administrative and maintenance personnel, expenditures for school supplies, and expenditures for the maintenance of school buildings.

(3) The term 'public elementary and secondary schools' means tax-supported grade schools and high schools which are under public supervision and control.

(4) The term 'number of children of school age in such State' means the number of children from five to seventeen years of age, inclusive, in such State. . . .

65. S. 1411, 81st Cong., 1st Sess. (1949).

66. The preeminence of the religious guarantees as the First Amendment is a historical accident. To begin with, only in the closing days and under much persevering prodding from Madison did the First Congress finally attend to the formulation of a bill of rights. *Cf.* Rutland, THE BIRTH OF THE BILL OF RIGHTS 1776-1791 (1955). When Madison first introduced his amendments, the two which dealt expressly with the subject of religion were fourth and fifth. The fifth amendment which restricted state action on religious conscience was dropped by the Senate and the fourth which regulated federal activity was altered by the House and was submitted to the states as the third of all the amendments actually proposed for ratification. Because the first two failed of ratification the third proposed amendment became our present First Amendment. Mr. Justice Jackson was not historically accurate when in his dissenting opinion in the Everson case he observed: "This freedom was first in the Bill of Rights because it was first in the forefathers' minds. . . ." Everson v. United States, 330 U.S. 1, 26 (1947).

67. Pierce v. Society of Sisters, 268 U.S. 510 (1925).

68. Cantwell v. Connecticut, 310 U.S. 296 (1940).

69. No little confusion is engendered by the reference to "church and state." Neither in the First Amendment nor elsewhere in the Constitution is there any mention of "church" or of "state" in the generic sense. Both the debates in the First Amendment and in the states at the time of the adoption of the First Amendment clearly show that the explicit intent of the Amendment was to effectuate a separation between the federal and state jurisdictions respecting religion and hardly at all raised the continental questions of union or separation of church and state. There was no dominant church vis-a-vis the federal government. The variety of state establishments at the time of the First Amendment, as well as the privileged position which the disestablished churches in the other states still retained and the prevailing numbers of a denomination in the three states which never had an established church made it practically impossible for the federal government to favor any one church by national establishment. Indeed, it is clear from Madison's rejoinders to objections raised at the First Congress, the amendment was not directed to interfere with state settlements on the subject of religion. Very often the amendment is quoted to read "respecting *the* establishment of religion" as if it prohibited the federal government to favor religious life whereas the literal meaning is "respecting *an* establishment of religion" — an accurate denial of legal preference for any one belief. A serious and very facile misconception is to identify government relation with religious education with church and state relationship. The state has no jurisdictional rights in matters of creed, worship and their free exercise, except to cooperate and encourage the freedom of the churches and of the individual believers. But the state has a jurisdictional right — though not an absolute and exclusive one — in education; a right which it has together with the parents and the churches. The separation of church and state which secures to each its own proper jurisdiction from encroachment by the other is consequently not applicable to education which fulfills authorized requirements and provides, besides, religious instruction. This is not therefore a theological question but a political one which the First Amendment fixes in constitutional, i.e., legal terms. The proper approach to a discussion of federal aid to education is to consider the responsibilities of the state for the education of its citizens in a manner consonant with civic and religious duties and liberties.

In such a sound perspective, civil and religious empowerments are kept by law inviolably separate. The distinct and correspondingly proportionate responsibilities of parents, church, and state in education upon one and the same subject, citizen-believer, unavoidably requires moral and material cooperation.

70. Pierce v. Society of Sisters, 268 U.S. 510, 535 (1925).

71. 60 Stat. 812 (1946).
72. The Court of Appeals in *Zorach v. Clauson* struck at the heart of the matter when it warned against exalting "no establishment" to the detriment of the "free exercise" clause: "We must not destroy one in an effort to preserve the other." 303 N.Y. 161, 172, 100 N.E. 2d 463, 468 (1951). And Judge Desmond in his concurring opinion:

The basic fundamental here at hazard is not, it should be made clear, any so-called ... principle of complete separation of religion from government. Such a total separation has never existed in America, and none was ever planned or considered by the founders. The true and real principle that calls for assertion here is that of the right of parents to control the education of their children, so long as they provide them with the State-mandated minimum of secular learning and the right of parents to raise and instruct their children in any religion chosen by the parents. Pierce v. Society of Sisters of the Holy Names of Jesus and Mary, 268 U.S. 510; Meyer v. State of Nebraska, 262 U.S. 390. . . . Packer Collegiate Inst. v. University of State of New York, 298 N.Y. 184, 192. . . . These are true and absolute rights under natural law, antedating, and superior to, any human constitution or statute.

I cannot believe that the Chief Justice of the United States, in his opinion for the Supreme Court majority in Dennis v. United States, 341 U.S. 494, 508 ... meant literally, what he wrote: that there are no absolutes and that all concepts are relative. Of course, even the constitutional rights of freedom of speech and freedom of religion are, to a degree, nonabsolute, since their disorderly or dangerous exercise may be forbidden by law. But embodied within 'freedom of religion' is a right which is absolute and not subject to any governmental interference whatever. Absolute, I insist, is the right to practice one's religion without hindrance, and that necessarily comprehends the right to teach that religion, or have it taught, to one's children. 303 N.Y. at 178, 100 N.E. 2d at 471.

73. Everson v. Board of Educ., 330 U.S. 1, 16 (1947). (Emphasis added.)
74. H.R. 7535, 84th Cong., 2d Sess. (1956).
75. ". . . (I)n the matter of erecting new school buildings, it's obvious that American children are entitled to the benefits of public-welfare legislation regardless of race, color or creed." Sheerin, *Eisenhower and Parochial Schools,* THE CATHOLIC WORLD 2 (April 1955).
76. Katz, *Freedom of Religion and State Neutrality,* 20 U. Chi. L. Rev. 426 (1953).
77. Madison's preoccupation for religious liberty carried him years later to a narrow logic. We find him noting in his Detached Memoranda constitutional doubts about the practice of governmental support of congressional chaplains which he as President had approved.

The establishment of the chaplainship to Congs. is a palpable *violation of equal rights,* as well as of Constitutional principles: The tenets of the chaplain elected ... shut the door of worship against the members whose creeds and consciences forbid a participation in that of the majority. To say nothing of other sects, this is a case with that of Roman Catholics and Quakers who have always had members in one or both of the Legislative branches. Could a Catholic clergyman ever hope to be appointed Chaplain? *To say that his religious principles are obnoxious or that his sect is small, is to lift the evil at once and exhibit in its naked deformity the doctrine that religious truth is to be tested by numbers, or that the major sects have a right to govern the minor."*

Fleet, *Detached Memoranda,* THE WILLIAM AND MARY QUARTERLY, Oct. 1946, p. 558. (Emphasis added.) Madison's fears of the majority's dictation to a minority deserves universal concurrence but his fears were in great part inspired by an overexaggerated notion of the relation of the congressional chaplain to the congressmen. These owe him no obedience. He is neither their ecclesiastical authority nor their teacher of sectarian dogma. He exercises neither a magisterium, properly speaking, nor a jurisdiction in matters of religious belief. Indeed the religious functions of the congressional chaplain whatever his denomination are characteristically, as discretion dictates, nonsectarian. The underlying significance of his office is the testimony it bears to one of the many traditional expressions of the official and authoritative protestations of the American need for invoking divine guidance in the governance of man.

78. Prince v. Massachusetts, 321 U.S. 158, 166, (1944).
79. 210 U.S. 50 (1908).

RELIGIOUS SCHOOLS AND SECULAR SUBJECTS*

Prior to the National Defense Education Act of 1958, the only federal financial assistance to reach elementary and secondary schools were noneducational child welfare benefits. Under the terms of the National School Lunch Act and the Special Milk Program of the Agricultural Act, the federal funds were appropriated for the provision of midday meals and milk to students attending schools of high school grade and under. Both these programs were administered with or without the concurrence of state agencies and reached without distinction both state and church-related schools. Where new or increased federal activities resulted in substantial increases in school membership, Congress provided funds for the construction and operation of school facilities in these federally affected areas. Apart from these exceptional circumstances, in which the enlarged educational needs of a locality had been brought about directly by activities of the national government, it was not until 1958 that any federal financial assistance was extended for educational purposes to the lower grade schools. Under the terms of Title III of the N.D.E.A., the federal government made available grants to state educational agencies and loans to nonprofit private schools so that they could acquire special equipment, suitable for use in providing education in science, mathematics, or modern foreign language, and for minor remodeling of the laboratory or other space used for such materials or equipment. Whether or not church-related schools have availed themselves of this provision to any great extent, their inclusion in the N.D.E.A. symbolized for them a gratifying acknowledgement by the federal government that they were a

---

*CONTINUUM. Vol. 1, 4, Winter 1964, pp. 445-497.

a part of national education and that they too should contribute to the objectives of national defense through educational programs.

The Presidential Special Message to Congress on February 20, 1961, on a general federal-aid program to education reopened wide the national controversey on the constitutionality of including children of parochial schools in such a program. Among the legislative precedents cited in their favor were the provisions of Title III, Section 305 of the N.D.E.A. The argument ran that similar provisions for the secular studies in church-related schools would not run counter to the constitutional requirements of the First Amendment.

In the spring of 1962, appeared the first press notice of the forthcoming publication of a study[1] which purported to demonstrate that the supposition on which the constitutionality of loans to parochial schools rested, the promotion of secular studies, was empirically false. An analysis of the textbooks used would disclose, it was alleged, many evidences of religious permeation. If the advocates of a nondiscriminatory federal-aid program to education had ever intended to develop an argument of prolongation which, proceeding from the alleged constitutionality of federal loans for science and language equipment, would extend to the advocacy of government loans for the construction of classrooms set aside for the study of these secular subjects designated in Section 305 of Title III,[2] the study had within the convolutions of its own argumentation a similar argument of extension but in reverse. If it could be shown by empirical evidence that the rationale of the purely secular subject premise on which the constitutionality of the N.D.E.A. loans allegedly rested was unfounded, then *a fortiori* federal loans for the construction of classrooms for parochial schools, and analogously, other educational aids, would wither on the constitutional vine. By striking at the roots the plant would never grow strong with an accumulation of substantive precedents. Either way the efficacy of the argument would be far-reaching and telling in its application. But the main difficulty with the study may prove to be that it was not radical enough. It did not enter into the nature and quality of the roots as thoroughly as it ought to have, and the detachment professed by its empirical methods was in fact a profound commitment to a philosophy of education of enormous magnitude.

While the purely secular subject concept is apparently accepted by George LaNoue, the author of the study, as his own personal conviction — he never raises critically the question of its validity either for himself or for others — the occasion for its legal supposition is supplied handily by two governmental sources. The first, is a passage from the "Memorandum on the Impact of the First Amendment to the Constitution upon Federal Aid to Education" which was prepared by the legal staff of the department of Health, Education, and Welfare in cooperation with the Attorney General in response to a request by Senator Morse in the aftermath of the President's Special Message to Congress.

> To what extent a special purpose provides constitutional legitimacy to assistance to elementary or secondary schools depends on the extent to which the specific objectives being advanced are unrelated to the religious aspects of sectarian education. The problem is complicated because assistance for one purpose may free funds which would otherwise be devoted to it for use to support the religious functions and thus, in effect, indirectly yet substantially support religion in violation of the establishment clause. At the present time, the National Defense Education Act permits the U.S. Commissioner of Education to make loans to private schools to acquire science, mathematics, or foreign language equipment. We believe such loans are constitutional because the connection between loans for such purposes and the religious functions of a sectarian school seems to be nonexistent or minimal.

Whether or not this passage may be said to rest the constitutionality for Title III, Section 305 loans under N.D.E.A. on a purely secular subject concept is an inference that is far from conclusive and beyond question. It states that the "constitutional legitimacy" of such assistance "depends on the extent to which the specific objectives being advanced are unrelated to the religious aspects of sectarian education." Does this mean that what matters is whether the specific objective is attained despite or together with or only in complete insulation from any religious reference? "Unrelated to the religious aspects of sectarian education." Does this mean, unrelated to the religious aspects of the general curriculum of education in a parochial school? Hardly; for how could that be? Unrelated to the religious aspects of formal sectarian religious instruction? That would be a clumsy tautology. Unrelated, that is to say, impervious to any moral-religious import of the secular subjects designated in Title

III? By no conscientious analysis of the passage may such a rationale be ascribed categorically to the authors of the Memorandum. Admittedly, on the other hand, the passage, thanks to its ambiguities, does not preclude the possibility of such an interpretation.

The second governmental source, however, does provide LaNoue with an unequivocal statement of the purely secular subject concept. Mr. Pucinski, Congressman from Illinois, in his interrogations of two witnesses appearing before the House Joint Subcommittee on Education and in his own testimony appearing as a witness before the House General Subcommittee on Education and Labor, allows no suspicion of a doubt in his personal commitment to the purely secular subject provision on which he categorically rests the constitutionality of the loan provisions of the N.D.E.A. to parochial schools.

> Mr. Pucinski. Mr. Witness, do you have any reason to believe, or do you have any evidence that would indicate, that these 162 loans that were approved by your Department, totaling more than two million dollars for the special purpose of science, language, or mathematics, that any of this equipment was used for courses and purposes other than purely secular instruction?
> Mr. Ludington. We have no such evidence at this time.
> Mr. Pucinski. Have you made any effort to ascertain that?
> Mr. Ludington. The loan application which is submitted by the interested school states that this equipment will be used for instruction in mathematics, science, or modern foreign languages.
> Mr. Pucinski. Therefore, you have no reason to believe that it is used for any other purpose except that the law provided.
> Mr. Ludington. Due to the types of equipment, I would find it difficult to find ways of using it in other types of courses.
> Mr. Pucinski. So, based on your experience with the act so far, you have no reason to believe that the lending of this money to private schools, although they may be church related, has in any way interfered with the separation doctrine?
> Mr. Ludington. I go by the applications and the kinds of equipment that they have listed on these applications, and it is our belief that these are held to math, science, and foreign language.[3]

As is apparent, Mr. Ludington's testimony assumes that the equipment requested was of such sort that it could be used only for the specific purpose prescribed by Title III.

Other witnesses, however, raised the question of the general permeation of religious influence in a church school and the pervasion of a particular religion in all of the subjects that are taught. To this pressing objection Mr. Pucinski insisted on knowing how religious doctrine could be brought into an algebraic formula.[4]

The Congressman from Illinois appearing as a witness before the House General Subcommittee on Education expressed his own convictions in a forthright statement:

> These loans should be made available for the specific purpose of developing science, math, and language facilities. And I certainly think that it would be in order to suggest that they include also loans for construction of facilities and physical fitness and perhaps cafeterias.
> We heard testimony yesterday from Coach Wilkinson who stressed the great importance of physical fitness in this country. And yet these are things that are completely divorced from any sectarian teaching. These are subjects that, as I have said many, many times, it would be extremely difficult to try to impugn, or to associate with these secular subjects any religious dogma.
> As a matter of fact, so far as I know, the textbooks which are used for the teaching of these subjects in the private schools, even though they may be church related, are the same textbooks that are being used by the secular, by the public schools. So there is no conflict there.[5]

Despite some questionable underlying assumptions of this statement, the paragraphs which immediately follow offered fruitful opportunity for second thoughts on what had just been stated.

> I believe that it is certainly fair to point out that we know from the youngsters going on to higher education that those youngsters who get their education in private schools, in these particular fields, are just as qualified to carry on their higher education in the scientific fields in colleges as youngsters who get their education in public schools. Certainly, then, if anyone was to presume that the training that these youngsters get in

these particular subjects is in some way deficient, or is in some different, or is in some way altered by religious dogma in the course of the educational process, this would very quickly be reflected when these youngsters go on to higher education. And yet we can show records and we can show proof and we can show evidence, and I am sure we can bring in thousands of cases of youngsters who have gotten their basic training in private schools, church related if they be so, and went on to college, and took courses over there, and graduated, and reached great positions of prominence in the scientific field.[6]

These statements might have suggested to both Mr. Pucinski and La-Noue (who admits quoting these two paragraphs) some profitable second thoughts on the preceding statements, namely, the controlling question should be whether the end result of the science courses in parochial schools satisfies the requirements of these sciences in higher grades in schools which are not church-related. This in turn may have suggested the consideration of the indefectibility of the subject matter of a science course in an educational process whose ultimate values are theistic and Christian. Mr. Pucinski's own illustration of athletic exercises as " completely divorced from any sectarian teaching" should easily have brought to mind parochial school children wearing religious medals and blessing themselves before plunging into the pool.

Apparently, LaNoue adopts the purely secular subject concept since he at no time examines the question of its validity either for himself or for others. Since the possibility of the neutrality of science courses must underlie any constitutional claim by whomsoever made for insisting on a neutral presentation, we shall have to examine that question. But before we do so we must make some preliminary observations.

First, the plan provisions of Title III are for equipment not textbooks. LaNoue dispenses with this difference in a footnote.

> Any claim that equipment as opposed to the other essentials of teaching is necessarily nonreligious is a meaningless distinction from a church-state point of view. It would be the same as claiming that the state could contribute bricks for a church building and wood for the pews because these two elements were in themselves not religious. The essential criterion is the

purpose for which the elements are used, be it church equipment or school equipment. To know that, one must examine the actual content of the subject matter. For an example of a court making this kind of analysis, see *Dickmen v. School District*, Oregon City, 366 P2d 553 (1961).[7]

The broad fact is that federal funds are expended for the construction of chapels on government property and for the provision of many of the instrumentalities of worship of the various faiths. There seems to be at present no real threat to this traditional congressional practice. The constitutional sensitivity on the part of opponents of federal aid to parochial schools seems to be for the most part restricted to the educational area and even at that largely to the infra-collegiate level. The religious purpose and sectarian uses to which brick, mortar, and wood are put in the construction of chapels at government expense is beyond all question. It seems doubtful to argue by analogy from the extensive aptitude of a subject matter for religious orientation to conclude to similar utilization of school equipment material. The illation from equipment to textbooks is provided by Mr. Pucinski. Furthermore, the federal government as the original and sole donor of outright grants for science equipment to public schools would have the right to stipulate for a reasonable time the exclusive purpose and use of the science equipment in the public schools. Nonprofit schools, on the other hand, in obtaining these science facilities through a government loan, to be repaid in full with interest, are from the very beginning co-owners and should not be denied all say in the use of these equipments.

Second, a word about the testimonies before the House Hearings. LaNoue makes no mention of those witnesses who did not, of their own accord, raise any objections to the continued inclusion of parochial schools in the N.D.E.A. program. It is safe to suppose, therefore, that the religious orientation of the curriculum of church-related schools was too broad a fact for them to be ignorant of. Among these witnesses were eminent educators and jurists. And while this is outside the time-limit of LaNoue's survey-study we could nonetheless also point to such students of our society as Walter Lippman and Robert Hutchins, and in some instances to reversals of position since the publication and wide publicity given to LaNoue's survey. Apparently the permeation argument has not weakened the conviction of many that the secular aspects and secular functions of science subjects remain inviolably intact for public purpose even though invested with religious values and judgments. For many the pedagogic distinction between theological instructions in a religion course and religious moral values in nontheological studies is too formidable to be obliterated by a nonblending formula.

Third, an impartial study would have inquired into the value permeations in public school textbooks and, in the light of Supreme Court ruling in *Torcaso v. Watkins,* raised the inevitable question of the role of public law in relation to the spiritual content of the educational process.

Fourth, at no time does LaNoue ask whether the science subjects are taught and learned proficiently in parochial schools according to existing empirical tests or by any standard of measurement that he could suggest, so as to satisfy the objective and national interest for which the N.D.E.A. was passed by Congress.

Since the time of Socrates pedagogues have conceived of the educational process as eminently a spiritual experience of the highest significance for the person and his community. Educators have differed on the ultimate premises and the substantive content of the moral ideas to which all learning is ordained. Political authorities no less than ecclesiastical officials have insisted on their interest in the education of their subjects. The stake of democratic societies in education is such that their survival is publicly professed to be dependent largely upon the loyalties engendered in school children to their free institutions. Totalitarian governments with logical consistency dictate not only the subject matters taught but define the ideals that are to be inculcated in the young. Any education worthy of its high purpose is above all else humanist and, therefore, supposes ultimates about human existence and destiny. And the serious-minded and well-intentioned construction in recent times of "neutral principles of adjudication" to help resolve the national controversy over the constitutional propriety of extending federal aid to church-related schools has not gone unchallenged. Even nonbelievers have had to admit this raw and unfair fact.

Professor Tussman of Syracuse University has observed in a recent publication:

> The charge that public education in its secular form is irreligious may have some substance. As a nonbeliever I may find this convenient. But I am not sure that it is altogether fair or that it justifies, in the name of "neutrality," the rejection of the claims of our religious citizens to public support for their efforts at

providing education that is religious in spirit. The neutrality of the public school should not, I suggest be considered beyond challenge.[8]

And from one who holds fast to absolute separation of church and state we hear a complaint of the uneven struggle for the spiritual control of public education.

If teacher-education colleges in the past generation in this country had attended more to the religious enlightenment of their students and had restricted themselves less exclusively to the thought and language patterns of a nonatheistic scientific naturalism, it is altogether possible that the churches would not have been driven to the only recourse that lay within their grasp. Their demand for sectarian religious education in the schools, and when possible, in teacher education, is a reasonable and democratic demand for just as long as the secularist insist on dominating the educational system and excluding, neglecting, or depreciating the religious dimension in American culture.[9]

To the best intentioned but nonetheless misguided efforts of those who seek a solution for public schooling in a purely secular education we must call to mind the militant secularism that has fought to prevail in our public schools from Francis Wright to Vivian Thayer.[10] There is no inclination on the part of secular humanists and ethical culturists to disown the spiritual content of their nonatheistic beliefs. It is precisely here that LaNoue's study falters badly. He does not give even a nod to the problem of value permeability in public schooling nor raise the constitutional question of government aid in support of these "religious" orientations.

THE MYTH OF THE PURELY SECULAR SUBJECT CONCEPT

The broad fact that most educators would acknowledge that the educational process as an integral whole is at its core pre-eminently spiritual and a commitment to value judgments of one sort or another does not, of course, settle *a priori* the distinct question, whether every subject matter for study is so permeated with moral ultimates. Nor does Mr. Pucinski's and Mr. LaNoue's assumption of the validity of the purely secular subject concept of specified branches of learning without any effort at demonstration (much less will a constitutional requirement) make it so. It is, therefore, imperative that we look into the meaning and content of secular studies in general and of secular subjects in particular to ascertain whether they are to be distinguished from religious studies and, if so differentiated, whether they bear within themselves any grounds for relations with sacral studies.

A subject of study is defined by its formal object, which, in turn, prescribes the appropriate methods of teaching which are conducive to an efficient learning. For example, spelling is the correct lettering of words. The method employed is oral or written exercises naming each letter component of the word. It is easily distinguishable as a natural science, *de naturalibus,* that is, it is not *de divinis,* not about the existence, nature, and attributes of a transcendental being. It reaches out to *all* words, inclusive of words that designate sacred subjects, such as God, the angels, the sacraments, items of worship and liturgy, and so on. The spelling of *sacral terms* does not convert spelling from a natural into a sacred study. We may safely conjecture that the number of sacral terms required for spelling exercises in a church-related school would be more extensive than what is required in a public school. Provided the list of words designating secular objects is not less than what is required by a state educational curriculum or what is necessary for daily concourse with people and for the needs of advancing in other subjects of study the greater inclusion of sacral terms is understandable and might be considered as an enlarged vocabulary. (Conversely, it would be equally understandable that fewer sacral terms would be included in a public school spelling list, though by the same token, fewer sacral terms are being learned.) Spelling does not become a religious subject because parochial school children are called upon to spell Trinity, Sacrament, Tabernacle, Host, Chalice, Extreme Unction, Rosary.

The formal object of the study of arithmetic is to add, subtract, divide, and multiply numerals. Numerals may be employed as substantives or as adjectives. Whether the things computed are potatoes or marbles or rosary beads the effective teaching and efficient learning of multiplication, division, subtraction, and addition remain unimpaired by the use of sacral illustrations. Arithmetic is not thereby transformed from a natural science to a theological science *nor does it as a natural science require the exclusion* of sacral illustrations. While spelling reaches out to all words, sacral and secular terms, the range of employment of sacral illustrations in arithmetic poses at most a question of intellectual temperance, restraint, balance, common sense.

There are, however, natural sciences where referrals to religious dogmas and morals, whether of reason or of revelational theology, may not be entirely excluded because they are patently relevant questions and they will unavoidably arise in class with direct reference to the subject matter. For example, in biology, the natural science of organic life, vegetable, animal, and human, the question of the ultimate origin of life may properly arise. The biology teacher in public schools as well as in church-related schools is faced with a choice. Either rule out the question or give an answer which is either theistic or nontheistic. The fact that some textbooks do not touch upon the question does not preclude it from the minds of the interrogating students. Whether or not the answer given in a public school classroom may be an affront to the religious conscience of some of the students is a problem that does not obtain in church-related schools.

Biology textbooks used in public schools make the dutiful distinction between voluntary and involuntary muscles. There is, however, generally no mention of free will and moral responsibility despite the discussion at times of the manner of change from a "bad habit" to a "good habit." The text simply notes that one habituation is reversible by the opposite habituation. There is an obvious restraint from mentioning freedom of choice and personal moral responsibility and hardly any explanation of what differentiates a "bad" habit from a "good" habit. Whether intentional or not a subtle form of naturalistic behaviorism pervades the public school textbooks. In church-related schools there is a frontal approach to these questions and the answers given constitute no concealed threat to the religious conscience of the studies. A natural science like arithmetic could refrain entirely from sacral illustrations without the subject matter or the student being the worse for it. But biology teaching and textbooks cannot block out completely from the minds of students in public and church-related schools all questions of religion and morality which are properly stirred by some lessons of the subject matter. In biology there are a number of points of study where the secular and religious aspects of a natural science are intertwined. There is some persistent talk among enlightened educators of the need for sensible sex instruction. At least, the instructions given in church-related schools on the morality of the use of sex faculties is in accordance with the religious conscience of the students and their parents.

There are subjects of study in the curriculum of public schools and church-related schools where the degree of religious permeability is such that it could not be disengaged without mutilating the subject matter itself. So many of the classic masterpeices and lesser works in sculpture, painting, architecture, and music give expression to a religious theme. If with Plato and other eminent educators we insist that schooling should include esthetics, then should Handel's *Messiah,* illustrations of world-renowned cathedrals and basilicas with their crucifixes and statues, and the prints of Michelangelo, Raphael, and many others be banned from schooling in order to satisfy constitutional eligibility for federal assistance? One could correctly reply that these are objects of study but let us note that with every gratifying appreciation of a religious work of art of undeniable beauty some attraction is experienced. That these questions are not raised to embarrass unduly a common-sense approach to the arts may be illustrated by the protests of the plaintiff in the Maryland Bible case which included among its complaints an illustration of the head of Christ by Velasquez in one of the public school textbooks.

The secular subjects in which religious factors are so much in evidence and so intimately intertwined with the subject matter as to constitute an integral part of it are literature and history. Many literary classics, poetry, drama, epics, essays, and novels have a religious story or are expressive of religious and moral values. Would the reading of selected excerpts from these classics entail a legal disability? History, above all, a uniquely secular study, is most permeated with religious facts and influences whose presentation cannot but entail religious interpretations, prepossessions, and loyalties. Surely history must be numbered among the necessary studies; and of all the subjects history is least capable of being expurgated of religious data without serious mutilation. Western history can scarcely avoid the advent of Christianity, the Crusades, the Inquisition, the Reformation, religious wars. In American history many of our basic national and organic documents are solemnly vibrant with religious professions and dedications.

The late Mr. Justice Jackson in his concurring opinion warned at some length those who might be encouraged by the court's ruling in *McCollum* to hope with the plaintiff for the insulation of every secular study from every religious connotation.

While we may and should end such formal and explicit instruction as the Champaign plan and at all times prohibit the teaching of creed and catechism and ceremonial and can forbid forthright proselytizing in the schools, I think it remains to be demonstrated whether it is possible, even if desirable, to comply with such demands as plaintiff's completely to isolate and cast out of secular education all that some people may reasonably regard as religious instruction. Perhaps subjects such as mathematics, physics, or chemistry are, or can be, completely secularized. But it would not seem practical to teach either practice or appreciation of the arts if we are to forbid exposure of youth to any religious influences. Music without sacred music, architecture minus the cathedral, or painting without the scriptural themes would be eccentric and incomplete, even from a secular point of view. Yet the inspirational appeal of religion in these guises is often stronger than in a forthright sermon. Even such a "science" as biology raises the issue between evolution and creation as an explanation of our presence on this planet. Certainly a course in English literature that omitted the Bible and other powerful uses of our mother tongue for religious ends would be pretty barren. And I should suppose it is a proper, if not an indispensable, part of preparation for a worldly life to know the roles that religion and religions have played in the tragic story of mankind. The fact is that, for good or ill, nearly everything in our culture worth transmitting, everything which gives meaning to life, is saturated with religious influences, derived from paganism, Judaism, Christianity — both Catholic and Protestant — and other faiths accepted by a large part of the world's peoples. One can hardly respect a system of education that would leave the student wholly ignorant of the currents of religious thought that move the world society for a part in which he is being prepared.

But how can one teach, with satisfaction or even with justice *to all faiths* (italics mine), such subjects as the story of the Reformation, the Inquisition, or even the New England effort to found "a Church without a Bishop and a State without a

King," is more than I know. It is too much to expect that mortals will teach subjects about their contemporaries with the detachment they may summon to teaching about remote subjects such as Confucious or Mohammed. When instruction turns to proselytizing and imparting knowledge becomes evangelism is, except in the crudest cases, a subtle inquiry.

The task of separating the secular from the religious in education is one of magnitude, intricacy, and delicacy. To lay down sweeping constitutional doctrine as demanded by complainant and apparently approved by the court, applicable alike to all school boards of the nation, "to immediately adopt and enforce rules and regulations prohibiting all instruction in and teaching of religious education in all public schools," is to decree a uniform, rigid, and, if we are consistent, an unchanging standard for countless school boards representing and serving highly-localized groups which not only differ from each other but which themselves from time to time change attitudes. It seems to me that to do so is to allow zeal for our own ideas of what is good in public instruction to induce us to accept the role of a super board of education for every school district in the nation...."[11]

It is well to note that the late Justice Jackson was discussing the unavoidable religious implications of secular studies in the elementary and secondary public schools of the state. The problem arises from the moral implications of the secular studies themselves in varying degrees of involvement, from the tangential to the necessary and the unavoidable. Public schools are confronted with an almost insuperable task of avoiding any offense to the rights of conscience of all the students and of their parents. Because of the religious identity of creed of the children attending church-related schools, a solution is realized which at least has the merit of offending no religious conscience. It is, therefore, puzzling to understand why their pedagogy should thereby raise constitutional questions.

Lastly, however neutral some natural sciences may be in themselves, such as physics and chemistry, once the products of these natural sciences are put to human use, they immediately become invested with a moral and spiritual import. One need only note in the various communication media the debates current in the national and international level on the moral aspects of the use of nuclear weapons, contraceptives, abortion of defective foetuses, birth control information, etc. The likelihood that such moral-scientific questions would arise in infra-collegiate studies should be gauged by the all-pervasive impact of the communications media—newspapers, magazines, cinema, radio and television programs which almost compel youngsters to take notice of these serious adult controversies.

For better or for worse neutrality in the educational process is a myth. The conversion of this myth into a constitutional principle would seem to be an unwarranted distortion of the function of public law. The assumptions of the purely secular subject concept on which some testimonies before the House Hearings apparently rested the validity of the loan provision of Title III are *false in themselves.* The data of the study simply discloses what may have been reasonably expected: that the spiritual orientation in religious schools would be in conformity with credal confessions while the moral context of public school education would have to contend with the authentic challenge of religious pluralism.

Before proceeding to a review of LaNoue's construction of the religious permeation in parochial school studies, let us first observe parenthetically that direct financial aid to formal religious activity seems to afford no serious constitutional challenge outside of the area of education. Tax support of chaplains in the armed forces and in state and national legislatures continues with the approval of the legislative and executive branches of the American government, and some justices of the United States Supreme Court have given reassuring explanations that these practices are not threatened by the court ruling in recent decisions on prayer and Bible reading. It it is technically correct to hold that tax exemption for religious institutions and their nonprofit religious social and educational enterprises is not a direct formal participation in government funds, it most assuredly constitutes an enormous governmental encouragement for religious activities in a manner no less concrete for the vitality and expansion of the religious apostolate. There is an undoubted *religious preferment* in the tax-exemption laws which is clearly distinguishable from the social welfare functions and services of the churches which nonreligious agencies also perform. Even in the educational area, opposition for the most part is directed in the lower levels. The higher institutions of learning with religious profession and affiliation—colleges, professional schools, universities—receive government subsidies in a wide variety of ways whether they reach the institution directly by construction loans, or indirectly through the student and research projects on the broad basis of a public purpose or utility. We have not yet brought completely to the surface all the nonrational forces beneath the formally rationalized opposition which denies to the parochial schools the same legal distinctions of direct, indirect, incidental, consequential benefits, secular aspects and functions which are not begrudged the higher institutions of learning despite the interdependence of all these church-related schools for their student enrollment.

AN ANALYSIS OF LaNOUE'S STUDY

LaNoue observes at the start that there was remarkable silence on the part of some witnesses who testified before the House Hearings in behalf of parochial schools about the religious permeation of the school curriculum in general and in the science subjects covered by Section 305. This, he notes, is in marked contrast to the forthright statements of Pope Leo XIII and Pope Pius XI on education for Catholics. One should seriously pause before suggesting that silence about an obvious broad fact known and easily knowledgeable to anyone was a calculated omission. Parochial schools are open for inspection by the state educational authorities and we may safely surmise that on occasion they have been visited by the appropriate officials. The textbooks used in parochial schools are not a guarded secret. The presence of religious garb, religious symbols, and of course, a uniformity of religious confession are factors which just do not evanesce as students go from one subject matter to another. It is simply that Catholics hold to the indefectability of secular aspects and functions of science studies in an integrated educational process which culminates for them in the primacy of religious ultimates. This philosophy of education has an ancient tradition reaching back even to Plato and it is still advocated in many reputable institutions of learning outside the Catholic Church. To talk of the religious pervasiveness of studies in parochial schools may be for many of us a pointless belaboring of the obvious.

LaNoue observes that the term "sciences" is nowhere precisely defined in the N.D.E.A. He assumes it is more likely that it refers to the natural sciences more than to the social sciences. He notes too there are borderline studies such as geography, physiology, and experimental psychology which would defy exclusive classification. Be that as it may, he intends to show that "even into subjects which are undeniably scientific, parochial schools inject a considerable amount of religious interpretation and even some sectarian doctrine."[12] By a rhetorical use of the verb "inject" he seems to suggest a forceable intrusion of religious considerations which are wholly alien to a science study. He finds that at the elementary school level most of the religion in textbooks is generally a simple theism. This is expressed in a variety of ways, use of religious symbols, scriptural quotations, and by repeated reference to God as creator. The theistic theme is specifically Christian in its view of the ultimate ends of man. Children are reminded in the textbooks that they are accountable to their Creator for the use they make of their bodies and souls. Children are given an integrated perspective of the harmonious relationship of religion and science, of the interdependence of creatures, of the orders of nature and grace, and of the personal responsibility they have as stewards of God's creatures. In a word, they are taught of the holiness of everything, and a veneration and grateful use of things of this earth.[13]

One need not apologize for teaching elementary school children a reverential regard for everything about them—by stressing the "importance of everything God made," "even the tiniest creatures"— much less admit to a legal disability for *inculcating a motive of conscience* for that responsibility and disciplined conduct that are so necessary for the proper behavior of energetic youngsters in a community. It is the task of all schooling, state and independent, to do this. To provide in addition *religious* reasons for that correct conduct on which the good order of the local community must rely would certainly seem to foster with greater moral strength the inculcation of the civic virtues. There is evidence to suppose that the Founding Fathers of our Republic welcomed religious motivation as an ally of public welfare. As for the purely theistic references as distinct from Christian theism, a great many of our national basic and organic documents are "permeated" with belief in and dependence upon Almighty God for the well-being of the nation: the Declaration of Independence, the preambles of our state constitutions, Presidential addresses and proclamations. LaNoue may correctly respond that these are not science treatises but what is to the *legal* point is that they are or may be subject matter of study at tax-supported public schools.

In Catholic parochial schools, a Christian motivation, that is, a compelling motive of conscience is provided for social conduct.

> In the pursuit of Catholic Action the spiritual and corporal works of mercy are the guide; in the pursuit of conservation the proper use of soil, water, minerals, forests and wildlife is the guide.[14]

Such teaching may prove to be more effective guidance than say, the posters in our city conveyances which depict "Papa Bear, Mamma Bear, and Baby Bear," begging us not to set the woodlands on fire while picnicking. Christianity is not behaviorism. Our sluggish natures need to be prodded as much from within our consciences as from without through fear of the law. Which of the motivations, religious or nonreligious, may prove to be the controlling factor in every instance of the actions of youngsters may be a matter of speculation. The law does expect that some motivation be inculcated in our school children for proper civic conduct. There is no reason to suppose that in view of the good effect intended it chooses between the religious and nonreligious. No value deleterious to society is being taught, no harm to our neighbors urged, nor any waste of natural resources encouraged by relating good conduct to a theistic creed. Intellectual temperance should counsel against unnecessary frequency or forced insertions. But surely there is nothing in the passages quoted, which relate human use of natural resources to a religious responsibility, that is against the national interest, that is bad pedagogy, or much less defeats the general and specific purposes of a publicly accredited education. To base civic conduct, that is warranted by the communal good, on a religious motivation might on the contrary be reasonably construed as a public service by religion rather than as a sectarian private interest liable to legal disabilities.

We cannot too strongly stress the high moral significance and imperative need in our times to call upon all the spiritual resources of the nation to eradicate the deep-rooted racial antipathies and animosities which are disturbing our society to its foundations. Let us consider, for example, the widely blazoned exhortation everywhere in public places for "brotherhood." Now, the wondering child may ask in perfect innocence, why is another person of a different color, of diverse ethnic origin, or another religious faith (or no faith) my brother? Children, of course, like adults are moved by a genuine *feeling* to give to the needy, even to those in faraway lands. But why are we brothers? Biologically we are all of the same species, at least by definition, but physical similtude varies amongst Caucasians, Orientals, Africans, Latins, Saxons, Nordics.

Apart from mixed racial marriages, a degree of affinity however thin and distant could not be postulated without supposing the unity of the human race and this reason and science unaided by divine teaching cannot establish categorically. Now for the Catholic, the brotherhood of men rests on revelational theology — that man was created in the image of God — on the unity of the human race, on the fall of man, on the redemption of mankind by the Incarnate Word, and on mankind's adoption by grace as children of God, the Father. Within the terms of these theological truths the Christian may be ready to hold that absolute and imperishable value of every human person whose sacredness may not be rightly disregarded by any power on earth: that every individual by virtue of his eternal destiny is at the core somewhat holy — touched by God, as it were, in the creation of his whole being, in the immortality of his soul, and by the special divine providence with which he is always surrounded. Freedom may enlarge the human capacity for equality and widen the prospects of mutual understanding and tolerance, but freedom and equality will not bring about fraternity. For this we must rise above our own devices to the spiritual bond with which we have been divinely united. Now other believers and nonbelievers may have their explanation for human brotherhood. What is not clear is whether LaNoue objects to these implied questions being raised at all or whether he objects to the *Catholic* or to any answer, or rather would insist that all the variety of answers be given to the youngsters in elementary and secondary schools. What unfortunately he seems to take no cognizance of in pointing to a sectarian — meaning a private religious interest — is that these teachings are ordained to make their contribution, along with other tenets alien to them, to the common good. He has not understood that the public welfare has many diverse spiritual tributaries. His concept of "sectarianism" is radically defective. The presence of a private desire and interest is not *eo ipso* to be opposed to a public need. Values to be gained by religious teaching are not merely private, and reasonable men and men of law can judge whether a faith has social significance. We would suppose that Christianity had long ago been acknowledged as the foundation of Western civilization even with full regard to the religious animosities of misguided Christians at variance with one another.

There have not been wanting eminent educators and jurists in our country who have stressed the need of public schools to teach the religious foundations (which have traditionally been affirmed since the Founding Fathers) of our American democracy. No less eminent a constitutional authority than the late Dr. Corwin has written:

> Primarily democracy is a system of ethical values, and that this system of value so far as the American people are concerned is grounded in religion will not be denied by anybody who knows the historical record. And that agencies by which this system of values has been transmitted in the past from generation to generation, the family, the neighborhood, the Church, have today become much impaired, will not be seriously questioned by anybody who knows anything about contemporary condition. But what this all adds up to is that the work of transmission has been put more and more upon the shoulders of the public schools. Can they then do the job without the assistance of religious instruction? At least, there seems to be a widely-held opinion to the contrary.[15]

Let us bear in mind that here the relevance of religious values to American Democracy is stressed in relation to *sectarian* religious instructions during a school hour in a public school classroom, which the Court disallowed in *McCollum*. And those who insist on released time programs for *sectarian* religious instruction *during* a school hour off public school property (a position sustained by the Supreme Court in *Zorach*) do so in order to stress the *nexus of religious instruction,* albeit sectarian, *to a public school education.* When then parochial schools include formal sectarian religious instruction in their general curriculum they are fulfilling one of the avowed educational purposes for sectarian instruction in a released program *during* a school hour, as well as serving their broader religious aspostolate as well. Further, there is an area of concordance between the general consensus, known as the religious heritage of America – tangibly discernible in our national historic documents – and what is taught in parochial schools. And what is in addition, specifically Catholic dogmas, give no evidence whatever of being adverse to the national interest, and there is much in them that fosters the fervent patriotism which has characterized these schools.

Christianity is not behaviorism: *Credo* means I believe. The charity that should distinguish the Christian will not ensue without deliberate personal effort and repeated spiritual exercise. To call forth this effort against the instincts of selfishness may require a strong doctrinal formation of the young conscience. Failure to live up to the ideals of the Christian faith for the benefit of society can be better remedied by an environment and schooling which integrate the educational process and infuse it with the high vocation of Christian dedication. A nontheistic humanitarian wonderfully generous in his daily living may be edified but not awed by Christ's warning: "Whatever you do to the least of mine, you do unto me." And if Catholics are to check their prejudice and bias they shall need more than their own instincts of generosity to urge them on to overcome deep-rooted social and moral infirmities. Whatever nonbelievers and non-Christians may consider to be "the way, the truth, and the life," Catholics are convinced that they can better serve their country as practicing Catholics. The religious orientation of parochial schools *is intended for the benefit of society* as well as for personal sanctification. "By their fruits shall you know them." This evangelical counsel might be profitably applied even by the law to the beneficent consequences of religious pluralism in America. It is not. to be sure, an equality of religious doctrine or an unconcern with dogmatic differences. Rather, with the passage of time, we have become the wiser and have succeeded in eliminating intercredal frictions and intolerances to a remarkable degree. More than that, we have come to acknowledge that each faith, firm in its own creed, can contribute from its own religious resources as so many diverse spiritual tributaries to the well-being of our country. LaNoue has entirely missed the full merits of religious life in schooling in confrontation with American public law and order. He has construed too narrowly sectarianism as a private interest in complete separation from the public interest *which depends upon it.*

If to be constitutionally eligible for federal aid, pedagogy were required to be stripped of all theistic reference and motivation, the resultant educational process might be not only a moral and legal affront to the religious conscience of the students but also a subtle assault upon the spiritual foundations of the nation. By subtraction if not by an openly formal instruction we would have a behaviorist psychology which through calculated omission might instill an apathetic amoralism in a youthful period of life when instincts and passions are most unruly. It is high time to recognize the moral role of religion in schooling for the public interest. The religious neutrality of public schools is not a good which is incidental to their educational process but rather a constraint which religious pluralism forces upon them.

At the high school level, religious doctrine is most prominent in the science textbooks when creation and evolution are discussed. This, we are told, follows upon a Catholic philosophical perspective which holds to the mutual compatability of science and religion because all verities — Catholic parochial school children are taught — originate in God. But this is an ancient inheritance. Long before Christianity the Psalmist had sung of God, Lord of all learning: *Deus, Dominus omnium scientiarum,* And through the centuries men not of the Catholic faith have held to this profound conviction. The point LaNoue is making is that the referred to compatibility between religion and science is that between the Catholic creed and the science teachings which Catholics hold.

It seems then that LaNoue is not questioning the propriety of discussing creation and evolutionary theory in science courses. The origin of life would be an obvious, albeit profound, question in biology — whether in its primal origination it was initiated by a divine creative act or by an eternal evolving mass of energy which at first generated the lower forms of life from which the higher forms emerge with the roll of centuries. What LaNoue raises as a basis for constitutional issue is that:

> certain interpretations given to the student are held uniquely by Catholics, or, at least, by Christians; and the context of the material is all Catholic. . . . Subjects like birth control, sterilization, and euthanasia are usually mentioned only in terms of the Church's judgements.[16]

What is not clear is what precisely generates the constitutional issue, whether the questions ought not to arise, whether they should be blacked-out or completely ignored, or whether, if an answer is given, that it is only the Catholic answer, or, which is more likely, whether not all the "answers" are given. If the latter then of course, the criticism ought to be directed toward every textbook in public schools as well. But just how comprehensive a sampling, and then, I suppose how fair and impartial the presentation of each position would have to be to make it acceptable for the lower levels of education may task the most earnest of pedagogues. These questions do arise not only from the very nature of the subject matter but also from the wide publicity given by the communication media to public discussion of deformed babies, abortion, and sterilization laws, use of contraceptives, etc., that can scarcely escape the attention of school youngsters. At least the answers given in parochial schools have the merit of being in conformity with the religious confession. No one can vouch with equal assurance that the answers given in public schools, however euphemistically expressed, may not be a subtle attack upon the religious conscience of the students. Surely if Darwin's evolution can have its day in class and in court, then too may creationist evolution fare with equal favor.

LaNoue quotes as an example of integration of religion and science: "...dependence on Divine Providence builds up healthy mental outlooks," and, "Prayer and the grace of God are powerful aids in overcoming bad habits." In public school biology testbooks we do find a dutiful distinction between voluntary and involuntary muscles and a remarkable restraint from mentioning free will and moral responsibility. At times there is mention of bad habits and good habits, and that one can change habits by a contrary habituation. What constitutes a "bad" or "good" habit is left undefined. Whether this adds up to a shallow behaviorist psychology, to a sterile noncommital moralism is a matter of serious conjecture. We are inclined to suppose that it is *the* knotty problem of religious pluralism, and in recent times, that it is the objections of the absolute dissenter which have withdrawn from public schooling any of the religious-moral answers that have their justifiable place in church-related schools. It is not the supposed ideal of neutral education that has immunized public schooling from religious-moral value judgments but rather an unresolved problematic. The absence of this problematic in church-related schools should not be turned to their disadvantage. One may note here that no legal disqualification for federal financial assistance is incurred under the Hill-Burton Act by church-affiliated hospitals which enforce a moral code of permissible surgeries.

LaNoue points to the cultural concentration in some elementary textbooks in geography on the Catholics contributions to Western civilization and culture.[17] For example, viewing the popes as patrons of science, noting the Catholic faith of a scientist, emphasizing Catholic features in various countries while passing over in silence the contributions of other faiths and churches. Here we should rather hope that LaNoue were making a good case for counseling intellecual temperance and for a comprehensive perspective, rather than rising apparently more evidence for the unconstitutionality of federal loans for science teaching. The question rightly framed is one of pedagogy not of law. However, difficult, the task of a balanced presentation which takes appreciative cognizance of all agencies for good living among men should be the overriding concern of all textbook writers. Moreover, one can sympathize with this Catholic cultural stance. Among the less enlightened and even in public school textbooks until as recently as the first World War, the Church directly or indirectly was pictured as an obscurantist, parochial society. Public school textbooks were wont to begin American history with the landing of the Pilgrims with scarcely any proportionate recognition of the Italian, Spanish, French Catholic discoverers, explorers, and missionaries who surely were among the first and principal settlers, and who helped open the new world to the old. On matters of religious intolerance and persecution in European and American history the weight was decidedly cast against the Church of Rome, despite the highly creditable record of Catholics from the Toleration Act of Lord Baltimore, and the consistent profession of Constitutional church-state relations by the Catholic hierarchy. In any public discussion of the two traditions of church-state relations, the major tradition which grants a preferred status in law to "true" religion and the minor one, which confers equality before the law, the preferred status position is more often than not identified with Catholics, despite the consistent disavowals of the Catholic hierarchy since the days of John Carroll. Yet both traditions have been supported by the other major faiths: Protestant (in Sweden today and in American society almost down to the Civil War), and Jewish Orthodox (State of Israel). Time was when the gallantry of the Anglo-Saxon Protestant adventurers shone in sharp contrast to the dark sinister Latin Catholic courtiers who were doing much the same thing: a contrast which even Hollywood enjoyed perpetuating. The criminal character was customarily, of course, an Oriental or a Latin. Clerics were identified with the Inquisition, that is to say the Spanish Inquisition, not the English High Court of Commission, or the other Protestant agencies of religious suppression and torture in Europe and colonial America. With time, and from mixed motives, public school textbooks have become responsive to Catholic protest, and Hollywood has in fact produced pictures of Catholic religious life of great popular attraction.

It is true one imbalance does not redress another, although it does bring about a change of sentiment. But when a people have been on the receiving end of a sustained, calculated campaign of professionally organized nativitism, portrayed as un-Americans or as suspect Americans, their churches, convents, and schools burned, their loyalty questioned despite a proud boast of American citizenship, enormous sacrifices in war, and a wide participation in public service and community life, then, partisan enthusiasm is easily understandable. LaNoue may recall that even on the higher levels of learning as recently as the first World War, scholars and historians were still referred to as Protestant and Catholic to designate the direction of their favorable prejudices and their adverse bias. Learning and scholarship was, openly or not, committed to an apologetic purpose. Persevering endeavors at intercredal dialogue have lessened much of this partisan championship of historic causes and brought about the brightest prospects of cooperative intellectual enterprises.

There will always be room for balanced writing of elementary and secondary school textbooks for private and public schools. Today voices are being raised for a fair and proportionate accounting in textbooks of the contributions to the American community by ethnic and racial minorities which have been completely neglected thus far. LaNoue's study on cultural and religious emphasis should stir serious thought in the direction of a truly *catholic* presentation. What is needed is not the obnoxious balancing of interest, but a balanced perspective correspondent with the broad sweep of history. LaNoue has posed an authentic problem which may prove highly troubling and overwhelming to resolve. But it is essentially and entirely a pedagogic problem better left to educators and scholars. Constitutional law and the judiciary have neither the jurisdiction nor the competence to serve as a national board of education. Would it be constitutionally eligible to narrate that Marquette paddled his canoe up and down the Mississippi and unconstitutional (for federal aid) to teach he went about preaching Christianity, baptizing and administering the sacraments of the Catholic Church? A religious fact is no less a fact of history than, say, Washington crossing the Delaware.

Perhaps subjects such as mathematics, physics, or chemistry[18] are, or can be, completely secularized. Religious facts, factors, and influences are so much a part of history, that they could not possibly be exorcised without maiming the subject matter. They are so prominent in esthetics that to concentrate on secular works of art is to study esthetics inadequately. And religious-moral value judgments and spiritual conflict cannot be completely banned from literature without deforming human experience. The science of biology, whenever it touches upon human action, however physical, cannot disengage itself from the spiritual dimension. Apart then from the products of mathematics, physics, chemistry, and engineering which raise at times inescapable moral questions when these products are put to human use or destruction—e.g., the hydrogen bomb and nuclear weapons—these natural sciences do not immediately, and certainly on elementary and secondary levels of education do not readily warrant any religious reference. The use of sacral illustrations in adding, subtracting, multiplying may be in bad taste or good taste but it certainly is not required by any degree of relevance (that we have seen in other subjects) by the subject matter itself. The reason is that numerals may be studied as substantives, 4 added to 3, or as adjectives, 4 potatoes plus 3 onions.

At best LaNoue has raised a question of intellectual temperance and I for one am inclined to believe that the use of sacral illustrations in mathematics is more likely to instill an aversion for religious reference, even in the minds of youngsters, than to foster religion itself. But the point remains that the use of sacral illustrations whether in good or bad taste, temperately or intemperately, does not raise a constitutional issue of eligibility for federal assistance in the study of these subjects. Only one question is all-controlling. Does the use of sacral illustrations in mathematics obstruct proficiency in the teaching and learning of the subject? Whether we add, multiply, divide, or subtract potatoes, marbles, or rosary beads, the question of the proficiency of learning mathematics remains, in my opinion, completely unaffected and this is and can be established, if needs be, by "secular" tests, that is by tests, entirely devoid of any sacral illustrations. But there is no legal point involved. I submit it is entirely beyond legal jurisdiction and competence. For example, would constitutional eligibility for federal assistance remain inviolate for computing, given the dimensions, the cubic feet of the United States House of Representatives and unconstitutional, to measure the cubic feet of the Immaculate Conception Shrine in Washington, D.C.? Would constitutional eligibility for government aid allow computing how long it would take to drive, given the road distance and car speed, from Washington's home in Mt. Vernon to the White House, and disallow computing the distance, given the road mileage and car speed, from St. Peter's Basilica to the Immaculate Conception Shrine at Lourdes? If in both instances, mathematics is learned whether the illustrations are religious or nonreligious, the purpose set down by Congress in Section 305 of Title III of the N.D.E.A. is truly and fully achieved. The insertion of law to determine constitutionally permissible illustrations in mathematics would be a grotesque and foolish function of law. Sacral illustrations do not convert mathematics into a sacral subject matter nor transform its purpose into a religious one. This is no more true than that muscular development through athletic exercises is in any way deflected from its natural course because the players bless themselves before the game, or before plunging into the swimming pool, or at the start of a relay race. At best LaNoue has raised a question of intellectual temperance which deserves to be heeded, and it is not improbable that his criticism may have already suggested corrections.

The teaching of modern languages[19] entails the teaching of grammar rules, spelling, and sentence structure. Here too the efficency with which these exercises are taught and mastered by the students remains unaffected by the cultural and religious emphasis that may be found in some textbooks. Whether one learns to translate into French "the cow jumps over the moon," or "St. Francis of Assisi spoke to the birds and the fishes," all these words are part of an language, and we have no reason to suppose in the absence of attested evidence that the modern language in parochial schools is being taught in such a way as not to prepare the students for the reading of literature without or with any cultural emphasis or religious theme.

In the expectation that "English is almost a certainty to be the first extension if the National Defense Education Act is expanded,"[20] LaNoue discusses the integration of religion in the study of the English language and literature in some parochial school textbooks. Now it seems to me that here LaNoue is belaboring the obvious. Langauge study whether foreign or domestic has among its classic works religious themes. Here too intellectual temperance and pedagogic prudence would counsel proportionate measure of literary exercise in religious and nonreligious themes. But it is difficult to see how the study, say, of sections from Francis Thompson's "Hound of Heaven," or excerpts from Chesterton and Belloc, Robert Southwell's "Burning Babe," classic translations of the canticles of St. Francis of Assi, of Dante's *Divine Comedy*, Milton's *Paradise Lost*, and any number of classic literary works with a religious theme in

English and foreign modern languages can be in less legal favor for federal loan assistance than, say, the study of Longfellow's "Evangeline," and "Hiawatha," selections from Blake, Wordsworth, Hemingway, or Steinbeck. What should be matter of consideration is not whether there is evidence of sacral themes studied in literature but rather whether there is such an excessive emphasis on them as to deprive students of acquaintance with the literary studies that are expected of a well-informed and properly educated elementary and secondary student. It is not so much the presence of the religious literary studies as the absence of nonreligious literature from the curriculum that should stir constructive cirticisms. At no time does LaNoue suggest that students in parochial schools are being kept in the dark about such literary studies as a well-rounded curriculum would require. On such a score a legal argument against aid to a schooling which state educational authorities found defective would hardly be contested.

One cannot argue for academic freedom on the one hand and on the other require the exclusion of religious themes in English and modern language studies in order to qualify for federal educational aid.

LaNoue tells us[21] that his study has concentrated on the integration of religion in Catholic science, mathematics, and language textbooks, first, because the Catholic parochial schools constitute by far the larger part of church-related schools and, second, because the church-related schools of other Christian or of Jewish faiths are opposed to "accepting public money for their schools on constitutional and policy grounds." This seems to me to avoid the question of law. Law does not require anyone to apply for government assistance. The question is whether the secular aspects and secular functions of formally nonreligious studies, the sciences and modern languages which congressional legislation offers to assist, can be realized in a Christian integration of learning. Further, the second consideration is whether Catholic parochial schools which enroll ninety-one per cent of all non-public school students, and one-sixth of the nations school children, are not such a significant part of national education that an exclusion of them from government assistance works to cross-purposes with the congressional intent to promote the knowledge of the sciences and languages among the students of America. Whether or not many Protestant and some Jewish organizations choose to receive government assistance may be likened to some extent to the action of Baptists who will apply "on principle" for loans and not for grants under the Hill-Burton Act for their church-affiliated hospitals.

Integration of religion in the science subjects of Protestant church-related schools is openly professed by their textbooks:

> A Lutheran elementary schoolteacher will insist that all areas of the curriculum reflect an adequate philosophy of Christian education. Thus he will select content and provide experiences that are consistent with such a philosophy.... Moreover, the Lutheran elementary schoolteacher will constantly search for materials that can be correlated with basic texts and that enable him to emphasize more fully a Christian point of view.

A very interesting comparison is the manner in which mathematics and religion are integrated by Catholic and Protestant textbooks. On the basis of the data which LaNoue provides, we saw that the manner in which Catholic textbooks integrated religion with mathematics was through the use of sacral illustrations. In a text published for use in schools established under the auspices of the Christian Reformed Church there is a far more intimate integration of religion and mathematics. We excerpt from two pages:

> Ideas of quantities and exact relationships have their source in God. God apparently used what in our language is called higher mathematics to plan the course of the stars, etc.

Repeatedly in successive statements mathematics is said to be part of God's revelation, part of the pattern of truth, and the study of it will "instill in the student a sense of wonder for the orderliness and beauty of God's creation as interpreted by mathematics."

Passages of the science textbooks used by the Seventh Day Adventists disclose a total integration of perhaps even a greater degree than in other church schools. They integrate, natural and social sciences, their theological tenets with the subject matter, relating all phenomenon, all human values and behavior to their Biblical construction. While LaNoue is careful to advise us that most Protestants object to federal aid (without mentioning the Orthodox Jews who are in favor of it) he seems to overlook the profound significance of the religious permeation of Protestant parochial schools, namely, that these confessions consider the state schools not sufficiently adequate to prepare their faithful morally and spiritually in those obligations that should rule their conscience in their private and community lives. In other words, they feel that the tax-supported state schools do not—perhaps because of the enormous difficulties—provide an educational process which has due regard for religious liberty in education. Further, while these Protestant groups may oppose federal aid to church-related schools, they would not, I am sure, allow the criticism that they are not fulfilling the requirements set down by the state educational agencies or that they are preparing their students less competently for their civic duties, or for further studies in other educational institutions. I do not suppose they would allow without angry challenge that in teaching the science and language subjects they are not achieving the secular aspects and functions of these studies even within the religious perspective of their textbooks.

It may be that the opposition of some Protestants to federal aid for parochial schools is re-enforced by the fact that the economic demands upon the financial resources of their faithful for the support of their church schools is relatively speaking not the great burden that the high percentage of Catholic parochial school children imposes upon the Catholic faithful. And it may also be that Catholics (together with some eminent non-Catholic constitutional jurists) hold not only that the extension of government subsidies to their school children is constitutionally permissible but also sound public policy. Undoubtedly an enormous federal aid program which excludes them would place them at greater economic disadvantage. Whether or not in the unreal hypothesis of financial self-sufficiency to cope with all their educational needs on a parity with state schools in the national interest, Catholics would still ask for federal aid, is a judgment they would surely make without disowning the constitutionality of such subvention. We see nothing in constitutional law which should place disabling consequences upon church-related schools—Catholic, Protestant, and Jewish Orthodox—for insisting upon a religious integration of the school curriculum, if it can be attested by existing devices or other means to be contrived that the secular studies in these schools are proficiently taught. And in the minds of many educators, secular studies as distinguishable from theological studies, are enhanced by religious permeation, rather than obstructed, are suffused with divine purposes and designs, and do provide a totality and coherence of moral and intellectual experience that can only offer helps to the manifold passions and volitional struggles which are the lot of everyone, and more so of the young. The young need more not less moral motivation and inspiration. The national government should welcome any educational process that may further not only its national-defense-through-education program but also the cultural and spiritual life upon whose vitality it must ultimately rely for the efficiency of its laws. Aristotle has said that a stone obeys laws and men form habits. Our governments, federal and state, it may be safely assumed, expect the cultivation of civic virtues in the elementary and secondary schools. The law *does not say* upon which motives of conscience the obligations to society must be founded. Least of all, may it prejudice the theistic or Christian or Judaic conscience in comparison with, say, ethical culture or humanism or some other ultimate commitment.

THE JUDGE AND THE SCHOOLMASTER

Unwittingly or not, LaNoue has stirred up more important questions for study than he has answered. And for the issues which he has chosen for his immediate attention, he has not gone to the roots. An extraordinary opportunity offered itself to him for a truly *catholic* study—the spiritual nature of the educational process, the degree to which various secular studies may entail religious consideration, the indefectibility of secular aspects and functions of the nontheological studies as taught in the parochial schools to the extent that the national interest requires, the common utility of these science and language studies, for an equality of religious liberty in education, and, let us say it, academic freedom about which so much more is heard in higher than in lower education. Academic freedom is more readily identified with the dissenter's freedom of choice than with the conformist's who for some strange psychological quirk is thought to be less reputable intellectually for being in agreement. But above all LaNoue has failed in his catholicity to inquire into the spiritual content of the textbooks used in tax-supported schools. There is one factor in the educational process, and at that, the principal one, which LaNoue took no cognizance of—the schoolteacher. If a scissor-and-paste job could purge parochial school textbooks of all the religious referrals in order to qualify for federal aid, how would LaNoue control the presentation, the moral and intellectual influence of the schoolteacher in any classroom of state or private schools? Neutrality in education has never been more than a hypothesis upon which constitutional reasoning can depend only too precariously.

Apart from LaNoue's failure to be truly *catholic* in his study, he has perhaps unknowingly initiated legal discourse, without setting down the ultimate grounds of relevance. The point I wish to make is that the court has neither the primary competence nor the jurisdiction to determine what should be constitutionally acceptable pedagogy. Apart from the incontrovertible right of local educational authorities to subject to examination the proficiency of teaching and learning in any publicly accredited school, the courts have not a primary competency in education except to review a possible *legal* challenge to the cancellation of such accreditation. What is or is not required in publicly accredited educations seems to be the function and obligation of educators not of jurists *qua* jurists. The court may take cognizance of the legal challenge before the bench to review the action of state educational officials in withdrawing an accreditation, and adjudicate whether such action was arbitrary or not. The distracting factor in these considerations is the hypothesis of "neutrality" which is supposed to prevail in public schools. As we have repeatedly insisted, neutrality in public schools is a necessitous course dictated by the conflicting claims of conscience; it is a negative retreat, not a positive affirmation of an ideal educational process. In its ultimate resultant it fails to satisfy the positive requirements of the religious conscience which finds itself a captive attendant by virtue of state compulsory school attendance laws and of its inability to afford a privately financed education in parochial schools. If the public school is striving earnestly for neutrality without hostility it cannot be said it has attained beyond question impartial neutrality.

But what of the court's competence and jurisdiction to pass upon parochial schooling for the benefit of federal aid. Would it be constitutional to tell the secular facts of Columbus' voyage to the New World, the intrigues at the Spanish court, his difficulties with the crew, and so on—but constitutionally disabling for federal aid to give at appreciable length excerpts from his writing so profuse with religious confession. Trinitarian and Christological, as the principal sustaining spiritual force behind his perseverance against discouraging odds. Why should creationist evolution in a biology course find less favor than non-creationist evolution?

What norms of constitutional interpretation would allow that the

"Ode on a Grecian Urn" should have more claim to federal aid than St. Francis' "Canticle to the Sun"? Would a selection of the religious professions in our American national documents and in the official utterances of our Presidents since the days of George Washington be less in legal favor than say a complete or relative silence about them, beyond the dutiful reading of the Declaration of Independence, without comment upon and without explanation of the religious premises of the document? Examples can be reasonably multiplied to the point of absurdity. When is emphasis without bias, silence without prejudice, omission without disparagement? We cannot expect the United States Supreme Court to review these questions as issues of law without conferring upon it the competence and jurisdiction of a national school board, which by law it does not have. Ethical culturists, secular humanists, and the educational "neutralists" are no less committed to a principle of integration for a school curriculum than the advocates of a religiously oriented educational process. None of these deny that value judgments and civic virtues should be taught to our students in our public schools. The court has neither the competence and jurisdiction to choose between one spiritual principle of integration and another. It has the competence and jurisdiction to ascertain that whatever spiritual principle of integration is employed, it should be conducive to good civic living. The law can inquire whether an educational process subserves a public good, fulfills a public function, and contributes to the public interest if it is to merit official public approval and share in its benefits. If the law knows no orthodoxy and no heresy, it is not unconcerned about orthodoxy and heresy. A number of court decisions, federal and state, attest to a public morality which no orthodoxy or heresy may violate. It is here that the educational "neutralists" engage in a pious deception. By all means, they insist, let there be religious liberty in education; and indeed they will admit to much good in parochial schools. But they insist too on identifying sectarian schools as private interests unrelated to a public interest. The supposition that the constitutional distinction between private and public interests will allow the public interest to be served by a private agency provided the primary public purpose is fulfilled even to a consequent benefit to the private agency is attested to by many federal subsidies of industrial, commercial, and agricultural enterprises for the national interest. So too, in *Everson*, Justice Black, in the opinion of the court, admitted that "to help parents get their children to school, regardless of their religion, safely and expeditiously to and from accredited schools" undoubtedly brought some incidental benefit to the church school. And similarly in the earlier *Cochran* case: "Individual interests are aided only as the common interest is safeguarded." It seems to be that this compatibility-of-interest doctrine while sufficient to sustain private performance of public services with the help of government funds (whether in hospital or social welfare work, in state provision of textbooks for school children, and in bus transportation of school children at public expense) ought not to suffer constitutional embarassment because in the very employment of a religious agency the public interest is colored by a moral and religious quality. The supposition that a private interest — here, a religiously oriented education in an accredited school — is far less related to public needs because it is invested with a religious conception of life has been seriously challenged by at least one authority who confesses to the nonrelevance of transcendental values to human purposes. In the aftermath of the *McCollum* decision, banning sectarian religious instruction in public school classrooms, Dr. Alexander Meiklejohn reflecting on the constitutional distinction between private and public interest on which *Everson* was based, argued that the private interest in a religious apostolate "to aid religious groups to spread their faith" ought not in *McCollum* have been considered without value to the public:

> As one questions the distinction here made, one is not denying that the parents have a private interest in religious teaching. But they have, likewise, a private interest in the physical safety of their children. In this respect the two cases are identical. *But the presence of a private desire does not prove the absence of a public need.* And the values to be gained by religious teaching are not merely private. To say that is to rob religious attitudes of all objective spiritual meaning. It is to reduce their significance to that of private personal idiosyncracies. As against such false sectarianism, surely the value of all our creeds, religious or nonreligious, lies in their common, though varied, attempt to interpret men and society and the world as to find in those interpretations, bases for human behavior, for human association. In relation to that common purpose, creedal differences are accidental. Our sects can live together in peace, not by ignoring each other as "private," but by recognizing and honoring one

another as fellows in a common cause. Just as the teaching of "geography" is public, so is the teaching of religion or nonreligion. In whatever varied ways are available, the general welfare requires that our young people learn the lessons which we call "spiritual."

The argument just stated seems to require that the writer of these words indicate, if not explain, his own "private" conviction. My own beliefs are definitely on the side of nonreligion. So far as I can see, human purposes have no extra-human backing. Yet, so long as half our people, more or less, are interpreting and conducting their lives, their family relationships, the upbringing of their children upon a basis of some religious belief, the *Constitution requires of us that those beliefs shall be given not only equal status but also positive status* in the public planning of education. The freedom of religion has the same basic justification as had the freedom of speech or of the press. In both sets of cases, a strong and passionate private desire is involved. But far deeper than this is a public necessity. When men are trying to be self-governing, no other single factor of their experience is more important to them than the freedom of their religion or of their nonreligion. The interpreting of our spiritual beliefs is a public enterprise of the highest order.

The shift in the meaning of Jefferson's "wall of separation" is a striking illustration of the change from the organic to the mechanical interpretation of a figure of speech. As one reads the words of the Rector of the University of Virginia, it is clear that the beliefs and attitudes of religion are, for him, "separated" from the other factors in education and in much the same way as is the bloodstream of a living body from its other structures and functions. That bloodstream must be kept separate by the walls of the circulatory system. A break in them is disastrous. And yet the blood performs its living function only as it nourishes the whole body, giving health and vigor to all its activities. It is some such organic meaning as this which seeks expression in Jefferson's "wall of separation." But men who claim to follow him have transformed his figure into one of mechanical divisions and exclusions. They speak of his wall as if it were made of brick or stone or steel. By so doing they cut off our spiritual education from its proper field of influence. They make "private" a matter of supreme "public importance." And the effect of that operation corresponds closely to what would happen if we should substitute for the living tissues which enclose the cortex, or the nerves, or the blood, casings of impenetrable steel.[22]

These reasoned and enlightened thoughts of Dr. Meiklejohn were, let us note, on formal sectarian religious instruction in public school classrooms. A *fortiori* they are pertinent to our present discussion and should encourage continuing reflection on the necessary immanence of spiritual values in the educational process, on the equal right of religion and nonreligion to exercise itself in education, and on their significance to the public interest. I for one do not think that any court test of a federal aid to religious schools will be determined wholly within the context of past decisional law. We have been warned that a categorical affirmation (within these narrow confines) one way or another will work to self-deception and to the deception of others. I am firmly convinced that the legal test whether openly acknowledged or not will be permeated — paradoxical as it may sound — by one or another concept of the educational process.

Plato in his *Republic* prescribed for the educational training of the young auxiliaries who were to guard the Republic against the assaults of the enemy. Superior to the physical exercise of bravery upon the battle field, he insisted on an intellectual training that would resist the spiritual subversion of the civic values which the Athenians were to hold dearer than life. Profession of loyalty alone will not long endure against the clever and cynical dialectic of the enemy nor against the comforting blandishments that weaken in the last resort loyalty to the City. There are many in our nation who find that the high call of patriotism must be rooted deeply in a religious grasp of the civic duties of a man to his country. And a neutral education, that is, one stripped of all theistic values, may not suffice to sustain this persevering loyalty.

Many today ask why the Churches have not been more effective in uprooting from their faithful racial bias and discrimination. To ask the parochial schools to immunize their courses against any or all religious orientation in order to be eligible for federal assistance is to compound beyond all hope the moral problem that weighs heavily upon the consciences of the nation. Religious faith tells us to love God with all our strength, our full hearts, and our whole minds. It will at times require no less than this full spiritual effort to shatter the hardened prejudices of generations. Whatever prayerful hope we all share for the social reconstruction of society this will not take place outside of the divine law of love and justice. Except the Lord build the house, they labor in vain that build it. Organizing peace on earth is a task too vast to rest on the one hand on a neutral educational process and on the other on the expectation that church and home can fulfill the responsibilities effectively and adequately without further assistance.

For some time we have heard with sonorous repetitiveness that religious formation is the task properly of the church and of the home. This is said so solemnly that it sounds at times as if that prerogative was in danger of violation. But the facts and requirements of law have so situated this prerogative that both the natural right and duty of parent can no longer be viewed quite so exclusively. When the state compels parents by public law under pain of legal judgment to send their children for the greater part of the day, for five to six hours, away from their immediate control and influence to a publicly accredited school, the duties of the parental prerogative are delegated and shared. And if those to whom the education of the children has been confined are approved by the duly constituted educational authorities of the state, then it is an affront to civilized thinking to withhold federal aid because the educational process is permeated with religious rather than with purely secular values. It is almost ironic to remind ourselves that the religious clauses of the First Amendment are no less operative upon the federal government than they are upon the states. The education of students in church-related schools is no less a governmental concern than the education of students in state schools. The education of any child in any school is part of the national education and national interest. To deny any sort of federal aid to parochial school children and their parents because their schooling is infused with religious values and ideals is not governmental neutrality but penalty and it ought to be acknowledged as such. I should very much wonder what the reactions of many would be if the present number of church-related schools were not so heavily Catholic but widely distributed among the various credal groups. Sympathies are engendered by personal interest and a widely distributed interest generates correspondingly a broader popular response.

At times we are unfortunately confronted with statistics of delinquents who are graduates of parochial schools. Just what this is supposed to prove has escaped me entirely. Is the cause of delinquency of a parochial or public school student traceable to some (nefarious) teaching or a (questionable) rule of conduct of that school? I for one have no hesitation in saying that any school, state, private, or church-related, that teaches the centrality of the God of love and justice and the universal sweep of his moral law has a superior offering than the school which does not. I for one must admit to the greater spiritual efficacy of obligations of conscience which are not of my own making and unmaking, of duties which are imposed upon me by the author of my being, for the good of society itself. With all the talk in the air about the integration of personality for contented and peaceful living, it may be that some will find this principle of integration in a naturalistic vision of man, while others will hold steadfast to a religious conception. If the interest of public law is in the conduct which issues forth into public order then it ought not to cast the full weight of its influence, power, and financial resources behind one type of formation as against another.

LAW, POLICY, AND POLITICS

The constitutional permissiveness of federal aid for parochial schools has in the past decade increasingly received the reasoned support from some of the nation's eminent jurists. And, on the other hand, the categorical charge of illegality made in high places has not gone without critical and at times caustic commentary. Some who have had second thoughts on the constitutional proscription of such aids have taken a new position, now arguing that it would not be a good policy to do so. At its best such an argument reflects serious concern for the future of public schools to which no American should be insensible. However, concern for the future of independent schools should strike an equally responsive chord among our citizens. But this interest in the future of public schools may cloak a fear of a truly democratic process: namely, what would be the free choice of all parents if they were economically free to send their children to a state school or to a religious school? Lately a remarkably novel approach to public policy has been enunciated. A non-Catholic spokesman affirms his opposition to federal aid for parochial schools in the name of the freedom and best interest of the Catholic Church itself! This new approach augurs intriguing prospects for intercredal relations or dialoguing. Perhaps such non-Catholics might come to allow that what the Catholic Church teaches as morally desirable for the public good, will no longer be viewed as the arbitrary interference of Roman Catholicism with the liberty of conscience of non-Catholics.

Not infrequently we hear too the complaint that Protestants should not pay for the education of Catholics. One would suppose that taxes paid to the public treasury are not tagged with the religious affiliation of the taxpayer. But allowing for the moment such a specious reasoning, the obvious answer is that Catholics are simply asking for an equitable return of *their* taxes paid into the public treasury. As one body of faithful they do constitute a very large body of taxpayers just as they are, even more so, one of the larger manpower resources for military service and — in time of war — casualties.

The only real public policy question before our national legislature is whether the church-related schools are in fact as well as *de jure* part of the American educational system and whether federal concern for educational needs and achievements should reach out to them as well as to state schools. To date, no opponent of federal aid to parochial school children has dared deny that these church-related schools are truly educational institutions.

Lastly, we should not discount in these discussions of constitutionality and public policy the hard consideration of politics as a motivation for much of the current thinking. It may not be, we respectfully submit, the religious orientation of the church-related schools but the numerical preponderance of the Catholic parochial schools which awakens in their opponents constitutional qualms of conscience.

THE CONSTITUTIONAL QUESTION

What, we ask, may we find in court decisions to shed light on the constitutionality of federal aid to a religiously oriented education. At the outset we shall have to admit to the same limitations as all prior polemicists on state, church, and school studies. Discussants of both sides select statements favorable to their cause excerpted from the same court opinions. There is no court ruling on this precise issue — of federal aid to a religiously oriented education so we shall have to review a series of cases customarily referred to state, church, and school controversies and ascertain what is the significance of a particular ruling or what are the implications of the statements in the court opinion for our discussion.

In 1899, the Supreme Court upheld in a unanimous decision the constitutionality of federal appropriation of funds for the construction of a building and public recompense for services rendered to a hospital owned and administered by a Roman Catholic Sisterhood. Presumably the Hill-Burton Hospital Survey and Construction Act which has been repeatedly renewed since its enactment in 1946 rests squarely upon the ruling in *Bradfield* that such federal subventions are not in violation of the no-establishment clause. Over one billion dollars of federal money has been spent to improve and enlarge the facilities of public and privately owned hospitals under the provisions of this law. Of the amount which has gone to religious affiliated hospitals about three fourths has gone to Catholic hospitals. One could scarcely argue conclusively from *Bradfield* that what is upheld in the noneducational area — hospital services and facilities — would necessarily apply to the area of education.

Allowing for the obvious differences between educational and medical situations nonetheless appropriations for an official recognized public service (performed in an undoubted religious environment: the religious garb, religious symbols, and the subjection to morally permissible surgeries and medical code of the religious profession of the Catholic Sister) might be favorably constructed into an analogous constitutional principle for gauging the public interest of an officially accredited schooling. Nor has any constitutional embarrassment come from acknowledging that some benefit does accrue to the private religious corporation, and in certain instances the benefit is almost incalculable to the fortunes of an affiliate educational institution of learning.

In *Quick Bear v. Leupp,* 210 U.S. 50 (1908) the Supreme Court sustained the legality of a contract made at the request of the Indians, to whom money was due as a matter of right under a treaty, for the payment of such money by the Commissioner of Indian Affairs for the support of Indian Catholic schools. We have here an arrangement somewhat similar to the *Zorach* case which did not find administrative cooperation between tax salaried officials and the churches forbidden by the no-establishment clause of the First Amendment.

In *Meyer v. Nebraska* 262 U.S. 390 (1923), the importance of the case is generally overshadowed by the momentous decision two years later of *Pierce v. the Society of Sisters* which in great part was prejudiced by the former. In 1919 Nebraska passed a statute governing the curriculum of its primary schools which provided that: 1. "No person, individually or as a teacher shall in any private, denominational, parochial, or public school, teach any subject to any person in any language other than the English language. 2. Languages other than the English language, may be taught as languages only after a pupil shall have attained and successfully passed the eighth grade as evidenced by a certificate of graduation issued by the county superintendent of the county in which the child resides." Meyer, a teacher in a parochial school affiliated with the Zion Evangelical Lutheran Congregation, was convicted by the state for using as a text a German Biblical history. The Supreme Court reversed the conviction which the Supreme Court of Nebraska had affirmed on appeal. The reasoning of the United States Supreme Court in reversing the conviction of Meyer and striking down the Nebraska statute does cast light on the tangled issues of the secular subjects as taught in parochial schools. Summarily, it strikes down pedagogic dictation by the state in any school, public or private, without denying it its legitimate and proper supervisory role over school curriculum. The quotations from the decision of the Supreme Court of Nebraska which the United States Supreme Court reversed are remarkably illuminating on the very problem before us and give depth in perspective to the court's own reasoning:

> On appeal to the Supreme Court of Nebraska, the conviction was affirmed, 107 Neb. 657, 187 N.W. 100. Parts of that opinion follow: "...it is clear that the reading from the textbook was *not, at least, solely, a devotional exercise. It was no religious worship, nor was it, primarily, religious instruction in itself. The textbook contained Biblical stories, but the subject matter of the text, used for the purpose of studying a language, does not alone control, nor indicate the object of the study.* The object was, as stated, "to have the children learn so much German that they could be able to worship with their parents." Defendant argues, then, that the teaching of the German language from this book containing Bible stories served a *double purpose,* in that it both taught the children the German language and also familiarized them with the Bible stories, and that the teaching, so characterized, was religious instruction. *It must be conceded,* even under that argument, that two subjects were

being taught — one the German language and one a religious text. If the law prohibited the teaching of the *German language as a separate and distinct subject,* then, certainly, the fact that such language was taught from a book containing religious matter could not act as a shield to the defendant. The teaching of the *German language, as a subject,* would come within the direct prohibition of the law, regardless of what text might be used in the book from which the language was taught. It does not appear that the German language is part of the religion of this church, nor that the services must, according to the particular faith be rendered in German.

Though every individual is at liberty to adopt and follow with entire freedom whatsoever religious beliefs appeal to him that does not mean that he will be protected in every act which he does which is consistent with those beliefs, for when his acts either disturb the public peace, or corrupt the public morals, or otherwise become inimical to the public welfare of the state, the law may prohibit them, though they are done in pursuance of and in conformity with the religious scruples of the offending individual.[23] (italics added)

The United States Supreme Court speaking through Mr. Justice McReynolds, ruled that the Nebraska statute, as applied, impaired the plaintiff's "right thus to teach and the right of parents to engage him so to instruct their children, we think, are within the liberty of the (Fourteenth) Amendment."

It is striking that the court in speaking of the high importance of education amongst the American people should choose to quote the Ordinance of 1787 which conjoins knowledge with religion and morality for the benefit of government and society. The high tribunal apparently agrees with the analysis of the case by the Nebraska Supreme Court — that two distinct and separate purposes remain intact — the teaching and learning of the proscribed German language and the teaching and learning of Bible stories. The two concurrent objectives are recognized to be separable and separate, and accordingly both the federal and state Supreme Courts see no constitutional right of religious liberty at issue before them. In a word, the German language is being taught even in the learning of Bible stories and it is on that precise issue that both court-rulings are made. Apparently the intermingling of religious matter in the teaching of a secular subject — a modern language — does not diminish nor impair the proficiency of teaching and learning the secular subject nor interfere with its achieving its own distinctive secular aspect and function. In upholding the fundamental rights of teachers, parents and students, the high tribunal denies the state exclusive pedagogic regulation even under the guise of police power.

> Evidently the legislature has attempted materially to interfere with the calling of modern language teachers, with the opportunities of pupils to acquire knowledge, and with the power of parents to control the education of their own.[24]

The court in forbidding pedagogic dictation does not deny the state its proper and legitimate supervisory role in education:

> The power of the state to compel attendance at some school and to make reasonable regulations for all schools, including a requirement that they shall give instructions in English, is not questioned. Nor has challenge been made of the state's power to prescribe a curriculum for institutions which it supports.[25]

Taking note of the laudable motive of promoting cultural assimilation in schools the court however expressed its aversion to the statute before it by reaching back to the Platonic and Spartan experiments by law of trying to mold the minds of the young by removing them entirely from parental care and submitting the youngsters to an educational process entirely controlled by the state.

PIERCE V. SOCIETY OF SISTERS 268 U.S. 510 (1925)

It is not without reason then that constitutional lawyers see *Pierce v. Society of Sisters* prejudiced in great part the *Meyers* ruling. In the consideration of *Meyer v. Nebraska,* the Supreme Court was aided by a brief amicus by counsel representing various religious and educational institutions. The purpose was not to take sides in the cause before the court but to bring to the court's notice "certain contentions of the parties and the implications which they may be said to involve" in respect to the validity of another statute, the Oregon Compulsory Education Act. That statute was not then before the court, but the brief pointed out that the controversy in regard to it was in danger of being prejudiced in the principal case. In the course of the oral argument, Justice McReynolds asked about the "power of a state to require children to attend the public schools." Thereupon a considerable part of the discussion at the bar was devoted to that question, thus injecting the validity of the Oregon statute (the subject of the next, the Pierce Case) into the argument on the Nebraska statute.

Though *Pierce* is generally cited for its celebrated pronouncement on the rights of parents, the issue before the court was the proprietary right of private corporations to engage in schooling in fulfillment of state compulsory school attendance laws. Actually, *Meyer* and *Pierce* were decided on the bases of the rights of teachers and of parents.

> Corresponding to the right of control, it is the natural duty of the parent to give his children education suitable to their station in life; and nearly all the states, including Nebraska, enforce this obligation by compulsory laws.[26]

But in *Pierce* the proprietary right of private corporations, secular, military, religious, to engage in publicly accredited schooling requires as a corresponding term the parental right to choose schools other than those owned and controlled by the state. The basic reason for the existence of independent schools is that they are differentiated, by a principle of integration of curriculum and a system of discipline, from state-owned schools while sharing in common with them a proficiency in required subjects and in the inculcation of civic virtues. The effect of the *Pierce* ruling is to deny any priority or superiority before the law to the state to compel parents to choose their schools.

> The fundamental theory of liberty upon which all governments in this Union repose excludes any general power of the state to standardize its children by forcing them to accept instruction from public schools only. The child is not the mere creature of the state; those who nurture him and direct his destiny have the right, coupled with the high duty, to recognize and prepare him for additional obligations.[27]

While there is no explicit discussion of a principle of integration in the school curriculum, the court seems to be not unmindful of it when it states that the reason that the parents may choose an accredited education in an independent school is that in the judgment of the parents *such* schooling is ordained to assist the student for "his destiny" and "additional obligations" beyond those presumably provided for in the state-owned schools. The profound significance of the *Pierce* ruling is that the proprietary right of independent schools to operate is related to the prime moral obligation of the parents to regulate the moral-educational process of their children, without denying the state a supervisory role and without removing from the independent schools their obligations to the public welfare. In a word, the court is not merely saying that a division of labor is legitimate, and so the state need not have an exclusive role in education nor that other agencies besides the state may not be equally competent to educate the young; rather the court affirms the proprietary right of independent schools and of the parents of the children to choose an educational process which serves the public welfare while inculcating virtues beyond those required for civic duties. It denies the state an exclusive role in education because it refuses to acknowledge that there may be only one standard of educational process. We may note that it is remarkable that both *Meyer* and *Pierce* were decided some time before the omnicompetence of the modern totalitarian state revealed itself in all its dimensions, and no one can scarcely say these decisions were prompted in great part by the experience of other countries.

While it is true that *Pierce* was decided a few days before the guarantees of the First Amendment were for the first time transferred to the states through the Fourteenth Amendment, its significance for federal legislation on national education is not without some meaning even after *Everson*. Surely if the court upholds the right and the competence of a private corporation to establish independent schools worthy of official approval, it admits to the comprehensive perspective that the education of the children of the nation depends on a variety of accredited schools. (We shall not, however, encounter the real stumbling block until we come to the court's construction of "no establishment" to mean "no aid" by federal and state governments to the *Everson* case.)

COCHRAN V. BOARD OF EDUCATION, 281 U.S. 370 (1930)

In 1930 the use of public funds to furnish nonsectarian textbooks to pupils in parochial schools of Louisiana was sustained. Let us observe that the Supreme Court noted that the Louisiana statute referred to "school children of the state" without any qualifying phrase narrowing the beneficiaries only to those attending state-owned schools. The court rejected the contention of the appellant that under the Fourteenth Amendment taxation for the purchase of schoolbooks constituted a taking of private property for a private purpose. "The purpose is said to be to aid private, religious, sectarian, and other schools not embraced in the public educational system of the state by furnishing textbooks free to the children attending such private schools." To all of this the court replied:

> What the statutes contemplate is that the same books that are furnished children attending public schools shall be furnished to children in private schools. . . . Viewing the state as having the effect thus attributed to it, we can not doubt that the taxing power of the state is exerted for a public purpose. The legislation does not segregate private schools, or their pupils, as its beneficiaries or attempt to interfere with any matters of exclusively private concern. Its interest is education, broadly; its method, comprehensive. Individual interests are aided only as the common interest is safeguarded.[28]

What light, if any, does *Cochran* cast upon the argument of permeability as we find it in LaNoue. While it is true, as the court noted, that the textbooks are not religious books, the obvious fact could not possibly escape the court any more than it did the appellant — the fact which LaNoue himself lists among the factors of permeability in parochial schools — namely, the religious confessions of the schools, the religious garb of the teachers, the religious symbols and exercises held in these schools, in a word, the general religious orientation of life-values in the educational process of private church-schools. Despite or in welcome acknowledgment of this broad fact, the extension to an educational facility for the promotion of an objective sought by the statutory provision was upheld to be for a public purpose. True, the religious clauses of the First Amendment were not brought to bear upon the issue as the plaintiff's challenge of constitutionality of state action did not require the court to do so. But the broad fact and the reason for church-related schools, the religious integration of school curriculum, was not on that account ignored by the court:

It is also true that the sectarian schools, which some of the children attend, instruct their pupils in religion and books are used for that purpose, but one may search diligently the acts, though without result, in an effort to find anything to the effect that it is the purpose of the state to furnish religious books for the use of such children. . . . *What the statutes contemplate is that the same books that are furnished* children attending public schools shall be furnished to children attending private schools. This is the only practical way of interpreting and executing the statutes, and this is what the state board of education is doing. Among these books, naturally, none is to be inspected, adapted to religious instruction.

The court upheld the extension of the same educational facility, nonreligious in itself, to state and independent school textbooks, without trying to insulate it constitutionally from the religious permeation of the school curiculum nor, more improbably still, immunize it from the teachers use of it. It seemed to be the court's understanding that the Louisiana legislature's intent could equally be realized in all the state schools, public and church-related, whatever the ethos permeating the general school curriculum. The use by religious-minded teachers of a neutral educational facility would not transform that instrumentality into a religious object nor the subject matter into a theological science. The *Cochran* court was not unaware that parochial schools are an integral part of the Catholic Church's intellectual and spiritual apostolate in the formation of a Christian way of life. It would not on that account hold with the plaintiff that a private interest rather than a public purpose was being served.

The purpose is said to be to aid private, religious, sectarian, and other schools not embraced in the public educational system of the state by furnishing textbooks free to the children attending private schools.

Reaffirming what *Pierce* had established *de jure* — the duality of national education — it concluded:

Viewing the statute as having the effect thus attributed to it, we cannot doubt that the taxing power of the state is exerted for a public purpose. The legislation does *not segregate* private schools, or their pupils, as its beneficiaries or attempt to interfere with any matters of *exclusively private concern. Its interest, is education broadly; its method, comprehensive.* Individual interests are aided only as the common interest is safeguarded.

The court in a word refused to act as the supreme national pedagogue and to define the educational process narrowly and to set down methods of instruction or the manner of the use of state-provided facilities. It is the only practical posture of legal adjudication that the court can take within its constitutionally defined competence and jurisdiction. State aid for a public interest is not nullified simply because the educational process is committed to religious orientation. Some state legislatures continue to provide textbooks to students schooled in an environment permeated by religious influence and values — religious teachers, religious garb and symbols, religious exercises — and the *Cochran* ruling seems fairly well entrenched in American constitutional law.

EVERSON V. BOARD OF EDUCATION, 330 U.S. 1 (1947)

In *Everson*, the court, speaking through Mr. Justice Black, upheld the constitutionality of a New Jersey statute which provided at public cost free bus transportation to school children, including by explicit mention children attending Catholic parochial schools. The court took cognizance of the fact that in making available free bus transportation to parochial school children, the church-related school undoubtedly was assured the attendance of school children whose parents might otherwise have them go to a public school:

> It is undoubtedly true that by the New Jersey program children are helped to get to church schools. There is even the possibility that some of the children might not be sent to the church schools if the parents were compelled to pay their children's bus fares out of their own pockets when transportation to a public school would have been paid by the state.[29]

The court justified this child-benefit provision on the premise that the education in the church school included, besides formal theological instructions, the study of secular subjects.

> It is much too late to argue that legislation intended to facilitate the opportunity of children to get a secular education serves no public purpose.[30]

And the court insisted that the validity of such a presumption can rest on an empirical test.

> This court has said that parents may in the discharge of their duty under state compulsory education laws, send their children to a religious rather than a public school, if the school meets the secular educational requirements which the state has power to impose.[31]

In *Everson* for the first time in American constitutional history, the court chose to acknowledge beyond the strict requirements of the issue before it the appellant's contention that the "no-establishment" clause forbade any governmental aid to religion.

> No tax in any amount, large or small, can be levied to support any religious activities or institutions, whatever they may be called, or whatever form they may adopt to teach or practice religion.[32]

Be that as it may, we must not isolate this absolute proscription of aid from the specific ruling of the *Everson* case, which acknowledges some undoubted aid to the church school, nor read it apart from the paragraph immediately following which calls to our attention that:

> On the other hand, other language of the amendment commands that New Jersey cannot hamper its citizens in the free exercise of their own religion. Consequently, it cannot exclude individual Catholics, Lutherans, Mohammedans, Baptists, Jews, Methodists, nonbelievers, Presbyterians, or the members of any other faith, *because of their faith, or lack of it* [italics by the court] from receiving the benefits of public welfare legislation. While we do not mean to intimate that a state could not provide transportation only to children attending public schools, we must be careful, in protecting the citizens of New Jersey against state-established churches, to be sure that we do not inadvertently prohibit New Jersey from extending its general state law benefits to all its citizens without regard to their religious belief.[33]

We have elsewhere maintained that an exclusionary rule for government benefactions based on religious profession ought to raise substantive constitutional questions about the legal consequences attendant upon the exercise of religious liberty. We cannot repeat too often that the only practical way of interpreting and executing legislative statutes reaching to a public interest and service without prejudice to religious liberty is the empirical test of acertaining whether secular aspects and functions of nontheological studies, the promotion of which the government has a direct interest, are in fact proficiently and competently realized to the public benefit. Such an empirical device or measurement can meet the impartial requirements of Justice Black's statement, "because of faith, or lack of it."

One cannot minimize the difficulties engendered by the absolute "no aid" formula not only in the light of the very decisions in which the court upheld an undoubted aid to religion but also in the great variety of governmental aids to religious life and institutions which the federal and state governments are still supporting with enormous financial resources. Yet despite the ambiguities which interpose between the affirmative decisions of *Pierce-Cochran-Everson* and some absolutists pronouncements, friendly and unfriendly polemicists on the constitutionality of federal aid to parochial schools see a constructive development that would seem to favor it. Thus Leo Pfeffer certainly a principal opponent of federal aid to church-related schools has admitted:

> When the Everson decision is coupled with the Cochran decision they lead logically to the conclusion that the state may, notwithstanding the First Amendment, finance practically every aspect of parochial education, with the exception of such comparatively minor items as the proportionate salaries of teachers while they teach the catechism.[34]

And Professor Paul Kauper who has argued for the constitutional permissibility of federal aid to parochial schools has done so by drawing into a reasonable coherence court decisions and legislative practices.

> But to distinguish on principle from this type of benefit (auxiliary) and the more substantial benefits that would accrue from

subsidies to pay teachers' salaries or to provide educational facilities presents difficulties, particularly when it is noted that in the *Everson* case the court emphasized that the state imposed a duty on all parents to send their children to some school and that the parochial school in question met secular educational standards fixed by the state. By hypothesis the school building and the instruction in secular courses also meet the state's requirements. When we add to this that education is appropriately a function of both government and religion, the question may well be raised whether the same considerations that govern the problems of bus transportation costs and textbooks, as well as the question of public grants to hospitals under religious auspices, do not point to the conclusion, whatever different conclusions may be reached under state constitutions, that the First Amendment, in conjunction with the Fourteenth does not stand in the way of governmental assistance for parochial schools.[35]

If education required by state law may competently take place in church-related schools *(Pierce)*, and nontheological textbooks provided by state funds may be used in religious schools *(Cochran)*, and the state may constitutionally finance the bus transportation of parochial school children to these schools, it would seem that it would not be unlikely that a protest directed against the religious permeation of the educational process may well have its hidden roots in a broad opposition to all the foregoing provisions.

PUBLIC SCHOOLS AND RELIGIOUS INSTRUCTIONS

The *McCollum* ruling of 1948 struck down the Champaign, Illinois, religious instruction program on school premises during a school hour. The court, which often quotes Jefferson and Madison, does not seem as yet to have placed these men in precise constitutional focus. Jefferson was one of the earliest advocates of formal religious worship and religious instructions at the state university of Virginia. What is not usually noted is that ex-President James Madison was one of the commissioners who concurred in Jefferson's educational plan of 1822. Believers were invited to "establish religious schools" on the confines of the university and university facilities for religious worship and instruction were readily made available, university regulations modified to give easy access to the students of the university and to the divinity students benefits each might seek from the others disciplines. "Such an arrangement would complete the circle of the useful sciences embraced by this institution, and would fill the chasm now existing, on principles which leave inviolate the constitutional freedom of religion, the most inalienable and sacred of all human rights. . . ." As for the elementary schools Jefferson was opposed only to religious instruction or exercises "inconsistent with the tenets of any religious sect or denomination." Some have used this text to justify in the name of Jefferson the exorcism of every religious influence in state elementary schools. The distinction between the higher and lower levels relating to religious instruction and exercises was intended by Jefferson to stress the necessity of safeguarding inviolable the religious conscience of the minor against indoctrination to an alien confession. This we take to mean not negative action of total abstention from all religious influence but a positive implementation, a contrivance of circumstances surely not beyond the ingenuity of state educational authorities to ensure the free exercise of religious expression. The chasm in a totally nonreligious elementary education would be no less repugnant to Jefferson than it would be in the higher institutions of learning. The mutual accommodations would from the very nature of the case be decidedly different.

Only within the concept of an educational process necessarily related to the higher duties of conscience can the insistence of a dismissed-time and/or released-time program for religious instruction make any sense. Why must religious instruction in one's own creed take place *during* a school hour? Parents who send their children to state schools are faced with a dilemma. They do not, obviously, want one sectarian faith taught in public schools to all. On the other hand, the education which is immunized against every spiritual and religious grounding is defective and without any of the ultimate motivations so necessary to give direction and inspiration to the formation of responsible conduct. Whether or not dismissed or released time religious programs effectively satisfy this moral expectation, many American communities insist on the official, that is, legal affirmation of the relevance or link of religious life to the educational process. It is also a frank if discouraging admission of the insufficiency of home and church to cope adequately with this problem when children spend the greater part of the day away from both by requirement of compulsory school attendance laws.

What is intriguing about Terry McCollum and other dissidents from community voluntary arrangements who have gone to court in this and subsequent cases is that they affirm their legally guaranteed rights not by exercising their own freedom of choice in accordance with the dictates of their own conscience but by obstructing the free choice of their neighbors who have agreed among themselves to let each choose as he will. The gratifying expectation that the exercise of religious liberty might issue forth into a broad intercredal agreement has rather enhanced for the majority of the community cordial and mutually respectful relations. Those who hold fast to ethical culture, secular humanism, or whatever nontheistic absolute or ultimate relativity, may do so with personal pride and should not complain of embarrassment. Witnesses to the rights of conscience will gather strength by being independently true to their own creed in the midst of others. The most effective way not to feel embarrassment is to take pride in one's own faith. The young McCollum could also have enjoyed the facilities of being instructed by an advocate approved by his parents.

McCollum did not allow the use of public classrooms for religious instructions even though no additional public expenditures were thereby incurred. *Zorach* permitted tax-salaried public school officials to cooperate with the released-time program conducted off school property. Whether Terry McCollum's embarrassment would be more tolerable in an arrangement under the New York plan where his classmates would be permitted to separate themselves from his companionship during a school hour and go to a church hall for religious instructions would entail a fascinating study of child psychology and of the subtle convolutions of law.

McCollum and *Zorach* do, however, suggest some favorable considerations to the permeation discussion. In released-time religious instructions programs a local community under permissive official ruling wants the public schooling — caught between conflicting claims of rights and conscience — to be related to religious training. It may be that, as we have already noted, this sort of relationship may prove to be very tenuous but its symbolic significance is profound. It is rooted in a tradition which first found official expression in Article III of the Northwest Ordinance of 1787.

> Religion, morality, and knowledge, being necessary to good government and the happiness of mankind, schools and the means of education shall forever be encouraged.

The conviction that religious instruction is part of an integral education is no less Jeffersonian than his metaphor of the "wall of separation." This underlying significance of the released-time program was not lost upon Justice Frankfurter who in his dissenting opinion noted:

> The court tells us that in the maintenance of its public schools. "(The state government) can close its doors or suspend its operations" so that its citizens may be free for religious devotions or instruction. If that were the issue, it would not rise to the dignity of a constitutional controversy. Of course, a state may provide that the classes in its schools shall be dismissed, for any reason, or no reason, on fixed days, or for special occasions. The essence of this case is that the school system did not "close its doors" and did not "suspend its operations." There is all the difference in the world between letting the children out of school and *letting some of them out of school into religious classes. If every one is free to make what use he will of time wholly unconnected from schooling required by law* — those who wish sectarian instruction devoting it to that purpose, those who have ethical instruction at home, to that, those who study music, to that, then of course there is no conflict with the Fourteenth Amendment. (Italics supplied). The pith of the case is that formalized religious instruction is substituted for other school activity which those who do not participate in the released-time program are compelled to attend.[36]

Mr. Justice Douglas' opinion for the court takes cognizance of the same issue approvingly but within a broader scope:

> When the state encourages religious instruction or cooperates with religious authorities by adjusting the schedule of public events to sectarian needs, it follows the best of our traditions. For it then respects the religious nature of our people and accommodates the public service to their spiritual needs. To hold that it may not would be to find in the Constitution a requirement that the government shows a callous indifference to religious groups.[37]

Strictly speaking, only *Bradfield, Cochran,* and *Everson* are directly relevant to the question of governmental provision of financial aid to church-related schools. The safe assumption is it should not be startling news to the court or anyone else that the whole curriculum in a church school is permeated by religion. The court evidently is equally aware that secular education which the public interest requires can be fulfilled in a religiously integrated educational process.

> It is much too late to argue that legislation intended to facilitate the opportunity of children to get a secular education serves no public purpose. *Everson v. Board of Educ.* 330 U.S. at 7 (1947).

The Sunday law cases, the Maryland public notary case, and the prayer case offer fruitful opportunities of further reflections which while not directly pertinent are broadly relevant to the question of benefit through governmental action to religion in education.

McGOWAN V. MARYLAND, 366 U.S. 420 (1961)

All of the court opinions in this and other Blue Laws cases admitted the religious origin of the Sunday day of rest. But in all of them the majority court opinion, even while aware that some state Blue Laws still literally refer to the Lord's day, held to the valid secular purpose which was said to emerge from and to prevail apart from its religious origins: "The proponents of Sunday closing legislation are no longer exclusively representatives of religious interests." There is no denial of the obvious fact, on the part of the court, that there is an intermingling of interests, of secular objectives and of religious advantage partial to Christians. But the court opinion refuses to allow that such concurrences of benefits, secular and religious, nullifies the valid secular purpose which government has a right and duty to secure:

> However, it is equally true that the "Establishment Clause" does not bar federal or state regulation of conduct whose reason or effect merely happens to coincide or harmonize with the tenets of some or all religions. In many instances, the Congress or state legislatures conclude that the general welfare of society, wholly apart from any religious considerations, demands such regulation. . . . *McGowan v. Maryland* 366 U.S. 420, 422 (1961).

Sunday Closing Laws, like those before us, have become part and parcel of this great governmental concern wholly apart from their original purposes or connotations. The present purpose and effect of most of them is to provide a uniform day of rest for all citizens; the fact that this day is Sunday, a day of particular significance for the dominant Christian sects, does not bar the state from achieving its secular goals. To say that the states cannot prescribe Sunday as a day of rest for these purposes solely because centuries ago such laws had their genesis in religion would give constitutional interpretation of hostility to the public welfare rather than one of mere separation of church and state.

With what force of logic and reason one may reflect in similar terms upon an analogous situation, the intermingling of secular functions and religious aspects of parochial school education, will depend for the most part on the recognition of a secular goal of education in the curriculum in which the state has a substantive interest, and this, we must emphasize again, can be ascertained empirically by the state educational authorities.

Justice Frankfurter who had dissented in *Everson* significantly relates his concurring opinion in the Sunday Law Cases to the *Everson* ruling:

(T)his court held in the *Everson* case that expenditure of public funds to assure that children attending every kind of school enjoy the relative security of buses, rather than being left to walk or hitchhike, is not an unconstitutional "establishment," even though such an expenditure may cause some children to go to parochial schools who would not otherwise have gone. The close division of the court in *Everson* serves to show what nice questions are involved in applying to particular governmental action the proposition, undeniable in the abstract, *that not every regulation some of whose practical effects may facilitate the observance of a religion by its adherents affronts the requirement of church-state separation* (366 U.S. at 467).

Linked with the issues raised by the appellants under the religious clauses of the First Amendment was an economic argument, namely, the disadvantage that was incurred by the Sabbatarians by observing their day of rest from religious motives and by keeping their business shops closed under compulsion of the state Blue Laws. Both the Chief Justice and Mr. Justice Frankfurter in his separate concurrring opinion took full cognizance of the economic argument raised by Sabbatarians and held that in the absence of a reasonable alternative, which was within the discretion of the legislature to determine, the economic disadvantage incurred by the personal observance of religious obligations which do not coincide with the valid secular goal does not thereby taint the constitutionality of the statute. As Chief Justice Warren expressed it:

> If the state regulates conduct by enacting a general law within its power, the purpose and effect of which is to advance the state's secular goals, the statute is valid despite its indirect burden on religious observance *unless a state may accomplish its purpose by means which do not impose such a burden.* (Emphasis supplied).

Mr. Justice Frankfurter, after repeatedly stressing that in some activities public and religious interests "overlap," "interplay," and that the history of Blue Laws has made them "the vehicle of mixed and complicated aspirations," inquired as to when a benefit to religion may be allowable if there is an intermingling of religious and civil objectives. Only, he concluded, when there is no other alternative for realizing the secular goals:

> Or if the statute furthers both secular and religious ends unnecessary to the effectuation of the secular ends alone — where the same secular ends could equally be attained by means which do not have consequences for promotion of religion — the statute cannot stand. . . . The close division of the court in *Everson* serves to show what nice questions are involved in applying particular governmental action the proposition, undeniable in the abstract that not every regulation some of whose practical effects may facilitate the observance of a religion by its adherents affronts the requirement of church-state separation.

Put negatively, the indirect burden that may be suffered by following a religious conscience positively considered, or the indirect benefit that may accrue to religion because of a valid secular purpose is in both instances allowable and constitutionally permissible if there is no adequate alternative means for effectuating the civil objectives.[38]

Proponents of federal aid to education on the lower levels have argued that the exclusion of the parochial schools from sharing in government aid would place them in such a disadvantageous position in the face of the enormous resources of the federal government that the educational facilities of the parochial schools might in comparison be reduced to a level of inferiority which could prove harmful to the education in these schools. Has the government no alternate means of avoiding this alleged damage to private schools? One may push the question further and ask if it is in the national interest to bring about, however indirectly, the imbalance? The root question to which we must always return is to ask of the government what precisely is the status of parochial schools (apart from their constitutional right to educate in fulfillment of state educational requirements) in the comprehensive national educational program: to ask whether in fact they can and do contribute to the national education of the country and whether the government may rely upon them as well as upon state-owned schools for its educational programs.

The underlying import of the economic aspect of the Sunday Law cases is that the state would be obligated to hold in check the free play of open market competition (even on the claim of religious conscience) if in effect it would obstruct or frustrate a valid *secular* goal. Whether or not the federal government may be economically unconcerned about the educational facilities of approximately six million parochial school children is a question that ought not to be settled out of hand without first determining their place in the scheme of the national interest.

In coming to a decision, the Congress ought first to make this frank confrontation of the crucial issue. But apart from the vast economic consideration is the evaluation of the educational process itself. Permeation means intermingled objectives — value-judgments, and motives, and religious and secular aspects of the science studies. May the national legislature any more than the courts choose one mode of value-inculcation against the others? Or, may it allow any value integration which is not offensive to the communal welfare, perhaps even tributary as a spiritual force, and which preserves intact the secular aspects and functions of the educational process that the public interest requires? If the indefectability of the secular studies is assured — and this, we must repeat may be ascertained empirically – then governmental aid ought not to be interdicted because of a religious consequential. The exercise of religious liberty should be no less inviolable in education and no less free of government prejudices and civil disabilities than in other public endeavors and enterprises – indeed even more so if its educational functions are officially accredited and in fulfillment of state law requirements.

The best that may be derived from a study of those court decisions that can reasonably be brought to bear on the constitutionality of federal aid to a religiously oriented public service in education are suppositional premises and inferential conclusions that are somehow lodged in the specific ruling and at other times logically implied in general statements of the court's opinions. These are the opportunities and uncertainties with which both sides of the discussants are faced. There has been as yet no direct raising of the constitutional issue of federal aid to a religiously oriented education before the Supreme Court. The problem is not in any manner helped by the contrary rulings of state courts on textbooks and bus transportation, and it is further complicated by the fact that the Supreme Court has refused to review state proscriptive decisions which were openly based on the *Everson* opinion with apparent disregard of the specific *Everson* ruling. Reluctantly both sides will have to admit that the hope for clarity must in great part rely on general speculation about law and not, as we might have equally expected, on any firm and consistent direction which the law should provide for a rational discussion of unresolved constitutional issues. And this uncertainty is further compounded by doubts as to the reach or extent of a logical thrust which is motivated more by public opinion than by the exigencies of law itself.

Of the cases customarily cited, only three are directly relevant to the precise issue of some benefit accruing to the private religious institution through government financing. Of these, *Bradfield* sustained the constitutionality of government funds supporting a private service in fulfilling a public need in a noneducational area. Permeability – that is, the presence and therefore the potential influence of religion – in hospital service is evident in the general environment of a hospital conducted by Catholic Sisters and certainly in the criteria of permissible surgeries, all according to the moral philosophy and theology of the religious institution. *Cochran* upheld the constitutionality of state provision of nonsectarian books. Here, too, the general religious environment, the religious factors of the pedagogy that one would expect to prevail in parochial schools, the answers to moral and religious questions that may at times arise in the teaching of secular subjects are undeniable suppositions of the situation. In fact, the contention of the appellants that a private purpose and not a public one was being aided was based in great part on the grounds that these schools were religious and sectarian. While it is true that the religious clauses of the First Amendment were not involved, the reasonable supposition of permeability did not deter the court from acknowledging that public purpose and not a purely private interest was being fulfilled. In fact, the appellant argued that under the Fourteenth Amendment "taxation for the purchase of schoolbooks constituted a taking of private property for a private purpose" with particular notice of the fact that the ownership was "religious, sectarian." In *Everson* the supposition of a religious permeation of the parochial school curriculum might reasonably be conjectured though it was certainly not the precise issue before the court, nor was it even explicitly noted by the court. Mr. Justice Black acknowledged, as we have seen, that undoubtedly some benefit accrued to the private interest of the religious school. And evidently the legislature of New Jersey and the educational authorities of the state were aware that a church school was indeed benefitted and that the justification was that the secular requirements of schooling were met. This is a fact that could be ascertained empirically by direct testing or presupposed by the approval of the transfer of students from one school to another and by their acceptance upon graduation at institutions that were not church related. And Mr. Justice Black relied on that supposition. "This court has said that parents may, in the discharge of their duty under state compulsory education laws, send their children to a religious rather than a public school *if* the school meets the secular education requirements which the state has power to impose." And it is not without legal significance that Justice Black referred earlier in his opinion to the *Cochran* case and observed: "It is much too late to argue that legislation intended to facilitate the opportunity of children to get a secular education serves no public purpose." It is indeed much too late to look legally askance at religious permeation in church schools which submit to state educational requirements — except to postulate, rather lately, the purely secular subject concept without inquiring into its validity.

From the cases which do not deal with the appropriation of tax funds for public services rendered by religious agencies, some inferences may be drawn not unfavorable to the permeation issue. *Meyers* denied to a state absolute power to prescribe the school curriculum and *Pierce* upheld the proprietary right and competency of private corporations to share in the responsibilities and objectives of public schooling whether these in turn were integrated around military disciplines or religious confessions. In *McCollum* and *Zorach* the correlation of religious instruction with the public school educational process during a school hour was not ruled out but was made to turn in part on the direct involvement of governmental, that is, tax-supported officials and facilities with exclusively formal theological indoctrination. Now if it be in accordance with the best traditions of our country, as *Zorach* held, to accommodate public service to the spiritual needs of school children, why should it be constitutionally offensive for sharing in a national education betterment program if the church schools besides teaching religious doctrines in their catechetical courses, should also teach secular subjects with relevance to their creed, so long as this does not impair the secular aspects and functions of the nontheological courses? The educational problematic is a stubborn one. Not every public service or secular objective can be rendered by legal fiat impervious to religious values, nor every academic query insulated against value judgments to which the human conscience bears correspondence. The ultimate question is whether we may rightly expect the court to have competence and jurisdiction *ex banco* to favor one set of principles of educational integration as against another. The court has on occasion disallowed such a prerogative for any other branch of government and is not likely to claim it for itself:

> If there is any fixed star in our constitutional constellation, it is that no official, high or petty, can prescribe what shall be orthodox in politics, nationalism, religion, or other matters of opinion. . . . *West Virginia State Bd. of Educ. v. Barnette* 319 U.S. 624, 642 (1943).

The prejudice which is engendered by the necessities of an *apologia* for the religious permeation in church schools would not suffer from its defensive stance if parents who are constrained by economic disabilities to send their children for moral and intellectual development to public schools were to raise similar questions of conscience within the terms of the religious clauses of the First Amendment about the presence or calculated absence of spiritual values in the classroom. In recent days voices have been raised about the ethnic and cultural imbalance of some public school textbooks. Questions might be asked for example, whether the religious heritage of America as embodied in our basic national documents is studied with an emphasis proportionate to its importance, or on what ultimate moral principles civic duties and social responsibilities are grounded — on a moral law or on prevailing mores, on general consensus or on divine decree. Questions ought to be asked on the legitimate modes of sexual conduct. Professional historians of England and the United States are presently engaged in a joint project financed by the Ford Foundation and Britain's Nuffield Trust to rewrite Anglo-American history with the intent of removing that nationalistic bias and misrepresentation upon which the good relationship between the two countries may founder. Similar readjustments might be made about early American colonial history. In Parkman's oft-quoted phrase, "Not a bay was turned nor a river entered but a Jesuit led the way."

Perhaps the present attempt by British and American scholars to revise the chapters on the War for Independence will serve as an impetus for further projects. For, as the scholars themselves have affirmed: "Fairness at the schoolbook level requires that reputable viewpoints should not be suppressed, relevant facts should be neither ignored nor exaggerated, and obvious myths should be laid to rest." Why is modern tyranny identified in the form of one totalitarianism and not as frequently in the other? The presentation of facts, their total or partial omission, the emphasis, the concentration, generate the spiritual attitudes of students and imperceptibly form the prejudices that may harden with time. The conventional portrayal of the Negro as a dependent, servile creature must give way to an acknowledgment of the real contribution of the Negro to American culture. His struggle for freedom must be viewed as a human struggle of men and therefore as a profound chapter in the American history of civil liberty. These and so many other questions on the spiritual formation of students in public schools may point to the unreality of the neutrality of the educational process in public schooling.

In *Torcaso v. Watkins* 367 U.S. 982 (1963) the right of a citizen to become a notary public without being required by law to make a public declaration of belief in God was upheld. It would have been more felicitous had the court not subsumed in a footnote, by an exercise of logical positivism, nontheistic beliefs into the meaning of religion in the First Amendment. It could have adequately rested its ruling on the Anglo-American tradition of law that the right to belief is a right to an internal area of absolute inviolability into which inner sanctum neither the law may inquire nor the coercive power of government force its disclosures. However, what does merge from *Torcaso* for the purpose of this discussion is that regardless of the *faith or lack of faith (Everson)*, what matters is that the public service of a public office (whether correspondent to the official's conscience or not) be in accord with the requirements of the duties of that office. If the conscience, religious or not, be tributary to, or at least conform with the civic virtues of public office, the law will not inquire further to ask on what theological grounds such conduct is based. The particulars of *Torcaso* mark it off by some distance from questions of federal aid to religiously integrated education. But it does suggest further reflections on the public benefit that the government expects and empirically ascertains in an educational process permeated by ultimates whether theistically grounded or not, whether Christian or not, etc. It also raises the correlative consideration whether the equality of religious liberty whether theistic or nontheistic should not ensue into an equality of treatment when confronted by government benefactions. The Maryland state courts in upholding the constitutional requirement had relied on the common law attitude toward atheists as a reasonable basis for excluding the appellant from the office of notary public. The state court determined that the distinction between believers and nonbelievers as a security for good conduct in office had not become so devoid of meaning that to adopt it would be arbitrary. The common law equated the ungodly with the untrustworthy. It was supposed, as Professor Wigmore had suggested, that the sanction of divine retribution for false swearing might add a stimulus to truthfulness whereever that was possible. While it may be cynical to suggest that many good men are not deterred from perjury because of moral dictates, it seems equally unreasonable to restrict an inducement to veracity to the believer. The equation of honesty with belief must in our day give way to the more conclusive evidence of the actual performance of civic duties.

A line of reasoning on the permeation issue might be constructed from *Torcaso* in this fashion. Whether the agent of a public requirement is motivated by theistic or nontheistic belief, whether he invests his work with moral or theological virtue, the service rendered must be judged on its own merits and by the canons properly applicable to that specific performance. Similarly, one may reason, whatever the spiritual permeation of an educational process — secular humanism, ethical culture, military discipline, theism, Christianity — the educational objectives in which the state has a public interest must be measured and evaluated by tests proper to the various intellectual disciplines. Has a student learned to spell, read, multiply? Does he learn in biology and history what the state educational authorities require of every schooling? In this wise the religious permeation of an accredited schooling would not disqualify from participation in a national program for the improvement of education.

When the Court said in *Watson v. Jones* "The law knows no heresy, is committed to the establishment of no religion, the support of no dogma," it did not mean to say the public law is indifferent to heresy or dogma. The First Amendment embraces two concepts, "freedom to believe and freedom to act. The first is absolute but, in the nature of things, the second cannot be." *(Cantwell v. Connecticut.)* ". . . In every case the power to regulate must be so exercised as not in attaining a permissible end, unduly to infringe the protected liberty." Since from the very nature of things not every public service and benefit is impervious to spiritual and religious values, public law must direct itself to the realization of its own interest whether its objectives and motives are intertwined with the objectives and motives of private interest, whether a private agency is religiously inspired or not. The public good is definable in itself and its efficacy for the public interest is not impaired — perhaps, on the contrary, enhanced — for being invested with religious insights. On this basis, a good start can be made for the substantive construction of a principle of neutrality, with prejudice to the rights of conscience of no one. Public law has indeed very much interest in the outward behavior of religious belief. It does not disdain to call upon the religious faiths for support of its own secular programs in times of peace and war. It has an interest in the ulterior motivation that religious life can provide for the conduct that is conducive to the harmonious peace and tranquil order of the commonwealth. In the crucial hour for the advancement of civil rights, public law looks to religious authorities and creeds to enlighten their faithful and help draw them out of those hardened and blind social prejudices which obstruct the free exercise of civil liberties and bring discord and violence to fellow citizens. If public law may turn to religious life for support of its own civic programs and for a resolution of many of its complex problems, then it ought not look askance upon an educational process which fuses the spiritual life of the student with his learning. We cannot departmentalize man by requirements of law and then ask him to conjoin — supposedly — his dual, concurrent lives as citizen and believer when the national benefit requires it. In a word, the law and government are not neutral and indifferent to the motivations provided in an accredited schooling.

When in *Meyers* and *Pierce,* the court determined that parents have the right coupled with the high duty of nurturing and educating their children for additional obligations, that is for responsibilities beyond civic duties, and reaffirmed in *Prince v. Massachusetts* the primary right of parental control of education, it was not simply denying exclusive monopoly to the state but rather affirming that both government and the church (parents) have a dual role in the educational process. The state sets its own requirements — relative to its own interest. This interest remains indefectible, subject to an empirical verification if need be, when inspired by religious beliefs. There are very many among us who hold that a religiously oriented education is highly beneficial to the common purpose and tributary to the spiritual resources of the American community. *Pro Deo et Patriae* is the proud calling of the parochial school.

There have been cases and conceivably circumstances may arise wherein the state can interfere to see that children are not taught beliefs, which would be at variance with the temporal welfare of the community. The state, for instance, may remove children from the custody of parents who refuse, on religious grounds, to give them the medical care which is normally taken for granted in our country. True, this is not strictly an interference with the rights of parents to teach their children. It is more an interference with the supposed right of the parents to deal with the child according to their religious faith. But the underlying truth cannot be stressed too strongly, namely, public law is far from indifferent to the public effects of religious belief. If an educational process conforms to officially prescribed standards, if students do learn to read, spell, multiply, etc., to the degree and in matters prescribed by state educational officials, the public interest has been met. And if this schooling is permeated with religious values which do not disturb the public order, which rather provide added stimulus to good citizenship, then it ought not to be disqualified for participating in a federal program of national betterment of education. The profound significance of *Torcaso* is the insistence that the government look to the service performed and not to the religious confession or lack of it. The "no aid" formula ought to be considered in the context of the particular situation of *Torcaso* — no preferential status of eligibility for sharing in a public service ought to be based on religious grounds. It argues for an equality of opportunity without prejudice to rights of conscience.

Admittedly, there are substantial points of disparity between *Torcaso* and the constitutional question of federal aid to education. In the disbursement of public financial benefactions a sound public policy may justifiably restrict its subsidies to a limited reach. Because privately owned services in industry and commerce — such as agriculture, airlines and railroads — may require government subsidies to sustain the public service it does not follow that every other privately owned and controlled public service must equally be a recipient of government subventions. The controlling consideration is the substantive national interest. And so we return to the original question which keeps recurring — whether or not parochial schools are part of the national education, whether parochial schools should share in federal programs for the advancement and improvement of educational facilities because they are part of the national interest.

The correspondence of probity and godliness which the common-law rule supposedly was really neither denied nor affirmed in *Torcaso*. What the court implicitly affirmed was that the test of office should be actual performance not a prior profession of a way of life. *Torcaso* seems to re-enforce the impartiality which *Everson* insisted upon in a passage which is less frequently quoted than its preceding passage on the "no aid to religion."

> On the other hand, other language of the amendment, commands that New Jersey cannot hamper its citizens in the free exercise of their own religion. Consequently, it cannot exclude individual Catholics, Lutherans, Mohammadens, Baptists, Jews, Methodists, nonbelievers, Presbyterians, or the members of any other faith, because of their faith or lack of it, from receiving the benefits of public welfare legislation.

We respectfully submit that the serious endeavor of the United States Supreme Court to arrive at a principle of neutrality is more likely to succeed if it is coupled with the principle of impartiality, or, as is more commonly expressed in law, an equal protection of laws. An interpretation that would see in *Torcaso* a public law disengagement from the influence and consequents of religious life — now broadly defined as a conscientious commitment to ultimates — would ascribe to the court a negative neutrality not borne out by the specifics of the case. What *Torcaso* seems to say is that public service must be validated on its own merits without prejudice to rights of conscience.

Engel v. Vitale and *Schempp* and *Murray* rulings deal with situations of religious exercises, Bible reading, and prayer in circumstances of conflicting claims of religious liberty, religious pluralism, and the alleged state support for those who choose as against those who do not. These cases highlight the need for giving positive substantive meaning to neutrality which the court "in accordance with the best of our traditions" may develop more constructively by the approach of impartiality under the formula of equal treatment as dictated by public need.

REFLECTIONS AND CONSIDERATIONS

The discussion of value permeability in school curriculum must take place within the broader dimensions of what constitutes national education. We must first ask what must a schooling provide to satisfy the national needs and expectations of education, or in other words, how may education be defined for the public interest so that the various schools, state, private, church-related, may be measured against those objectives. The *Pierce* ruling does not simply say that military and religious schools may also exist by sufferance of the state. Rather, its import is that public law legitimizes what the courts acknowledge to be the prior and primary rights of parents to direct the education of their children, a right that inheres in the very nature and vocation of parenthood *(Prince v. Massachusetts)*, subject of course to the supervisory role of the state, The national Congress must squarely confront the question of the place and role of church schools in the national education. Are they an integral part of a dual system of education or not? It will not do to acknowledge only their legal status under the *Pierce* ruling — namely, their right to exist in fulfillment of state compulsory school attendance laws. The import and underlying broad significance of *Pierce* must be fully explored and weighed. Namely, are all publicly accredited schools that comply with officially prescribed standards of teaching, curriculum, and facilities fulfilling the educational needs of the nation? By virtue of the end result of their educational process are they all equally eligible to participate in some way in a federal program for the advance and promotion of the nation's educational facilities?

The second consideration which seems to obstruct rational thinking about federal aid to schools is how absolute is the "no aid to religion" formula in the lights of *Bradfield, Pierce, Cochran,* and *Everson*. In each of these court determinations the undeniable public service of private religious institution was the controlling fact on which the ruling of law was based.

Third, is the principle of compatibility of interests, which prevails unchallenged when undoubted economic advantages accrue to private commercial and industrial interests which the government subsidizes in the public interest, not equally applicable to private religious institutions fulfilling educational needs?

Fourth, where public and private motives and objectives intermingle, as the court found in the Sunday Law cases, may not the secular aspects and secular functions of education be preserved indefectible whatever the infusion of value judgments, whatever the principle of spiritual and religious integration? A twofold test may be applied, the primary one, an empirical test to ascertain the competence of the learning, and second, whether spiritual values taught are tributary to the public good or harmful. It is *ultra vires* to require that a public service should otherwise be officially impervious to any spiritual permeation.

Fifth, it would prove to be a very helpful approach if it were borne in mind that educational responsibility is tripartite. The primary rights of parents with which the law of nature has endowed them to direct the education of their offspring, the supervisory role of government to require minimal standards of teaching, curriculum, and facilities in its own public interest, and the high expectations of religion, whether institutionalized or as dictates of individual consciences, all must be acknowledged not only in terms of moral and legal claims of religious liberty but also as an essential spiritual resource for the good republic. An exclusive control by one or other of these agencies would threaten not only academic freedom but also the very integrity of the educational process.

Sixth, man does not live by bread alone. Civil society does not survive solely by its own political and legal determinations. It will not do to speak of civic virtues and the high duties of patriotism without reference to the spiritual life of the citizen and the spiritual heritage of a nation. Values to be gained by religious teaching are not meant to be confined wholly to an inner sanctum of spiritual life, nor can they be. Religious pluralism will have an added significant and truly unique meaning for society if it means that all faiths and churches are tributary to the good dispositions, the proper inclinations, and the civil sensitivity for obedience to the law – all with a view to that peace and concord among fellow citizens which is the distinguishing mark of the good republic. This spiritual interdependence of the political and moral order does not need to be prescribed by law. It emerges from the very nature of things. Separation of church and state which the religious clauses of the First Amendment are intended to insure bears no contrariety to a mutual accommodation of purposes and objectives for the vitality of both. Separation is not insulation. Neutrality must be understood in terms of independence and impartiality. Only on such firm foundations may the proper relationships between free institutions and free churches become possible of formulation. Within the correlative terms of discernible public service and freedom of religion in education no prejudice should operate to the disability of religion to fulfill a public interest because it is infused with religious values.

Seventh, in the judicial interpretation of the religious clauses of the First Amendment no less emphasis ought to be given to religious liberty than to the establishment clauses. And the rights of consentients should not be less inviolable than those of dissidents. "Coercive" has been one of the middle terms by which the establishment clause has been made to bear upon a litigated issue. Even in such instances where the court declared that violation of the establishment clause did not depend on the factor of coercion it would nonetheless take notice of it in either or both forms, the embarrassment allegedly suffered by the plaintiff or the prestige, power, or influence of the government was said to be weighted to one side by its permissiveness of certain religious exercises in public schools. The court's determination of just when an embarrassment may be construed to be a substantive hurt which warrants wiping out a whole program of voluntary participation willed by the majority of the local community, or when an accommodation in the best of our traditions amounts to the proscribed establishment has not been above all rational criticism. Be that as it may, the problematic of rights of conscience in education in both state and independent schools poses questions which are unique to each situation. The conformity of creed in a parochial school cannot be legally viewed to its disadvantage without concretely infringing upon religious liberty. The tendency towards a neutrality of abstention, which the peculiarities of religious pluralism in public schools forces upon the court, should scarcely be expected in ruling upon constitutional questions that are raised about federal aid to church-related schools. The controlling principle subject to empirical verification is whether learning in the prescribed studies of interest to the national congress is completely realized.

Eighth, in his concurring opinion in *McCollum,* the late Justice Jackson — forewarned about the legal presumptions which the court might risk assuming if the complainant's petition for a complete separation of secular from the religious in public schools were acknowledged — wrote:

> The task of separating the secular from the religious in education is one of magnitude, intricacy, and delicacy. To lay down a sweeping constitutional doctrine as demanded by complainant and apparently approved by the court, applicable alike to all school boards of the nation to immediately adopt and enforce rules and regulations prohibiting all instruction in and teaching of religious education in all public schools, is to decree a uniform rigid and, if we are consistent an unchanging standard for countless school boards representing and serving highly localized groups which not only differ from each other but which themselves from time to time change attitudes. It seems to me that to do this is to allow zeal for our ideas of what is good in public instruction to induce us to accept the role of super board of education for every school district in the Nation. . . .

A fortiori it would seem even less warranted to require purely secular subject studies in circumstances where religious liberty in education should be paramount.

CONCLUSION

Mr. LaNoue has initiated a study which if broadened into its full dimensions would be highly enlightening in approaching constitutional questions of state, education, and religion in all schools. Unfortunately, he bases a constitutional argument on an assumption of the purely secular subject concept without inquiring into its validity. Nonetheless he could have turned a discussion of the purely secular subject concept into a very profitable opportunity for an analysis of the educational process that *de facto* or *ex professo* obtains in state, church-related, and other independent schools, and he might then have inquired whether the public requirements and interests were being served. He might have proceeded further to show how each educational process imbued with a spiritual content might be tributary to the spiritual resources upon which the faithful performance of civic duties must depend. Instead of simplifying the problem by absolute insulations (for eligibility for federal aid) he might have enlightened the complexities of religious pluralism and the multi-school system of the nation that confronts our legislatures and courts. With light and understanding the approach to the constitutional questions of federal aid to education would perchance be less burdened by partisan polemics of law, education, and religion.

FOOTNOTES AND REFERENCES

1. "Parochial Texts Called Bar to Aid," *New York Times*, May 11, 1962, pp. 1, 38. The survey-study was made by George R. LaNoue, at that time a doctoral candidate at Yale University, Department of Political Science, at the request of the Department of Religious Liberty, Division of Christian Life and Work, of the National Council of the Churches of Christ in the U.S.A. On May 18, 1962, the Department of Religious Liberty made available photo-offset copies of an abbreviation of the original lengthy report. A substantial exposition with more detailed documentation and examples appeared in the June issue of the *Phi Delta Kappan* titled, "The National Defense Education Act and 'Secular' Subjects." A lengthier version appeared in the *Harvard Educational Review*, Vol. 32, No. 3, Summer 1962, titled, "Religious Schools and 'Secular' Subjects," pp. 255-291. All references will be to this publication.

2. National Defense Education Act, P.L. 85-864, Sec. 305; 20 U.S.C. 445.

3. Joint Subcommittee on Education of the House Committee on Education and Labor, *Hearing*, on H.R. 6774, H.R. 4253, H.R. 7378, 1961 Part 1, pp. 121-122.

4. *Ibid.*, Part 1, p. 280.

5. *Ibid.*, Part 2, p. 471.

6. *Ibid.*, Part 2, pp. 471-472.

7. LaNoue, *op. cit.*, p. 259, n. 11.

8. *The Supreme Court on Church and State*, ed. by Joseph Tussman, Oxford Press, 1962, p. XXIV.

9. *Teacher Education and Religion*, by A. L. Sebaly, E. R. Collins, E.S. Cooper, E. E. Dawson, K. G. Hill, E. J. Kircher, H. K. Schilling, American Association of Colleges for Teacher Education, 1959, pp. 95-96 (by E. J. Kircher).

10. *American Education and Religion: The Problem of Religion in the Schools*, ed. by F. Ernest Johnson, Harper, 1952. Secularism is "a faith that conflicts with the tenets of

traditional religion ... we should recognize it for what it is: an affirmation of faith, a religion, if you will, which entitles it to the right of competition in the marketplace, with all the privileges and limitations that apply to the propagation of other religions." Vivian Thayer, p. 30.

11. *McCollum v. Board of Education*, 333 U.S. 203, 235-236 (1948).
12. LaNoue, *op. cit.*, p. 262.
13. *Ibid.*, p. 236.
14. *Ibid.*, p. 263.
15. "The Supreme Court as National School Board," by Edward S. Corwin in *Law and Contemporary problems*, Vol. 14, No. 1, Winter 1949, p. 21.
16. La Noue, *op. cit.*, pp. 264-265.
17. *Ibid.*, pp. 271, 273-280.
18. *Ibid.*, pp. 271-273.
19. *Ibid.*, pp. 273-276.
20. *Ibid.*, pp. 276-280.
21. *Ibid.*, pp. 280-288.
22. "Educational Cooperation Between Church and State," by Alexander Meiklejohn in *Law and Contemporary Problems*, Vol. 14, No. 1, Winter 1949, pp. 66-67, 69.
23. Quoted in Dowling, *Cases on Constitutional Law*, 5th ed., Foundation Press, 1954, pp. 1060-1062.
24. *Meyer v. Nebraska*, 262 U.S. 390, 401 (1908).
25. *Ibid.*, at 402.
26. *Ibid.*, at 400.
27. *Pierce v. Society of Sisters*, 268 U.S. 510, 534 (1925).
28. *Cochran v. Board of Education*, 281 U.S. 370, 375 (1930).
29. *Everson v. Board of Education*, 330 U.S. 1, 17 (1947).
30. *Ibid.*, at 7.
31. *Ibid.*, at p. 18.
32. *Ibid.*, at 15-16.
33. *Ibid.*, at 16.
34. *Church, State, and Freedom*, Beacon Press, 1953, p. 476.
35. Paul O. Kauper, *Frontiers of Constitutional Liberty*, Ann Arbor, University of Michigan Law School, 1956, p. 136.
36. *Zorach v. Clauson*, 343 U.S. 306, 320 (1952).
37. *Ibid.*, at 312.
38. However, compare with the court ruling in *Sherbert v. Verner*, 373 U.S. 83 (1963), the South Carolina case decided the same day as *Schempp* and *Murray*. This was an unemployment benefits case. A Seventh Day Adventist was out of work because she would not work on Saturdays. The court held that she must be given unemployment benefits on the grounds "that South Carolina may not constitutionally apply the eligibility provisions so as to constrain a worker to abandon his religious convictions." Although this case does not overrule the decision in the Sunday Closing Law cases as the dissenting opinion of Mr. Justice Harlan, whom Mr. Justice White joined, insisted it did, it is an important qualification of that decision. Mr. Justice Stewart agreed with the result but disagreed with the court's opinion. He rightly, it seems to me, pointed to the "dilemma posed by the conflict between the Free Exercise Clause of the Constitution and the Establishment Clause as interpreted by the court" for the disjunctive and at times contrary considerations of religious liberty and secular, public law purpose, when the two are inextricably bound together in the concrete.

PRAYER IN PUBLIC SCHOOLS*

It is well at the outset to define with precision the constitutional issue involved in *Engel v. Vitale*.[1] The issue was not simply prayer in public schools. No legal power can prevent a student from reciting privately his prayers while sitting in the school library or standing in the schoolyard provided he does not interfere with any academic assignments or with prescribed recreational employments. All prayer is personal, all prayer is a religious exercise, wheresoever it is said, in private or public institutions, and on every occasion. No description of prayer as ceremonial deprives it of its religious nature and meaning. Only the internal dispositions and, secondarily, the outward demeanor of a private individual or of a public official, determine whether he is truly praying or not. Prayer is always and on every occasion a religious exercise or it is not prayer at all. A ceremonial prayer which is not a religious act is a contradiction in terms.

Prayer may be individual when one prays by himself or even in the midst of others for his own intentions. And prayer may also be corporate as when several pray together in unison for one another, or for a purpose common to all of them. Corporate prayer may be at home as when a family prays together, or in a house of worship when a congregation professing the same creed takes part in a common liturgy. Corporate prayer may also be civic as when fellow citizens voluntarily unite to pray to God for divine blessings upon their country. From the earliest days of our history, it has been a time-honored and cherished tradition for our people to respond in prayer at the official request of government authorities on solemn public

---

*THE CATHOLIC LAWYER. Vol. 8, n. 4. Autumn 1962, 269-281. Based upon an address delivered to jurists at the Red Mass celebrated in St. Charles Borromeo Church, Brooklyn, New York, on September 20, 1962.

occasions, in times of impending peril, during war and in peace. Men, women and children of different religious confessions and church affiliations united by the common bond of belief in God have joined their hearts and minds in a corporate act of prayer for the preservation, survival and prosperity of America. Civic corporate prayer has been one of the most effective unifying spiritual bonds in our national history.

In the case before the high tribunal, no one disputed that prayer was a religious act. The Court admitted the absence of regulatory compulsion and punitive coercion.[2] The prayer in its simple wording was a solemn declaration of belief in the existence of Almighty God and a public acknowledgement of our dependence upon God as a nation as well as individually. There was no intent or effect of "teaching" a new belief in God.[3] The prayer was an open affirmation of a faith already possessed by every participant. The approval of the parents incontestably upholds this fact. The prohibition against any comments on the prayer was to ensure this fact. Voluntary participation and liberty of exemption gave the widest possible scope to personal response of conscience.

An Establishment of Religion

The Supreme Court ruled that because the prayer had been composed by a governmental agency it fell under the ban of the no establishment clause. Now this cardinal argument of the Court on governmental composition may not really be as telling as it seems. If by composition it is understood that the prayer originated in wording and meaning wholly with the New York Board of Regents and entirely on their own initiative then the argument is without foundation. The New York educational authorities were motivated in part by the broad public consensus authentically embodied in our national documents on the religious foundations of our Republic and, in part, by the rights and anxieties of religious-minded parents of students in the public schools. They were guided in the writing of the prayer in context and in words by state constitutions, by congressional resolutions and laws, by presidential acts, and by practices in the judiciary. Fifty state constitutions, in one way or another, acknowledge their dependence upon Divine Providence, express their gratitude to God as the Author of our civil and religious liberties, and pray for His continuing guidance and counsel in their government deliberations. In addition to legislative and military chapels and chaplaincies, acts of the national Congress and other deliberative assemblies have called for days of prayer through executive proclamations. The day after the national Congress passed the proposal which became the first amendment, it passed a resolution calling for the designation of "a day of public thanksgiving and prayer." This tradition of civic corporate prayer at the invitation of government officials has been, with but two exceptions, unbroken from the days of George Washington to the present administration. More precisely to the issue at hand, the Congress has officially prescribed and adopted the divine invocation on our coinage and currency, in the national anthem and motto, and in the Pledge of Allegiance to the flag. What the New York Board of Regents did was neither novel nor original. Only in a minimal sense — almost only in the capacity of an amanuensis — may it be said to be *their* composition. They simply gave expression to what the American people and their duly elected representatives have ratified and adopted in every decade of our national history.[4]

Some few reassuring voices insist that the Court decision might not proscribe the optional recitation of a prayer composed by nonofficials. But the fact and the law are that whatever takes place permissively in a state school under official supervision or conduct necessarily involves governmental responsibility to some degree or another. It is respectfully submitted that the high tribunal overexaggerated the significance of the role of the New York Board of Regents in the construction of the prayer and foresaw potential dangers to Church and State wholly out of proportion to its real intent. It may be said that not every and any government involvement in a religious act is *eo ipso* suspect and tainted with unconstitutionality. One must look to the context, purpose, and concrete circumstances of the religious act to ascertain its constitutional propriety. One would suppose that an officially prepared civic corporate prayer, publicly known, approved and consented to in advance, might have been favorably viewed as a calculated precaution to ensure the necessary constitutional safeguards against any surprise encroachments upon a sectarian conscience by the impromptu prayer of a well-meaning student or teacher. Of two likely opposing interpretations, the Court chose the negative one. The pivotal question may well have turned on the rights of religious-minded parents and school children to choose freely to participate in an official prayer modeled on our national documents, in an educational program, to impress upon the school children the moral and spiritual values which have been recognized as the basis of our free society.

Ancient History and Modern Law

As if to give substance to its fears about an official prayer, the Court reached back to sixteenth-century England and the Common Prayer Book which the Established Church imposed upon a nation. The employment of history in the determination of cases should be subject to more rigorous canons of constitutional relevance than was exercised in the ruling on prayer. The Common Prayer Book and its succeeding amended versions was composed by the Established Church of England with the deliberate attempt of effectuating revolutionary doctrinal changes — at first upon those unsuspecting faithful who still cling to articles of faith according to papal teaching after the breach with Rome, and in the following century, upon alert and vigorously resisting Puritans. It was deliberately designed not only to change ancient ceremonial administration of the sacraments, but its wording was calculated to instill in the people the new theological doctrines of the Episcopal Church touching upon the meaning, substance, and validity of the sacramental rites. The Common Prayer Book was an instrument of radical credal changes prescribed for the willing and the unwilling, for the knowledgeable and the unknowing, and the English government was a party to this.[5]

The New York prayer was not a surprise encroachment upon sectarian confessions; it conformed with beliefs already held, it was imposed on no one, it was recommended to all, it was freely adopted by the local school board, and in the instant case, voluntarily participated in by all school children with the approval of their parents, with but one exemption — the highest degree of near unanimity possible.

The constitutional relevance of sixteenth- and seventeenth-century English history was without any substantive analogy to the New York case. The resort to the historical past does not enlighten if it serves to evoke ancient fears and premonitions out of tune with our times and our sensibilities. Americans have a right to fashion their own constitutional history in church-state relations without being burdened by the memories of religious wars and animosities of their distant forebears.

Perhaps in an effort to bolster the weakness of the historical analogy, the Court sought to bridge the span of centuries and the disparity of national experiences by the use of a "bad tendency" rule together with an agreement based on indirect coercive pressure. The majority opinion said that "a union of government and religion tends to destroy government and to degrade religion." To which we would add that when government encourages religious life as part of its spiritual heritage, it strengthens itself and enhances religious liberty. And both the dark and bright lessons of history will illustrate that the governments which show impartial accommodations for the exercise of religious liberty to all are the wonder of mankind and the hope of all churches. As for the indirect coercive pressure, it is no more – perhaps even less – than what might be inferred from voluntary salute to the flag with or without the divine reference, in the singing of the national anthem and in the program of released time for religious instruction.

It is no small cause for wonder that in all of the first amendment cases touching upon education and religion, at no time does the Court, in resorting to Jefferson, ever consider Jefferson's own plans for lower and higher education which he drew up for his own state of Virginia upon his retirement from the presidency. His educational plans of 1814[6], 1817[7], 1818[8], 1822[9], and 1824[10] disclose three principles to be permanent in Jefferson's mind. First, that a totally non-religious education is defective. Secondly, government is to offer impartial encouragement and, if need be, accommodations to expressions of religious life in state schools. Thirdly, in the manner of mutual accommodation and cooperative relationship, neither government nor religion is to lose any measure of its proper competence and independent jurisdiction. Jefferson never construed such cordial arrangements and mutual adjustments as tantamount to a union of Church and State which tends to destroy the one and degrade the other. If the high tribunal was in search of Jefferson's mind on a practice that bore some substantial constitutional analogy to the New York prayer it might have examined his draft for the establishment of state elementary schools which the Virginia Assembly enacted into law in 1817. In the eleventh provision of the act we read:

The said teachers shall, in all things relating to education and government of their pupils, be under the direction and control

> of the visitors; but no religious reading, instruction or exercise shall be prescribed or practiced *inconsistent with the tenets of any religious sect or denomination.*

For Jefferson there was only one absolute and all controlling restriction on any religious exercise or instruction in the elementary grades; that it be not inconsistent with the confessional tenets of the school children. He was most anxious to guard the religious conscience of all minors against the more learned persuasion of adult instructors. All of his educational plans insist upon a positive doctrine of impartial and mutually beneficent accommodation between the religious conscience and the state schools. The New York prayer gave offense to no denominational confession. On the contrary, it was willingly recited precisely because it was in full accord with professed beliefs. We do not say that Thomas Jefferson should be considered the constitutional oracle of government relations with religion in education. But if the Supreme Court chooses to quote him, it ought to have recourse to the very documents that give his own explicit direct and pertinent testimony. Whether the Court might then be still willing to follow him remains at this time an open question.

One of the most engaging enterprises of the high tribunal is the frequency with which it employs James Madison's justly famed *Memorial and Remonstrance Against Religious Assessments* of 1785 and the ease with which its meaning is bent beyond its authentic purpose. In 1784, Patrick Henry proposed to the Virginia Assembly a "Bill Establishing a Provision for Teachers of the Christian Religion" with the expectation that such a comprehensive tax support would find acceptance with all Christians to take place of the abrogated provision for the support of the Anglican ministers alone. It was against this preference through tax support of *a* religion, a broadly defined christianity under the benign mantle of the Anglican Establishment, that Madison directed his famed *Memorial.*

> Who does not see that the same authority which can *establish Christianity*, in *exclusion* of all other Religions, may establish with the same ease any *particular* sect of Christians, in *exclusion* of all other Sects? That the same authority which can *force* a citizen to contribute three pence only of his property for the support of any one establishment, may *force him to conform* to any other establishment in all cases whatsoever.[11]

The New York prayer was singularly free of any of these Madisonian premonitions. It allowed Christians of every denomination and non-Christians of any confession to join in a unifying corporate prayer wholly of their own choice and in accord with their own religious conscience. Fifty signers of the Declaration of Independence— 34 Episcopalians, 13 Congregationalists, 6 Presbyterians, 1 Baptist, 1 Quaker, and 1 Catholic—confessed publicly to self-evident truths in the common patrimony of human nature which the Creator had endowed with certain inalienable rights. And Paul of Tarsus, Jewish Apostle of Christianity among the Gentiles, taught that knowledge of God is open to human reason apart from the teachings of divine revelation.

As for the Court's reference to James Madison, one may note that, apart from its misleading use of his *Memorial*, it scarcely takes any cognizance of Madison's own unequivocal explanation of the scope and meaning of the no establishment clause recorded in the congressional debates.[12] And further, it takes no note of the significant fact that ex-President Madison was one of the Commissioners for the University of Virginia for whom Jefferson drafted the educational plan of 1818 for submission to the legislature of the state which declares that:

> [T]he proofs of...God, the creator, preserver, and supreme ruler of the universe, the author of all the relations of morality, and of the laws and obligations these infer, will be *within* the province of the *professor of ethics*; to which adding the developments of these moral obligations, of those *in which all sects agree*, with a knowledge of the languages, Hebrew, Greek, and Latin, a basis will be formed *common to all sects*.

Psychology and Law

The establishment clause, the Supreme Court said, does "not depend upon any showing of direct governmental compulsion and is violated by the enactment of laws which establish an official religion whether the laws operate directly to coerce the nonobserving or not." It may be that the Court was simply saying that, as in England today, direct governmental compulsion need not be a necessary incidence of proscribed establishment even though it almost always entails at least indirect coercive pressure. In a word, the Court ruled the element of compulsion to be constitutionally non-relevant and not as controlling as it had held in the *McCollum* and *Zorach* cases.

Indirect coercive pressure upon the religious nonconformist is everywhere in the air we breathe, apart from those circumstances where there is governmental provision for religious expression in public institutions. It takes its strongest emotional experience in a constraining feeling of embarrassment. This is generally the concomitant of most acts of dissent and nonconformity. Public law is committed to the defense of individual rights, to the remedy and redress of hurt rights, not hurt feelings unless the hurt is such that it effectively impedes the free exercise of personal choice. Public law is not required to convert the psychology of dissent into a constitutional principle. It is not the function of law to remove the situations wherein contrary choices may engender contrary feelings. The dissenter must be the first to acknowledge that the condition for his own dissent is to live and let live. Good will in a community rests in great measure on people leaving others to their own choices. No man is an island to himself in society. Robinson Crusoe was seemingly free from any social inhibitions until one day he noticed the footprints of another and from that moment on, the law of mutual adjustment and tolerance set in. The right of the conscientious objector is to shield his own conscience, not to strike down the religious rights of his neighbors. We are all conscientious objectors and none of us should enjoy an exclusive privilege to the prejudice of others.[13]

If words have substantive meaning, a "captive audience" is an audience whose involuntary presence is forcibly detained or whose involuntary participation is compelled. To have denied the school children the choice of joining in the recitation of the prayer was to deny them the opportunity of sharing in the spiritual heritage of our nation. The governmental denial of freedom of choice is as much coercion as the imposing of an action. The argument that public law is required to ensure the conscientious dissenter impervious to indirect coercive pressure, divisiveness, and the likelihood of social stigma and isolation that may possibly follow upon a governmental program of religious accommodation, bears within itself a premise of assault upon the salute to the flag in our public schools to which the Jehovah Witnesses oppose their religious conscience.

We have travelled a full and truly *vicious* circle. From religious persecution, intolerance and church establishment to benign tolerance — to disestablishment — to equality of all faiths before the law — to equality of belief and nonbelief before the law — and now to the secularist and the religious dissenter's intolerance of religious belief in public law. The wry irony is that this is being done, we are told, in the name of and for the sake of religious liberty.

We are losing by default. We have taken our spiritual heritage for granted. We have allowed a creeping gradualism of secularism under one specious pretext after another to take over our public schools. A vociferous and highly organized pressure group is exerting its own form of indirect coercive pressure upon the American community. Determined to deflect our national traditions and heritage from their authentic historic course, it is cutting a devisive swath across the nation, advertising for clients to challenge in court what is obnoxious to them. Whoever works for the destruction of the positive doctrine of accommodation and mutual adjustment must shoulder the blame for uprooting the bonds of concord and friendship and forcibly injecting bitter antagonisms in our pluralistic society. Political and legal action *alone* cannot create the moral and social impulses which are the conditions of harmony in a community. With full regard for the radical and primary rights of *all* parents to guide the education of their children in public schools, as well as in independent private schools, members of a local community can strive with persevering good will to find a reasonable accommodation and mutual adjustment of one another's choices. In this way law becomes — as it ought — the formal expression of the practical wisdom of a self-regulating community. Dissidents and consentients should be motivated to the exercise of *cultivated* rights of men living in fellowship and not as strangers in a contest of absolute and conflicting claims.

The more we examine the context of the New York prayer and the circumstances attending its optional recitation, the more we discern the vast possibilities it offered for the increase of friendly community life.

First, the children and their approving parents of different faiths and church affiliations came together in a prayer based on the common bonds of their religious beliefs. Their religious sectarianism was in no way experienced as a barrier to the brotherhood of all men under the Fatherhood of God. One would suppose that with all the adult incantations about the intercredal relations and the counsels — on all sides — of charity and good-will against divisiveness, here indeed was a truly unitive bond of intercredal relations in the most sensitive time of the school children's formative years.

Second, it provided an opportune and excellent educational training and habituation to the exercise of individual choice in the midst of others according to the vaunted American boast of individualism and free self-expression. Religious differences are a very broad fact even for the most enlightening adults, and social adjustment in this matter is essential to good community relations. Should not the youngsters mature gradually in this delicate experience with civility toward one another without resentment and without inhibition? The circumstances for the corporate prayer provided an early schooling both for the dissidents and the consentients to advance in mutual reverence for one another's religious choices.

Third, the dissenter and the minority must surely be shielded from majoritarian imposition. So too must the majority be protected from the unilateral dictation of the absolute dissenter. It is indeed a strange pathology of our time that when people in increasing numbers freely choose to act agreeably in unison there is less cause for public gratification than in the uncompromising protestations of the dissenter. The numerical superiority of a consensual agreement should not be constitutionally suspect, and if conformity is the flower of human freedom, the wider the area of religious consensus among the variety of religious confessions, the greater will be the harmony among men of good will. Only when the dissenter treasures the liberties of others as his own and insists on equal freedom and the same legal immunity for opposing choices that he demands for himself, then will we be sure that he acts in the name of law and justice.

No one can deny that public law is burdened with an almost insurmountable task when it is confronted with the problems of religious pluralism. We are of the opinion that the voluntary nondenominational prayer was possibly one of the best, and at that, a minimal resolution of this thorny moral-legal problem.

Separation and Relation

Separation of Church and State in American law is uniquely an American experience. Its meaning derives from our own constitutional history from the days of the Northwest Ordinance to the recent construction of the chapel at the Air Force Academy in Colorado. Our separation of Church and State is a positive affirmation not a negative protestation. Its paramount purpose is to preserve unimpaired and inviolable the freedom and independence of both Church and State. It is but the counterpart of an orderly and harmonious relationship of friendly powers, a relationship of cordial cooperation and of benevolent accommodation, not a relationship of mutually exclusive isolation. In *Everson*[14] the Court held for benevolent impartiality for believers and unbelievers equally alike. In *Zorach*[15] a positive doctrine of accommodation was opposed to a neutrality of total abstention, of indifference, suspicion and hostility. The New York prayer was indeed a reasonable and proper accommodation to the spiritual needs of our people in accordance with the spiritual heritage of our country. What absolute right has a dissenter to protest against such an orderly harmony when the government acts to foster the relevance of religion to our national existence according to the cherished traditions of our country? To what purpose then may a court reason, "If this is allowed to take place, dire consequences will *therefore* inevitably follow." Politics, social relations, and public law cannot be regulated solely by narrow legal ergotisms. Each human experience is invested with sensibilities of its own times and the present may presage a future wholly alien to the heavy hand of the past. The law of progress is applicable to public law as to other human enterprises. Far from being a dark beginning, a first experiment on our liberties, a portent of dangers to come, the New York prayer was, on the contrary, a refined product of American constitutional history on Church-State relations, sensitive to the rights of conscience of all – of parents and their children, of participants and nonparticipants, of equal neutrality between believer and nonbeliever, of impartiality among all the religious confessions, with due regard to the government's role to foster in public schools the relevance of belief in God to our national existence – and all above with immunity for personal choice.

Every generation of Americans has admitted to the role of the government in attesting to the religious foundations of our republic and official composition or adoption of divine invocations has been one of the traditional government practices in a great variety of government-supported religious exercises: the Presidential proclamations of days of prayer and thanksgiving, the prayerful invocation in fifty state constitutions, the prayer which opens each day's session of the Supreme Court, the religious inscription on our coinage and currency,[16] in our national anthem and motto, and in the salute to the flag — not to mention the public financing of legislative and military chapels and chaplaincies by the state and national governments. Now if federal and state government officials and public institutions may engage in religious activity why should the first amendment operate to greater duress upon a local school board and the school children who wish to say a prayer together? The New York prayer was no more a violation of the no establishment clause in public school activities than the optional participation in the singing of the national anthem, the Pledge of Allegiance, the released time religious instruction program, and in court proceedings, the statutory alternate of testifying under oath or by affirmation. In *Zorach,* we were told that the "problem, like many problems on constitutional law, is one of degree." But in the prayer case, the Court perceived an absolutizing principle which posed a threat to government and religion.

One Nation Under God

It is not in any way intimated that a civic corporate prayer so much in evidence in our public institutions and in our national documents would, if excluded from our public schools, bear within itself a "bad tendency" rule that might inexorably work to the development of a godless state in America. But in our times we have seen a highly civilized society whose government gradually restricted in their civil institutions the official profession of belief and dependence upon God and withdrew religious exercises exclusively to churches and homes. But when the tragic hour of conflicting allegiances bore upon its citizens, they obeyed with passioned submission and gratified acquiescence a supreme and absolute statal authority to the complete destruction of the state and to the enduring shame of their religious confessions. Perhaps the United States Supreme Court might have allowed a "good tendency" rule to be immanent in the civic corporate prayer to impress on all alike — on the participants and the nonparticipants — that there is a higher allegiance to God under which men must rule, that no patriotism may obey against the moral law, that personal immunity against arbitrary power is a divine mandate. It is not without profound symbolism that public authority should be a party to an acknowledgement of dependence upon God.

Thomas Jefferson once wrote:

Can the liberties of a nation be thought secure, when we have removed their own firm basis, a conviction in the minds of the people that these liberties are the gifts of God?[17]

Public schools should share in the task of transmitting to our school children the relevance of a free order among men to the Divine Author of all liberties and accordingly allow this conviction to abide and deepen among the rising generation of Americans.

FOOTNOTES AND REFERENCES

1. 370 U.S. 421 (1962).

2. Justice Douglas made these detailed admissions in his concurring opinion: "First a word as to what this case does not involve. Plainly, our Bill of Rights would not permit a State or the Federal Government to adopt an official prayer and penalize anyone who would not utter it. This, however, is not that case, for there is no element of compulsion or coercion in New York's regulation requiring that public schools be opened each day with the... prayer.... The prayer is said upon the commencement of the school day, immediately following the Pledge of Allegiance to the flag. The prayer is said aloud in the presence of a teacher, who either leads the recitation or selects a student to do so. No student, however, is compelled to take part. The respondents have adopted a regulation which provides that 'neither teachers nor any school authority shall comment on participation or non-participation... nor suggest or request that any posture or language be used or dress be worn or be not used or not worn.' Provision is also made for excusing children, upon written request of a parent or guardian, from the saying of the prayer or from the room in which the prayer is said. A letter implementing and explaining this regulation has been sent to each taxpayer and parent in the school district. As I read this regulation, a child is free to stand or not stand, to recite or not to recite, without fear of reprisal or even comment by the teacher or any other school official. In short, the only one who need utter the prayer is the teacher; and no teacher is complaining of it. Students can stand mute or even leave the classroom if they desire."

3. Mr. Justice Douglas, in his concurring opinion, stated: "In the present case, school facilities are used to say the prayer and the teaching staff is employed to lead the pupils in it. There is, however, no effort at indoctrination and no attempt at exposition. Prayers of course may be so long and of such a character as to amount to an attempt at the religious instruction that was denied by the *McCollum* case. But New York's prayer is of a character that does not involve any element of proselytizing as in the *McCollum* case."

4. While the majority opinion written by Mr. Justice Black pivots the decision technically on governmental composition of the prayer, construed as one of the exercises of a proscribed state-established church under the ban of the first amendment, Mr. Justice Douglas, on the other hand, settles upon governmental financing of religious exercises. Both the majority and concurring opinions isolate elements of state-church establishment, elements which by themselves are not necessarily derivative of nor conducive to state-church establishment. Indeed a governmental composition of a prayer – *not any prayer* – and certain governmental financing of religious exercises may be justifiably sustained by the religious liberty clause. (In the instant case, there was greater use of what was already financed. An additional specific expenditure of public funds was not entailed by the optional recitation of the New York prayer.) In severing these elements from one another, the way is paved for absolutizing an isolated element into a constitutional barrier whether or not anyone suffers an infringement of religious liberty and without regard to the equal protection which the law should extend to all, believer and nonbeliever, consentient and dissident. Such an absolutizing process gradually expands from a narrow legalism to a broad

premise of proscription. Only recently, the New York Commissioner of Education ruled that a part of The Star-Spangled Banner may not be used as a school prayer. The radical source of the antinomies which have been inserted by court interpretation into the religious clauses of the first amendment is the as yet unsettled legal question (historically, there appears to be less doubt about it) whether the two clauses, dealing with no establishment and free exercise, are so correspondent to one another that an adjudication under one clause may not be at the expense of the legal guarantees of the other, or whether the two clauses may be interpreted in exclusive isolation to one another. Until and unless this question of the interrelationship of the two clauses is resolved, the absolutist construction of the no establishment clause which Mr. Justice Rutledge put forth in his dissenting opinion in *Everson* and which the Court adopted in *McCollum* is likely to prevail over the original authentic meaning of no establishment as explained by James Madison in his rejoinders to questions put to him in the debates of Congress. The danger involved in the absolutist interpretation is that the judiciary may over-reach itself by preempting the democratic political process and embodying on its own initiative public policy into constitutional law. In *Zorach*, the possibilities of relating the two religious clauses to one another harmoniously in specific programs of mutual accommodation seemed an implementation of Mr. Justice Black's assertion in *Everson* about "the interrelationship of these complementary clauses" and his warning against interjecting a religious discriminatory norm into the first amendment.

Another source of ambiguity is the fear of the extent to which government aid to religion may go. To date, the Court has not yet formulated practical norms beyond which the political process may not extend. The wide variety of legislative precedents from the beginning of the Republic to this day of governmental financing of religious life directly, indirectly, and incidently offers the greatest obstacles to the judicial construction of such norms. Perhaps in the last resort, public opinion may provide the practical wisdom to which intercredal dialogues hope to make sensible contributions. Some constitutional lawyers have opposed a "neutral principle" to the principle of neutrality in the area of federal aid to education. This neutral principle looks to the standard of public function and will not allow religion to be *the* cause for action or inaction because the religious clauses of the first amendment prohibit classification that would entail conferment of a benefit or the imposition of a burden. Under this neutral principle, the prayer case might have turned on the question whether civic corporate prayer was indeed a constitutionally justifiable exercise for the promotion of an educational program to foster in school children moral and spiritual values which have been traditionally part of our national heritage. The determination of this precise issue would in turn rest on the ulterior question whether it is a part of the public function of tax-supported schools to transmit the spiritual heritage of the nation *as it is authentically embodied* in the official acts and the authoritative documents of American history.

5. 2 Hughes, THE REFORMATION IN ENGLAND 111-13, 121-26 (1954).

6. Jefferson, *Plan for An Educational System*, in THE COMPLETE JEFFERSON 1064-69 (Padover ed. 1943) [hereinafter cited as Padover].

7. Jefferson, *An Act for Establishing Elementary Schools*, in Padover 1072, 1076.

8. Jefferson, *The University of Virginia, Aim and Curriculum*, in Padover 1097, 1104.

9. Jefferson, *Freedom of Religion at the University of Virginia*, in Padover 957-58.

10. Jefferson, *Regulations for the University*, in Padover 1106-11.

11. 2 THE WRITINGS OF JAMES MADISON 184-88 (Hunt ed. 1901). (Emphasis added.)

12. 1 ANNALS OF CONG. 727 (1789).

13. Jewish Orthodox want an exception for their ritual slaughter of animals in humane slaughter laws. Jehovah's Witnesses are exempt from the salute to the flag. Pacifists object to combatant and noncombatant military service. Christian Scientists are excused from hygiene courses. One atheist child wiped out a voluntary cooperative arrangement of five years standing by eight hundred Protestants, about twenty Catholics, and thirty Jews for religious instruction in public schools. Sabbatarians oppose Sunday Laws. Catholics oppose the use of public funds for the promotion of birth control instructions at home and in any foreign aid program. The Amish raise religious objections to the Social Security tax. These are but a handful of the instances of legally and politically effective protests. Is there any room for conscientious protest against godless education in public schools? Would Thomas Jefferson's protest be heeded today?

14. "New Jersey cannot consistently with the 'establishment of religion' clause of the First Amendment contribute tax-raised funds to the support of an institution which teaches the tenets and faith of any church. On the other hand, other language of the amendment commands that New Jersey cannot hamper its citizens in the free exercise of their own religion. Consequently, it cannot exclude individual Catholics, Lutherans, Mohammedans, Baptists, Jews, Methodists, non-believers, Presbyterians, or the members of any other faith, *because of their faith or lack of it,* from receiving the benefits of public welfare legislation. While we do not mean to intimate that a state could not provide transportation only to children attending public schools, we must be careful, in protecting the citizens of New Jersey against state-established churches, to be sure that we do not inadvertently prohibit New Jersey from extending its general state law benefits to all its citizens without regard to their religious beliefs." Everson v. Board of Educ., 330 U.S. 1, 16 (1947).(Emphasis added.)

15. *"We are a religious people whose institutions presuppose a Supreme Being.* We guarantee the freedom to worship as one chooses. We make room for as wide a variety of beliefs and creeds as the spiritual needs of man deem necessary. We sponsor an attitude on the part of the government that shows *no partiality* to any one group and that lets each flourish according to the zeal of its adherents and the appeal of its dogma. When the state *encourages* religious instruction or *cooperates* with religious authorities by adjusting the schedule of public events to sectarian needs, *it follows the best of our traditions.* For it then respects the religious nature of our people and *accommodates* the public service to their spiritual needs. To hold that it may would be to find in the Constitution a requirement that the government show a *callous indifference* to religious groups. *That would be preferring those who believe in no religion over those who do believe."* Zorach v. Clauson, 343 U.S. 306, 312 (1952). (Emphasis added.)

In the *Zorach* opinion which Mr. Justice Douglas wrote, he listed, with apparent approval and as giving substance to his argument, several tax-supported religious exercises by public officials and in public institutions: "Prayers in our legislative halls; the appeals to the Almighty in the messages of the Chief Executive; the proclamations making Thanksgiving Day a holiday; 'so help me God' in our courtroom oaths – these and other references to the Almighty that run through our laws, our public rituals, our ceremonies, would be flouting the First Amendment. A fastidious atheist or agnostic could even object to the supplication with which the Court opens each session: 'God save the United States and this Honorable Court.'" In *Engel v. Vitale,* Justice Douglas has forgotten the fastidious objector and attached himself to an absolutizing principle of government financing of religious activity (and every governmental action is tax-supported) that would abrogate the multitude of governmental involvements in religious exercises which he had cited with approval in *Zorach.* Now, apparently, a taxpayer may have stronger claims before Justice Douglas as a fastidious financier than as a fastidious conscientious objector.

16. Occasionally one hears and reads of statements (recently, by Rev. Dean Kelley of the Department of Religious Liberty, Council of the Churches of Christ) that religious inscriptions on coins and currency are a profane use of divine invocations. Really, no one may argue conclusively that there *must* be religious inscriptions on our coinage. But given the fact by congressional enactment, one may question the charge of impropriety of the employment of divine references on our currency. Radically, it is a question of asceticism. Optimistic asceticism affirms that the original goodness of divine creation forever retains the image of godliness against any evil doing. All things remain sacred and for this reason St. Paul wrote that all creation calls out "Abba Pater" and our Divine Lord said that the stones would cry out in His praise if the jubilant shouts of the children had been stifled. Through the centuries men have quarried stones and marble to raise magnificent houses of worship. Most of the tangible articles used in divine services are of gold, silver and the finest raiment. There is too a somber asceticism once prevalent among the English and American Puritans which saw the danger of distraction or interference in these instrumentalities to the direct communication of the human heart with God. This view, however, is not relevant to the issue. The charge of profane use rests logically upon a presupposition of Manichaeism which considers corporeal and material things as somehow vitiated, tainted, and imbued with a radical principle for evil in eternal contest with the spiritual principle of Goodness for the allegiance of men. In this view, material things in no way can give glory to God. Optimistic asceticism affirms, on the contrary, that the source of evil does not spring from things – *falsitas non ex rebus sed ex peccatis* (St. Augustine) but from a love that is not

God-centered — *non faciunt bonos vel malos mores nisi boni vel mali amores* (St. Augustine). Now, optimistic asceticism does not demand nor require that there be divine invocations on currencies. But it does deny that such inscriptions on coinage are a profane use. They are in accord with the dominical prayer for daily bread and may serve as a telling reminder that commercial instruments of exchange are not to be debauched by dishonest trafficking. Also, religious-minded citizens may wish divine blessing and providence for our national economy.

17. Quoted by Morris, CHRISTIAN LIFE AND CHARACTER OF THE CIVIL INSTITUTIONS OF THE UNITED STATES DEVELOPED IN THE OFFICIAL AND HISTORICAL ANNALS OF THE UNITED STATES 35 (1864).

WHOLESOME NEUTRALITY: LAW
AND EDUCATION*

In September, 1963, a suit was filed in Anne Arundel circuit court, Annapolis, Maryland, titled, *The Horace Mann League of the United States of America et al,* plaintiffs, v. *J. Millard Tawes, Governor et al,* defendants, which set into motion the judicial process on a critical question of law whose ultimate determination will bear far-reaching consequences for education in America. After a year of pretrial depositions the court trial opened in November, 1964, with Judge O. Bowie Duckett presiding. At issue was the constitutionality of an appropriation by the Maryland legislature of $2.5 million for four Maryland church-related colleges — $750,000 to Notre Dame of Baltimore, $750,000 to St. Joseph's College of Emmitsburg for science buildings, $500,000 to Methodist-related Western Maryland College in Westminister for a science building and dining hall, and $500,000 to Hood College in Frederick, related to the United Church of Christ, for a dormitory.

The Maryland case represents a change in political and legal tactics for the opponents of public support for educational institutions under religious auspices. In the preceding years, they concentrated their instrumentalities of influence upon members of the national and state legislatures. But aid in one form or another and for a variety of specified purposes which were identified as a legislative concern of public interest were extended to educational facilities under church sponsorship. They were judged to be no less efficacious and competent than the nonreligious institutions of learning in realizing the educational objectives set down by the

---

*NORTH DAKOTA REVIEW. Vol. 43, N. 4. Summer 1967, pp. 605-658.

legislators. Besides, the nationwide debate on the constitutionality of these subventions in law journals, before congressional committees, and on televised forums, brought to the fore the fact that scholars, jurists, and men of high public repute were to be found no less on the side which upheld their constitutionality as there were in the opposite camp. Surveys and polls of public opinion showed a steady decline in the public persuasion and political influence of the opponents. With a shift of preponderance from one side to the other, the opponents hopefully concentrated on winning the legal battle in the courts. In the legal forum there is a change of tactic too. Whereas Mr. Marbury, the chief counsel for the defendants in the Maryland case argued that several Supreme Court decisions established a precedent that public aid is constitutionally permissable if a church-related institution performs "a legitimate secular function that does not advance or prohibit religion," Mr. Pfeffer contended for the plaintiffs that Judge Duckett must apply a different constitutional test — that tax support cannot be given to institutions "which either teach or practice religion." The Maryland case was carefully chosen by Mr. Edgar Fuller, an official of the Horace Mann League, and his associates. First, inasmuch as the grants involved are made directly from the state to the colleges the more appealing student-benefit argument may be avoided. Secondly, the four institutions represent two Protestant affiliations as well as two Catholic and in this wise the usual concentration of legal attack upon Catholics subtly suggestive of discriminatory bias is shunned.

On March 11, 1965, Judge O. Bowie Duckett handed down his ruling that the Statutes mentioned in the Bill of Complaint are valid and constitutional.[1] On June 2, 1966, the Court of Appeals of Maryland in a four to three decision[2] reversed for three of the colleges but upheld the constitutional permissiveness of the state grant to Hood College on the basis of tests which weighted the degree of relationship of the educational institution to church or religious regulation. The Supreme Court has declined to review the ruling of the Maryland Court of Appeals. In the expectation that eventually a similar issue will come before the high tribunal we here undertake to examine pertinent cases of the United States Supreme Court and try to ascertain what constitutional premises may be controlling on this great issue of governmental financial aid to church-related institutions of learning. For the moment, the refusal to review the Court of Appeals ruling leaves us with a presumption in favor of that ruling but it is a rebuttal presumption and in the hope that it may someday be contravened by the Supreme Court of the United States we undertake to discuss this issue at length. It takes only a modicum of perception to see how epoch-making the Supreme Court decision on such an issue would be. The alternatives which the Supreme Court may have to consider are three: (1) whether the colleges in question are essentially educational institutions despite or together with their religious affiliation and therefore they may receive tax funds; (2) whether such tax support is violative of the nonestablishment prohibition of the First Amendment and therefore they may not be recipients of government subventions; (3) whether a line must be drawn, as the Court of Appeals of Maryland did, between church relationship and church control — admittedly, an extremely difficult canon of application.

A FREE STATE AND A FREE CHURCH

Some prefatory reflections must be stated in order to be alert to distracting or misleading considerations customarily made in a discussion of this problem.

The Constitution does not mention the word "church" nor "state" in the generic sense except in the Second Amendment, in which a "well regulated militia" is asserted to be "necessary to the security of a free state." The principle of separation of church and state and the "wall of separation" are nonlegal terms which better fit the European (and Middle East and Oriental) historic experience from which Americans have gradually disengaged themselves since colonial times. The resort to the historical past does not enlighten if it serves to evoke fears and premonitions out of tune with the times and popular sensibilities. Americans have a right to fashion their own constitutional history in church-state relations without being burdened by memories of religious wars and animosities of their distant forebears. Many of the foreboding nuances of the historic church-state relations might be avoided if we spoke more accurately of the relations between the temporal and spiritual lives of the American community to the extent that they come under the regulations of public law in America. We have religious pluralism and a multiplicity of churches with none of which any of our fifty-one state and federal governments have a concordat or legal establishment as state religion. But the term, "separation of church and state" is here to stay by popular usage. Strictly speaking, church-state relations are not in any positive way defined or formulated by the Constitution. The twin religious clauses of the federal First Amendment and similar provisions in state constitutions are stated in negative terms—what these governments may not do—between the confines of these prohibitions and the courts, both state and federal, have evolved the positive affirmations of permissive and required relations between state and the religious conscience. The controversy which has been raging in recent times must be dated with the celebrated dictum of Justice Black in *Everson v. Board of Education*:

> The 'establishment of religion' clause of the First Amendment means at least this: neither a state nor the Federal Government can set up a church, nor can pass laws which aid one religion, aid all religions, or prefer one religion over another. Neither can force or influence a person to go to or to remain away from church against his will or to profess a belief or disbelief in any religion. No persons can be punished for entertaining or professing religious beliefs or disbeliefs, for church attendance or non-attendance. No tax in any amount, large or small, can be levied to support any religious activities or institutions, whatever they may be called or whatever form they may adopt to teach or preach religion. Neither a state nor the federal government can, openly or secretly, participate in the affairs of any religious organization or groups and *vice versa*. In the words of Jefferson, the clause against establishment of religion was intended to erect 'a wall of separation between church and state.'[3]

Several summary observations may here be made. It is Justice Black's broad interdiction against any aid to religion which is contrary to a great variety of governmental legislative provisions for religion, religious activities, and public services conducted by religious agencies and institutions and offers the greatest difficulty of constitutional construction unless its literal comprehensiveness becomes less than absolute when contracted by the constitutional permissiveness of the specific ruling. Secondly, some of the doctrinaire generalizations have inserted unresolved antinomy between members of the Court. In *Everson*,[4] *McCollum*,[5] and *Zorach*,[6] the Court with the exception of Justice Reed, subscribed to the formulation of non-establishment by Justice Black but then split five to four in this specific ruling in *Everson* and in *Zorach* in the particular application.

Thirdly, Justice Black's interpretation of the nonestablishment clause includes elements that properly are inherent to the free exercise of religion guarantee. This is not without significance for in succeeding cases the Court is alert to the fact that the nonestablishment prohibition is not to be so understood or applied as to infringe upon the equally inviolable constitutional guarantee of religious liberty. This conduces the Court to a competing of interests calculation in particular instances and weighs its favor to the religious liberty concept. Fourth, the sum total of the prohibitions does constitute *absolute* separation between the government and the spiritual life of the American community. It denies to the government both competence and jurisdiction to operate a church, to define dogma, or to participate in the internal affairs of the church. And conversely, it denies by implication that it is the function of the churches to run the government. These negations are those constitutionally guaranteed conditions which serve the cause of freedom – freedom and independence of the state and its legitimate activities from dictation and imposition by the churches on political governance – freedom and independence of the churches from governmental interposition in church government, in the definition of creeds, and the right to proselytyze without coercive power – freedom of the individual to believe or not to believe, to attend or not to attend church services except as his conscience impels him to do so. It is not a separation that spells indifference. On the contrary, external conduct attributed to religious creeds are not outside the reach of the police powers of the state.

No government in modern history has affirmed so frequently in corporate and individual official pronouncements on the most memorable and solemn occasions belief in and dependence upon God as the author of its liberties and reliance upon divine providence for civic peace, order, and good government, as has the American government.

This moral nexus between religious and civic life enjoys preferment status in law. Churches, seminaries, monasteries, convents, synagogues, and rabbinical schools are given tax preferment and tax deductible benefits by law, the clergy and students of the ministry are exempt from military service, both in peace and war, state and federal governments provide for chaplains to invoke God's blessings and guidance upon legislative deliberations. These preferment benefits are an acknowledgement by law that religious life is a necessary beneficient influence for the promotion of civic virtue and religious institutions are considered as tributory to civic peace, law, and order. The legal preferments through tax exemption and tax deductible benefits in favor of religious life are to be clearly distinguished from similar benefits that educational and social welfare affiliates of the churches enjoy under a statutory law in common with other non-profit organizations. Legislative chaplaincies and military exemptions for students of the ministry as well as for the ordained clergy bears no other parallel with secular institutions.

The plain fact is that the state and federal governments and the churches are mutually reliant upon one another in order to enjoy the freedom and independence that results from "separation." The churches are no less beneficiaries of the facilities of the administration of justice than other associations, commercial, industrial, cultural, etc. Where church schools have not adequate recreational facilities, municipal authorities have roped off the streets for their students to play, deflecting the unrestrained flow of public traffic. Public proselytizing in parks, street corners, and distribution of religious literature in person even to the inconvenience of tenants has been upheld by the courts. In turn, the churches are called upon to testify before congressional committees to give their counsel on domestic and foreign affairs, and to assist in the moral enlightenment of their congregations on the inviolability of the rights of others against deeply rooted bias and prejudice. We may note here that it is misleading to refer to all litigations as church-state cases. The generality of cases are not between the juridical entities but between a government and an individual who in his moral character as the subject of natural rights invokes his rights of conscience under the religious liberty clause and between the government and a citizen, or corporation, as the subject of legal rights claiming he ought not to be excluded as a beneficiary from general welfare provisions because of his exercise of religious liberty in the fulfillment of a civic purpose defined by the government.

There is too, a concurrence of identical interests between government and religious agencies. Historically, the care of the poor, the infirm, and of dependents and other works of corporal mercy have been the principal burden of churches and religious organizations. Gradually, the state has assumed more and more of these temporal cares but not with the intent of preempting the field. Rather, it has subsidized on a *pro rata* basis, the care of the aged, the infirm, incurables, the blind, deaf, mutes, the orphaned, and the wayward under the care of religious agencies, and acknowledged the need of religious solace for the sorely afflicted. In 1894, the State of Louisiana invited Catholic Nuns, the Daughters of Charity, to help care for the afflicted at the leprosarium at Carville. When the federal government took over in 1921, the Sisters remained in this charitable employment. The federal Hill-Burton Act makes grants for the new construction and expansion of hospital facilities to all qualified hospitals, and of those under religious auspices constitute a major number of the total.

There is, too, a concurrence of functions between government and religious agencies because both jurisdictions fall upon one and the same subject in his dual capacity, the individual person, as believer and citizen. This occurs, for example, in the areas of marriage and divorce laws, education and birth control programs. This mutual involvement of civic and ecclesiastical jurisdictions is unavoidable because such matters touch upon personal conscience and the outward conduct correspondent to religious confession. It is not difficult to see in what sense there is absolute separation of church and state—there is to be no jurisdictional, institutional, or functional fusion of the two authorities, civil and religious. This separation is to ensure freedom of conscience for the believer (and nonbeliever) and for the churches and their religious apostolate and activities. It is a freedom which makes possible a cooperation that is vigorous because independent of interference from the other. Cooperation may and does take expression in a variety of forms. It may be an accommodation that is required because its denial would restrict the exercise of religious liberty (as in the *Jehovah Witnesses*[7] and *Sherbet v. Verner*[8] cases); an accommodation that is prohibited because it is considered to be constructively an establishment of religion (as in *McCollum, Engels,*[9] and *Schempp*[10] cases); an accommodation which is permitted because it assists religious life without entailing the constitutionally forbidden establishment (*Everson, Zorach*). Where a public service is involved, the government must not use a religious exclusionary norm (*Bradfield,*[11] *Cochran, Everson, Torcaso*[12]) but must observe strict neutrality as between believer and nonbeliever. Nor may a religious exclusionary norm be used if the secular, i.e., civic general welfare purpose is achieved in such a way that it unavoidably does entrail as an overflow a discernible benefit to the religious life (*Bradfield, Pierce,* [14] *Cochran, Everson,* the

Sunday Closing Laws cases). One cannot deny that religious life does enjoy a variety of public privileges which may rightly be said to encourage religious life if not confer upon it a privileged status. And where a conflict between competing interests emerges between the interplay of the twin religious clauses, the Court has weighed the scales in favor of the free exercise of religion.

CANONS OF CONSTITUTIONAL CONSTRUCTION

Bearing in mind that there are a number of concurring functions of interest between governments and religious agencies and unavoidably an interplay of the two religious clauses involving the individual both as a believer and as a subject of the government we ask what may we find in court decisions of the past to shed light on the constitutionality of federal aid to church schools. There is no court ruling on this issue. While *Bradfield v. Roberts*,[15] *Cochran v. Board of Education*,[16] and *Everson v. Board of Education*,[17] are the only three decisions of the Supreme Court which bear more relevance to our discussion than do the others, we will review a number of other cases in order to ascertain if in any reasonable way our precise issue is at least broadly adumbrated in the reasonings of the opinions of the Justices.

Bradfield v. Roberts

In 1899, the Supreme Court upheld in a unanimous decision the constitutionality of federal appropriations of funds for the construction of a building and public recompense for services rendered to a hospital owned and administered by Roman Catholic Sisters. Presumably the Hill-Burton Hospital Survey and Construction Act which has been repeatedly renewed since its enactment in 1946 rests squarely upon the ruling in *Bradfield* that such federal subventions are not in violation of the nonestablishment clause. One cannot argue conclusively from *Bradfield* that what is upheld in the noneducational area—hospital services and facilities—would necessarily apply to the area of education. But allowing for the obvious differences between educational and medical situations nevertheless appropriations for an officially recognized public service might be favorably constructed into an analogous constitutional principle for gauging the public interest of an officially accredited schooling. Nor has any constitutional embarrassment come from acknowledging that some benefit does accrue to the private religious corporation, and in certain instances the benefit is almost incalculable to the fortune of an affiliate educational institution of learning.[18] *Bradfield* supplied the constitutional rationale in an area of concurrent or overlapping functions. Federal and state governments in disbursing funds and property for specified objectives that come within their powers to provide and spend for the general welfare, have extended financial assistance impartially to all agencies and institutions, religious[19] or secular, who can fulfill the legislative intent and so service a public purpose. This rationale has been explained by subsequent state court decisions to counter the customary two objections of the religious character of an institution and the overflow of benefits to it.

In 1955 the highest court of New Hampshire upheld the constitutionality of a statute giving state aid to denominational hospitals for the education of nurses:

> The purpose of the grant... is neither to aid any particular sect or denomination nor all denominations, but to further the teaching of the science of nursing.... The aid is available to all hospitals offering training in nursing without regard to the auspices under which they are conducted or to the religious beliefs of their managements, so long as the aid is used for nurses' training 'and for no other instruction or purpose'.... If some denomination incidentally derives a benefit through the release of other funds for other uses, this result is immaterial.... A hospital operated under the auspices of a religious denomination which receives funds under the provisions of this bill acts merely as a conduit for the expenditure of public funds for training which serves exclusively the public purpose of public health and is completely devoid of sectarian doctrine and purposes.
>
> The fundamental position that public moneys shall be used for a public purpose has not prevented the use of private institutions as a conduit to accomplish the public objectives.[20]

In Kentucky the Court of Appeals upheld the federal statute against the contention that the federal-state grant to church-affiliated hospitals violated both federal and state constitutions.

> ...(4) private agency may be utilized as the pipe-line through

which a public expenditure is made, the test being not who receives the money but the character of the use for which it was expended.... The fact that members of the governing board of these hospitals, which perform a recognized public service to all people regardless of faith or creed, are all of one religious faith does not signify that the money allotted the hospitals is to aid their particular denominations... courts will look to the use to which these funds are put rather than the conduits through which they run. If that use is a public one... it will not be held in contravention of sec. 5 merely because the hospitals carry the name or are governed by members of a particular faith.[21]

The difference between religion and public health and religion and education is not so broad as to warrant, despite certain obvious dissimilarities, a contrary attitude toward those who approve of government aid to church-affiliated schools. What the state court rulings of New Hampshire, Kentucky, Mississippi and others have stressed is that a public purpose can still be served through a private agency despite or together with its patent religious profession and environment and even allowing for incidental benefits to the religious institution itself.

Meyer v. Nebraska[22]

The importance of *Meyer* is generally overshadowed by the momentous decision two years later of *Pierce* which in great part was prejudiced by the former. In both cases, the Supreme Court made similar observations touching upon the rights of parents to direct the education of their children, the contractual rights of schools and of the teaching profession as restrictions upon the state's provisions and requirements regulating state compulsory school attendance laws. Both cases deny state monopoly of the educational process either by an absolute control of school curriculum or by compulsory attendance at public elementary schools for all children. But scarcely any notice has been taken of the court's consideration of the multiple aspects of a language study which does cast light on the tangled issues of the secular subjects as taught in church-related schools. It quotes at length from the decision of the Supreme Court of Nebraska that underscored the indefectibility of the study of the German language even in the very employment of Biblical stories.

The question of the constitutionality of the state statute proscribing the teaching of German in elementary schools remains without prejudice should any appeal be made to the freedom of religious beliefs. The high tribunal apparently agreed with the analysis of the case by the Nebraska Supreme Court — that two distinct and separate purposes remain intact — the teaching and learning of the state proscribed German language and the teaching and learning of Bible stories. The two concurrent objectives are recognized to be separable and separate, and accordingly, both the federal and state Supreme Courts see no constitutional right of religious liberty at issue before them. In a word, the German language is being taught even in the reading of Bible stories and it is on that precise issue that both court-rulings are made. Apparently the intermingling of religious matter in the teaching of a secular subject — a modern language — does not diminish nor impair the proficiency of teaching and learning the secular subject nor interfere with achieving its own distinctive secular aspect and function. Taking note of the laudable motive of promoting cultural assimilation in schools the Court however expressed its aversion to the statute before it by reaching back to the Platonic and Spartan experiments by law of trying to mold the minds of the young by removing them entirely from parental care and submitting the youngsters to an educational process entirely controlled by the state. It is striking that the court in speaking of the higher importance of education among the American people should choose to quote the Ordinance of 1787 which conjoins knowledge with religion and morality for the benefit of government and society.

Pierce v. Society of Sisters[23]

Though *Pierce* is generally cited for its celebrated pronouncement on the rights of parents, the issue before the Court was the proprietary right of private corporations, secular, military, and religious, to engage in schooling in fulfillment of state compulsory attendance laws. The Court's affirmation of the primacy of parental rights is more than a *dictum* because it is the necessary term correspondent to the inviolable exercise of the private corporations' right to engage in public education. Their rights, the Court noted, are dependent upon patronage, "the free choice of patrons, present and prospective." In ruling upon both cases together, the Court in effect denied that the religious affiliation of the parochial school distinguished it from the private school as an educational institution. The significance of *Pierce* is sharply defined when projected against the background of forces which brought about the enactment of the Oregon statute. Those who worked for its enactment argued that:

> The assimilation and education of our foreign-born citizens in the principles of our government, the hopes and aspirations of our people, are best secured by and through attendance of all children in our public schools.[24]

The Court rejected this underlying premise that state schools are better educational instrumentalities for inculcating civic virtues and patriotism. We might observe on this point that church-related schools are, on the contrary characteristically more noted for their patriotism. *Pierce* affirms the *right* of *private* corporations, whether religious, military or secular, to operate schools for the same public intent as the state schools. They exist not by privilege nor sufferance of the political power. The basic reason for the existence of the independent schools is that they are differentiated, by a principle of integration of curriculum and a system of discipline, from state-owned schools while sharing in common with them a proficiency in required subjects and in the inculcation of civic virtues. The effect of the *Pierce* ruling is to deny any priority or superiority before the law for the state to compel parents to choose the state schools.

> The fundamental theory of liberty upon which all governments in this Union repose excludes any general power of the state to standardize its children by forcing them to accept instruction from public schools only. The child is not the mere creature of the state: those who nurture him and direct his destiny have the right, coupled with the high duty, to recognize and prepare him for additional obligations.[25]

It is true that the First Amendment was never argued or even mentioned in the *Pierce* ruling. But this is precisely what constitutes its unique merit. In ruling upon both cases together, the Court in effect denied that the religious affiliation of the parochial school distinguishes it from the private (military) school as an educational institution capable of fulfilling a public purpose as prescribed by state educational laws. Both are subsumed as private corporations with equally inviolable property rights *not merely in education but in public education.*

Private proprietary title and church affiliation do not derogate from nor diminish the ability to fulfill public law requirements of school curriculum, standards of teaching, and other educational facilities, nor render the educational process less competent, less truly public in purpose and achievement. By denying to the state a monopolizing role in education, it implicitly affirms that parents, church, and the state are all contributors to public education. Strictly speaking, it is not the religious and nonreligious conscience that is made to prevail but it is the parental right, (correspondent to rights of private corporations in public education), whether exercised out of religious motivation or not, that limits the state to a partnership, and denies it an exclusive role in public education. At the same time, while there is no explicit discussion of a principle of integration in the school curriculum, the court seems not unmindful of it when it notes that the reason that parents may choose an accredited education in an independent school is that in the judgment of the parents such schooling is ordained to assist the student for "his destiny" and "additional obligations" beyond those presumably provided for in the state-owned schools. The profound significance of the *Pierce* ruling is that the proprietary right of independent schools to operate is related to the prime moral obligation of the parents to regulate the moral educational process of their children, without denying the state a supervisory role and without removing from the independent schools their obligation to the public welfare. In a word, the court is not merely saying that a division of labor is legitimate, and so the state need not have an exclusive role in education nor that other agencies besides the state may not be equally competent to educate the young; rather the court affirms the proprietary right of independent schools and of its "patrons, present and prospective," to be co-participants with the state in the educational requirements of public welfare. We cannot too strongly emphasize the fact that of those private church-affiliated schools who do not ask for a share in governmental aids, none will permit critics to say they are not fulfilling the purposes of public education, none will admit that their schools are unAmerican, divisive, undemocratic, none will agree that their educational process is defective. The reason why they exist at all is precisely because they are firmly persuaded that the state schools are wanting in the fullness of intellectual and spiritual development. They make this criticism respectfully not to disparage the state schools but with full awareness of the complex problems which religious pluralism engenders in those circumstances. The religious neutrality in state schools is not the definition of an educational ideal but a compromise, an abstention which constitute the very reason why parents who can afford to do so send their children to church-affiliated schools.

Cochran v. Board of Education[26]

Whereas in the *Pierce* ruling the principal stress was upon the correlation of real rights, parental rights and proprietary rights of private corporations to participate in public education in the *Cochran* case the Court upheld the identifiable common purposes of a total view of pluralist public education as the legitimate objective in a general welfare benefaction. The appellant had brought suit to restrain the Louisiana state officials from expending any part of the severance tax fund in purchasing textbooks and in supplying them free of cost to parochial school children, contending that utilization of state funds for private uses contravened the mandate of the due process clause of the Fourteenth Amendment. In support of this federal judicial question they argued that:

> The courses of study and the school books prescribed by the private, religious, and other schools aforesaid *not embraced* in the public educational system of the State of Louisiana, are different from those prescribed and used in the free public schools of this State, and the Louisiana State Board of Education has no right or authority to prescribe the course of study or the school books to be used by the children attending schools *constituting no part* of the public educational system of the State of Louisiana, and petitioners show that there is a large number of such private and sectarian or denominational schools in the State of Louisiana where religious instruction is included in the course of study, and many of the school books selected, used and required in such schools, are designed and employed to aid and promote religious beliefs, and to foster and encourage the principles of faith, and to teach the tenets of the creed, mode of worship, and ecclesiastical policy of the respective churches under whose respective control the said schools are conducted.[27] (Italics supplied.)

Further, the petitioners asserted that Section 4 of Article I and Section 8 of Article IV of the Constitution of Louisiana forbade "the taking of money from the public treasury for the purpose of teaching, religion, and in aid of churches, sects, or denominations of religion." The respondents acknowledged all the alleged facts but contended to the contrary:

> That it is not their intention nor purpose to furnish free, or otherwise, any sectarian or denominational textbooks to the *school children of the State of Louisiana* . . . and that respondents only propose to furnish such books to the *educable school children of the State attending schools, curricula of which have been approved by the State Board of Education of Louisiana.*[28] (Italics supplied.)

The state further expanded upon the comprehensive conception of all publicly accredited schooling by asserting:

> That the private schools of the State of Louisiana thus become and are *agencies of the state,* aiding in the education of its children and making it possible to educate many thousands who would otherwise be deprived of educational advantages.... That the primary policy of the aforesaid acts of the legislature is providing free testbooks for the *educable school children* of the State, *without discrimination* as to race, sex, religion or creed, and respondents aver that if any children of the State are denied the privilege of obtaining free school books from the State of Louisiana because of the fact that such children are attending private or sectarian schools, such discrimination would be arbitrary, unjust and illegal, as well as unconstitutional, and incapable of legal enforcement.[29] (Italics supplied.)

It was the Supreme Court of Louisiana, however, which enlarged upon the child-benefit concept and related it to state-care for all educable school children.

> One can scan the acts in vain to ascertain where any money is appropriated for the purchase of school books for the use of any church, private, sectarian, or even public school. The appropriations were made for the specific purpose of purchasing

school books for the *use of the school children of the state,* free of cost to them. *It was for their benefit and the resulting benefit of the state* that the appropriations were made. True, these children attend some school, public or private, the latter, sectarian or non-sectarian, and that the books are to be *furnished to them for their use, free of cost, whichever they attend.* The schools, however, *are not the beneficiaries of these appropriations.* They obtain nothing from them, nor are they relieved of a single obligation, because of them. *The school children and the state alone. are the beneficiaries.* It is also true that the sectarian schools, which some of the children attend, instruct their pupils in religion, and books are used for that purpose, but one may search diligently the acts, though without result, in an effort to find anything to the effect that it is the purpose of the state to furnish religious books for use of such children. In fact, in view of the prohibitions in the Constitution against the state's doing anything of that description, it would be legally impossible to interpret the statute as calling for any such action on the part of the state. . . .[30] (Italics supplied.)

The United States Supreme Court, in an opinion by Mr. Chief Justice Hughes, took cognizance of the nondiscriminatory language of the state statute which authorized without any religious exclusionary clause "supplying school books to the school children of the state" and the directive to the Board of Education to provide "school books for school children free of cost to such children." After quoting the language of the majority set out above, it concluded:

Viewing the statute as having the effect thus attributed to it, we cannot doubt that the taxing power of the state is exerted for a public schools, or their pupils, as its beneficiaries or attempt to interfere with any matters of exclusively private concern. Its interest is education, broadly; its method, comprehensive. Individual interests are aided only as the common interest is safeguarded.[31]

The ruling of the Louisiana state courts stresses the *patria potestas* of the state for all its educable children without distinguishing in the reach of its care between the children who attend state and privately operated schools. They reject the contention of the plaintiffs that the non-governmental schools are "not embraced in the public educational system of the State of Louisiana," that these schools "constitute no part of the public educational system of the State of Louisiana." On the contrary, they agree with the state "that the private schools of the State of Louisiana thus become and are, agencies of the State, aiding in the education of its children." The reach of the state concernment is for all educable school children without discrimination as to race, sex, religion or creed. The intent and reach of the legislative benefaction, as the Supreme Court of Louisiana, stresses, is the benefit of the educable child and its consequent benefit to the State. "It was for their benefit and the resulting benefit to the State that the appropriations were made." The United States took cognizance of the nondiscriminatory language of the state statute which authorized without any religious exclusionary norm "supplying school books to the school children of the state" and the directive to the Board of Education to provide "school books for school children free of cost to such children." It is the firm persuasion of this writer that any federal aid program for the betterment of national education ought to confront the question squarely and affirm or deny whether or not education in private, religious schools is or is not achieving those objectives of schooling that are in the interest of general welfare. This fact is in practice acknowledged by the schools themselves both on the intracollegiate, and university levels. Students may transfer from one school to another in midterm or after graduation with due acknowledgement of the academic record. Ought not the law admit what the academy itself has never denied? Obviously, governmental aid to church-related schools would be directed and proportionate to the public function of these schools, (namely, the mastery of the secular and natural sciences) and a formal explicit acknowledgement of the secular goals and achievements of the church-related schools so long acted upon in a multiplicity and diversity of federal aid programs is long overdue.

Everson v. Board of Education[32]

Whereas in *Pierce,* the Court affirmed the legal right of private corporations, whether religious, secular, or military, to participate in public schooling together with state schools as a necessary correspondent to the inviolable moral right of parents to direct the education of minors, and in *Cochran* the Court denied that the religious profession of parochial schools constituted an exclusionary norm to forbid state provision of secular educational facilities to all educable school children. In *Everson* the Court through the majority opinion of Mr. Justice Black, declared in italicized words — as if to emphasize the firmness of its conviction — that no religious exclusionary rule may be applied to recipients of state welfare benefits. The *Everson* ruling is a study of symmetry of dialectic with inbuilt antinomies that can be explained only by subordinating an absolute premise to a particular determination rather than by relating the specific ruling to the general premise. A taxpayer of the township of Ewing brought suit against the reimbursement to parents for the cost of transportation of children to Catholic schools which were being made pursuant to a resolution of the school board of Ewing in accordance with a state statute authorizing such provisions. It is not without significance that Mr. Justice Black, speaking for the majority of five, disposed of the argument that the payments were illegal because they required the taking of some persons' property for the private use of others, by rejecting the contention that the religious affiliation of the parochial schools withdrew them from the area of public education. This he did both at the beginning of his opinion and at its conclusion.

> It is much too late to argue that legislation intended to facilitate the opportunity of children to get a *secular* education serves no public purpose. . . . The same thing is no less true of legislation to reimburse needy parents, or all parents, for the payment of fares of their children so that they can ride in public busses to and from schools rather than run the risk of traffic and other hazards incident to walking or 'hitchhiking'.[33] (Italics supplied.)

And

> Its legislation, as applied, does no more than provide a general program to help parents get their children, regardless of their religion, safely and expeditiously to and from *accredited* schools.[34] (Italics supplied.)

Everson reaffirms *Cochran* in holding to the public function and character of the educational process and facilities of private, religious-affiliated schools. It is the core of the ruling composed of two solemn declarations, one succeeding the other, that has stirred an almost endless controversy on the permissible and impermissible tax benefits that are constructively in accord with or in contravention of the non-establishment clause of the First Amendment and the complete proscription of any religious exclusionary in the application of governmental benefits. In a word, there is an apparent contrariety between two absolutes which is resolved differently by two opposing schools of interpretation. The advocates of absolutely no aid subordinate the second absolute to the first; the advocates of aid in support of a legislatively defined secular goal, qualify the first absolute by the second.

> We must consider the New Jersey statute in accordance with the foregoing limitations imposed by the First Amendment. But we must not strike that state statute down if it is within the state's constitutional power even though it approaches the verge of that power. New Jersey cannot consistently with the "establishment of religion" clause of the First Amendment contribute tax-raised funds to the support of an institution which teaches the tenets and faith of any church. On the other hand, the other language of the amendment commands that New Jersey cannot hamper its citizens in the free exercise of their own religion. Consequently, it cannot exclude individual Catholics, Lutherans, Mohammedans, Baptists, Jews, Methodists, Non-believers, Presbyterians, or the members of any other faith, *because of their faith or lack of it,* from receiving the benefits of public welfare. While we do not mean to intimate that a state could not provide transportation only to children attending public schools, we must be careful, in protecting the citizens of New Jersey against state-established churches. To be sure that we do not inadvertently prohibit New Jersey from extending its general state law benefits to all citizens without regard to their religious beliefs.[35]

The italics in the above passage are the Court's (an unusual occurrence in the Court's opinions) and clearly reject an exclusionary religious test in the definition of general welfare benefits. And then as if to link together *Pierce* and *Cochran* with *Everson,* Justice Black adds:

The Court has said that parents may in the discharge of their duty under state compulsory education laws, send their children to a religious rather than a public school, if the *school meets the secular education requirements which the state has power to impose.*[36] (Italics supplied)

The Court does not deny that some undoubted benefits do accrue to the parochial schools by the extension of transportation facilities set by the state, but this does not constitutionally interdict that neutrality on religious matters which permits the state to direct its assistance to a secular purpose that is being realized under the state's own supervisory educational regulations by religious institutions.

Of course cutting off church schools from these services, so separate and indisputably marked off from the religious function, would make it far more difficult for the schools to operate. But such is obviously not the purpose of the First Amendment. That Amendment requires the state to be neutral in its relations with groups of religious believers and nonbelievers. It does not require the state to be their adversary. State power is no more to be used so as to handicap religions than it is to favor them.[37]

Everson like *Cochran* affirms the principle that government may assist public service aspects of an educational process which fulfills the secular educational requirements which the state has power to impose. Indeed, their accreditation depends upon this compliance. In at least three different instances does the Court acknowledge the secular education that obtains in religious schools and finds it almost tiresome to doubt it. "It is much too late to argue that legislation intended to facilitate the opportunity of children to get a secular education serves no public purpose."

We maintain in this study that an exclusionary rule for government benefactions based on religious profession ought to raise substantive constitutional questions about the legal consequences attendant upon the exercise of religious liberty in education. We cannot too often repeat that the only practical way of interpreting and executing legislative statutes reaching to a public interest and service without prejudice to religious liberty is the empirical test of ascertaining whether the secular aspects and functions of non-theological studies, in the promotion of which the government has a direct interest, are in fact proficiently and competently realized to the public benefit. Such an empirical device or measurement can meet the impartial requirement of Justice Black's statement, "because of faith, or lack of it."

Unfortunately the passage which precedes the one we have been analyzing is more often quoted because it provides another "absolute" held in the particular ruling. The Court took cognizance of the appellant's contention that the provision of transportation at public expense for children who attend church-affiliated schools constituted an aid to religion in violation of the no establishment clause of the First Amendment. Said Mr. Justice Black:

> The "establishment of religion" clause of the First Amendment means at least this: Neither a state nor the Federal Government can set up a church. Neither can pass laws which aid one religion, aid all religions, or prefer one religion over another. Neither can force nor influence a person to go to or remain away from church against his will or force him to profess a belief or disbelief in any religion. No person can be punished for entertaining or professing religious beliefs or disbeliefs, for church attendance or nonattendance. No tax in any amount, large or small, can be levied to support any religious activities or institutions, whatever they may be called, or whatever form they may adopt to teach or practice religion. Neither a state nor the Federal Government can, openly or secretly, participate in the affairs of any religious organizations or groups or *vice versa.* In the words of Jefferson, the clause against establishment of religion by law was intended to erect "a wall of separation between church and state."[38]

A careful weighing of these propositions discloses that nonestablishment is simply not a disengagement from religious life of the American Community but directed to ensuring the exercise of religious liberty without any coercive interference touching upon the individual choice to believe or not believe, to attend religious services or not. Other propositions must be historically viewed as against those incidences of state-establishment of church or religion, which by legislative preference for a creed visited civil disabilities and punitive consequences upon dissidents and nonconformists and imposed taxes upon them for the support of a faith or church not of their choice or confession. What has provided the occasion of much controversy is the implication of the literal statements which seem to proscribe *any* aid to religion, even on a nondiscriminatory basis, "in *any* amount, large or small, to support any religious activities or institutions." While the language admittedly lends itself to a formula of absolutely no aid at all to religion a reading of it in context saddles such an interpretation with many difficulties. The demarcation of a secular education in church-related schools to which both *Cochran* and *Everson* admit, is held to be constitutionally eligible for government support proportionate to the fulfillment of the purpose. In such a context, then, an educational process that is so defined and supportable by tax funds is not constructively aid for any religious *activities* or *institutions* that teach or practice religion, even if as a consequence there is an overflow of some benefit to the religious agency itself. One cannot control the consequence of multiple effects in this matter no more than in any other human enterprise. And the legislative record of state and federal tax support, large and small, in a variety of forms, with no prejudice to religious affiliation is a constant witness to this official conviction. Grants and contracts for research projects, scholarships, fellowships, tuition grants, and loans for educational facilities and building constructions, fiscal provision for remedial and special pedagogy for the mentally retarded, for disadvantaged children, funds for language institutes and training programs and numerous other programs by a variety of government agencies constitute one of the most gratifying etceterations of government use of all educational instrumentalities for the sake of general welfare without any religious exclusionary rule. Where an identity of the secular goals of education and a compatibility of interest has existed, national and state legislatures have made appropriations in support of those achievements. This is not to say that the same identical provisions in kind and degree are extended in every form of governmental aid in support of the secular goals of education in state and nonstatal schools. Some, such as scholarships and tuition grants, fellowships, matching grants, research grants and contracts, student loans at low interest are generally extended on equal basis. Government funds for educational equipment and building construction of science buildings, campus centers, and dormitories, generally take the form of long-term loans at low interest when extended to church-affiliated schools.

The legislatures of the nation have established a long standing consensus on the competence and effectiveness of the educational process in nongovernmental schools without prejudice to religious affiliation. As for the interdiction of any aid to religion impartially extended, such as tax exemptions and tax deductible benefits to churches and religious institutions and agencies, the support of military and legislative chaplains, the income tax laws which permit housing allowances for ministers, exemptions from military service of conscientious objectors, of students of divinity, and of clergy in peace and war, whatever the underlying rationale justifying or challenging these preferment benefits of public law, the secular goals and achievements of these institutions of learning which are accredited and comply with state educational requirements should not be equally subsumed under the same general discussion. If the *Everson* decision indicates any direction of application it points favorably in the direction of the educational concernment of governments.

If the two classic passages on non-aid – at all – and the religious exclusionary rule mean anything it is that the two absolutes must be jointly considered and related to one another. Undoubtedly the first absolute would deny tax support of sectarian teaching and practices. The second absolute should deny the exclusion of religious sectarian agencies and institutions from government aid in the achievement of secular goals in which the government has a substantive interest to promote. The Court has upheld this federal involvement in *Bradfield* in the area of hospital care in the educational field, the provision of textbooks by the state to all educable children by the *Cochran* ruling.

McCollum v. Board of Education[39]

The *McCollum* ruling of 1948 struck down the Champaign, Illinois, religious instruction program which was conducted on the school premises by outside teachers representing the various faiths to students whose parents had requested these religious classes. The Court through the majority opinion of Mr. Justice Black, found the arrangement to be a utilization of tax-supported public school system and its compulsory attendance machinery for the dissemination of sectarian religious doctrine that is proscribed by the nonestablishment clause of the First Amendment.

This specific ruling has no bearing on the issue before us. In fact a comparison of the two considerations would be as a matter of factual situation and the controlling legal principles would be more notable for its sharp contrasts than for similarities.

Zorach v. Clauson[40]

The impartiality of the *Everson* ruling which refused to allow the religious affiliation to be made the basis of an exclusionary rule seemed to some constitutional jurists to have been reduced to a questionable neutrality of total abstention in *McCollum*, was restored in *Zorach* with such affirmations as to lead some scholars to hold that *McCollum* was to a considerable extent checked by a more positive construction of government neutrality. *Zorach* permitted tax-salaried public school officials to cooperate with the religious released time program conducted off school property. If it is a cause for some reflection why the absolute separatism passage in *Everson* is cited more often without the accompanying absolute interdiction of a religious exclusionary rule of the succeeding paragraph, it is even more surprising why it is quoted more frequently than the more positive formula of *Zorach,* which was a later ruling, as if the earlier formula were the only one to control church-state relations in education. *Zorach* like *McCollum* does not concern itself with government funds in support of education in church-related schools. It does, however, affirm broadly certain propositions on relations between the government and the religious life of the American community. Mr. Justice Douglas, speaking for the majority, distinguished *Zorach* from *McCollum* on two grounds — there was no utilization of tax-supported property premises and there was no evidence of any coercion being exercised upon the children by state officials. It does make statements which are intended to make more clear the absolute prohibition of the non-establishment clause.

> The First Amendment... does not say that in every and all respects there shall be a separation of Church and State. Rather, it studiously defines the manner, the specific ways, in which there shall be no concert or union or dependency one on the other. That is the common sense of the matter. Otherwise the state and religion would be aliens to each other — hostile, suspicious, and even unfriendly. Churches could not be required

to pay even property taxes. Municipalities would not be permitted to render police or fire protection to religious groups. Policemen who helped parishioners into their place of worship would violate the Constitution. Prayers in our legislative halls; the appeals to the Almighty in the messages of the Chief Executive; the proclamation making Thanksgiving Day a holiday; "so help me God" in our courtroom oaths — these and all other references to the Almighty that run through our laws, our public rituals, our ceremonies would be flouting the First Amendment. A fastidious atheist or agnostic could even object to the supplication with which the Court opens each session: "God save the United States and this Honorable Court."[41]

And then there follows that memorable passage in which neutrality of total abstention is disowned for a benevolent impartiality that finds expression in reasonable accommodations. It is not without profound significance that this passage is introduced with the statement: "We are a righteous people whose institutions presuppose a Supreme Being." Here in the solemnity of the highest judicial review on the constitutionality of official actions and law, the high tribunal was not simply observing that as a broad, undeniable historical fact the American people have been traditionally religious, God-fearing and God-loving men. Rather, it is said with calculated particularity that the public institutions of the American Republic rested on religious belief in God.

> We are a religious people whose institutions presuppose a Supreme Being. We guarantee the freedom of worship as one chooses. We make room for as wide a variety of beliefs and creeds as the spiritual needs of man deem necessary. We sponsor an attitude on the part of government that shows no partiality to any one group and that lets each flourish according to the zeal of its adherents and the appeal of its dogma. When the state encourages religious instruction or cooperates with religious authorities by adjusting the schedule of public events to sectarian needs, it follows the best of our traditions. For it then respects the religious nature of our people and accommodates the public service to their spiritual needs. To hold that it may not would be to find in the Constitution a requirement that the government show a callous indifference to religious

groups. That would be preferring those who believe in no religion over those who do believe. Government may not finance religious groups nor undertake religious instruction nor blend secular and sectarian education nor use secular institutions to force one or some religion on any person. But we find no constitutional requirement which makes it necessary for government to be hostile to religion and to throw its weight against efforts to widen the effective scope of religious influence. The government must be neutral when it comes to competition between sects. It may not thrust any sect on any person. It may not make a religious observance compulsory. It may not coerce anyone to attend church, to observe religious holiday, or to take religious instruction. But it can close its doors or suspend its operations as to those who want to repair to their religious sanctuary for worship or instruction. More than that is undertaken here.

This program may be unwise and improvident from an educational or a community viewpoint. That appeal is made to use on a theory previously advanced, that each case must be decided on the basis of "our own repossessions." . . . Our individual preferences, however, are not the constitutional standard. The problem, like many problems in constitutional law, is one of degree. . . .[42]

The *Zorach* ruling like that of *McCollum* was not concerned with the issue of government funds for secular goals in religious education. *Zorach* is nonetheless significant in its stress upon a principle of benevolent impartiality as within the permissible governmental relations with religion that are not forbidden by the nonestablishment clause. Against a neutrality of total abstention the Court sets a formula of a cooperative and reasonable accommodation that gives scope to the religious life of the American community without placing constraints upon anyone, believer or nonbeliever. There is implied in the specific settlement of the case a point which is explicitly stressed by Mr. Justice Frankfurter's dissenting opinion and which carries with it a meaning not openly stated in the majority ruling. Justice Frankfurter would have no constitutional qualms if there were a general dismissed time program whereby the public school once a week dismissed all students an hour earlier than the general hour of the end of the school day. In such an arrangement the students may then spend that hour as they choose, to sectarian instruction, to ethical instruction, to the study of music, etc. But the provision of the New York Legislature for released time within the regular school day would seem to imply that a nexus be affirmed between the educational process and religious and spiritual values in an arrangement that does no violence to the diversities of religious conscience.

There is an undoubted difference of attitude and approach between *Zorach* and *McCollum*. It seems to overlap *McCollum* while adhering to that specific ruling, — to *Everson* and repeat in different language some of its proscriptions of government activity that fall under the ban of the nonestablishment clause. Government may not finance religious groups, must be neutral between sects, cannot undertake religious instruction or force religion, religious instruction, or religious observance on anyone. These proscriptions leave untouched the support by government of carefully defined secular goals of education by whomsoever they are realized. The support of educational programs which are not religious subjects but are identifiable as citizen education are objectives which can be fulfilled by competent and official educational agents and facilities. To preclude some of them because of their religious confession or affiliation is to do violence to the absolute proscription of an exclusionary rule affirmed so categorically in *italics* in *Everson*. At the same time the absolute proscriptions of the nonestablishment clause does not preclude a reasonable measure of accommodation for specifically religious practices and teachings. To what extent public law accommodations for religious teachings and practices are permissible — such as the New York released time program and the sectarian religious holidays during school years — and when they are forbidden will depend on the degree of governmental involvement that the Court decides in each instance to be within the complementary boundaries of the two religious clauses of the First Amendment.

Zorach made no mention of the Jeffersonian metaphor, "wall of separation," which other members of the Court cited in their several opinions in the earlier *Everson* and *McCollum* cases. Rather, the Court strove sedulously to contrive a formula of separation of church and state without resorting to the metaphor on masonry and its connotation of complete and permanent separation.[43] As Mr. Justice Frankfurter was to observe later, the separation is one of friendly fences between neighbors that allows and encourages cordial and cooperative relations.

SUNDAY CLOSING LAW CASES

McGowan v. Maryland[44]

All of the court opinions in this and other Blue Laws cases admitted the religious origin of the Sunday day of rest. The majority Court opinion, while aware that some state Blue Laws still literally refer to the Lord's day, held to the valid secular purpose which was said to emerge from and to prevail apart from its religious origins even if it still operated in such a manner as to favor the dominican and to the disadvantage of the sabbatarian religious confessions. "The proponents of Sunday closing legislation are no longer exclusively representatives of religious interest." There is no denial of the obvious fact, on the part of the court, that there is an intermingling of interests, of secular objectives and of religious advantage partial to Christians. But the court opinion refuses to allow that such concurrence of benefits, secular and religious, nullifies the valid secular purpose which government has a right and duty to secure:

> However, it is equally true that the "Establishment Clause" does not bar federal or state regulation of conduct whose reason of effect merely happens to coincide or harmonize with the tenets of some or all religions. In many instances, the Congress or state legislatures conclude that the general welfare of society, wholly apart from any religious considerations, demands such regulations.[45]
>
> Sunday Closing Laws, like those before us, have become part and parcel of this great governmental concern wholly apart from their original purposes or connotations. The present purpose and effect of most of them is to provide a uniform day of rest for all citizens; the fact that the day is Sunday, a day of particular significance for the dominant Christian sects, does not bar the state from achieving its secular goals. To say that the states cannot prescribe Sunday as a day of rest for these purposes solely because centuries ago such laws had their genesis in religion would give constitutional interpretation of hostility to the public welfare rather than one of mere separation of church and state.[46]

With what force of logic and reason one may reflect in similar terms upon an analogous situation, the intermingling of secular functions and religious aspects of church-school education, will depend for the most part on the recognition of a secular goal of education in the curriculum in which the state has a substantive interest and which can be ascertained empirically by the state educational authorities. The precise holding of Chief Justice Warren's opinion is that governmental action directed to a valid public purpose does not become invalid because it operates simultaneously to other effects — the promotion of religious interests, either generally or of a particular group. The court opinion holds to its exposition of nonestablishment by referral to *Everson* which had upheld the expenditure of public funds to transport children to parochial schools as a legitimate service for a valid secular purpose. This secular purpose was not solely the safe transportation of the school children but, as Justice Black noted, a *safety means* to the secular educational goals which the state requires and accredits in religious schools. The fulfillment of these secular purposes are not annulled or vitiated because it also advances and helps a program of religious education. Mr. Justice Frankfurter's concurring opinion adds to the Chief Justice's rationale:

> To ask what interest, what objective legislation serves, of course, is not to psychoanalyze its legislators, but to examine the necessary effects of what they have enacted. If the primary end achieved by a form of regulation is the affirmation or promotion of religious doctrine-primary in the sense that all secular ends which it purportedly serves are derivative from, not wholly independent of, the advancement of religion — the regulation is beyond the power of the state. This was the case in *McCollum.* Or if a statute furthers both secular and religious ends by means unnecessary to the effectuation of the secular ends alone — where the same secular ends could equally be attained by means which do not have consequence for promotion of religion — the statute cannot stand. A state may not endow a church although that church might inculcate in its parishioners moral precepts deemed to make them better citizens, because the very raison *d'etre* or a church, as opposed to any other school of civilly serviceable morals, is the predication of religious doctrine. However, inasmuch as individuals are free, if they will, to build their own churches and worship

in them, the State may guard its people's safety by extending fire and police protection to the churches so built. It was on the reasoning that parents are also at liberty to send their children to parochial schools which meet the reasonable educational standards of the State, *Pierce v. Society of Sisters,* 258 U.S. 510, that this Court held in the *Everson* case that expenditure of public funds to assure the children attending every kind of school enjoy the relative security of busses, rather than being left to walk or hitchhike, is not an unconstitutional 'establishment,' even though such an expenditure may cause some children to go to parochial schools who would not otherwise have gone. The close decision of the Court in *Everson* serves to show what nice questions are involved in applying to particular governmental action the proposition, undeniable in the abstract, that not every regulation, some of whose practical effects may facilitate the observance of a religion by its adherents, affronts the requirement of church-state separation.[47]

Mr. Justice Frankfurter after repeatedly stressing that in some activities public and religious interests "overlap," "interplay," and that the history of Blue Laws has made them "the vehicle of mixed and complicated aspirations," inquired as to when a benefit to religion may be allowable if there is an intermingling of religious and civic objectives. Only, he concluded, when there is no other alternative for realizing the secular goals:

> Or if the statute furthers both secular and religious ends to the effectuation of the secular ends alone – where the same secular end could equally be attained by means which do not have consequences for promotion of religion – the statute cannot stand.

This passage precedes Justice Frankfurter's concatenation of *Pierce, Everson,* with the ruling in *McGowan* and therefore invites a legitimate argument by analogy with the mixed objectives in education. It is a misconstruction to frame the problem simply as – the government cannot financially take over the entire educational facilities of the country and therefore the only alternative is for the government to assist to some extent the education of its children that attend church-sponsored schools. The simple answer to that would be – that such an alternative is possible. The problem is correctly formulated in terms of the right of the student (and of his parents) to attend a schooling of the lower and higher levels in accordance with the dictates of his conscience. There can be no feasible alternative to these church-related schools to this compounded right other than for the government to allow the teaching of religious dogma and philosophy in an all-comprehensive government system of education by tax paid teachers, not excluding the clergy. This supposition would not be seriously contemplated either as a matter of American policy or of constitutional law.

But the economic argument does come into play when related to the corporate proprietary rights of the church-related schools. Proponenets of federal aid to education on the lower levels have argued that the exclusion of the parochial schools from sharing in government aid would place them in such a disadvantageous position in the face of enormous resources of the federal government that the educational facilities of the parochial schools might in comparison be reduced to a level of inferiority which could prove harmful in these schools. Has the government no alternate means of avoiding this alleged damage to private schools? One might push the question further and ask if it is in the national interest to bring about, however indirectly, this imbalance? The root question to which we must always return is to ask of the government what precisely is the status of parochial schools (apart from their constitutional right to educate in fulfillment of state educational requirements) in the comprehensive national educational program: to ask whether in fact they can and do contribute to the national education of the country and whether government may rely upon them as well as upon state-owned schools for its educational programs.

The underlying import of the economic aspect of the Sunday Law cases is that the state would be obligated to hold in check the free play of open market and competition (even on the claim of religious conscience) if in effect it would obstruct or frustrate a valid *secular* goal. Whether or not the federal government may be economically unconcerned about the educational facilities of approximately six million parochial school children and the status of eight hundred church colleges is a question that ought not to be settled out of hand without first determining their place in the scheme of the national interest.

In coming to a decision, the Congress ought first to make this frank confrontation of the crucial issue. But apart from the vast economic consideration is the evaluation of the educational process itself. Permeation means intermingled objectives — value judgments, and motives, and religious and secular aspects of the science studies. May the national legislature any more than the courts choose one mode of value-inculcation against the others? Or, may it allow any value integration which is not offensive to the communal welfare, perhaps even tributary as a spiritual force, and which preserved intact the secular aspects and functions of the educational process that the public interest requires? If the indefectibility of the secular studies is assured — and this, we must repeat may be ascertained empirically — then government aid ought not to be interdicted because of a religious consequential. The exercise of religious liberty should be no less inviolable in education and no less free of government prejudices and civil disabilities than in any other public endeavors or enterprises.

Torcaso v. Watkins[48]

In *Torcaso* the right of a citizen to become a notary public without being required by law to make a public declaration of belief in God was upheld. It would have been more felicitous had the court not subsumed in a footnote, by an exercise of logical positivism, nonatheistic beliefs into the meaning of religion in the First Amendment. To have preserved even in legal interpretation the traditional meaning of religion as the relation of man to a transcendental being, God, would not have precluded the right of a non-theistic (non-religious) conscience from the protective mantle of the First Amendment religious clauses. *Torcaso* could have adequately rested its ruling on the Anglo-American tradition of law that the right to belief is a right to an internal area of absolute inviolability into which inner sanctum neither the law may inquire nor the coercive power of government force its disclosures. However, what does emerge from *Torcaso* for the purpose of our discussion is that regardless of *the faith (Everson)* what matters is that the public service of a public office (whether correspondent to the official's conscience or not) be in accord with the requirements of the duties of that office. If the conscience, religious or not, be tributary to, or at least conform with the civic virtues of public office, the law will not inquire further to ask on what theological grounds such conduct is based. The particulars of *Torcaso* mark it off by some distance from questions of federal aid to religiously integrated education. But it does suggest further reflections on the public benefit that the government expects and empirically ascertains in an educational process permeated by ultimates whether theistically grounded or not, whether Christian or not, etc. It also raises the correlative consideration whether equality of religious liberty whether theistic or nontheistic should not ensue into an equality of treatment when confronted by government benefactions. The Maryland state court in upholding the constitutional requirement had relied on the common law attitude towards atheists as a reasonable basis for excluding the appellant from the office of notary public. The state court determined that the distinction between believers and nonbelievers as a security for good conduct in office had not become so devoid of meaning that to adopt it would be arbitrary. The common law statute equated the ungodly with the unworthy. It was supposed, as Professor Wigmore had suggested, that the sanction of divine retribution for false swearing might add stimulus to truthfulness wherever that was possible. While it may be cynical to suggest that many good men are not deterred from perjury because of moral dictates, it seems equally unreasonable to restrict an inducement to veracity to the believer. The equation of honesty with belief must in our day give way to the more conclusive evidence of the actual performance of civic duties.

A line of reasoning on the permeation issue might be constructed from *Torcaso* in this fashion. Whether the agent of a public requirement is motivated by theistic or nontheistic belief, whether he invests his work with moral or theological virtue, *the service rendered must be judged on its own merits and by the canons properly applicable to that specific performance. Similarly, one may reason, whatever the spiritual permeation of an educational process* — secular humanism, ethical culture, military discipline, theism, Christianity — *the educational objectives in which the state has a public interest must be measured and evaluated by tests proper to the various intellectual disciplines.* Has a student learned to spell, read, multiply? Does he learn in biology and history what the state educational authorities require of every schooling? In this wise the religious permeation of an accredited schooling would not disqualify from participation in governmental programs for the improvement of education.

When the Court said in *Watson v. Jones*[49] "The law knows no heresy, is committed to the establishment of no religion, the support of no dogma," it did not mean to say the public law is indifferent to heresy or dogma. The First Amendment embraces two concepts, "freedom to believe and freedom to act." *(Cantwell v. Connecticut)*[50] ". . . In every case the power to regulate must be so exercised as not in attaining a permissible end, unduly to infringe the protected liberty." Since from the very nature of things not every public service and benefit is impervious to spiritual and religious values, public law must direct itself to the realization of its own interest whether its objectives and motives are intertwined with the objectives and motives of private interest, whether a private agency is religiously inspired or not. The public good is definable in itself and its efficacy for the public interest is not impaired — perhaps, on the contrary, enhanced — for being invested with religious insights. On this basis, a good start can be made for the substantive construction of a principle of neutrality, with prejudice to the rights of conscience of no one. Public law has indeed very much interest in the outward behavior of religious beliefs. It does not disdain to call upon the religious faiths for support of its own secular programs in time of peace and war. It has an interest in the ulterior motivation that religious life can provide for the conduct that is conducive to the harmonious peace and tranquil order of the commonwealth. In the crucial hour for the advancement of civil rights, public law looks to religious authorities and creeds to enlighten their faithful and help draw them out of those hardened and blind social prejudices which obstruct the free exercise of civil liberties and bring discord and violence to fellow citizens. If public law may turn to religious life for support of its own civic programs and for a resolution of many of its complex problems, then it ought not look askance upon an educational process which the state has accredited because it fuses the spiritual life of the students with his learning. We cannot departmentalize man by requirements of law and then ask him to conjoin — supposedly — his dual, concurrent lives as citizen and believer when the national benefit requires it. In a word, the law and government are not neutral and indifferent to the ethical values and religious motivations provided in an accredited schooling.

Admittedly, there are substantial points of disparity between *Torcaso* and the constitutional question of government aid to education. In the disbursement of public benefactions a sound public policy may justifiably restrict its subsidies to a limited reach. Because privately owned services in industry and commerce — such as agriculture, airlines and railroads — may require government subsidies to sustain the public service it does not follow that every other privately owned and operated public service must be equally a recipient of government subventions. The controlling consideration is the substantial national interest. And so we return to the original question which keeps recurring — whether or not religious institutions of learning are not truly educational facilities and as such are part of national education, whether these schools should share in federal programs for the advancement and improvement of their educational process because they are part of the national interest. Only in this wise will the twin clauses of the First Amendment operate to promote the freedom of the believer and the freedom of the unbeliever in the performance of a public service. To the absolutist school of interpretation, we suggest that adherence to the supposed principle that Government cannot aid religion may well discriminate against religion and impair its free exercise.

School District of Abington Township, Pennsylvania v. Schempp[51]

In the light of the court ruling in Engel v. Vitale[52] holding unconstitutional a school board's action in prescribing the daily recitation of the New York Regents' non-sectarian prayer, the findings of the Court in Schempp, concerning the laws and regulations requiring Bible reading without comment and the recitation of the Lord's Prayer at the beginning of the public school day, were almost a certainty to predict.

If a nondenominational prayer could be struck down as a violation of the nonestablishment clause, the use of the Lord's Prayer, as taught by the Founder of Christianity, would be more vulnerable to the charge of unconstitutionality. Bible reading posed a new question. While the court followed the finding of the trial court of a Bible reading without comment at the beginning of the school day was a religious exercise in itself and in fact was so intended by the state, it admitted that the Bible could be a legitimate study and a legitimate object of study for its literary and historic qualities appropriate to the secular and civic purposes of public schools. Just as many have considered *Zorach* a judicial reaction to the absolutists strictures of *McCollum* in response to the public furor that the latter aroused, so too many have felt that both the tone and attitude of *Schempp,* while negative in its specific settlement, showed great concern for the adverse public criticism that followed upon the *Engel* decision. Mr. Justice Clark's majority opinion repeats Mr. Justice Douglas' proposition in *Zorach* that "we are a religious people whose institutions presuppose a Supreme Being." He underscores gratefully and profound significance of religious life in the American community and in evidence details a number of public religious exercises. The seventy-nine page concurring opinion of Mr. Justice Brennan discourses about the related meanings of the religious clauses of the First Amendment, the caution in the use of historical referrals, the contemporary problematics of religious pluralism, the particularities of public schooling, the constitutional principles in appraising the historic practices of Bible reading and prayer, and, significantly, six different categories of permissible cooperation or accommodation between government and religion. The tone of *Schempp* is not characterized by the peremptoriness of *Engel*. Both the majority opinion and the concurring opinion of Mr. Justice Brennan are sensitive to the public concern on the interrelationship between government and religion by reassuring that some of the traditional government practices in favor of religion are not being imperiled by the instant decision.

But *Schempp* differs from *Engel* in a more significant way than in its tone of concern and reassurance. The Court could have settled the issue in *Schempp* on a narrow meaning of the establishment clause in that the Lord's prayer favored Christians and Bible reading favored believing Jews and Christians. Instead it struck down these sectarian religious practices on the broad interpretation first defined in *Everson,* and then applied in *McCollum,* and relied on in *Engels.* Government support of any sort of religious activity in public schools is constructively an establishment of religion.

The element of coercion which was stressed in some of the opinions in *McCollum* and was apparently abandoned as a controlling factor in *Engel,* has now been succeeded by a consideration of the degree of governmental involvement even in an arrangement that rests upon voluntary participation. Mr. Justice Douglas noted in *Zorach* that the "problem, like many problems in constitutional law, is one of degree," a consideration which underlay the permissibility of indirect aid to a religious school in *Everson.* In *McCollum* and *Engel,* the governmental involvement was found to be equal to establishment of religion. What emerges from *Schempp* is a resolution to the problem of weighing the neutrality principle that has been repeatedly reaffirmed since *Everson* by the degree of government involvement and this solution is made to derive from a newly formulated principle that distinguishes between primary and secondary purposes and effects of legislative enactment. The rationale upon which *McGowan* was based is now explicitly translated to the area of education in *Schempp*.

The neutrality principle as formulated in these more precise terms is set forth by Mr. Justice Clark as follows:

> The test may be stated as follows: what are the purpose and the primary effect of the enactment? If either is the advancement or inhibition of religion then the enactment exceeds the scope of legislative power as circumscribed by the Constitution. That is to say that to withstand the strictures of the Establishment Clause there must be a secular legislative purpose and a primary effect that neither advances nor inhibits religion.[53]

Mr. Justice Clark prefaces this passage with the notice that in order to avert a collusion of government and religious functions or a dependency of one upon the other, it is necessary to apply "the wholesome neutrality" of preceding cases.

The neutrality which was expressed in absolutist terms — no aid in any amount or form — which was related to *Everson* to a rejection of a religious exclusionary norm — and reaffirmed in *Zorach* in terms of impartiality between believer and nonbeliever and benevolent accommodations, is now spoken of as a "wholesome neutrality." Further, the Court's opinion begins with a recital of governmental practices that undoubtedly favor religious life whose constitutionality the Court does not call into question but which at the same time seems literally to be at variance with the proposition that the legislative provision neither advances nor inhibits religion. How then may this apparent ambivalence be resolved if we are to spare the court opinion from the charge of inconsistency. The Court speaks of *"the* primary effect" and of *"a* primary effect." It is one thing to say that the primary effect of a legislative enactment is secular and therefore constitutionally correct even if there are incidents of benefit to religion and another to speak of *"a* primary effect" that is secular but which does not preclude a concomitant primary effect which advances or inhibits religion. In view of the specific ruling of *Schempp* the second interpretation seems unwarranted.

The appellants had contended that while Bible reading and the recitation of the Lord's payer were religious in purpose and effect a no less principal purpose and effect was the promotion of moral values designed to serve appropriate secular purposes. The Court rejected this contention and besides it was vulnerable for other reasons, namely, both religious exercises were patently sectarian in nature. It is more correct to say that the secular primary purpose must be effectuated by a secular means. The legislation's validity cannot be impugned even if there follows from its provisions an incidental consequence which either advances or inhibits religion. At its core this rationale seems to be the identical one upon which both *McGowan* and *Schempp* are based. But following upon this secular primary purpose and effect — secular means formula, Mr. Justice Clark takes cognizance of practices which are undoubtedly religious and both as means employed and effect intended obviously advance religion. If the *wholesomeness* of neutrality being fashioned by the Court covers under its constitutional mantle all these instances with no evident sense of embarrassment and inconsistency, it would be better counsel to speak of the principle of neutrality in terms of specific determination rather than in an all comprehensive doctrinaire construct to be imposed *a priori* on conflicting claims. It may be, however, that there is really less incongruity in the position of the Court than appears at first and far more basic consistency. The key to the solution of these apparent ambivalences may be found in *Zorach* where Mr. Justice Douglas observed that the problem is one of degree. A circumstantial fact which seems to have favored the absolutist interpretation has been that in recent years these problems have been raised under the establishment clause of the First Amendment which provided the occasion for firm and absolute affirmations against any governmental action that at least constructively added up to establishment. The earlier cases, on the contrary, were based on claims of religious liberty and in these the Court manifested no less zeal in affirming — a great latitude of freedom against a competing interest. If we conjoin the Court's specific rulings and general propositions in favor of religious liberty of the earlier cases with those against the establishment cases, in the latter cases, there does emerge a viable formula that guards with equal zeal and firm conviction the twin religion clauses of the First Amendment. What at first appeared as inconsistencies in the rationale and specific determinations of the Court were actually a diversity of positions concentrating on the protections of rights and against the dangers of establishment. The Court has upheld exemption from military service on religious and nontheistic claims of conscience in the Selective Draft and *Seeger* cases. In the *Jehovah's Witnesses* cases, the Court upheld a latitude in religious proselytizing that protected it against the requirements of permits *(Marsh v. Alabama,*[54] 1946; *Kunz v. New York,*[55] 1951), against the claims of privacy and convenience of house owners *(Martin v. Struthers,*[56] 1943), prohibited the imposition of a tax on the distribution of religious literature *(Murdock v. Pennsylvania,*[57] 1943), and upheld proselytizing on public streets against claims based on common law and state statutory safeguards for the peace *(Cantwell v. Connecticut,*[58] 1940), and has repeatedly declined to review lower court approval of the constitutionality of tax exemptions for religion.

The concept of neutrality must then comprehend within itself not only the strictures against establishment but also the affirmations in vindication of the right of religious liberty. While in some instances these judicial determinations are made independently under one or other of the two religion clauses at other times they overlap and still at others they have competed with one another. In these latter instances, the Court has more often than not deferred in favor of free exercise. In conjoining then the judicial determinations on claims of conscience, religious proselytizing, and tax preferment benefits under the free exercise clause to the rulings under the establishment prohibition, the neutrality which the Court has fashioned is more nearly benevolent and accommodating than one of total and absolute abstention.

But the principle of accommodation like that of neutrality is also one of degree. The Court has distinguished between three sorts of accommodation: the required, the permissive and the prohibitive. We have detailed instances of each sort. Even when the Court is engaged in weighing competing interest under the religious clauses the subordination of the establishment interdicts to the free exercises of religion is also a matter of degree beyond which the prohibition falls absolutely. The accommodation of public services to the spiritual needs of a community is an exercise of legislative discretionary judgement which then in turn is regulated by a pragmatic decision of the Court in each instance. To fix upon the concept of neutrality divorced from specific Court rulings as a self-operating concept is to ignore the fact that members of the court have agreed to the same literal formula of neutrality and differed five to four in the same case or in succeeding cases. Mr. Justice Brennan senses this division within the Court when in *Schempp* he lists practices of necessary and allowable accommodations by the government for religion in the very act of ruling against the state law requirement of Bible reading and the Lord's prayer in public schools.[59] The degree of accommodation under the free exercise clause must stop short of the strictures of establishment and the prohibitions of the establishment clause must not in effect become hostile to the rights of religious liberty.

The accommodation theory is a slide rule which is guided by a pragmatic calculation of the degree of government involvement. In *Zorach* the professed neutrality is sensitive to a sort of neutrality which may border on hostility to religion. This sensibility reappears in *Schempp* in the court opinion of Mr. Justice Clark and in the concurring opinion of Mr. Justice Brennan. These advisory cautions on the neutrality concept are more sharply edged in Mr. Justice Stewart's dissenting opinion when he states that true neutrality between believer and nonbeliever should rather find its expression in the freedom of choice to participate in religious exercises or not. Their complete exclusion by state authority would amount to "establishment of a religion of secularism, or at least, as government support of the beliefs of those who think that religious exercises should be conducted entirely in private."[60] The judicial insistence on the secular objects of a public schooling however is not to operate to the promotion of secularism. Mr. Justice Stewart's dissenting opinion is all the more meaningful when projected against *Torcaso* which adumbrated nontheistic convictions together with theistic beliefs and morally grounded values and accordingly brought both not only under the protective mantle of the free exercise of religion but also submitted each equally to the strictures of nonestablishment.

Even *Schempp* reveals that a strongly influential determinant of the decision was the degree of official involvement in the religious exercises. The specifics of the state arrangements were considered to exceed accommodation.[61] *Schempp* is more nearly in line with *McCollum* which seemed to involve the government in religious teaching to a greater degree than was ruled permissible in *Zorach*. If neutrality is hedged in by considerations of accommodations, accommodation in turn is hedged in by a permissible and nonpermissible degree of governmental involvement. So considered, neutrality serves as a balancing instrument between the two religious clauses of the First Amendment which in the concrete means a weighing of competing interests toward a reasonable pragmatic determination. The absolute formula of no aid actually works to undermine strict neutrality. Aid may be given provided it does not involve the government itself to a questionable degree in religious teaching and practices. *Schempp* provides a formula that is relevant to governmental relations to religious education on two grounds. The legislative power may not be exercised either to advance or inhibit religion. If this be neutrality it is better designated as a benevolent neutrality rather than a neutrality of abstention. If the government has defined certain specific educational goals whose primary purpose and effect are secular, then a "wholesome neutrality" precludes it from ruling out of its reach these same objectives as they are to be found in accredited religious schooling. The question then of the degree of governmental involvement in religious teaching and practices should not logically rise at all in the state's promotion and advancement of secuular goals of education which are pursued in church-related schools. Indeed, even the concept of accommodation does not strictly enter into this primary consideration. Government may spend public money for public purposes whether in the area of social welfare, health, or education as these purposes are fulfilled by the severalty of instrumentalities, without excluding any of them on religious grounds, or because of their religious affiliation. To do so is to contravene that neutrality and impartiality repeatedly reaffirmed by the Court.

Sherbert v. Werner[62]

Sherbert v. Werner which was decided on the same day as *Schempp* gives strength of confirmation to our reflections.

Adell Sherbert, an adherent of the Seventh-day Adventist Church, was denied unemployment compensation under the terms of a South Carolina statute because she would not work on Saturday, the Sabbath day of her faith. The South Carolina Unemployment Compensation Act denied unemployment benefits to persons who would not accept employment that required work on Saturdays unless it be for a good cause. The statute did not specify adjectivally what would be considered a good cause. On its face, the statute did not require work on Saturday. The claim of religious conscientious objection on the part of the Sabbatarian was considered by the Employment Security Commission as an insufficient personal reason without any referral to the religious category. While in intent and formulation the statute was strictly neutral in its construction, it operated in practice to favor those who were opposed to work on Sunday on religious grounds. The United States Supreme Court reversed the rulings of the South Carolina courts and held that the religious convictions of the appellant respecting a day of worship must be considered by the state in deciding whether unemployment compensation benefits should not be granted to the applicant. The opinion of the court and of concurring justices reinforces the suggestion that the neutrality of *Schempp* was greatly influenced by the degree of actual governmental involvement in religious exercises. In *Sherbert,* the deference to the free exercise of religion clause did not entail such intimate involvement and posed no real danger of establishment. While *Sherbert* calls to mind the preferred position given to religious conscience and activities in the Jehovah's Witness cases, and in the Selective Draft Law cases, *Sherbert* implies a greater latitude than these other cases. In the holding for exemptions from regulatory and tax laws, the Court was relieving religious proselytizing in those cases from a direct burden in the public conduct of the religious apostolate. In *Sherbert,* the state statute, wholly neutral and nondiscriminatory in its terms, was at most operating an indirect burden on the individual Sabbatarian and the Court ruled nonetheless that the state defer to her precisely on religious grounds. We cannot too strongly underscore the significance of *Sherbert*. The Court ruled that in the application of an authentic neutral statute, the state must in its application take into consideration the religious claim of the appellant and give it a preferred position as against the indirect burden that the statute placed on religious liberty. Mr. Justice Stewart who wrote a concurring opinion, and Mr. Justice Harlan and Mr. Justice White who dissented, thought that *Sherbert* was not distinguishable from *Braunfield* and in effect overruled it. But the Court opinion and the concurring opinions were convinced that the Sunday Closing Laws which *Braunfield* upheld operated a much less direct burden on the free exercise of religion rights and, besides, the greater dimensions of public welfare together with the complex difficulties of granting exemptions to a uniform day of rest posed problems of application not consequent to the exemption here granted to the Sabbatarian.

When we consider *Sherbert's* insistence upon the religious factor in the application of a state unemployment compensation act together with the various acknowledgements of the practical interrelationships between government and religion and its admonitions against a neutrality that may be hostile to the freedom of religious life in *Schempp* decided on the same day, it does not offend reason to say that the Court is far from committed to a strict neutrality concept as some of opponents of government aid to religion have argued. Mr. Justice Brennan's court opinion would not allow that special preference or exemption on religious grounds was constitutive of establishment.

> ... plainly we are not fostering the "establishment" of the Seventh-day Adventist religion in South Carolina, for the extension of unemployment benefits to Sabbatarians in common with Sunday worshippers reflects nothing more than the governmental obligation of neutrality in the face of religious differences, and does not represent that involvement of religious with secular institutions which it is the object of the Establishment Clause to forestall. ... Nor does the recognition of the appellant's right to unemployment benefits under the state statute serve to abridge any other person's religious liberties.[63]

Mr. Justice Stewart, who had dissented in *Schempp*, could not resist admonishing his brethren on the Bench against the "mechanistic concept of the Establishment Clause" which he declares to be offensive both to history and to law and warns of its dangers to the harmony of the twin religious clauses.

> For so long as the resounding but fallacious fundamentalist rhetoric of some of our Establishment Clause opinions remains on our books, to be disregarded at will as in the present case, or to be undiscriminatingly invoked as in the *Schempp* case ... , so long will the possibility of consistent and perceptive decision in this most difficult and delicate area of constitutional law be impeded and impaired.[64]

The neutrality principle on which *Engel* and *Schempp* were based is to be related to the appropriate degree of abstention which should keep governmental relations with religion from being too intimately involved, so that it becomes itself, as it were, an agency of religious practice and teaching. *Sherbert* raises for our consideration the question whether or not government may deny on the basis of religious exclusionary rule financial aid proportionate to secular goals of education which are no less the objectives of church-affiliated schools as they are of other private and governmental schools. *Sherbert* may offer prospects of encouragement for an affirmative answer since it *required* the state to consider the religious factor even though in its application the statute operated no more than an indirect burden on the free exercise right as contrasted with the preferred position for religious activities vindicated for the Jehovah's Witnesses who suffered a direct burden by state regulatory and taxing requirements.

On March 11, 1965, Judge O. Bowie Duckett, Associate Judge of the Fifth Judicial Circuit, gave his decision in *The Horace Mann League of the United States of America, Inc., et al v. J. Millard Tawes, Governor et al.* upholding the validity and constitutionality of the Maryland grants to be matched by four church-connected colleges.[65] The crux in the Court opinion was the extent of the church relationship, whether one or more of these four institutions is legally sectarian as contrasted to secular. In ascertaining the measure of the extent of this relationship the opinion briefly summed up the relevant data.

Hood College is controlled by a Board of 30 Trustees of whom seven are selected by the United Church of Christ with which the college is affiliated. With the exception of the chaplain there is no requirement that any of its administrative officers or faculty members be of the same religious confession. In an enrollment of 676, the students are widely distributed among a variety of faiths. No courses are required as training for the ministry. Two semester courses are mandatory in biblical studies. Hood "makes some attempt to require its students to attend approximately 14 Wednesday evening services in the Chapel and seven Sunday evening services also in the Chapel per semester." Hood receives approximately $45,000 annually from the United Church of Christ for operational services and a number of government grants from the National Science Foundation, the Atomic Energy Commission and other public agencies.

Western Maryland College is associated with the Methodist Church. There is no religious test for the admission of any student, teacher or officials. One more than one-third of 40 Trustees are required to be Methodist ministers. No courses are given specifically for training in the ministry. Studies in biblical literature are mandatory and a certain percentage of chapel services must be attended. The Methodist Church annually contributes $40,000 toward the operational costs of the college. All its Presidents have been Methodists. In a faculty of 76, 64 are Protestant, five Catholic, one Jewish, one Mohammed and five unaffiliated. In a student enrollment of 755, there is a distribution of religious confession. Children of Methodist Ministers receive a 50 per cent reduction in tuition. Students must attend at least five of 10 required chapel services and studies in biblical literature is mandatory.

The College of Notre Dame of Maryland was originally organized by the School Sisters of Notre Dame, a religious community of the Roman Catholic Church. Of the seven on the Board of Directors, five are required to be Sisters of Notre Dame. No religious affiliation is required for the admission of students but approximately 98 per cent of them are Roman Catholic. Of a faculty of 85, 44 are members of religious orders and of the 41 lay teachers eight are Non-Catholic. They are required courses in philosophy and theology.

St. Joseph's College was founded by Mother Seton in 1809. In 1902 the College was empowered by the State of Maryland to confer degrees for liberal arts and sciences and nursing. While the Board of Trustees may include two laymen, it is customarily composed of the Sisters. Of the 13 administrative officers all are Catholic, 10 of them religious and three lay. Thirty-seven of the 72 teachers belong to religious orders and of the 35 lay teachers eight are non-Catholic. Over 98 percent of the students are Catholic. Non-Catholics are not required to attend religious courses nor religious services.

Mr. Justice Bowie ruled that the Horace-Mann League has no standing to sue because as a non-profit corporation it pays no taxes and does not suffer any other injured interest.[66] However, he found that individual taxpayers who have brought suit not only in their own name but also on behalf of all other taxpayers of the State do have sufficient standing to sue. The Plaintiffs in question are real and personal property taxpayers and therefore have a special interest in the appropriations, different from that of the general public and even from other classes of taxpayers. To this must be added the acknowledgement that the question at issue is of such importance and urgency that it is ripe for decision.

On the "subordinate question" does the Maryland Constitution forbid grants of public money to church connected institutions, Justice Bowie relied on the repeated decisions of the Court of Appeals, Maryland's highest court, that little or no distinction intervenes between a sectarian or secular institution receiving an appropriation, provided the money is used to perform a public service as, for example, health, education, and general welfare of the citizens of the state.[67]

Addressing himself to the main question, does the First Amendment to the United States Constitution prohibit these grants to church connected colleges, Justice Bowie applies Mr. Justice Clark's test in *Schempp*—a secular legislative purpose and a primary effect that neither advances nor inhibits religion. As to the legislative purpose, he observes that the Maryland legislature[68] was in no way concerned with religion in making the appropriation because the language of the Acts themselves show that the grants were intended for science buildings, dormitories, dining halls, and classroom buildings, all of a secular nature. To the more difficult question, is the primary effect of one or more of the enactments to advance religion, he notes that the appropriations are for the construction of secular college buildings in no way connected with religion, that there is no training for the ministry at any of these four colleges, that there is no religious test for faculty members nor for the admission of students. Noting that there are some requirements for the study of religion and attendance at religious services for students of the same religious confession as the college and a greater distribution of religious professions at Hood and Western Maryland than at the two Catholic colleges, he said that if an adult chooses an institution where religious instruction is mandatory, he is merely asserting his constitutional right to the freedom of religion.

Justice Bowie takes cognizance of five factors[69] advanced by the complainants and admits that they do take the measure of the extent of the relationship of the institutions of learning with religion. But this, he points out is a foregone conclusion since, to begin with, the litigation is about church connected colleges. The "real issue" he emphasizes, is whether the primary effect of providing the means for the construction of secular buildings at these institutions advances religion. He concludes that the stated purpose and formal pronouncements in the college catalogues, especially of the two Catholic colleges, which declare the centrality of theology and philosophy in their educational process does not annul the actual achievements of these institutions in the secular studies for non-Catholic as well as for Catholic students.

> The buildings sought to be constructed are for secular purposes and the testimony in this case clearly establishes that the secular courses, such as science, English and mathematics, taught in these Institutions are practically identical with the courses at non-religious colleges.
> ... non-Catholic students and faculty are freely admitted to both institutions, and no attempt is made to convert non-Catholic students and faculty or to interfere with the free exercise of their religion. *If we distinguish between church related colleges on the basis of the degree of their relationship to a particular denomination, we would discriminate between different religions which is likewise prohibited by the First Amendment.* (Italics supplied)

Justice Bowie concluded by identifying the providential motive behind the secular legislative purpose and primary effect of the enactment.

> Most of us know that the Government maintains Military, Naval and Air Academies, but that it lacks a science academy. All of our scientists, therefore, must come from the public and private institutions of higher learning. According to the testimony of this case there are a total of approximately 1189 private institutions of higher learning in the United States and of this total, 817 are church related. Our source for obtaining scientists would be very limited if confined to the small number of non-religious institutions. ... It would therefore seem to me that the scientific education of college students is most vital to our public safety and welfare, perhaps more so than training juveniles at St. Mary's Industrial School even though it did produce Babe Ruth.[70]

Justice Bowie upheld the state of Maryland's appropriations as valid and constitutional.

There are a number of reflections I wish to note on Justice Bowie's ruling. In determining the constitutionality of financial assistance to church-affiliated schools we must identify the "real issue." The direct purpose to which these appropriations are applied must be such as are within the rights and duties of the legislative power to provide for—security of state, general welfare, etc. The fulfillment of these purposes are not vitiated, deflected, or rendered less acceptable to state authority because they are realized through agencies that are motivated by religious convictions. Nor are they less competently taught nor less efficient in the end result because of the philosophy of education which correlates all the various disciplines of learning to a religious source. The actual achievement can be empirically ascertained. The degree then of involvement of religious persons in the governance of the educational institution is not relevant to the constitutional determination no more than its avowed philosophy of education. The real issue is whether the legislative secular purpose and primary effect is fulfilled. The primary effect of providing the means for the construction of secular buildings at these institutions is not to advance religion. Unquestionably, such an assistance for secular goals in a church-related college is an advantage to the educational institution but only because its students are obtaining at these institutions these secular studies that they would otherwise have to seek elsewhere. Whoever raises the question that such aid "advances religion" as a legitimate consideration must also raise the correlative question whether its denial because of the institution's religious affiliation does not constitute an inhibition of religion. In all court rulings the phrase "neither advances" is always coupled with "nor inhibits religion." Only in such wise can we strive for that "wholesome neutrality" that Justice Clark wrote of in *Schempp* and for the impartiality—"because of faith or lack of faith"—which Justice Black set down in *Everson*.

It is high time that there be openly admitted on all sides that the educational process is preeminently a spiritual process and that the law does not prescribe what that spiritual integration be—theistic, non-theistic, Catholic, Christian, Hebraic, Ethical-Culture, etc. The real issue is whether the philosophy of education professed in any way diminishes the content and methodology of the secular subjects taught at these church-connected institutions. We have already pointed to a very broad and highly significant fact that the academy itself does not discriminate between the state, private, and religious schools in their mutual acceptance of students and graduates. If law be concerned with the realities of national education, how then may the law not admit the same evidences of academic achievement?

Church-related colleges are essentially educational institutions, not religious enterprises, and they can contribute to the state's interest in educational accomplishment. The religious piety which these religious colleges may actively foster by their environment, courses in theology, and attendance at chapel services is never considered by them as a substitute for competence in learning. Those who fail their examinations are not the less pious and those who do pass are not necessarily numbered among the saints. The avowed aims that appear in their college catalogues to integrate the collection of the various disciplines of learning into an integrated whole is ostensibly to invest the whole educational process with moral values and religious motivations for the benefit of the student and of the community in which he will live. This religious investiture is intended to keep science and its achievements preminently *human*, that is, subject to moral judgment and evaluation, to couple freedom with responsibility, and to ordain through human effort the stark realism of arbitrary human conduct to the ideals that elevate by faith, hope and charity. It is surely not an unwarranted usurpation much less a legal prohibition that educators teach the meaning of life and the destiny of man as a salutary accompaniment to immediate secular pursuits. It is the answer to Tertullian's question "What has Athens to do with Jerusalem?"

The church affiliated schools enjoy the singular advangage of providing instruction on the relations between man and God, the want of which constituted for Jefferson a "chasm in a general institution of the useful sciences." It is for this reason that Jefferson in his education plans for the state of Virginia entrusted this responsibility "to each society of instruction in its own doctrine" and extended facilities to them on the grounds of the state university or adjacent to it.[71] It is a facile but misleading construction to translate the constitutional neutrality between believer and nonbeliever into a neutral educational process. The first is a legal act; the second is a myth. If the educational process is to be adumbrated within constitutional neutrality, then the correct formula is that the constitution is neutral on value judgments that invest all educational processes with the reasonable and necessary reservation that the general welfare is not harmed thereby. Indeed, it will be found that there are a diversity of value-judgment systems that are contributory to the commonwealth.

The plaintiffs appealed the ruling of the lower court and the Court of Appeals of Maryland[72] by a 4 to 3 vote reversed in part by upholding the constitutionality of the matching grants for Hood but denying them to the other three colleges. The ruling of the court revolved on the contention of the appellants that while some degree of relationship to church or religion may exist in an educational institution without rendering it "sectarian," a relationship which is "substantial" renders the institution sectarian and thereby constitutionally ineligible to receive public funds. The appellees, on the contrary, held that the degree of relationship to religion, however substantial, does not render that educational institution legally ineligible to receive grants for educational purposes. For the lower and higher court there seems to have been two different "real issues." The Court of Appeals did not consider whether the buildings to be constructed were for secular purposes and whether secular courses "such as science, English and mathematics, taught at these institutions are practically identical with the courses at nonreligious colleges." It chose rather to apply the five standards that the plaintiffs had proposed in ascertaining the degree of connection of the college with religion and by this calculation determining whether each college was truly an educational institution or a sectarian institution and *as such* disqualified under the nonestablishment clause of receiving governmental assistance in its educational programs identical with the interest of the state. By inserting this dichotomous leverage between the "objective" nature of the subject studies and services and the religious affiliation and government of the school, it disengaged the educational instrumentality and facility from its educational achievements.

Prefatory to these considerations, the Court of Appeals has an "extended" lengthy disquisition on the "historical background of the First Amendment" beginning with Pliny's letter to the Roman Emperor Trajan in 112 A.D., no less! One would have hoped by this time that the American gradual disengagement from ancient animosities and historical complexities would warrant that the American community can now fashion its own history of state-religion relationships as a unique experiment in "wholesome neutrality," of accommodation and impartiality, ever sensitive to encroachments upon religious liberty and prejudicial establishments whether on theistic or nontheistic grounds. The usefulness of historical references should not be marred by an implied sense of historical determinism and a Hegelian logism that works out inevitably to foreordained consequences. Governmental grants to specific educational goals defined in terms of the public interest in no way diminishes the mutual independence of the state or of the religious institution nor confer upon the public authority religious functions nor upon the religious institution any political power. The Court is completely silent about the mutual exchange of students by state, private, and church-connected schools on all levels during a school term or upon graduation. Nor is there any awareness of the eligibility, without discrimination, of students for scholarships and fellowships from public and private sources. The "real issue" is deflected in the application of the five factors plus one which measure the degree of school-church connection. (1) the stated purposes of the college; (2) the college personnel, which includes the governing board, the administrative officers, the faculty, and the student body; (3) the college's relationship with religious organizations and groups; (4) the place of religion in the college program; (5) the result of "outcome" of the college program; such as accreditation and the nature and character of the activities of the alumni; and (6) the work or image of the college in the community. After applying these criteria to each of the colleges, the Court concluded that three of the colleges may not constitutionally receive the state grants. Hood College was adjudged not to be "sectarian in a legal sense under the First Amendment, or to a degree that renders the grant invalid thereunder." Further, the Court did admit that the Maryland state statute making available public funds to a private institution for a public purpose was not violative of any of the controlling articles of the Maryland state constitution, namely, Articles 23, 15 and 36.

In corroboration, the Court then quotes at length from the dissenting opinion of Judge Parke in *Board of Education v. Wheat*[73] which in its literal expression would seem to uphold the constitutionality of such state grants to all four the colleges. This is in fact what the dissenting opinion of the three justices pointed out, in repeating the very same quotation:

Neither the payment of money by the State to a private person, whether corporate or otherwise, nor the nature and occupation of that person, is determinative of the purpose of the payment. Thus the appropriations by the General Assembly of public funds are customarily made and paid to various bodies and institutions through the state, which are privately owned and managed, and which are, in many instances, of sectarian origin and character. It will be found, upon examination, that this employment of public moneys has been sanctioned by the decision of this court. If an incidental or direct benefit result to the recipient, this resultant advantage becomes immaterial and negligible because of the paramount public and essential nature of the service rendered and out of the further factor that the State has either not undertaken or not fully assumed the performance of the public service or function involved. (citation). *The validity of such grants, when so limited, is not affected by any sectarian circumstance.* (citation). Thus, *grants to educational institutions* which supply instruction and training in learning and mechanical, industrial, agricultural and other arts, of which the State does not offer or undertake to afford universal service, are freely made without reference to whether the recipient be denominational or otherwise. (citation of Maryland cases and legislative grants). Similarly, the grants in aid of the hospitalization of patients for care and treatment in sickness, injury and disease (citation) for chronic alcoholism, (citation) for homes for the aged and infirm, for orphans, for children, for the blind, for crippled children, for reformatories and for other purposes which are within the functions of the State as conducive to the welfare of its inhabitants, and pursuant to the mandate of the Declaration of Rights: "That the Legislature ought to encourage the diffusion of knowledge and virtue, the extension of a judicious system of general education, the promotion of literature, the arts, sciences, agriculture, commerce and manufactures, and, the general amelioration of the condition of the people." Article 43.

In these grants the State advisedly *makes no distinction between denominational and non-denominational institutions,* nor has it limited its appropriations to race or color. The grants so made for special public purposes find at once their justification and vindication in the promotion of the general welfare in those matters of public concern in respect of which the government had not theretofore undertaken completely to perform. In short, although paid to a private person, the money is appropriated and expended for a public use.[74] (Emphasis added.)

Both the majority and the minority opinion quote Justice Parke but what makes the majority's use of this passage so intriguing is that the italicized words and lines are supplied by the majority and not by the minority. And the italicized sections are the very portions of the passage that would have warranted on the part of the majority a contrary decision, an affirmative one for all of the four colleges.

The dissenting opinion of Justice Hammond, in which Justice Horney and Justice Marbury concurred, pointed to the historical record of the state of Maryland which has for over a hundred and eighty years followed a general, systematic and non-discriminatory pattern of financial assistance to private institutions furnishing a higher secular education. These grants, the minority opinion stressed, were under both Maryland law and federal constitutional standards for a public use and purpose. It quoted, as we have already indicated, the same passage from Justice Parke which literally would warrant rather than interdict them as constitutionally permissible provisions. It turned to *Everson* for its major premise: "It is much too late to argue that legislation intended to facilitate the opportunity of children to get a secular education serves no public purpose." While the provision for free bus transportation to a parochial school is in itself a safety welfare measure properly within the exercises of state police power, the Court had linked that secular means of travel to an educational process which is religiously orientated and called it a means to a secular education on the implied grounds that the parochial schooling was effectively fulfilling the secular requirements. Translating this valid interpretation to the case at hand, the minority opinion made its application with convincing evidence:

> the four donee colleges here involved all furnish a secular liberal arts education comparable to that furnished by other first rank liberal arts colleges in the United States and are accredited by standard accrediting agencies. The courses taught in the four donee colleges are taught in substantially the same manner as at other similar colleges, for example, Johns Hopkins or Goucher, and are not used as vehicles for religious indoctrination; the text books are chosen by individual teachers for their merit in supplying knowledge of the course and are not chosen for their religious orientation or because of the religion of the author and, in most instances, are the same texts that are used at other

public and private colleges. No doctrine, dogma or other teaching of any church enters into or interferes with the teaching of the secular subjects that are taught. Graduates of the four donee colleges go on to take graduate studies and obtain the degrees on an individual basis with graduates of other public and private colleges at universities offering the best post graduate courses, such as Johns Hopkins and Columbia. There are no religious requirements, oral or written, for admission of students to the donee colleges and, finally, the buildings to be erected with the funds granted will be places which will furnish the secular training offered by the colleges and not used for religious ceremonies or instruction.[75]

If law should be attendant to the meaning of facts, should it disregard the universal experience among all colleges and universities of America whose students may transfer from one to another public, private, and church-connected college, — before the completion of an educational process after graduation? The minority opinion then describes the vast national need that private colleges have helped to fulfill and what a large percentage of these the church-connected colleges constitute. And in testimony of this broad fact, more than two billion dollars from the federal government is currently going to private colleges for research contracts, loans, and outright grants without prejudice to their religious affiliation.

Justice Hammond reviewed the preceding Supreme Court decision and finds in Justice Clark's test enunciated in *Schempp* a summary focus of the guidelines by which we are to evaluate what aids are not constitutive of establishment — a secular means to a public purpose which is primary in intent and effect of the legislative provision. There is, lastly, the argument on alternate means from *McGowan*. The minority opinion quotes from a Note in the *Harvard Law Review:*[76]

> To exclude these 800 institutions of higher learning from federal aid would seriously hamper the effort to increase enrollment capacity to the point where colleges will be able to handle the expected demand of 1970 and distort the present educational allocation of students between denominational and nondenominational schools. . . . Such pragmatic considerations would be irrelevant if the command of the Constitution were clear; the remedy would then be a constitutional amendment. However,

the lack of an effective alternative should be highly relevant when a plausible constitutional defense can be made and where, in an area of church-state overlap, criteria can be formulated which minimize governmental intrusion into religious concerns without paralyzing governmental attempts to cope with urgent national problems.

On the question of constitutionality, the author, at pp. 1356-57 says:

On the other hand, the opinions of Justice Clark and Brennan in *Schempp* indicate that federal aid to education would be considered constitutional. For example, Justice Clark enunciated the test of constitutionality to be a secular legislative purpose and a primary effect that neither advances nor inhibits religion. Similarly Justice Brennan would draw the line at legislation employing the organs of government for essentially religious purposes or using essentially religious means to serve governmental ends where secular means would suffice. Under either test, the act would appear to be free from constitutional flaws.[77]

PROSPECTUS

On November 14, 1966 the United States Supreme Court declined to review[78] the Court of Appeals decision and that in effect left the court's rule controlling in the State of Maryland. Opponents of federal grants to church colleges have been unable to obtain a court test because of the Supreme Court's rule announced in 1923 in the case of *Massachusetts v. Mellon*.[79] This ruling held that federal taxpayers lacked standing to challenge, in court, expenditures of United States funds. In the Maryland courts, however, state taxpayers were allowed to contest state grants. The Higher Education Facilities Act has authorized federal grants for construction of certain types of buildings at church-related colleges. One can only speculate why the United States Supreme Court refused to hear the Maryland case. It may be because it involved only Maryland law. The federal government was not a party to the litigation in any way. According to the federal program of assistance to higher and lower levels of education, grants may be made to private and church-related colleges to help finance institutes under the National Defense Education Act and to such schools under the developing college program. It is a fair conjecture that the federal programs involved in these assistances and financial subventions add up to $1.6 billion dollars to private colleges and a $1 billion dollar plan for aid to elementary and secondary education. In the expectation that someday the United States Supreme Court will agree to review this momentous question on governmental aid to church-connected schools, whether of the higher or lower level, we here submit certain criteria derived from preceding court decisions in the light of which we may conjecture the ultimate determination of this controversial issue.

First, both government and religious communities have concurrent interests and functions in many areas of general welfare, including education. Second, the identity of goals, the competence and efficiency of the religious educational instrumentalities may be tested and ascertained empirically. Third, the public law should take cognizance of the broad and long-standing experience of the academy itself which gives witness to the identity of secular goals realized in the diversity of publicly accredited schools by the mutual exchange of students during a school term and after graduation. To this too must be added the government confirmed belief in the competence of state, private and church-connected schools to fulfill its goals by granting to the diversity of the schools without any discrimination on basis of religion those grants and research contracts. Fourth, an unreal objection often arises to distract from concentrating on the real issue, the secular services and studies of the church-connected schools. It is said that such aids benefit the institution itself. Undoubtedly! Negatively considered, deny all governmental assistance to these church colleges and universities and extend them only to state and private secular institutions and the series of consequences to their disadvantage may be easily conjectured. Positively considered, extend these benefactions to these religious institutions in the government's own interest and that of its citizens, and the consequent benefit to the enrollment, to students, and the faculty can scarcely be denied. The objection is unreal because it blinds itself to the nature and operation of almost all human acts and conduct, whether private or public. Fifth, there is more often than not multiple effects rather than singleness of outcome. Nor can one constrain all efficiency to a predetermined end. There is generally an overflow of consequences. Good and evil, private or governmental, are diffusive of themselves. If the legislative secular purpose and primary effect is realized through an agency that admits to a religious confession then one would suppose all the better for it. To insert a religious exclusionary rule because of an overflow of benefits offends civility no less than common sense. Sixth, *Everson* denied that such a religious exclusionary rule may interject between the recipients of a governmental assistance directed to secular education in church-schools. Whoever than invokes the phrase "neither advances religion" must give in its complementary entirety the Supreme Court's own proposition, "that neither advances nor inhibits religion." Only in this wise will it be possible to achieve the delicate balance of preserving on the one hand religious liberty in education and on the other forbid what constitutes establishment. Seventh, the neutrality between believers, on the one hand, and between believers and non-believers on the other, affirmed in *Torcaso,* will be absolute, showing favoritism neither to one nor the other by weighting government power, influence, and prestige on the side of one educational process. The "wholesome neutrality" of which Mr. Justice Clark spoke of in *Schempp,* will be regulated by identifying the governmental interest wheresoever it is done with no prejudice to the exercise of religious liberty in education. Eighth, in the use of historical precedents on the union of church and state, of Altar and Throne, of state church establishments with all their incidents of civil disabilities and oppression to dictates of conscience, we counsel caution against an implied sense of historical determinism and a species of Hegelian *a priori* ergotisms. The American community and its political and legal institutions have gradually disengaged themselves from the social-political-religious inheritance of their European forebears. They have a right as well as the awesome responsibility of fashioning their own church-state relations without evoking ancient fears and animosities. There is discernible an "American way" of doing things and it is this unique pragmatic American approach and not the dead heavy hand of the past that should guide our decisions. In conclusion, we suggest that in order to dispel the incubus of the logic of past events and to affirm our own freedom of force and action, the time has come for the United States Congress to make a full and complete evaluation of the church schools and ascertain to its own satisfaction whether or not they may participate as authentic educational facilities in the goals of national education and whether they are beneficial to our democratic institutions.

We are convinced that properly defined relationships of mutual cooperation where there is an identity of goals, a concurrence of functions and of interests, is a proper implementation of the unique American experiment in the separation of church and state. And we are firmly convinced that by these arrangements both church and state will remain free and unhampered by each other in the performance of their divinely-ordained and constitutional functions.

FOOTNOTES AND REFERENCES

1. The Horace Mann League of the United States of America, Inc. v. J. Millard Tawes, Governor et al. No. 15, 850 Equity, March 11, 1965, Judge O. Bowie Duckett.
2. Horace Mann League of the United States of America, Inc. v. Board of Public Works of Maryland, 242 Md. 645, 220 A. 2d 51 (Ct. App. 1966).
3. Everson v. Board of Education, 330 U.S. 1, 15-6 (1947).
4. *Ibid.*
5. McCollum v. Board of Education, 333 U.S. 203 (1948).
6. Zorach v. Clauson, 343 U.S. 306 (1952).
7. West Virginia State Board of Education v. Barnette, 319 U.S. 624 (1943).
8. Sherbert v. Verner, 374 U.S. 398 (1963).
9. Engel v. Vitale, 370 U.S. 421 (1962).
10. School District of Abington Township, Pennsylvania v. Schempp, 374 U.S. 203 (1962).
11. Bradfield v. Roberts, 175 U.S. 291 (1899).
12. Cochran v. Board of Education, 281 U.S. 370 (1930).
13. Torcaso v. Watkins, 367 U.S. 982 (1963).
14. Pierce v. Society of Sisters, 268 U.S. 510 (1925).
15. *Supra* note 11.
16. *Supra* note 12.
17. *Supra* note 3.
18. Yeshiva, Book 396, note 105. Notes 105-109 for a discussion of the contractual arrangement between the City of New York and Yeshiva University. *Cf.* Costanzo, THIS NATION UNDER GOD, 257-260, 396 (1964).
19. The Court meticulously observed in what sense the Catholic Hospital must be understood to be a church-affiliated institution and what relevance that has on public service: the federal government expected from it no less. The Court pointedly makes these observations: (1). the hospital was owned by a corporation, chartered by the government and consequently, legally speaking, the corporation was subject solely to the control "of the government which created it." Under this aspect the corporation was secular and nonsectarian. (2). the fact that the hospital was conducted under the Auspices of the Catholic Church meant "That the church exercises great and perhaps controlling influences over the management of the Hospital." (3). the stockholders of the corporation were all nuns, Bradfield v. Roberts, 175 U.S. 291, 298 (1899). In the light of these admissions of fact the Supreme Court's ruling in Bradfield means that a direct appropriation of government funds for the performance of a public function conducted under the auspices "and perhaps controlling influence" of an institution with religious professions is not in contravention of the non-establishment clauses of the First Amendment. The Court too noted the error of confounding a "law respecting an establishment of religion" with "a law respecting a religious establishment."
20. Opinion of the Justices, 99 N.H. 519, 113 A 2d 114, 116 (1955).
21. Kentucky Building Commission v. Effron, 220 S.W. 2d 836 (Ky. 1949).
22. Meyer v. Nebraska, 262 U.S. 390 (1923).

23. *Supra* note 14.

24. The principal forces behind the Americanization campaign were led by the Imperial Council, A.A.O. Nobles Mystic Shrine. *Cf.* Oregon School cases: Complete Record 732 (1925). An interesting comment upon this motivation will be found in the brief amicus curiae filed in the case by Louis Marshall on behalf of the American Jewish Committee. "Recognizing in the main the great merits of our public schools system, it is nevertheless unthinkable that public schools alone shall, by legislative compulsion rather than by their own merits, be made the only medium of education in this country. Such a policy would speedily lead to their deterioration. The absence of the right of selection would at once lower the standards of education. If the children of the country are to be educated in accordance with an undeviating rule of uniformity and by a single method, then eventually our nation would consist of mechanical robots and standardization Babbitts. *Id.* at 615 . . . The private and parochial schools which exist throughout the country are conducted on the same patriotic lines as are our public schools." *Id.* at 618. For a sharp rejection of the charges of divisiveness leveled at parochial schools, *Cf.* Marshall, *Id.*, at 621-22.

25. Pierce v. Society of Sisters, 268 U.S. 510, 534 (1925).
26. 281 U.S. 370 (1930).
27. Record, p. 4, Cochran v. Board of Education, *supra* note 26.
28. *Id.* at 13.
29. *Id.* at 16.
30. Borden v. Louisiana State Board of Education, 168 La. 1005, 1020, 123 So. 655, 660 (1929).
31. Cochran v. Board of Education, *supra* note 26.
32. 320 U.S. 1 (1947).
33. *Id.* at 7.
34. *Id.* at 18.
35. *Id.* at 16.
36. *Id.* at 18.
37. *Id.* at 16.
38. *Id.* at 15, 16.
39. 333 U.S. 203 (1948).
40. 343 U.S. 306 (1952).
41. *Id.* at 312-3.
42. *Id.* at 313-4.

43. Justice Frankfurter, in his concurring opinion in the *Sunday Law* cases, states: "But the several opinions in *Everson* and *McCollum* and in Zorach, 343 U.S. 306, makes sufficiently clear that 'separation' is not a self-defining concept." McGowan v. Maryland, 336 U.S. 420, 461 (1961).

44. 386 U.S. 420 (1961).
45. *Id.* at 422.
46. *Id.* at 444-45.
47. *Id.* at 465-67.
48. 367 U.S. 982 (1963).
49. Watson v. Jones, 80 U.S. (13 Wall.) 679 (1871).
50. Cantwell v. Connecticut, 310 U.S. 296 (1940).
51. 374 U.S. 203 (1963).
52. 370 U.S. 421 (1962).
53. *Supra* note 51 at 222.
54. Marsh v. Alabama, 326 U.S. 501 (1946).
55. King v. New York, 240 U.S. 290 (1951).
56. Martin v. Struthers, 319 U.S. 141 (1943).
57. Murdock v. Pennsylvania, 319 U.S. 105 (1943).
58. *Supra* note 50.

59. These are as follows: (1) cases of conflicts between establishment and free exercise, including provision for churches and chaplains at military establishments for those in armed services and chaplains in penal institutions; (2) prayers in legislative chambers and appointment of legislative chaplains; (3) non-devotional use of the Bible in public schools; (4) uniform tax exemptions incidentally available to religious institutions; (5) religious con-

sideration in public welfare programs; (6) activities, like Sunday closing laws, which, though religious in origin, have ceased to have religious meaning. 374 U.S. 203, 294-304 (1963).

60. *Id.* at 246. So also Mr. Justice Goldberg who wrote that "untutored devotion to the concept of neutrality can lead to invocation or approval of results which partake . . . of a brooding and pervasive devotion to the secular as a passive or even active, hostility to the religious." *Id.* at 306. Such results "are not only compelled by the construction, but, it seems to me, are prohibited by it." *Id.* at 306.

61. Mr. Justice Goldberg, observed that the "pervasive religiosity and direct governmental involvement entering in the prescription of prayer and Bible-reading in the public schools, during and as a part of the curricular day, involving young impressionable children whose school attendance is statutorily compelled and utilizing the prestige, power and influence of school administration, staff and authority, cannot realistically be termed simply accommodation. . . ." 374 U.S. 203, 307 (1963).

62. Sherbert v. Werner, 374 U.S. 398 (1963).

63. *Id.* at 409.

64. *Id.* at 416-417. Even Mr. Justice Harlan, who dissented would see no constitutional objection under the establishment clause if the state statute had provided for accommodations to religious claims. The constitutional concept of neutrality would not have suffered thereby.

65. Chap. 546, Acts of 1963 granted $5000,000 to West Maryland College toward the construction of a science wing and dining hall. Chap. 545, Acts of 1963 granted to St. Joseph's College $750,000 toward the construction of a science building. Chap. 88, Acts of 1962 granted $500,000 to Hood College toward the construction of a dormitory and classroom building. Chap. 66, Acts of 1962 granted $750,000 to the College of Notre Dame of Maryland toward the construction of a science building. Each act provided that the recipient would privately obtain elsewhere an equal and matching sum for the aforesaid buildings.

66. Besides, Justice Bowie felt bound to abide by the ruling of Sun Cab Co. v. Cloud, 162 Md. 419, 159 A. 132 (1932), which the Maryland Court of Appeals, its highest court, had only the year before cited with acceptance. Citizens Committee v. County Comm., 233 Md. 398 (1964).

67. Article 36 of the Maryland Declaration of Rights provides in part: ". . . nor ought any person be compelled to . . . maintain, or contribute . . . to maintain any place of worship, of any ministry; . . ." . Justice Bowie quotes the Court of Appeals in St. Mary's Industrial School v. Brown, 45 Md. 310, 336: "The fact that the institution may be under denominational or religious control, can in no manner affect their qualification for assuming such relation to the City, or for the full and faithful discharge of the duties that they may contract to perform. Charity, to say the least of the matter, is quite as likely to be fully and faithfully administered under such auspices as it could be under any other. It could, therefore, be no objection that the institutions are or may be under the control and influence of those belonging to any particular church or denomination." *Cf.* Finan v. M. & O.O. of Cumberland. 154 Md. 563, 141 A. 269 (1928), in which the Court of Appeals upheld the validity of a municipal appropriation in aid of the construction of a hospital operated by a group of Roman Catholic Nuns. See also, Board of Education v. Wheat, 174 Md. 314, 199 A. 628 (1934).

68. Justice Bowie also noted that the Maryland legislature for the past 175 years has made similar grants to private colleges and universities including many denominational institutions. In holding fast to the concept of neutrality first formulated in *Everson,* Justice Bowie notes by citing a long litany of federal governmental programs that this neutrality has not been an absolute neutrality but one which has been as sensitive against taking a hostile stance against religion as it has against indifference to the establishment clause.

69. (1) stated purpose of the college; (2) college personnel; (3) colleges' relation to religious organization; (4) place of religion in the college program; (5) the result and outcome of the college program.

70. The Plaintiffs conceded that public grants to religious institutions, such as hospitals, orphan asylums and other non-educational institutions are valid when affecting health, safety and welfare of our citizens.

71. Costanzo, THIS NATION UNDER GOD 170-76 (1964).

72. Horace Mann League of the United States of America, Inc. v. Board of Public Works of Maryland, 242 Md. 645, 220 A. 2d 51 (Ct. App. 1966).
73. Board of Education v. Wheat, 174 Md. 314, 199 Atl. 628 (1934).
74. *Id.* at 637.
75. Horace Mann League of the United States of America, Inc. v. Board of Public Works of Maryland, *supra* note 72, at 78.
76. *Constitutionality of Federal Aid to Church Related Colleges,* 77 Harv. L. Rev. 1353, 1358 (1964).
77. Horace Mann League of the United States of America, Inc. v. Board of Public Works of Maryland, *supra* note 72, at 81.
78. Horace Mann League of the United States of America, Inc. v. Board of Public Works of Maryland, 242 Md. 314, 220 A. 2d 51 (Ct. App. 1966), *cert. denied,* 385 U.S. 97 (1966). The Court also refused to review the decision informing Hood College of the request of the Horace Mann League.
79. Massachusetts v. Mellon, 262 U.S. 447 (1923).

ACADEMIC FREEDOM AND
THE INTELLECTUAL*

Discussions of the past decade on academic freedom have brought to the surface not only the many issues therein involved but also the divergent vantage points from which they may be considered and, supposedly, resolved. Prevailing through most of these discussions is a persistent, ever-recurring charge that Catholics, whose religious convictions are allied to a teaching authority outside and above the individual can scarcely pretend to intellectual liberty. Surely, it is said, a unity of Faith through obedience to Authority will not allow the Catholic scholar the same degree of uninhibited intellectual freedom as the mind who is not subject to papal teaching on Faith and Morals. Such a prior commitment in conscience, it is alleged, is bound to restrict intellectual inquiry, scientific research, and experimentation. And when one recalls all the incidences of adherence to Catholic orthodoxy, such as ecclesiastical review, imprimaturs, censorship, and the Index, the submission to papal teaching amounts we are told almost to intellectual servitude. The act of obedience to the Church's *magisterium* is considered objectionable because the faithful thereby give intellectual assent to certain propositions as dogmatically unerring. Instead of the Truth, as Our Divine Lord said, making us free, we are told that we are made captive by it. In a word, religious dogma and academic freedom are mutually opposed.

A frontal approach should be made to the innuendo lodged in the proposition that the Catholic intellectual cannot be academically free — an innuendo which says that as a sociological fact,

---

*CORK UNIVERSITY PRESS (Ireland) 1960, pp. 1-16. Lecture given at University College, under the auspices of the U.S. Department of State.

academic freedom in a community will be in inverse proportion to the Catholic population. Where Catholics — or more precisely — Catholicism prevails, academic freedom will be extremely narrow if not well-nigh extinct.

Obviously, we Catholics may not be indifferent to these imputations. Surely we should examine them because they are sometimes made by intellectuals who bear us good will as well as by those who do not. Now these suppositions, may I presently point out, rest on a misconception and on a controverted question. The misconception is that dogmas are only religious. On the contrary, dogmas are unconditional truths — as distinguished from conjectures, opinions, theories, and hypotheses. They are declarative of a truth to which the mind adheres with a degree of certainty that precludes all reasonable doubt. Every science has its dogmas, theology, philosophy, and all the natural sciences. Dogmas are not only the ultimate answers to some questions; they prompt further questioning and research. Since indeed science is the cumulated knowledge of the necessary and universal — of what is not accidental and merely transient — the scientist is not at all embarrassed to admit to scientific axioms.

The controverted question is how should the libertarian end be defined. It is not sufficient to inquire simply what is freedom or to engage in the endless debate whether freedom is to be defined absolutely in a negative way as freedom *from* all external restraints or primarily in a positive way as freedom *for* what. The prior question is freedom *of* whom — only in this wise shall we begin to distinguish instinctual jungle freedom and freedom of physical movement from the specifically *human* freedom, the spiritual faculties of man, his intellect and will.

But history is a stubborn witness against the protestations of libertarian rationalism. At a time when Western Christendom was united by the bond of the Catholic Faith, the Middle Ages produced its most unique and original achievement, the universities. Antiquity knew the schools of Athens and Alexandria, the Academy and the Lyceum of the Peripetetics, and the Porch of the Stoics. But the institutional embodiment of an educational ideal, the organization of the various faculties of arts and sciences, the interdependence of all the sciences to the full complement of learning and wisdom — this was a distinctly medieval creation of which our own universities are the modern heirs. What glowing memories are brought to mind when we recall the universities of Paris, Oxford, and Cambridge, the universities of Padua, Naples, and Bologna, the universities of Valencia, Salamanca, and Valladolid. Though the medievalists considered theology the central and supreme science, it was far from being dominating and exclusive. The medieval universities singly distinguished themselves for their faculties of law, medicine, and liberal arts as well as for philosophy and theology. Bologna was preeminent for its faculty of law, Paris was eminent in philosophy and theology, Salerno was the great center of medicine. Before the revolt of Luther, eighty-one universities were dispersed throughout Christendom; the majority of them were founded by papal charters. The major universities numbered from five to twenty thousand students, lay and ecclesiastic. Under the presidency of the theology of a universal faith, sciences flourished in medieval universities and thousands of students crowded to its lecture halls.

THE MEDIEVAL UNIVERSITIES

What does history record of academic freedom in the universities when the Catholic Faith was all-prevailing? What effect did religious dogma and obedience to the *magisterium* of the Church have upon the intellectual life as exemplified in the medieval universities? Unlike the *mysteries* of pre-Christian pagan religions which were occult, not open to rational inquiry, scarcely cognoscible even by their custodians, the dogmas of Christian revelation broke upon new visions of truth heretofore unknown to man. St. Augustine, taking up St. Peter's exhortation to the early Christians "to give reason for their Faith," gave added impetus to intellectual inquiry by his dictum "fides quaerens intellectum" which St. Anselm in turn enlarged to mean "credo ut intelligam." For the first time in the history of religions, Christian revelational dogma initiated the intellectual inquiry by human reason left to its own connatural powers into the existence, nature, and attributes of God and His creation. The Christian conception of divine mysteries was far from an inhibiting one. Paradoxical as it may seem, medieval theologians for example, considered the greatest of all divine mysteries, the Blessed Trinity, the most fruitful for speculation.

One can very easily enlarge upon the increased and broadening opportunities for intellectual inquiry into the nature and purpose of human existence which the Christian dogmas of supernatural elevation, Original Sin, the Redemption, salvation through Faith and Charity, as to the nature, extent, and limits of human free will for salvation. We have come to know about man through Christian revelation what we would not otherwise have guessed. Only the myopic mind of a libertarian rationalist could insist that a wholly secular education was necessary for academic freedom. The medieval universities give lasting testimony to the exuberance, originality and resourcefulness of intellectual activity which revelational theology animated and inspired. In Dante's Divine Comedy, Divine Wisdom is compared to "Light intervening between Truth and intellect" — "che lume fia tra il vero e l'intelletto." This was but the poetic exultation of the Psalmist's "Dominus illuminatio mea et salus mea" — an illumination which burst upon us with the advent of the Light of the World.

The Age of Faith was the Age of Reason. Christian revelational dogma far from being repressive of intellectual inquiry under the magisterial authority of the Church, unleashed a vigorous, intensely curious, and penetrating intellectual activity. Between Faith in this life and the Beatific Vision in the next, there is an intermediary which is the understanding of Faith. In this striving, the Medievalist could scale heights which the pagan philosophers had dimly glimpsed. The medieval intellectual did not confuse credibility with credulity and though many articles of Faith are transrational, above reason, yet reason was impelled by the innermost dynamism of Faith to strive to comprehend according to its capacities what it would otherwise have never known. St. Augustine expressed the thought of all Christian philosophers and theologians when in a letter to Consentius he wrote (Ep. 120.3: *ad Consentium*): "Far be it from us to suppose that God abhors in us that by virtue of which He has made us superior to other animals. Far be it, I say, that we should believe in such a way as to exclude the necessity either of accepting or requiring reason since we could not even believe unless we possessed rational souls." Like Jacob, it was given to them to wrestle with God. Religious unity of the Catholic Faith did not then, nor ought at any time, put a quietus on intellectual inquiry. To the medieval mind Faith presupposed reason, grace presupposed nature, and revelation presupposed that God be known to reason.

Some would allow that if only Catholic intellectuals would keep their religious dogmas somehow departmentalized and isolated within their minds they might still enjoy some measure of academic freedom. But unfortunately, the objection continues, they admit to philosophical doctrines. Here, too, misconception gives direction to the criticism.

Philosophical doctrines are, like religious dogmas, unconditional truths, such as, man has an immortal soul, man is a moral agent subject in conscience to the moral law of a personal God according to which he must regulate his life and which holds him accountable for all eternity. But unlike religious dogmas which are characteristically authoritarian, that is to say, intellectual assent is given to a proposition because of the veracity and infallibility of the divine disclosures — philosophical doctrines are held through the compelling force of rational conviction motivated solely by the evidence of the truth affirmed.

Scholastic philosophy as medieval speculation is called is the most conspicuous example of a philosophy animated and inspired by religion. Yet it maintained its intellectual independence. Whatever the role of authority in matters of revelational theology, in philosophy, as the medieval maxim went, authority was as good as its reason. Far more than the seventeenth and eighteenth century, the Age of Faith was the Age of Reason. Abelard's method of inquiry, the *Sic et Non*, the Thomistic *videtur quod non*, and the *ego autem contra* of the schoolmen were characteristic rather of scepticism than of credulity, and it was by these critical, probing methods that the most important systems of knowledge, the medieval *Summas*, were constructed. It was a time of *controversiae, disputationes, quaestiones, argumenta*, distinctions and contradistinctions. It was of the medieval universities that John Henry Newman wrote: "If ever there was a time when the intellect went wild and had a licentious revel, it was at the date I speak of." But the most remarkable phenomena of the medieval universities which flourished under the unity of the Catholic Faith was the divergent schools of philosophy, Augustinianism, Scotism, Thomism, and later on, Suarezianism, and the variations within each school. We are not making an appeal for a return to medieval intellectual life. In the ensuing centuries giant strides in the various branches of learning — if not always in wisdom — have been made. Knowledge and mastery of the forces of nature and their utilization have given us amazing inventions and discoveries undreamed of in the Middle Ages.

INTELLECTUAL REALISM

Perhaps the principal difference between their intellectual life and that of modern times is that their desire for knowledge was motivated by the rational conviction that human reason could know the intelligible universe and read therein the natural revelation of the divine intentions imprinted in all creation. Our quest for wisdom may not be as relentless as theirs. In contrast to the modern world, the medievalists were fully convinced that there was an order of absolute religious truths, of absolute ethical goodness, of absolute political and social justice, to which differences had to submit and by which they had to be judged. And in this quest for wisdom they did not disdain to turn to Greek and Roman pagan philosophers for assistance and enlightenment. Might not the pagan mind of today emulate this desire to know by seeking whatever assistance and enlightenment he might obtain from Christianity? We have resorted to history to bear witness against the charge that the Catholic intellectual is restrained in academic freedom to the measure of his Catholicism and the concomitant innuendo that academic freedom in the community at large bears inverse proportion to the prevalence of Catholicism. The unity of Faith which was universal in Western Christendom in the Middle Ages gave impulse and new life to intellectual inquiry. Far from imposing a quietus on intellectual activity and a blind conformism in thought, Catholicism was vibrantly combative in controversies and confidently independent in self-expression. An exuberant diversity of philosophical inquiry prospered within the unifying framework of the Faith.

In all fairness we must admit that the allegations made are not personal, they are not directed against individuals who are Catholics. In all nakedness we must recognize them to be what they are – an assault upon intellectual realism. They have their roots in religious agnosticism and philosophical scepticism and relativism even though paradoxically they are often made by intellectuals who are church-affiliated or who profess a religious belief, and who live their daily lives with many presumptions of dogmatic certitude. There are those, too, who *would* admit to intellectual realism save for some unresolved doubts and lingering fears about the consequences that philosophical dogmatism might entail.

These fears rationally formulated are basically three: first, a mind that admits to religious dogmas and philosophical doctrines is no longer an "open" mind; secondly, dogmatic convictions preclude or impede progressive inquiry. And thirdly, a dogmatist is prone to be intolerant with those who disagree with him.

Let us acknowledge at the outset what is undeniably true and is partly the basis for the popular currency of these suspicions. Who has not met those who claim they know the truth and are antagonistic towards those who supposedly do not; minds who are too positive to be cautiously critical, too combative to be understanding and fair, too confident to be persuasive, and much too incompetent, really, to recognize a partial truth, a penetrating objection, or an enlightening criticism? They unfortunately bring disfavour upon their beliefs rather than upon themselves as they deserve. They cast their own shadows between their auditors and the truth that might otherwise have appeared. But we must also readily allow that these mental distempers are subjective: they not infrequently stem from personal incompetence and from inexperience in the rational exchanges of the dialogue. There is, too, the limitation common to so many of us – the inability to appreciate another mind's genuine difficulties. But we can dispense with these distempers and incompetencies in our consideration because we are concerned with the virtues that ought to obtain amongst the enlightened, not with the failures to which all flesh is heir.

THE "OPEN MIND"

When we speak of an open mind, we generally mean a mind willing to be informed, to be corrected, eager to learn more, willing to submit acquired judgments to critical re-examination. Greek philosophy began with a sense of wonder about reality and the intellectual curiosity to know all that could be known. It did not rest satisfied with sense knowledge nor with a manner of living based on such knowledge. For the Greeks the actual was real and the real was intelligible and human intelligence is self-transcendant. Greek speculation – *spokeo* – was the affirmation of intellectual insight into the transempirical, the eternal verities, first causes and ultimate principles, and the absolutes, natures, essences, substances and forms. The excellence of intelligence – its *arete* – consisted in the mind finding its complement in valid knowledge. For the Greek the mind was open to knowledge of reality, and found its fulfillment and perfection therein. An open mind is one that is open to whatever is humanly cognoscible that it might adhere to it when once acquired. An open mind admits to ignorance, to insufficiency and perhaps even dissatisfaction about knowledge already possessed; but its pursuit of learning starts with the rational conviction in the capacity of human intelligence to know. When reason affirms categorically that this is true, it does not claim it knows the whole truth nor all about that particular partial truth but simply that the direct and specific contradictory is not true. An open mind that claims not only that it is ignorant but further than cannot know anyhow is not open at all to anything. Intellectual impotence can scarcely be the virtue of the academic and hardly the basis for any right to freedom. When human reason is confronted unmistakably with objective evidence, it cannot but register the dictates of reality. Such a judgment is dogmatic if the truth it affirms is unconditional. It does not mean that it is unquestionable and above controversy. Rather through reflection, the prior judgment is reviewed, validated, corrected, or abandoned. A mind incapable of knowing with certitude is not open; it is empty — save for the one exempt dogma of agnosticism and skepticism about the nature of the mind itself.

The justification of the Academic life is to search out truths *in order to discover* truths. It is not the *quest* for truth that is important but the discovery and thereafter the transmission of truth. Just as the educational experience of recorded civilization has yielded certain conclusions, it has yielded certain conclusions in the realm of values. We are as certain that Communism errs as we are that the whole is equal to the sum of its parts. And we wonder at the anti-intellectualism of those who, in the name of the intellect, show so little respect for the human mind that they cannot credit it with the power to come to any reliable conclusion.

Last June thirty university professors gathered at an American University to discuss problems of human freedom and political economy. After ten days, it became apparent not only how vastly almost all of us differed from one another but also how startlingly uncertain most minds were about the fundamental questions of the meaning and significance of human existence. On the last day, in the process of summing up, what impressed me most was how many seemed to exult in the expressions of disagreement and uncertainty so freely and abundantly manifest throughout the whole conference. Never had I witnessed so much pride taken in the failure of individuals to have attained so few personal convictions which one might rationally and persuasively communicate to other intelligences.

The second allegation, a dogmatic mind is a closed mind. It does not allow for progress in learning. Certitude is somehow opposed to it. Now progress in learning I take to be an increase of knowledge quantitatively and qualitatively. There is not only always so much more but also the constant abiding need to deepen and broaden our knowledge, to re-examine and explore anew many more realities in the universe because only in this wise do our insights deepen and multiple interrelations of the order of different natures become increasingly apparent. When therefore human reason affirms that it knows, it does not pretend to know all reality or all about one reality or any more than partial reality. Nature does not leap. Neither does knowledge. The progress is not from the known into the unknown but — apart from accidental discoveries — always from the less known toward the more. As long as dogmatism is correspondent with realism, it will not be stationary, fixed, self-satisfied. There is a congenital impulse of thought that will not rest satisfied with any but the whole truth. There is an ever-recurring disquiet characteristic of intellectual finalism, an essential discontent which prevents man not only from clinging to any stable form but from being satisfied — to progress always in the direction of more truth and more of truth. Knowledge already possessed is the point of departure for the further enterprises of the intellect and an enlightened exploration of the less known. Our sciences are but an accumulation of acquired knowledge and apart from theories, hypotheses, and experiments, each science has its own deposit of firmly established facts and laws. There can be no advance in any branch of learning without continuity of knowledge. Doctrinal certainty is inherently progressive because it is correspondent with reality, whose many splendored truths are inexhaustible. To affirm and to deny is to say that we know. How can knowledge, the complement of intelligence, be its own frustration. There is a subtle sort of intellectual escapism in the skeptics' "open" mind. They fail to see that disagreement is impossible if agreement is improbable. Both in disagreement and agreement the appeal is to the evidence of reason; both in certitude and probability the evaluating judgment addresses itself to the presence or absence of conclusive evidence.

DOGMAS AND INTOLERANCE

The third allegation, the dogmatic mind is intolerant. I suppose the best way to discuss intellectual tolerance and intolerance is to turn to the world of science. I cannot imagine any university employing a professor of science who refused to admit to certain undeniable truths about the very science he professes to teach. I cannot conceive of a medical board passing a student who did not recognize some uncontroverted facts and laws about the health of the human body. We all recall the ever current story of the medical professor who questioned his student in class. After giving an answer, the student thought better of it and gave another answer which the professor recognized to be the correct one. But the professor also observed – alas – in the short interim the imaginary patient had died. And yet no one would think of calling the universities, the state medical boards, and the professor intolerant. The fact is that valid knowledge is intolerant of error, of falsehood, and of quackery. No one will use a means of conveyance, train, plane, bridge, automobile, boat, except on the rational supposition that it was reliably built by competent engineers, nor will anyone have his prescriptions fulfilled by a quack pharmacist. We are all intolerant of error, of incompetence, and of quackery. Our charity for our fellowmen does not blind us to falsehood.

We do not tolerate what is false nor are we free to tolerate what is true. Tolerance is not an intellectual virtue. We are not expected to accept falsehood but to denounce it; we are expected to accept truth. No one respects the man who deliberately intends falsehood for himself, and by communicating it intends the deception of others. Tolerance is a moral virtue whereby we tolerate men whom we know to be in error because they too are sincerely striving for the truth. No one respects the man who deliberately intends falsehood for himself, and by communicating it intends the deception of others. Properly speaking, only he who knows the truth is capable of tolerance for the person who is in error. More specifically, tolerance is an exercise of the virtue of charity which is directed to our fellowmen, not to ideas.

No scientist is wantonly free to disregard the terms of his science. Scientists distinguish quite rightly opinions, conjectures, theories and hypotheses from axioms, the dogmas of the world of science. Why should the scientist's intolerance of error and falsehood and his insistence on the knowledge of scientific dogmas — the laws of nature — for which we revere him — become so unwelcome and obnoxious in the philosopher? The dogmatic scientist does not claim he knows it all, nor all about what he is certain of; neither does the dogmatic philosopher. Investigation and research imply an earnest intention to get at the truth. All the natural sciences are committed. They are bound by the methods, manner of demonstrations, and objectives settled upon by the consensual agreement of the community of scientists in each field of learning. An invasion of an alien field is allowable only by complying with the terms set by that community of scientists. This is true of all the branches of learning. The theologian who is not an astronomer is not equipped to speak for astronomy. The eminent law expert may not speak for the philosopher nor the latter for the chemist. And in all sciences the objective in general is the "find," "the discovery" of a fact of reality, its laws of operation and reaction. When consequent to the findings of scientists the community at large wishes to utilize the benefits of human mastery of natural energies, both the scientists and the community must come to terms with the dictates of nature. It may be more appropriate to say we must first accommodate ourselves with nature, cooperate with it before it responds to our needs and desires. The natural sciences are not embarrassed by its categorical "it is" "it is not."

They measure the advance of scientific learning by the accumulation of dogmatic axioms about the laws of nature. They are no totalitarian agnostics or skeptics amongst scientists or — if there are some who profess to be — no one wants to risk his life or goods or even education to their employment. Indeed it ought to be axiomatic that scientific dogma is the condition of life. I cannot think usefully — say — for my biological — or mechanical purposes — if I do not think what is true. And the remarkable thing is that those who suppose that certitude for knowledge does not allow for freedom of intellectual inquiry to the philosopher are ready to admit that the certitude of the natural sciences enhance the possibilities of human freedom. When thoroughly understood, mechanism, for example, instead of shutting in on every hand, constitutes the means at our disposal for acting upon things and obtaining power over them. Certitude about the fundamentals of human existence, its meaning, significance, and destiny provides the principles of a just peace and a righteous order founded upon the dignity of man that makes human coexistence not only possible but also enjoyably necessary. There can be no tolerance of error in any field of sciences and learning in the face of acquired valid knowledge deserving of servitude. But let us not overlook some serious and real dangerous occasions for intolerance towards persons.

INTOLERANCE TOWARDS PERSONS

The danger is that those who claim they have the truth and rightly are opposed to error may transfer a legitimate intolerance toward error to the person. The transition from thought to the thinker is not always deliberate or malicious. It may insert itself quite subtly so that the opposition we have for a false judgment may convert itself into a resentment towards the advocate of such judgments. Now intolerance towards persons though psychologically understandable is morally inexcusable. The prevailing and prior presupposition should always be unless otherwise disillusioned — that each thinker sincerely means what he says and that he too is striving for the truth. Indeed this reverence for those who disagree with us derives from the human dignity with which all humans are divinely invested. We reverence the person in error because even in the course of his error he seeks truth he deserves to know, as we too have often been as we sought for truth. The history of religious persecutions could have been spared many of its wasteful tragedies had it been borne clearly in mind that, theologically, an act of faith is invalid unless free; that by sound moral philosophy the individual conscience, firmly convinced of the righteousness of its own persuasion, is bound by the dictates of that conscience, and that sociologically, political allegiance is not contingent upon religious conformity. One of the enduring embarrassments of human rationality is that the fallacy of spiritual enlightenment through compulsion was not apparent for centuries. Indeed even Plato, the high idealist, failed to grasp it. I suppose it is because it is not enough to be men of good principle in order to be good men, and that good will — charity — as the angelic choir sang at the Birth of Christ, is the required disposition for peace amongst men. The first imperative is charity — prompted by — fraternity. "By this shall men know you are my disciples that you love one another." Charity is one of the strongest credentials for the bearer of truth, and the *reddere benevolos* of the rhetorician is a first imperative in the art of persuasion.

So we see that the opposition whether of the agnostic or anti-Catholic to intellectual dogma while not reasonable has a rationale that must be carefully examined and reverently answered because indeed there are certain dangers attendant upon a dogmatic mind. In the three suppositions underlying the opposition to dogma, theological and philosophical — scientific dogma seems to be silently excepted — was that a dogmatic mind is not open, that certitude is opposed to freedom of inquiry, and that dogmatic convictions engender intolerant attitudes. And we have answered that a mind is open to knowledge and the mind is kept open by knowledge by an inner dynamism of the mind which pursues the inexhaustible riches of reality. Certitude far from being opposed to free inquiry is a necessary condition for free inquiry; unless it be certain that we can know there is no sense in wanting to know what we cannot designate as true and false; and thirdly, certain knowledge is by its very nature opposed to error and falsehood. It is truth which is intolerant of error.

But going more deeply beneath this triple supposition is the fear that to allow a claim for truth is to expect conformity of minds to truth and with this expectation a right to impose that conformity forcibly. Though the logic is patently specious history discloses tragic instances of the influence of that line of thinking. Here again we must disengage ourselves of personal motives and motivations, of subjective mental distempers and incompetences of individuals, and ask ourselves whether the claim to truth implies any such right to impose and coerce. It is my contention that such a right is not only non-existent but impossible. Knowledge like an act of the will is the most inward human act. When therefore I claim that I have true knowledge, the burden is on me to persuade you to the same judgment. This supposes that all men are invested connaturally with reason and that reason will affirm a categorical judgment only — when by its own light it is confronted with the objective evidence that warrants a judgment which precludes all reasonable doubt and opposes its contradictory as true to false. The best I may achieve when I undertake to persuade you is to help bring that evidence to the light of your own reason so that it may then freely and in the light of its own powers acknowledge the truth which is manifest to me in the light of my own intellect. Objective evidence is not always immediate. Indeed primary truths are not always the most easily accessible to human reason; but however long and intricate the process of thought, a valid judgment is legitimately posited only with the final disclosure of objective evidence. We agree because each in the light of his own intellect has seen the same truth. The agreement is one by concurrence. There is no question at all here about forced imposition, coercion, or any manner of compulsion or intimidation. When such coercion is exercised there is exacted lip service, servile compliance, or at best brainwashing.

It is in the very nature of a valid intellectual assent that it be necessitated only by the evidence of reality. The only reasonable way that a philosophical doctrine may be presented for acceptance is to disclose to the auditors the full clarity and intelligibility of its evidence. The ability to see evidence by the light of reason is the common patrimony of mankind and this makes possible the art of persuasion, the likelihood of communication, of agreement and disagreement, of discourse, the dialogue, the debate, in fact every manner of discourse. The appeal is to reason. There is no imposition because there cannot be. Intellectual assent is wholly interior and into this sanctuary no force can enter.

WHAT IS INTELLECTUAL FREEDOM?

We have at the last come to answer the question which from the beginning has been tumbling at our feet — what is intellectual freedom? It is the ability of reason to see freely for itself — how much soever assisted by others — the conclusive evidence necessitating a categorical judgment. It is the freedom which human reason must have in order that it may see objective evidence for itself. It is freedom from any compulsion which either tries to impose a dogma or attempts to interfere with the full avenue to truth. To see in dogma, theological, philosophical, and scientific a stoppage to intellectual inquiry, an inhibition and restraint upon academic freedom is to misconstrue the original question, namely, may human reason know reality. If human intelligence is meant to know truths about God, the universe, our fellowmen, and about societies — then the knowledge of these truths is possible because the human mind is *open to them,* the increase of knowledge is ensured, not damaged, by certitude, and truth far from being divisive is meant to be the spiritual source of agreement amongst men.

There can be no significant doubt except upon the presumption of actual knowledge or in its expectation. The charge that the

Catholic intellectual by reason of his religious dogmas and philosophical doctrines is inhibited or impeded in his academic freedom covers a multitude of presuppositions which deserve to be patiently analyzed and studied and weighed. We hope to have cast some light on these misgivings. The core of the allegations, fears, etc. is an assault on reason itself, on the cognoscibility of God and of His revelation, of the intelligibility of the Universe, and the ability of men to reach these truths, to discourse and communicate to one another their theological and philosophical findings just as scientists do not hesitate to do in science. The charge that the Catholic intellectual by the very reason of his Catholicism does not enjoy academic freedom conceals several extremely dubious presuppositions and highly questionable premises. The real question is the critical problem; what is the nature and finality of intellectual activity? Can human reason attain to the world of nature and the laws of operation? Can human intelligence ascertain the meaning and purpose of human existence? Those who take their stand with the skeptics and agnostics make a pretense to live practically in a dreamworld of actualities. Truth to say, their dreamworld is the dreamworld of their minds to which the universe of facts, natures, laws, and principles presents a hard irresistable confrontation. If they ever dared not to conform their actions to the immutable dictates of realities, the forces of nature would punish them immediately. Realism brooks no denial — truth and consequences.

On the higher order of moral life — the disastrous consequences of a false philosophy of man may not be instantaneous because the spiritual nature of man is never beyond spiritual remedy, restoration, and regeneration. In this ever abiding capacity for human regeneration is rooted the virtue of hope, which activated by faith in God, the author of our being, engenders the bond of friendship amongst men through charity. Truth is perfective of reason and certitude is but the consciousness of its possession.

THE ACADEMY AND THE CITY*

Today we are witnessing a world-wide rivalry for the allegiance of the mind. Though free societies and servile states are relentlessly racing for material advantage and technological superiority underground, on earth, and in outer space neither side entertains the illusion that conquest or victory is enduring without the allegiance of the mind and souls of men. And for obvious reasons, — communities and societies look to the intellectual for guidance and leadership and place their destinies into their hands. Lenin, master-mind of revolutions, implemented Marxist theory with the practical technique of control by the few of the many through exclusive possession of the instruments of power. So too — especially where the absence of geographic contiguity renders forceful invasion and take-over less likely — the foreign conquest of a people through its own intellectuals has proven to be one of the most effective ways of undermining and subverting political and social institutions.

It is therefore not an unwarranted suspicion that makes communities at times anxious about the intellectual activities of their institutions of learning. The radical source of this concernment is the fact that an intellectual like every other citizen is bound to patriotic duty and beyond that, a dedication, a loyalty, if you will, to arts and science that transcend political definition. An academic, as scientist, philosopher, historian, literateur, aesthete may rightly claim and merit unrestricted activity for the advancement of learning not only for its own sake but also that society may profit thereby spiritually and materially. A problem arises when he requires as a condition for academic freedom an immunity from political restraint in *any* oral

---

*CORK UNIVERSITY PRESS 1961. Lecture given at University College (Ireland) at invitation of U.S. Department of State.

or written expression of his convictions in the lecture-room or off campus. When under the protective cloak of academic freedom fealty to one's own country is effectively minimized in favour of an alien political allegiance which in its high sounding pretensions to universal allegiance from everyone on earth is said to be superior to national patriotism then it becomes imperative to weigh the respective loyalties for the Academy and for the City as well and discover if scholastic and political universalism might not concur for the benefit of all mankind.

I take an Academy to be a community of minds who are associated together by the common objectives of the intellectual search and united by consensual agreement on the methodology, demonstrations and experiments suitable to each science. Scholars, scientists and philosophers hold that whenever one of their members ventures beyond the boundaries of professional competence into other provinces of learning he must respectfully abide by their rules. A theologian may lecture on astronomy expertly only as an astronomer and an astronomer may write about theology knowledgeably only as a theologian. A claim then to academic freedom is always bounded by the canons of each science.

Since it is of *human* freedom we speak, not of the instinctual or physical movement of anyone, it will not simply do to give primacy either to freedom *from* restraints or to freedom *for* positively defined goals. Academic freedom derives from the rationality of man who is thereby uniquely set above and apart from the rest of the universe. Its meaning is correspondent to the nature and purpose of the intellectual activity of man to whom God has entrusted dominion and stewardship of this earth. Either we hold with the Greeks and the Schoolmen that the actual is real and the real intelligible and that man can know with his senses and his intelligence, phenomenon and being or we shall be forced to suppose out of the desperation born of agnosticism and skepticism that we must conduct ourselves as if they were so though really they are not. This philosophical make-belief helps us find our way conjecturally and pragmatically like the blind man who gropes his way by tentative touch and reaction.

I take academic freedom to mean at least this, unimpeded access to evidence. Every science reaches out to an alteriety in order that it may know it and thereby come to terms with it to man's own benefit and enjoyment either by contemplation, utility or mastery.

Academic freedom is therefore both purposive and responsible. It has its own in-built rules. Only certain types of methodology, demonstrations, and experiments are suitable to each intellectual pursuit of being. Every inquiry is conditioned by a predefined direction. The moral right to academic freedom then arises from the inviolability of proper action necessary to scientific employment as well as from its original source, the connatural inner dynamism of human intelligence. Implied in this moral right to immunity of action is the freedom to err. Not indeed that an individual may deliberately intend to err but that the moral right to seek out truth does not always proceed successfully and infallibly.

One might add that the right to err is an incidence of the various forms of experimentation, of trial and error so that by a process of exclusion multiple hypothesis and alternatives are narrowed and reduced to the more probable. Right to err is wholly medial; it is a necessary incidence of that freedom understood as accessibility to evidence. Strictly speaking, neither truth nor error have rights. Persons do. Things, on the other hand, may be said to be truthful — they are incapable of error, nor can they deceive. Their realism and fixity of purpose and operation provide the conditions for safe living and the means of prospering. When thoroughly understood, mechanism, for example, instead of shutting us in on every hand, constitutes the means at our disposal for acting upon things and obtaining power over them. Realism and intelligence are the prerequisites of free living in the midst of cosmological necessitarianism. But there is a higher world of which we humans are a part and on earth the most significant part, the life of the human spirit. What is man himself and all the social, cultural, and political associations which he projects as embodies enlargements of his spiritual capabilities. These, too, and above all else are profound inquiries for men of learning.

The gravity of these inquiries no one will call into question today when the free world is interlocked in a death and life struggle with international forces for world domination. Daily events make increasingly clear the role of the intellectual in the fortunes and outcome of this gigantic combat. Both sides admit that it is primarily a spiritual contest for the minds and souls of men and that with all the material and technological massing of forces their main efforts are directed to human persuasion. Both protagonists recognize the close and dynamic correspondence between the Academy and the City, and deeply appreciate the efficacious instrumentality of the intellectual in every community.

The question how the prerogative of academic freedom can help preserve free society without prejudice to itself takes on immense importance. In totalitarian states there is no freedom of expression and no academic loyalty independent of party fealty. This is not to deny that scientists under total mobilization of resources and supervision may achieve extraordinary feats in technological advance — but at the cost of many personal moral and legal liberties and to the extinction of the spiritual legacies of a free Academy. A free society is recognized by the legal and practical opportunities for a broad popular share in the direction and ultimate determination of government. And where there is not yet a condition of complete equality there is at least an equality of conditions. Such a society is democracy, and it owes its existence to human aspirations asserting themselves affirmatively against the pretensions of the omnicompetent ruler. And these aspirations take on formidable expression, as Athenian and modern European history bears testimony, in the protests of the intellectual who refines the agonizing struggles of a populace into resounding echoes of eternal verities. The birth, life and freedom of democratic society draws from the life and freedom of the Academy.

I am not suggesting that the Academy must be democratic if society is to be democratic. On the contrary, facts, judgments, laws, principles, theories and formulae are true or false, not democratic. The Academy at its best is an aristocracy, a word which despite its lingering political resonance still retains the original meaning of excellence. The point I wish to stress is: if indeed a free society draws its first breath of life from a free Academy, once in existence and prospering, the Academy may not cease to keep ablaze the truths that set a nation free. Now the ascertaining duty and proper function of these truths falls squarely upon the shoulders of philosophers and political philosophers.

It is the prerogative and grave responsibility of the philosopher to ascertain by the light of reason the meaning and purpose of human existence, and the substantive truths within which we must govern our conduct and relations with one another. Man is determined as to his end but indeterminate as to the means for realizing his end. Herein lies the opportunity and need of the statesmen to acknowledge these doctrinal premises and establish within these terms the allowable prudential choices in the governance of the political order.

The moral law is the law of human nature, not the law of men. It is no more the invention of men than fire, and justice amongst men is but the conformity of human choice to the principles of moral justice. Human laws do not constitute justice; they have no other purpose save to embody it. And human laws may command man's obedience only to the extent that they express a right inherent in nature, that is the end which has been appointed to man, and over which man has no control. This is what the ancients and medievalists meant by the necessary, universal, immutable verities which invested man with a unique meaning in the universe. This too is the message of Christianity, the absolute and imperishable value of the individual; that every individual by virtue of his eternal destiny and divine vocation is at the core somewhat holy and indestructible even in relation to the highest power on earth; that the least amongst men has an undiminished value of his own, and not merely because he is a part of a whole; that every man is to be regarded by every community, never as a mere instrument, but all equally as an end. And history records the relentless human struggles to surround this sacredness with legal guarantees variously denominated as franchises, liberties, privileges, immunities till finally the *homo legalis* became consonant with the *homo liber*.

Should the philosophers default in their proper task of keeping clearly defined the divine laws of human nature for the regulation of human life singly and in community — then there is great peril that the State may assume such a *magisterium* to itself. Not that the State and the political governors should be unconcerned about the moral and supreme vocation of man and society; on the contrary, it is their duty never to ignore them. But it is not their proper competence nor within their jurisdiction to determine what these ends are. The omnicompetence of the totalitarian state is not to be primarily identified with its capacity to concentrate all power within its grasp and to regulate unfettered all human conduct; but rather with its arrogant claim that it has supreme authority and exclusive competence to say what is man and what is his place in society. This is unquestionably true of Marx, Lenin, Stalin and their heirs. This was no less true of the mad hatter of Berchtesgaden. In the face of such a claim by the absolute state, philosophical agnosticism and skepticism can offer no resistance. The apathy of the German intellectuals to withstand as a group the absolutist pretensions of Nazism must be attributed to their failure to formulate for the benefit of the German people a sound political philosophy. The frank fact must at last be admitted that philosophical doctrine is the rational barrier against the political dogmatism of the totalitarian state. The proper functions of political authority in furthering the common good are wholly limited to the realm of experience. They are mostly prudential choices of the suitable and wise means for the actualization in concrete historical circumstances of the substantive goals of justice, peace, order, unity, security, prosperity and freedom.

If so much of human destiny depends on the philosophers' role as teachers, a political *magisterium* on the contrary is fraught with dire consequences for man and society. In competence, method and objective the two agencies vastly differ.

The philosopher who claims he has the right philosophy of life has the burden to convince others of the same truth by appealing to the reason of his auditors and help make manifest to their intelligences the evidence that confronted his own reason. The appeal to reason is the only avenue of persuasion and evidence is the whole force of truth. The only authentic witness to intellectual conviction is personal conscience. The philosopher's approach presupposes that all men are connaturally endowed with reason as he is and though his facility and experience as a thinker is superior to theirs, he nonetheless holds fast to the truth that each intelligence must see the evidence in the light of its own reason before it will acknowledge the same truth. Indeed intellectual freedom as to the same truth is simply concurrence of different minds as to the same evidence seen in the light of each one's reason and assented to free of any compulsion save the compelling force of evidence. Needless to say, any other compulsion may exact at most a lip service judgment but it cannot bring a personal intellectual assent. Failing persuasion, there is no free disagreement or no general agreement.

When the State arrogates to itself the *magisterium,* it first appeals to reason but in a manner restrictive of its freedom, by impassioned propaganda. When it fails to achieve conformity and unanimity of mind amongst its subjects, it resorts to force. The dogmatizing totalitarian state will not tolerate dissent nor a free rational inquiry by its subjects into its philosophical pretensions, much less any public and open criticism. Its appeal to reason is only a temporary expediency. Its ultimate weapon of persuasion is force and at best a conformity of outward compliance. The dogmatizing state wants certain propositions held as true not because they are true, but because they subserve the ends of the Party. The existence of the Party depends on universal political conformism. That is why there is no academic freedom in a totalitarian state. For its own sake it must eliminate and root out any contrary political ideologies.

Communism is emphatically not a skepticism. Marxists will have nothing to do with a theory of knowledge which denies all certainty and they relentlessly war against the followers of Hume. In his *Materialism and Empirio-Criticism*, Lenin made repeated and continual attacks upon Humean agnosticism and its progenies. To say then as is sometimes averred that philosophical dogmatism engenders political intolerance is to ignore the history of politics as well as to misconstrue the meaning of philosophy. To those who would deny the possibility of certitude, it can only be said that, while they may be entitled to their point of view, they are definitely not entitled to the privilege of feeling moral indignation at evil and abuse of power which they cannot be sure ever took place, or which, if it did take place, cannot be called either right or wrong since they cannot be sure there is a distinction between right and wrong or that anything specifically is ever right or wrong. Totalitarianism breeds on intellectual insecurity and fattens on the philosophical agnosticism and skepticism of the academy. If the philosophers cannot be validly sure of the meaning of human intelligence, then how can anyone be sure of the error of Marxism and what would be the sense of fighting it even at the cost of life and possessions. Philosophical dogma is not only the prize achievement of the free academy; it is also the condition for a free society.

Hence the dire consequences that follow from the definition of the libertarian end as primarily procedural to the complete disregard of a fixed commitment to substantive truths. They think as John Dewey wrote, to

"find security in methods of inquiry, of observation, experiment, of forming and following working hypothesis. Such persons are not unsettled by the upsetting of any special belief, because they retain security of procedure. They can, borrowing language from another context, though this method slay my most cherished belief, yet I will trust it. The growth of this sense, even if only half-consciously, is the cause of the increased indifference of large numbers of persons to organized religion. It is not that they are especially excited about this or that doctrine, but that the guardianship of truth seems to them to have passed over to the *method* of attaining and testing beliefs. In this latter fundamental they rest in intellectual and emotional peace."

Instead of substantive truths they settle for "felt needs", "shared effort", "creative values", "made truths". The value of action is to be judged by the stream of consequences and so a new morality is born, the morality of efficiency.

Ideas, indeed, do have consequences. But here the philosophic skeptic falters. *What* ideas and *What* consequences? Freedom of expression and teaching is a valuable liberty, something to be cherished and defended. But certainly not because of the relativist and libertarian claim that, since we can never be sure of the truth, no one has any right to impose one point of view on another. That sort of argument can quickly be turned around to justify the extinction of the formal liberties. The repudiation of all certitude invites the conclusion that, if truth and value do not make right, then might makes it very well. It is precisely for this reason that I have never found the **expression of Justice Oliver Wendell Holmes, the open market of ideas, felicitous**. It is rudely suggestive of the hawking of the market place and the triumph of the fast sale in free competition. The enduring question is, does it not matter what ideas emerge triumphant? If not, why should it matter *how* they come to prevail?

If truth is constituted by majoritarian acceptance, if there are no eternal verities and absolute values superior to the fortunes of popularity, then what is the sense of national mobilization against the threat of Communism except the intellectual conviction that it is a false philosophy of life and a dehumanization of man? Further, let it be noted there is a deceptive fallacy hidden in the slogan "open market of ideas and free competition." It supposes that the contest between truth and error remains purely on the intellectual level and always amongst equals. The most easily advertised and appealing ideas are those which promise a minimum of responsibility and propaganda is a dangerous instrument which the unscrupulous and ambitious wield with dreadful success. Primary truths are not always easily accessible to human understanding nor easily understood and the process of correct logical reasoning can be an onerous discipline.

Substantive truths are not always popular because they may lay claim to controlled human conduct.

The sad lesson of history is that truth does not always conquer error in a free competition. In an optimistic liberal era, farseeing Coventry Patmore could write with realistic cynicism: "Today there is no certainty at all that truth can overcome falsehood in an unrefereed fight, with the latter using brass knuckles, hitting below the belt, and inciting its own interested supporters to riot, the while speakers about the ring become so confused they cannot tell one contestant from the other." It is primarily the responsibility of the philosopher of the Academy in circumstances of equal debate and serene critical discourse to ascertain the substantive truths about the meaning of human existence. They may then patiently and persuasively enlighten society at large to arrive to the same judgments by an appeal to their reason. Such a people will then be better able to withstand the initial blandishments, the messianic promises, and spurious doctrines of the totalitarian advocate.

Freedom of expression and teaching may require regulation under certain circumstances, but not because coercion is a higher value in itself than liberty. The free act towards a good end is always better than a compulsory act towards a good end, even though both may achieve the same result. And self-regulation and discipline is more virtuous than that required by duly constituted authority. Liberty itself is inherently a restricted thing. Liberty is a product of order. It has responsibilities as well as rights for its own preservation and vigorous exercise. Liberty itself needs protection.

Regulation from within will ensure the Academy from regulation from without and all the dangers attendant thereupon. Most professions and associations of learning set up standards of scholarship and scientific research and a code of professional ethics. Medicine and law, for example, will not tolerate quacks amongst them. Why should teachers? Without freedom of expression — the legal protection of academic freedom — the other political liberties will not long endure. But if the Academy allows for the possibility of its own extinction then it will scarcely help preserve the very political freedoms wherein its own academic freedom may exist and flourish.

Is it not a question, rather of Truth and Consequences? For example, no one can deny that the most profound influence upon political and legal institutions has been the affirmation or denial of the doctrine that man is created in the image of God and destined for eternal happiness. The American Constitution does not explicitly say man is a child of God. But in those lands whose governments explicitly or in effect deny man is a child of God we shall look in vain for the proper securities for man's immunity from governmental arbitary action. We need only compare the trial of Cardinal Mindzenty and the trial of the Communist leaders under Judge Medina to appreciate the vast differences which derive from ultimate theological convictions. The theology of man does not say that there must be a writ of habeas corpus; it does say that the law must never disregard the dignity of the human person. The writ of habeas corpus asserts the right of an individual; but a right presupposes a value outside the reach of a power to cancel. Due process means that persons, rights, and possessions must be treated with reverence even when they are chargeable with crime.

National Patriotism and Scholastic Universalism

And now the crucial question which was acutely focussed in the last two decades by the cry of protest by members of the academy against the restrictions imposed upon them by loyalty tests and security laws, by political governments and by the institutions of learning themselves. Save those who see freedom as opposed to authority, scarcely anyone would reasonably deny the necessity for such measures for the sake of national security not only in time of war but also in that novel, agonizing oddity of peacetime, known as "cold war". Generally disagreements are generated by the questions of the timely opportuneness of such measures, the manner of their application, the extent of consequences, and their wisdom. Briefly, granting for the sake of argument, that there is real danger for subversive activity against our national security, do the measures established achieve the desired good or do they unlease disadvantages disproportionate to the good contemplated. This is a pressing subject for serious study, very complex and not easily resolved. Granting further for the sake of argument that wise measures of loyalty and security are possible of formulation, may be formulated and prudently applicable, let us go forward and examine *the radical* question: whether there is an contrariety between the scholar's civic patriotism and his scholastic universalism. Do these two allegiances conflict with one another? In the supposition of a conflict one would easily surmise that the universal scholastic allegiance is the higher duty, and that it should take precedence over the expectations of local patriotic allegiance, and that therefore the supposed need for loyalty test and security laws is subordinate to the higher vocation of the intellectual.

It seems to me that the problem viewed in this manner is artificially contrived and at best an artificial answer could ensue. The artificiality arises from the supposed opposition between freedom and authority. The antimony is not between liberty and law but between liberty and bad laws, or between abuse of liberty and good laws. There is an orderly relation between national patriotism and scholastic universalism. We may describe patriotism as that human devotion which a citizen bears for his country for the manifold and constant benefits which accrue to him under his country's protection and general providence and for which he in justice as well as in gratitude owes support to the social order of which he is a beneficiary. To say then that an intellectual should be loyal to his country is to say simply that he is not an exempt citizen. Nor do the loyalties to a free society — the responsible participation of an active citizenry — need in any way intervene in or diminish scholastic universalism. We have already said as much when we have denied to political authority a *magisterium* in the sciences.

Our problem is far from speculative. And as a practical urgency it demands recognition for what it actually is. May an intellectual of a free society admit to Communism — the only existing state which calls for universal political allegiance to itself — let us say to the degree that allegiance to his own country is subordinated to the higher fealty to the Kremlin — in the name of academic freedom itself? I hold without reservation that such a superior political allegiance to Marxist universalism is itself destructive of academic freedom as well as of the free society. This is the stubborn fact wherever the Red imperium has extended.

The members of the Academy have duties toward the society of which it is itself a beneficiary. I am motivated by a deep conviction that academic freedom should not be entrusted to those who would work for its destruction by subverting the free society within which a free academy may exist and flourish and which they deny wherever they are in dominant control. No one may reasonably claim the right to work for the denial of these rights to others. We are not obliged to tolerate, in the Academy or out of it, those who would not tolerate us if they had the power; nor are we obliged to tolerate those who would subvert the civil social order under the cloak of freedom of study and teaching. Academic freedom, like the Bill of Rights, is not a suicide pact. To define liberty solely as the absence of restraint is to define all restraint as a curtailment of liberty. From such negative premises human intelligence can only reason in a void. But liberties are enjoyed, not in a void but through and by human interrelations and interdependence. Their rights are not more inviolable than ours, and respect for one another's rights is the achievement of an *ordered* freedom.

The profession of Communism bears within itself the duty to destroy free societies in which a free academy may exist and flourish. Such a profession cannot be justified in the name of academic freedom itself. They would arrogate to themselves the kind of liberty over others that they deny others over themselves. The Red State has upturned and reversed the roles of political local allegiance and scholastic universalism. It demands a new universalist political allegiance and a local scholastic dedication – to the Kremlin. Red Party allegiance absorbs scholastic allegiance. A free society asks for a patriotic allegiance, which is local and national and leaves unrestrained scholastic universalism. The Red Absolute State demands universalist political allegiance and a local scholastic dedication. A free academy no more than a free City need tolerate a nest of subversives whose total intellectual envelopment is a political way of life, supreme and universal. The best things in human existence are above politics. The German scientists who were captured by an elite corp of the Russian Army were forcibly detained within the boundaries of Red Russia.

Academic freedom is *unimpeded access to evidence* and the freedom to be publicly articulate about the findings of research and investigation, and the reasonings therein involved. There is no question here of the necessity to be well informed about the philosophy, ideology and world-wide program and tactics of Communism. But teaching about Communism is at opposite poles to teaching *for* Communism. A Communist is *unfit to* teach because he is *not himself free.* His mental servitude to Party dictation, paradoxical as it may seem, is made by his rejection of the ethical and moral values of Christian civilization. Morally uninhibited, he is exhorted to any manner of deception and deceit to achieve the one supreme objective, the triumph of the Party. A Communist teacher exploits the privileges of academic freedom because by training, purpose, and dedication he intends not to teach but to twist and torture the truth. He is neither reliable nor trustworthy.

The Communist teacher is *useless*. Bound to the Party line, he compromises the scholarly standards of each branch of learning, shutting off avenues of approach to an all comprehensive study and critique. They cannot be fair teachers of Communism or of anything else. Thirdly, it is a falsification of man: They strike at the origin of all human freedom, the spiritual value of man and his eternal destiny. How can man be educated into machines and economic factors? God made man a little less than the angels; Marxists make man much less a man. And lastly, the Communist teacher is treacherous to academic freedom itself. Wherever it has prevailed it has drawn the Iron Curtain on minds as well as bodies. The dedication of Party membership is in the realm of conduct not mere belief. The prerogatives and responsibilities of the Academy are lofty and priceless. When therefore it protects itself against the abuse and betrayal of its professional trust it is guarding against the subversion of its own freedom as well as the freedom of the City.

It is neither fair nor correct to hold that the libertarian desires the rise of totalitarian government. The fact is the libertarian and the totalitarian Communist are at opposite poles in their basic philosophy. The former defining academic freedom as wholly procedural, as the open market and free and peaceful competition of ideas, with cavalier unconcern for substantive truths, represents unrestrained freedom, moral and intellectual. The latter, the most rigid thought-behaviour control ever contrived by man. *But* the libertarian leaves open the opportunity of an intellectual and moral vacuum into which the heavy-booted dogmatizing state with its powerful myths will step unchallenged. The libertarian fails the free society at the very time when the free society needs him most. He is not only — by his own avowal — intellectually impotent to unmask the arrogant usurpations of the dogmatizing state but he is helpless to assert any valid and authentic rights for the academy and society. He can only confront the situation with Delphic ambiguity: 'right either way'. If the positive guarantees of liberty are to be claimed on the grounds of consent then its exercise must conduce to the principled direction of that consent which originates and perpetuates the free society. One need only recall the unrestrained use of liberty by the Nazi Party prior to 1933 to the extinction of the liberties of the Weimar Republic to appreciate the appalling failure and shame of the German intellectuals to formulate a sound philosophy of freedom in accord with the spiritual nature of man.

The best regulation of human conduct is of course self-regulation. It is most desirable that governmental measures for national security be kept at a minimum, and that society has confidence in the integrity of the Academy. Let the academy set its own standards of scholarship and scientific excellence and professional code of ethics. Let the academy exercise its own supervision within the terms of a freedom which does not tolerate its own destruction. The Free Academy has a right to self-preservation. This it cannot do unless it first acknowledges certain substantive truths about the meaning of human existence before which all differences must submit. Giant strides in the various branches of learning have led man to an amazing mastery over the forces of nature. But it is not given to man to make, to forge his own destiny. This arrogant ambition would usurp a role which is not his, but the right of God.

Made in the image of God, His Creator, man has the high calling of being artist and artisan. A creature in the image of God, His Lord and Master, he is also called upon to lord over the things of this earth and to master the forces of the universe for his own benefit as stewards of God, but surely, not to transform them. Man is morally impelled by divinely endowed law of his nature to establish societies but not without due regard for the order of eternal justice; it is given to man to become a creature of his own making, civilized and cultured, but hardly in defiance of those moral laws which elevate his mind and will above mere functional faculties. In his longing for liberation from the occult forces of nature which advanced learning and scientific achievement are to bring him, man must not dare deny everything which makes him a dependent being. In imitation of His Creator whose image he bears he too can be creative, but he will never cease to be a creature. But if he suffers the deceptive and maddening illusion that he is free to forge his own destiny and chart his own eternal course independently by his own will, then his destiny will be forged by the stronger force. A freedom which is a revolt and rejection of the Fatherhood of God is but the prelude to servitude. Knowledge is power — but only over the material universe. It is indeed a wise intelligence which discovers the limitations of reason as well as its horizon. Superman is a patently absurd contradiction. To be free man must transcend himself as well as the things of the earth by the very faculty that makes him capable of surpassing himself and keep company with God — Who is above all — and supremely free. The deepest frustrations of individuals and societies have been the endeavour for self-fulfillment through self-sufficiency.

Academic freedom is one important aspect of the general problem of freedom in society. We are led necessarily in conclusion to the original question of human freedom.

Can man be free without God? If we deny God of whom man is the living reflection, where shall we find the principle of human dignity and the infinite value of every human soul? Where else can we find a principle of freedom save in Him Who is not immersed in matter and Who has neither equal nor superior?

The Marxist Humanity offers no liberation to the present living generation of real people who are sacrificed to a perpetual dialectical alternation of contradictories. The Utilitarian with his mathematical calculus of the greatest happiness of the greatest number abandons the minority to their own misery. The Libertarian shouts his fatuous independence of Omnipotent God — but only to be swallowed whole by the omnicompetent State.

Men will be free as they bear witness to the divine imagery within them, to that spirituality which lifts them above cosmic captivity, and invests them with inviolability before the exercise of any human power.

The root cause of freedom is spiritual. Man is capable of freedom because his mind and will are not matter nor like matter — they are like God. Man is rational not because he thinks but because he can think if he tries. Man is capable of freedom because he can recognize the difference between right and wrong and can choose to do the right against strongly attractive temporal advantages to the contrary. In the Mass for the Confessors—the priests read in the Introit—*Potuit facere mala sed fecit bona.* Man's freedom is rooted in his divine vocation — the ability with God's grace to keep company with God. In sharing the divine trascendence — man is free, as the Psalmist sang — *adhaerere Deo* — clinging to God. Freedom is life and life is union with the author of life. I am the Vine, You are the branches, Abide in Me and I in you.

A discussion which touches upon any expression of human freedom must be radical in order to authenticate its position. We can get to the roots of the problem only by asking the original questions whether man can be free in any capacity and association, as a member of the Academy and a subject of the City within the terms of a philosophy of freedom which rejects or ignores or blandly questions the existence of God and His universal moral order or whether in such a philosophy of negation, man risks rather the hazards of greater numbers and predominant force, the pragmatic test of consequences, of man-made values — in a word — the new morality of efficiency.

We are of the dogmatic mind that only in sharing the divine transcendence will man be truly free. By adhering to absolute truths, he is superior to the transient and relative. By acknowledging and submitting to absolute goodness and divine moral laws, he will be elevated to the freedom of the Children of God, by recognizing objective standards of social and political truths, will man be able to live freely in an order that makes freedom possible.

Truth and Consequences! There are three basic truths which must serve as the philosophic foundations upon which the superstructure of a free society can be constructed: The spiritual immortality of man and God as his ultimate end; the connatural moral duties and rights which are inviolable before any human exercise of authority and with which all claims upon human obedience must correspond; thirdly, political authority is a service for the higher ends of man, not an end in itself.

The struggle between a free society and the powers of domination will not be decided in the stratosphere of the sputniks but in the minds and hearts of men who inhabit the earth. The eventual outcome will rest in no small measure on the convictions and religious formula of the intellectuals of the free society. What will be their glory or shame — time will tell.

THE DIVIDED ALLEGIANCE OF THE CATHOLIC*

It is an unpleasant experience in American politics that the Catholic Faith of an American citizen becomes a stirring issue almost solely when he runs for the highest magistracy of the land, the office of the president of the United States. The national debates of 1924, 1928, and 1960 have made this incontestably clear. There seems to be no insurmountable problem about any other office of public trust, military or civil, federal, state, or foreign service, legislative, judicial, executive. But let an American Catholic aspire to the presidency and the air is filled with refined insinuations and raucous warnings. At its worst, anti-Catholicism is a witches' brew of blinding bias, inherited prejudices, and stubborn prepossessions. On a much higher plane, it seems possible to disengage anti-Catholicism from crude forms of bigotry and from the clutter of irrational motivations which inspired and characterized the Nativist and Know Nothing movements of the pre-Civil War period, from the American Protective Association movement after the Civil War and the repellant vulgarities of the Ku Klux Klan after World War I. Many non-Catholics of deep piety and great learning who are respectful friends of the Catholic Church have unresolved doubts and anxieties about a Catholic in the White House. We owe it to them in charity to explain ourselves just as we ought to acknowledge that they are honest in their criticisms and fears.

Anti-Catholicism in its rational core is a composite of three apprehensions: a Catholic, it is said, by reason of his spiritual allegiance to the papacy, as his Faith prescribes, is subject to the foreign

---

*PROBLEMS AND PROGRESS. The Newman Press, 1962. Pages 17-39. Public lecture given at Fordham University prior to John F. Kennedy's election to the U.S. Presidency.

jurisdiction of the pope, who is also a temporal sovereign. This obedience to the papacy in faith and morals, it is alleged, can and may operate in conflict with the American citizen's oath to uphold and obey the laws of his country. Secondly, the religious dogmatism of Catholicism is dialectically incompatible with political democracy. Doctrinal dogmatism and intolerance conduce to political dogmatism, civil intolerance, and absolutism, while, on the contrary, religious and philosophical relativism promotes civil tolerance and political democracy. Thirdly, the growth of Catholicism poses a grave threat to the existence of Protestantism. A numerically superior Catholic electorate might be tempted to change the Constitution in order to restrict the exercise of religious freedom for non-Catholics.

None of these suppositions is flimsy, nor will a satisfactory explanation dispel all lingering doubts and suspicions. The Catholic and non-Catholic worlds (and they are distinct worlds) have too long been divided by diverse histories which have engendered adverse habits of biased appraisals of one another.

First, then, let us consider the divided allegiance of the Catholic. In its most acute form this is a relatively modern problem that arose with the emergence of the national secular state and deepened with the Reformation. Historically, the early Christians were the first to protest against the overweening pretensions of a pagan omnicompetent state, that "we ought to obey God rather than men," without denying Caesar's due. For centuries thereafter, long before legal positivism hammered its shattering blows, all men held fast to the universal supremacy of the moral law, to the primacy of the spiritual over the temporal, to the moral and practical necessity of a plurality of allegiances complementary to one another. No one questioned the moral-legal continuum.

In the fifth century Pope Gelasius distinguished the separate spheres of jurisdiction for the spiritual and temporal empowerments. Both authorities are from God, each superior to and independent of the other in the legitimate exercise of power over the proper objects of its competence. Unfortunately, a turbulent history, the unsettling of legal and political institutions by the barbarian invasions, and the blending of the two powers in the same hands, now secular, now ecclesiastic, did not provide the tranquil conditions for the evolution of Church-State relations envisioned by the Gelasian formula. The enormous religious and political problems that followed upon the breakup of the unity of medieval Christendom were complicated almost beyond hope by the generally prevailing consensus on all sides that political allegiance depended upon and demanded religious uniformity. The Peace of Westphalia in 1648 simply froze the question without solving it by the expedient arrangement of *cuius regio eius religio.*

Our American colonists were heirs of these religious-political tensions. Many of them came to the new world to escape religious persecution and civil disabilities inflicted by the State-Church establishments of the old world and then, with a remarkable loss of memory, proceeded to set up their own Church establishments, often with intolerable restrictions for dissenters in their midst.

The fear of foreign domination through an ecclesiastical agency was widely evident during most of the colonial period and became increasingly acute as the movement for political independence gained momentum. It was in no way exclusively or even mainly an anti-Catholic bias. Seven of the ten established churches were of the Church of England. For a complex of reasons these were without bishops during the entire colonial period despite the genuine need for their spiritual ministrations. It was feared that English bishops, being sworn supporters of the crown and members of the House of Lords, would be unlikely to support the colonies in political issues. Besides, the defection of a number of their leaders who sympathized with the British government to loyal British colonies in Nova Scotia and other parts of Canada did not endear them to the rank and file of the people as the revolutionary cause became more clearly defined. There was too much opposition from those disaffected with the course of the Reformation in the Church of England. Presbyterians, Congregationalists, and Baptists viewed with alarm the prospects of an Anglican prelacy in their midst with all its historic ties with the crown and reminiscent of the persecutions they had fled from in the homeland. It is within the context of this all-pervading opposition to the presence of a foreign prelacy in the colonies that we must view the Laity Remonstrance of 1765 in which two hundred and fifty Catholic laymen of Maryland protested against the appointment of the Bishop of Quebec as their apostolic vicar. Charles Carroll of Annapolis, father of Charles Carroll of Carrolton, wrote at the time to Bishop Challoner:

> Your Lordship must know, yet for many years past attempts have been made to establish a Protestant bishop on this conti-

nent, and yet such attempts have been as constantly opposed through the fixed aversion the people of America in general have to a person of such character. If such is the aversion of Protestants to a Protestant bishop, with what an eye will they look upon an Apostolic Vicar?

In 1784 the Maryland clergy addressed a memorial to Pope Pius VI in which they advised against the designation of a bishop, reporting that a superior *in spiritualibus* would suffice for the spiritual needs of the faithful. Father John Carroll, in a letter to Cardinal Antonelli (dated February 27, 1785), perhaps gave the most acute expression to the colonial aversion to a foreign bishop when he urged that Rome permit the Catholic clergy to select their own native ecclesiastical superior. He called attention to the sixth of the Articles of Confederation that "no one who holds office under the United States shall be allowed to receive any gift, office or title of any kind whatsoever from any king, prince or foreign government."

Carroll was of the opinion that this prohibition extended only to those appointed to public office in the republic but added significantly "it will perhaps be wrested by our opponents to apply also to ecclesiastical offices."

Though the construction which was rightly placed upon the Anglican bishop's tie to the British Crown should not have applied to the Catholics' religious allegiance to the papacy, nevertheless the Catholic colonials were eager not to give any grounds to this misconception. With political independence, the Protestant Episcopalian Church in the United States was freed from its oath of fealty to the Crown and gradually became entirely self-governing in its ecclesiastical jurisdiction, though it continued in regular communion with all branches of the Anglican Church. While Catholics on their part developed a native American hierarchy, the fear of popery continued to linger in American minds and at different times and for varying reasons would come to the surface and even erupt into open violence. Such occasions were the rising rate of Catholic immigration, disputes about Bible reading and sectarian religious indoctrination in public schools, episcopal requests for tax support of Catholic parochial schools, and legislation about divorce, birth control, and sterilization.

What shall we say about the implications of foreign jurisdiction in the Catholics' allegiance to the pope, who is also a temporal sovereign? Does this imply that the Catholic's patriotism is not entire but divided? Apart from the official doctrinal response to this charge by ecclesiastical authorities, there is an objective approach, that is to say, a consideration which transcends or cuts across religious lines, namely, the status accorded to the Holy See in international law by the practice of states.

States which in their public law grant preferential status to different faiths — Protestant, Catholic, Islamic, Oriental — and states which profess religious neutrality have for decades recognized the Holy See to be a general, permanent and perfect subject of international law. As such the Holy See has *in its own capacity* always enjoyed the rights of active and passive legation and concluded agreements (concordats) with states. In addition, the Holy See can conclude normal international treaties on behalf of her temporalities, before 1870 for the Papal State, and since 1929 for the City of the Vatican. The unique status of the Holy See in general international law consists in the fact that it is precisely as a spiritual sovereign that she enjoys the rights of sovereignty ordinarily accorded to national political sovereignty and that no other Church or religion has known the same status in the world community of states.

Sovereignty and international personality is vested with the Holy See precisely as a spiritual authority, independently of the existence of a papal state. From 1870 to 1929 when she was without territories her unique status remained unchanged and she continued to exercise her customary rights in international law. The reason for the existence of the State of Vatican City is wholly derivative and contingent upon the presupposition that the free exercise of a supranational spiritual sovereignty by the Holy See is better ensured by an independent territorial jurisdiction of its own. Prior to 1870 and subsequent to 1929, there have been two subjects of international law, the Papal States, or the State of Vatican City, and the Holy See. The pope united in his own person these two distinct subjects of international law, and of the two obviously the more important and primary is that of the Holy See. Papal nuncios and apostolic delegates are accredited by the Holy See, not by the papal state. Diplomatic relations by the states of England, Netherlands, Finland, Japan, Egypt, Indonesia, and others are established with the Holy See and not, as is popularly supposed, with the Papal State. Their diplomatic representatives are accredited to the spiritual sovereignty and not to the temporal jurisdiction. None of these states suffers any qualms about divided allegiance or contrary allegiances and it is patently absurd to suppose that their diplomatic relations with the Holy See import a confessional bias.

What then precisely is the significance of the state of Vatican City? A study comparing it with the Holy See may make this clear. Both of them are subjects of general international law. The Holy See is a nonterritorial personality; Vatican City is a territorial international personality. The Holy See is not a state but it exercises sovereign prerogatives, including sovereignty over the Vatican State. Some writers on international law call Vatican City a "vassal" state. It is not autonomous, its existence is wholly derivative, and it is subordinate to and subserves the purposes of the Holy See. Even as a territorial personality, Vatican City is wanting as a state, for it does not meet the Greek requirement of self-sufficiency. There are no industrial, agricultural or commercial enterprises that could sustain an economy. Actually, the state of the Vatican City, and for that matter, of the Holy See is almost wholly dependent for its financial resources upon worldwide contributions of its faithful for maintenance and administration. Furthermore, it barely fulfills the Roman law requirement of territorial definition and a coterminous jurisdiction. Because of its small size and because its activities and purposes are totally different from those of national political states, it does not enjoy membership as a state in the United Nations. Its constitution derives wholly from the necessity of the Holy See to be independent and free from any political domination. The spiritual office of all papal representatives is symbolically attested to by the honorary precedence that they enjoy in the diplomatic corp over all political diplomats.

International law does not, of course, commit itself to any theological position. Its recognition of the non-territorial international personality of the Holy See precisely as a spiritual sovereign cannot be construed as having any confessional implication whatever. That being so, we may add that Catholic ecclesiology, which understandably is not acceptable to non-Catholics, should be reassuring to them on this matter. The pope or bishop of Rome is acknowledged by Catholics to be the Vicar of Christ on earth. In virtue of the apostolic succession the Roman pontiff exercises a primacy of jurisdiction over all bishops and over all the faithful. His jurisdiction extends not only to faith and morals, but also to those matters which pertain to the discipline and law of the Church throughout the world. It is clearly necessary that the Holy See enjoy complete immunity from the influence, dictation, or interference of any national political sovereignty in the exercise of its spiritual authority over its faithful who are citizens of different national governments throughout the world. In matters touching upon faith and morals, the pope is never a foreigner. Wherever the Catholic faithful are, there too is the pope as Vicar of Christ, present by the universal extension of his divinely invested spiritual office.

Now there are non-Catholics who readily admit to the purely spiritual allegiance of Catholics to the Holy See but who fear that this may be the very vehicle through which papal or hierarchical influence or "pressure" may be exerted upon the religious conscience of a Catholic in the exercise of his presidential duties. This fear is emphasized by the difference between the dominance that Protestant theology gives to private judgment as the ordinary guide of conscience and the deference which Catholics ordinarily and normally show to the authoritative direction of the Church. The difficulty is further confounded by the misconception about the extent of papal authority, which is considered to be so absolute and complete that a Catholic president would be inhibited in making any independent political judgments by an apparent conflict of the two allegiances. One would think that John Henry Newman had disposed of this lingering ghost by his reply to the identical allegations of Mr. Gladstone:

> When, then, Mr. Gladstone asks Catholics how they can obey the Queen and yet obey the Pope, since it may happen that the commands of the two authorities may clash, I answer that it is my *rule,* both to obey the one and to obey the other, but that there is no rule in this world without exceptions, and if either the Pope or the Queen demanded of men an "absolute obedience" he or she would be transgressing the laws of human nature and human society. I give an absolute obedience to neither. Further, if ever this double allegiance pulled me in contrary ways, which in this age of the world I think it never will, then I should decide according to the particular case, which is beyond all rule, and must be decided on its merits. I should look to see what theologians could do for me, what the bishops and clergy around me, what my confessor; what my friends whom I revered; and, if after all, I could not take their view

of the matter, then I must rule myself by my own judgment and my own conscience.

And in another place in the same letter:

The Pope's infallibility indeed and his supreme authority have in the Vatican *capita* been declared matters of faith; but his prerogative of infallibility lies in matters speculative, and his prerogative of authority is no infallibility, in laws, commands, or measures. His infallibility bears upon the domain of thought, not directly of action, and while it may fairly exercise the theologian, philosopher, or man of science, it scarcely concerns the politician.

All moral obligations descend from God. A reasonable person will generally in difficult cases consult those invested with the proper authority and competence to ascertain the correct course of action. To be bound in conscience is to be bound by one's own conscience. That is not to say that it is a self-imposed obligation. Rather it is the free personal acknowledgment of what ought to be done.

Almost all theologians and political philosophers hold that the province of faith is that of the Church and that politics is the proper domain of the state. Almost all agree that morality is the common concern of both jurisdictions because man as citizen and believer acts as a moral agent. This provides the potential source of conflict and friction between the two authorities, religious and secular, and it may be attributed not so much to the mutual denial of jurisdiction as to the priority and extent of its exercise.

The objectives of civil society are eminently moral: social justice, public order, security, peace, the legal protection of natural rights which it is not in the power of the state to deny or abrogate, such as the right to religious freedom. The distinction between positive law and morality is that of a part to the whole. The performance of a human act is always under the jurisdiction of the universal moral law. The problem arises in the pluralist interpretation and opposing application of the moral law to an action of public law. Political authority may not shirk its responsibilities in assisting the moral life of its subjects and yet on the other hand should not arbitrarily impose one moral philosophy rather than another upon its citizens. Reason would require that the political authorities should expect and welcome the efforts of all duly constituted religious authorities such as the Board of Rabbis, the Protestant Council of Churches, and the Catholic Bishops, as well as private citizens to express themselves on grave moral questions affecting the public order as becomes their duty. In turn the public at large has the right to weigh the justice and reasonableness of these authoritative pronouncements, with sensitive regard for the rights of all consciences and the exigencies of public order. Where contrary and conflicting positions are affirmed then public discussion and debate should proceed on the basis of reason and with an appeal to reason. The natural law, which is the law of human nature and not the law of men, offers the most optimistic possibility for civilized men to discourse their way to agreement. The natural law remains unalterably the unitive bond of all men of different faiths, and at the same time the proper context in which to view the legitimate role of public power. I take the source of the difficulty to be generally a flight from reason, the fear that an agreement might be reached which the absolutist dissenter might be required to respect.

Now on the American scene three specific issues are raised about the Catholic in the White House: provisions for a birth control program in a foreign aid bill, diplomatic relations with the Holy See, and federal aid to all publicly accredited schools, including of religious schools.

It is the unique genius of the American Constitution that it guarantees the exercise of religious freedom for the president of the United States without thereby impairing the operations of the political process or imposing forcibly by virtue of presidential authority his moral conscience upon others. Should a Catholic president, then, in response to his moral convictions about birth control, refuse to approve it, the congressional bill might still become law automatically without his signature after the passage of the constitutionally prescribed time or by congressional action overriding the veto. Every presidential action must always be viewed within the context of the political process. One might add, too, a *sotto voce* reflection that obedience to one's own personal conscience is not always and necessarily in conformity with the publicly avowed dictates of its religious profession. Not every Quaker public officer subscribes to pacifism.

Federal aid to religious schools and formal diplomatic relations with the Holy See are nonreligious questions. They are political decisions dependent upon congressional action which is sensitively respondent to the public and ultimately subject to judicial review. No one may reasonably *insist* that there *must* be formal diplomatic relations with the Holy See. But to insist that they must never be established at any event for any reason may well conceal a symbolic affront to Catholics not unlike that shown to this day to a Catholic presidential candidate. The practice of Protestant, Buddhist, Hindu, Moslem states with legally established religions and of states with separation of Church and State contradicts the misconception that formal diplomatic relations with the Holy See imply a preferential status for one Church or discrimination against other Churches.

Our second consideration is about the alleged incompatibility of the philosophical and religious dogmatism of Catholicism and political democracy. The common Protestant assumption is that Luther and the Reformation brought freedom into the world, that American liberty is a late product of the Reformation of the same type as those liberties so loudly advertised on the European continent by anti-Catholic liberals throughout the nineteenth century. Hence it can be an occasion of sincere and agreeable surprise to discover that the American Catholic can be loyal to his country. This assumption is uncritical and wholly gratuitous because it is invalid both historically and sociologically. The freedoms proclaimed by Luther and spread by the Reformation may not be isolated from the theological and political syntheses of the various Protestant theories: justification by faith, the servile will, the debased value of human 'reason, the concentration in the sovereign of all external powers even where ecclesiastical matters were concerned imply rather politico-religious intolerance and a rigid religious-political structure of communities. Luther and Calvin were logical when they maintained the right of banishing or burning heretics, sectarians, and all those who by denying one of the dogmas resulting from the common interpretation of the Bible denied at the same time the new Christian society and the basis of social power. As for the American experience we should not blithely forget that many of our colonial immigrants fled from persecution in Protestant State-Church establishments of the old world and that they in turn persecuted religious dissenters in the new world. The historical process leading to religious toleration has other theoretical and historical roots than Protestantism.

The rational misconception derives from the false juxtaposition of two different levels of human experience as though the relation between the two — and related they are — was of an arithmetic or geometric proportion. It is argued that philosophical and religious dogmatism engenders habits of intolerance for what is believed to be false, and is therefore conducive to political absolutism and civil intolerance. Such an equation misconstrues as equivalent the ends and purposes of religious and civil life. Man is determined as to his end and indeterminate as to the means for realizing his end. It is the rightful province of theologians and philosophers to ascertain the meaning of human existence and to yield intellectual assent to conclusive evidence. They are free to inquire but not free to fashion man's destiny. It is the proper domain of statesmen to contrive apt means and multiple courses of action from which a choice may be made for the governance of the civil order, ever mindful and respectful of the religious conscience of its subjects. Dogmatism in any science is an intellectual achievement; it is the goal toward which all learning strives and upon whose certainties rest the possibilities of a life of convenience without fear. For example, dogmatism in the natural sciences, instead of shutting us in on every hand, constitutes the means at our disposal for acting upon things and for obtaining power over them. A knowledge of the laws of things enables us to control them; consequently instead of checking our freedom, natural physical laws make it efficacious. Religious dogmatism frees us from the phantom world of blind fate and the mythical world of demons by assuring us that we are children of God, for whose sake the world of forces and life has been created. Philosophical dogmatism tells us that men have been created equal by God and that therefore no one has by nature a right to govern another, save by his consent. Historically, revolutions for political freedom have been fought by men who were willing to sacrifice their possessions and their lives for their beliefs. Conversely, theological and philosophical skepticism and relativism deprive a people of the spiritual and intellectual resources with which to withstand the pretensions of the omnicompetent state. As modern history only too patently proves, the totalitarian state steps into this intellectual vacuum and makes the arrogant claim to dogmatize (with force, if necessary) not only politically but theologically and philosophically as well. If the theologians and philosophers cannot be validly sure of the meaning of human existence then how can anyone be sure that Marxism is an error? What would be the sense of fighting it at so great a sacrifice? Dogma is not only the prize achievement of human intelligence; it is also the condition for a free society.

The third consideration focuses on the fears that many Protestants have about a numerically superior Catholic electorate. Might it not be tempted to change the Constitution to restrict the religious freedom of non-Catholics? The source of these fears, European history, past and present, and our own colonial period, is creditable to neither side. Broadly speaking, there have been in both religious camps two traditions on Church-State relations. The major tradition would have public law confer a preferential status to the "true" religion and civil restrictions upon or civil tolerance for the dissenters. The minor tradition affirms that civil society is an exigency of the divine natural law and that it prescinds from the prerogatives of revelational theology. It maintains that both religious and secular empowerments are each independent of the other and superior in their own proper domain. It is forced to recognize that there are certain common areas of morality wherein both jurisdictions converge, which provide the potential source of conflict as well as the occasion of harmonious cooperation. In America the minor tradition has gradually emerged as the major one, for Catholics and Protestants alike, in the post-Civil War period.

The Catholic record in American history beginning with Lord Baltimore's Act of Toleration of 1649 and continuing to this day is remarkably reassuring. The Catholic hierarchy, since the days of Bishop John Carroll, has without exception repeatedly professed great devotion to and grateful appreciation of the American Constitution, particularly the religious clauses of the First Amendment. Catholics as private citizens and in public office have given no cause for us to doubt their patriotism. In matters political, there is no instance of an ecclesiastical call for Catholic political solidarity. Catholics in both Houses of Congress do not vote *en bloc*. And in surveys of state and municipal elections there is no consistent pattern that large concentrations of Catholic voters are committed to Catholic candidates. Catholic political solidarity is a myth.

But what of a Catholic bloc vote understood as a conscientious response to a religious position on a public law issue such as birth control and sterilization? Such controversies are inevitable wherever there is religious pluralism and the possibility of a bloc vote involves Protestant and Jew no less than Catholic. Now the political process of democratic society settles public issues through the presumably reasonable procedure of majority decision. In the rational and tentative expectation that the formal reason for the numerical majority be outside itself — in reason — this procedure, subject to review and reversal, allows for peaceful change and progress while at the same time it serves to express corporate capacity and responsibility. If then a group, religious or not, should express the solidarity of its convictions through the voting process, this is the expectation or hazard if you will, inherent in the process of arriving at majority decision. The problem incumbent upon all is so to condition this democratic process that there does not ensue an arbitrary majority rule over a minority. The only possible way of resolving this dilemma in a rational manner is by recourse, through reason, to the unitive bond of the divine natural law which is the law of man and not of men. Doctrinal positions are generally affirmed authoritatively from opposing camps. Despite the agreement about the necessity and desirability of intercredal dialogue there is not in evidence as much collective and cooperative discussion as is needed. Round table discussions by theologians, philosophers, statesmen, which prescind without disavowing religious dogmas, might inquire into the moral laws of human nature and ascertain what, in the political order, would be in accord with them. Such collective thinking might reveal that there is much more substance than shadow in the natural law and, further, might provide the political authorities with that general consensus which legislation should recognize. What of the obdurate and exceptional dissenter? It is a strange pathology of modern politics that it abhors the absolute dictator, totalitarian democracy, majoritarian rule but cannot place in proper perspective the absolutist dissenter.

In conclusion may I suggest that a Catholic candidate for the presidency might choose, even at the cost of votes, not to confine himself to a series of disclaimers on hypothetical issues. He might take a more positive approach and explain how his Catholic Faith would enrich his subjective dispositions in the performance of public duties. He might, without embarrassment, point to papal teaching on social justice, on the social responsibilities of labor and capital not only to one another but also to the community at large, on the principle of subsidiarity which Pope Pius XI opposed to the monolithic state. He might call attention to the contributions of Pope Pius XII on international relations and institutions. He might explain how his faith encourages foreign aid for deeper reasons than expediency. He might explain that the opposition between Catholicism and Communism is profoundly theological and humanist; he might point out papal teaching on the necessity of never acknowledging as final the captivity of certain peoples. He might point to the remarkable agreement of certain central Catholic dogmas with the American Declaration of Independence, how the Church insists on the moral basis for education, patriotism, the fulfillment of all civic duties. The Catholic conception of the social order supports and promotes legislation for the betterment of labor conditions, of housing facilities, for economic provisions for the aged and the needy. All of these and many others are not exclusively Catholic doctrines but nonetheless Catholic they are and they should inspire the faithful in the promotion of a better and more expansive life for the whole community. If a Catholic candidate for president is challenged on matters of his Faith then he might welcome the opportunity to make it better known and perhaps better understood. Surely, one would suppose that the historical record of over two centuries would disclose convincing and conclusive evidence of the patriotism of the Catholic, his devotion to the laws of his country, and his full share of sacrifice in her behalf.

PUBLIC LAW AND THE UNIVERSITY CAMPUS*

When the states incorporated the Bill of Rights into the Constitution, the first amendment guarantee of "the right of the people peaceably to assemble, and to petition the Government for a redress of grievances" left undefined the place where such activities could legally be conducted. But thanks to the religious zeal of the Jehovah's Witnesses, the labor picketing protests of the 1930's and the 1940's, and the civil rights demonstrations of the 1960's, the Supreme Court spelt out the conditions of constitutionally protected freedom of expression on public property — a reasonable regard for time, place, manner of conduct and compliance with narrowly drawn restrictions which public order, safety and convenience dictated.

It is a strange pathology of our times that a lone felon would be brought before the bar of justice but a conspiratorial or casual group perpetrating or attempting to perpetrate any action subject to civil and criminal liability is somehow endowed with higher exculpatory motives of righteous anger for the redress of grievances. Here we set down our reflections on the reach of public law and its protective insurance to such illegal conduct as has obtained on so many of the state-owned universities, *mutatis mutandis* they would be substantially applicable to privately owned universities.

Limits Campus Civil Liberties

Campus students enjoy fully the same freedoms of expression as do individuals in off-campus activities. Yet, I submit that their liberties *should not properly* coincide with the same constitutional

---

*VIRGINIA LAW WEEKLY, *Dicta*, Vol. XXII, No. 2 (1969).

latitude that others may have on street corners with legal impunity and protective coverage. Profanity, insulting the parentage of university officers, immoral allegations and insinuations are hardly conducive to rational discourse and scarcely accord with the civility that becomes the Academy. In exercising freedom of the press in campus journals, it is not a restriction upon the communication of argumentative ideas and challenging criticism for student publications to emulate the highest canons of journalism and not the style of tabloids. The voices of dissent and discontent and the clamor for reform will be heard more clearly and persuasively if they are free of vulgarity, abusive language and the threat of intimidation.

It is misleading to equate student militancy and disruptive tactics with the American revolutionaries, with the struggle of labor unions, the civil rights movement and resistance to totalitarian regimes. The colonists were denied basic rights and liberties as Englishmen and subjected to intolerable duresses, not the least of which was compulsory quartering of troops in private domiciles. Student dissidents have not been denied basic liberties and rights. On the contrary, they have interfered with the rights and liberties of other students who choose to attend to their studies. Legislative and decisional law guarantee labor unions the right to strike, picket, boycott and walk off the premises of employment until the alleged grievance is redressed. Discontented students are free to do the same.

Decries Violence

In 1939 the Supreme Court ruled that forcible occupation of factories was not distinguishable from the legally proscribed physical assaults upon an employer and from illegal seizure of his property. It is intolerable that the dictates of righteous conscience of the militant activtists, which allegedly justify their course of obstructive conduct, be allowed to prevail upon the conscience of their fellow students by interfering with their open access to university facilities. Acts of civil disobedience were performed in violation of a local or state law in order to initiate a court test of constitutionality in the light of a higher law, a federal statute or a provision of the Constitution and with the expectation of submitting to the punitive sanction and the recourse of the appellate process. Labor unions acknowledge the right of employers to fire an employee for cause. Student activists, on the contrary, demand advance immunity from court action as a precondition to terminating their disruption of the normal educational process. To interject memories of Nazism borders on the facetious. There is no extinction of civil rights and liberties in America, on or off the campus, nor do federal and state governments dominate the universities as Hitlerite Germany did. Further, the probabilities of reforming and updating the American universities are enhanced by the wide exposure our communication media seem only too eager to provide to the student dissidents — an enormous advantage wholly nonexistent under totalitarian regimes.

To hold members of the faculty and university administration hostage is under public law actionable for false imprisonment. An attack upon a university official is assault and battery. Seizure of property is actionable under laws governing extortion. Rifling confidential files is common thievery. The destruction of property and defamation of character is criminally liable. Barricading school buildings is justiciable under trespass laws. Concessions extracted from university officials in forced circumstances would scarcely be upheld as binding in a court of law. Yet university authorities feel bound to abide by extorted promises. What public law would not tolerate off campus should not go unpunished when done on campus. Students are not exempt citizens.

A free and independent university is not only one which is immune from external dictation but one whose internal freedom derives from the freedom of students and scholars to pursue their studies, communicate their learning and engage in relentless research and reexamination. It also means at least this — that campus militants have no greater right of freedom of expression than those in disagreement with them or those who refuse to be part of their demonstration. No one, for example, is under any compulsion to join the R.O.T.C. program. No one has the superior right of denying others the option of joining. The R.O.T.C. is the militants' catspaw. If students should not be impeded from demonstrating against war in Vietnam, neither should those who support our government's commitment there be denied the option of preparing themselves for military service through an on-campus program. The presence of the S.D.S. on university campus with its non-negotiable demands, its unilateral dictation of views, and coercive and disruptive tactics should hardly be more tolerable than the R.O.T.C. and its open option. Subjecting the university to the promotion of one partisan view will provide no general principle, moral or legal, for denying such a precedent of intolerance to opposing advocates. The underlying rationale of open option as a derivative of a free and independent university and equal rights and liberties for all students and faculty members applies no less validly to job recruiting and research projects.

Recommends Legal Remedies

It has been argued in some quarters that the only warrant for summoning the local police onto the campus should be the clear and present danger to persons and property. It is curious that the Holmesian norm which has receded from decisional law for almost two decades in favor of the "balancing of interests" has been resurrected in an inappropriate circumstance. The rights of students go far beyond security of person and property. They have a vested property interest — an expression that has a pejorative intonation nowadays — in study, learning, attendance at lectures, use of library and laboratories, completion of courses, advancement from year to year to graduation — in a word, an immunity from the arbitrary on campus no less than off campus. The question what is the reasonable employment of physical force on the part of the police in disengaging the obstructionists from armed occupation of buildings deserves serious consideration, but one which should not be used to confuse the original issue with one that is consequent to it. University grounds are not extraterritorial reservations beyond the protective mantle of public law.

Recourse to the courts for an injunction restraining militant students from disrupting the university educational process has relieved university authorities, who are hedged in by many extralegal circumstances, of the responsibility of calling the police for the restoration of order and transferred it to the courts. Obedience to court orders are a hard American commitment and popular sympathies are thereby shifted to the majesty of the court and its employment of law enforcement officers.

Defiance of court injunctions is chargeable with criminal contempt. The penalties for criminal contempt are, under state laws, generally more severe than for criminal trespass charges brought on by school officials. Trial for contempt of court may be with a jury, the penalty may extend to a month's confinement in jail and a monetary fine as well. Further, the prospect of sanctions imposed by the court are not subject to advance promises for criminal amnesty. The due process of courts is a matter of public record and can only be challenged by appellate recourse. Some courts have refused to drop charges of criminal trespass notwithstanding the requests of university officials that these charges be dropped. Court injunctions also obviate the adverse reaction that is likely attendant upon the cutoff of federal aid to students who disrupt university education. Another but less likely expectation is for the local community to initiate grand jury hearings and in the process bring charges of criminal trespass against militant students.

Some state legislatures have enacted laws which require colleges and universities to submit to the state department of education rules and regulations governing public order on campus. They must define types of impermissible conduct, set down specific penalties, establish procedures for hearings and adjudication, and set up a machinery for immediate and effective response to disruptive activities. State aid to colleges and universities who are eligible for such aid is made contingent on compliance with such pre-established rules of self-governance. Effective self-discipline is much to be preferred to the provisions of a variety of bills presently contemplated by a number of other state legislatures which place the principal responsibility for containing and penalizing disruptive student demonstrations on state governmental action.

Compares Academy and City

Force does exact some change. But it is misleading to suppose that it is the only way, or to deny that there is a better way to effectuate the resultant changes. Students' participation in university affairs did not require the violation of the rights of others, destruction of property, arson, vandalism, forced occupation of school buildings, personal injury or threat of injury, defamation of character and scurrilous language. Militant students have not pre-empted the moral capacity of America to be sensitive to poverty, racism, wars, misery and hunger. They may in fact be laboring under the self-deception of a romantic illusion of instant transformation of society. The righteous indignation is not all pervasive. They have not demonstrated in ghetto areas against the conniving villainy of theft of millions of dollars from anti-poverty funds.

We must accept the postulate that the American people and their regional and national governments *can* remedy, however sluggishly, injustices and inequities by the process of law as embodied in our political and legal institutions or we shall have to speak within the context of a revolution wherein a people opposes with armed force a government and its supporters or within the context of a civil war wherein a nation is divided in half and each strives to prevail by force of arms. The American Republic has known both experiences.

The Academy is within the City but it is not one with it. Nor ought it to be equated with it. Violence may be morally and legally justifiable as a last resort in political societies because rational and reasonable settlement is seemingly beyond hope. As centers of hope and light, the universities should be inviolably free from all those nonrational coercive instrumentalities by which political societies try to impose their "solution" of conflicting claims upon the vanquished. The Academy is not the City.

PACIFISM IS NOT PEACE*

The nationwide public debates over the war in Vietnam have revolved usually around the moral and legal correctness of American commitments to the Republic of South Vietnam, the validity of the domino theory, the expediency or wisdom of so deep a regional involvement weighed against the larger global strategy for containing Communist aggression and expansionism, and the risks of escalating the conflict into a nuclear war with China. But offstage, and more often in private discourse, the argument of the doctrinaire pacifist is pressed in genuine earnestness and will not be stilled. The reason is that the pacifist argument reaches some of the more difficult problems of Christian morality.

The Christian holds that war should be waged only as an assertion of moral right — that it is rooted in the inherent right of individual and collective self-defense. According to this view, when every possible exertion of reason has been expended, when every appeal to morality, to legal right, even to self-interest, and every call to neutral nations to intervene has proved unavailing — then war may be a justifiable or even obligatory means of defending a nation's rights: its security, its independence, its freedom from external aggression and domination. It will not do to say war settles nothing. For better or for worse it does. World War II has set the course of history for the present and for the foreseeable future. And although many might question the attribution of moral right and wrong to one side or the other in that war there are many more who would not have wished for a different outcome.

Now the principled pacifist who advocates non-resistance need

---

*TRIUMPH, November 1966, pp. 18-21.

not deny the inherent right of self-defense. His argument may proceed along two distinct lines.

For one, he may accept the theoretical possibility that in resorting to violent means a good end, and one which is not outweighed by an evil consequent to it, can be attained. But in modern warfare, he will argue, the destruction of lives among the military and the civilian populace, together with their property, is so vast that this possibility can be called unlikely. This line of reasoning does not contend that war is intrinsically evil, but rather that one of the key moral presuppositions of the "just war" can scarcely be maintained today. So reasonable is this argument that in the several armed conflicts which have occurred since World War II every effort has been made to limit them and to end hostilities as soon as possible.

For another — and this is the second argument — the pacifist position need not be restricted to a purely utilitarian weighing of survival and subjugation against the havoc of war, which might cancel out an intended vindication of violated right. Pacifism may be related to higher premises — to Christianity itself. The appeal may be to the Christian ethic, the Christian spirit, to the teaching and life of Christ. (Note here that the principled pacifist, regardless of which of the two arguments he makes, is to be distinguished from the part-time pacifist who objects to a particular war on "moral" grounds that in fact amount to an ideological bias, or an ethnic and historical predisposition, or simply a dread of military combat.)

The principled Christian pacifist asserts that love will conquer hatred and injustice; the meek of heart will inherit the earth; non-resistance will disarm the barbarian and tame the savage. Nor is he discouraged from these idyllic expectations by centuries of hard history.

But putting aside the disparity between the pacifist's expectations and the rude facts of history, the pacifist's argument — his appeal to "The Christian spirit" — ought to be examined seriously. Does an authentic understanding of Christ's doctrine as recorded by the evangelists really yield the pacifist ideal? Does the life and the crucifixion of Christ require the Christian to practice non-resistance at whatever cost to himself and to those dependent on him?

There is an undeniable suggestion of pacifism in the New Testament. We are exhorted to forsake the old ways — an eye for an eye, a tooth for a tooth — and take on the new — love thy enemies and pray for those who persecute you. Did Christ not repeatedly refuse to use force to protect Himself and his followers? Did He not by word and deed inspire us to suffer all tribulations in his name, to turn the other cheek, and to carry our cross in his likeness?

In weighing this counsel and example, let us recall the precise issue here. It is not whether war should be banned — we may agree that nothing could better benefit mankind than to be able to outlaw war effectively, for all time. The issue, as posed by the pacifist, is whether those threatened by aggression and domination must refrain from taking up arms, no matter what the consequences to themselves and to others. The issue is whether the Christian spirit, as reflected in these passages of the New Testament, exhorts us to endure the loss of personal and civil liberties — to submit to tyranny — as a means of avoiding the destruction and horrors of war. For make no mistake about it: loss of liberty and rule by brute force is frequently the *sure* consequence, insofar as human wit can foretell, of non-resistance. There are times in history when governments, supported by their people, including a sizeable number of intellectuals, are recognizably impervious to reasonable persuasion. Such governments are firmly set upon the use of force as the means of fashioning the present and future course of history for themselves and for others. Hitler and his enthusiastic followers could be appeased only by acceding to the Nazis' rapacious demands. The Communists are frankly dedicated to dominating whatever they can without risking certain destruction for themselves. No one can seriously doubt that the armed might of the Soviet Union would sweep across Europe, save for the deterrent nuclear power of America.

The Sermon on the Mount Had a Civic Environment

It seems to me that the words and deeds of Christ referred to above must be understood not only in their own context but also in the context of his other recorded teachings. To begin with, the appeal to the Christian spirit must be made with full acknowledgement that God, the Author of our human nature, willed that men live in *civility,* and under public laws designed to maintain a social order dedicated to the requirements of *justice.* If, then, civilized living (which distinguishes civil men from savages, who are a law unto themselves) is the fulfillment of divine intent, it follows that there is a divinely ordained natural-law right and obligation to preserve civilization. He who said, "Give to Caesar what is Caesar's and to God what is God's," was not presenting us with an embarrassing and difficult dichotomy, but with distinct duties which, though discharged on different levels, nevertheless cohere. The commandment of love does not abrogate the demands of justice, but rather presupposes them.

When Christ exhorted the rich young man to sell all he had and to follow Him, He was not excusing the man from paying his debts to the grocer, the doctor, to his business associates, to the tax-collector. At another time Christ instructed the apostles to pay their taxes with the pearl found in the fish they caught.

The Sermon on the Mount was not an invitation to disregard the hard necessities of civilization. Christian missionaries go to distant lands, first to teach the Good News and what must be done to live justly on earth and to attain eternal beatitude. But they also teach habits of personal hygiene, modesty of dress, public sanitation; they set up dispensaries, build schools, instruct converts in improved techniques of agriculture. The Jesuits in Paraguay taught the Indians whom they converted how to defend themselves against savages who were intent upon their destruction, and to that end instructed them in the production of gunpowder, and in the manufacture of firearms. In a word, the commandment of love and the Christian spirit of forbearance do not annul the obligations of natural and legal justice.

In our day priests still assert, by their example, the right of self-defense. In Binh Hung, on the Camau Peninsula of Vietnam, Father Hoa recently organized an effective regional defense against the Viet Cong terrorists. Because of him, the peasants, many of whom were refugees from Red China, succeeded in repelling Communist guerrilla forces. Indeed, they reclaimed much territory. President Kennedy wrote the editor of the *Saturday Evening Post*, expressing the wish that this inspiring story be told publicly; it appeared on May 30 1961, under the title "The Report the President Wanted Published."

No scholar will deny the complexity of motives and causes that brought about World War II, nor be so naive as to picture the Allies in the spotless role of St. George and the opposing forces in the guise of the Dragon. But when Winston Churchill pleaded with his countrymen not to lose heart because they were engaged in a life and death struggle for Christendom, those who heard him understood that if Christendom, whatever its shortcomings, did not prevail, a very dark and fearful future lay ahead for all men. It is therefore spurious to characterize those who seek to defend themselves and civilization by recourse to arms, as hawks, and those who recommend negotiation, or even acquiescence in the demands of an aggressor, as doves. The hawk is rapacious and quick to kill. The harmless dove survives in protected circumstances not of his own making, and is hardly appropriate as the symbol of earthly peace. It better symbolizes supernatural peace, of which God is the unfailing warrantor. "My Peace I give to you . . . which no man can take away."

One Man's Heroism Can Be Another Man's Cowardice

There are fates worse than death. The Jews were unwilling to allow the Seleucids to dishonor their religion and their national rights; they chose to fight to the death. The Filipinos made the hard choice for war's devastation and the sacrifice of their youth rather than acquiesce in a "peaceful" submission to Imperial Japan. The Hungarian freedom-fighters gave their lives against overwhelming odds in what may have seemed to the pacifist a senseless sacrifice.

To the question, "Who is my neighbor?," Christ answered, "He who has need of you." In his letter of December 14, 1961, to President Diem, President Kennedy wrote angrily of "the deliberate savagery of the Communist program of assassination, kidnapping and wanton violence," of "the campaign of force and terror . . . supported and directed . . . by the authorities of Hanoi." When the United States government, by its solemn pledges of help and actual assistance, encouraged the South Vietnamese to resist the aggressor, was America not going to the aid of its "neighbor"?

The Gospels tell the story of the Good Samaritan. A traveller is set upon by bandits, beaten, robbed, left to bleed on the roadside. A priest and Levite from Jerusalem, both pass him by. A Samaritan, an alien, chances upon the scene and takes the traveller to a nearby inn for care. Had the Samaritan come by when the bandits were assaulting the traveler, and swung his staff with great force to bruise and repel the aggressors (and perhaps in the process risk his own safety or life), would he have been less good? I think his goodness would have been still greater. "He who lays down his life for his friend will find it." If the appeal is to the Christian spirit, it must also make reference to the life beyond death as well as to life on earth. The pacifist, like the priest and Levite, passes by.

Those who equate with pacifism the appeals of Popes John and Paul for universal peace do little honor to those pontiffs. Neither of the popes, nor any of their predecessors, ever denied the inherent right of individual and collective self-defense. When Pope Paul addressed the UN General Assembly, and through it the entire world, he called for *universal* disarmament. "Let the weapons of destruction fall from your hands." He did not say, "You, Americans, do so first; perhaps others will follow your example." I venture to guess, subject to correction, that His Holiness would be gravely concerned and fearful of what might happen should the United States, the only power capable of checking Communist expansionism, disarm unilaterally.

In the evangelists' record of the several encounters between Christ and soldiers, there is a striking absence of any denunciation of the military. Nor are the soldiers exhorted to shed their arms and turn to pacific employments. And early Christian writers such as Lactantius and Augustine pointed with pride to the military service and valor of the Christian soldier in the Roman army.

Pacifism is not peace. St. Augustine defined peace as the "tranquillity of order," and for Augustine order without justice was not peace. St. Thomas warned us not to identify peace with mere concord, for concord that rests upon fear or coercion is not truly peace. Tacitus counselled against confusing the quiet of a subjugated people with peace *(Agricola: ubi solitudinem faciunt, pacem apellant).*

A people that chooses not to submit to the social engineering of a statist government, preferring to work out its destiny freely through self-determined processes — such a people should not be compelled to "negotiate" with foreign aggressors or to admit their representatives into a coalition government. Paradoxically, peace is not only the precondition for human progress, notably for advancement in moral and legal justice; it is also the worthy object of justifiable war with all its horrors. We do well to bear in mind that it is God who has set us in two Cities and placed on us the awesome responsibility of coping with the requirements of each.

Undoubtedly it is better for a Red to be alive than dead. But God has given men the high vocation not merely of choosing how to live, but also of choosing how to die. Moreover, history teaches that the more clearly a people makes it known that it will not submit, no matter what the cost, the greater prospect that people has of both survival *and* freedom — of avoiding the forbidding alternatives, Red or dead.

Human Way of "Imitation"

The teaching of Christ, then, does not make a convincing case for pacifism. However, the principled pacifist had yet another argument—namely that the Christian spirit invites us to imitate the *example* of Christ, especially in that supreme outpouring of love in which Christ allowed His enemies to nail Him to death. The question now posed is to what extent we humans may imitate Christ, apart from his miraculous powers and works. "He was led as a lamb to the slaughter and opened not his mouth." "Come and follow me for I am meek and humble of heart." Were we not all asked to carry our cross in his likeness?

The reply must be that the Redemptive Act ratified by the Resurrection is entirely and exclusively Christ's own to fulfill. He alone could offer to the Divine Majesty condign satisfaction for the original insolence of man, and it is through his merits that we are restored to the benefits of grace in the supernatural life. We do not in any efficient manner share in the Redemptive Act, nor can we imitate it. Neither natural nor legal justice requires or permits an innocent man to serve another man's jail sentence, nor to die for him in expiation of a capital offense. A citizen may pay another's fine or provide funds for the settlement of a civil suit, but this is scarcely vicarious action; financial means are simply made available to another in order to satisfy a court's judgment. True, in the Garden of Gethsemani, Christ told Peter to put away the two swords; but this rejection of natural and supernatural weapons must be related to the uniqueness of the Redemption which was Christ's principal mission on earth and His alone to accomplish.

We may and should imitate Him in behavior that it is in accord with our humanity and with our vocation in life. Contrariwise, there are many morally correct human actions — indeed duties — which I, for one, find extremely difficult to imagine Our Lord performing. For example, I can imagine Christ as a carpenter assisting St. Joseph. I cannot imagine Him as a hangman. I cannot imagine Christ as a policeman shooting a criminal who is assaulting an innocent person. Yet civilized society cannot endure without officers of the law armed with guns — or, even like English Bobbies, with clubs — who are obliged to capture criminals, and bring them to the processes of justice.

The Heroism of Contemplating the Consequences

What of human heroism? An individual is about to be assaulted and robbed. He is likely to be seriously hurt, even killed. Should he "turn the other cheek," offer no resistance, accept meekly the damaging blows? If he is free of temporal, familial, civic, or military responsibilities, if he has not been entrusted with the safety and welfare of others, he may choose to do so. Nuns, priests, and missionaries, who have separated themselves from family responsibilities by religious vows and the superior duties of a religious vocation, ordinarily do not retaliate and fight. They may have taught others how to defend themselves through armed resistance; but for themselves they choose to submit to torture, and to die as martyrs. It is otherwise with laymen. As the father of a family is morally bound to defend himself and his own, no statesman or government may meekly turn over a nation, "in the name of Christianity," to the domination of an aggressor. Englebert Dollfuss chose to die rather than acquiesce in Hitler's "peaceful" takeover of Austria. History records countless instances of patriots who chose to die rather than betray their country.

A further word is in order concerning religious martyrdom; to which principled pacifists sometimes refer. Men who die for their religious faith do not actively seek opportunities for martyrdom. They are typically in hiding, or go about, like early Christians, without visible signs of identification. They meet in secrecy, in catacombs. They make earnest efforts to avoid detection while always avoiding cowardice. If they are apprehended, jailed, or tortured, it is not because they have sought out these afflictions. They were obliged to avoid being caught; their martyrdom consists in having preferred death to apostasy.

The pacifist who objects to all wars on "principle" is, at least, consistent (though he is content to enjoy the safety that others earn for him by their sacrifices). But what of the "part-time pacifist," mentioned earlier?

Doubtless, there are some who are truly convinced that a particular war is unjust, or that, in the weighing of evils, submission in this particular case is morally preferable to violent resistance. And of course no one denies that, guided by the lights of conscience, such persons are morally bound to "obey God rather than men." But note that such men enjoy all the advantages of democracy without any of its liabilities. They approve the democratic processes of an open society; they approve the idea of the people electing a government charged with the awesome responsibility to guide the domestic and international affairs of the nation through its presumably superior knowledge and competence (always subject, of course, to public criticism and accountability). Yet, unlike the rest of the nation, they refuse to defer to the government in time of crisis. They reserve to themselves the right of ultimate judgment as to the moral and legal correctness of governmental decisions. Granted, a genuine conflict may arise between government policy and a subjective conscience. But ought not the constitutional and statutory immunities from government compulsion that the objector enjoys be so exercised as not to give scandal? Should he discredit the public authority by open acts of defiance — e.g., by burning draft cards, exhorting and instructing others in how to evade the draft, obstructing the movement of troops? Why should the dictates of *his* conscience be invested with superior sanctity? The conscientious objector can sometimes overstate his case.

A troublesome question is frequently asked. If resort to armed force for the deliverance of an aggrieved nation like, say, Vietnam, is morally and legally justified, are we then, by parallel agrument, committed to defend all nations in equally grave need of help? The moral law does not require a nation, any more than an individual, to do *all* good. That is beyond human capabilities and possibilities. But the moral law does require that whatever we do *be* good. If a nation is helpless to cope with an aggressor, we are not strictly bound to provide assistance to the point of participating in actual combat, unless we have given solemn pledges which led that nation to believe that its own sacrifices would not be in vain. Without such pledges the attacked nation might have chosen to submit rather than resist hopelessly.

Pacifism is not peace. Nor will it prevent war. It may be that isolationism, appeasement, a negotiated settlement based upon a "neutral" coalition government that includes representatives of the aggressor force, will gradually satisfy the expansionist appetite of the Communist powers and bring about in Vietnam a condition that goes by the name of "peace." But before we adopt that course we are advised to recall Winston Churchill's reflections at the close of the Second World War. ". . . if you will not fight when your victory will be sure and not too costly, you may come to the moment when you will have to fight with all the odds against you and only a precarious chance for survival. There may even be a worse case. You may have to fight when there is no hope of victory, because it is better to perish than live as slaves."

CONSCRIPTION AND THE CONSCIENTIOUS OBJECTORS*

Conscription — Western Europe

Prior to the French Revolution, the system of universal military training and service was unknown. Liability to military duty by every able-bodied male citizen is as ancient as the civil society that wills to survive against conquest or defeat by foreign forces. This call to duty has always rested on the principle that everyone who chooses to enjoy the benefits of civil peace, order, and security, is reasonably obligated to come to the defense of that community. As George Washington observed:

> It may be laid down as a primary position ... that every citizen who enjoys the protection of a free government, owes not only a portion of his property, but even of his personal services to the defense of it.

In the middle of the fifteenth century, Charles VII organized from the mercenaries who had served under him in the Hundred Years' War, the *compagnies d'ordonnance,* and thereby laid the foundation of the national standing army in France.[1] In Spain, the regular army developed with the Italian wars of the sixteenth century. Atkinson notes: "The oldest regiments of the present Spanish army claiming descent from the *tercios* date from 1535." The organization of regular armies at the disposal of the sovereign, trained in accordance with professional standards of military experience, and adaptable to

---

*UNIVERSITY OF WYOMING LAW REVIEW, Vol. vi, n. 2, 1971, pp. 587-660. A lecture addressed to the MILITARY OFFICERS CONFERENCE, Fort Meade, Maryland.

needs as defined in a nascent military science occurred in both France and Spain during the sixteenth century.

The development of standing armies in Europe proceeded at first differently in the various nation states but each was quick to learn and imitate from the undoubted military effectiveness of the other countries. Spain maintained a "relatively high" effective peace strength. The only regular troops in France down to 1660 were comprised of royal guards, some squadrons of "gendarmerie," and some regiments of infantry called significantly "les vieux." In most other countries the only permanent forces kept under arms by their sovereigns included select personal guards, small garrisons, and not infrequently a limited regular army to serve as a nucleus.

If France is to be credited with the rudimentary beginnings of the national standing army, to her must also be attributed important radical innovations in military organization which were undertaken under the direction of the Marquis de Louvois, the celebrated Minister of War, upon the accession of Louis XIV to the French throne.

The all-out effort of the French Revolutionaries to guard their new born Republic against threatened invasion from a coalition of encircling inimical forces as well as against internal peril brought about a radical innovation in French military history that may be labelled as "the nation in arms." Subject to the regular army and navy forces poised against foreign armed might and the troops assigned to internal policing, the First Republic enrolled all citizens and children capable of shouldering arms in the national guard which could be summoned to supplement the public force. The debates in the French Assembly especially from 1789 to 1793 reveal the dilemma posed on the one hand by the insistence of the French libertarians such as Mirabeau, the Duc de Liancourt, and others to recruit a regular army by volunteer enlistment most of whom had never had any previous military training and service, and on the other, the dire necessity of obviating the patent defects of such a plan by compulsory universal training and service—in a word, by national conscription. By 1793 the libertarian plan had been tried and found gravely ineffective. On August 23, 1793, the French Convention decreed[2] what may rightly be designated as the first formal official plan of compulsory military training and service. Ironically, national conscription was born of the need to defend the liberty and security of the French Republic and not from the demands of an all powerful royal sovereign. There is no doubt but that this national conscription and mobilization of French manpower resources must be credited with the survival of the French Republic and the complete collapse of foreign danger.

With the security of the Republic now beyond doubt its aggressive capabilities became manifest by Bonaparte's successes of 1796. Certain apparent inequities of recruitment of the decree of 1793 were corrected by the law of September 5, 1798 in which the term "conscription" was first used to describe compulsory military service.

If France has to this point been responsible for the succession of military organizations that culminated in the system of conscription, it was left to Prussia to develop and perfect the system as a permanent peacetime program. After Napoleon crushed the Prussian armies at Jena in 1806, he sought to make sure that Prussia would not regenerate her former military strength by limiting her armed forces to a mere 42,000 by the terms of the Treaty of Tilsit of 1807. But these restrictions were ingeniously circumvented by the "Krumper system" contrived by General Scharnhorst. The limit of 42,000 set by the Treaty of Tilsit was never exceeded at any one time but by the device of substituting three to five new recruits for an equal number withdrawn each month, Prussia had by 1813, a reserve of 270,000 trained soldiers. When the new Prussian army had attested by its military triumphs to the effectiveness of the short-term compulsory service and reserves, several important advantages, civilian in character, were also vindicated. A truly broad national army had been formed whose patriotism for the Fatherland proved to be superior in ardor and dedication to that of the traditional professional lifetime soldier. Further, by its process of gradual turnover, civilian commitments, personal and familial were not disrupted seriously for any intolerable length of time, nor were any of the industries and requirements of commerce and agriculture seriously thrown off balance. What had been an emergency contrivance of Scharnhorst to circumvent the restrictions of the Treaty of Tilsit became the first scientific military law for universal peacetime military service on September 3, 1814.[3]

If any persuasion was needed to point to the superior effectiveness of the Scharnhorst-Boyen military system, it was painfully and most convincingly borne home by the Prussian victories over Denmark (1864), Austria (1866), Napoleon III (1870). One after the other European states adopted the program of peacetime conscription so that, with the exception of England, practically every country drawn into the vortex of World War I had a sizeable army of citizen soldiers already trained for combat through peacetime conscription. The standing reserve of large national forces trained and ready for combat by peace-time conscription and built up by a short term turn-over program had served more than one advantage. On the one hand, it avoided the prohibitive cost of maintaining large armies of long-term professional volunteers; and, on the other, it was a silent show of strength in the diplomatic power plays. But like a two-edged sword, these advantages gave way to armageddon when ready trained forces were mobilized by rival nations crowding each other geographically.

England

Great Britain alone of all the Great Powers of Europe has partly owing to reliance on its maritime ascendency and to its separation from contiguous foreign borders, and partly from a supposed aversion to conscripted standing armies[4] relied almost entirely upon volunteer enlistment for her needs of land warfare and upon impressment in the navy for her requirements of her farflung empire. The two conscription bills of 1704 and 1707 were rejected by Parliament as unconstitutional. But in the 1750's, Parliament adopted two acts for the forcible induction of vagrants, "the idle poor and disorderly, without means of support." Whether the exemption of the nobility and the gentry, and of the middle class who had a vote in the election of members of Parliament should suggest that conscription was unbecoming for such as these, free and economically *independent* men, and, on the other hand, becoming and beneficent for free but *burdensome* Englishmen, is a matter of conjecture. In 1914 volunteer recruitment failed to fulfill the higher quotas necessary for continental warfare and England stumbled to compulsory military training and service through a succession of poorly conceived and administered experiments at raising troops by the draft system. With the conclusion of the war, England reverted to the volunteer system until April 27, 1923, when England again had recourse to compulsory training and service after the signing of the Munich Pact.

United States

The history of military service in the United States has steadily veered from the earlier prevailing tradition of volunteer recruitment to the draft in time of war until it has become today generally an unquestioned policy of national defense. The sore point of contemporary controversy is compulsory training and service in peacetime in an undeclared war. The American colonials, heirs of the traditional English loose system, were for the most part satisfied with the ability of colonial militia to cope with enemy assaults upon closely-grouped settlements. That volunteer military service even in time of war was the prevailing mind is attested to in several ways by the set of grievances in the Declaration of Independence protesting not only the presence of standing armies in times of peace without the consent of colonial legislatures, the independence and superior status of the military over the civil, and the quartering of armed troops among the colonials, but also — more to the point — "He has constrained our fellow-citizens, taken captive on the high seas, to bear arms against their country. . . ." But the experience of the American Revolution made only too patent the weakness of the militia system for united defense. At least nine of the States adopted constitutions during the Revolutionary War which sanctioned compulsory military service.[5] But with the exception of Massachusetts and Virginia, which resorted to conscription, the American Revolutionary War was fought and won by volunteer recruits. However, the weaknesses of the militia system for united defense, for the more complex organizational requirements of maneuvering against an enemy marshalled in large numbers and proceeding according to planned military strategies, were almost tragically revealed during the American Revolution.

The Continental Congress authorized a regular force, but did not (could not) compel recruitment. At best, their authorizations carried no more weight than urgent recommendations to the colonies that they provide for the common cause. Undoubtedly, the Revolutionary War would have been concluded in less time and with less casualties, had Washington's protest against the militia system been heeded. Surely, a permanent armed force with substantially the same men trained and disciplined for combat and committed for the war's duration was to be preferred to the annual shift of fresh recruits, untrained and inexperienced in the contemporary military engagements. The Articles of Confederation spoke of the necessity of a minimal "body of forces" for the defense of each state in time of peace (Article VI) and of land forces "raised by any state for the common defense" (Article VII) without specifying how each state should recruit and without conferring upon the Confederacy any power of recruitment. The Constitution of 1789 set down that the Congress shall have power to declare war, raise and support armies, provide and maintain a navy, call forth the militia and provide for their organization and arming (Article I, Sec. 8) without explicitly saying whether that meant a national recruitment, voluntary or compulsory, separate from and in addition to the "calling forth of the state militia." This inattention may be due, as Story explained *(Commentaries,* No. 1187), to the mind at the Federal Convention that the legislative branch of government be designated as the sole power to raise armies[6] in time of peace as well as during a period of armed conflict. Even so, a sort of check was placed upon the Congress by the constitutional provision that "no appropriation of money to that use shall be for a longer term than two years." (Article I, Sec. 8, cl. 12). We may note here that Rhode Island, which was the last of the thirteen original states to ratify the Constitution, made earnest effort to get an amendment that would bar conscription.

Scarcely a year after his inauguration, President Washington, who had known the dangerous uncertainties of an impermanent and inexperienced army during the War of Independence, proposed to the Congress on January 21, 1790, the cultivation of a well-regulated militia through universal training for young men between eighteen and twenty. The trainees were to spend approximately a month in camp for the first two years and only ten days, the third year. Congress was not amenable to the presidential recommendation.[7] The War of 1812 disclosed only too patently the tragic shortcomings of the untrained volunteers of the militia. But the proposal in 1814 for the conscription of men for the Army by James Monroe, then Secretary of War, was strongly attacked by Daniel Webster in the Senate and widely unpopular with the people. The war ended with the Treaty of Ghent (Christmas Eve, 1814) before the bill could be enacted.[8] A summary presentation of the challenge to the constitutionality of conscription can be found in the Report and Resolutions of the Hartford Convention of January 4, 1815.[9]

The war with Mexico in 1847 proved again the inefficacy of short-term volunteers. While General Scott was halfway to Mexico City approximately 40 per cent of his men returned home because their enlistments had expired. While he waited for replacements, Santa Anna was able to recoup his badly beaten army and again a war had been needlessly prolonged for want of a trained army.

At the outbreak of the Civil War, the States had their militia and the Federal Government a standing army of 16,000 troops, which were stationed mostly on the frontier. Congress was not in session and would not convene for three months. President Lincoln called for 75,000 volunteers for three months service, scarcely adequate time to train men for actual combat. By April, 1862 the Southern Confederacy acknowledged it had failed to realize its military requirements by volunteer enlistments for a full year's service and adopted universal conscription. The failure of the Union states to provide the necessary militia forced the Congress a year later to pass the Enrollment Bill on March 3, 1863, the "Draft Act" as it was called.[10] Riots broke out in New York City and elsewhere. Ninety-eight Federal registrants were killed or wounded in the first four months as they attempted to enforce the registration and enrollment. Although by the conclusion of the war, 1,120,000 were drafted by the Federal Government, only 42,347 were actually inducted into service. The preponderance of the Union forces were volunteers who had joined either in anticipation of the draft or in expectation of generous bounties.

Prior to America's participation in the first World War, efforts were made to provide some stabilized resource of volunteer military service, notably by the Act of 1903[11] and the National Defense Act of 1916.[12] The first war-time conscription in American history was established by the Selective Service Act of May 18, 1917. In addition to the nearly three million who were inducted through the Selective Service Act, approximately one million enlisted voluntarily in the Army, while almost the entire Navy and Marine Corps as well were made up of volunteers. Volunteer recruiting has always been and still remains the primary source and the core of American military manpower as a matter of traditional and cherished *principle;* conscription is designed to supplement it and is by now a fixed *policy* of national defense in time of war, questioned only by those who would restrict such a policy to the status of a declared war but not agree to it for an undeclared war. The Act of 1940 was the first peacetime selective service law enacted in the shadow of war. Apart from the second World War, American combat participation in Korea and Vietnam has taken place under the status of undeclared wars. Active military combat by United States armed forces in undeclared wars are not a rarity in American history. But the military requirements of manpower were always sufficiently provided for without any recourse to compulsory service. What distinguishes our contemporary combat service is that it takes place in that gray area of "peacetime" and undeclared war status by the requirements of a compulsory military training and service law. This has contributed to doubly compound the problematics of the conscientious objector, as we shall observe later on. Be that as it may, consideration of peacetime conscription has been cast within a modern context of the multiple mutual defense treaties, numbering almost fifty, by which our nation through its Presidents and the Senate has committed itself to go to the military defense of its signatory allies in the interest of national security. The precarious peace that may be and has been instantly shattered at different places without any formal declarations of war and at times even against reasonable expectation has made even more urgent the need for preparedness for such eventualities. While our draft policy has emerged almost exclusively from actual wars, today it is related to the immediate prospects of undeclared wars. Whatever tentative conclusions one may come to as to the compatibility of compulsory military training and service laws in peacetime for a democratic society, it would be a serious and misleading misconstruction of the question to relate these laws to a chauvinist militarism or militant nationalism or the arrogance of power of nineteenth century Europe and of ancient Empires.

The Constitutionality of Conscription

The discussion about the constitutionality of conscription is directed to two distinct problems. The first raises the question whether Congress has the constitutional power to enact such laws. The second, while conceding that Congress is empowered by the Constitution to enact compulsory military training and service laws, insists that the exercise of such a power must not violate personal rights guaranteed to the individual by the same Constitution.

Kneedler v. Lane, 45 Pa. St. 238 (1863)[13]

First, the question whether Congress is invested by the Constitution with the legal power to conscript men into military service.

The Civil War draft law of 1863 was put into operation without any challenge in the federal courts, but it was brought before the bar of the Pennsylvania State Supreme Court in a proceeding that may be unmatched for its bizarre turn of circumstances. Henry S. Kneedler, Francis B. Smith and William Francis Nickels sought injunctions to restrain the Enrolling Board of the Fourth Congressional District of Pennsylvania from inducting them into the Union army. They contended that the conscription act of 1863 was unconstitutional because the Federal Government was without power to compel military service by direct action upon a citizen, an action which only the states could lawfully take in recruiting state militias. The constitutional empowerment of Congress to raise armies, they maintained, operates upon the citizen only by volunteer enlistment.

On November 9, 1863, all five members of the Pennsylvania Supreme Court wrote separate and lengthy opinions and split three to two against the constitutionality of the draft act. Chief Justice Lowrie, in the opinion of the court, maintained that the congressional power to raise armies (Art. I, Sec. 8, cl. 12) and the "ancillary power to pass 'all laws which shall be necessary and proper for that purpose'" (cl. 18) were the directly relevant premises controlling the constitutional issue. He found that not even the necessity to suppress insurrection and to repeal invasions constitutionally warranted the federal government to conscript armed forces since even these emergencies were explicitly and specifically provided for by "calling forth the militia." (cl. 15) The Tenth Amendment sets down that "powers not delegated to the United States... are reserved to the States respectively...." Arguing on a narrow construction of the Constitution, he concluded that powers not granted are reserved and none should be implied. In a word, any forced levy of the military by the Congress must be through the States from the state militias under their own state officers and not by any direct action upon the citizens. He also considered the issue independently of the emergency situations of rebellion and invasions (for which cl. 15 specifies the definite mode of federal suppression). Forced levies, he wrote, in order to recruit the regular army, is still not warranted by any constitutional grant of power. Exploring the question further, he would not allow that the mode of coercion of the draft law of 1863 to be constitutional even if *arguendo* it be assumed that the regular army may be recruited from the forced levies. The ultimate catalyst is really the lurking argument of implied powers which the court's opinion rejects in its narrow construction in accordance with the rule of the common law. One would have supposed that by 1963 the Hamiltonian-Marshall doctrine of implied powers had surely by then become unquestioned. Perhaps in an effort to ward off this supposition, he held that the explicit provisions of the Constitution were such on this matter that an implied power interpretation was foreclosed. Chief Justice Lowrie resorted to history. The militia was a state institution and it was called "the militia of the several states." (Article II, Section 2, cl. 1) The right of the states to its own militia was unaffected by the constitutional grant of powers to the federal government. On the contrary, the Constitution specifically defines the manner of suppressing insurrections and repelling invasions by "calling forth the militia." Chief Justice Lowrie objected that the draft law was "an unauthorized substitute for the militia of the states." Its provision, whereby all able-bodied men within certain age groups "are 'declared to constitute the national forces'. . . , covers the whole ground of the militia, and exhausts it entirely." On the telling question of the jurisdiction of the state supreme court to adjudicate the litigation, he maintained that a federal officer no less than a state officer could be sued in the state courts. Besides, President Lincoln's suspension of the privilege of the writ of habeas corpus removed the federal avenue to the United States Supreme Court and only the state courts were available to afford relief.

Both of the concurring opinions of Justices Woodward and Thompson stressed the undoubted influence of the English tradition upon the thinking of the framers of our constitution. "Assuredly!" wrote Justice Woodward, "the framers of our constitution did not intend to subject the people of the states to a system of conscription which was applied in the mother country only to paupers and vagabonds. On the contrary, I infer that the power conferred on Congress was the power to raise armies by the ordinary English mode of voluntary enlistments." Besides, he emphasized, the true test of constitutional government is to preserve its provisions in the very time of crisis.

> Times of rebellion, above all others, are the times when we should stick to our fundamental law, lest we drift into anarchy on one hand, or into despotism on the other. The great sin of the (present) rebellion consists in violating the constitution, whereby every man's civil rights are exposed to sacrifice.[14]

Justice Thompson repeated much the same argument, the continuity with the English tradition, and wrote with expression of deeply felt emotion how on his recent visit to the slopes of Runnymede, the memory of the English past "sent a thrill to my heart in admiration of those old barons who stood up there and demanded from a tyrannical sovereign that the lines between power and right should be then and there distinctly marked.... Our forefathers marked those lines in the federal constitution. I must adhere to them"[15]

Both of the separate dissenting opinions of Justices Strong and Reed argued, on the contrary, to the constitutionality of the draft with reliance upon the doctrine of implied powers. They would not allow that the federal government could have a lesser power to draft men than the states had. They noted that while there are limitations upon the means which may be used for the support of the army the government, for example, could not arbitrarily seize private property for the maintenance of the army nor could an appropriation be longer than the explicitly prescribed two year span there were no restrictions set upon the means of raising an army.

The *Kneedler* case is a bizarre curiosity in the history of constitutional law. The restraining injunctions set by the Pennsylvania Supreme Court majority upon the federal offices on November 9, 1863 were vacated on January 16, 1864 by the conversion of the former minority into a new majority when Justice Agnew succeeded to the bench upon the retirement of Chief Justice Lowrie. To the despair of the hapless new minority, the court now held by benefit of the newly formed majority that the state did not have the legal power to interfere by injunction, even if the draft law were deemed beyond the constitutional delegation of power to the Congress. As to the propriety of vacating a court decree by a numerical shift of concurrence after the decree has been put into final form and without benefit of new facts to warrant reconsideration, we leave that to the academic disquisitions of scholars of American law. The *Kneedler* case was the only court test of the legality of the first wartime military draft and the action of the federal government prevailed simply by a routine exchange of personnel on the bench. Despite the fact that the *Kneedler* case covers approximately one hundred pages in the Pennsylvania reports, it received no more than a short allusion to it from Chief Justice White in his opinion in the *Selective Draft Law Cases* in 1918 and without any notice at all of the bizarre reversal of the first decision by the second.

Selective Draft Law Cases — World War I

It was not until 1918 that the constitutional power of the federal government to conscript able-bodied men into the armed forces was upheld by the United States Supreme Court ruling in the *Selective Draft Law Cases*.[16] Conscription was attacked on several grounds: it operated to preempting the states of their right to "a well-regulated militia," that the power which the constitution confers upon the Congress to require compulsory service is that of "calling forth the militia" which is immediately related to three specifically designated objectives— "to execute the laws of the union, suppress insurrections and repel invasions" (Article I, section 8, cl. 15) without any mention of military combat service abroad, and thirdly, that conscription imposes involuntary servitude in violation of the Thirteenth Amendment. In addition, it was contended that the Draft Act was in contravention of the religious clauses of the First Amendment, since the Act provided exemption to religious conscientious objectors and to ministers of religion and theological students. (This later charge was summarily rejected out of hand by the Court without any direct confrontation with and consideration of the issue raised.[18]) The Supreme Court responded that the powers of the states to raise militia must be viewed subject to the superior power of the federal government to raise and support armies; that the congressional power to raise an army is a separate empowerment from the constitutional authorization for "calling forth the militia" and being independent of it, is in no way limited by it. (The *a minus a maius* argument of *Kneedler* appears here reversed for a more effective defense of national power.)

The constitutionality of conscription is based then squarely upon the power of the Congress "to raise and support armies," an empowerment that the Supreme Court declares to be separate and independent of the constitutional delegation of power to the Congress "to provide for calling forth the militia to execute the laws of the union, suppress insurrections and repell [sic] invasions." A great number of litigations while conceding the validity of compulsory service have challenged the legality of a specific law because it was alleged it violated certain constitutional rights. In every instance lower federal courts have upheld the constitutionality of the law and its application.[19]

CONSCIENTIOUS OBJECTORS UNDER AMERICAN LAW

A Historical-Legal Conspectus

In discoursing on conscientious objectors, we are focusing primarily on the moral claim they make upon legal protection for the immunity and inviolability of their claim of conscience, which, practically, means not to be coerced to combat duty. There are of course other related questions, whether they ought also to be excused from noncombat participation in military operations, or even against assignment to civilian services outside the military. There is too the very troublesome question of selective conscientious objection to a particular war. Cognate to the discussion but not agnate to it is the question of the preferential status that follows upon ministerial exemption. This too poses a vexing constitutional problem. If on the one hand, religion is defined in the traditional sense of ontological and moral relations of man to God, a transcendental Being, the Creative Author of all reality, who is to be worshipped, loved, and obeyed, then a minister or divinity student of such a creed who is exempted from military service is surely being preferred over leaders of or official representatives of non-religious congregations, v.g. such as the Secular Humanist. If on the other hand, religion be widely understood as ultimate belief without any requirement that the ultimate be related to an Absolute Being distinct from and superior to the human conscience, as was first proposed directly in *Torcaso v. Watkins*,[20] and earlier and less directly in the dictum in *Everson v. Board of Education*,[21] then a different complexus of problems arise.[22]

Prior to the formation of the National Government, sensitive concern for the inviolability of the religious conscientious objector to the bearing of arms reaches back to the earliest collective resistance on the part of the colonies. Scarcely two weeks after the First Continental Congress had issued its Declaration of the Causes and Necessity of Taking Up Arms (July 8) for the protection of their rights, the Congress on July 18, 1775 passed a resolution advising— (it could do no more)—the colonists to respect the rights of conscience of those who were opposed to the bearing of arms because of their religious beliefs. Since it would yet be another year before the Colonists would break definitely with England this respectful counsel to exemption takes on added significance when projected against the need of an effective resort to armed resistance to secure their rights. But this should not be too surprising. The Continental Congress was acting within a traditional frame of mind on the matter which was already widely expressed during the earlier revolutionary period by constitutional provisions or by statutes.[23] The proffered exemption—in some instances restricted to christians and in others extended to non-christians—was accompanied by the requirement that the beneficiary of this exemption engage in some charitable or purely civil service as the circumstances warranted. Strikingly anticipatory of the first federal draft act of 1863, the exempted conscientious objector was generally required to obtain a substitute or provide funds in order to pay for a substitute.[24]

The Annals of the First Congress, which undertook, at Madison's insistence, to fulfill the pledge given on a Bill of Rights, disclose nothing more than tentative considerations on incorporating a provision for religious conscientious objectors each of which was cancelled by critical objections that prevailed over the proffered suggestions.[25] Whether or not the final rendering of the religious clauses of the first amendment embodied any congressional intent for the protection of those conscientiously scrupulous of bearing arms is a question that receives some light but no definite settlement from the amendment which the House tagged on to the Senate Federal Draft Bill of 1814 which James Monroe as Secretary of War had proposed to the Congress for the more effective prosecution of the War of 1812. The House amendment stipulated exemption from military conscription for the religious conscientious objectors because of their membership in a "religious sect or denomination of Christians."[26] Though the proposed Draft Act did not pass both houses of Congress, the overwhelming vote of the House of Representatives to the amended Senate version would suggest that the near contemporaries of the founders of the Republic had not inherited a conclusive mind on the specific coverage of the conscientious objectors by the first amendment.

At the outbreak of the Civil War, both the Union and the Confederacy gathered the manpower for its armed forces indirectly by stipulating the quotas that each state must provide from its militia. Consequently the conditions for exemption from military service were regulated by the state constitutions or statutory laws. As we have already noted, the ineffectiveness of this circuitous system of fulfilling the requirements of military manpower was first acknowledged by the Southern Confederacy when it resorted to universal conscription in April, 1862, and a year later by the Union, when it passed the Enrollment Bill on March 3, 1863. In the debates on the first federal draft act of 1863, broadly three approaches were discussed on how to cope with the problem of the conscientious objector. Should the federal government be regulated by the already existent state proviso on the matter; should the federal government have its own law providing exemption for those whose consciences on military participation was regulated by the creed of a religious sect; the third approach, more involved than the first two, required that the conscientious objector should first petition a federal court and seek relief upon proof of sincerity.[27] None of these approaches to the problem survived the critical objections levelled against each and consequently the Act of March 3, 1863 became law without any exemption for the conscientious objector save that of substitution or commutation upon payment of $300.00. In response to wide public protest against the monetary commutation clause, the Act was amended the following year, February 24, 1864 to provide for noncombatant service to the conscientious objector who has given sufficient proof of his religious motivation.[27]

Less than a year before the United States entry into World War I, the Congress enacted the National Defense Act of June, 3, 1916, which, in view of the gathering probability of American involvement in the European theatre, surprisingly did not establish the machinery or the organization for an overall national mobilization. The Act authorized exemption from military service for religious ministers and conferred upon the President the power to regulate the exemption for objectors who are motivated by religious beliefs and whose claim could be reasonably ascertained to be conscientiously authentic. Such a one was nonetheless required to fulfill certain designated noncombatant services.

The Draft Act of May 18, 1917 was the first wartime *national* conscription in American history as compared with the sectional conscription of the Southern Confederacy and of the North during the Civil War. It committed the nation to a full mobilization of manpower and resources. Its broad basis was the "liability to military service of all male citizens" and its plan was a "selecture draft" of citizens between 21 and 31 years of age for military service for the duration of the emergency. It authoritatively disowned once and for all the earlier practices of bounties, substitutions and fiscal commutation for the payment of a substitute. There were several categories of the exempted: ministers, students of divinity, some higher public officials, men engaged in essential occupations as the President might in his discretion regulate, and serious obligations of dependency. As to the conscientious objector in the bearing of arms, the Draft Act of 1917 restricted their exemption to those religious scruples which were related to membership in a recognized pacifist sect.[28] The Act authorized the President to designate noncombatant services which the exempted could be required to fulfill. The obviously narrow restriction of the exempted to affiliation with an historic pacifist church was considerably widened by presidential regulation which defined the noncombatant military services to which the exempted could be assigned and which was expressed in such a way as to include religious conscientious objectors without the concomitant requirement of membership in a historic pacifist sect.[29]

On August 3, 1919 almost a year after the signing of the Armistice (on November 11, 1918), Newton Baker, then Secretary of War, recommended to the Congress a bill which proposed three months of compulsory military training for those between the ages of 18 and 19. Representative Julius Kahn and Senator Chamberlain at first urged that all young men undergo six months training and to be subject to additional training for five more years. Later, as a part of the Army Reorganization Act, which they too sponsored, the requirements were reduced to four months military training for 19 year olds and enrollment in the organized reserves for five years with subsequent refresher courses for two summers, but they were not liable to any military service. These provisions were defeated along party lines.[30] In what eventually became the National Defense Act of 1920, the compulsory provisions were replaced by voluntary enlistments.

The Act of 1940 was the first peacetime selective service law. It differed from the 1917 Draft Act in several aspects. It lacked the urgency of the World War I Act which was passed after the declaration of war. Consequently, it was a training and service act with emphasis on training. But what is more to our study, the word "deferment" in the Act of 1940, with its implication of an abiding duty to serve, replaces the employment of the word "exemption" which had appeared in earlier draft law of 1917. Since the two Supreme Court decisions that are related indirectly or directly to the conscientious objector are the 1917 and the 1948 draft acts and several lower court rulings are interpretive of the 1940 draft law, it suffices to note now that since 1917 there have been the 1940, 1948, and recently, the Military Selective Service Act of 1967, which took cognizance of the Supreme Court's constructive interpretation of religious scruples in the *Seeger* case of 1964. Congressional legislative provisions on conscientious objectors will be examined in the light of judicial review.

The Conscientious Objector and the Decisional Law

The constitutionality of the 1917 Draft Act was challenged in the *Selective Draft Law Cases*. In declaring that act constitutional, the United States Supreme Court summarily dismissed the argument that the exemption clause was violative of the first amendment's establishment and free exercise clauses.

> We pass without anything but statement the proposition that an establishment of a religion or an interference with the free exercise thereof repugnant to the First Amendment resulted from the exemption clause of the act . . . because we think its unsoundness is too apparent to require us to do more.[31]

Since in fact the 1917 Act provided for religious objectors affiliated with a historic peace church, and a claim under that statutory definition would be upheld, it is interesting to conjecture what regard the Court would have for the inviolability of the religious objector to war whose religious denomination or church did not forbid participation in war in any form. Or, further, whether the legislative phrase of a member "of any *well-recognized* sect or organization" (whose "existing creed or principles forbid its members to participate in war in any form") was not a precarious contingency on the significance of a believer's sect to others not of his sect. Or, again, what of the churches whose creed did not forbid arms bearing but who adopted vigorous statements in support of the right of individual Church members to be conscientious objectors.[32] Since none of these issues were directly placed before the Court for review, the summary disposition of the conscientious objector in the complex problematics that could be raised under the religious clauses of the First Amendment is tolerably acceptable since it was technically correct. That particular issue was not directly before the Court. To the charge that conscription was violative of the Thirteenth Amendment proscription of involuntary servitude the Court, as if to express its opinion of how seriously it thought it should regard this constitutional challenge, disposed of this issue in the concluding part of its opinion.

> Finally, we are unable to conceive upon what theory the exaction by government from the citizen of the performance of his supreme and noble duty of contributing to the defense of the rights and honor of the nation, as a result of a war declared by the great representative body of the people, can be said to be the imposition of involuntary servitude in violation of the prohibitions of the Thirteenth Amendment, we are constrained to the conclusion that the contention to that effect is refuted by its mere statement.

To begin with, the response obviously skirts around the question of the conscientious objector, which technically is not before the Court. The reference to duty to defend a nation in a declared war, while prima facie may raise a distinction between the sense of duty for a declared war and an undeclared war, would by today be an academic question. True, in the past, voluntary enlistments were able to cope with any number of undeclared wars. Today, that would be seriously questionable. Further, whether a declared war has greater demands than an undeclared war, might be hedged today with a number of collateral considerations. The immediacy with which the Commander-in-Chief may have to respond to an obligation incurred under a mutual defense treaty, and the subsequent congressional enactment of draft laws and monetary appropriations directly related to the bellicose engagement, may have reduced the solemnity and technicality of a formal declaration of war to less than an invalidating norm.[33] Chief Justice White did allude to the Civil War *Kneedler* case and found therein an identity of ruling with the instant one. He did not aver, as we have already noted earlier, to the bizarre way in which the first ruling in *Kneedler* was reversed by a sudden shift of court personnel. Though he did not mention that *Kneedler* preceded the Thirteenth Amendment, a fact that would not have any significant bearing on the question of conscription, the referral of the 1863 decision to a formal declaration of war as compared with present day conscription for an undeclared war would not, again it seems to us, hold any telling significance upon the merits of the issue.

A number of Supreme Court and lower court rulings intervening between the *Selective Draft* cases of 1918 and the Selective Training and Service Act of 1940[34] have established that decisional law holds to date that exemption from bearing arms because of religious scruples is a matter of congressional grace and not a constitutional right whose inviolability is guaranteed by the first amendment. Historically, there is much that is debatable and on either side of the question, a position of inference may be drawn neither of which may be said to be conclusively persuasive. The fragmentary and summary accounts of the debates on the conscientious objector in the first Annals of Congress which formulated the Bill of Rights leads us to no certainty on the matter. It was thought of and discussed and dropped for the legislatures to decide as a matter "of benevolence" — whether that benevolence was a tactical posture to counter all practical objections or a denial of constitutional right cannot be settled with any degree of certainty. The House amendment to the proposed federal draft act of 1814 provided exemption from conscription for the conscientious objector who was scrupulous of bearing arms because of his affiliation with a religious sect. This may indicate, on the one hand, that the Congress of 1814 did not think that the first amendment provided such a protective coverage for the dissenter, and, on the other, it may be that the House took upon itself to resolve what the first Congress did not resolve. How much of the widespread opposition to the contemplated conscription act of 1814, which never actually became law, and in particular the strongly worded remonstrance against it by the Hartford Convention express what the constitutional law was understood to be or should be is again an unresolved question. The provision for substitution or exemption upon payment of $300.00 in the conscription law of 1863 may be used as an argument for either side. It might indicate a constitutional right to exemption conditioned by some compensatory action or it simply affirms the right of the government to require a certain number of servicemen no matter how forthcoming. The emendation of a year later in the Act of February 24, 1864 which allowed the dissenter the alternate of noncombat service again does not settle for either side. Court rulings however have been less hesitant in affirming that exemption from bearing arms because of conscientious scruples is dependent upon the grace of benevolence of the legislature. A chronological study of the Supreme Court and lower court rulings on issues which indirectly or directly bear upon the conscientious objector will disclose that the predominating and still prevailing judicial doctrine is the emphasis upon the general duty to defend the fatherland as against the protest of the dissenting conscience and the gradual elevation of the dissenting conscience to greater significant notice and inviolability but within the context of a congressional grace.

United States v. Schwimmer, 279 U.S. 644 (1929)

In 1929 the Supreme Court ruled that an applicant for naturalization could be denied her request because of her pacifist confession,[35] according to the provisions of the Naturalization Act of 1906.[36]

> That it is the duty of citizens by force of arms to defend our government against all enemies whenever necessity arises is a fundamental principle of the Constitution. (ibid. at 650)

> Whatever tends to lessen the willingness of citizens to discharge their duty to bear arms in the country's defense detracts from the strength and safety of the Government. And their opinions and beliefs as well as their behavior indicating a disposition to hinder in the performance of that duty are subjects of inquiry under the statutory provisions governing naturalization and are of vital importance, for if all or a large number of citizens oppose such defense the "good order and happiness" of the United States can not long endure. (ibid. at 650, 651.)

> The fact that she is an uncompromising pacifist with no sense of nationalism but only a cosmic sense of belonging to the human family justifies belief that she may be opposed to the use of military force as contemplated by our Constitution and laws. And her testimony clearly suggests that she is disposed to exert her power to influence others to such opposition.

> A pacifist in the general sense of the word is one who seeks to maintain peace and to abolish war. Such purposes are in harmony with the Constitution and policy of our Government. But the word is also used and understood to mean one who refuses or is unwilling for any purpose to bear arms because of

conscientious considerations and who is disposed to encourage others in such refusal. And one who is without any sense of nationalism is not well bound or held by the ties of affection to any nation or government. Such persons are liable to be incapable of the attachment for and devotion to the principles of our Constitution that is required of aliens seeking naturalization. (ibid. at 651, 652)

Apart from the fact that the applicant for naturalization was a woman forty-nine years of age, a most improbable subject to be called upon to bear arms in defense of the United States, the reasoning of the Court discloses an undefined but none the less overly alarming fear of the corrosive effect of pacifism upon devotion to the Constitution and upon fellow citizens. Though free speech was not the issue before the Court, the Court's premonitions that the applicant "is disposed to exert her power to influence others to such opposition (to war)" discloses the Court's mind on the efficacy of speech to be in accord with its earlier rulings under the Espionage Act of 1917 and the state criminal anarchy statutes.[37]

United States v. Macintosh, 283 U.S. 605 (1931)

Two years later, the Supreme Court, on a five to four split, ruled that Douglas Macintosh, a Canadian by birth and a professor of theology at Yale, whose application for naturalization had been declined by the lower courts, could not be admitted because, though not a pacifist, he would not give a definite pledge in advance to fight in any war in which the country should engage.[38] In response to the query of the Naturalization Act of 1906, "Are you willing to bear arms in defense of the United States?", he wrote: "Yes, but I should want to be free to judge of the necessity." *Macintosh* clearly sets forth the apparent antinomy between a claim of inviolability of conscience on the bearing of arms and the general patriotic duty to come to the defense of the fatherland. The question is with whom does the ultimate decision on the righteousness of war rest?[39]

The *Macintosh* case is clearly distinguishable from the earlier *Schwimmer* case. In the latter case, there was an apparent contrariety between an uncompromising pacifism and the duty implied in the manifold benefits that a citizen enjoyed under the Constitution to fight if necessary for its survival. Actually, the Court in *Schwim-*

mir veered more to the bad tendency latent in a free speech advocacy of pacifism. In *Macintosh* the Court was confronted with the age-old problem of ultimate and absolute allegiances, to God and to country, and in this instance, it was not an abstract question, but concretely, the United States of America with high credentials as a democratic and generally speaking, a beneficent governance. We must note that though *Macintosh* is a conscientious objector case, it is not the customary one. To begin with, he is not a citizen of the United States but seeks citizenship. Further, he is not objecting to all wars — he had served as a chaplain of the Canadian Expeditionary Force in World War I — but more precisely, he refuses to commit himself *a priori* to underwrite the moral righteousness of any war in which America may be a participant and to bear arms at her calling. In a word, he claims the right of conscience to be a selective conscientious objector as a citizen of the United States. While he was anticipating the more common issue of today, that of the selective conscientious objector, he was at the same time proceeding from a less firm position, that of an applicant to citizenship, a privilege which the American government need not "bargain" about with any alien.

Justice Sutherland gave the majority opinion denying the right to citizenship:

> In effect, he offers to take the oath of allegiance only with the qualification that the question whether the war is necessary or morally justified must, so far as his support is concerned, be conclusively determined by reference to his opinion.

> When he speaks of putting his allegiance to the will of God above his allegiance to the government, it is evident, in the light of his entire statement, that he means to make his own interpretation of the will of God the decisive test which shall conclude the government and stay its hand. We are a Christian people according to one another the equal right of religious freedom, and acknowledging with reverence the duty of obedience to the will of God.

> But, also, we are a nation with the duty to survive; a nation whose constitution contemplates war as well as peace; whose government must go forward upon the assumption, and safely can proceed upon no other, that unqualified allegiance to the nation and submission and obedience to the laws of the land,

Conscription and the Conscientious Objectors 421

as well those made for war as those made for peace, are not inconsistent with the will of God.

The applicant here rejects that view. He is unwilling to rely, as every native-born citizen is obliged to do, upon the probable continuance of Congress of the long established and approved practice of exempting the honestly conscientious objector, while at the same time asserting his willingness to conform to whatever the future law constitutionally shall require of him; but discloses a present and fixed purpose to refuse to give his moral or armed support to any future war in which the country may be actually engaged, if, in his opinion, the war is not morally justified, the opinion of the nation as expressed by Congress to the contrary notwithstanding....

It is not within the province of the courts to make bargains with those who seek naturalization. They must accept the grant and take the oath in accordance with the terms fixed by law, or forego the privilege of citizenship. There is no middle choice. If one qualification of the oath be allowed, the door is open for others, with utter confusion as the probable final result.

There is no intimation of any probability of an unjust war by the United States, but rather, on the contrary, the unquestioned deference to be shown to the morally unfailing democratic process by which a nation is committed through congressional declaration of war. It may be that America is viewed as the light of the world. Communism and Facism had already emerged on the Continent as a threat to the European democracies and the awesome lesson of the Nuremburg was still in the future. But as far as the constitutional issue was concerned — could Macintosh invoke a constitutional right under the first amendment to refuse to bear arms because of religious conscientious objections? *Macintosh* states unequivocally for the first time the doctrine which to this date has persisted and seems likely to endure unchanged that exemption from military service because of religious scruples is not a constitutional right but a matter of congressional grace.

This, if it means what it seems to say, is an astonishing statement. Of course, there is no such principle of the Constitution, fixed or otherwise. The conscientious objector is relieved from the obligation to bear arms in obedience to no constitutional provision, express or implied, but because, and only because, it has accorded with the policy of the Congress thus to relieve him. The alien, when he becomes a naturalized citizen, acquires, with one exception, every right possessed under the Constitution by those citizens who are native born.... The privilege of the native-born conscientious objector, to avoid bearing arms comes not from the Constitution but from the acts of Congress. That body may grant or withhold the exemption as in its wisdom it sees fit; and if it be withheld, the native-born conscientious objector cannot successfully assert that privilege. No other conclusion is compatible with the well-nigh limitless extent of the war powers as above illustrated, which include, by necessary implication, the power, in the last extremity, to compel the armed service of any citizen in the land, without regard to his objections or his views in respect to the justice or morality of the particular war in general.[40]

The startling fact of the majority opinion in *Macintosh* is its affirmation about the "well-nigh limitless extent of the war powers."

From its very nature, the war power, when necessity calls for its exercise, tolerates no qualifications of limitations, unless found in the Constitution or in applicable principles of international law.[41]

Chief Justice Evans Hughes gave the celebrated minority opinion concurred in by Justice Holmes, Brandeis, and Stone. The majority opinion upheld the constitutionality of the Naturalization Act even while understanding its requirement of a promise to bear arms to be unconditional and absolute. The dissenting opinion, on the contrary, would not call into question the constitutionality of the Naturalization Act because it read its commitment to bear arms not to be absolute, but rather a requirement subject to higher moral imperatives, a supposition demanded by the constitutional guarantee of religious liberty of conscience.

While it has always been recognized that the supreme power of the government may be exerted and disobedience to its commands may be punished, we know that with many of our worthy citizens it would be a most heartsearching question if they were asked whether they would promise to obey a law believed to be in conflict with religious duty. Many of their most honored exemplars in the past have been willing to suffer imprisonment or even death rather than make such a promise. And we also know, in particular, that a promise to engage in war by bearing arms, or thus to engage in a war believed to be unjust would be contrary to the tenets of religious groups among our citizens who are of patriotic purpose and exemplary conduct. . . . Much has been said of the paramount duty to the state, a duty to be recognized, it is urged, even though it conflicts with convictions of duty to God. Undoubtedly that duty to the state exists within the domains of power, for government may enforce obedience to laws regardless of scruples. When one's beliefs collides with the power of the state, the latter is supreme within its sphere and submission or punishment follows. But, in the forum of conscience, duty to a moral power higher than the state has always been maintained. The reservation of that supreme obligation, as a matter of principle, would unquestionably be made by many of our conscientious and law-abiding citizens.

The essence of religion is belief in a relation to God involving duties superior to those arising from any human relation. . . . One cannot speak of religious liberty, with proper appreciation of its essential and historic significance, without assuming the existence of a belief in supreme allegiance to the will of God.

Professor Macintosh, when pressed by the inquiries put to him, stated what is axiomatic in a religious doctrine. And, putting aside dogmas with their particular conceptions of deity, freedom of conscience itself implies respect for an innate conviction of paramount duty. The battle for religious liberty has been fought and won with respect to religious beliefs and practices, which are not in conflict with good order, upon the very ground of the supremacy of conscience within its proper field. What that field is, under our system of government, presents in part a question of constitutional law and also, in part, one of legislative policy in avoiding unnecessary clashes with the dictates of conscience. *There is abundant room* for enforcing the requisite authority of the law as it is enacted and requiring obedience, and for maintaining the conception of the supremacy of law as essential to orderly government, without demanding that either citizens or applicants for citizenship shall assume by oath an obligation to regard allegiance to God as subordinate to allegiance to civil power.[42] (emphasis supplied.)

At this point, it is well to bring into focus and note how much that is said in opposition is not disowned but rather resolves into a coherent, complementary proposition. Morally, the conflict between patriotic duty to defend the country and, on the other, to be true to the dictates of conscience in obedience to God, is complicated by the fact that in either claim of duty there is a presumption of moral correctness, a supposition of course that is rebuttable. We shall have to return to this moral problematic in the concluding part of our discourse which will inquire into the polarity of claims of conscience and of the moral-legal claims of a political community upon its citizens. For the present, we make these observations: exemption from military service for scruples of conscience is by congressional grace. Since *Macintosh* this proposition has not been brought into doubt by the Supreme Court nor by any lower court. However startling it is to read of the limitless extent of the war powers, *salus populi suprema lex*, remains broadly an uncontested affirmation. It is within these two positions that in fact the courts have worked out to the present decisional law on conscientious objectors. Granting the congressional provisions for conscientious objectors, the preferential status formerly given to theistic believers, has by now since the construction of no-establishment in *Everson* and of novel latitudinarian meaning of religion to adumbrate nontheistic beliefs since *Torcaso* and *Seeger,* the right of government to compel every able bodied person to participate in a war effort *somehow* – either by assignment to noncombatant service in the military or to civilian service outside the military – remains undiminished. And we may well conjecture whether with all the moralizing and legal thinking, it has been the realism of the situation that makes possible the course of moral and legal development on the conscientious objector. Namely, *there is abundant room* (in the words of the dissenting opinion) – there is the pragmatic experience that in time of war, a government can rely upon the patriotism of its people for a sufficiency of military manpower both from voluntary and coercive enlistment with all the numerical allowances made for the exempted conscientious objector. The only alternate is a morally justifiable resistance and insurrection against a government committed to war.

Though the 6 to 3 majority of *Schwimmer* dwindled in two years to a 5 to 4 in *Macintosh* (and *Bland*), it was not until fifteen years later that the dissenting opinions would emerge for the majority in *Girouard v. United States*.[43] The Court, in effect, reversed the three earlier[44] cases, by holding that Girouard may be admitted to citizenship because he was willing to take the oath of allegiance and to serve in the army as a non-combatant, but who, because of his religious scruples — he was a Seventh Day Adventist — was unwilling to bear arms. The Court reasoned *a maiore ad minorem* by noting that similar religious scruples would not bar a citizen from public office, that of congressman not excluded, and surely, the national legislature could not have intended stricter requirements for aliens requesting citizenship than for public officials who legislate and administer law. In 1950 the Court went further and would admit to citizenship a man who would not serve in the Army in any capacity.[45] Strictly speaking, the *Girouard* ruling does not of course deny that Congress has the right to require military service as a prerequisite for naturalization but rather conditions it with alternate equivalents with due regard for the immunity of conscience guaranteed by the religious clauses of the first amendment.

Intervening Lower Federal Court Reasonings Conducive to the Seeger Decision of 1965

Deference to rights of conscience is a sensitivity which American law has gradually and in increasing extensions reached to a variety of claims. But in almost all such protests of conscientious scruples a limit is set that somehow subordinates an absolute immunity to the interests of national security or in a weighing of interests a superior claim of general welfare. This is noted for example in the concurring opinion of Mr. Justice Cardozo in *Hamilton v. Regents of the University of California*,[46] who notes that the exercise of private judgment is not beyond all restriction. Similarly, the exercise of free speech and press in times of war will undoubtedly be subordinated to national security and defense whatever the reappraisal in retrospect of the reality of the dangers to the national war effort and of the appropriate canon of constitutional construction of "danger" in the first World War cases.[47] Be that as it may, the duty to participate in the defense of the nation *in someway,* provided for by the national compulsory military training and service, is evident in the very provisions on conscientious objectors — there is to be some form of authoritatively stipulated and assignable service. There is no constitutional right to exemption[48] and the mandatory alternates to actual combat service underscore what *Macintosh* and succeeding court rulings have established as a principle beyond doubt. But there has been a gradual enlargement of the category of the conscientious objector from the first World War Draft Act of 1917, which provided for conscientious objectors who were members of "any well-recognized sect or organization...whose creed or principles forbid its members to participate in war in any form," to a consideration of the religious scruples of one not a member in a recognized pacifist sect by the broader terms of an Executive Order.[49] During the congressional committee hearings on the Burke-Wadsworth Conscription Bill in 1940[50] witnesses urged exemption for non-theistic conscientious scruples against the bearing of arms of those who were affiliated with organizations committed to pacifist profession and on such non-religious grounds. It seems that the affiliation with a publicly noted organization as a test or ostensible sign of sincerity of conscientious protest was undoubted on both sides, the theist and non-theist rule of conscience. Though the argument for members of non-theist pacifist organizations did not then prevail, the outcome of the *Seeger* case fifteen years later was to allow for the non-theist without any such membership the same identical protection given to the theist-grounded scruples under the religious clause of the first amendment by an apparently arbitrary enlargements of the conventional meaning of religion. To this end-result, lower federal court opinions contributed by setting in opposition contrary constructions of religious scruples, an opposition which the Supreme Court in *Seeger* would resolve by affirming that there may be no opposition before the law between the ultimate determinants of different individual consciences.

Lower Federal Court Construction of "Religion"

The Burke-Wadsworth Conscription Bill was enacted prior to the American entry into World War II and is known as the Selective Training and Service Act of 1940.[51] The religious scruples against the bearing of arms obviously would rest on the religious liberty clause of the first amendment. But the objector whose conscientious scruples were not rooted in theistic belief could only hope to gain equal consideration before the law by charging preferential treatment of the theistic protestor in violation of the no establishment clause. Nonetheless, despite the basic reasonableness of their rationale, the Act of 1940 only broadened its allowance for exemption from combat training those whose objections were related to religious training and belief.[52] The Act did not limit exemption to members of recognized pacifist sects, but rather extended it to any person "who, by reason of religious training and belief, is conscientiously opposed to participation in war in any form." It in effect legislated what had been permissible during World War I by virtue of the broad terminology of the Executive Order that implemented the 1917 Draft Act. It was, however, an improvement upon the precedent in another regard, — surrogate civilian service was now placed under civilian direction and as a corollary removed the conscientious objector assigned to these civilian tasks from military supervision and from military court martial proceedings. The disengagement of religious scruples from a required affiliation to a historic pacifist sect would of course remove the presumption of an objective test of sincerity. What was now required in order to allow the same claim of subjective conscience for the non-theist was either to reverse the *Macintosh* ruling that exemption was by congressional grace and affirm it to be a constitutional right under the first amendment or, somehow adumbrate under "religion" the nontheistic claim of conscience in order to avoid the challenge to establishment of religion in diminution of the religious liberty clause. These prima facie antinomies were to emerge in fact in lower federal court reasonings and rulings in a polarization between the narrow and broad construction of the meaning of "religion" and so force eventually the Supreme Court to resolve this crucial problem. And so in fact it came about.

The first breach in the traditional meaning of religion which the Congress and the courts[53] had consistently adhered to even against mounting pressures against the narrow construction of the definition of "religion" occurred in 1943, in *United States v. Kauten*,[54] when Justice Augustus Hand set forth one of those *dicta* that eventually courses its way into constitutionality.[55] Kauten had refused to report for induction as required by the Selective Service Act of 1940. His objections to military conscription were not based on religious grounds nor for that matter on moral claims of conscience as he might have done so even as an atheist. Rather, he charged that the American involvement in the war was President Roosevelt's way of coping with the rising rate of unemployment. Obviously, since his protest was political, he could not claim exemption under the religious conscientious objector provisions of the Selective Service Act, and in fact, the circuit court ruled against him. Nonetheless, Judge Augustus Hand in the course of his opinion proceeded without any necessity for the disposition of the case and, contrary to the clear intent of Congress,[56] to reconstruct the federal statute broadly so that "religious" "take into account the characteristics of a skeptical generation and make the existence of a conscientious scruple against war in any form, rather than allegiance to a definite religious group or creed, the basis of the exemption."[57] It is interesting to note that Judge Augustus Hand would uphold the legitimacy of a nontheistic moral claim against all wars but does not allow that a selective conscientious objection — to a particular war — is deserving of equal consideration. Rather, he strongly intimates that generally speaking objection to a particular war is more likely than not political. He concludes with the proposition that is later adopted in the *Seeger* ruling of 1965 which equates the ultimate non-theistic conscientious persuasion to conscientious scruples related to theistic dogmas.[58]

Judge Hand's *dictum* in *Kauten* must have impressed his associate justices because that same year, the same court of appeals ruled in *United States ex rel. Phillips v. Downer*[59] that a stricter view than that expressed by Judge Hand, namely, that which demanded a belief sanctioned by one of the historic peace churches, would restore in essence the requirement of the Act of 1917 which the 1940 Act deliberately set out to amend. An analysis of the circuit court's reasoning will disclose that it was more distinguished for its enlightening and expansive mood than for its accuracy. A reading of the Hearings on the proposed Selective Service Act of 1940[60] reveals that the congressional committees pointedly rejected to allow non-religious protests against war, couched in philosophical and humanitarian terms, to be eligible for exemption from combat service. But the Circuit Court nonetheless was ready to denote philosophical and humanitarian conscientious objections as "religious" — contrary to a consistent traditional use by the courts themselves up to that time of "religious" as connoting theism; further, to identify arbitrarily the "religious" with church membership, and thirdly, by this unjustifiable device, read into the 76th Congress, an intent contrary to their very explicit distinction between the religious scruples against the bearing of arms unrelated to membership (which the Congress now wished to include among the exempted) and the religious protestor who was a member of a historic pacifist sect to whom alone the 1917 Act restricted the exemption.[61] So it was that the second circuit of appeals reasoned by an intellectually uncomfortable amalgam of an innovation in lexicography, by a contrary to fact reconstruction of congressional intent, and by an unreflecting identity of the "religious" with a church-member.

Three years later, the court of appeals of the Ninth Circuit was confronted with the same problem in *Berman v. United States*[62] and after deliberating at length on the *dictum* of *Kauten* refused to adopt it. Judge Stephens noted the similarity, at least in principle, between the situations in the Second Circuit cases and in *Berman* and immediately stated that the court took "divergent views from those expressed in those cases." The court correctly read the congressional intent in the provision "of religious training and belief" to mean training in theistic beliefs and related this meaning to the double purpose that the 76th Congress embodied in the statute, namely, to distinguish between the nontheistic moralist objection to war and the religious, that is, a dictate of conscience related "to an authority higher and beyond any worldly one."[63] These latter the Congress of 1940 wished now to include within the coverage of exemption whether or not they were affiliated with a pacifist church or not. In a word, the Ninth Circuit court noted the obvious that had unaccountably escaped the Second Circuit court, namely, the statute of 1940 was drawing a distinction precisely to provide exemption for the religious, i.e., theistic, scruples of one not a member of a historic pacifist church, and to distinguish such a one from the objector on merely philosophical, sociological or moral grounds, whose belief did not relate to a deity, and not to include the latter within the exemption because he was not a "religious" objector within the meaning of the statute. The Supreme Court refused *certiorari*[64] and left the antinomy between the Second and Ninth Circuit Courts of Appeal to Congress to settle.

The 80th Congress responded to the Court's inaction on the *Kauten-Berman* antinomy by unequivocally agreeing that *Berman* had indeed correctly understood its "plain language" and "specific purpose" of the 1940 statute. In order to dispel any further ingenious reconstruction of its intent such as the Second Circuit Court of Appeals had forged in *Kauten* and *Downer*, it specifically defined the meaning of "religious training and belief," something the Congress had not bothered to do[65] because supposedly it was intelligible in the traditional context of religion as related to Deity, as the Courts themselves had until then so understood.

> Religious training and belief in this connection mean an individual's belief in relation to a Supreme Being involving duties superior to those arising from any human relation, but does not include essentially political, sociological or philosophical views or a merely personal moral code.[66]

But if the Selective Service Act of 1948 determined to abide by the traditional meaning of religion, those whose moral convictions were not theistically grounded and were accordingly excluded from the congressional grace extended to the religious scruples of theists, now shifted their tact and challenged the constitutionality of the statutory provision by raising claims under the guarantees of the First Amendment, issues which until then, had emerged before the court only indirectly[67] and were either summarily dismissed or met by collateral considerations other than those of the religious clauses of the First Amendment.

During the decade and a half following the 1948 Draft Act, the Second, Third[68] and Ninth Circuits construed the statute in keeping with the criteria set down in *Berman* and adopted by Congress in the Draft Act of 1948. Both the Second and Ninth Circuits upheld the constitutionality of the 1948 amendments against First Amendment challenges. In 1952, the Ninth Circuit court was confronted with the charge that the exemption provision of the 1948 Draft Act was an interference with the religious liberty clause or a violation of the no-establishment prohibition of the First Amendment. Here surely would have arisen the opportunity to challenge the Supreme Being clause by pointing to the statutory preference of theistic believing conscientious objectors over non-theistic protestors. But the fact that the defendant was a believer in God denied him the personal claim to make such an assault upon the constitutionality of the exemption provision.[69] Nonetheless, the court chose to discourse about the constitutionality of the exemption as restricted to theistic believers and argued that since the exemption was a matter of legislative benevolence and not of constitutional right, the Congress could set conditions to the exemption at will. Since arbitrary determination might import unreasonableness, as the court itself allowed,[70] such a view would be of doubtful validity in the light of the *Speiser* ruling of 1958.[71]

Though the Court had disposed of the challenge to the constitutionality of the discriminatory exemption of the act of 1948, on the *Macintosh* doctrine of legislative grace and discretionary selectivity, it did nonetheless, take cognizance of the defendant's charge that the exemption provisions did violence to the religious clauses of the First Amendment. The Court pointed to the fact that Congress had formally adopted in 1948 the traditional meaning of "religion" as generally understood "in American society" "and the manner in which it has been defined by courts," namely, "in terms of the relationship of the individual to a Supreme Being." Such a clear understanding underlying "religious training and belief" was easily distinguishable from "political, sociological, philosophical and ethical grounds for opposing the war," and the Congress, even prescinding from the plenary power to provide for the defense of the country, to which the Supreme Court had referred in *Macintosh*, could make a discriminatory classification based upon that distinction without offending the due process clause.[72]

Four years later, the Ninth circuit court was directly confronted with the constitutional issue posed by the First Amendment in *Clark v. United States*.[73] The defendant had been denied exemption from military service because he had not based his scruples upon belief in God. He buttressed his argument by adding to the guarantees of the religious clauses of the First Amendment, the proscription of a "religious test" provision of Article VI of the Constitution. The circuit court dispensed with the appeal to the First Amendment by referring to its own ruling in *George* and discounted the invocation of Article VI as "specious reasoning."[74] Both in *George* and *Clark* the Supreme Court denied *certiorari*.[75]

We have so far observed that the provision of the 1917 Draft Act for religious conscientious objectors related religious scruples to the bearing of arms to membership in a historic pacifist church or sect, a provision that was broadly construed by an executive order in implementation of the statute. The Selective Draft Law Cases of 1918 upheld the constitutionality of the act. The 1940 Draft Law extended the exemption to religious objectors whose scruples were not conditioned by affiliation with a well-known pacifist church or sect. Though the two draft acts provided exemptions to scruples based on "religious beliefs" (1917) and on "religious beliefs and training" (1940), neither statute explicitly and formally mentioned that the religious belief be in God. It is safe to surmise that the traditional meaning of religious belief in a Supreme Being was too obvious to spell out and besides the courts themselves had explicitly or implicitly so understood the term "religion."[76] Having disengaged religious scruples from church-affiliation or confession to any congregational creed, the conscientious objectors then proceeded to attack the constitutionality of the exemption provision for restricting it to scruples which were prompted by religious, that is, theistic belief. When the United States Supreme Court refused to resolve the antinomy between the construction of religion by the Second and Ninth Circuit courts, Congress, in 1948, formally and explicitly adopted the traditional meaning of religion as a relation to theistic doctrine and refused to include within the exemption provision conscientious scruples against arms not based on a belief in God as is abundantly clear from the congressional committee Hearings on the matter.

Whereas the first two challenges were directed against the preferential status conferred by the 1917 and 1940 draft laws upon theistic believers and church affiliation, the third assault was ingeniously construed — once the disengagement from church-affiliation had paved the way — *under* the protective coverage of "religious beliefs" and by entering *within* the meaning of religion. To this ultimate successful challenge, in *Seeger* (1965), propositions originally set forth as dicta in *Everson* and *Torcaso* were to contribute the ideas of "non-preference, "impartiality" and "equivalence" for the latitudinarian mutation of the lexicographical meaning of "religion."

With the dislodgment of the church-membership requirement and the reaffirmation of theism as the core meaning of "religious beliefs" in the statute of 1948, the only course left against congressional intransigence on religious, that is, theistically, motivated scruples against the bearing of arms, was to induce the Supreme Court to subsume non-theistic conscientious protests under the same literary connotation of "religion" as the theistically rooted scruple. The Court could be induced to this purpose by facing it with a dilemma for which the Court itself had paved the way in the last twenty years. The restriction of exemption to pacifist theists was a frankly preferential benevolence denied to non-theist pacifists. But prior to 1947, inspite of the almost general proscription of state financial aid to religious institutions, not only the federal government but even state governments under one form or another, by one justifying rationale or another, provided fiscal benefits to religious institutions and agencies in a large variety of ways. Why is 1947 the origination of that course of dialectical gymnastics that conduced with reasonable expectation the outcome of *Seeger* in 1965?

The First Amendment to the Constitution, of itself, binds only the Federal government. "Congress," says the Amendment, "shall make no law respecting an establishment of religion or prohibiting the free exercise thereof." The States were left free by the Amendment to regulate the regulation between government and religion as they chose. But most of the areas in which religion comes into contact with government lie within the jurisdiction of the States rather than of the Federal government. Such are marriage and the family, public morals, the protection of life and health, some parts of criminal and civil law and, supremely, education. In 1925, however, the Supreme Court began to interpret the Fourteenth Amendment as meaning that the First Amendment was binding on the States as well as on the Federal government. It was not until 1947 that the Court for the first time undertook to apply the establishment of religion clause of the First Amendment to the States and their administrative subdivisions, such as counties, municipalities and school districts. Prior to 1947, the Court had decided only three cases under the establishment clause. All three had involved the Federal government, and in each of these cases the Court upheld the government against the charge that it acted in such a way as to establish religion.

The clause in the First Amendment that "Congress shall make no law respecting an establishment of religion" was first invoked in *Bradfield v. Roberts,* 175 U.S. 291 (1899), where the Supreme Court sustained a federal appropriation for the construction of a public ward to be administered as part of a hospital under the control of Sisters of the Roman Catholic Church. The Court found no prohibited aid to religion but rather a valid appropriation in aid of a group of privately incorporated individuals whose religious affiliations and beliefs were beyond the scope of judicial inquiry. Federal appropriations were again challenged in *Quick Bear v. Leupp,* 210 U.S. 50 (1908), where the Supreme Court distinguished between federal funds held in trust for the beneficial use of Indian wards, at whose request such funds could be used to reimburse the religious schools which they attended, and funds from the public treasury which could not be paid to any sectarian group for educational purposes. The Court, though holding that such use of trust funds in no way violated the First Amendment (citing *Bradfield v. Roberts,* supra), declined to comment on the extent to which the Amendment might forbid a similar expenditure from public funds. In *Selective Draft Law* cases, 245 U.S. 366 (1918), the Supreme Court upheld the Selective Service Act of 1917 over the objection, inter alia, that the clause, exempting ministers and members of religious sects whose tenets deny the moral right to engage in war, constituted an establishment of religion D.6th ('59)

In 1947 the Court upheld the constitutionality of a New Jersey statute which provided at public expense bus transportation to all school children whether they attended governmental schools or non-governmental schools, as a legitimate exercise of state police power.[77] Not content with satisfying the requirements of law, the Court, in acknowledgment of the appellant's contention, also considered whether public aid to religion was constructively a violation of the First Amendment. It pronounced:

> The establishment of religion clause of the First Amendment means at least this: Neither a state nor the Federal Government can set up a church. Neither can pass laws which aid one religion, aid all religions, or prefer one religion over another.... No tax in any amount, large or small, can be levied to support any religious activities or institutions, whatever they may be called, or whatever form they may adopt to teach or practice religion.[78]

What apparently at its face seemed to many jurists at most a *dictum* as far as the precise issue before the Court was in time officially adopted as a constitutional law proposition,[79] and in its light the meaning of the establishment clause has changed considerably from what had been understood by such leading authorities of constitutional law as Storey, Cooley and Corwin.[80] What matters for our discourse is that the Court was putting forth a proposition that has been variously described as one of absolute separation of church and state, of governmental neutrality, of governmental impartiality between believers, and between believers and non-believers. Apart from its implications on governmental fiscal aids to religious institutions, it sets down a proposition which advocates of the "rights" of non-believers, whether for themselves or in denial of governmental action toward others, could use as a premise for the evolution of the notion that the non-believer should have equal status with the believer within the protective coverage of the religious clauses of the

First Amendment. Encouraged then by the *Everson dictum* and undeterred by the reaffirmation of the traditional meaning of religion by the Draft Act of 1948, they succeeded in inducing the Court to make such an admission 14 years later in *Torcaso v. Watkins* (1961) again by a dictum, though not as prominently incorporated within the text of the opinion as in *Everson*, at least appended as a footnote.

In *Torcaso*[81] the right of a citizen to become a notary public without being required by law to make a public declaration of belief in God was upheld. It would have been more felicitous had the court not subsumed in a footnote,[82] by an exercise of logical positivism, nontheistic beliefs into the meaning of religion in the First Amendment. To have preserved even in legal interpretation the traditional meaning of religion as the relation of man to a transcendental being, God, would not have precluded the right of a nontheistic (non-religious) conscience from the protective mantle of the First Amendment religious clauses. *Torcaso* could have adequately rested its ruling on the Anglo-American tradition of law that the right of belief is a right to an internal area of absolute inviolability into which inner sanctum neither the law may inquire nor the coercive power of government force its disclosures.[83] The prolongation of the propositions of *Everson* — originally a dictum — become apparent in the passage in *Torcaso* to which the footnote-dictum is appended.

> Neither (a State nor the Federal government) can constitutionally pass laws or impose requirements which aid all religions as against non-believers, and neither can aid those religions based on a belief in the existence of God as against those religions founded on different beliefs.[84]

Just as it was the antinomy to legal interpretation between the broad construction of "religion" in the Draft Law of 1940 by the Second Circuit court opinions in *Kauten v. United States* (1943) and *United States ex rel. Phillips v. Downer* (1943) and the traditional meaning of religion by the Ninth Circuit court opinion in *Berman v. United States* (1946) that forced Congress to specifically include the Supreme Being requirement in its definition of religious belief in the Selective Service Act of 1948 — in default of judicial review by the United States Supreme Court, so too, it is the antinomy between the opinions of the Second Circuit court — a route understandably favored by the litigants and their lawyers — and the Ninth Circuit court, that would confront the Supreme Court to decide whether the Supreme Being requirement may adumbrate under its dictionary meaning non-theistic believers, as *Torcaso* seemed to augur, or whether it may abide by the traditional meaning of Supreme Being, as the Ninth Circuit court had consistently adhered to. The contest between the *Kauten*[85] (all moral conscientious objectors) and the *Berman*[86] line (theistic religious scruples) was to be resolved not by opposing one against the other with the weight of congressional specification on the *Berman* side, but by gaining entrance into a more expansive (even if uncomfortable) meaning of theism and religion by relating (or equating) Supremacy of Being to Supremacy of conscientious reference.

In collating the trilogy of *Seeger, Jakobson, and Peter*[85] for final review the United States Supreme Court was faced with an impasse from which it was able to extricate itself only by rising above the constitutional challenges. For such an effort the Court has had a persevering tradition of guidelines to exert every ingenuity to safeguard the constitutionality of a legislation short of a judicial denial of a clear constitutional right.[86] Mr. Justice Douglas' concurring opinion is remarkable for its frankness on this point.

> The legislative history of this Act leaves much in the dark. But it is, in my opinion, not a *tour de force* if we construe the words "Supreme Being" to include the cosmos as well as an anthropomorphic entity. If it is a *tour de force* so to hold, it is no more so than other instances where we have gone to extremes to construe an Act of Congress to save it from demise on constitutional grounds. In a more extreme case than the present one we said that the words of the statute may be strained "in the candid service of avoiding a serious constitutional doubt." *United States v. Rumely,* 345 U.S. 41, 47.[87]

The majority opinion of Court delivered by Mr. Justice Clark, on the other hand, is more confident about the propriety of its construction and in fact, proceeds to relate its ingenious interpretation to congressional intent and even to the implications of the *Berman* ruling. And as if to render its interpretation theologically respectable, it even quotes knowledgeably from Tillich and other "modern" theologians and the Ecumenical Council no less.[88] Much is made of the disparity between the explicit use of the appellation "God" in *Macintosh* and *Berman* and on the other hand the employment rather of "Supreme Being" in the Act of Congress of 1948 to reason that Congress intended by this substitution to refrain from the narrow connotation and to deliberately intend a broadened meaning by "Supreme Being." And all this is done, it seems, with the blessing of Chief Justice Hughes whose definition of religion as "a relation to God involving duties superior to those arising from any human relation" had been relied upon in part by the *Berman* ruling. But the passage[89] which the Court quotes from the dissenting opinion of Chief Justice Hughes in *Macintosh* can lend support to *Seeger* only by considering it in itself, severing it from the rest of the succeeding passages even though Justice Clark reads it as an interpretative commentary upon the later statement with the appellation "God." Generally a commentary follows upon a passage to be so interpreted, or if it precedes it — contrary to the usual usage it would pointedly forewarn that the succeeding passage is to be understood by the preceding propositions.

Be that as it may, the Court had a purpose in radically redefining the term "religion," for, in this way, it could avoid the issues raised by the First Amendment cases of *School District of Abington v. Schempp,* 374 U.S. 203 (1963), the ruling on the Bible and the Lord's Prayer, and *Engle v. Vitale,* 370 U.S. 421 (1962) on a voluntary school prayer, and more especially, by *Torcaso v. Watkins,* 367 U.S. 488 (1961), the Maryland notary public oath case, where, after stating that "neither a State nor the Federal Government can constitutionally force a person to profess a belief or disbelief in any religion," (at 495) the Court noted that there are religions which are not predicated upon a conventional belief in God. (at 495 n. 11) In addition to the First Amendment problems which would arise under the *Berman* view of the test, a problem would present itself as to the denial of due process which is guaranteed by the Fifth Amendment. In fact, the court of appeals in *Seeger* held that the exemption clause was violative of the due process guarantee in that it established an impermissible classification.[90] As we have already noted, it is a fundamental rule of the judicial process that a statute should be construed so as not to draw its constitutionality into question, but in *Seeger* the Court's intellectual maneuvering was patently a failure to confront the real, hard issue, that has only been delayed and only time can bring about another unavoidable confrontation — the question whether the free exercise or establishment clause of the First Amendment or the due process guarantee of the Fifth Amendment was possibly violated. The Court was careful to note — as it skirted the constitutional issue — that none of the individuals involved were atheists and that it was not deciding that question.[91] The Court avoided the problem presented by the *Berman* ruling by interpreting the Senate Report[92] on the 1948 Act in such a way as to conclude that, "rather than citing *Berman* for what it said 'religious belief' was, Congress cited it for what "religious belief' was not."[93] This sort of interpretation is not likely to offer the most assuring prospects of ascertaining legislative intent. Much less persuasive was Mr. Justice Clark's notice that the Senate Report "was intended to reenact" substantially the same provisions as were found "in the 1940 Act."[94] To have pointed out, as he does, that statute, of course, refers to "religious training and belief *without more*,"[95] is not to eliminate effectively the significance of the Senate's specific citation of *Berman* (with its appellation "God") as the Senate's construction of the 1940 Act's "religious training and belief" phrase. The "substantial reenactment" in 1948 of the 1940 provisions could more reasonably mean that the original reference contained that traditional meaning (if not word) of God-man religious belief which the 1948 points to by its citation of *Berman*. Perhaps the expediency of weakening an obvious historical legislative record prompted the less likely construction.

Under the *Seeger* test, the only statutorily excluded claims are those based upon (1) scruples which are essentially political, sociological or philosophical *and* are accompanied by a disavowal of religious belief as it is defined by the Court, and (2) a personal moral code which is the only basis for objection and has no relation whatsoever to a Supreme Being.

The dubiety of the new test is not centered in the Court's positing of those who are explicitly excluded from exemption, but rather in the novel understanding of what constitutes religion. It would now seem that any conscientious objector may benefit from the exemption from service clause provided he is evidently sincere in his avowed scruples and does not explicitly disavow theism — however they may be understood. Besides, the objector need not disown political, sociological, or philosophical rationales provided these are not the sole basis of his claim for the classification. One might cynically observe that a person clever enough to simulate sincerity and intelligent enough to formulate his objection to military service in language as to fit with the legal requirements as interpreted by *Seeger* would have an advantage over the avowed atheist who is sincerely convinced of the uselessness or wrongfulness of modern war. But then too the same cynic ought to allow that even with the benefit of external norms of sincerity, which formerly prevailed in 1917 as membership in a historic pacifist church and in 1940 religious scruples without any such affiliation, that even such a claim could be made expediently without inner profound commitment. These reflections are made to suggest that the practical effect of the *Seeger* ruling is to compound the difficulties with which a Local Draft Board must cope in deciding whether a protestor is truly eligible for the exemption.[96]

IN SUMMATION

Now, to purse together what is allowable under statutory and decisional law. Exemption to the "bearing of arms" based on religious scruples is dependent upon an act of congressional grace and not upon a claim of constitutional right. Once the categories of exemption are established by the supreme legislature, its terms must not be violative of constitutionally guaranteed rights or the due process clause of the Fifth Amendment by a show of discriminatory preference. The direct challenge to a claim of a preferential status of a definition of religion in disregard of the no-establishment and free exercise of religion was avoided by enlarging upon the traditional meaning of religion to include what is equivalently ultimate in every man's conscience, provided that such a profession is not accompanied by an explicit formal affirmation of atheism or is exclusively identical in its rationale with philosophical, political, economic or sociological considerations concerning the justice or utility of war. The line between religious scruples which stop short of denying human relations to a "Supreme Being" and whose belief is sincere and meaningful in the sense that it "occupies a place in the life of its possessor parallel to that filled by the orthodox belief in God" and accordingly "qualifies for the exemption" is but for that denial or restraint from denial, scarcely discernible from a philosophical moral objector who openly avows atheism. Be that as it may, a conscientious objector whose dissent is honored as sincere and meaningful by the civilian draft boards may choose to serve in the armed forces in a noncombat function or serve his country in civilian work outside the military, contributing to the maintenance of the national health, safety and interest. Obviously, test for a ministerial exemption differs from that of a lay conscientious objector. A claim of ministerial exemption is a factual question susceptible of exact proof by evidence of membership in a pacifist church or sect. The validity of a "belief" cannot be questioned.[98] Local Boards, and for that matter the courts, may not pry into the "truth" of a belief or reject it as being incomprehensible. But it is their responsibility to ascertain where the "belief" is "truly held." In every case then, as the Court admits, the question that must be resolved is the one of sincerity. The burden of proof is clearly upon the conscientious objector above all of the *Seeger* type and there are more demands made upon such a one than say upon the dissenter who is a member of a historic pacifist church or even of one whose religious scruples are premised upon theism.

> Since the ultimate question is sincerity, the registrant cannot, like the minister-registrant, rely solely on objective facts, but in his case objective facts are relevant only in so far as they help determine the sincerity of the registrant in his claimed belief. The registrant has the burden to show clearly that he is entitled to classification as a conscientious objector, and the burden is not shifted by his statement as to his belief. In a word, he must establish credibility of his claim of conscience apart from testimonies by witnesses or his own statements as to his beliefs. In this writer's judgment, if this was a difficulty with religious scruples related to theistic premises but with no relation to a pacifist church or sect, the difficulty of proof would seem to be even greater for the dissenter who relates his conscience to a "Supreme Being" without committing himself to belief in a personal God.

The rulings of the civilian boards are not subject to judicial review except as a defense against criminal prosecution. Their determinations are final and may not be reversed by the courts.[99]

Recourse to the courts by defendants is generally predicated on a claim — as in the past — of the unconstitutionality of the statutory exemption or — as in our times — the unconstitutionality of our combative involvement in Vietnam. On the latter question the Supreme

Court has at least in two cases refused to grant certiorari[100] by civilian complainants and by complainants in military service. It is well to stress that any deferment, whether for occupational reasons or for religious scruples, are given only when they serve the national interest. This is patently obvious in regard to the former. The exemption that covers conscientious objectors is intended to fulfill a double purpose, – the claim of conscience and a civilian service "in the National health, safety, of interest."

SUMMATION AND ADDENDA

Successive steps at which a justiciable action may arise for conduct in violation of the requirements of the Military Service Act of 1967 and the Uniform Code of Military Justice Act of 1968 may be set down as follows:

(a) those eligible refuse to submit to registration with their local draft board.
(b) registrant refuses to report for induction.
(c) registrant reports for induction but refuses to be sworn in.
(d) serviceman in noncombat military camp refuses to perform normal military assignments that are unrelated to combatant engagement.
(e) serviceman in noncombat military post refuses to fulfill an assignment that is related to combat services of others, e.g., train pilots.
(f) serviceman refuses to go to combat area.
(g) serviceman deserts upon receipt of orders assigning him to combat area.
(h) serviceman in combat area refuses to perform combat duties.
(i) serviceman in combat area deserts in order not to participate in combat operations.
(j) serviceman in combat area refuses to carry out a specific combat assignment.

We will limit our concluding considerations to those litigations upon which the United States Supreme Court has ruled as a valid claim of conscience and discourse in part about the regulations on protest and dissent activities of servicemen as these activities may be subsumed under the freedom of expression rights of the first amendment. Apart from the Captain Levy case, consideration of the legitimate invocation of the Nuremburg doctrine on Crimes Against Humanity, Crimes Against Peace, War Crimes, and Conspiracy to commit any of the foregoing crimes, cannot possibly be contained within narrow bounds and deserves for the complexities of the issues involved and the controversies about them a comprehensive and independent study.

Absolute (universal) Conscientious Objectors

Our historical survey of the origins of conscription have been related to the American constitutional history of the conscientious objector to military service and combat. The constitutional premise is still in the construction of the Court an exercise of congressional grace; its statutory provisions until the *Seeger* ruling, membership in a historic pacifist church or sect. The *Seeger* ruling expanded from within the meaning of "religion" to include nontheistic ultimate referrals that in effect stop short of openly avowed atheism. We have noted elsewhere that the high tribunal could have avoided this judicial interpolation in lexicography which has its original inspiration in footnote 10 of *Torcaso*.

> It would have been more felicitous had the Court not subsumed in a footnote, nontheistic beliefs into the meaning of religion in the First Amendment. The Court could have adequately rested its ruling on the Anglo-American tradition of law that the right to belief is a right to an internal domain of absolute inviolability, into which inner sanctum neither the law nor the coercive power of government force its disclosure.[101]

The national judiciary had steadfastly with but one exception held to the meaning of religion as an orthodox belief in God in accord with the highest tribunals understanding of the term in *Davis v. Beason* (1889), *Church of the Holy Trinity v. United States* (1892), *United States v. Macintosh* (1930), *Hamilton v. Regents of California* (1934). The one exception occurred in a lower federal court *dictum* of Justice Augustus Hand who in *United States v. Kauten* (1943) undertook to redefine "religion" in the Selective Service Act of 1940 in a manner that strongly suggests the latitudinarian construction of *Seeger* even though the Supreme Court makes no such acknowledgment of indebtedness. This *dictum,* which we may note was not actually necessary for the disposition of the litigation in *Kauten* was, however, adopted by the same Second Circuit Court of Appeals that same year in *United States ex rel. Phillips v. Downer.* The Ninth Circuit Court of Appeals, in contrast, clung to the traditional and prevailing meaning of religion in its *Berman* ruling.

The Supreme Court's abiding intention to preserve whenever possible the constitutionality of congressional law would have served in the long run a more positive purpose in constitutional interpretation had this paramount intent been subordinated to the necessity and advantages of preserving the identity of meanings of words even at the hazard of striking down the constitutionality of #6 (j) of the Universal Military Training and Service Act by submitting it to the tests of the twin religious clauses of the First Amendment, the nondiscriminatory requirements of the equal protection of laws, and the due process clause of the Fifth Amendment. In such an eventuality, the problem would have been referred back to the Congress on how to relate the moral prerogative of immunity of conscience to a legal status without endangering on the one hand national security and on the other, without exposing a legal favor to abuse. For not every claim of conscience is a conscientious claim. Mr. Justice Clark's latitudinarian interpolation of "Supreme Being" expression in the Universal Military Training and Service Act is made to rest on a supposed motivation when the Congress did not use the designation "God," – despite the explicit reference to *Berman* in the Senate Report on the 1948 Act. This was an ingenious exercise of professing to understand and follow the authentic legislative intent contrary, we respectfully submit, to its patent purpose.

The *Seeger* ruling, despite its explicit intent to hold the line against "essentially political, sociological, or philosophical views" and from "merely personal moral code", in fact weakens the distinction by which the cut-off of exemption from military duty may be maintained. First, the restraint from an open avowal of atheism is too tenuous to have any great practical significance. Atheists and secular humanists need not find it conscientiously intolerable to phrase their conscientious objection to war as did the defendants in *Seeger.* Secondly, a "merely personal moral code," sincerely avowed, is scarcely distinguishable from *Seeger's* "belief in and devotion to goodness and virtue for their own sakes, and a religious faith in a purely ethical creed." *(Jakobson* held to the "belief in a Supreme Reality" and *Peter* in the existence of a universal power beyond that of man.) Thirdly, why should a moral philosophical conviction on the immorality of war be distinguishable from a sincere and meaningful belief whose saving grace seems to be that it does not formally avow atheism, as *Seeger* chose not to commit himself one way or the other. Fourthly, does not a moral imperative presuppose a conscientious evaluatory judgment of human realities — not excluding the political, sociological, and economic? Men do not act on principle but on motivations (practical judgments) in the light of a principle. There are general principles of morality but not general morality. Morality inheres in each particular concrete human act. It seems to this writer that once the conscientious objection is disengaged from its theistic referral, both practically and rationally, for better or for worse the line cannot be logically held.

In *Oesterreich v. Selective Service System Local Board,* 393 U.S. 233 (1938), the Court ruled that the grant of draft-exempt status to a divinity student was not revocable under the delinquency regulations and unconditioned by activities that are unrelated to the original grant of exemption. "When Congress has granted an exemption and a registrant meets its terms and conditions, a Board (cannot) . . . withhold it from him for activities or conduct not material to the grant or withdrawal of the exemption." The draft board had declared Oesterreich delinquent because he protested United States participation in the Vietnam war by returning his draft card to the Government. The delinquency procedure, the Court ruled, was "without statutory basis and in conflict with" Oesterreich's explicit statutory right to an exemption.

Selective Conscientious Objector

One would suppose that if the "religious" conscience of the absolute pacifist can lay claim to draft-exemption, the claim of conscience based on a discriminating evaluatory judgment on the justice or injustice of a particular war would commend itself with greater reasonableness to the legislature. It is safe to say that the generality of mankind does distinguish between just and unjust wars and whatever the merits of the sincere subjective conscience of the absolute pacifist, a free and independent political community would not long survive against an aggressor without the ultimate recourse to arms. But the absolute pacifist has the legal advantage of not subjecting his religious scruples and the validity of his beliefs to inquiry by the government whereas the selective objector, precisely because his moral evaluatory judgment is related to a factual situation, would have to demonstrate the correctness of his moral stance. Besides, this pragmatic difficulty is doubly compounded by the danger of converting draft boards into Inquisitions—unless both statutory and decisional law would hold the SCO equally with the ACO to the test of sincerity and not to the demonstrative force of the evaluatory judgment as SCO are in some continental countries, where draft exempt provision is extended to them.

Selective Conscientious Objector—Classified but not yet inducted

Draftees who have registered and been classified by the local draft board have expressed their selective protest against the American involvement in the Vietnam war by burning their draft card or turning it in to the draft board.

In *United States v. O'Brien*, 391 U.S. 367 (1968), the defendant publicly burned his Selective Service Registration certificate in order to influence others to adopt his antiwar protest. The defendant was convicted under the provisions of the 1965 Amendment to the Universal Military Training and Service Act of 1948, (Section 462 (b)(3) of Title 50 App. of the United States Code), whereby Congress subjected to criminal liability not only one who "forges, alters, or in any manner changes" but also one who "knowingly destroys, (or) knowingly mutilates, or in any manner changes any such certificate." Chief Justice Warren, in the opinion of the Court, upheld the constitutionality of the 1965 Amendment. To the defendant's claim that his act was 'symbolic speech' under the protective coverage of the First Amendment, the Chief Justice responded:

> We cannot accept the view that an apparently limitless variety of conduct can be labelled 'speech' whenever the person engaging in the conduct intends thereby to express an idea. However even on the assumption that the alleged communicative element in O'Brien's conduct is sufficient to bring into play the First Amendment, it does not necessarily follow that the destruction of a registration certificate is constitutionally

protected activity. This Court has held that when 'speech' and 'nonspeech' elements are combined in the same course of conduct, a sufficiently important governmental interest in regulating the nonspeech element can justify the incidental limitations on First Amendment freedoms. To characterize the quality of the government interest which must appear, the Court has employed a variety of descriptive terms: compelling; substantial; subordinating; paramount; cogent; strong. Whatever imprecision inheres in these terms, we think it clear that a governmental regulation is sufficiently justified if it is within the constitutional power of the government; if it furthers an important or substantial government interest; if the governmental restriction is unrelated to the suppression of free speech; and if the incidental restriction on alleged First Amendment freedom is no greater than is essential to the furtherance of that interest. We find that the 195 Amendment to #462(b) (3) of the Universal Military Training and Service Act meets all these requirements.

Distinguishing the present ruling from that in *Stromberg v. California*, 283 U.S. 359 (1931), the Court stressed that "both the governmental interest and the operation of the 1965 Amendment are limited to the noncommunitative aspect of the defendant's conduct and that the governmental interest and scope of the 1965 Amendment are limited to preventing a harm to the smooth and efficient functioning of the Selective Service Act.

In response to a memorandum circulated to the local draft boards by the then Selective Service Director Lieut. General Lewis B. Hershey, counselling the draft boards to apply the delinquency regulation of the Selective Service Act against draftees who engaged in "illegal" forms of protest – v.g. sit-ins in local draft board offices, turning in registrant's certificates, – the Supreme Court ruled on the validity of these delinquency regulations under which, in one case, the defendant's induction was accelerated and in the other, the defendant incurred loss of deferment.

In *Gutknecht v. United States* decided January 19, 1970, the Court stated through Mr. Justice William Douglas that:

There is nothing to indicate that Congress authorized the Selective Service System to reclassify exempt and deferred registrants for punitive purposes and to provide for accelerated induction of delinquents.... If federal and state laws are violated by registrants they can be prosecuted. If induction is to be substituted for these precautions, a vast rewriting of the draft act is needed.

David Earl Gutknecht had been classified 1—A and was appealing his draft board's refusal to classify him as a conscientious objector. During a protest demonstration he threw his draft credentials at the feet of a United States marshal at the Federal Building in Minneapolis. He was declared delinquent and was ordered to report for induction in five days. When he refused to be inducted he was convicted of refusing to perform a duty required of him by the Selective Service laws and was sentenced to four years imprisonment. In overturning his conviction, the Court stressed that Congress had not set down statutory standards for the acceleration of induction and that the asserted discretion of draft boards to do so constitute a "broad, roving authority, a type of administrative absolutism not congenial to our lawmaking traditions."

In response to complaints in Congress that the Federal courts were interfering with the Selective Service System's efforts to discourage illegal activities which physically obstructed recruitment, sit-ins at local draft boards, draft card burning, turning in registrant's certificate,—by reclassifying the protestors, Congress passed a law in 1967 which permitted draft registrants to challenge their reclassifications in court in one of two ways. One was to submit to induction and then obtain release through habeas corpus proceedings. The other was to refuse to serve and then raise the objection to the reclassification as a defense to the Government's criminal prosecution. On January 26, 1970, the Court ruled in *Breen v. United States* that this provision does not apply in the revocation of a student deferment. In *Oesterreich*, the preceding year, the Court had declared that Congress could not have intended to bar those with draft exemptions specifically granted by Congress—such as men studying for the ministry—from going to court promptly in a civil suit to challenge a draft board's attempt to take the exemption away. In *Breen* the Court said it was "unable to distinguish" any legal difference between an exemption and deferment. Until 1967, exemptions were different from deferments in that they were absolute declarations by Congress that men in certain categories could not be drafted. Student deferments were subject to the discretion of individual draft boards. But when Congress amended the law in 1967 it also wrote into the statute specific standards for student deferments making them similar to statutory exemptions. The Court reasoned in *Breen* that Congress could not have intended at the same time to give local draft boards broad power to cancel these student deferments free of judicial interference. The defendant, Timothy J. Breen, an undergraduate at the Berkeley School of Music in Boston lost his 2–S deferment and was reclassified 1–A after he gave his draft card to a clergyman as an act of protest. On the second issue, the Court ruled that the Selective Service System lacks legal authority to declare students delinquent and to reclassify them 1–A as punishment for turning in their draft credentials. On this point, the *Breen* ruling is but a prolongation of the ruling in *Gutknecht* which denied statutory basis for accelerating induction.

Protest, Dissent, and Conscientious Objectors in Military Service

Protest and Dissent by Military Personnel

On May 28, 1969, the Department of the Army set forth through the Office of the Adjutant General, *Guidance on Dissent*. Acknowledging that the right to express opinions on matters of public and personal concern is "secured to soldier and civilian alike by the Constitution and the laws of the United States," it noted that the exercise of these rights is not absolute but subject to constitutional, statutory, and regulatory provisions relevant to the status of the subjects.

The constitutional coverage is in the First Amendment guarantee of freedom of speech, press, assembly, and right of petition. Restrictive statutory provisions applicable to all persons, military and civilian relate to activities subversive of military service and the performance of military duties: (1) Enticing desertion, 18 U.S.C. Sec. 1381; (2) Counselling insubordination, disloyalty, mutiny, or refusal to carry out duties, 18 U.S.C. Sec. 2387; (3) Causing or attempting to cause insubordination, 18 U.S.C. Sec. 2388; (4) Counselling evasion of the draft, 50 U.S.C. App. Sec. 462. Statutory restrictions which are specifically applicable to members of the Army are: (1) 10 U.S.C. Sec. 917 (Article 117, UCMJ)–Provoking speech or gestures; (2) 10 U.S.C. Sec. 882 (Article 82, UCMJ) — Soliciting desertion, mutiny, sedition or misbehavior before the enemy; (3) 10 U.S.C. Sec. 904 (Article 104, UCMJ) — Communication or corresponding with the enemy; (4) 10 U.S.C. Sec. 901 (Article 101, UCMJ) — Betraying a countersign; (5) 10 U.S.C. Sec. 888 (Article 88, UCMJ) — Contemptuous words by commissioned officers against certain officials; (6) 10 U.S.C. Sec. 889 (Article 89, UCMJ) — Disrespect toward his superior commissioned officer; (7) 10 U.S.C. Sec. 891 (Article 91, UCMJ) — Disrespect toward a warrant officer or non-commissioned officer in the execution of his office; (8) 10 U.S.C. Sec. 892 (Article 92, UCMJ) — Failure to obey a lawful order or regulation; (9) 10 U.S.C. Sec. 934 (Article 134, UCMJ) — Uttering disloyal statements.

In addition to constitutional and statutory provisions, there are Army regulations that may relate to "soldier dissent". These are (1) AR 210-10, par. 5-5 Dissemination of publications; (2) AR 360-5, par. 9b Submission for review of unofficial writings or speeches; (3) AR 380-5 Divulgence of National Security Information; (4) AR 600-20 Political Activities (par. 42) and participation in demonstrations (par. 46); (5) AR 600-20, par. 31 Appearance and conduct; (6) AR 604-10 Discharge of personnel who are active members of subversive organizations; (7) AR 670-5 Wearing of unauthorized items on the uniform.

Within the context, then, of the constitutional, statutory, and specifically Army regulatory provisions, *Guidance* delineates the following norms of conduct:

Concerning the possession and distribution of political materials, a commander may delay distribution of a specific issue of a publication which reaches servicemen through official facilities (Post Exchanges and Post Libraries) only if he determines that the specific publication presents a clear danger to loyalty, discipline, or morale of the troops and concurrently with the delay submits a report to the Department of the Army. A commander may require prior approval be obtained for the distribution on the post of publications which reach servicemen through other than official transits. Denial of permission for distribution must be related to illegal content (counselling disloyalty, mutiny, etc.,) or to the manner of its circulation which impedes training or troop formation. Mere possession of a publication may not be prohibited unless in direct violation of of post regulations governing unauthorization and distribution.

Attendance by members of the Army at Coffee Houses should not be barred because of the First Amendment guarantee of freedom of association and expression. If, however, it can be demonstrated that activities therein include illegal acts calculated to have an adverse effect on soldier health, morale or welfare, e.g., counselling soldiers to refuse to perform duty or to desert, — commanders may declare such places "off-limits."

Mere membership in "Servicemen's Union" could not constitutionally be prohibited. But commanders are not authorized to acknowledge or to bargain with them. Specific acts by individual members of a "servicemen's union," which constitute offences under UCMJ or AR, e.g., refusal to obey orders, — may be dealt with appropriately.

"Underground Newspapers" may not be published on post, with Army facilities, and during duty hours. On the other hand, such publications off post during off duty hours and with private resources comes under the protective coverage of the free press and speech clauses of the First Amendment, subject only to such restrictions of federal law which make certain utterances punishable (e.g., 10 U.S.C. Sec. 2387 or the UCMJ). On post distribution requires the prior approval of the commander according to AR 210-10.

On post demonstrations by soldiers is presently prohibited by AR 600-20 and 600-21. These same regulations prohibit members of the Army to participate in off-post demonstrations if they are in uniform or during duty time, or in a foreign country, — if the activity constitutes a breach of law and order, or if there is reasonable expectation of violence as a consequent.

Refusal to Obey Orders (to teach)
Captain Levy

The court martial of Captain Howard Brett Levy on charges of wilful disobedience of orders and seeking to promote disloyalty and culpable negligence, ended on June 3, 1967 when he was sentenced to three years of hard labor and dismissal from the service. His court-martial is particularly significant. It was the first time that the war crimes doctrine of Nuremburg was raised as a defense for wilful disobedience of an order to train aidsmen of the Green Beret in the treatment of skin diseases in Vietnam. It marked too the first attempt to cite medical ethics as a defense for wilful disobedience. After chief defense counsel, Charles Morgan, Jr., cited the Nuremburg War Crimes trials and ruling there that any soldier must disobey an order he knows will result in war crimes or crimes against humanity, Colonel Brown, the Army's senior trial judge, ruled that the defense could present evidence attempting to prove that the Special Forces (Green Berets), an elite counter-insurgency unit, were guilty of war crimes and crimes against humanity. The original publicly avowed intent of the defense was to plead the defense of truth by proving that since the Green Beret medics were cross-trained in combat, they were killers first and healers second. Despite wide advertisement through the communication media, the defense was unable to produce a live witness with first-hand knowledge of an atrocity committed by a Green Beret medic. In an out of court hearing, Colonel Brown ruled that the evidence proffered was insufficient:

While there have been, perhaps, instances of needless brutality in this struggle of Vietnam, about which the accused may have learned through conversations or publications, my conclusion is that there is no evidence that would render the order to train men illegal on the ground that eventually these men would become engaged in war crimes or in some way prostitute their medical training by employing it in crimes against humanity. Consequently on this issue, the accused's subjective beliefs may be heard only in mitigation of punishment if the trial reaches that stage. (New York Times. May 26, 1967).

The defense counsel then invoked medical ethics as a defense. He noted that Captain Levy's remark that medicine was being "prostituted" because Green Beret medics used it as a "handmaiden of politics" to convert Vietnamese peasants to loyalty to the Saigon regime. The supposition that a humanitarian act becomes somehow vitiated morally and suspect because by its advantages and goodness it engenders friendliness and invites loyalty in the recipients left the ten career officers who sat in judgment unmoved — and for obvious reasons of basic sanity and common sense.

On the issue of freedom of speech, Col. Brown stated that any member of the armed services had the right to express opinions, privately and informally "on all political subjects and candidates — and in strong and provocative words." An officer can disagree with foreign policy, especially the Vietnam war, as strongly as he wants, so long as his words do not have the clear intent of creating insubordination and mutiny. The defense counsel's argument that "If he's a subversive, he's pretty ineffective subversive" was in this writer's opinion a misconstruction of casual intent with efficacy, since the inefficacy of a deliberate calculated intent to subvert may well be a testimonial to the patriotism and firm convictions of the auditors.

On June 1, 1967, Captain Howard Levy was found guilty by a general court-martial of disobedience, seeking to promote disloyalty and of culpable negligence. On November 13, 1967, the United States Supreme Court denied petition for review filed by the American Civil Liberties Union for Captain Levy.

Captain Dale E. Noyd

The court-martial of Captain Dale E. Noyd is similar to that of Captain Levy in that both were officers who refused to teach as ordered but the two cases are marked off more by their disparities. Capt. Levy of the United States Army, refused to teach medic aidemen whose military assignment would be functionally noncombatant while Capt. Noyd of the United States Air Force refused to train fighter pilots whose service would clearly be combatant. Capt. Levy charged that the war in Vietnam was immoral because of alleged atrocities and he therefore pleaded defense under the Nuremburg doctrine on war crimes and wars against humanity. Under this major premise – moral (international) legal doctrine, he justified his exercise of free expression under the protective coverage of the first amendment guarantees when he urged servicemen not to fulfill their military duties. Capt. Noyd made no such charges nor was he charged similarly. Rather, his protest was that of the selective conscientious objector to American participation in a war of aggression in Vietnam, while avowing his readiness to fight for his country in a defensive war. He asked the Air Force either to accept his resignation or to assign him to noncombat service. His recourse to the civil courts for an injunction to compel the Air Force to accept either alternative was unsuccessful. The Federal District Court (Denver) ruled that civil courts must refrain from interfering with the military and had no jurisdiction until all the available administrative remedies of the military had been exhausted. Judge William E. Doyle said:

It is not unreasonable to require him to exhaust his remedies within the (military) establishment before coming to court. He has enjoyed its benefits and it is not unreasonable to require him to face its burdens. (New York Times, April 26, 1967)

The United States Court of Appeals for the Tenth Circuit affirmed. With the refusal of the United States Supreme Court to act, Capt. Noyd faced court martial proceedings.

The Defense Department has procedures for releasing servicemen who become conscientious objectors after entering service, but the Air Force turned down Capt. Noyd's selective conscientious objection for release to noncombatant duty. While the courts have recognized a serviceman's right to alter his beliefs after his enlistment, they have not ruled that he has a right to object to a particular war.

A nine-member general court-martial found Capt. Noyd guilty of wilful disobedience of a lawful order in refusing to train a student pilot to fly in Vietnam.

Col. Harold R. Vague, who presided as law officer of the court, had ruled that religious convictions would constitute a defense only if they caused a "mental compulsion" that affected Capt. Noyd's capacity "for specific intent" to disobey the order. But both the attorneys for the defendant and Capt. Noyd himself explicitly refused to use any defense that might imply a plea of insanity. The exchange between the presiding officer and the defendant discloses only moral compulsion:

Col. Vague: During that time, were you suffering from any mental disease, defect or derangement that would prevent you from knowing the difference between right and wrong and adhering to the right?

Capt. Noyd: When I was up against that order and that was the ultimate confrontation of what had been going on for a year and a half, I could not obey that order. It was conscious and voluntary, but in a sense I would say I had no choice because I knew it was what I must do.

In response to Col. Vague's question if the captain was at that time "mentally capable," of obeying the order, the defendant said: "Yes sir. If I could have brushed aside everything I believed, I could have obeyed the order." (New York Times, March 9, 1968. Captain Is Convicted for Refusal To Train Pilot for Vietnam War.)

Both the Levy and the Noyd cases raise a moral-legal consideration which neither the civil nor military courts have attended to because the military law itself does not give basis for that consideration. But extra-judicial reflections might raise the issue of an argument of greater presumption for obedience in career officers and professional soldiers than in enlisted men, and even to a lesser degree in draftees. This question must be weighed not in the abstract but in the concrete circumstances of an open society dedicated to public challenge and debate, and to disclosure, not only by private individuals but also by members of the government in unofficial capacities as well as in official hearings of congressional committees. Military obedience and discipline cannot reasonably be restricted only to duties with which military personnel agree. Surely these officers are aware of the forty or more mutual defense pacts of their government with other governments and that the final determination rests with the highest officials of the national government. I am not now ready to resolve this question satisfactorily. But may the mutuability of private judgment on the morality of a war invite less and less credence in professional soldiers and career officers who, apart from enjoying certain privileges for years in military life, are in a sense expected to defer with greater expectation to the order of higher officials?

Refusal to Obey Combat Orders

Under the Uniform Code of Military Justice as most recently amended by the Military Justice Act of 1968, military personnel who refuse to obey the order of a superior officer, e.g., to board a troop ship or having reached the area of military operations, refuse to move out to a combat area with a unit, — are subject to the provisions of Article 90. Article 99 details nine specific categories of grave offenses in the presence of the enemy in wartime. A formal declaration of war is not essential because the courts have held since Korea that combat operations in the presence of the enemy are legally equivalent. The maximum penalty is death. Such an extreme punishment is rare and most unlikely. In World War II only one man out of approximately 13 million under arms was executed for military dereliction of duty. A sentence of death would have to pass through six legal stages of investigation and review, culminating automatically in a personal review by the President. Before a death penalty can be handed down, however, there must be a full investigation under the provisions of the 32d Article of War with rights for "representation, cross-examination and presentation" (Art. 32, Sec. 832, a,b,c). If that investigation ascertains that a lawful order by a superior officer has been refused, the offender is liable to trial by a locally convened general court-martial. The court's judgment is next reviewed in the field by officers of the Judge Advocates Office. It then passes to Washington for further review by the Judge Advocate General of the military service concerned, and from there to the Court of Military Appeals, — the military equivalent of the United States Supreme Court, and finally, before sentence can be carried out, to the President. (cf. Articles 59-76)

The above discourse is clearly unrelated to the serviceman who is in the area of military operations but prior to commitment to actual combat makes a plea of becoming a general conscientious objector before proper authorities and asks for assignment to noncombat service — even if need be in combat area.

CONCLUSION

Not every moral right and obligation is translated into legal rights and obligations nor, even when desirable, is any moral right and obligation easily translatable into a legal guarantee. We see no rational difficulty in affirming the moral right of a subjective conscience to protest a discriminating, selective conscientious objection. We do not thereby affirm with equal title that such moral right must be a legal right. We do approach the vexing problem in terms of tolerable, pragmatic considerations. To date, the actual expectancy of selective conscientious objectors in countries which allow military service-exemption to them, has not been of such high incidence as to pose a threat to the requirements of self-defense. Secondly, every war cannot be supported by a nation under arms without necessary services of civilians and to such capacities and functions the selective conscientious objector may be assigned. Thirdly, even in combat areas a significantly high proportion of the men under arms never participate in combat duties. The selective conscientious objector in the military may be assigned to these necessary services, — caring for the wounded, transportation, maintenance, food distribution, postal service, etc. One need not be committed to the desirability or even the necessity for granting exemption status to the selective conscientious objector in holding, as does this writer, that the prolongation of the rationale of *Seeger* logically leads to this consideration.[101]

FOOTNOTES AND REFERENCES

1. Atkinson, II, ENCYCLOPEDIA BRITTANICA, 592-625 (ed. 11, 1910); D'Aumale, Duc, LES INSTITUTIONS MILITAIRES DE LA FRANCE (Paris, 1867). THE ANNALS OF THE AMERICAN ACADEMY (1945); Atkinson, A HISTORY OF GERMANY (London, 1908) Maude, CONSCRIPTION, in ENCYCLOPEDIA BRITANNICA (11 ed.) Phipps, THE ARMIES OF THE FIRST FRENCH REPUBLIC.
2. Anderson, CONSTITUTIONS AND OTHER SELECT DOCUMENTS ILLUSTRATIVE OF THE HISTORY OF FRANCE, 184-185 1789-1907, (Minneapolis, 1908).
   (1.) "From this moment until that in which the enemy shall have been driven from the soil of the Republic of France, all Frenchmen are in permanent requisition for the service of the armies. The young man shall go into battle; the married men shall forge arms and transport provisions."
   (2.) "The levy shall be general. The unmarried citizens and widowers without children from eighteen to twenty-five years, shall march first."
3. Ford, *Boyen's Military Law*, AMERICAN HISTORICAL REVIEW, April, 1915. The law is usually referred to as "Boyen's Law".
4. Taswell-Langmead, ENGLISH CONSTITUTIONAL HISTORY, 747-756 Houghton Mifflin, (1946) May, Thomas E. *Constitutional History of England* (cf. p. 219).
5. Selective Draft Law Cases (Arver v. United States), 245 U.S. 366, 380 (1918); Cox v. Wood, 247 U.S. 3 (1918).
6. Undoubtedly English History motivated the delegates at the Federal Convention to our constitutional formula. In England, prior to the Revolution of 1688, the King's prerogative power to raise armies in times of peace posed real threats to the exercise of liberties. The Bill of Rights of 1688, resolved the problem not by prohibiting standing armies altogether in times of peace but by making their existence and maintenance contingent upon Parliamentary consent.
7. Palmer, WASHINGTON, LINCOLN, WILSON: THREE WAR STATESMEN (Doubleday, Doran, 1930).
8. Selective Draft Law Cases (Arver v. United States), 245 U.S. at 385.
9. Dwight, HISTORY OF THE HARTFORD CONVENTION, p. 368 ff.
   The effort to deduce this power from the right of raising armies is a flagrant attempt to pervert the . . .Constitution. The armies of the United States have always been raised by contract, never by conscription, and nothing can be wanting in a government possessing the power thus claimed to usurp the entire control of the militia in derogation of the authority of the states, and to convert it by impressment into a standing army.
10. While the conscription system both for the North and South made available larger resources of manpower and offered obviously better opportunities for discipline and training, it was marred by serious defect — substitutions for service, monetary commutation in lieu thereof, exemptions for religious conscientious objectors. In the North, the oppressive nature of the draft was unfortunately underscored by assigning its operation to the military. Modern draft systems have completely eliminated the military from local administration of the draft and assigned to local civilian boards the task of determining the order of service and the application of exemptions.
11. The Act of 1903, defined the militia as inclusive of all able-bodied male citizens, from the age of 18 to 45, and every able-bodied male alien within the same age range, who had declared his intention to become a citizen. The militia was distinguished into two categories, the Organized Militia and the Reserve Militia. The former comprised the National Guard of the States whose components were to be trained in encampments and drills. Military schools for the training of officers were to be established. The Organized Militia was the first actual similitude to George Washington's plan of January 21, 1790, for a "trained militia". The Reserve Militia comprised all male citizens from 18 to 45 years and in its comprehensiveness it is suggestive of a selective service system. The President of the United States was empowered to call any part of the militia for active service up to nine months for the purposes of executing Federal law, repel invasion or suppress rebellion.
12. Though this Act was passed scarcely a year before America's entry into the war, it still did not provide for national mobilization.

13. Cf. Bernstein, *Conscription and the Constitution: The Amazing Case of Kneedler v. Lane,* 53 A.B.J. 708-712, August, 1967. I have relied on this article for the excerpts from the *Kneedler* case.

14. Excerpts are taken from the lengthier quotations in Mr. Berstein's article.

15. *Id.*

16. *Cf.* Arver v. United States, 245 U.S. 366, 380 (1918); Cox v. Wood 247 U.S. 3 (1918).

17. It is interesting to note that the objections raised by the defendants are strikingly similar to the ones raised in the *Kneedler* case of 1863.

18. The court evidently felt satisfied that it had already disposed of this sort of argument completely to its own satisfaction by anticipating it in an earlier ruling prior to the American entry to the First World War. Butler v. Perry, 240 U.S. 328, 333 (1916). On the intent of the Thirteenth Amendment to it had said:

It introduced no novel doctrine with respect of services always treated as exceptional, and certainly was not intended to interdict enforcement of those duties which individuals owe to the State, such as services in the army, militia, on the jury, etc. The great purpose in view was liberty under the protection of effective government, not the destruction of the latter by depriving it of essential powers.

19. *See* LEGAL ASPECTS OF SELECTIVE SERVICE, Revised January 1, 1963, Selective Service System, Washington, D.C., pp. 3-5.

"Unquestionably the Congress has the power to enlist the manpower of the nation by conscription both for the prosecution of the war and for a peace-time army, and it may subject to military jurisdiction those who are unwilling as well as those who are eager to come to the defense of their nation. It is within the power of Congress to call everyone to the colors, and no one under the jurisdiction of the sovereign nation, whatever his status, is exempt from military service except by the grace of the Government. Aliens may properly be required to forfeit any future opportunity to become citizens of the United States, in order to secure exemption.

Furthermore, the Congress has power to seek information through registration or otherwise in peacetime, to prepare for an intelligent exercise of the power to raise armies by conscription; and in the present phase of history, marked by wars undeclared, failure to register the manpower of the country would be a failure to provide for the common defense.

The power to wage war successfully is not limited to combat action, but extends to every matter and every activity related to war which affects its conduct and progress, and the Congress is the judge as to whether a clear and present danger exists requiring the enactment of a selective service law.

The selective service law does not violate the constitutional principle that equality of duties is based on equality of rights, nor does it violate the constitutional provision against involuntary servitude. It does not provide for an invalid delegation of powers, either with respect to conscientious objectors or otherwise, and it does not deny freedom of religion, freedom of speech, or due process of law. Neither is it objectionable as class legislation. An assignment to civilian work is not in violation of the Thirteenth Amendment. *Cf.* footnote reference to specific court decisions, numbers 32 to 49".

20. *Cf.* Torcaso v. Watkins, 367 U.S. 488, (1961).

21. *Cf.* Everson v. Board of Education, 330 U.S. 1, 15-16 (1947).

"The establishment of religion clause of the First Amendment means at least this: Neither a state nor the Federal Government can set up a church. Neither can pass laws which aid one religion, aid all religion, or prefer one religion over another."

Cf. Corwin, "THE SUPREME COURT AS NATIONAL SCHOOL BOARD", 14 *Law and Contemporary Problems,* 3, 10 (1949) for a critical appraisal of these statements.

22. Among which, must be included, by an ironic twist of logical precession, the question, what happens to the wall of separation of the absolute separationists? Separation supposes some significant distinction which the undifferentiated monism of the novel meaning of religion now excludes as a preferential status for the purposes of law.

23. *Cf.* Macintosh v. United States, 42 F. 2d 845, 847-848, rev'd, 283 U.S. 605 (1931), wherein the circuit court refers to numerous colonial statutes and constitutional provisions.

24. *Cf.* Kurland, THE BIRTH OF THE BILL OF RIGHTS, University of North Carolina

Press, 1955, p. 15, conscription for military service outside the colony was barred by the Massachusetts Body of Liberties (1641), p. 47. Conscientious dissenters were exempted from military service upon payment of a fee by the Pennsylvania Declaration of Rights (1776) Article VIII. p. 62, New York Constitution (1777) excused Quakers from militia duty, as non-believers in armed resistance, upon the payment of an exemption fee. Cf. SOURCES OF OUR LIBERTIES. Edited by Richard L. Perry. American Bar Foundation, 1952, p. 329. A Declaration of the Rights of the Inhabitants of the Commonwealth, or State of Pennsylvania. Article VIII. "Nor can any man who is conscientiously scrupulous of bearing arms, be justly compelled thereto, if he will pay such equivalent. . . ." As early as 1673 those who had conscientious scruples were exempted from military service in Rhode Island very likely because it had come largely under the control of Quakers. Cf. Thomas and Richard, HISTORY OF THE SOCIETY OF FRIENDS IN AMERICA, (American Church History Series, Vol. XII), p. 211.

25. Cf. Kurland, THE BIRTH OF THE BILL OF RIGHTS, on Madison's championship of a Bill of Rights against the sluggish reaction of his fellow congressmen in the House of Representatives.

Madison initiated the discussions on the amendments on Monday, June 8, 1789, Cf. 1 Gales, Annals of Congress 424 ff.

"The right of the people to keep and bear arms shall not be infringed; well armed and well regulated militia being the best security of a free country: but no person religiously scrupulous of bearing arms shall be compelled to render service in person." The wording of Madison's proposal 'in person' would on its face allow substitution or fiscal commutation to pay for service by another.

On Monday, August 17, 1789, the House resolved itself into a committee with Mr. Boudinot presiding. The whole discussion on religious dissenters to the bearing of arms is dispensed with in approximately two columns. Cf. Gales, ibid., 749-751. Mr. Gerry proposed to confine the exemption "to persons belonging to a religious sect scrupulous of bearing arms." Mr. Jackson, while he did not expect everyone to "turn Quakers or Moravians", some would be defenders of the others. So he recommended that the exemption be conditioned "upon paying an equivalent to be established by law". Mr. Smith thought that the religious objectors "were to be excused provided they found a substitute". Mr. Sherman countered that the religious objection of the dissenters "are equally scrupulous of getting substitutes or paying an equivalent. Besides, he noted that exemption on credal sectarian grounds would not be fair to Quakers who would choose to fight for their country. Mr. Benson brought the whole summary exchange to a close by moving that the whole clause be omitted. He would rather that the matter of religious scruples to the bearing of arms be left "to the benevolence of the Legislature". The whole clause was voted out, 24 to 22. So much for the debates on conscientious objectors at the time of the Bill of Rights were being formulated in the first Congress.

26. 28 Annals of Congress 774-775 (1815) (1789-1824).

27. Cf. CONG. GLOBE, 37th Congress, 3d Session 994, 1389-90 (1863).

27a. Cf. Wright, CONSCIENTIOUS OBJECTORS IN THE CIVIL WAR, Philadelphia, (1931), p. 301, notes that figures are not available to show the total number of conscientious objectors in the different denominations. Mennonites seem to predominant, with the Friends, second.

28. Act of May 18, 1917, ch. 15, 4, 40 Stat. 78. That the exemption was available only to those whose objecting conscience was religiously ground can be reasonably inferred with certainty from the fact that a proposed amendment which founded exemption upon a broader basis other than the specifically defined as membership in "any well-recognized sect or organization . . . whose existing creed or principles forbid its members to participate in war in any form. . . ." ibid.

29. Exec. Order No. 2823, March 20, 1918. Undoubtedly the terms of the Draft Act in specifically restricting exemption to adherence to a sect conferred a preferential legal benefit to religious objectors who were members of a pacifist church as against religious objectors who were not. That however was not the intent of the Congress. The intent of the Congress was to provide some objective norm of sincerity and presumptively membership in such a sect seemed to provide some such evidence.

30. *Cf.* Dickinson, THE BUILDING OF AN ARMY, (1922) Ch. XI, "The Army Act of 1920". Also, Palmer, AMERICA IN ARMS (1921).
31. Selective Draft Law Cases is the title given by the official reporter to five consolidated appeals (Arver v. United States), 245 U.S. 366, 389-390, (1918).
32. This did constitute an actual concrete problem from 1930 to 1940. *Cf.* III Stokes, CHURCH AND STATE IN THE UNITED STATES, 294. Among such churches who defend the right of individual Church members to be conscientious objectors in public statements whose official creed did not forbid participation in war were: The American Unitarian Association, 1933, 1940; the Northern Baptist Convention, 1934; the Presbyterian Church of the United States of America, 1934, the Protestant Episcopal Church, 1934, the Congregational Christian Churches, 1939; the International Convention of the Disciples of Christ, 1939; the Methodist Church, 1939, 1940; the Reformed Church in America, 1939; and the United Lutheran Church in America, 1940.
33. In an earlier ruling, the Supreme Court took direct cognizance of the relation of the Thirteenth Amendment to duties that a government may impose upon those within its jurisdiction. *See* Butler v. Perry, 240 U.S. 328, 333 (1916):
"It introduced no novel doctrine with respect of services always treated as exceptional, and certainly was not intended to interdict enforcement of those duties which individuals owe to the State, such as services in the army, militia, on the jury, etc. The great purpose in view was liberty under the protection of effective government, not the destruction of the latter by depriving it of essential powers."
34. 54 Stat. 885.
35. United States v. Schwimmer, 279 U.S. 644 (1929).
36. U.S.C. Title 8, 381.
"He (the applicant for naturalization) shall, before he is admitted to citizenship, declare on oath in open court. . . that he will support and defend the Constitution and laws of the United States against all enemies, foreign and domestic, and bear true faith and allegiance to the same."
37. Notably the *Schenck* (1919), *Frohwerk* (1919), *Debs* (1919), *Abrams* (1919), *Gitlow* (1925), *Whitney* (1927) Cases.
The dissenting opinion, written by Justice Holmes and concurred in by Justice Brandeis, was quick to distinguish such fears of influence in wartime from those that the Court shared in *Schenck*. *Cf. id.* at 654, 655.
38. The Naturalization Act #4, 34 Stat. 596 (1906).
39. In a memorandum, Macintosh stated:
I am willing to do what I judge to be in the best interests of my country, but only in so far as I can believe that this is not going to be against the best interests of humanity in the long run. I do not undertake to support "my country, right or wrong" in any dispute which may arise, and I am not willing to promise beforehand, and without knowing the cause for which my country may go to war, either that I will not "take up arms in defense of this country", however, "necessary" the war may seem to be to the Government of the day. *Cf.* United States v. Macintosh, 283 U.S. 605, 618 (1931). Professor Macintosh has served as a chaplain in the Canadian Expeditionary Force during World War I.
40. 283 U.S. at 623-24.
41. *Id.* at 622.
42. *Id.* at 633-634.
43. 328 U.S. 61 (1946).
44. There are slight discrepancies between *Schwimmer, Macintosh,* and *Girouard* which do not affect the substantial basic issue. *Schwimmer* was a woman, who is not traditionally inducted into military service in the United States. Besides, the naturalization act of 1906 had not specifically required willingness to bear arms in the defense of the country but literally, an oath of allegiance and support, a provision, however, which the Supreme Court construed to an equivalence to the bearing of arms and equivalence further debilitated by the Court's fear that the Hungarian pacifist's use of free speech against war might influence the duty of patriotism of others. *Macintosh* was willing to take the oath to "support and defend the Constitutional laws of the United States against all enemies, foreign and domes-

tic", provided he reserved to himself to judge of its necessity and morality. *Girouard* prescinded from the issue raised by Macintosh and was content to limit his duty to defense to noncombabtant service in the army. The *Girouard* ruling simply reversed the narrow statutory construction of the Naturalization Act. In *Macintosh* with a non-absolutist interpretation which allowed alternate service.

45. Cohnstaedt v. Immigration and Naturalization Service, 339 U.S. 901 (1950). By the Immigration and Naturalization Act of June 27, 1952 (66 Stat. 163), which codified much previous legislation, terminated the policy of denying the privilege of naturalization to conscientious objectors. The present controlling law on conscientious objectors *cf.* 8 U.S.C. 1451 (c): "(5) (A) to bear arms on behalf of the United States when required by law, or (B) to perform noncombatant service in the Armed Forces of the United States when required by law, or (C) to perform of national importance under civilian direction when required by law."

Hamilton v. Regents of the University of California, 293 U.S. 245 (1934) is interesting for the conditions and limitations that may be set to a conscientious objector short of the requirements of war. It distinguishes a circumstance of grace, the benevolence of free higher education provided for under the Morrill Act of 1862 in Federal land-grant colleges, to which no one is obliged by law, with the requirement of compulsory instruction in military science unaccompanied by any pledge of military service from military service.

Even so, the Federal government leaves it up to each state how to comply with the Morrill Act requirement of military training. States may require it absolutely as a condition for admission in these Federal land-grant colleges or allow an alternate course, e.g., in physical exercise, for those opposed to any instruction in arms, and provide some other training that would prepare the student for noncombatant service in time of war.

46. In controversies of this order courts do not concern themselves with matters of legislative policy, unrelated to privileges or liberties secured by the organic law.... Instruction in military science is not instruction in the practice or tenets of a religion. Neither directly or indirectly is government establishing a state religion when it insists upon any such training. Instruction in military science, unaccompanied here by any pledge of military service, is not an interference by the state with the free exercise of religion when the liberties of the constitution are read in the light of a century and a half of history during the days of peace and war.

Manifestly a different doctrine would carry us to lengths that have never yet been dreamed of. The conscientious objector, if his liberties were to be extended, might refuse to contribute taxes in furtherance of a war, whether for attack or for defense, or in furtherance of any other and condemned by his conscience as irreligious or immoral. The right of private judgment has never yet been so exalted above the powers and the compulsion of the agencies of government. One who is a martyr to a principle – does not prove by his martyrdom that he has kept within the law.

293 U.S. 245, at 268 (1934). Justices Brandeis and Stone concurred in this opinion.

47. Notably, Schenck v. United States, 249 U.S. 47 (1919), Frohwerk v. United States, 249 U.S. 204 (1919), Debs v. United States, 249 U.S. 211 (1919), Abrams v. United States, 250 U.S. 616 (1919), Schaefer v. United States, 251 U.S. 466 (1920), Pierce v. United States, 252 U.S. 239 (1920), Gitlow v. New York, 268 U.S. 652 (1925), Whitney v. California, 274 U.S. 357 (1927).

48. *Cf. In re* Summers, 325 U.S. 561 (1945) State of Illinois Bar Committee on character and fitness recommended that Summers not be allowed to practice law in Illinois because Summers would not swear to support and defend the constitution of Illinois by arms. Summers based his refusal on grounds of religious conscience but the United States Supreme Court upheld the decision of Supreme Court of Illinois on the basis of the *Macintosh* and *Hamilton* rationale and in effect rejecting the plea that the refusal to bear arms because of religious scruples was protected by the religious clauses of the First Amendment. The dissenting opinion of Justice Black concurred in by Justices Murphy, Douglas, and Rutledge, would have allowed Summers' plea a consideration under the First Amendment religious liberty clause. That the dissenting opinion of Justice Black may have disposed the Court the following year to the Girouard construction of the Naturalization Act may be indicated by the narrow margin of 5 to 4 re Summers.

49. Executive Order No. 2823, March 20, 1918, which, while stipulating the non-

combatant services to which objectors could be assigned, extended the exemption to include those who, although they were not members of "any well recognized sect or organization" opposed to the bearing of arms, were motivated by personal religious dictates against service in the armed forces.

50. Cf. Hearings on S. 4164 before the Senate Committee on Military Affairs, 76th Congress, 3d Sess. 1 (1940): Hearings on H. R. 10132 before the House Committee on Military Affairs, 76th Congress 3d Sess. 1, (1940).

51. 54 Stat. 885.

52. The Act of 1940 was the first peacetime selective service law with emphasis on training. Its provision for exemption read: "Nothing contained in this act shall be construed to require any person to subject to combatant training who, by reason of religious training and belief, is conscientiously opposed to participating in any form." Ch. 720, 5 (g), 54 Stat. 889.

53. In addition to the state and federal statutes (to which we have already referred) that consistently understand religion to be as Jefferson had expressed it "the relations which exist between man and his Maker, and the duties resulting from those relations". *Cf.* Costanzo, THIS NATION UNDER GOD, CHURCH, STATE, AND SCHOOLS IN A-MERICA, (Herder and Herder 1964); the Supreme Court rulings which understood "religion" in this man-God relationship are Davis v. Beason, 133 U.S. 333, 342, (1890), Church of the Holy Trinity v. United States, 143 U.S. 457 (1892), Macintosh v. United States, 283 U.S. 605 (1931), dissenting opinion of Chief Justice Hughes at 633-34.

54. 133 F. 2d 703 (2d. Cir. 1943).

55. Such for example as the dictum in Everson denying any financial aid in any form, in any amount to religion which the Court subsequently refused to consider merely a dictum.

56. *Cf. supra* note 50.

57. *Cf. supra* note 54, at 708. The relevant statutory provision reads: "Nothing contained in this act shall be construed to require any person to be subject to combatant training who, by reason of religious training and belief, is conscientiously opposed to participating in war in any form." (Selective Training and Service Act of 1940, ch. 720 5 (g), 54 Stat. 889.)

58. There is a distinction between a course of reasoning resulting in a conviction that a particular war is expedient or disastrous and a conscientious objection to participation in any war under any circumstances. The latter, and not the former, may be the basis or exemption under the Act. The former is usually a political objection, while the latter, we think may justly be regarded as a response of the individual to an inward mentor, call it conscience or God, that is for many persons at the present time the equivalent of what has always been thought a religious impulse. *Cf. supra* note 54 at 709.

59. 135 F. 2d 521 (2d Cir. 1943). *See too*, United States *ex rel.* Reel v. Badt, 141 F. 2d 845 (2d Cir. 1944).

60. *Cf. supra*, note 50.

61. 135 F. 2d 521 (2d Cir. 1943) at 524: But if a stricter rule than was announced in the *Kauten* case is called for, one demanding a belief which cannot be found among the philosophers but only among religious teachers of recognized organizations, then we are substantially, or nearly back to the requirement of the Act of 1917 of membership in a well-recognized religious sect or organization whose existing creed or principles forbid its members to participate in war in any form.

62. 156 F. 2d 377 (9th Cir.), *cert. denied*, 329 U.S. 795 (1946).

63. It is our opinion that the expression "by reason of religious training and belief" is plain language, and was written into the statute, for the specific purpose of distinguishing between a conscientious social belief, or a sincere devotion to a high moralistic philosophy, and one based upon an individual's belief in his responsibility to an authority higher and beyond any worldly one. . . . There are those who have a philosophy of life, and who live up to it. There is evidence that this is so in regard to appellant. However, no matter how pure and admirable this standard may be, and no matter how devotedly he adheres to it, his philosophy and morals and social policy without the concept of deity cannot be said to be religion. (*Id.* at 380-81.)

64. *Cf. supra* at 62.

65. *Cf. supra* note 57.

66. Section 6(j), 62 Stat. 612 (1948), 50 U.S.C. App. 456(j), 1958. We may note here that while both the 1940 and 1948 statutes speak of both "religious training and belief" both the courts and Congress have not followed the lead of Justice Stephens who stressed the requirement of "religious training" no less than "belief" in *Berman*.

Cf. Universal Military Training and Service Act, 62 Stat. 609 (1948), 50 U.S.C. App. 451-73 (1958). In fact, the congressional explanation of "religious training and belief" really only defines what Congress understands "belief" to be while actually being entirely mute on the meaning of "religious training". In 1948 one *might* reasonably find corroborating evidence of congressional meaning of "religious" from the 1940 and 1948 provisions for ministerial exemptions which patently favored theistic believers as against non-believers. But in the light of the *Seeger* ruling in 1965, such an interrelated rationale ceases to be meaningful. The statutory ministerial exemption is surely by now, consequent to *Torcaso* and *Seeger* – constitutionally *sui generis* and must be upheld by a reasoning unique to itself.

67. *For example,* in Kramer v. United States, 245 U.S. 478 (1918) the defendant's conscientious objection to the 1917 Draft Act was not based on religious grounds but on philosophical, social, or humanitarian persuasions. Consequently the first amendment religious guarantees were not apparently directly before the Court. But when earlier, in Arver v. United States (Selective Draft Law Cases), 245 U.S. 366 (1918), the challenge was made that the 1917 Act was in violation of the First Amendment because by its ministerial exemptions the conscription act was establishing or interfering with religion, the Court summarily rejected it out of hand as not deserving serious consideration. "We think its unsoundness is too apparent to require us to do more." Id. at 390. In *Macintosh*, the Court could do no better with the defendant's claim of conscience than to point to the "limitless extent of the war powers". . . which include, by necessary implication, the power, in the last extremity, to compel the armed services of any citizen in the land, without regard to his objections or his views in respect to the justice or morality of the particular war in general." United States v. Macintosh, 283 U.S. 605, at 624 (1931). In *Schwimmer* (1929) the claim of conscience was swallowed up in the bad tendency of the exercise of free speech upon the wartime obligations. In *Hamilton* (1934) the conscientious protest was engulfed in the bad tendency of an unbridled exercise of private judgment. In *Girouard* (1946) and *Cohnstaedt* (1950), the claim of conscience was met by a broadened statutory construction of the Immigration and Naturalization Service laws, in a reversal of *Macintosh, Bland,* and *Schwimmer* rulings.

68. In United States v. De Lime, 233 F. 2d 96 3d Cir. 1955) the defendant, by his own avowal, an agnostic, could hardly sustain his claim in accordance with the congressional statutory explanation of "religious training and belief" as related to the individual's belief to a Supreme Being.

69. George v. United States, 196 F. 2d 445, 452 (9th Cir.). *Cert. denied,* 334 U.S. 843 (1952).

70. "It is established constitutional doctrine of long standing that exemptions of this character do not spring from the constitution but from the Congress. . . . This being so, there is brought into play the familiar principle that whatever the Government, State or Federal, may take away altogether, it may grant only on certain conditions. Otherwise put, whatever the Government may forbid altogether, it may condition even unreasonable." *Id.* at 449-50.

71. Speiser v. Randall, 357 U.S. 513 (1958). Supreme Court would not allow a veteran's property tax exemption to be conditioned by a loyalty oath as required by Articles XIII and XX of the California Constitution. See too the companion cases, First Unitarian Church v. Los Angeles, Valley Unitarian-Universalist Church, Inc. v. Los Angeles, 357 U.S. 545 (1958), disposed of on the same grounds as Speiser. The churches had contended that to condition property tax exemption accorded to churches upon the required disclaimer of forbidden advocacy was a denial of due process.

72. *Cf. supra* note 69 at 451-52.

73. Clark v. United States, 236 F. 2d 13 (9th Cir.), *cert. denied,* 352 U.S. 882 (1956).

74. *Id.* at 23-24.

75. *Cf. supra* notes 69 and 73.

76. *Cf.* Davis v. Beason, 133 U.S. 333, 343 (1890): "the term religion had reference to one's views of his relations to his Creator, and to obligations they impose of reverence for his being and character, and of obedience to his will." *See too,* Church of the Holy Trinity v. United States, 143 U.S. 457, 470-471 (1892), Macintosh v. United States, 283 U.S. 605, 627 (1931) dissenting opinion of Chief Justice Hughes: "The essence of religion is belief in a relation to God involving duties superior to those rising from and human relation". "Allegiance to God is superior to allegiance to civil power, passin . . . passin. Holmes, Brandeis, Stone concur in the Chief Justice's dissent.

77. Everson v. Board of Education, 330 U.S. 1 (1947).

78. *Id.* at 15. For a personal study of the issues involved, particularly as related to education under religious auspices or religious practices in public schools confer, Costanzo, THIS NATION UNDER GOD, CHURCH, STATE AND SCHOOLS IN AMERICA (Herder and Herder 1964).

79. *Cf.* McCollum v. Board of Education, 33 U.S. 203 (1948) where the dictum is repeated, and Torcaso v. Watkins, 367 U.S. 488 (1961) where it is affirmed as a proposition of constitutional construction.

80. The study on the historical-legal meaning of the no-establishment clause is one of the most agitated and prolific in the last two decades in publications on constitutional law and outside the scope of our paper.

81. Torcaso v. Watkins, 367 U.S. 488 (1961).

82. "Among religions in this country which do not teach a belief in the existence of God are Buddhism, Taoism, Ethical Culture, Secular Humanism and others." *Id.* at 495 n. 11. Two reflections on this proposition may provide pause on the soundness of the statement as a correct proposition theologically speaking and secondly suggest serious doubts as to its viability as a constitutional principle. First, though the oriental beliefs differ in their concept of theism from the western creeds — the personality of the divine being, its trainitarian nature, its eternal immutability, its transcendence as well as its immanence, the order of creation, the eternal distinctiveness of the personal immortality of humanism the afterlife — still the far eastern oriental faiths — whatever the concept of absorption of human realities into the absolute, or the belief on reincarnation, or the eternal procession of absolute being in time and space in manifold phenomenal manifestations, or the unreality of temporal-spatial realities — none of these faiths denied the objectivity of the Absolute, of the Permanent Reality and its distinctiveness from the subjectivity of worshippers or non-worshippers — and would scarcely merit being linked with atheism or the nontheism of Ethical Culture and Secular Humanism. Eastern religious confess to, not deny, a Supreme Being.

Secondly, if the Court intended neutrality between believers and non-believers, between theists and non-theistic believers, as it purported to do in the opinion to which the footnote is appended, then it has placed itself in a truly uncomfortable posture if such a neutrality were to be applied to the area of education, that area on which these presuppositions may not be taught — in public schools to underly those — the inculcation of moral and civic values which the state expects the public school children to learn — then in effect the Court is underwriting the teaching of Ethical Culture and Secular Humanism in these tax-supported schools and conferring upon these non-theistic "beliefs" a preferred status in contravention of the no-establishment clause of the First Amendment. It would seem at this time that the Court in order to avoid conferring a preferential status upon Secular Humanism in its consideration of the question of tax aid to church-affiliated institutions of learning, infra-collegiate and collegiate, may have to fix upon the secular achievements in these religious schools without prejudice to its religious affiliation and its religious teachings. Only in this way can neutrality and impartiality be hyphenated to comport with both religious clauses of the First Amendment.

83. *Cf.* Costanzo, *Wholesome Neutrality: Law and Education,* 43 N.D. LAW REV. 605, 633-34 (1967).

84. *Cf. supra,* note 81 at 495. On writs of Certirori to the United States Court of Appeals for the Second Circuit. United States v. Jakobson, 325 F. 2d 409 (2d Cir. 1963), United States v. Seeger, 326 F. 2d 846 (2d Cir. 1964). In Jakobson, the Second Circuit espoused the view that the Supreme Being clause must be liberally interpreted to prevent constitutional difficulties which might arise from protecting the "free exercise" of only a

few favored religious. *Id.* at 415. Jakobson, while recognizing an Ultimate Clause or Creator of all existence, contended there were two basic views of man's relationship to his Creator: the conventional "vertical" image which conceived of God as being on a higher plane than man, and the "horizontal" view which pictured the Creator as man's partner, allowing mortals to share in the grandeur and joy of the universe. He maintained that *only* the horizontal perspective led to the love for one's brethren which made war abhorrent and unallowable. *Id.* at 413. Unable to believe that Congress meant to exclude views of this character, or to require draft boards to distinguish between "vertical and horizontal transcendence", the court concluded that the statute must be broad enough to embrace Jakobson's views. *Id.* at 416. By refusing to perpetuate unduly restrictive concepts of a Supreme Being, the Second Circuit in Jakobson set the stage for *Seeger,* which squarely posed the issue of whether the requirement of belief in a Supreme Being could validly be employed at all. To arrive at its conclusion, the Seeger court, assuming arguendo that Congress could constitutionally withdraw the conscientious objector provision (of Macintosh and Hamilton cases), reasoned that the conditions which it could place upon exercise of the privilege were subject to constitutional limitations. Having established the proposition that Congress could not constitutionally condition a privilege which it could constitutionally withdraw, the court proceeded to find the Supreme Being requirement an unconstitutional limitation. 326 F. 2d at 854. For support the court relied on Speiser v. Randall, 357 U.S. 513 (1958), which held that while a state legislature was not required to give a property tax rebates to veterans, it could not condition such a grant on a procedure which amounted to less than due process, *i.e.,* the signing of loyalty oaths. The application of the *Speiser* principle to *Seeger* necessitated an extension of the former, since in Speiser an error on the part of the state could have resulted in denial of a constitutional right, whereas a similar mistake in *Seeger* situation could not abridge the nonexistent right to a draft exemption. Neither the deistic nor the nondeistic conscientious objector is *entitled* under the Constitution to a draft exemption. (cf. Macintosh and Hamilton and to federal circuit court of appeals which relied on the Macintosh and Hamilton rationale on congressional grace).

However, the extension was not unwarranted, given the traditional definition of religion of section 456 (j) of the Universal Military Training and Service Act of 1948.' "While the problem of discrimination falls historically within the proscription of the Fourteenth Amendment, it is settled that most, if not all, aspects of equal protection are embodied in the due process requirement of the Fifth Amendment. Therefore, in the words of the Seeger circuit court, "a line such as is drawn by the 'Supreme Being' requirement between different forms of religious expression cannot be permitted to stand consistently with the due process clause of the Fifth Amendment." 326 F. 2d at 854. Whether or not the line drawn by the statute is violative of the Fifth Amendment depends on its reasonableness, in the light of the purpose sought to be attained. Arguably, down to the Supreme Court ruling in Seeger (1965), the Supreme Being requirement was a reasonable implementation of a valid legislative purpose because confession to Supreme Being, or to theistic transcendence, provided an objective norm, however dubious, that pragmatically at least served as an external shield of defense against arbitary objections, whether sincerely or insincerely professed, based on allegedly political, sociological, and other nonreligious grounds. Even Mr. Justice Augustus Hand had distinguished his broad concept of religion in *Kauten* from political objections. If however, as it not appears in the light of the *Seeger* ruling of 1965, the subjective test of sincerity proceeding from an avowal of broadly religious conscientious scruples can be as reliable or suspect as the formerly objective tests of membership in a historic pacifist church or profession of religious pacifism, the way has undoubtedly been paved that cannot be marked off by a line, the distinction between religious scruples however God, now understood from purely moral conscientious scruples which openly affirm atheism or formally denies God even in the broad understanding of *Seeger.* What undoubtedly encouraged the Second Circuit court to its *Seeger* rationale were the neutrality and impartiality affirmations in *Everson* and, more pertinently in *Torcaso,* in order to avoid the charge of favoritisms among religions, however religion and theism is now legally to be understood.

85. United States v. Seeger, 380 U.S. 164 (1965); United States v. Jakobson, 380 U.S. 164 (1965); Peter v. United Sttes, 380 U.S. 164 (1965); Nos. 50, 51, and 29 October Term 1964. Ruling rendered on March 8, 1965.

86. *Cf.* Ashwander v. Tennessee Valley Authority, 297 U.S. 288 (1936) concurring

opinion of Mr. Justice Brandeis at 346-348. For a remarkably similar set of rules set down ten years previously cf. the eminent constitutional jurist, Ed Ward S. Corwin, Judicial Review in Action, U. of Pa. L. R. 639 (1926).

87. *Cf. supra* note 85, Mr. Justice Douglas concurring opinion, at 1. (refers to 85 of this page).

88. *Cf. supra* note 85 at 14-20.

89. *Cf. supra* note 85 (of this page) at 12. (P)utting aside dogmas with their particular conceptions of deity, freedom of conscience itself implies respect for an innate conviction of paramount duty. The battle for religious liberty has been fought and won with respect to religious beliefs and practices, which are not in conflict with good order, upon the very ground of the supremacy of conscience within its proper field.

Macintosh v. United States, 283 U.S. 605, 632 (1931). Mr. Justice Clark might have considered that in "putting aside dogmas with their particular conceptions of deity" Chief Justice Hughes was not putting aside the deity but particularity of differing conceptions of the deity and further that the "supremacy of conception" that Chief Justice Hughes here speaks of is a "supremacy" that is related to those "duties superior to those arising from any human relation" because of the relation of these duties to "God" which is apparently what Chief Justice Hughes meant in the succeeding passage. *Id.* at 633-634.

90. United States v. Seeger, 326 F. 2d 846, 854 (2d. Cir. 1964).

91. *Cf. supra* note 85 (I) at 10: "No party claims to be an atheist or attacks the statute on this ground. The question is not, therefore, one between theistic and atheistic beliefs. We do not deal with or intimate any decision on that situation in this case. Nor do the parties claim the monotheistic belief that there is but one God; what they claim (with the possible exception of Seeger who bases his position here not on factual but on purely constitutional grounds) is that they adhere to theism, as opposed to atheism, which is "the belief in the existence of a god or gods: belief in the superhuman powers or spiritual agencies in one or many gods." *Our question here, therefore, is the narrow one: Does the term "Supreme Being" as used in   6 (j) mean the orthodox God or the broader concept of a power or being, or a faith,"* to which all else is subordinate or upon which all else is ultimately dependent"?

92. S. Rep. No. 1268 80th Cong., 2d Sess. 14 (1948).

93. *Cf. supra* note 85 (I) at 12-13.

94. *Id.*

95. *Id.*

96. The enlargement of the difficulties are not eased by Mr. Justice Clark's confidence in the provision of the Act for "a comprehensive scheme for assisting the Appeals Board in making this determination (of whether a belief is truly held) — placing at their service the Federal Bureau of Investigation, hearing examiners and other facilities of the Department of justice." *Cf. supra* note 85 (I) at 21-22. The rulings of the civilian boards are not subject to judicial review except as a defense against criminal prosecution, is a relevant question but one which is not directly pertinent to our discourse and so need not detain us here.

97. What constitutes a church or who is an "ordained" minister is a relevant question. *Cf.* Legal Aspects of Selective Service. Revised January 1, 1963, pp. 19-24. Ministerial Classification in General.

98. "Some theologians, and indeed some examiners might be tempted to question the existence of the registrant's "Supreme Being" or the truth of his concepts. But these are inquiries foreclosed to Government." *Cf. supra* note 85 (I), p. 21.

99. "The provision making the decisions of the local boards 'final' means to us that Congress chose not to give administrative action under this Act the customary scope of judicial review which obtains under other statutes. It means that the courts are not to weigh the evidence to determine whether the classification made by the local boards was justified. The decisions of the local boards are made in conformity with the regulations are final even though they may be erroneous. The question of jurisdiction of the local board is reached only if there is no basis in fact for the classification which it gave the registrant." Estep v. United States, 327 U.S. 114 (1946) quoted in *Seeger* at 21-22.

100. *Cf.* United States v. Johnson, United States Court of Military Appeals, September 26, 1967, *per curiam,* 18 N.S.C.M.A. 246. Case No. 401 on the appellate docket for the

1967 term of the United States Supreme Court. Mora v. McNamara. Lower Federal Courts have traditionally waived this challenge aside since the conduct of war, whether by congressional declaration of war or by presidential powers is considered as purely a political and military act and therefore outside the judicial determination. Strictly speaking, the Supreme Court can legally review the acts of the Commander in Chief. Technically, its power of judicial review extends to all Federal constitutional questions. Its refusal to grant certororari stems from a longstanding judicial reluctance to challenge the President in wartime over the legality of his wartime actions. Historically, the Supreme Court has a record reaching as far back as the Civil War, of permitting highly questionable acts by the Executive during wartime. Occasionally, it has declared those or similar acts, illegal — but only after the war has ended. Not until after the Civil War was over, did the Court declare that President Lincoln had overstepped his authority in suspending habeas corpus by trying civilians in military courts. It similarly waited until peace came before declaring unconstitutional the martial law imposed on Hawaii during World War II (and the confinement of American born Japanese citizens in segregated camps during the war on the west coast). The sole notable exception (to judicial refrain without effective consequence) occurred at the very beginning of the Civil War, after the right of habeas corpus had been suspended in Maryland under authority granted by President Lincoln to his generals. Chief Justice Taney, act *in camera* for the Supreme Court in *Ex parte Merryman* granted a writ of habeas corpus to a lieutenant of a secessionist drill company who had been imprisoned by the military in Fort McHenry. When General Cadwallader, commanding the fort, refused to release Merryman, the Chief Justice issued a writ of attachment for contempt against the general. When the Federal Marshall attempting to serve the writ was refused to admittance to the fort, Taney had to contend himself with filing his option. In it he argued that only Congress could suspend the rights of habeas corpus, that even it could not do so if the civil courts in the area were open, and that the suspension had therefore been an act of military usurpation. It may well be that since the conduct of a war is an exercise of war that as much, once it is initiated, it cannot be as easily constrained by the rule of law and is therefore not deemed justiciable — susceptible to resolution in the courts. This note is, however, not revelatory of whether this writer does in fact personally question the legal basis for the American involvement in Vietnam, but is descriptive of Supreme Court conduct.

101. The question of the legality of selective conscientious objector to a particular war is before the United States Supreme Court now in the case of John H. Sisson, Jr., whose conviction for refusing induction was overturned in April, 1969, by Chief Judge Charles E. Wyzanski of the United States District Court for Massachusetts. U.S. v. Sisson, 297 F. Supp. 902, 1969 found the 1967 Selective Service Act unconstitutional on the ground that it discriminates against non-theists, religious or not, with profound moral convictions.

> The sincerely conscientious man, whose principles flow from reflection, education, practice, sensitivity to competing claims, and a search for a meaningful life, always brings impressive credentials. When he honestly believes that he will act wrongly if he kills, his claim obviously has great magnitude. That magnitude is not appreciably lessened if his belief relates not to war in general, but to a particular war or to a particular type of war. Indeed a sensitive conscientious objector might reflect a more discriminating conscience, and a deeper spiritual understanding.

VITA (Reverend Joseph F. Costanzo, S.J.)

September 3, 1913	Born of Maria Theresa and Federico Costanzo in New York.
	Attended DeWitt Clinton High School, Moshulu Parkway, New York.
	Awarded the *Arista Pin* in his Junior Year what was as a rule conferred in Senior Year.
	First violinist in the school's orchestra in his Senior Year.
	Attended Fordham College for a year and a half.
September 16, 1931	Entered the Novitiate of St. Andrew of the Society of Jesus at Poughkeepsie, New York.
September 16, 1933	Professed first religious vows at St. Andrew Novitate at Poughkeepsie, New York.
1933 - 1935	Classical Studies at St. Andrew Novitiate at Poughkeepsie, New York
	Classical and Philosophical Studies at Sacred Heart Seminary, Woodstock, Maryland, affiliated with Georgetown University.
June, 1938	Received B.A. Degree at Georgetown University.
June, 1939	Received Master of Arts Degree in Political Philosophy at Fordham University.
1939	Taught at Regis High School while attending Fordham Graduate School for a doctorate in Political Philosophy.

1941 - 1945	Theological Studies at Sacred Heart Seminary, Woodstock, Maryland.
June 18, 1944	Ordained to the Priesthood, Sacred Heart Seminary, Woodstock, Maryland.
1944 - 1945	Post Military Chaplain at Letterkenny Ordnance Depot, Chamberburg, Maryland.
1945 - 1946	Tertianship at Jesuit Martyrs Shrine, Auriesville, New York.
	Licentiate in Sacred Theology - *magna cum laude*.
June, 1949	Ph.D. Fordham University - Doctoral Dissertation - THE HISTORICAL AND JURIDICAL SIGNIFICANCE OF ST. AUGUSTINE'S POLITICAL THOUGHT.
February 2, 1949	Final Solemn Vows, Fordham University Chapel Feast of the Presentation of Our Lord.
September, 1949 through June, 1952	Member of the Faculty of Fordham University. Lectured on Historical Jurisprudence, American Constitutional Law, and the History of Political Philosophy.
1952 - 1955	Visiting Professor of Constitutional Law and History of Political Philosophy at the Graduate School of Georgetown University.
1953	Received the Scholarship Award *Alpha Theta Beta Pi*, American Historical Society for series of articles on *Politeia*.
September, 1955 through June, 1970	Fordham University Graduate School. 1970
September, 1955	Chairman of the Political Science Program of the American Political Science Association convened at the University of Colorado.

1960	Lectured in Germany and Ireland as an "American Specialist" at the invitation of the United States Department of State.
1964	The publication of THIS NATION UNDER GOD, CHURCH, STATE AND SCHOOLS IN AMERICA (Herder and Herder).
1979	The publication of THE HISTORICAL CREDIBILITY OF HANS KUNG: AN INQUIRY AND COMMENTARY.
1980	Currently in composition: (1) HANS KUNG'S PROTAGOREAN CHRISTIAN (2) A FAMILY APOLOGETICS: A SCRIPTURAL STUDY. Co-author, Sister Mary Ruth Murphy CCVI.

Invitation Lectures in American Higher Institutions of Learning

Address to Annual Conference of Military Chaplains, Fort Meade, Maryland
American Historical Association – Panelist
Ateno Puertorriqueno (San Jose, Puerto Rico)
Catholic Teachers' Association
Colgate University
College of New Rochelle
Columbia University
George Washington University
Immaculata College
Johns Hopkins University
Long Island University – Principal Discussant
Loyola College (Montreal)
Loyola University (New Orleans)
Loyola University School of Law (New Orleans)
Manhattan College
McGill University (Montreal)
Mercy College (Dobbs Ferry, New York)
National Strategy Seminar, United States Army War College, Carlisle, Pennsylvania
New York Bar Association
New York University
Radford College (Virginia)
Red Mass, Brooklyn Diocese, New York
Red Mass Address, Rockville Center, New York
Red Mass Address, Westchester County, New York
Sacred Heart University (Bridgeport, Connecticut)
Seventh Centenary Commemorative Lecture in honor of Dante Alighieri, Villanova University

Spring Hill College (Alabama)
Syracuse University
Tulane University
United States Department of State Lectures in Germany and Ireland
University of Colorado
University of North Carolina
University of Notre Dame
University of Southern Illinois
University of Wyoming
University of Wyoming School of Law
Xavier College (Nova Scotia)

Publications in America and Europe

Catholic Lawyer
Catholic Mind
Catholic World
Christopher Publishing House
Congressional Record
Continuum
Cork University Press (Ireland)
Duquesne Review
Fordham Law Review
Great Books Series
Giornale di Metafisica (Italy)
Herder and Herder
Humanitas (Italy)
Journal of Public Law (Emory University Law School)
La Civilta Cattolica (Italy)
L'Osservatore Romano (Italy)
Loyola Law Journal
Loyola Law Review
New Catholic Encyclopedia
Newman Press
North Dakota Law Journal
St. John's Law Journal
The American Journal of Jurisprudence (Notre Dame)
The New Scholasticism
Thomist
Thought
Triumph
University of Detroit Law Journal
University of Wyoming Law Review
Virginia Law Weekly

LIBERTY UNIV SCHOOL OF LAW
LYNCHBURG, VA